# Global Health Justice and Governance

# Endorsements

In this vigorously reasoned analysis of the injustices in the global health situation today, Jennifer Ruger provides both insightful causal investigations and identification of promising ways and means of overcoming the problems that have to be addressed. Combining conceptual and analytical concerns with critically assessed proposals of remedial reforms, Ruger has made a major advance towards a better understanding of some of the most distressing aspects of the unequal world in which we live. This is an essential reading not only for health care specialists but also for concerned citizens across the world.

Amartya Sen, Thomas W. Lamont University Professor,
Professor of Economics and Philosophy, Harvard University, US
Nobel Laureate in Economic Sciences

Building on her influential health capability paradigm, Ruger here deepens its normative grounding, elaborates a global division of responsibilities for seeing to it that health justice is achieved, and pinpoints where the relevant agents are falling short on these responsibilities. She proposes and defends specific reforms of international law and of the ways that global institutions, nation-states, and individuals go about securing health. Only Ruger, equally at home with foundational normative arguments, theories of governance, and epidemiology, could have built such a formidable and compelling edifice.

Henry S. Richardson, Professor of Philosophy,
Georgetown University, US

Jennifer Prah Ruger has launched nothing less than a devastating critique of the shameful way human society tolerates unequal life-chances and allocates health resources world-wide. Her vision of shared health governance will strike some as idealistic, but it is a bold moral response to the global patchwork-of-a-system that has left so many people's lives at early risk.

Beth A. Simmons, Andrea Mitchell University Professor of Law,
Political Science and Business Ethics, University of Pennsylvania, US

Inequalities in health abound within and between countries and are the major challenge of global health. Why should we act on them, and how should we bring various actions together? This work of both humanity and truly impressive scholarship puts human capabilities and flourishing at the centre and builds outwards. It is exactly the book I needed to give both theoretical structure and practical action for global health.

> Sir Michael Marmot, Professor of Epidemiology,
> University College London, UK
> Chair of WHO Commission on Social Determinants of Health

This book will be an invaluable resource to a range of intersecting readerships, including students, analysts, and policy makers in global health, global justice and global institutions. The author gives a comprehensive account of how the current system works, its shortcomings, principles for redesign, and practical ways forward. She brings rigorous scholarship to bear on one of the major policy issues of our time.

> Ravi Kanbur, T.H. Lee Professor of World Affairs and
> International Professor of Applied Economics and Management,
> Cornell University, US

At a time when many relatively poor countries have decided to move seriously towards Universal Health Coverage while a rich one is trying to move farther away from it, Ruger's encyclopedic treatise on the ethical, justice and global dimensions of healthcare is pertinent and illuminating.

> Ernesto Zedillo, Frederick Iseman '74 Director,
> Yale Center for the Study of Globalization,
> Professor of International and Area Studies,
> Yale University, US; Former President of Mexico

# Global Health Justice and Governance

Jennifer Prah Ruger

OXFORD
UNIVERSITY PRESS

# OXFORD
UNIVERSITY PRESS

Great Clarendon Street, Oxford, OX2 6DP,
United Kingdom

Oxford University Press is a department of the University of Oxford.
It furthers the University's objective of excellence in research, scholarship,
and education by publishing worldwide. Oxford is a registered trade mark of
Oxford University Press in the UK and in certain other countries

© Jennifer Prah Ruger 2018

The moral rights of the author have been asserted

First Edition published in 2018
Impression: 1

Published in the United States of America by Oxford University Press
198 Madison Avenue, New York, NY 10016, United States of America

British Library Cataloguing in Publication Data
Data available

Library of Congress Control Number: 2017957868

ISBN 978–0–19–969463–1

Printed and bound by
CPI Group (UK) Ltd, Croydon, CR0 4YY

I dedicate this book to Margaret, Henry and Helen

# Preface

In a world beset by serious and unconscionable health disparities, by dangerous contagions that can circle our globalized planet in hours, by a bewildering confusion of health actors and systems ... in this world, humankind desperately needs a new vision, a new architecture, new coordination among renewed systems to ensure central health capabilities for all. *Global Health Justice and Governance* lays out this vision and its ramifications.

If, as Aristotle proposed, the fundamental responsibility of society is to ensure human flourishing, then health, vital to flourishing, places a unique claim on our public institutions and resources. And ensuring health requires ensuring central health capabilities, to avoid premature death and preventable morbidity. In its simplest terms, this is the vision at the heart of *Global Health Justice and Governance*, to ensure that all people on Earth can avoid premature death and unnecessary illness and injury.

Making this vision a reality will require an alternative theory of global health justice—*provincial globalism* (PG). PG rejects the prevailing modus operandi that has resulted in such suffering in the world and focuses instead on human flourishing and capabilities, the effective agency of individuals, and the responsibility of individuals both for their own health and that of others.

Making this vision a reality will also require an alternative, overarching global health architecture—not global government, but a collaborative global health enterprise in which individuals, providers, institutions, insurers, non-profit organizations, public–private partnerships (PPPs), foundations, United Nations (UN) organizations, and government agencies at every level work together to ensure human flourishing and central health capabilities. Along with existing actors, it will require new institutions for coordination and research. *Shared health governance* (SHG), an alternative theory of governance, brings these many actors together. State governments will be the cornerstone in this architecture. With the authority to raise revenue, shape policy, and enact and enforce laws, they will be the locus of effective health legislation and law. Where other existing organizations play useful roles, they will integrate into SHG. Those organizations whose effectiveness has diminished can either be reformed and reinvigorated or phased out.

Creating this enterprise requires fostering *public moral norms*. Seventy years after the UN declared a right to health in 1948, many nations around the world, including the United States with all its wealth, have failed to make it a reality. As in social movements for civil rights, the environment, and gender equality, and other efforts to create a more just and sustainable world, public education and dialogue about health's centrality in a strong and prosperous society will be key in fostering a commitment to health capability for all. Ensuring health capabilities will require a redistribution of resources and a willingness on the part of the wealthier to support health services for the disadvantaged. Public moral norms are critical in engendering this support.

*Global Health Justice and Governance* builds on my previous book, *Health and Social Justice*, which offered an alternative model, the *health capability paradigm* (HCP), for analysis of health disparities, addressing complex issues at the inter-section of economics, ethics, and politics in health. But it also grows out of a decades-long research program, beginning with my doctoral studies at Harvard University where, under the supervision of Amartya Sen and also Joseph Newhouse and Jerry Green, I wrote two essays and a dissertation[1] and delivered a presentation[2] addressing health, its special moral importance, and health capability. These and subsequent works also examined a theory of a right to health, a moral justification for risk pooling and management through universal health insurance, social choice theory, including incompletely theorized agreements, and mechanisms for achieving health equity, shortfall inequality for measurement, and economic evaluation to assure efficient resource allocation.

Since then, our research group has advanced this examination further, researching on global health justice[3] and health governance,[4] developing PG and SHG as alternative theoretical frameworks for social cooperation focused on public moral norms and a just allocation of responsibilities.[5] We have exposed inadequacies in traditional health economics and bioethics approaches. We have developed theoretical foundations for claiming the injustice of health inequalities, the moral imperative to reduce them, and the priority due to disadvantaged groups, and for determining the conditions

---

[1] J. P. Ruger, 1995. "Health, Health Care and Incompletely Theorized Agreements." Mimeographed. Harvard University; J. P. Ruger, 1995. "Value Formation, Democratic Choice Process, and Health Care Rationing." Mimeographed. Harvard University; J. P. Ruger, "Aristotelian Justice and Health Policy: Capability and Incompletely Theorized Agreements." PhD dissertation, Harvard University, 1998.

[2] J. P. Ruger, "Social Justice and Health Policy: Aristotle, Capability and Incompletely Theorized Agreements." Health Policy Doctoral Seminar Series, Harvard University, 1997.

[3] J. P. Ruger, "Global Health Justice," *Public Health Ethics* 2, no. 3 (2009): 261–75.

[4] J. P. Ruger, "Governing Health," *Harvard Law Review Forum* 121 (2008): 43–56; J. P. Ruger, "Shared Health Governance," *American Journal of Bioethics* 11, no. 7 (2011): 32–45; N. Y. Ng and J. P. Ruger, "Global Health Governance at a Crossroads," *Global Health Governance* 3, no. 2 (2011): 1–37.

[5] J. P. Ruger, "Global Health Justice and Governance," *American Journal of Bioethics* 12, no. 12 (2012): 35–54.

for just allocation of societal resources.[6] We have argued for governing for the common good, ensuring that all people have opportunities to flourish, for which health capabilities are indispensable.[7] We have examined reflective solidarity and its relationship to PG and SHG.[8]

We have compared health inequalities globally,[9] employing clustering analyses to stratify countries into mortality groups and assessing economic, social, and health sector variables associated with inequalities among countries. We have assessed the relationships between health and democratic institutions[10] and development as it relates to health,[11] and we have explored the ethics of development assistance for health.[12]

We have developed the case for health capabilities, conceptualizing and operationalizing them,[13] and have examined various instruments through this lens, including the UN's Millennium Development Goals (MDGs),[14] accomplishing them and their successor Sustainable Development Goals (SDGs) requires a renewed, just, and transparent global health governance system. Likewise, we used this lens to analyze the Framework Convention on Tobacco Control (FCTC),[15] arguing that it can serve as an example for multifaceted efforts to improve health. We have explored further the centrality of both public moral norms and health agency, and the ability to participate in and navigate the health system to ensure one's own central health capabilities.[16]

On a more pragmatic level, we have expanded on the use of shortfall inequalities to measure health disparities, arguing that current intergroup inequality comparisons can mask deficits in health care quality, and proposing threshold levels—for life expectancy, for example—as the standard against which to measure inequality.[17] We have conceptualized and analyzed costs,

[6] J. P. Ruger, "Ethics and Governance of Global Health Inequalities," *Journal of Epidemiology and Community Health* 60, no. 11 (2006): 998–1003.

[7] J. P. Ruger, "Governing for the Common Good," *Health Care Analysis* 23, no. 4 (2015): 341–51.

[8] M. DiStefano and J. P. Ruger, "Reflective Solidarity as to Provincial Globalism and Shared Health Governance," *Diametros* 46 (2015): 151–8.

[9] J. P. Ruger and H.-J. Kim, "Global Health Inequalities: An International Comparison," *Journal of Epidemiology and Community Health* 60, no. 11 (2006): 928–36.

[10] J. P. Ruger, "Democracy and Health," *Quarterly Journal of Medicine* 98, no. 4 (2005): 299–304.

[11] J. P. Ruger, "Health and Development," *The Lancet* 362, no. 9385 (2003): 678.

[12] J. P. Ruger, "Ethics of Development Assistance for Health," *Hastings Center Report* 45, no. 3 (2015): 23–6.

[13] J. P. Ruger, "Health Capability: Conceptualization and Operationalization," *American Journal of Public Health* 100, no. 1 (2010): 41–9.

[14] J. P. Ruger, "Millennium Development Goals for Health: Building Human Capabilities," *Bulletin of the World Health Organization* 82, no. 12 (2004): 951–2.

[15] J. P. Ruger, "Global Tobacco Control: An Integrated approach to Global Health Policy," *Development* 48, no. 2 (2005): 65–9.

[16] J. P. Ruger, "Good Medical Ethics, Justice and Provincial Globalism," *Journal of Medical Ethics* 41, no. 1 (2015): 103–6.

[17] J. P. Ruger, "Measuring Disparities in Health Care," *British Medical Journal* 333 (2006): 274.

studying emergency department use,[18] the costs of motivational interviewing to reduce tobacco use,[19] the real resource costs of a National Institutes of Health HIV intervention among drug-using women,[20] and new methodologies for estimating opioid dependence treatment costs in nations worldwide.[21] To promote efficiency in reducing health disparities, we have explored cost-minimization and cost-effectiveness, investigating the cost-effectiveness of motivational interviewing to help low-income pregnant women stop smoking[22] and of peer-delivered substance abuse interventions among women,[23] among other such studies.

We have analyzed financial protection in health, proposing universal risk protection to reduce disparities in vulnerability to natural disasters[24] and a multidimensional financial protection profile that more accurately measures heath costs' impacts.[25] We have studied health insurance empirically in places as disparate as Morocco, where we analyzed insurance reforms;[26] South Korea, where we investigated out-of-pocket health spending among the poor and chronically ill;[27] and Vietnam, where we studied insurance's impact on health care treatment and costs as well as strategies to cope with health costs.[28]

[18] J. P. Ruger, C. J. Richter, E. L. Spitznagel, and L. M. Lewis, "Analysis of Costs, Length of Stay, and Utilization of Emergency Department Services by Frequent Users: Implications for Health Policy," *Academic Emergency Medicine* 11, no. 12 (2004): 1311–7.

[19] J. P. Ruger, K. M. Emmons, M. H. Kearney, and M. C. Weinstein, "Measuring the Costs of Outreach Motivational Interviewing for Smoking Cessation and Relapse Prevention among Low-Income Pregnant Women," *BMC Pregnancy and Childbirth* 9 (2009): 46.

[20] J. P. Ruger, A. B. Abdallah, and L. Cottler, "Costs of HIV Prevention Among Out-of-Treatment Drug-Using Women: Results of a Randomized Controlled Trial," *Public Health Reports* 125 (Suppl. 1) (2010): 83–94.

[21] J. P. Ruger, M. Chawarski, M. Mazlan, C. Luekens, N. Ng, and R. Schottenfeld, "Costs of Addressing Heroin Addiction in Malaysia and 32 Comparable Countries Worldwide," *Health Services Research* 47, no. 2 (2012): 865–87.

[22] J. P. Ruger, M. C. Weinstein, S. K. Hammond, M. H. Kearney, and K. M. Emmons, "Cost-Effectiveness of Motivational Interviewing for Smoking Cessation and Relapse Prevention among Low-Income Pregnant Women: A Randomized Controlled Trial," *Value in Health* 11, no. 2 (2008): 191–8.

[23] J. P. Ruger, A. B. Abdallah, C. Luekens, and L. Cottler, "Cost-Effectiveness of Peer-Delivered Interventions for Cocaine and Alcohol Abuse among Women: A Randomized Controlled Trial," *PLoS One* 7, no. 3 (2012): e33594.

[24] J. P. Ruger, "Social Risk Management: Reducing Disparities in Risk, Vulnerability and Poverty Equitably," *Medicine and Law* 27, no. 1 (2008): 109–18.

[25] J. P. Ruger, "An Alternative Framework for Analyzing Financial Protection in Health," *PLoS Medicine* 9, no. 8 (2012): e1001294.

[26] J. P. Ruger and D. Kress, "Health Financing and Insurance Reform in Morocco," *Health Affairs* 26, no. 4 (2007): 1009–16.

[27] J. P. Ruger and H.-J. Kim, "Out-of-Pocket Healthcare Spending by the Poor and Chronically Ill in the Republic of Korea," *American Journal of Public Health* 97, no. 5 (2007): 804–11.

[28] K. T. Nguyen, O. T. H. Khuat, S. Ma, D. C. Pham, G. T. H. Khuat, and J. P. Ruger, "Coping with Health Care Expenses among Poor Households: Evidence from a Rural Commune in Vietnam," *Social Science & Medicine* 74, no. 5 (2012): 724–33; K. T. Nguyen, O. T. H. Khuat, S. Ma, D. C. Pham, G. T. H. Khuat, and J. P. Ruger, "Impact of Health Insurance on Health Care Treatment and Cost in Vietnam: A Health Capability Approach to Financial Protection," *American Journal of Public Health* 102, no. 8 (2012): 1450–61.

We have examined the World Bank's Safe Motherhood project in Indonesia[29] and health capability in rural India.[30]

We have also examined existing global institutions, including the World Health Organization (WHO),[31] addressing both its key roles and its failures and inadequacies; and the World Bank,[32] which has assumed a vastly larger role in global health. We have studied the proliferation and impact of actors in the global health landscape.[33]

Given the inadequacies of existing institutions, we have conceptualized an integrated, collaborative global governance structure in which states are the central actors but individual, local, and global actors all play key roles.[34] An overarching Global Health Constitution (GHC) shapes this structure[35] and a Global Institute of Health and Medicine (GIHM) enables decision-making to be evidence based and free of undue influence. We have studied elements of SHG empirically, as evidenced in Malawi,[36] and assessed the role of emerging nations in global health governance.[37]

Global health law is critical in this discussion; we have argued for a normative foundation for global health law to achieve health equity, recognizing the complex relationship among law and policy, global and domestic.[38] We

---

[29] J. L. Baird, S. Ma, and J. P. Ruger, "Effects of the World Bank's Maternal and Child Health Intervention on Indonesia's Poor: Evaluating the Safe Motherhood Project," *Social Science & Medicine* 72, no. 12 (2011): 1948–55.

[30] C. H. Feldman, G. L. Darmstadt, V. Kumar, and J. P. Ruger, "Women's Political Participation and Health: A Health Capability Study in Rural India," *Journal of Health Politics, Policy and Law* 40, no. 1 (2014): 101–64.

[31] J. P. Ruger, "International Institutional Legitimacy and the World Health Organization," *Journal of Epidemiology and Community Health* 68, no. 8 (2014): 697–700; J. P. Ruger and D. Yach, "The Global Role of the World Health Organization," *Global Health Governance* 2, no. 2 (2009): 1–11.

[32] J. P. Ruger, "The Changing Role of the World Bank in Global Health," *American Journal of Public Health* 95, no. 1 (2005): 60–70; J. P. Ruger, "What Will the New World Bank Head Do for Global Health?" *Lancet* 365, no. 9474 (2005): 1837–40; J. P. Ruger, "Global Health Governance and the World Bank," *The Lancet* 370, no. 9597 (2007): 1471–4; J. P. Ruger, "The World Bank and Global Health: Time for a Renewed Focus on Health Policy," *Journal of Epidemiology and Community Health* 68, no. 1 (2014): 1–2.

[33] S. Pallas and J. P. Ruger, "Does Donor Proliferation in Development Aid for Health Affect Health Service Delivery and Population Health? Cross-Country Regression Analysis from 1995–2010," *Health Policy and Planning* 32, no. 4 (2017): 493–503; S. Pallas and J. P. Ruger, "Effects of Donor Proliferation in Development Aid for Health on Health Program Performance: A Conceptual Framework," *Social Science & Medicine* 175 (2017): 177–86.

[34] J. P. Ruger, "Shared Health Governance," *American Journal of Bioethics* 11, no. 7 (2011): 32–45; J. P. Ruger, "Global Health Governance as Shared Health Governance," *Journal of Epidemiology and Community Health* 66, no. 7 (2012): 653–61.

[35] J. P. Ruger, "A Global Health Constitution for Global Health Governance," *Proceedings of the Annual Meeting (American Society of International Law)* 107 (2013): 267–70.

[36] C. Wachira and J. P. Ruger, "National Poverty Reduction Strategies and HIV/AIDS Governance in Malawi: A Preliminary Study of Shared Health Governance," *Social Science & Medicine* 72, no. 12 (2011): 1956–64.

[37] J. P. Ruger and N. Y. Ng, "Emerging and Transitioning Countries' Role in Global Health," *Saint Louis University Journal of Health Law & Policy* 3, no. 2 (2010): 253–89.

[38] J. P. Ruger, "Normative Foundations of Global Health Law," *Georgetown Law Journal* 96, no. 2 (2008): 423–43.

have also exposed its failures, studying the root causes of the breakdown in domestic and global law revealed in the Andrew Speaker case, an accumulation of individual and government errors that together posed a grave threat from multi-drug-resistant tuberculosis.[39]

A quest for justice, to enable all people to flourish, has underlain these efforts to understand how health governance has gone awry, to ground health justice theoretically, and to develop the institutions and processes to effectuate it. The current health landscape is dangerously inadequate, unsustainable, unfair, and, for far too many, manifestly harsh. We can do much better. I hope this book helps show the way.

---

[39] J. P. Ruger, "Control of Extensively Drug-Resistant Tuberculosis (XDR-TB): A Root Cause Analysis," *Global Health Governance* 3, no. 2 (2010): 1–20.

# Acknowledgments

Many people have provided invaluable help with this project. I owe my greatest debt to Amartya Sen, who has inspired and encouraged me throughout this project and many prior ones. He has been an extraordinary teacher, from whom, along with Eric Maskin and Robert Nozick, I have learned about social choice theory, welfare economics, and rational choice theory, among many important topics. I am indebted as well to Hurst Hannum, my professor at Tufts University's Fletcher School of Law and Diplomacy, and Jerry Mashaw and Jed Rubenfeld, my professors at Yale Law School, for teaching me, respectively, about international human rights law, administrative law, and constitutional law.

The International Studies Association Annual Meeting Roundtable on Global Health Justice and Governance in 2017 focused on this book, and Stefan Elbe, Sophie Harman, and Jeremy Youde provided excellent commentary.

*The American Journal of Bioethics* published my article "Global Health Justice and Governance" in 2012, followed by an editorial and six open peer commentaries. They were extraordinarily helpful. For these contributions and comments, I thank Rajaie Batniji, Jasper Doomen, Patrick Heavey, Bandy X. Lee, Matthew Lindauer, Ruth Macklin, David Magnus, Kayhan Parsi, Katherine Pettus, Paul Wise, and John L. Young.

The Global Health Ethics, Politics, and Economics class I co-taught with Thomas Pogge at Yale University yielded thoughtful critiques and rich discussion with him, seminar participants, and our students. Participants included Tom Beauchamp, Thomas Bossert, William (Terry) Fisher, Julio Frenk, Larry Gostin, Aidan Hollis, Charles King, Noah Novogrodsky, James Orbinski, Peter Walker, and Paul Wise in spring 2009; Christoph Benn, Arthur Caplan, Einer Elhauge, Ann Ginsberg, Alex John London, David Magnus, Harvey Rubin, Ted Ruger, and Michael Selgelid in fall 2010; Anne Becker, Barry Bloom, Dan Brock, Allen Buchanan, Esther Duflo, Frances Kamm, Ruth Levine, Donald Light, Christopher Murray, Richard Parker, Haun Saussy, and Dan Wikler in spring 2010; Anita Allen, Kenneth Arrow, Ronald Bayer, Lisa Berkman, Jo Ivey Boufford, Alex Capron, Gary Darmstadt, Javier Guzman, Ichiro Kawachi, Isabel Ortiz, and Jeff Sachs in spring 2012; and Joseph Fins, Christine Grady,

Nancy Kass, Felicia Knaul, Ruth Macklin, Mary Moran, Arti Rai, Peter Singer, Paul Starr, Jeremy Sugarman, and Harold Varmus in spring 2013.

Additional help from Yale came from the members of our Global Citizenship Initiative (Robert Evenson, Rafael Fernández de Castro, Rajiv Kumar, Nicoli Nattrass, Gus Ranis, T. N. Srinivasan, Michael Teitelbaum, and Jay Winter).

Participants in the Greenwall Faculty Scholars Meetings also helped me think through important questions. I am indebted particularly to Jennifer Blumenthal-Barby, Baruch Brody, Robert Burt, Alta Charo, Farr Curlin, James Curran, Neal Dickert, Barbara Evans, Gidon Felsen, Lori Freedman, Thomas Gallagher, Jeremy Greene, Sherine Hamdy, Lisa Harris, Karla Holloway, Steve Joffe, Jason Karlawish, Aaron Kesselheim, Scott Kim, Bernard Lo, Debra Matthews, Amy Lynn McGuire, Michelle Mello, Maria Merritt, Douglas Opel, Efthimios Parasidis, Kimani Paul-Emile, Jeffrey Peppercorn, Jessica Roberts, Charmaine Royal, Margaret Schwarze, Alexander Smith, Daniel Sulmasy, Jon Tilburt, Keith Wailoo, Douglas White, David Winickoff, and Leslie Wolf.

The Values and Moral Experiences in Global Health Conference: Bridging the Local and the Global at Harvard University in 2007 produced useful discussion and insights. I am especially grateful to George Annas, Homi Bhabha, Allan Brandt, Paul Farmer, Julio Frenk, Richard Horton, Dean Jamison, Jerry Keusch, Jim Kim, Arthur Kleinman, Richard Parker, Kearsley Stewart, and Strom Thacker.

Other conferences where colleagues offered invaluable suggestions on my presentations include the AcademyHealth Annual Research Meeting, the Biennial Conference of the American Society of Health Economists, the World Congress of the International Health Economics Association, the Society for Medical Anthropology of the American Anthropological Association International Conference, and the Harvard Petrie-Flom Center for Health Law Policy, Biotechnology, and Bioethics Annual Conference.

For probing discussions, I am indebted to Sudhir Anand, Uwe Bittlingmayer, Robert Black, Mylène Botbol-Baum, David Cutler, Edward Epstein, Marcia Inhorn, Ilona Kickbusch, Felicia Knaul, Barbara Koenig, Melissa Lane, Michael Marmot, Michael Merson, Robert Pollak, Bridget Pratt, Ken Scheve, Richard Smith, Al Tarlov, Catherine Wilfert, and Ernesto Zedillo; participants in the Joint Colloquium in Bioethics at the National Institutes of Health (particularly David DeGrazia, Joseph Millum, and Alexander Voorhoeve); and participants in Villanova University's tenth Annual Anthropology Lecture Series.

A great many participants in seminars and workshops have helped me refine my work. These include colleagues at the Yale Law School Information Society Meeting (particularly Jack Balkin and Yochai Benkler); Yale Interdisciplinary Center for Bioethics; Quinnipiac University Law School (particularly Jennifer Gerarda Brown, Stephen Latham, and Linda Meyer); Columbia University; the

High-Level Workshop in Development Assistance at the European Investment Bank; Emory University; Harvard Law School; University College London (particularly Shepley Orr, James Wilson, and Jonathan Wolff); Yale Law School; India–Yale Parliamentary Leadership Program; Northeastern University School of Law (particularly Kristin Madison and Wendy Parmet); the Yale Global Justice Seminar; the Princeton Ira W. DeCamp seminar (particularly Angus Deaton, Elizabeth Harman, Robert Keohane, Henry Richardson, Jason Schwartz, and Paul Starr); Harvard Petrie-Flom Center for Health Law Policy, Biotechnology, and Bioethics at Harvard Law School (particularly Glenn Cohen and Christopher Robertson); University of Chicago Neubauer Collegium for Culture and Society Symposium (particularly Daniel Brudney, Sarah Conly, Varun Gauri, Matthew Liao, James Nickel, David Ready, Gopal Sreenivasan, Daniel Sulmasy, and John Tasioulas); and the Center for Global Public Health at the University of California, Berkeley (particularly William Dow, Jodi Halpern, and Katharine Hammond).

My thanks as well to participants in seminars, workshops, and colloquia at the World Bank (particularly James Wolfensohn); Harvard University Kennedy School of Government Annual International Development Conference; the Yale Rudd Center for Food Policy and Obesity (particularly Kelly Brownell and Derek Yach); Georgetown University; Ritsumeikan University (particularly Reiko Gotoh); American Political Science Association Annual Meeting (particularly Jeremy Shiffman and James Raymond Vreeland); US Institute of Medicine/National Academies of Science; the Council on Foreign Relations (particularly David de Ferranti, Laurie Garrett, Margaret Hamburg, Yanzhong Huang, and Kelley Lee); Yale Center for Faith and Culture (particularly Jennifer Herdt and Miroslav Volf); the Pan American Health Association; University of Toronto Faculty of Law Health Law, Ethics, and Policy Seminar Series (particularly Rebecca Cook, Bernard Dickens, and Trudo Lemmens) and the Global Health Summit (particularly Abdallah Daar, Jennifer Gibson, Prabhat Jha, Jillian Kohler, and Ross Upshur); University of Richmond Jepson Colloquium on Leadership and Global Justice (particularly Gillian Brock, Simon Caney, David A. Crocker, Douglas A. Hicks, Waheed Hussain, Mathias Risse, and Thad Williamson); Johns Hopkins Bloomberg School of Public Health (particularly David Bishai); University of North Carolina (particularly Paula Braveman, Mara Buchbinder, Eric Juengst, Carla Keirns, J. Paul Kelleher, Nicholas King, Eva Feder Kittay, Anne Drapkin Lyerly, Jonathan Oberlander, Michele Rivkin-Fish, Carolyn Rouse, and Rebecca Walker); American Society of International Law Annual Meeting (particularly Philip Alston, Gian Luca Burci, Jacob Katz Cogan, David Gartner, and Benedict Kingsbury); Consortium of Universities for Global Health Annual Conference (particularly Larry Gostin and Thomas Novotny); University of Edinburgh (particularly Graeme Laurie); the Human Development and Capability Association Annual Conference (particularly

# Acknowledgments

Paul Anand, Enrica Chiappero-Martinetti, David Clark, Andrew Crabtree, Ravi Kanbur, Sophie Mitra, Martha Nussbaum, Philip Pettit, Antonella Picchio, Antoanneta Potsi, Mozaffar Qizilbash, Ingrid Robeyns, Lorella Terzi, and Polly Vizard); the Priorities in Global Health 2020 Workshop (particularly Matthew Adler, Marion Danis, Ezekiel Emanuel, Marc Fleurbaey, Dean Jamison, Kjell Arne Johansson, Reidar Lie, Joseph Millum, Ole Norheim, Trygve Ottersen, Larry Temkin, Stéphane Verguet, and Alexander Voorhoeve); Suffolk University Law School (particularly Sara Dillon, Renée Landers, and Patrick Shin); American University; University of Florence (particularly Mario Biggeri); University of Sydney; and the Economic Research Department at the Bank of Italy (particularly Andrea Brandolini).

I am grateful to have delivered the Labelle Lectureship and to members of McMaster University's Centre for Health Economics and Policy (particularly Julia Abelson, Stephen Birch, and John Lavis) and the Bob Jones Memorial Lecture.

Faculty and students in courses in which I have lectured have also been most helpful. These courses include Introduction to Global Health at Yale School of Medicine (Nora Groce); Interdisciplinary Perspectives in Global Health at the University of North Carolina (Margaret Bentley); Social and Behavioral Influences on Health at Yale School of Medicine (Jeannette Ickovics); Global Health Elective Course at Yale School of Medicine (Michele Barry); International Trade Law in a Globalizing World at Yale Law School (Dan Esty); and, at the University of Pennsylvania Perelman School of Medicine, courses in Public Health Policy and Management (Walter Tsou), Effective Public Health Programs Using a Human Rights Approach (Wendy Voet), Empirical Bioethics (Scott Halpern and Peter Reese), Issues in Global Health—Addressing Health Disparities (Carol McLaughlin), and Global Bioethics (Ezekiel Emanuel and Harald Schmidt), as well as my own course in Global Health Policy: Justice, Governance, and Reform.

I am grateful for constructive conversations among University of Pennsylvania colleagues in the Department of Medical Ethics and Health Policy at Penn's Perelman School of Medicine, including Anne Barnhill, Ezekiel Emanuel, Alex Guerrero, Jonathan Moreno, Govind Persad, Harald Schmidt, and Dominic Sisti, and in other departments, including Cristina Bicchieri, Bill Burke-White, Devesh Kapur, Julia Lynch, Beth Simmons, Rogers Smith, and Kok-Chor Tan.

My students ask dependably original and provocative questions, and discussions with them, inside the classroom and out, have helped hone my work through the years. Special thanks to Jarrad Aguirre, John Baird, Candace Feldman, Jason Gerson, Matthew Kavanagh, Benjamin Mason Meier, Kim Nguyen, Sarah Pallas, Takudzwa Shumba, Atheendar Venkataramani, and Catherine Wachira.

For their research assistance and useful comments, I am grateful to Michael DiStefano, Bryant Huang, Joshua Jordan, Emily Karsch, Christina Lazar, Ruth T. Lee, Mayookha Mitra-Majumdar, Nora Ng, Rupa Palanki, Trudel Pare, Ana Rancic, and Yusra Shawar.

I thank Betsy Rogers for editing services.

I am most grateful, of course, to my family, my parents, Sharon and Harry Prah, my husband, Ted Ruger, and my children, Helen, Henry, and Margaret, my sister and brother-in-law, Heidi and Chris Richter, and my nieces, Madeline and Natalie, for their support.

My work was supported in part by an Investigator Award from the Patrick and Catherine Weldon Donaghue Medical Research Foundation, the Greenwall Foundation, the MacMillan Center for International and Area Studies at Yale University, and the John Simon Guggenheim Memorial Foundation Fellowship.

I thank Oxford University Press, particularly my editor (Adam Swallow) and assistant editors (Katie Bishop and Aimee Wright) for their excellent guidance throughout this project.

# Table of Contents

## Part IV:  The International Order and Global Institutions

# List of Figure, Tables, and Box

**Figure**

**Tables**

**Box**

# Part I
# Problems in Global Health and Governance

# 1

# Global Health Problems

On December 6, 2013, a 2-year-old boy in Guinea's Guéckédou region fell ill, and thus began the Ebola outbreak that claimed roughly 11,000 lives and transfixed a world frightened by this virulent and deadly disease.

The first confirmed case of Ebola came in March 2014 in Guinea. By late June, this hemorrhagic fever had raged through Guinea, Sierra Leone, and Liberia, and the international relief nongovernmental organization (NGO) Médecins Sans Frontières (MSF), by default a lead organization in the global response, declared the outbreak "out of control."[1] It had overwhelmed states and their public health systems: Liberia, according to President Ellen Johnson Sirleaf, had fifty doctors for its entire population of 4.4 million.[2] By early fall 2014 the disease had spread to Senegal, Nigeria, and beyond Africa to Spain and the United States.

The epidemic was afflicting the very people most needed to help in the crisis. By mid-September, 318 health care personnel had contracted Ebola and 151 died in Guinea, Liberia, Nigeria, and Sierra Leone.[3] In a critique of the global response, MSF acknowledged that its care centers had been "overwhelmed."[4] Laurie Garrett, Senior Fellow for Global Health at the Council on Foreign Relations, described medical workers in Africa as exhausted, terrified, and burned out.[5]

Observers identified numerous reasons for the Ebola crisis. It erupted in states with little or no capacity to deal with it. "[I]ncredibly weak health systems, with few staff, little equipment, and poor facilities" made "disease surveillance, isolation, and supportive care virtually impossible without external assistance," *The Lancet* editorialized.[6] Cross-border traffic among the three

---

[1] "Ebola: A Failure of International Collective Action," *The Lancet* 384 (2014): 637.
[2] E. J. Sirleaf, "The Long-Term Cure for Ebola: An Investment in Health Systems," *Washington Post*, October 19, 2014.
[3] WHO, "Ebola Response Roadmap Situation Report" September 18, 2014.
[4] T. Nierle and B. Jochum, "Ebola: The Failures of the International Outbreak Response," *Le Temps*, August 27, 2014.
[5] Council on Foreign Relations, "The Ebola Outbreak," Transcript, August 5, 2014.
[6] "Ebola: A Failure of International Collective Action," 637.

countries spread the disease quickly. Cultural factors—burial practices, widespread mistrust of government workers, and religious beliefs—all confounded efforts to find and treat the ill.

Finger-pointing extended beyond these suffering nations. Observers criticized aid-stingy Western and emerging nations, especially China and Russia.[7] The pharma industry came under fire: the *Lancet* observed that "a vaccine would probably exist today if Ebola affected a large number of people in high-income countries, making research and development financially attractive to drug companies," and quoted John Ashton, former President of the UK Faculty of Public Health, who saw in this situation "the moral bankruptcy of capitalism."[8]

But the World Health Organization (WHO) sustained the most withering criticisms. WHO's Constitution charges it with directing international health efforts, battling epidemics, and helping in emergencies. Facing an imploding budget and rising debt, however, it had essentially abdicated these roles. Its allocations for disease outbreaks had been slashed and its regional emergency outbreak experts reduced from more than twelve to three for all of Africa.[9] Director-General Dr. Margaret Chan told the *New York Times* that WHO lacked the material and human resources to lead the anti-Ebola effort, and argued that "[i]t was a fantasy... to think of the W.H.O. as a first responder ready to lead the fight against deadly outbreaks around the world."[10]

More specifically, critics faulted WHO for its failure to enforce the 2007 revised International Health Regulations (IHR), which require all member states to report "events that may constitute a public health emergency of international concern" and develop "core public health capacities" by 2012, with a possible two-year extension.[11] But the IHR implementation process left countries to self-report their progress and didn't provide additional financing to expand core capacities[12]—a sure recipe for failure.

The epidemic undercut whatever medical services were available. MSF noted that "health systems in the affected region have imploded," and that while patients are dying of Ebola, they are also succumbing to "malaria, diarrhoea or complicated deliveries due to the absence of effective medical care."[13]

Ebola damaged regional economies and threatened national stability in West Africa as well. "We transformed our country from a failed state into a stable democracy, rebuilding its infrastructure and its education and health systems, and enjoying one of the most promising growth records in Africa,"

[7] S. Tisdall, "UN Gets Tough on Ebola Shirkers," *The Guardian*, October 17, 2014.

[8] "Ebola: A Failure of International Collective Action," 637.

[9] S. Fink, "Cuts at W.H.O. Hurt Response to Ebola Crisis," *The New York Times*, September 3, 2014.

[10] Ibid.

[11] "Ebola: What Lessons for the International Health Regulations?" *The Lancet* 384 (2014): 1321.

[12] Ibid.

[13] Nierle and Jochum, "Ebola."

Liberia's President Sirleaf wrote in *The Washington Post*. "Then Ebola swept in, threatening to tear apart that progress. It is a terrifying reminder of the destructive power of infectious disease . . . "[14]

Ebola offers an exceptionally tragic example of global health inequalities, externalities, and cross-border issues, but it is certainly not the only one.

## 1.1 Global Health Inequalities

The remote Wakhan Valley in Afghanistan is a narrow corridor of land lying between Tajikistan and Pakistan, stretching to China. High mountain ranges surround it. There, ethnic Kyrgyz nomads lead an isolated life on what has been called the "the roof of the world." Doctors and clinics are distant, and a trip to the closest town with a hospital can take up to four days. Kyrgyz children die at what is perhaps the world's highest rate: a staggering 50 percent do not survive to age 5. Maternal mortality during childbirth is alarmingly high.[15]

In Mali, parents live in dread of malaria, where approximately one in five deaths before age 5 are due to the disease. Indeed, men, women, and children in this western African nation of about 17 million are at risk of contracting malaria, its debilitating fevers, and, in severe cases, its neurological and respiratory complications; 2.5 million clinical cases were reported in 2014. Mali's climate, so congenial to the *Anopheles* mosquitoes that carry malaria, is partly to blame, but in Ecuador, with a climate similarly conducive to malaria, the rate of infection is vanishingly low, and the disease no longer regularly claims lives. Clearly, Mali's intractable malaria problem involves more than climate.

And consider the United States, where people in parts of the South and in the Dakotas can expect to die as much as twenty years sooner than their fellow Americans in central Colorado, and where life expectancy has been actually decreasing in much of Appalachia.[16] America's large cities encompass similarly dramatic health disparities: Loop residents of Chicago can live as much as sixteen years longer than their not-so-distant neighbors on the city's south side in Washington Park. In Richmond, Virginia, Gilpin residents can expect to live twenty years less than those in Westover Hills.[17] And in a telling example of racial and socioeconomic differences in the distribution of risk

---

[14] Sirleaf, "The Long-Term Cure for Ebola."
[15] M. Finkel, "Stranded on the Roof of the World," *National Geographic*, February 2013: 84–111.
[16] C. Ray, "Life Expectancy Declines in Appalachia," *Renew Appalachia*, June 20, 2011.
[17] VCU Center on Society and Health, "Mapping Life Expectancy," *VCU Center on Society and Health*, September 26, 2016 and November 12, 2015.

and vulnerability, the Katrina disaster revealed America's continuing struggle with health inequalities.[18]

These and countless other examples illustrate the grim reality: the burden of disease and ill health falls with profound inequality upon the world's peoples. That this reality is well known, covered in the press, and studied by scholars makes it no less appalling. While there has been much progress toward improving global health outcomes over the past several decades, global inequalities in adult and child mortality remain extreme; the gap is far from being closed, and the distribution of health burdens and benefits is drastically unequal. Mortality gaps between the richest and poorest countries are wide. Worldwide 99 percent of maternal deaths occur in developing countries.[19]

Although the average global life expectancy has increased by roughly twenty years in the past five decades, up from 48 in 1955, some of the poorest countries still lag behind, with average life expectancies of 55 or less (for example, Chad, Nigeria, Lesotho, Somalia, Côte d'Ivoire, Central African Republic, Angola, Sierra Leone). Mortality before the age of 5 in Somalia is over forty times higher than in Singapore; in Sierra Leone, a newborn girl will live thirty years fewer, on average, than one in Japan. Countries with high young-child mortality are making only slow progress toward reducing it.[20] Young adults in those states face the same likelihood of premature death, and some countries with the lowest life expectancies have actually lost ground, exhibiting a slower rate of improvement since 1990 than in some previous decades.[21] In countries like Lesotho and Swaziland, life expectancy actually decreased by at least ten years after 1990. The vast global inequality in HIV/AIDS prevalence and associated disability represents a global health failure in disease prevention, despite the significant and multilayered regime that evolved to address the pandemic and its consequences, especially in Africa.[22]

Various economic, social, political, and health sector variables, global and domestic, are associated with global health inequalities. Countries with high child mortality or low life expectancy, for example, have had on average lower mean incomes, more extreme poverty, lower investment in human and physical resources, higher inflation, less effective disease prevention, worse educational outcomes, more people living in rural areas, and greater health risk factors.[23]

---

[18] K. Wailoo, K. O'Neil, J. Dowd, and R. Anglin, *Katrina's Imprint: Race and Vulnerability in America* (Piscataway, NJ: Rutgers University Press, 2010).

[19] WHO, "Maternal Mortality, Fact Sheet," updated November 2016.

[20] World Bank, "Mortality Rate, Under-5," *World Development Indicators (WDI)*, 2017.

[21] World Bank, *World DataBank: World Development Indicators*, 2017.

[22] S. Harman, "15 Years of 'War on AIDS': What Impact has the Global HIV/AIDS Response had on the Political Economy of Africa?" *Review of African Political Economy* 42, no. 145 (2015): 467–76; A. S. Patterson, ed., *The African State and the AIDS Crisis (Global Health)* (London: Ashgate, 2005).

[23] J. P. Ruger and H.-J. Kim, "Global Health Inequalities: An International Comparison," *Journal of Epidemiology and Community Health* 60, no. 11 (2006): 928–36.

More specifically, these countries have had some of the world's highest percentages of populations living on less than a dollar per day; female adult illiteracy rates that approach, and sometimes exceed, 45 percent; and gross national income per capita that is hardly more than 2 percent of the United States'. Some countries have fewer than one hospital bed per thousand people, lower numbers of outpatient visits and doctors, and many among their rural populations have no access to decent sanitation. While Organisation for Economic Co-operation and Development countries spent approximately $1,000–9,000 (purchasing power parity) per capita on health care in 2015, the Central African Republic spent $25 in 2014. Among the fifteen countries with the highest neonatal mortality worldwide, fourteen experience political instability or chronic conflict.[24]

Health inequalities can be widespread and dramatic not just between countries but within them as well.[25] People living in rural areas in middle- and low-income countries have experienced higher rates of under-5 mortality as compared to those in urban settings.[26] Inequalities in childhood health can have an impact on inequalities in health and economic status well into adulthood.[27,28] Differences in life prospects by socioeconomic status threaten the viability and sustainability of domestic economic systems, as poverty, disease, hunger, and accompanying social ills simultaneously reduce government revenues and require more government programs. Such findings demonstrate that the wide inequality in both child and adult mortality reflects gaps in living conditions and standards as well as health care and public health systems between and within the richest and poorest countries. The recent Zika virus epidemic, for example, exposed significant inequalities in the Brazilian health care system, particularly in its treatment of women.[29] It is important to address health needs on multiple fronts with an integrated set of strategies, especially in countries where poverty, hunger, gender discrimination, unsafe occupational and travel conditions, inadequate education, and environmental ruin are prominent and deleterious social determinants of health.

[24] P. H. Wise and G. L. Darmstadt, "Confronting Stillbirths and Newborn Deaths in Areas of Conflict and Political Instability: A Neglected Global Imperative," *Paediatrics and International Child Health* 35, no. 3 (August 2015): 220–6.

[25] P. Braveman and E. Tarimo, "Social Inequalities in Health within Countries: Not Only an Issue for Affluent Nations," *Social Science & Medicine* 54 (2002): 1621–35.

[26] G. Fink and K. Hill, "Urbanization and Child Mortality: Evidence from the Demographic and Health Surveys," Commission on Investing in Health Working Paper, 2013.

[27] A. Case and C. Paxson, "Causes and Consequences of Early-Life Health," *Demography* 47 (2010): S65–85.

[28] M. M. Black, S. P. Walker, L. C. Fernald, C. T. Andersen, A. M. DiGirolamo, C. Lu, et al. "Early Childhood Development Coming of Age: Science through the Life Course," *The Lancet* 389, no. 10064 (2016): 77–90.

[29] D. Diniz, S. Gumieri, B. G. Bevilacqua, R. J. Cook, and B. M. Dickens, "Zika Virus Infection in Brazil and Human Rights Obligations," *International Journal of Gynecology & Obstetrics* 136, no. 1 (January 2017): 105–10.

Interest in health inequality among countries has grown substantially over the past several decades. WHO,[30] World Bank,[31] United Nations Children's Fund (UNICEF),[32] Pan American Health Organization,[33] United Nations Development Programme (UNDP),[34] UK Department of International Development,[35] and the broader global health community[36] have made this issue a priority. Almost two decades ago, the Rockefeller Foundation report *Challenging Inequities in Health: From Ethics to Action* published results from the Global Health Equity Initiative examining social inequalities in health in thirteen countries.[37] In 2000 the WHO Commission on Macroeconomics and Health was created and chaired by Jeffrey Sachs, and in 2005, WHO formed its Commission on Social Determinants of Health, chaired by Michael Marmot, concentrating on identifying interventions and policies to reduce global health inequalities.

Much work has focused on health inequality within and between both industrialized and developing countries. Research has examined the determinants of average health, the global burden of disease,[38] the conceptualization and measurement of poverty worldwide,[39] global health convergence,[40] differences in health outcomes among population groups from an epidemiological perspective,[41] and the relationship between the social determinants of

[30] WHO, *How Health Systems Can Address Health Inequities Linked to Migration and Ethnicity* (Copenhagen: WHO Regional Office for Europe, 2010); WHO, *The World Health Report 1999: Making a Difference* (Geneva: WHO, 1999).

[31] World Bank, *World Development Report 2006: Equity and Development* (New York: Oxford University Press, 2005); 2005; O. O'Donnell, E. van Doorslaer, A. Wagstaff, and M. Lindelow, *Analyzing Health Equity Using Household Survey Data: A Guide to Techniques and their Implementation* (Washington DC: World Bank, 2008); D. Gwatkin, "Health Inequalities and the Health of the Poor: What Do We Know? What Can We Do?" *Bulletin of the World Health Organization* 78, no. 1 (2000): 3–17.

[32] I. Ortiz and M. Cummins, "Global Inequality: Beyond the Bottom Billion—A Rapid Review of Income Distribution in 141 Countries," UNICEF Social and Economic Policy Working Paper, 2011.

[33] Ministers of Health of the Americas, *Health Agenda for the Americas 2008–2017* (Panama City: Ministers of Health of the Americas, 2007).

[34] UNDP, *Humanity Divided: Confronting Inequality in Developing Countries* (New York: UNDP Bureau for Development Policy, 2013); UNDP, *Human Development Report 2011: Sustainability and Equity—A Better Future for All* (New York: UNDP, 2011).

[35] UK Department for International Development (DFID), *Health Position Paper: Delivering Health Results* (London: DFID, 2013).

[36] Special Theme - Inequalities in Health, *Bulletin of the World Health Organization* 78, no. 1 (2000).

[37] The Rockefeller Foundation, *Challenging Inequities in Health: From Ethics to Action* (New York: Swedish International Development Cooperation Agency, 1999).

[38] Institute for Health Metrics and Evaluation (IHME), *Global Burden of Disease (GBD)* (Seattle: University of Washington, 2017).

[39] A. Sen, *Inequality Reexamined* (Cambridge, MA: Harvard University Press, 1992); World Bank, *World Development Report (WDR) 2000/2001: Attacking Poverty* (New York: Oxford University Press, 2000); World Bank, *WDR 2006: Equity and Development* (New York: Oxford University Press, 2005).

[40] D. T. Jamison, L. H. Summers, G. Alleyne, K. J. Arrow, S. Berkley, A. Binagwaho, et al., "Global Health 2035: A World Converging within a Generation," *The Lancet* 382 (2013): 1898–955.

[41] C. L. Murray, K. F. Ortblad, C. Guinovart, S. S. Lim, T. M. Wolock, D. A. Roberts, et al., "Global, Regional, and National Incidence and Mortality for HIV, Tuberculosis, and Malaria during

health and observed health inequalities,[42] among many important topics.[43] Despite many declarations about global health equity in publications,[44] reports,[45] statements,[46,47] and official policy documents,[48,49,50,51] however, the concept of global health equity in public health has been fraught with normative indeterminacy, with little "actionable normative guidance to public health policy-makers, practitioners and researchers."[52] These theoretical problems lead to unpredictable and contradictory efforts to address global health inequalities, and paradoxically maintain or even exacerbate them.[53]

"Language [about health equity] is important,"[54] Michael Marmot and Jessica Allen note. One public health definition states that health inequities are health differences which are "unnecessary and avoidable, but in addition, are considered unfair and unjust," a definition that sounds reasonable but still requires an account of what inequalities should be seen as unjust or unfair.[55] Forming a foundation for guiding research and public policy requires theoretical work on equity, justice, and responsibility in global health.

A critical underpinning is discerning questions of justice raised by global health. The mere mention of the words "equity," "justice," or "fairness" does not constitute such critical scrutiny; nor do public actions such as humanitarianism

1990–2013: A Systematic Analysis for the Global Burden of Disease Study 2013," *The Lancet* 384, no. 9947 (2014): 1005–70.

[42] M. Marmot, "Social Determinants of Health Inequalities," *The Lancet* 365, no. 9464 (2005): 1099–104.

[43] R. G. Wilkinson, *Unhealthy Societies: The Afflictions of Inequality* (London: Routledge, 1996); J. P. Mackenbach, A. E. Kunst, A. E. Cavelaars, F. Groenhof, and J. J. M. Guerts, "EU Working Group on Socioeconomic Inequalities in Health: Socioeconomic Inequalities in Morbidity and Mortality in Western Europe," *The Lancet* 349, no. 9066 (1997): 1655–9; A. E. Kunst, J. J. M. Geurts, and J. den Berg, "International Variation in Socioeconomic Inequalities in Self-Reported Health," *Journal of Epidemiology and Community Health* 49, no. 2 (1995): 117–23.

[44] F. P. Grad, "The Preamble of the Constitution of the World Health Organization," *Bulletin of the World Health Organization* 80 (2002): 981–4.

[45] WHO, *World Health Report 2003: Shaping the Future* (Geneva: WHO, 2003).

[46] WHO, Declaration of Alma Ata (Alma-Ata: International Conference on Primary Health Care, 1978).

[47] H. Mahler, "The Meaning of 'Health for All by the Year 2000'," *World Health Forum* 2 (1981): 36–8.

[48] WHO, *Basic Documents, Forty-fifth Edition, Supplement, October 2006, Constitution of the World Health Organization* (New York: WHO, 2006).

[49] UN Committee on Economic, Social, and Cultural Rights, *General Comment No. 14: The Right to the Highest Attainable Standard of Health* (Geneva: Office of the UN High Commissioner for Human Rights, 2000).

[50] UN, *International Covenant on Economic, Social and Cultural Rights* (New York: United Nations, 1966).

[51] CDC, *CDC Health Disparities and Inequalities Report, 2013* (Atlanta: CDC, 2013).

[52] M. J. Smith, "Health Equity in Public Health: Clarifying our Commitment," *Public Health Ethics* 8, no. 2 (2014): 173–84.

[53] Ibid.

[54] M. Marmot and J. J. Allen, "Social Determinants of Health Equity," *American Journal of Public Health* 104, no. S4 (2014): S517–9.

[55] Smith, "Health Equity in Public Health," quoting M. Whitehead, "The Concepts and Principles of Equity and Health," *International Journal of Health Services* 22, no. 3 (1992): 433.

adequately address inequalities without a strong theoretical footing. Grounding the empirical study of cross-national health inequalities in an ethical approach—for example, employing clustering techniques to stratify countries into mortality groups of different levels (better off, worse off, mid-level) and examining inequality-associated risk factors from a normative reference point—enables the international community, including multilateral institutions like WHO and the World Bank, to devise multifaceted policies and interventions to reduce the mortality gap between countries. It is important to examine what empirical evidence regarding health inequalities reveals about injustices in health and well-being.[56] Building on work that examined and sought to clarify the normative and empirical structure of social justice to guide domestic health policy,[57] this current book researches such features of global justice to guide global health policy.

It is important to understand why global health inequalities are morally troubling, if they are at all; why efforts to reduce them are morally justified; how they should be measured, evaluated, addressed, and prevented;[58] how much priority disadvantaged groups should receive; and what roles and responsibilities global and national actors must assume.[59]

## 1.2 Problems of Global Health Externalities

In November 2002, a mysterious illness, described as atypical pneumonia, broke out in China's Guangdong province. By mid-February 2003, hundreds of Guangdong residents had fallen ill, and several had died. On February 21, a Chinese doctor who had treated Guangdong patients checked into the Metropole Hotel in Hong Kong. He developed symptoms and died several days later. Meanwhile, a Chinese-American businessman, who occupied a room across the hall from the Guangdong doctor, left Hong Kong for Hanoi, where he too became ill and died in mid-March. Two weeks later, Dr. Carlo Urbani, an infectious disease specialist who attended the businessman at the Hanoi hospital, also died—in Bangkok, where he was attending a medical conference. Dr. Urbani had been the first to report the new disease to WHO.

---

[56] A. Deaton, "What Does the Empirical Evidence Tell Us about the Injustice of Health Inequalities?" Social Science Research Network Working Paper Series, 2011.

[57] J. P. Ruger, "Aristotelian Justice and Health Policy: Capability and Incompletely Theorized Agreements," PhD dissertation, Harvard University, 1998; J. P. Ruger, "Health and Social Justice," *The Lancet* 364, no. 9439 (2004): 1075–80; J. P. Ruger, "Social Justice and Health Policy: Aristotle, Capability and Incompletely Theorized Agreements," Paper presented at Health Policy Doctoral Seminar Series, Harvard University, Boston, MA, November 25, 1997; J. P. Ruger, *Health and Social Justice* (Oxford: Oxford University Press, 2009).

[58] J. P. Ruger, "Ethics and Governance of Global Health Inequalities," *Journal of Epidemiology and Community Health* 60, no. 11 (2006): 998–1003.

[59] J. P. Ruger, "Global Health Justice," *Public Health Ethics* 2, no. 3 (2009): 261–75.

On March 12, WHO issued a global health alert about severe acute respiratory syndrome (SARS). Three days later, it issued a travel advisory after Singapore and Canada joined the list of affected nations. By March 24, the USA had identified thirty-nine suspected cases of the new illness. "At this moment," an April 11 WHO status report said, "public health authorities, physicians and scientists around the world are struggling to cope with a severe and rapidly spreading new disease in humans, severe acute respiratory syndrome, or SARS. This appears to be the first severe and easily transmissible new disease to emerge in the 21st century. Though much about the disease remains poorly understood...we do know that it has features that allow it to spread rapidly along international air travel routes. As of 10 April, 2781 SARS cases, with 111 deaths, have been reported to WHO from 17 countries on three continents."[60] By summer 2003, SARS appeared to have run its course.

In May 2007, for the first time since quarantining a smallpox patient in 1963, the United States government isolated a man under Centers for Disease Control and Prevention (CDC) auspices. Officials believed Andrew Speaker, from Atlanta, Georgia, had extensively drug-resistant tuberculosis (XDR-TB). XDR-TB is transmissible by air to others nearby and is deadly, especially when coupled with another illness; one South African study found that it killed approximately 98 percent of its victims.[61]

Speaker's extensive travels complicated the case. His itinerary included two transatlantic flights, five flights within Europe, and at least one cross-national car ride. He travelled from the USA through France, Greece, Italy, Czech Republic, and Canada before returning home.[62] During his flights, he could have infected other passengers, especially those within two rows of his seat. Even before he left on his trip, county and federal health department officials and Speaker himself believed he had multidrug-resistant TB (MDR-TB). Fulton County health officials claim he disregarded their warning that he could be a danger to others.[63] Speaker says county officials told him he was not contagious.[64] Officials issued a written directive against travel, but because Speaker allegedly moved his departure date up two days, they did not deliver it to him before he left.[65]

---

[60] WHO, "Update 27: One Month into the Global SARS Outbreak," *Global Alert and Response (GAR)*, April 11, 2003.

[61] N. R. Gandhi, A. Moll, A. W. Sturm, R. Pawinski, T. Govender, U. Lalloo, et al., "Extensively Drug-Resistant Tuberculosis as a Cause of Death in Patients Co-Infected with Tuberculosis and HIV in a Rural Area of South Africa," *The Lancet* 368, no. 9547 (2006): 1575–80.

[62] US CDC, "Flight Itinerary of U.S. Traveler with Extensively Drug-Resistant Tuberculosis (XDR TB)," *CDC*, May 30, 2007.

[63] J. Schwartz, "Tangle of Conflicting Accounts in TB Patient's Odyssey," *New York Times*, June 2, 2007.

[64] D. Grady, "TB Patient Says Officials Are Trying to Blame Him to Cover Mistakes," *New York Times*, June 9, 2007.

[65] Schwartz, "Tangle of Conflicting Accounts."

After his departure, health officials concluded that he had the even more serious XDR-TB, an extremely rare disease: the USA recorded only forty-nine cases between 1993 and 2006.[66] (Doctors publicly downgraded Speaker's diagnosis from XDR-TB to MDR-TB in July 2007.) After the diagnosis, the CDC contacted him in Rome, reportedly telling him not to take commercial flights. Speaker left Rome by commercial flight to Montreal and drove into the USA. An agent at the Canadian–USA border permitted him to pass, despite knowing that health authorities sought him.

The SARS and XDR-TB cases illustrate clearly how today's globalized world has swept aside the barriers that once might have protected us from a disease outbreak on the far side of the Earth. Across hotel hallways, in the air of an international flight, through the care of a health worker unknowingly infected, in the cells of people traveling worldwide, pathogens can circle the globe with startling speed and kill indiscriminately.

Globalization offers both opportunities and challenges for global health and its distribution.[67] It enhances prospects for health improvement through the spread of medical and public health knowledge and technology from one part of the globe to another, in the sharing of best practices, health promotion and prevention strategies, and medical treatments.[68] Further, all countries can benefit from international norms and standards and sustained global advocacy for health. Outside the health sector, the benefits of globalization range from progress on gender empowerment and human rights to better prospects for trade, information technology,[69] and economic growth.[70]

But globalization has also accelerated the spread of infectious diseases, as the rapid outbreaks of SARS, influenza A (H1N1), Ebola, and Zika show, and raises other threats, as in the Speaker case. Infamously, the failure to prevent HIV/AIDS led to a pandemic of historic proportions. These increasingly potent health externalities are pressing and pose significant and potentially deadly health threats to all, regardless of nationality. The spread of disease across borders presents substantial challenges beyond the capacity of individual states to manage. Globalization also facilitates biological, chemical, and

[66] MMWR, "Extensively Drug-Resistant Tuberculosis: United States, 1993–2006," *Morbidity and Mortality Weekly Report* 56, no. 11 (March 23, 2007): 250–3.

[67] E. Zedillo, ed., *The Future of Globalization: Explorations in Light of Recent Turbulence* (New York: Routledge, 2014); D. Yach and D. Bettcher, "The Globalization of Public Health I: Threats and Opportunities," *American Journal of Public Health* 88, no. 5 (1998): 735–8.

[68] V. Govindarajan and C. Trimble, *Reverse Innovation: Create Far from Home, Win Everywhere* (Boston, MA: Harvard Business Review Press, 2012); World Bank, *WDR 2000/2001*.

[69] UNDP, *Human Development Report 1999: Globalization with a Human Face* (New York: Oxford University Press, 1999).

[70] P. Samimi and H. S. Jenatabadi, "Globalization and Economic Growth: Empirical Evidence on the Role of Complementarities," *PLoS One* 9, no. 4 (2014): e87824; W. D. Savedoff and T. P. Schultz, eds., *Wealth from Health: Linking Social Investments to Earnings in Latin America* (Washington, DC: Inter-American Development Bank, 2000).

radiological warfare, which raise a host of ethical challenges.[71] It has fostered global marketing of unhealthy consumption patterns and products and exposed failures in influenza vaccine access across the globe. And the challenges of twenty-first-century globalization link to global inequality, not just in health but other economic and social indicators as well.

The distribution of health benefits from the globalization process depends significantly on preexisting economic, social, and political conditions within countries, the fairness of trade and investment agreements, existing political economy, and the strength of the multilateral global health system. Globalization's substantial problems exceed the management capacity of individual states. Avoiding the perpetuation of a group of countries excluded from most of the global economy's benefits requires multifaceted and sustained effort by the international community. The problems of global health are linked with global justice and the institutions governing the international order.

The international spread of pathogenic health risks reflects global health governance failures to respond effectively and to prevent local health harms from becoming worldwide risks. They threaten individuals' ability to be and stay healthy, and in many cases even to survive. These arbitrary negative externalities are morally troubling; together with health inequalities, they present compelling moral imperatives. International and national responses to health externalities should arise from ethical values about risks to health and their distribution. Ethical claims have the power to increase understanding of and commitment to principles; to delineate duties and responsibilities; and to hold global and national actors morally responsible for achieving common goals. Prior efforts toward health cooperation around specific communicable diseases—plague, cholera, and yellow fever, for example—were grounded largely in concerns about trade, travel, national and global security, and the national interests of wealthy countries. They did not establish a sound normative basis for global health.

## 1.3 Cross-Border Problems in Global Health

The European Union (EU) illustrates yet a third category of global health problems. In accordance with the EU's subsidiarity principle, its nation-members, integrated in many ways, nevertheless remain independent states, each with a unique approach to health and health care provision. This subsidiarity principle limits union-wide legislation only to those areas where it is either uniquely capable of acting or more effective than national, regional, or

---

[71] J. D. Moreno, ed., *In the Wake of Terror: Medicine and Morality in a Time of Crisis* (Boston, MA: MIT Press, 2003).

local action. (The related proportionality principle declares that EU action can only extend to the level necessary to reach agreed-upon goals.)

Consider, then, the Hungarian who suffers a heart attack while on business in the Netherlands. He carries a European Health Insurance Card, which guarantees medically necessary care for him and reimbursement for the provider. But Hungary, his country of insurance, reimburses less than €1,000 for acute myocardial infarction treatment, while the Netherlands reimburses nearly €9,000 for the same procedure. How much will the Dutch provider be reimbursed? Indeed, will the Dutch provider hesitate or even refuse to treat the Hungarian traveler, if she believes the reimbursement will be just a fraction of the bill? Across the EU, there are wide reimbursement differences for many health needs and little clarity about how the responsibility for reimbursement should be managed. "A standardized 'European' accounting methodology right down to provider level might be justified and 'necessary', but enforcing one methodology conflicts with the principle of subsidiarity."[72]

Patients in EU nations seek care elsewhere in the Union for a variety of reasons. Capacity in their home countries might be limited, causing lengthy waiting periods for needed surgery. Northern Europeans retire to the south but remain citizens of their native countries. Vacationers fall ill on holiday. Border-area residents are often closer to medical facilities in neighboring countries than in their own. Quality of care might be higher in an adjacent country. Inequalities in health outcomes remain high across the zone: infant mortality in some EU states is more than five times the rate in others; life expectancy varies as much as fourteen years for men and eight years for women.[73] Health governance and health system capacity, including the quality and quantity of health workers, can differ significantly among states.

For these reasons and others, member states' health systems, their patients and providers confront tough and sometimes unanswerable questions. When a citizen of France needs care in Germany, does the French "benefits basket" apply, or the German? What about countries without universal health care: Is care provided elsewhere to their citizens reimbursed? What procedures must a patient follow before accessing services in another country? Can a transborder patient select among all providers, or are there limits? Does the patient pay for care in another country and then seek reimbursement, or does the provider bill the home country insurance directly? What about cost-sharing: Does the patient co-pay at the level of the country of insurance or the country of

---

[72] R. Busse, E. van Ginneken, J. Schreyögg, and M. V. Garrido, "Benefit Baskets and Tariffs", in *Cross-Border Health Care in the European Union*, ed. M. Wismar, W. Palm, J. Figueras, K. Ernst, and E. van Ginneken (Copenhagen: WHO, 2011), 91–120; 107.

[73] Commission of the European Communities, "Solidarity in Health: Reducing Health Inequalities in the EU," Communication from the Commission to the European Parliament, the Council, the European Economic and Social Committee and the Committee of the Regions, 2009.

service? How do health systems oversee training, process, and outcome quality?

Additional problems with counterfeit drugs, health worker migration, and the overuse of antibiotics represent significant differences across countries in access to and the quality of health care and public health goods and services. And medical tourism,[74] as well as organ allocation and transplantation,[75] are related phenomena that extend worldwide.

The EU thus paints a clear continental picture of a global reality: where one falls ill or sustains an injury might well mean the difference between quality care, substandard care, or no care at all; between full recovery, permanent ill effects, and death. Public health and health care systems capacity and governance vary considerably across the globe. Like rapidly spreading contagions and global inequalities, this arbitrary patchwork of health systems and services is morally troubling. Yet again, reality prods our collective conscience: How and why might these conditions be unjust? Does justice require a conception of global health citizenship by which any individual on the planet can be in any country with the assurance that conditions exist to promote her health and prevent disease and injury? Global health citizenship entails equal guarantees to the opportunity to be healthy, and quality public health services and health care everywhere. While this goal is not currently within reach, it is an important aspiration for a global health theory.

---

[74] I. G. Cohen, *Patients with Passports: Medical Tourism, Law, and Ethics* (New York: Oxford University Press, 2015).

[75] I. G. Cohen, "Organs without Borders? Allocating Transplant Organs, Foreigners, and the Importance of the Nation-State(?)," *Law and Contemporary Problems* 77, no. 175 (2014): 175–215.

# 2

# Global Health Governance Problems

## 2.1 Global Institutions

Each of these sets of global health problems—inequalities, externalities, cross-border issues—has a potential resolution in the behavior of global and domestic actors. While the state remains the most important actor in both domestic politics and international relations, global actors, both state-based and nongovernmental, play an increasingly important role. The United Nations (UN) system itself, including the World Bank and World Health Organization (WHO), is responsible for a number of global arrangements that directly and indirectly impact the global health problems described in Chapter 1. Yet different actors have different levels of interest in these global health problems. States approach global health problems in terms of foreign policy, concerned with those that most directly affect their national interests, and are amenable to minimal interventions through bilateral action; multilateral collective action is a second choice. They focus on externalities that pose direct and dangerous threats of transmission to their own populations. Other problems, embedded in global health inequalities and cross-border issues, involve more difficult solutions such as the development and good governance of public health and health care systems.

This book presents a theoretical framework for evaluating global and domestic policies, practices, and institutions. How do they distribute benefits and burdens? What are their priorities and how are disagreements about priority setting resolved? Are these distributions and the associated policies, institutions, and practices just? Are they based on evidence of effective investments or on political priorities? Do certain diseases or conditions, such as HIV/AIDS or other communicable diseases, receive a disproportionate share of resources and consideration? If the global institutional order is not just, how might it be reformed, or gaps be filled by the creation of new institutions and policies?

Are existing institutions, along with relevant processes and rules, sufficient to address contemporary and future global health problems? Global health governance (GHG) produces suboptimal results in both individual and population health. How can we move our world toward a more just set of global and domestic actions and arrangements?

## 2.2 From International Health Governance to Global Health Governance

For many decades in the nineteenth and twentieth centuries, international health was the purview of states and multilateral organizations with state members, beginning with a focus on cooperation among states to control the spread of communicable diseases—yellow fever, cholera, and the plague—to protect trade and travel. Thereafter collective action focused on specific health problems related to cross-border issues such as military victims, trade in alcohol, border-area water pollution, and, later, occupational safety and health exposures and injuries, none of which were foremost in states' foreign policies.[1] Health funding flowed between donor and recipient governments. National ministries had responsibility for health services delivery.

In 1948, WHO was established and has since advanced the rhetoric of "Health for All" and of the right to the highest attainable standard of health. Mired in powerful states' political interests and its own ineffectiveness, however, WHO has largely failed to effectuate these ideals. A limited set of partners has coordinated effectively with WHO on global efforts like smallpox eradication, successfully eliminating the disease, and on onchocerciasis, yaws, and global immunization programs. WHO has also used the International Health Regulations (IHR) to manage international reporting and disease outbreaks.[2] For some decades, the international health architecture—more recently termed "the multilateral health regime,"[3] or "horizontal germ governance"[4]—was relatively uncomplicated, with significantly fewer actors and straightforward responsibilities. Health efforts required less coordination, because emerging and re-emerging infectious diseases did not spread globally as they do now, and WHO achievements in smallpox gave it credibility and authority; states therefore followed WHO's lead. Advanced states applied their medical and

---

[1] D. P. Fidler, "The Globalization of Public Health: The First 100 Years of International Health Diplomacy," *Bulletin of the World Health Organization* 79, no. 9 (2001): 842–9.

[2] S. E. Davies, A. Kamradt-Scott, and S. Rushton, *Disease Diplomacy: International Norms and Global Health Security* (Baltimore, MD: Johns Hopkins University Press, 2015).

[3] M. W. Zacher, "Part II—Global Challenges and Responses: The Transformation in Global Health Collaboration since the 1990s," in A. Cooper, J. Kirton, and T. Schrecker, eds., *Governing Global Health: Challenge, Response, Innovation* (Burlington, VT, and Aldershot: Ashgate Publishing, 2007), 15–27.

[4] D. P. Fidler, "Germs, Governance, and Global Public Health in the Wake of SARS," *Journal of Clinical Investigation* 113, no. 6 (2004): 799–804.

administrative capacities to control outbreaks and defend their borders.[5] The system operated—for powerful Western states—but critics have suggested it neglected the interests of other countries.[6]

On another front, the Declaration of Alma-Ata in 1978, calling for universal access to primary health care, was unsuccessful. As a humanitarian effort, this approach failed to create a new international order, but rather reflected existing geopolitical concerns of powerful states and significant East–West friction in international relations. "Health for All" and international health more generally were not major foreign policy issues for powerful countries. Thus, neither the great powers nor the multilateral system gave international health significant priority.

WHO's first decades showed that the old structures were inadequate for a swiftly globalizing planet, where national economies are increasingly interdependent and people and products move rapidly worldwide. Infectious diseases emerging or re-emerging anywhere can have repercussions everywhere, and such contagions quickly became national and global security issues. Thus began the more complex GHG era, in which new actors, programs, initiatives, and regimes have proliferated and new funding has exploded. Very often these activities are uncoordinated and their effectiveness is questionable. Multiple different regimes impacting international health have evolved in human rights, labor and trade, the environment, economic development, and humanitarianism. Only in the past several years have scholars attempted a definition of "global health."[7]

Multiplying non-state actors have emerged. For example, the Global Fund to Fight AIDS, Tuberculosis and Malaria (Global Fund) includes non-state actor representatives on its board of directors, and the revised WHO IHR includes surveillance information from nongovernmental sources. GHG's diffuse, non-hierarchical nature is evident in the language observers use—"post-Westphalian,"[8] "nodal,"[9] "open-source anarchy,"[10] a "regime complex,"[11] and

---

[5] M. W. Zacher, "The Transformation in Global Health Collaboration since the 1990s," in A. Cooper, J. Kirton, and T. Schrecker, eds., *Governing Global Health: Challenge, Response, Innovation* (Burlington, VT, and Aldershot: Ashgate Publishing, 2007), 16–29.

[6] O. Aginam, "Between Isolationism and Mutual Vulnerability: A South–North Perspective on Global Governance of Epidemics in an Age of Globalization," *Temple Law Review* 77 (2004): 297; N. Howard-Jones, "Origins of International Health Work," *British Medical Journal* 1, no. 4661 (1950): 1032–7.

[7] J. P. Koplan, T. C. Bond, M. H. Merson, K. S. Reddy, M. H. Rodriguez, N. K. Sewankambo, et al., "Towards a Common Definition of Global Health," *The Lancet* 373, no. 9679 (2009): 1993–5.

[8] Aginam, "Between Isolationism and Mutual Vulnerability," 308.

[9] S. Burris, P. Drahos, and C. Shearing, "Nodal Governance," *Australian Journal of Legal Philosophy* 30 (2005): 30–58.

[10] D. Fidler, "Architecture amidst Anarchy: Global Health's Quest for Governance," *Global Health Governance* 1, no. 1 (2007): 1–17.

[11] K. Raustiala and D. G. Victor, "The Regime Complex for Plant Genetic Resources," *International Organization* 58, no. 2 (2004): 277–309.

a "complex adaptive system."[12] Non-state actors, including the media, have begun to provide information to international organizations, in the cases of severe acute respiratory syndrome (SARS) and avian flu, for example, even contradicting state actors such as China, Thailand, and Indonesia. By providing important information, non-state actors' surveillance information incidentally has assisted WHO as it seeks to manage these global pandemics.

Disease-specific programs mushroomed particularly around HIV/AIDS (the Global Fund and Joint United Nations Programme on HIV/AIDS (UNAIDS)) and tobacco control with the Framework Convention on Tobacco Control (FCTC). Rather than building on prior UN and WHO programs, political interests created and drove new initiatives. This expansion of actors has injected new resources and ideas, different processes and principles, but it also "blur[s] lines of responsibility"[13] and encourages a scramble for resources and leadership. It further challenges WHO's role as an institution responsible for collective action, technical assistance, and normative principles. Though some claim this multiplication of actors results in enhanced cooperation, competition among non-state, state, and intergovernmental actors permeates these complex relationships.

As a result, GHG lacks any clear structure. It does not clearly delineate roles for states, UN organizations (UNOs), international organizations, civil society organizations (CSOs), and public–private partnerships (PPPs). These actors often serve simultaneously as program funders, initiators, implementers, monitors, and evaluators. As just one example: the Global Fund, financed by state governments, philanthropic foundations, nongovernmental organizations (NGOs), and corporate initiatives, disburses resources to national governments, which work with donors and CSOs to design plans, and may implement those plans with these actors' assistance. Some argue that there is simply "no architecture of global health."[14] Others characterize GHG as three concentric circles of actors: the World Bank and WHO at the center; countries, the International Monetary Fund (IMF), and other UNOs in the next ring; and NGOs, multinational corporations (MNCs), epistemic communities (or networks of experts), and individuals in the outermost ring.[15]

[12] P. Hill, "Understanding Global Health Governance as a Complex Adaptive System," *Global Public Health* 6, no. 6 (2010): 593–605.

[13] I. Kickbusch, "The Development of International Health Policies: Accountability Intact?" *Social Science and Medicine* 51, no. 6 (2000): 979–89.

[14] B. Bloom, Dean of Harvard University's School of Public Health, cited in J. Cohen, "The New World of Global Health," *Science* 311, no. 5758 (2006): 162–7.

[15] N. Drager and L. Sunderland, "Public Health in a Globalising World: The Perspective from the World Health Organization," in A. F. Cooper, J. J. Kirton, and T. Schrecker, eds., *Governing Global Health* (Burlington, VT, and Aldershot: Ashgate Publishing, 2007), 67–78.

Indeed, GHG often seems more like a three-ring circus than three concentric circles: the operational chaos is indisputable. A burgeoning landscape of fragmented global health processes impedes an effective and efficient integration of resources, interests, and approaches to address global health problems. The WHO World Health Assembly (WHA) is now just one process for global health decision-making. In many respects the WHA is eclipsed by newer mechanisms that work bilaterally (for example, the President's Emergency Plan for AIDS Relief (PEPFAR)), regionally (for example, the European Union (EU)), or through alternative structures (for example, Gavi, the Global Alliance for Vaccines and Immunizations; Global Fund; or the Bill and Melinda Gates Foundation). Fierce competition among actors and priorities results in end runs around national governments and the UN system. Disruptions in national planning, duplication, and waste plague GHG. If actors don't get what they want in one venue, they move to another: failing to get favorable intellectual property (IP) protections for medicines from WHO, for example, actors simply moved to the World Trade Organization (WTO). UN agencies, too, compete for funds, so often no objective, impartial organization exists to seek the common good or agree upon global health processes. Even as non-state actors increasingly define GHG, traditional international health governance (IHG) actors prove difficult to displace and continue to dominate health governance. NGOs and PPPs can be flexible, innovative, cost-effective, and more accountable, but these actors exhibit their own dysfunctions and may create new complications even as they solve others.[16]

GHG is increasingly political and decreasingly technical and scientific. The theories and methods of foreign policy and international relations are eclipsing those of science, epidemiology, medicine, and public health. In the USA, for example, the Obama administration used global health as a component of its smart power in foreign policy,[17] and an Institute of Medicine Committee, co-chaired by Thomas Pickering and Harold Varmus, recommended that the USA improve internal and external coordination, increase global health financial contributions, and make global health an important component of American foreign policy.[18]

---

[16] For an introduction to global health governance, see S. Harman, *Global Health Governance* (Oxford: Routledge, 2012), and for a description of the evolution of global health governance, see J. Youde, *Global Health Governance* (Cambridge: Polity Press, 2012).

[17] M. Otero, *Smart Power: Applications and Lessons for Development* (Washington DC: American University, 2010).

[18] H. Varmus, "U.S. Commitment to Global Health," David E. Barnes Lecture in Global Health, US National Institutes of Health, 2008.

## 2.3 Development Assistance for Health[19]

Development assistance for health (DAH) a form of foreign aid, has grown massively over the past few decades. Levels of and contributors to global health financing have increased at an unprecedented pace, with an emphasis on funds for HIV/AIDS; maternal, newborn, and child health; malaria; and tuberculosis. DAH nearly quintupled from 1990 to 2012 (from $5.7 billion to $28.1 billion),[20] though now may have peaked. Proliferating DAH actors now number 175-plus major global health agencies and organizations, 15 percent of which are private entities, such as the Bill and Melinda Gates Foundation, other not-for-profit organizations, and PPPs. Governments are still DAH's largest source.

While increased aid is essential and welcome, these DAH system developments raise numerous ethical questions. The failure to demonstrate these investments' effectiveness is a major GHG problem. Other questions: Are these resources sustainable? Are expenditures focused correctly on key priorities? Who should decide and how should these decisions be made? Who should pay and receive these funds? How might the system address the epidemiological transition in many developing countries, where increasingly prevalent non-communicable diseases (NCDs) are adding to persistent inequalities in communicable diseases? Emerging nations' political and economic transitions also require attention as these countries claim greater independence in addressing their own health financing needs and extend their influence beyond their borders. The poorest countries depend most heavily upon DAH and suffer most from asymmetries in information and in power vis-à-vis the donor community. This context shapes global justice concerns. The debates about a post-Millennium Development Goals (MDG) and Sustainable Development Goals (SDG) health agenda have failed to analyze DAH's issues adequately, specifically whether DAH conforms to basic global justice principles.

The existing DAH system grew out of the post-World War II period of reconstruction and decolonization in which neoliberal principles of national interests, charity, or enlightened self-interest guided foreign aid from donors to recipients within a hierarchical and asymmetric relationship. Empirical evidence on donor priorities suggests that these motivations persist today. While proposals for DAH system changes have emerged, they have focused on more practical issues and have not adequately addressed critical global justice concerns. DAH's main problems, such as failure to enable developing

---

[19] This section stems from J. P. Ruger, "Ethics of Development Assistance for Health," *Hastings Center Report* 45, no. 3 (2015): 23–6.

[20] IHME, *Financing Global Health 2012: The End of the Golden Age?* (Seattle: IHME, 2012).

countries to help themselves, lie in its underlying values.[21] Addressing ethical questions thus requires changing fundamental DAH features.

### 2.3.1 *Foreign Aid, Public and Private*

Foreign aid, a key global governance function, involves transferring goods and services or money from donors to recipients in a foreign country as a donation, grant, or favorable-terms loan. These favorable terms include lengthy repayment schedules, grace periods, and below-market interest rates. Indeed, sometimes this aid is altogether unavailable commercially. Official Development Assistance (ODA) is the term the Organisation for Economic Co-operation and Development (OECD)'s Development Assistance Committee uses. The OECD defines ODA's main objective as the "promotion of the economic development and welfare of developing countries."[22]

Donor organizations are both public and private, the latter including foundations, corporations, and other private entities. Private aid involves voluntary donations from organizations and individuals to recipient individuals and groups. Governments comprise the public sector. Public aid can be either bilateral aid, government to government assistance, or multilateral aid, whereby aid is distributed by an organization through which donors contribute funds. Government tax revenues fund public sector bilateral and multilateral aid. The largest public aid donors in terms of volume are the United States, United Kingdom, Germany, Japan, and France. Sweden, Norway, Denmark, Luxembourg, Germany, and the United Kingdom gave 0.7 percent ODA or more as a percentage of gross national income.[23] The largest single multilateral agency for development assistance remains the World Bank Group through the International Development Association (IDA) and International Bank for Reconstruction and Development (IBRD).[24] IDA provides zero or very low interest interest long-term loans (called credits) to the lowest income countries, and IBRD offers slightly below-market interest rates and medium-term loans to other developing countries, primarily middle-income ones. Given sufficient funds, development assistance, unlike humanitarian relief, can serve long-term goals to develop sustainable national systems.

---

[21] A. Deaton, *The Great Escape: Health, Wealth, and the Origins of Inequality* (Princeton, NJ: Princeton University Press, 2013); J. E. Stiglitz and B. C. Greenwald, *Creating a Learning Society* (New York: Columbia University Press, 2014); W. R. Easterly, *The White Man's Burden: Why the West's Efforts to Aid the Rest Have Done So Much Ill and So Little Good* (New York: Penguin Press, 2006).

[22] OECD, *Glossary of Statistical Terms: Official Development Assistance* (Paris: OECD, August 2003).

[23] OECD, "Development Aid Rises Again in 2016 but Flows to Poorest Countries Dip," *OECD* November 4, 2017.

[24] OECD, *Multilateral Aid 2015: Better Partnerships for a Post-2015 World* (Paris: OECD, July 2015).

## 2.3.2 Reasons Why Donors Provide Foreign Aid

Empirical research on donor motivations reveals multiple reasons and framings of the issue. First, while recipient need—as measured by disease prevalence, mortality rates, food security status, or a country's overall degree of poverty—can evoke sympathetic concern and beneficence and does motivate donors to provide aid, these are not the only or dominant motivations for donor assistance, nor does altruism necessarily produce effective aid.[25] Some benefit may accrue to the recipient under an altruism framing, and the recipient may be (although is not necessarily) better off with the aid than without it. But aid evaluation criteria rarely specify what type and how much benefit must result from foreign assistance. This framing does not require engaging the recipient country in determining its own needs and the best way to address them. Capacity constraints in many countries may hamper aid effectiveness, while countries with stronger policy environments may be better able to deploy foreign aid effectively.[26] Enhancing competencies in recipient countries is missing from this perspective, yet capacity building is critical to helping recipients get the most benefit from resources.

Recipient merit is a second framing for development assistance, but it too is not the dominant motivation. Donors conceptualize recipient merit variously in terms of human rights, anti-corruption,[27] or historical ties such as sharing a colonial past.[28] Similarly, a donor country might want to aid a country with a shared culture or language. This framing in part captures the desire to rectify past wrongs that have harmed a recipient country. Yet normative criteria don't exist against which to evaluate this type of aid. To what objective should donors direct such reparative efforts? Is restoring recipient countries to pre-harm conditions ethically acceptable or even possible?

Thirdly, some donors are motivated by development ideology, or simply follow what other countries or peer institutions do to gain credibility in the donor community. Development ideology is donor-driven, not recipient-driven.

---

[25] S. Feeny and M. McGillivray, "What Determines Bilateral Aid Allocations? Evidence from Time Series Data," *Review of Development Economics* 12, no. 3 (2008): 515–29; G. Greco, T. Powell-Jackson, J. Borghi, and A. Mills, "Countdown to 2015: Assessment of Donor Assistance to Maternal, Newborn, and Child Health between 2003 and 2006," *The Lancet* 371, no. 9620 (2008): 1268–75; C. Kuhlgatz, A. Abdulai, and C. B. Barnett, "Food Aid Allocation Policies: Coordination and Responsiveness to Recipient Country Needs," *Agricultural Economics* 41 (2010): 319–27; J. Youde, "The Relationships between Foreign Aid, HIV and Government Health Spending," *Health Policy and Planning* 25, no. 6 (2010): 523–8.

[26] P. Nunnenkamp and R. Thiele, "Targeting Aid to the Needy and Deserving: Nothing but Promises?" *The World Economy* 29, no. 9 (2006): 1177–201.

[27] B. Ouattara, J. A. Amegashie, and E. Strobl, "Moral Hazard and the Composition of Transfers: Theory with an Application to Foreign Aid," Proceedings of the German Development Economics Conference No. 24, Frankfurt am Main, 2009; W. Easterly, "Are Aid Agencies Improving?" *Economic Policy* 22, no. 52 (2007): 635–78.

[28] A. Alesina and D. Dollar, "Who Gives Foreign Aid to Whom and Why?" *Journal of Economic Growth* 5 (2000): 33–63.

It can focus on basic needs, poverty reduction, participatory approaches, or, as in the recipient-merit framing, on a good recipient policy environment. It can draw on development principles embodied in the OECD's Paris Declaration (2005) and Accra Agenda for Action (2008), which stress recipient involvement and ownership. A dominant development ideology for much of the post-World War II period has been the neoliberal "Washington Consensus" with its focus on free markets. The Washington Consensus and its variants have come under significant criticism recently, even among development economists.[29] Fluctuating development ideologies, which are often unsupported by empirical evidence, can do more harm than good.

Finally, empirical research overwhelmingly finds that donors provide aid for economic, military, and political reasons. Geopolitical power, regional peace and security, and trade relations are common motivations.[30] Gaining economically from aid allocations is a strong motivation, especially when donors seek access to natural resources or export markets[31] or to ensure contracts for their businesses in recipient countries. Security interests such as combating terrorism, ensuring a ceasefire, or supporting strategic alliances[32] pervade foreign aid. Donors deploy geopolitical power to support certain regimes and thus influence regional or global affairs both bilaterally, as was done during the Cold War, or through international organizations of the UN, World Bank, or IMF.[33] Analyses of the geographic distribution of aid by the World Bank and Asian Development Bank found linkages between these distributions and US geopolitical and commercial interests. UN Security Council temporary membership has been linked with greater access to IMF programs.[34] These motivations reflect a neorealist and neoliberal view of international relations.

---

[29] W. Easterly, "Was Development Assistance a Mistake?" *American Economic Review* 97, no. 2 (2007): 328–32; C. Gore, "The Rise and Fall of the Washington Consensus as a Paradigm for Developing Countries," *World Development* 28, no. 5 (2000): 789–804; J. Stiglitz, "Challenging the Washington Consensus," *The Brown Journal of World Affairs* 9, no. 2 (2003): 33–40.

[30] E. Balla and G. Y. Reinhardt, "Giving and Receiving Foreign Aid: Does Conflict Count?" *World Development* 36, no. 12 (2008): 2566–85; J. Berthélemy, "Bilateral Donors' Interest vs. Recipients' Development Motives in Aid Allocation: Do All Donors Behave the Same?" *Review of Development Economics* 10, no. 2 (2006): 179–94; P. J. Schraeder, "Clarifying the Foreign Aid Puzzle: A Comparison of American, Japanese, French, and Swedish Aid Flows," *World Politics* 50, no. 2 (1998): 294–323.

[31] E. Mawdsley, "China and Africa: Emerging Challenges to the Geographies of Power," *Geography Compass* 1, no. 3 (2007): 405–21; J. Younas, "Motivation for Bilateral Aid Allocation: Altruism or Trade Benefits?" *European Journal of Political Economy* 24, no. 3 (2008): 661–74.

[32] F. Y. Owusu, "Post-9/11 U.S. Foreign Aid, the Millennium Challenge Account, and Africa: How Many Birds Can One Stone Kill?" *Africa Today* 54, no. 1 (2007): 2–26.

[33] A. Dreher, P. Nunnenkamp, and R. Thiele, "Does US Aid Buy UN General Assembly Votes? A Disaggregated Analysis," *Public Choice* 136, no. 1/2 (2008): 139–64.

[34] A. Dreher, J. E. Sturm, and J. R. Vreeland, "Global Horse Trading: IMF Loans for Votes in the United Nations Security Council," *European Economic Review* 53, no. 7 (2009): 742–57.

These foreign aid frames do not recognize the moral claims of individuals or allocate moral responsibility for addressing such claims. All foreign aid cannot be assumed to be good or ethically desirable. There is good aid and bad aid, and distinguishing between them requires evaluative criteria rooted in normative theory.

### 2.3.3 The DAH System: Critiques and Proposals

Given these varying motivations for foreign aid, the empirical literature's mixed results on DAH's effects are not surprising. Some studies find that health sector aid has either no significant effect or a negative effect on health outcomes, while others find positive effects. In one study, health aid is found to have no significant effect on immunization coverage, life expectancy, death rate, or infant mortality,[35] while another study finds a significant positive effect on the latter.[36] Other studies have found significant positive effects of health sector aid on diphtheria-tetanus-pertussis immunization coverage in countries with low corruption control,[37] of US aid for HIV/AIDS on reducing AIDS-related deaths (although aid in general did not reduce new HIV infections),[38] and of aid for malaria in increasing insecticide-treated mosquito net distribution and reducing under-5 mortality in African recipient countries.[39] Nor is the greatest amount of DAH consistently allocated to countries with the lowest income and highest disease burden. One study found that of the top ten countries receiving DAH (all of which are low-income countries) only four fall in the top ten in terms of disease burden, measured by DALYs (disability-adjusted life years, a standard measure).[40]

Criticisms of the DAH system abound and reflect varied concerns. First, the total DAH levels are considered inadequate,[41] the volatility of overall health financing exacerbates recipients' uncertainty, and DAH may actually crowd out domestic health financing. These problems undermine recipient countries' ability to finance sustainable health systems. Second, concerns about the

[35] C. R. Williamson, "Foreign Aid and Human Development: The Impact of Foreign Aid to the Health Sector," *Southern Economic Journal* 75, no. 1 (2008): 188–207.

[36] P. Mishra and D. Newhouse, "Does Health Aid Matter?" *Journal of Health Economics* 28, no. 4 (2009): 855–72.

[37] S. Dietrich, "The Politics of Public Health Aid: Why Corrupt Governments Have Incentives to Implement Aid Effectively," *World Development* 39, no. 1 (2011): 55–63.

[38] P. Nunnenkamp and H. Öhler, "Throwing Foreign Aid at HIV/AIDS in Developing Countries: Missing the Target?" *World Development* 39, no. 10 (2011): 1704–23.

[39] Y. Akachi and R. Atun, "Effect of Investment in Malaria Control on Child Mortality in Sub-Saharan Africa in 2002–2008," *PLoS One* 6, no. 6 (2011): e21309.

[40] J. Dieleman, C. Murray, and A. Haakenstad, *Financing Global Health 2013: Transition in an Age of Austerity* (Seattle: IHME, 2014).

[41] WHO Macroeconomics and Health Commission 2001 and Task Force on Innovative International Financing for Health Systems 2009.

locus of DAH decision-making and priority setting are long-standing issues, with donor-driven development still the dominant paradigm. Third, lack of coordination among an increasingly fragmented set of DAH actors creates and exacerbates inefficiencies in health administration, delivery, and processes in recipient countries. Fourth, DAH lacks effective accountability mechanisms to ensure that both donors and recipients are accountable, not just for the use of funds and their impact, but for the overall DAH system. While efforts have tried to include recipients in decision-making processes, coordinate donors, and hold actors accountable for performance and results, the main problem is that no clearly recognized global normative framework exists for DAH. The legitimacy and accountability of the DAH system as a whole are questionable.

Numerous DAH system reforms have been proposed in several areas. First are financing proposals in the form of international taxes (for example, airline ticket levies, billionaire and sin taxes, financial transaction taxes), financial mechanisms (Advance Market Commitments, the International Finance Facility for Immunisation (IFFIm) in support of Gavi's immunization programs, the Global Fund's Debt2Health program), and products in the private sector (for example, (PRODUCT)[RED] fundraising through product labeling). Second are coordination and accountability mechanisms in the form of sector-wide approaches (SWAps), other "One" or "Unified" initiatives (for example, "Three Ones" for HIV/AIDS, "One United Nations"), the Paris Declaration on Aid Effectiveness and the Accra Agenda for Action, the International Health Partnership, Poverty Reduction Strategy Papers (PRSPs), Health 8, and Health 4+ for maternal and child health. The third area comprises UN commissions and international laws and treaties (for example, the UN Commission on Information and Accountability for Women's and Children's Health, the FCTC, the Framework Convention on Global Health, Framework Convention on Obesity Control, Global Fund for Social Protection, and proposed international conventions on research and development (R&D) and on alcohol). Critics of reform-based framework conventions say they fail to provide a convincing rationale for states to pursue such reforms and lack binding obligations in international law.[42]

But the DAH system reform debate has not adequately considered the relationship between DAH and global justice. Reforms have focused on practical issues and have framed the DAH system within a neoliberal view. These solutions thus fail to scrutinize critically the donor/recipient hierarchy. Indeed, some have argued that the current development paradigm has created as many problems as it has sought to address.[43]

---

[42] D. P. Fidler, "The Challenges of Global Health Governance," Council on Foreign Relations Working Paper, May 2010.

[43] L. Garrett, "The Challenge of Global Health," *Foreign Affairs*, January/February 2007.

## 2.4 Actors and Regimes in Global Health Governance[44]

### 2.4.1 *States*

Many agree that states remain the primary actors with ultimate responsibility in health governance, national and global.[45] The greatest single source of global health assistance remains bilateral funding, alongside the UN system,[46] and even in low- and lower middle-income countries, national resources account for nearly 40 percent of total health expenditure.[47] National governments' capacity and decisions determine disease surveillance and control, despite their global implications; the Chinese government's attempted suppression of SARS news in 2003 and China and Mexico's handling of H1N1 years later are just two examples of national interference in these vital functions. States decide what to negotiate internationally and implement domestically.[48] Member states fund organizations like WHO. Powerful states also set WHO priorities and limit permitted actions. For example, WHO's surveillance authority has been described as what Western states allow.[49] Furthermore, wealthy countries can impact health by influencing bilateral trade agreements to strengthen IP rights, limit drug access, and protect pharmaceutical, tobacco, and food industry interests. The Agreement on Trade-Related Aspects of Intellectual Property Rights (TRIPS), an international pact imposing standards for IP regulation, is a prime example. Globalization purportedly breaks down national boundaries and diminishes the state's importance, but the Westphalian model is still relevant.[50] There is no global health system, as the SARS, Ebola, and H1N1 examples demonstrate, that bypasses state measures. Some observers suggest that GHG actually promotes "re-territorializations."[51]

---

[44] This section stems from N. Y. Ng and J. P. Ruger, "Global Health Governance at a Crossroads," *Global Health Governance* 3, no. 2 (2011): 1–37.

[45] WHO, *The World Health Report 2000* (Geneva: WHO, 2000); I. Kickbusch and K. Buse, "Global Influences and Global Responses: International Health at the Turn of the 21st Century," in M. Merson, R. Black, and A. Mills, eds., *International Public Health* (Gaithersberg, MD: Aspen Press, 2000), 701–37; A. Buchanan and M. Decamp, "Responsibility for Global Health," *Theoretical Medicine and Bioethics* 7, no. 1 (2006): 95–114; S. Gruskin, "Is there a Government in the Cockpit: A Passenger's Perspective or Global Public Health: The Role of Human Rights," *Temple Law Review* 77 (2004): 313–33.

[46] "Who Runs Global Health?" *The Lancet* 373, no. 9681 (2009): 2083; IHME, *Financing Global Health 2009: Tracking Development Assistance for Health* (Seattle: University of Washington, 2009).

[47] See Table 7: Health Expenditures in WHO, *World Health Statistics 2014* (Geneva: WHO, 2014), 150.

[48] A. L. Taylor, "Governing Globalization of Public Health," *Journal of Law, Medicine & Ethics* 32, no. 3 (2004): 500–8.

[49] S. Davies, "Securitizing Infectious Disease," *International Affairs* 84, no. 2 (2008): 295–313.

[50] O. Aginam, "From Westphalianism to Global Governance: The G8, International Law, and Global Health Governance through Public–Private Partnerships," Paper presented at Annual Convention of the International Studies Association, Chicago, February 28–March 2, 2007.

[51] R. Keil and H. Ali, "Governing the Sick City," *Antipode* 39, no. 5 (2007): 866.

The primacy of states is evident in other ways. Around the world, public health systems designed and operated by state governments tend to achieve health equity more effectively than private sector systems.[52] Country-level efforts have also yielded major public health successes, including Morocco's trachoma control campaign, Chile's folic acid fortification of flour for neural tube defect prevention, and HIV/AIDS programs in Brazil and Thailand.[53] And states have primary responsibility as well for the social determinants of health—those factors outside the health sphere that nonetheless affect health, such as housing, sanitation, education, economy, and the environment. The US government's role in regulating the food industry,[54] for example, is evidenced by public policy measures such as taxation on sugared beverages,[55] and restricting marketing to children and the availability of junk food in schools.

Global policies in any domain will not gain significant traction without industrialized states' support. The USA and other G8 countries arguably have considerable, even hegemonic, clout.[56] By insisting on IP rights and thus limiting drug access, do the USA and EU exacerbate infectious disease threats? Do they have moral obligations in addressing those risks? Protecting other US industries—especially tobacco—also undermines global health. Should the USA use its global influence to establish a global health agreement?[57] Is the G8 the logical emerging global health governor?

Finally, emerging countries, especially Brazil, Russia, India, China, and South Africa, are also assuming a larger GHG role. They are increasingly providing financial and technical assistance, examples (both good and bad) of health system development, and medical services and supplies, including generic drugs. Emerging nations are challenging trade and IP rules that hinder

---

[52] S. Basu, J. Andrews, S. Kishore, R. Panjabi, and D. Stuckler, "Comparative Performance of Private and Public Healthcare Systems in Low- and Middle-Income Countries: A Systematic Review," *PLoS Medicine* 9, no. 6 (2012): e1001244.

[53] R. Levine and What Works Working Group, *Millions Saved: Proven Successes in Global Health* (Washington, DC: Center for Global Development, 2004); J. Lopez-Camelo, I. M. Orioli, M. G. Duntra, and E. E. Castilla, "Reduction of Birth Prevalence Rates of Neural Tube Defects after Folic Acid Fortification in Chile," *American Journal of Medical Genetics: Part A*, 135A, no. 2 (2005): 120–5; S. Okie, "Fighting HIV: Lessons from Brazil," *New England Journal of Medicine* 354, no. 19 (2006): 1977–81.

[54] L. L. Sharma, S. P. Teret, and K. D. Brownell, "The Food Industry and Self-Regulation: Standards to Promote Success and to Avoid Public Health Failures," *American Journal of Public Health* 100, no. 2 (2010): 240–6.

[55] K. D. Brownell and T. R. Frieden, "Ounces of Prevention: The Public Policy Case for Taxes on Sugared Beverages," *New England Journal of Medicine* 360 (2009): 1805–8.

[56] I. Kickbusch, "Influence and Opportunity: Reflections on the U.S. Role in Global Public Health," *Health Affairs* 21, no. 6 (2002): 131–41; O. Aginam, "Salvaging Our Global Neighbourhood: Critical Reflections on the G8 Summit and Global Health Governance in an Interdependent World," *Law, Social Justice and Global Development Journal* 7 (2004): 1, no. 1 (2004).

[57] I. Kickbusch, "SARS: Wake-Up Call for a Strong Global Health Policy," *YaleGlobal*, April 25, 2003.

drug access, and through them the developing world is finding a greater voice in the global arena.

### 2.4.2 United Nations Organizations

The importance of WHO and other health-related UNOs in GHG has diminished as non-state actors—PPPs, NGOs, foundations, G8, and MNCs—and their initiatives have proliferated.[58] WHO inefficiency and ineffectiveness arguably contributed to the emergence of these non-state actors.[59] WHO lost its purview over major diseases, for example, to the Global Fund and UNAIDS.[60]

Criticisms of the UN and WHO abound. In the absence of a UN "master plan" for health, UN agencies compete and duplicate efforts.[61] Influence and political pressure diminish WHO's role as the "global health conscience."[62] WHO lacks enforcement powers. It is, according to critics, too focused on the Global Fund and UNAIDS,[63] technical matters and vertical programs, too bureaucratic, and insufficiently engaged with civil society.[64] Furthermore, WHO plays conflicting roles as advisor and evaluator, also eroding its effectiveness.[65] Some believe its private sector partnerships undermine its reliability in setting norms and standards.[66] Unable to use international law in the past, it is still reluctant to use it today.[67] WHO must now compete with numerous other global health actors for influence and for DAH, including recipient countries, NGOs, other UN actors such as the WTO and World Bank, PEPFAR,

---

[58] "Who Runs Global Health?" *The Lancet*; K. Lee, "The Pit and the Pendulum: Can Globalization Take Health Governance Forward?" *Development* 47, no. 2 (2004): 11–17.

[59] K. Buse and G. Walt, "Globalization and Multilateral Public–Private Health Partnerships: Issues for Health Policy," in K. Lee, K. Buse, and S. Fustukian, eds., *Health Policy in a Globalising World* (Cambridge: Cambridge University Press, 2002), 41–62.

[60] F. Godlee, "WHO in Retreat: Is It Losing Its Influence?" *British Medical Journal* 309, no. 6967 (1994): 1491–5.

[61] K. Lee, S. Collinson, G. Walt, and L. Gilson, "Who Should be Doing What in International Health: A Confusion of Mandates in the United Nations?" *British Medical Journal* 312, no. 7026 (1996): 302–7.

[62] A. Whyte, D. McCoy, and M. Rowson, eds., *Global Health Action: Global Health Watch Campaign Agenda* (Umea: Russell Press, 2005–6), 19.

[63] W. Hein and L. Kohlmorgen, "Global Health Governance: Conflicts on Global Social Rights," *Global Social Policy* 8, no. 1 (2008): 80–108.

[64] Global Health Watch, *Global Health Watch 2005–6: An Alternative World Health Report* (London: Zed Books Ltd, 2005); G. Walt, "WHO under Stress: Implications for Health Policy," *Health Policy* 24, no. 2 (1993): 125–44; "A Vital Opportunity for Global Health," *The Lancet* 350, no. 9080 (1997): 750–1.

[65] S. J. Hoffman and J. A. Røttingen, "Split WHO in Two: Strengthening Political Decision-Making and Securing Independent Scientific Advice," *Public Health* 128, no. 2 (2014): 188–94; C. L. Murray, A. D. Lopez, and S. Wibulpolprasert, "Monitoring Global Health: Time for New Solutions," *British Medical Journal* 329, no. 7474 (2004): 1096–100.

[66] K. Buse and A. Waxman, "Public–Private Health Partnerships: A Strategy for WHO," *Bulletin of the World Health Organization* 79, no. 8 (2001): 748–54.

[67] L. Gostin, "A Proposal for a Framework Convention on Global Health," *Journal of International Economic Law* 10, no. 4 (2007): 989–1008.

MNCs, and foundations. Powerful countries have bypassed WHO in setting up new institutions and regimes such as UNAIDS, the Global Fund, the Advanced Market Commitments for vaccines, and the IFFIm.

Many of these criticisms were validated in WHO's response to the 2014 Ebola outbreak. WHO was criticized for failing to mount an effective first response, only declaring the Ebola epidemic a public health emergency of international concern on August 8, 2014, five months after it was first reported.[68] A gap is growing between the world's view of WHO as a first responder and WHO's view of itself as a technical, standards-setting organization.[69] WHO's budgetary issues are widening this gap. To address a US$300 million deficit in 2010, WHO chose to cut its "outbreak and crisis response" funds by 51 percent from $469 million to $228 million. Moreover, in recent years over 75 percent of WHO's funding has come from voluntary contributions from member states and other donors, which are typically earmarked for specific priorities. This extra-budgetary funding is not WHO's to allocate as it would choose, thus leaving its hands tied during outbreaks like Ebola or 2016's Zika epidemic.

But despite its many flaws, the world continues to look to WHO as the obvious global health governor; real alternatives don't exist. Many believe WHO is uniquely positioned to organize disease surveillance,[70] and alone combines legal authority, public health expertise, and mandate.[71] And in the face of WHO's budgetary weaknesses,[72] many argue for strengthening it financially and politically, giving it enforcement powers and a stronger mandate, rather than creating or enhancing alternative institutions.[73] Overall, numerous observers think multilateral UNOs and WHO, as more neutral forums than bilateral arrangements, should play a greater role in globalization.[74] Theoretically, the UN and WHO, as public sector entities, are more

---

[68] MSF, "Ebola: The Failures of an International Outbreak Response," *MSF*, August 29, 2014.

[69] S. Fink, "Cuts at W.H.O. Hurt Response to Ebola Crisis," *New York Times*, September 3, 2014.

[70] T. W. Grein, K. B. O. Kamara, G. Rodier, A. J. Plant, P. Bovier, M. J. Ryan et al. "Rumors of Disease in the Global Village: Outbreak Verification," *Emerging Infectious Diseases* 6, no. 2 (2000): 97–102.

[71] "Who Runs Global Health?" *The Lancet*; Ministers of Foreign Affairs of Brazil, France, Indonesia, Norway, Senegal, South Africa, and Thailand, "Oslo Ministerial Declaration—Global Health: A Pressing Foreign Policy Issue of Our Time," *The Lancet* 369, no. 9570 (2007): 1373–8; A. Taylor, "Global Governance, International Health Law and WHO: Looking Towards the Future," *Bulletin of the World Health Organization* 80, no. 12 (2002): 975–80; L. Gostin and E. Mok, "Grand Challenges in Global Health Governance," *British Medical Bulletin* 90, no. 1 (2009): 7–18; S. Harmon, "International Public Health Law: Not So Much WHO as Why, and Not Enough WHO and Why Not?" *Medicine, Health Care and Philosophy* 12, no. 3 (2009): 245–55.

[72] D. Sridhar, "Post-Accra: Is there Space for Country Ownership in Global Health?" *Third World Quarterly* 30, no. 7 (2009): 1363–77.

[73] K. Lee, D. Sridhar, and M. Patel, "Trade and Health 2: Bridging the Divide: Global Governance of Trade and Health," *The Lancet* 373, no. 9661 (2009): 416–22; I. Kickbusch and L. Payne, "Constructing Global Public Health in the 21st Century," Paper presented at Meeting on Global Health Governance and Accountability, Harvard University, Cambridge, MA, June 2–3, 2004.

[74] G. Walt, "Globalisation of International Health," *The Lancet* 351, no. 9100 (1998): 434–7.

objective, more equitable, and less subject to corporate influence and bottom-line compulsions. On the ground, of course, the picture is not nearly so convincing. And WHO's need now to compete with other actors for influence and DAH dollars challenges its normative neutrality and scientific integrity.

### 2.4.3 Economic Organizations and Coalitions: World Bank, World Trade Organization, G8, and G20

Global economic organizations have extended their reach beyond economics and development into health governance in recent decades. The WTO trade regime, with its impact on drug access and health services and on major risk factors such as tobacco, food safety, unhealthy diets, and, by extension, NCDs, has expanded the WTO's role in health affairs. Some have argued for greater involvement by the health community with Doha Round negotiations and the WTO above and beyond the typical IP focus.[75] The WTO is becoming increasingly important in GHG.[76] (Though the WTO has a major impact on GHG, an in-depth analysis of it is beyond this book's scope.)

The World Bank, recognizing the importance of health to development, has also asserted a major role. The Bank is well positioned to stress health system strengthening (HSS) and financing and to provide technical and policy advice. With superior resources, it has challenged WHO's agenda-setting role in health since the 1990s, especially in poor countries.[77] But some still call on the World Bank to offer more effective leadership,[78] support WHO functions,[79] collaborate with WHO to lessen free trade's negative health effects,[80] and address global public goods.[81] The World Bank's critics charge it with undemocratic and pro-privatization policies,[82] opaque and

[75] J. Scott and S. Harman, "Beyond TRIPS: Why the WTO's Doha Round is Unhealthy," *Third World Quarterly* 34, no. 8 (2013): 1361–76.

[76] O. Williams, "The WTO, Trade Rules and Global Health Security," in Alan Ingram, ed., *Health, Foreign Policy and Security: Towards a Conceptual Framework for Research and Policy* (London: Nuffield Trust, 2004), 73–87.

[77] K. Abbasi, "The World Bank and World Health: Changing Sides," *British Medical Journal* 318, no. 7187 (1999): 865–9; C. Thomas and M. Weber, "The Politics of Global Health Governance: Whatever Happened to 'Health for All by the Year 2000'?" *Global Governance* 10, no. 2 (2004): 187–205.

[78] J. P. Ruger, "What Will the New World Bank Head Do for Global Health?" *The Lancet* 365, no. 9474 (2005): 1837–40.

[79] D. T. Jamison, J. Frenk, and F. Knaul, "International Collective Action in Health: Objectives, Functions, and Rationale," *The Lancet* 351, no. 9101 (1998): 514–17.

[80] E. Baris and K. McLeod, "Globalization and International Trade in the Twenty-First Century: Opportunities for and Threats to the Health Sector in the South," *International Journal of Health Services* 30, no. 1 (2000): 187–210.

[81] R. Kanbur, "What is the World Bank Good For? Global Public Goods and Global Institutions," CEPR Discussion Paper, 2017.

[82] A. E. Birn and K. Dmitrienko, "The World Bank: Global Health or Global Harm?" *American Journal of Public Health* 95, no. 7 (2005): 1091–2.

inefficient management,[83] and a narrow focus on performance rather than outcome and impact evaluation.[84]

Some observers have discussed the G8 nations as a potential global health governor,[85] or one of last resort,[86] suggesting this coalition could be GHG's "emerging centre."[87] The G8's membership is task-oriented, builds public–private collaborations, and works from shared values.[88] These assets, coupled with its intragroup accountability,[89] might make G8 more effective than other global institutions. Essentially an informal network, however, G8 may lack the organizational capacity to lead GHG as a "global health apex institution,"[90] and questions arise as to whom this coalition is accountable. Still, the influence of its members could be an asset,[91] and this government network can be a mechanism for achieving global governance results.[92] The G8 also has greater flexibility in its work, operating outside constraining global health bureaucracies. Soliciting funds for specific work is also more ably accomplished through G8 auspices than, for example, by WHO, given the coalition's access to its own national financial and human resources. The Global Fund, for example, was a G8 project. But these powerful countries are likely to pursue their own interests first. Despite the concerning global effects of smoking,[93] the G8's inaction on tobacco, and its inadequate redistribution efforts,[94] have revealed its priorities.

[83] D. Tarullo, "Prepared Statement for the Hearing on Reforming Key International Financial Institutions for the 21st Century," Senate Subcommittee on Security and International Trade and Finance of the Committee on Banking, Housing, and Urban Affairs. Washington, DC, August 2, 2007.

[84] A. Wagstaff and Y. Shengchao, "Do Health Sector Reforms Have their Intended Impacts? The World Bank's Health VIII Project in Gansu Province, China," *Journal of Health Economics* 26, no. 3 (2007): 505–35; J. Baird, S. Ma, and J. P. Ruger, "Effects of the World Bank's Maternal and Child Health Intervention on Indonesia's Poor: Evaluating the Safe Motherhood Project," *Social Science and Medicine* 72, no. 12 (2011): 1948–55.

[85] N. Bayne, "Managing Globalization and the New Economy: The Contribution of the G8 Summit," in J. Kirton and G. von Furstenberg, eds., *New Directions in Global Economic Governance: Managing Globalization in the Twenty-First Century* (Aldershot: Ashgate, 2001): 171–88.

[86] A. Price-Smith, *Plagues and Politics: Infectious Disease and International Policy* (New York: Palgrave, 2001).

[87] J. Kirton, N. Roudev, and L. Sunderland, "Making G8 Leaders Deliver," *Bulletin of the World Health Organization* 85, no. 3 (2007): 192–9.

[88] Ibid.

[89] InterAction, "Accountability: Building on Progress in 2012," *G8 Background Policy Brief*, March 2012.

[90] M. Reich and K. Takemi, "G8 and Strengthening of Health Systems: Follow-Up to the Toyako Summit," *The Lancet* 373, no. 9662 (2009): 508–15.

[91] Ibid.

[92] A. M. Slaughter, "The Power and Legitimacy of Government Networks," in Alfred Herrhausen Society for International Dialogue, ed., *The Partnership Principle, New Forms of Governance in the 21st Century* (London: Archetype Publications, 2004).

[93] R. Jha and R. Peto, "Global Effects of Smoking, of Quitting, and of Taxing Tobacco," *New England Journal of Medicine* 370 (2014): 60–8.

[94] R. Labonte and T. Schrecker, "Committed to Health for All? How the G7/G8 Rate," *Social Science and Medicine* 59, no. 8 (2004): 1661–76.

Perhaps the G20, an expanded G8, could take a role. It is an intergovernment group whose member governments have authority and accountability to their populations; it represents more than 60 percent of the global population; participants are chiefly finance ministers with access to funding. And it is a "broadly representative leaders-level grouping."[95] However, the G20's 2009 summit was virtually silent on the poverty and suffering resulting from the 2008 world financial meltdown. Some doubt that the G20 can deliver fundamental reforms;[96] still, arguments for global cooperation among the G20 and broader community are building.[97]

### 2.4.4 Civil Society Organizations and Nongovernmental Organizations

Conventional wisdom suggests that NGOs and CSOs can be more flexible, democratic, cost-effective, and expert in accessing remote communities, and thus can outperform governments as service providers.[98] NGOs have been involved in many proven successes in global health. The Task Force for Child Survival and Development; Bangladesh Rural Advancement Committee; Carter Center; Clark, Gates, and Hassan II Foundations; Helen Keller International; and the International Trachoma Initiative are just a few. NGOs, rather than governments, receive much of PEPFAR's funding. Some argue that CSOs give voice to and empower aid recipients,[99] particularly the poor, helping them grasp issues and define negotiating positions. NGOs turned a spotlight on drug access during the WTO Doha Round;[100] many think they helped propel the FCTC negotiations.[101]

But others challenge the conventional wisdom.[102] Time and experience have revealed NGOs' own pathologies. They compete amongst themselves for donor funding, turf, and attention; adverse effects on program design,

---

[95] C. Bradford, "Reaching the Millennium Development Goals," in Cooper, Kirton, and Schrecker, eds., *Governing Global Health*, 79–86.

[96] A. Guise, D. Woodward, P. T. Lee, R. De Vogli, T. Tillman, and D. McCoy, "Engaging the Health Community in Global Economic Reform," *The Lancet* 373, no. 9668 (2009): 987–9.

[97] E. Zedillo, "The Mounting Challenge of Global Governance," Lecture delivered at the Graduate Institute of Geneva, Switzerland, February 24, 2016.

[98] A. Clayton, P. Oakley, and J. Taylor, "Civil Society Organizations and Service Provision," Civil Society and Social Movements Programme Paper No. 2, October 2000.

[99] B. Tomlinson, "Civil Society and Aid Effectiveness: A Synthesis of Advisory Group Regional Consultations and Related Processes," Paper presented at the Advisory Group, January 28, 2008.

[100] E. 't Hoen, "TRIPS, Pharmaceutical Patents, and Access to Essential Medicines: A Long Way from Seattle to Doha," *Chicago Journal of International Law* 3, no. 1 (2002): 27–46.

[101] R. Lencucha, R. Labonté, and M. J. Rouse, "Beyond Idealism and Realism: Canadian NGO/Government Relations during the Negotiation of the FCTC," *Journal of Public Health Policy* 31, no. 1 (2010): 74–87.

[102] C. Doyle and P. Patel, "Civil Society Organisations and Global Health Initiatives: Problems of Legitimacy," *Social Science and Medicine* 66, no. 9 (2008): 1928–38.

implementation, and interorganization coordination result.[103] Ideology sometimes drives NGO priorities and can diminish effectiveness—religious beliefs, for example, obstruct condom use and promotion[104]—though real needs often overcome ideology on the ground.[105] CSOs receive funding not just from civil society, but also from states and businesses, and therefore reflect those interests.[106] Though they often claim to represent the public interest, NGO and CSO actors are not elected, and one does not necessarily know whom they represent or to whom they are accountable. NGO service delivery also bypasses and can undermine elected governments; and higher NGO salaries can cause health-worker brain drain, thus damaging public sector organizations.[107] Beyond these varied issues, some observers question the whole notion of a global civil society.[108]

### 2.4.5 Public–Private Partnerships

The emergence of PPPs has raised hopes of bringing together civil society with the public and private sectors to correct market failures. Many believe that private sector management skills, abundant financial and in-kind resources, an innovative culture, and efficiency equip PPPs to be uniquely effective.[109] They are also, arguably, unavoidable in some contexts: the private sector "own [s] the ball"[110] in drug R&D, for example. Merck's ivermectin donation and Pfizer's trachoma programs are among successful PPPs. Studies show that PPPs can reduce disease at low expense.[111] They also typically target the most menacing diseases and the neediest countries.[112]

But skeptics suggest that PPPs place the risks on the public sector while the private sector reaps profits, and that corporations use PPPs to burnish corporate

---

[103] A. Cooley and J. Ron, "The NGO Scramble: Organizational Insecurity and the Political Economy of Transnational Action," *International Security* 27, no. 1 (2002): 5–39.

[104] S. Woldehanna, K. Ringheim, C. Murphy, and T. Perry, *Faith in Action: Examining the Role of Faith-Based Organizations in Addressing HIV/AIDS* (Washington, DC: Global Health Council, 2005).

[105] K. Joyce, *Seeing is Believing: Questions about Faith-Based Organizations that are Involved in HIV/AIDS Prevention and Treatment* (Washington, DC: Catholics for Choice, 2010).

[106] Lencucha, Labonté, and Rouse, "Beyond Idealism and Realism."

[107] Doyle and Patel, "Civil Society Organisations."

[108] Ibid.

[109] K. Buse and G. Walt, "Global Public–Private Partnerships Part II: What are the Health Issues for Global Governance?" *Bulletin of the World Health Organization* 78, no. 5 (2000): 699–709.

[110] Walt, Buse, "Global Public–Private Partnerships: Part I," *Bulletin of the World Health Organization* 78, no. 4 (2000): 549–61, 552 citing personal communication: A. Lucas, July 13, 1999.

[111] Bill and Melinda Gates Foundation, *Developing Successful Global Health Alliances* (Seattle: Gates Foundation, 2002); E. Sinanovic and L. Kumaranayake, "Financing and Cost-Effectiveness Analysis of Public–Private Partnerships: Provision of Tuberculosis Treatment in South Africa," *Cost Effectiveness and Resource Allocation* 4, no. 11 (2006).

[112] K. Caines, K. Buse, C. Carlson, and R. Sadanandan, *Assessing the Impact of Global Health Partnerships* (London: DFID Health Resource Centre, 2004).

images and expand markets.[113] Because PPPs involve specific companies and industries, they tend toward vertical programs with their attendant problems. Nor do they particularly target poverty: they have excluded impoverished countries with big populations, for example, or countries with unpopular governments or inadequate infrastructure.[114] PPPs are often opaque and unaccountable, untethered to lines of responsibility.[115] Northern actors tend to dominate; the Global South has been underrepresented,[116] though that imbalance has begun to shift.[117] PPPs may also weaken governments and multilateral organizations, by distorting the public sector's normative focus. And they can compromise international organizations' values and thus their norm- and standard-setting authority.[118]

## 2.5 Where Global Health Efforts Succeed

The global eradication of smallpox throughout the 1970s, under IHG, was one of the most noteworthy global health successes. WHO coordinated and member states implemented eradication programs. Help came from donor governments such as the USA, the Soviet Union, and Sweden, and from Wyeth Laboratories' invention of the bifurcated needle. Fourteen years after the program began in 1966, smallpox was officially declared eradicated.[119] More recently, success stories under GHG show that the multiplication of new actors does not preclude effective work. National governments, international organizations, CSOs, the private sector, and individuals have collaborated fruitfully. WHO's African Programme for Onchocerciasis Control, begun in 1995 to eliminate river blindness in central, southern, and eastern Africa, exemplified these collaborations. It included the governments of nineteen African

---

[113] E. Ollila, "Global Health Priorities: Priorities of the Wealthy?" *Globalization and Health* 1, no. 1 (2005): 6.

[114] Buse and Walt, "Global Public–Private Partnerships: Part II."

[115] Y. Zwi, "International Health in the 21st Century: Trends and Challenges," *Social Science and Medicine* 54, no. 11 (2002): 1615–20; J. A. Alexander, M. E. Comfort, and B. J. Weiner, "Governance in Public–Private Community Health Partnerships: A Survey of the Community Care Network Demonstration Sites," *Nonprofit Management & Leadership* 8, no. 4 (1998): 311–32; D. Tarantola, "Global Health and National Governance," *American Journal of Public Health* 95, no. 1 (2005): 8.

[116] K. Buse and A. Harmer, "Power to the Partners? The Politics of Public–Private Health Partnerships," *Development* 47, no. 2 (2004): 49–56.

[117] S. Bartsch, "The South in Global Health Governance: Perspectives on Global Public–Private Partnerships," Paper presented at the annual meeting of the International Studies Association, San Diego, California, March 21–25, 2006.

[118] K. Buse and G. Walt, "Global Public–Private Partnerships: Part I: A New Development in Health?" *Bulletin of the World Health Organization* 78, no. 4 (2000): 549–61.

[119] D. Hopkins, *The Greatest Killer: Smallpox in History* (Chicago: University of Chicago Press, 2002); D. A. Henderson, "Principles and Lessons from the Smallpox Eradication Programme," *Bulletin of the World Health Organization* 65, no. 4 (1987): 535–46; see timeline from WHO, "The Smallpox Eradication Programme—SEP (1966–1980)" *WHO*, May 2010.

countries; twenty-seven donor countries, institutions, and foundations; more than thirty CSOs; and more than eighty thousand rural African communities that distributed the medication locally.

Polio and guinea worm eradication and lymphatic filariasis elimination campaigns have likewise brought together many national, international, non-profit, and corporate players, including WHO, Pan American Health Organization, United Nations Children's Fund (UNICEF), US Centers for Disease Control and Prevention (CDC), Gates Foundation, Carter Center, Merck, and DuPont, in successful programs.[120] Dramatic global declines in measles since 2000 are the fruit of regional campaigns undertaken by national governments and entities such as WHO, UNICEF, US CDC, and American Red Cross.[121] The PARTNERS project on multidrug-resistant tuberculosis (MDR-TB) is a collaboration among Partners in Health, its sister Peruvian group Socios en Salud, US CDC, WHO, the Task Force for Child Survival and Development, and national governments. It demonstrated that MDR-TB treatment could be successfully scaled up in resource-poor settings, and WHO integrated MDR-TB into its TB policy as a result.[122]

Diverse actors can provide more of the elements necessary for good global health performance—adequate and sustained funding, political leadership and commitment, technical expertise, innovation, and managerial and logistical skills.[123] Partners with common interests and complementary skills can surmount competing agendas, conflicting requirements, and turf disputes if they develop mutual trust; agree on goals, measurements, and strategies; and establish an appropriate collaborative structure.[124] Third parties can also foster international cooperation: the Carter Center brought the Dominican Republic and Haiti together to eliminate malaria and lymphatic filariasis as part of its larger International Task Force for Disease Eradication.[125]

Still, the challenges in global health far exceed the successes. Meeting these challenges continues to vex GHG. Though the MDGs and SDGs offer a basis

---

[120] Levine et al., *Millions Saved*; R. Voelker, "Global Partners Take Two Steps Closer to Eradication of Guinea Worm Disease," *Journal of the American Medical Association* 305, no. 16 (2011): 1642; D. Molyneux, "Lymphatic Filariasis (Elephantiasis) Elimination: A Public Health Success and Development Opportunity," *Filaria Journal* 2 (2006): 13.

[121] W. J. Moss and D. E. Griffin, "Global Measles Elimination," *Nature Reviews Microbiology* 4 (2006): 900–8; WHO, "Global Elimination of Measles: Report by the Secretariat," provisional agenda item 5.1., Executive Board 125th Session, April 16, 2009.

[122] M. L. Rosenberg, E. S. Hayes, M. H. McIntyre, and N. W. Neill, *Real Collaboration* (Berkeley: University of California Press, 2010).

[123] Levine et al., *Millions Saved*.

[124] Rosenberg et al., *Real Collaboration*; McKinsey & Company, *Developing Successful Global Health Alliances* (Seattle: Bill and Melinda Gates Foundation, 2002); C. Wachira and J. P. Ruger, "National Poverty Reduction Strategies and HIV/AIDS Governance in Malawi: A Preliminary Study of Shared Health Governance," *Social Science & Medicine* 72, no. 12 (2010): 1956–64.

[125] The Carter Center, "Catalyzing the Elimination of Malaria and Lymphatic Filariasis from the Caribbean," *The Carter Center*, 2017.

for cooperation, the absence of either a universally accepted coordinating body or a unified vision for global health thwarts best efforts to solve global health problems.

## 2.6 GHG: Major Issues and Challenges

### 2.6.1 *Approaches to Global Health Challenges: Vertical and Horizontal*

Most efforts to address health challenges today are either vertical and selective (disease-specific) or horizontal and comprehensive such as broad-based HSS and development. WHO's 1978 Health for All initiative exemplifies the horizontal approach; current global health initiatives tend to be vertical. Some are calling for a "diagonal" third way.[126]

Vertical efforts show results: performance and outcomes are readily measurable. Assessing results in horizontal programs, on the other hand, is more difficult and takes longer. And where the absence of disease is the measure of success, population-based preventative efforts are at a disadvantage in demonstrating results. These broader systemic efforts are also more likely to become unmanageable. Donors therefore tend to prefer vertical programs. Many of global health's proven successes have emerged from vertical programs: examples are smallpox and polio eradication; onchocerciasis, trachoma, TB, measles, and Chagas disease control; and guinea worm reduction. Some believe vertical projects are "what works" in global health programming.[127]

But the vertical approach has evident failings. Critics argue that many vertical programs exhibit and exacerbate global health's enduring governance challenges—poor coordination, duplication and waste, short-term funding, unsustainability, and inadequate performance assessment. Further, laser focus on specific diseases constructs a hierarchy in which certain ailments like HIV/AIDS receive extraordinary attention while other conditions go untended.[128] Vertical programs drain human and material resources away from population-wide preventative functions. The vertical approach also ignores broader equity issues and the socioeconomic determinants of health. Other critics argue that vertical programs are technocratic and skewed in favor of some populations while neglecting others.[129] They can overlook investments in broader health

---

[126] J. Frenk, "Bridging the Divide: Comprehensive Reform to Improve Health in Mexico," Paper presented at WHO Commission on Social Determinants of Health (CSDH), Nairobi, Kenya, June 29, 2006.

[127] Levine et al., *Millions Saved*; Rosenberg et al., *Real Collaboration*; Hopkins, *The Greatest Killer*.

[128] A. Swidler and S. C. Watkins, "Teach a Man to Fish: The Sustainability Doctrine and Its Social Consequences," *World Development* 37, no. 7 (2009): 1182–96.

[129] L. Magnussen, J. Ehiri, and P. Jolly, "Comprehensive versus Selective Primary Health Care: Lessons for Global Policy," *Health Affairs* 23, no. 3 (2004): 167–76.

systems necessary to their own success.[130] Vertical programs might also distort national health priorities; some argue they reduce states' policy autonomy.[131] On the other hand, some observers believe that in countries with weak health systems, a logical first step is funding disease-specific programs, in hopes that they will foster health infrastructure development as a second stage.[132]

Overall, an emerging consensus supports action on health care, public health systems development, and universal coverage, increasingly acknowledged as essential to improving health, precisely because systems failings are thwarting vertical program objectives and achievement of the MDGs[133] and SDGs. Observers are arguing for strong commitments, funding, and technical support for developing health infrastructure, ensuring access, and addressing inadequacies in human resources and data systems.[134] The lack of data systems is a considerable global concern, particularly in the areas of global child health.[135] The World Bank's role in these endeavors is receiving particular attention. Many believe WHO's focus on developing health systems driven by primary care is essential for meeting developing countries' health challenges.[136] Still, despite reported successes in the 1980s in Mozambique, Cuba, and Nicaragua, the horizontal approach's potential remains "largely unexploited."[137] Strategies for building a strong health system vary, and a clear choice remains to be seen.[138]

Some have proposed a diagonal approach,[139] which deploys vertical intervention measures to drive horizontal HSS. This approach allocates resources to improve health system components relevant to specific diseases burdening a

---

[130] R. S. Northrup, "Critical Elements for Improved Global Health," *Health Affairs* 24, no. 3 (2005): 879–80.

[131] J. Youde, "Is Universal Access to Antiretroviral Drugs an Emerging International Norm?" *Journal of International Relations and Development* 11, no. 4 (2008): 415–40.

[132] D. Yu, Y. Souteyrand, M. A. Banda, J. Kaufman, and J. H. Perriëns, "Investment in HIV/AIDS Programs: Does it Help Strengthen Health Systems in Developing Countries?" *Global Health* 4 (2008): 8.

[133] WHO, *Everybody's Business: Strengthening Health Systems to Improve Health Outcomes—WHO's Framework for Action* (Geneva: WHO, 2007).

[134] J. Y. Kim and P. Farmer, "AIDS in 2006: Moving toward One World, One Hope?" *New England Journal of Medicine* 355, no. 7 (2006): 645–57; L. Garrett and K. Schneider, "Global Health: Getting it Right," in *Health and Development: Toward a Matrix Approach*, ed. A. Gatti and A. Boggio (London: Palgrave Macmillan, 2008), 3–16.

[135] P. H. Wise and G. L. Darmstadt, "The Grand Divergence in Global Child Health: Confronting Data Requirements in Areas of Conflict and Chronic Political Instability," *JAMA Pediatrics* 170, no. 3 (2016): 195–7.

[136] R. Koskenmaki, E. Granziera, and G. L. Burci, "The World Health Organization and Its Role in Health and Development," in *Health and Development*, ed. Gatti and Boggio, 16–55.

[137] Magnussen, Ehiri, and Jolly, "Comprehensive versus Selective Primary Health Care," 169.

[138] P. Travis, S. Bennett, A. Haines, T. Pang, Z. Bhutta, A. Hyder et al., "Overcoming Health-Systems Constraints to Achieve the Millennium Development Goals," *The Lancet* 364, no. 9437 (2004): 900–6.

[139] M. Rabkin, W. El-Sadr, K. De Cock, "The Impact of HIV Scale-Up on Health Systems: A Priority Research Agenda," *Journal of Acquired Immune Deficiency Syndromes* 52 (2009): S6–S11; J. Frenk, "The Global Health System: Strengthening National Health Systems as the Next Step for Global Progress," *PLoS Medicine* 7, no. 1 (2010: e1000089).

given country.[140] GAVI-HSS, an initiative from the Gavi alliance in 2006, embodies the diagonal approach, seeking to improve immunization by strengthening health systems.[141] Health ministries in participating countries identify health system weaknesses where GAVI-HSS help is needed. Research into the program so far supports developing an HSS approach starting with specific programs.[142]

## 2.6.2 Health: A Multisectoral Issue

Increasingly, scholars and policy-makers recognize that health is a multisectoral issue, connected to other sectors, especially in a globalizing world.[143] Integrating health into broader policy-making requires greater coordination across sectors to ensure coherent policies protecting health interests.[144] For example, the globalization of unhealthy diets and sedentary lifestyles exacerbates NCDs such as cancer, heart disease, and diabetes.[145] Tobacco's spread to developing markets and its importance for many developing economies (for example, China, Turkey, Zimbabwe) worsens the NCD threat.[146] Wealthy philanthropists such as Michael Bloomberg and Bill and Melinda Gates have supported global anti-tobacco campaigns,[147] but individual and environmental factors also affect NCDs, requiring multisectoral action and partnerships, beyond the work of any one organization.[148]

---

[140] Gatti and Boggio, *Health and Development*.

[141] J. Naimoli, "Global Health Partnerships in Practice: Taking Stock of the GAVI Alliance's New Investment in Health Systems Strengthening," *International Journal of Health Planning and Management* 24, no. 1 (2009): 3–25.

[142] B. Galichet, L. Goeman, P. S. Hill, M. S. Essengue, N. Hammami, D. Porignon, et al., "Linking Programmes and Systems: Lessons from the GAVI Health Systems Strengthening Window," *Tropical Medicine and International Health* 15, no. 2 (2010): 208–15.

[143] B. J. Plotkin and A. M. Kimball, "Designing an International Policy and Legal Framework for the Control of Emerging Infectious Diseases: First Steps," *Emerging Infectious Diseases* 3, no. 1 (1997): 1–9; P. Piot and A. M. Coll Seck, "International Response to the HIV/AIDS Epidemic: Planning for Success," *Bulletin of the World Health Organization* 79, no. 12 (2001): 1106–12.

[144] J. P. Ruger, "Global Tobacco Control: An Integrated Approach to Global Health Policy," *Development* 48, no. 2 (2005): 65–9; J. P. Ruger, "Ethics of the Social Determinants of Health," *The Lancet* 364, no. 9439 (2004): 1092–7.

[145] J. Collin, K. Lee, and K. Bissell, "The Framework Convention on Tobacco Control: The Politics of Global Health Governance," *Third World Quarterly* 23, no. 2 (2002): 265–82; B. M. Meier and D. Shelley, "The Fourth Pillar of the Framework Convention on Tobacco Control: Harm Reduction and the International Human Right to Health," *Public Health Reports* 121, no. 5 (2006): 494–500.

[146] Food and Agriculture Organization (FAO), *Projections of Tobacco Production, Consumption and Trade to the Year 2010* (Rome: FAO, 2003).

[147] Gates Foundation, "Gates Foundation, Bloomberg Commit $500 Million to Global Anti-Tobacco Campaign," *Philanthropy News Digest*, July 24, 2008.

[148] S. Nishtar, "Time for a Global Partnership on Non-Communicable Diseases," *The Lancet* 370, no. 9603 (2007): 1887–8; R. S. Magnusson, "Rethinking Global Health Challenges: Towards a 'Global Compact' for Reducing the Burden of Chronic Disease," *Public Health* 123, no. 3 (2009): 265–74.

The health–trade nexus is particularly challenging. Economic globalization and trade liberalization have both positive and negative potential for health. They can promote NCDs and limit access to drugs and health care technologies.[149] But globalization and trade can also spur economic growth, essential for health systems development and sustainability.

Incentives for R&D, pricing, and IP rules can all affect drug access. Most pharmaceutical R&D occurs in developed markets and targets health conditions affecting those countries' populations; poor countries lack the spending power to make immense R&D investments worthwhile to private industry.[150] Profit-driven R&D neglects tropical diseases because the developing countries they affect are unlikely to yield sufficient return on investments.[151] The Drugs for Neglected Diseases *initiative* (DND*i*),[152] and orphan drug acts in the USA, Japan, and the EU, attempt to promote more equity in R&D.[153]

When drug prices are too high, often the result of IP rules, they limit access.[154] Large price differences exist between countries where drugs are patented and thus subject to IP protection and those where generic versions are available.[155] On the other hand, when pricing in wealthy countries subsidizes lower prices in the developing world, this international price discrimination can foster greater access—if separate markets are maintained and accepted politically. Parallel importing and compulsory licensing, allowing the import and manufacture, respectively, of generic products, can also improve access. But pharmaceutical companies and interest groups in rich countries oppose developing countries' attempts to use these instruments. Some of these opposing actions fail (South Africa and Brazil, for example, successfully fought off pharma attempts to limit generics), while others have succeeded in curbing generics' manufacture and importation.[156] But whether

---

[149] Baris and McLeod, "Globalization and International Trade," 187–210.

[150] B. Pécoul, P. Chirac, P. Trouiller, and J. Pinel, "Access to Essential Drugs in Poor Countries: A Lost Battle?" *Journal of the American Medical Association* 281, no. 4 (1999): 361–7.

[151] N. Dimitri, "R&D Incentives for Neglected Diseases," *PLoS One* 7, no. 12 (2012): e50835.

[152] DND*i* 2017, "Diseases & Projects," DND*i*. Available at: https://www.dndi.org/diseases-projects/ (accessed February 24, 2018).

[153] R. R. Shah, "Regulatory Framework for the Treatment of Orphan Diseases," in *Fabry Disease: Perspectives from 5 Years of FOS*, ed. A. Mehta, M. Beck, and G. Sunder-Plassmann (Oxford: Oxford PharmaGenesis, 2006).

[154] A. Banerjee, A. Hollis, and T. Pogge, "The Health Impact Fund: Incentives for Improving Access to Medicines," *The Lancet* 375, no. 9709 (2010): 166–9.

[155] N. A. Bass, "Implications of the TRIPS Agreement for Developing Countries: Pharmaceutical Patent Laws in Brazil and South Africa in the 21st Century," *George Washington International Law Review* 34, no. 1 (2002): 191–222.

[156] F. Cheru, "Debt, Adjustment and the Politics of Effective Response to HIV/AIDS in Africa," *Third World Quarterly* 23, no. 2 (2002): 299–312; D. Matthews, "WTO Decision on Implementation of Paragraph 6 of the Doha Declaration on the TRIPS Agreement and Public Health: A Solution to the Access to Essential Medicines Problem?" *Journal of International Economic Law* 7, no. 1 (2004): 73–107.

drug patents actually limit access to essential medicines is an unresolved question. Some argue that most drugs that WHO considers "essential" are not patented,[157] that drug companies often do not patent formulas even when they could, and that in practice, patents do not limit access to certain therapies—antiretroviral treatment in Africa, for example.[158] In this view, the fundamental problem is that individual states have not established a right to essential medicines, a problem that revising IP rules would not solve.

Along with inequitable access to drugs and health services, the research gap is another major health inequality: although the developing world suffers large parts of the global disease burden, a small fraction of research expenditures specifically targets that burden. This gap resists remediation both because the private sector has little market incentive to make the investments and because developing countries lack the capacity to conduct and access research.[159] Technological and scientific advances such as genomics, nanotechnology, and proteomics in developed countries are likely to widen the gap even more.[160] Augmenting research capacity in developing countries, information sharing to improve knowledge access, and fair global rules to direct technology toward the health needs of the poor could help bridge this divide.[161]

Another trade–health nexus with implications for developing countries appears in the WTO General Agreement on Trade in Services (GATS). GATS aims to liberalize trade in health services, and foster market competition and privatization. The impact on health and health care is unclear. GATS criticisms are numerous, charging that it helps MNCs to extend their reach,[162] and that health services privatization will cost more, generate inequitable two-tiered systems, widen health gaps, and obstruct universal access.[163] Others worry that progressive liberalization will only bring more privatization of health systems and health care provision, thus hindering development of public health services and limiting future government options in health system design.[164] GATS could also worsen the brain drain problem as workers

[157] A. Attaran, "How do Patents and Economic Policies Affect Access to Essential Medicines in Developing Countries?" *Health Affairs* 23, no. 3 (2004): 155–66.

[158] A. Attaran and L. Gillespie-White, "Do Patents for Antiretroviral Drugs Constrain Access to AIDS Treatment in Africa?" *Journal of the American Medical Association* 286, no. 15 (2001): 1886–92.

[159] N. Pakenham-Walsh and C. Priestley, "Towards Equity in Global Health Knowledge," *Quarterly Journal of Medicine* 95, no. 7 (2002): 469–73.

[160] V. Ozdemir, D. Husereau, S. Hyland, S. Samper, and M. Z. Salleh, "Personalized Medicine beyond Genomics: New Technologies, Global Health Diplomacy and Anticipatory Governance," *Current Pharmacogenomics and Personalized Medicine* 7, no. 4 (2009): 225–30.

[161] WHO, *Genomics and World Health* (Geneva: WHO, 2002).

[162] R. Labonte, T. Schrecker, D. Sanders, and W. Meeus, *Fatal Indifference: The G8, Africa and Global Health* (South Africa: University of Cape Town Press, 2004).

[163] C. Blouin, N. Drager, and R. Smith, eds., *International Trade in Health Services and the GATS: Current Issues and Debates* (Washington, DC: World Bank, 2005).

[164] K. Lee and M. Koivusalo, "Trade and Health: Is the Health Community Ready for Action?" *PLoS Medicine* 2, no. 1 (2005): e8.

move from the public to the private sector and from developing to developed countries.[165]

The relationship between the trade and health sectors has been the focus of much debate, particularly about the strength of the world trade system as compared to the global health system. The global system for trade is more formalized and unified with legal, enforceable obligations, and thus is more powerful and effective than GHG with its "unstructured plurality."[166] Countries are willing to join the WTO and adhere to its rules since their economic success depends on participation in an effective international trade system. By contrast, WHO lacks enforcement power and bases its authority primarily on technical expertise.[167] WHO, with the WHA and external financing, must deal with diverse actors with minimal reciprocal obligations. Though WTO proceedings and policies impact health, WHO has limited access to trade commissions, where business representatives outnumber health officials. And while trade policy impacts health, adequate systematic assessment and monitoring of these impacts does not occur. GHG lacks a unified vision, further compromising health's standing vis-à-vis trade. Some advocate coordination between trade and health to achieve policy coherence:[168] WHO can bring its scientific and technical capacities to bear in assisting countries as they study, negotiate, and draft trade laws.[169] For example, WHO can help them understand the health impacts of trade policy and the effects of global brands marketing. It could push harder to effectuate the FCTC,[170] and to monitor large-scale agricultural production. Others argue for direct transnational corporation regulation to protect health from international commerce effects.[171]

Health intersects with other sectors as well. Health ties into development, and links to extreme poverty and other development indicators. WHO argued for incorporating health more into PRSPs and SWAps,[172] and health has become a significant component of the World Bank's global economic role. Yet large-scale development projects often proceed without adequately

---

[165] E. Friedman, *An Action Plan to Prevent Brain Drain: Building Equitable Health Systems in Africa* (Boston, MA: Physicians for Human Rights, 2004).

[166] D. P. Fidler, N. Drager, and K. Lee, "Managing the Pursuit of Health and Wealth: The Key Challenges," *The Lancet* 373, no. 9660 (2009): 325–31.

[167] Ibid.

[168] WHO and WTO, *WTO Agreements and Public Health: A Joint Study by the WHO and the WTO Secretariat* (Geneva: WHO/WTO, 2002).

[169] C. Thomas, "Trade Policy and the Politics of Access to Drugs," *Third World Quarterly* 23, no. 2 (2002): 251–64.

[170] K. Lee, "Global Health Promotion: How Can We Strengthen Governance and Build Effective Strategies?" *Health Promotion International* 21(Suppl. 1) (2006): 42–50.

[171] J. Frenk, J. Sepúlveda, O. Gómez-Dantés, M. McGuinness, and F. Knaul, "The Future of World Health: The New World Order and International Health," *British Medical Journal* 314, no. 7091 (1997): 1404–7.

[172] WHO, *Health and the Millennium Development Goals* (Geneva: WHO, 2005).

assessing their health effects.[173] Growing economic prosperity is important, but heedless development that damages air or water quality harms rather than benefits health. Development has other potential health impacts—worker exploitation, the use of harmful chemicals in agriculture, threats to animal health and meat, and the loss of biodiversity to sustain life—to which global health efforts must attend.[174]

### 2.6.3 Neoliberalism and Global Health

Neoliberalism is a broader theme underlying health's multisectoral connections and globalization's health impacts. Neoliberalism seeks global economic liberalization, market competition, privatization, and the pursuit of efficiency. Its application has health impacts. Infectious disease outbreaks multiply during human migrations believed to be associated with economic globalization.[175] Economic growth, foreign direct investments, and urbanization affect NCD mortality rates.[176] Although open trade can promote economic growth and poverty reduction, it also produces both winners and losers. Equitable health care does not necessarily result from liberalization;[177] devolving responsibility for health to the individual level, when health's determinants are also global and national, does not necessarily improve health.[178]

Some scholars note that international institutions such as the IMF, WTO, and the World Bank promote a neoliberal agenda,[179] favoring capital and overriding national democratic institutions. Their tools—structural adjustment programs (SAPs), debt repayment arrangements, and PRSPs—have failed, according to observers, to account for the social, health, and economic costs of

---

[173] R. Shademani and Y. von Schirnding, *Health Impact Assessment in Development Policy and Planning: Report of an Informal WHO Consultative Meeting* (Cartagena: WHO, 2001).

[174] C. Corvalan, S. Hales, and A. McMichael, *Ecosystems and Human Well-Being: Health Synthesis* (Geneva: WHO, 2005); M. Parkes and P. Horwitz, "Water, Ecology and Health: Ecosystems as Settings for Promoting Health and Sustainability," *Health Promotion International* 24, no. 1 (2009): 94–102; M. Jay and M. G. Marmot, "Health and Climate Change," *The Lancet* 374, no. 9694 (2009): 961–2.

[175] B. Gushulak and D. W. MacPherson, "Globalization of Infectious Diseases: The Impact of Migration," *Clinical Infectious Diseases* 38, no. 12 (2004): 1742–8.

[176] D. Stuckler, "Population Causes and Consequences of Leading Chronic Diseases: A Comparative Analysis of Prevailing Explanations," *Milbank Quarterly* 86, no. 2 (2008): 273–326.

[177] E. Missoni, "Understanding the Impact of Global Trade Liberalization on Health Systems Pursuing Universal Health Coverage," *Value in Health* 16, no. 1 (2013): S14–18.

[178] P. E. Farmer, B. Nizeye, S. Stulac, and S. Keshavjee, "Structural Violence and Clinical Medicine," *PLoS Medicine* 3, no. 10 (2006): e449; W. Hein and L. Kohlmorgen, eds., *Globalisation, Global Health Governance and National Health Politics in Developing Countries: An Exploration into the Dynamics of Interfaces* (Hamburg: Deutschen Ubersee-Instituts, 2003).

[179] I. Kawachi and S. Wamala, eds., *Globalization and Health* (Oxford: Oxford University Press, 2006).

adjustment.[180] They charge that health care suffers from policies such as spending cuts and user fees,[181] designed to reduce government health expenditures. Indeed, some would exempt health spending from international financial institutions' fiscal restraints, because neoliberal globalization "simultaneously maximizes the need for social intervention," and minimizes the political and strategic options available to achieve the public good.[182]

Neoliberalism pursues efficiency and consumption at the cost, some believe, of equality.[183] Clarifying which countries and which citizens within each country benefit or suffer under neoliberal agendas will help assess neoliberalism's impacts. A literature review of empirical studies of SAPs' consequences for health, for example, found both positive and negative effects.[184]

### 2.6.4 Country and Local Capacity and Ownership

When short-term orientation and uncoordinated efforts undermine health programs, complicate national planning, and strain national and local resources, recipient countries and local communities suffer. Local ownership better represents and addresses local needs,[185] and community health improves when communities have greater control over local programs.[186] Local ownership and engagement in global health initiatives are key to development and sustainability,[187] and governments in poorer countries have funded and led proven successes in global health.[188] They have contributed, for example, to recent successes against guinea worm, onchocerciasis, and malaria.[189] The WHO Healthy Cities initiatives, first launched in 1986,

---

[180] W. Eberlei, "Poverty Reduction Strategies between Global Governance and National Politics," in *Globalisation, Global Health Governance and National Health Politics*, ed. Hein and Kohlmorgen, 63–75; Global Health Watch, *Global Health Watch 2005–6*.

[181] N. Poku, "Confronting AIDS with Debt: Africa's Silent Crisis," in *The Political Economy of AIDS in Africa*, ed. N. Poku and A. Whiteside (Burlington, VT: Ashgate, 2004), 33–51.

[182] J. Brodie, "Globalization, In/Security, and the Paradoxes of the Social," in *Power, Production and Social Reproduction: Human In/Security in the Global Political Economy*, ed. I. Bakker and S. Gill (New York: Palgrave Macmillan, 2003), 60.

[183] J. Y. Kim, J. V. Millen, A. Irwin, and J. Gershman, eds., *Dying for Growth: Global Inequality and the Health of the Poor* (Monroe, ME: Common Courage Press, 2000).

[184] A. Breman and C. Shelton, "Structural Adjustment and Health: A Literature Review of the Debate, Its Role-Players and Presented Empirical Evidence," CMH Working Paper Series, Paper No. WG6:6, WHO, Geneva, 2001.

[185] L. Trubek and M. Das, "Achieving Equality: Healthcare Governance in Transition," *DePaul Journal of Health Care Law* 7, no. 2 (2004): 245–79.

[186] S. Burris, "Governance, Microgovernance and Health," *Temple Law Review* 77 (2004): 335–62.

[187] M. Dybul, "Lessons Learned from PEPFAR," *Journal of Acquired Immune Deficiency Syndromes* 52 (Suppl. 1) (2009): S12–13.

[188] Levine et al., *Millions Saved*.

[189] G. T. Keusch, W. L. Kilama, S. Moon, N. A. Szlezák, and C. M. Michaud, "The Global Health System: Linking Knowledge with Action—Learning from Malaria," *PLoS Medicine* 7, no. 1 (2010): e1000179.

exemplify efforts to foster local ownership in certain contexts.[190] Other key elements are country leadership, harmonization, and the alignment of global health initiatives with national plans.[191] Efforts targeting country ownership and coordination include the Paris Declaration on Aid Effectiveness,[192] PRSPs, UNAIDS' "Three Ones" initiative,[193] GAVI-HSS, Committee C of the WHA,[194] and the International Health Partnership and related initiatives. Still, barriers exist to local and national ownership of projects. Financial and human resources capacities might be insufficient.[195] Key stakeholders might or might not be included. Regulating activities of better-resourced actors is challenging for poor countries,[196] and some country governments are incompetent and/or corrupt. Donors' reluctance to give up pet initiatives and long-standing procedures also thwarts country ownership.[197] Strengthening local and country capacities and ownership is a major task.

### 2.6.5 Research Gaps in Global Health Governance

Knowledge deficiencies about governance itself also undermine GHG. The global health community might well have an insufficient evidence base for the most important global health tasks—strengthening health systems and improving public health. Many global health initiatives lack an evidence base. Interventions to improve health among the poor are often untested,[198] particularly as to whether specific interventions can successfully move from one geographic context to another.[199] Developing more knowledge about interventions'

---

[190] T. Hancock, "Healthy Cities and Communities: Past, Present, and Future," *National Civic Review* 86, no. 1 (1997): 11–21; I. Kickbusch, "Global + Local = Glocal Public Health," *Journal of Epidemiology and Community Health* 53, no. 8 (1999): 451–2; R. J. Lawrence and C. Fudge, "Healthy Cities in a Global and Regional Context," *Health Promotion International* 24 (Suppl. 1) (2009): i11–8.

[191] WHO and The World Bank, *Resources, Aid Effectiveness and Harmonization Issues for Discussion: Session 2*, High-Level Forum on the Health Millenium Development Goals, December 2003.

[192] UNDP, *Implementing the Paris Declaration on Aid Effectiveness* (New York: United Nations, 2011).

[193] UNAIDS, *"The Three Ones" in Action: Where We Are and Where We Go from Here* (Geneva: United Nations, 2005).

[194] I. Kickbusch, W. Hein, and G. Silberschmidt, "Addressing Global Health Governance Challenges through a New Mechanism: The Proposal for a Committee C of the World Health Assembly," *Journal of Law, Medicine, & Ethics* 38, no. 3 (2010): 550–63.

[195] Caines et al., *Assessing the Impact*.

[196] L. Kumaranayake and S. Lake, "Regulation in the Context of Global Health Markets," in *Health Policy in a Globalising World*, ed. Lee, Buse, and Fustukian, 78–96.

[197] S. Maxwell, "Can the International Health Partnership Deliver a New Way of Funding Health Spending?" *Overseas Development Institute*, September 7, 2007.

[198] P. Buekens, G. Keusch, J. Belizan, and Z. A. Bhutta, "Evidence-Based Global Health," *Journal of the American Medical Association* 291, no. 21 (2004): 2639–41.

[199] J. J. Furin, H. L. Behforouz, S. S. Shin, J. S. Mukherjee, J. Bayona, P. E. Farmer, et al., "Expanding Global HIV Treatment: Case Studies from the Field," *Annals of the New York Academy of Sciences* 1136 (2008): 12–20.

costs and effectiveness is essential. What works and does not work in health policy design and implementation also requires more study.[200] Research on the effectiveness of private sector contracting and its impact on the poor;[201] biotechnology relevant to disease, agriculture, and the environment;[202] and GHG institutions and processes is also important. Improving treatment adherence among patients with limited literacy and numeracy also needs further study,[203] given the need for complicated HIV/AIDS treatments in some of the world's poorest places. More fundamentally, norms must be established for allocating resources across health needs.[204] If global health research is to maximize usefulness, it must both address priority health needs and contribute to policy formulation.

## 2.7 Global Health Governance's Key Problems Persist

The most striking GHG theme is the persistence of its key problems. With the exception of proven successes in global health, primarily in disease-specific programs, the international problems in health governance Charles Pannenborg listed in 1979 still persist today.[205] In 1979, IHG weaknesses included: (1) lack of coordination between donor governments, NGOs, and recipient countries; (2) confusion of norms and activities due to different ideas regarding health rights and obligations; (3) lack of coordination between WHO, World Bank, other UNOs, and multilateral organizations; (4) lack of national health plans in recipient countries, or plans that do not provide for donor coordination; (5) donor neglect of recurrent expenditures; (6) donors' short-term orientation, ignoring middle- and long-term commitments; (7) tying health aid to donors' or recipients' foreign policies or to purchases of supplies from donor countries; and (8) criteria of "self-reliance" and past performance,

---

[200] N. Szlezak, B. Bloom, D. Jamison, G. Keusch, C. Michaud, S. Moon, et al., "The Global Health System: Actors, Norms, and Expectations in Transition," *PLoS Medicine* 7, no. 1 (2010): e1000183.

[201] R. England, *Experience of Contracting with the Private Sector: A Selective Review* (London: DFID Health Systems Resource Centre, 2004).

[202] P. A. Singer and A. S. Daar, "How Biodevelopment Can Enhance Biosecurity," *Bulletin of the Atomic Scientist* 65, no. 2 (2009): 23–30.

[203] B. J. Powers, J. V. Trinh, and H. B. Bosworth, "Can This Patient Read and Understand Written Health Information?" *Journal of the American Medical Association* 304, no. 1 (2010): 76–84.

[204] S. Moon, N. Szlezák, C. Michaud, D. Jamison, G. Keusch, W. Clark, and B. Bloom, "The Global Health System: Lessons for a Stronger Institutional Framework," *PLoS Medicine* 7, no. 1 (2010): e1000193.

[205] C. Pannenborg, *A New International Health Order: An Inquiry into the International Relations of World Health and Medical Care* (Alphen aan den Rijn: Sijthoff & Noordhoff, 1979); G. Walt, A. Spicer, and K. Buse, "Mapping the Global Health Architecture," in *Making Sense of Global Health Governance: A Policy Perspective*, ed. K. Buse, W. Hein, and N. Drager (New York: Palgrave Macmillan, 2009), 74–113.

channeling aid away from the most needy countries. Why these problems persist, and how to solve them, are core questions that this book addresses.

Today, one of the most salient issues remains the lack of coordination among donors and between donors and recipient governments.[206] GHG's proliferation of initiatives, funding sources, and actors has exacerbated this problem. Many donors lack long-term commitment,[207] and issues of accountability and sustainability as well as performance-based evaluations persist in distorting program design, implementation, and the choice of funding recipients. Furthermore, donor economic, political, and strategic self-interests continue to determine bilateral health aid.[208] Multiple competing principles associated with different regime clusters and associated processes in global health lack coherence and generate overlap, redundancies, and conflicts. Enumerations of these problems are routine, yet GHG solutions remain elusive after nearly four decades. And now, with the scope and complexity of the social determinants of health and the effects of globalization overwhelming state and non-state actors, bringing coherence and coordination to countless unconnected players is increasingly difficult.

### 2.7.1 Summary of Global Health Governance Problems

In sum, several key problems vex GHG. First, hyperpluralism and fragmentation produce incoherence, disorder, and inefficiency; no single regime governs health. Two, blurred lines of responsibility undercut accountability and compliance, making it hard to hold actors—including the WHO—responsible. Three, the proliferation of new actors with divergent interests increases competition and reduces incentives for long-term, prevention-oriented investments in health, health care, or public health systems. Four, uncertainty reigns about normative principles and processes guiding global health in the absence of a genuine agreement on common goals and procedures. Five, key components of global health analyses and planning are lacking: a master health plan, an analysis of global health problems, policy solutions that include an evidence base for their effectiveness and cost-effectiveness, and a global health strategy with global health priorities. Six, powerful countries and institutions exercise excessive political influence, control finances, and manipulate decision-making, and injustice results. Seven, credible compliance and dispute resolution mechanisms are lacking. Eight, inadequate global

---

[206] D. Sridhar, "Seven Challenges in International Development Assistance for Health and Ways Forward," *Journal of Law, Medicine & Ethics* 38, no. 3 (2010): 459–69.

[207] I. Kickbusch, "Action on Global Health: Addressing Global Health Governance Challenges," *Public Health* 119, no. 11 (2005): 969–73.

[208] P. Hirvonen, "Stingy Samaritans: Why Recent Increases in Development Aid Fail to Help the Poor," *Global Policy Forum*, August 2005: 14–28.

standards and rules, other than the IHR, fail to govern the system effectively. Finally, a façade of ethics whose content is charity, not justice, conceals narrow self- and national political interests, operating under the prevailing rational actor model. The current approach is reactive with an ex post or after-the-fact orientation. GHG needs an alternative approach that is proactive, preventative, and ex ante oriented. Addressing health problems after they become global pandemics, as in the 2014 Ebola and 2016 Zika crises, is ineffective and in fact unconscionable in the suffering it fails to avert; it is the wrong approach to global health.

The relatively few success stories notwithstanding, overall the state of GHG points to continuing, decades-old problems of insufficient coordination, the pursuit of narrow national and organizational self-interest, inadequate recipient participation, and sheer lack of resources. Both state and non-state actors continue to oppose governance reforms that would constrain their pursuit of their own interests.

The world needs a new way forward, and shared health governance (SHG) provides a conceptual and operative framework. As a theoretical approach to GHG, SHG calls for developing a shared vision of health and health provision by amalgamating values among global, national, and local actors. Such shared understanding aims to foster agreement on goals and strategies to promote program design, coordination, implementation, and evaluation. SHG is compatible with different framings of health, and can potentially bring the frames together. SHG also advances health agency for all; involving affected but marginalized groups in national and global health initiatives is critical for addressing aid recipients' needs effectively and for reining in powerful industry and national interests. The global community should recognize health as an entitlement, the realization of which will require voluntary resource redistribution from rich to poor, in order to narrow the vast and unjust gaps in health and health services. Actors internalize public moral norms for equity in health and commit to meeting the health needs of all.

SHG envisions an institutional structure for the reduction of global health injustices and greater realization of health equity. While different policy realms touch on health, and health's expansive policy relevance for multiple sectors is important, a unified global health infrastructure is crucial. But though health is broad and multifaceted, a complicated regime complex is not necessary at either the domestic or global level. Successful health governance is focused on preventing people from getting sick and injured and then on treating them as efficiently as possible. Effective prevention and treatment come from creating and sustaining integrated, rational, and harmonized structures, as in many national contexts. A major focus of global and national health systems should be control of health issues that occur every day in human lives and on managing infectious and chronic conditions with limited

49

resources. Building and sustaining national and local public health and health care systems that interface with integrated global health systems should be the foundation.

The current global system, including WHO, is inadequate. Effective governance demands new solutions, a framework for solving global health problems. Scholarly investigations in this area have been as uncoordinated and fragmented as the global health architecture itself. GHG has been framed in dissimilar ways, as an issue of national security, human security, human rights, and global public goods.[209] Global health's increased political prominence in international relations has led powerful state and non-state actors to use health even more as a political tool for geostrategic purposes, and has decreased their willingness to cede control to other bilateral and multilateral actors, including WHO. The Gates Foundation, for example, is now viewed by many as more powerful than WHO in global health. Emerging nations act no differently. Public health and health policy actors are sidelined or politicized in these processes. The current characterization of GHG's purpose in terms of global security,[210] global commerce, global preparedness, response, individual rights, its constitutional outlines,[211] and even philanthropy serves the interests of powerful state and non-state actors. This multiplicity of frames has failed to provide a sufficient basis for strong domestic public health and health policy, to ground a sustainable global health policy, or to motivate a commitment to global health justice.

## 2.8 Why a Theory of Global Health Justice and Governance?

The literature has been essentially untethered to a theorized framework able to illuminate and evaluate GHG in accordance with moral values. Global and national responses to health problems must derive from ethical values about health: ethical claims have the power to create greater understanding and commitment; to motivate; to delineate principles, duties, and responsibilities; and to hold actors morally responsible for achieving common goals. Since addressing inequalities requires redistributing societal benefits and burdens

---

[209] For more on various global health frames, see C. McInnes, A. Kamradt-Scott, K. Lee, D. Reubi, A. Roemer-Mahler, S. Rushton, et al., "Framing Global Health: The Governance Challenge," *Global Public Health* 7(Suppl. 2) (2012): S83–94.

[210] For ethical issues and political consequences related to the international security frame, see S. Elbe, "Should HIV/AIDS Be Securitized? The Ethical Dilemmas of Linking HIV/AIDS and Security," *International Studies Quarterly* 50, no. 1 (2006): 119–44; and S. Elbe, *Virus Alert: Security, Governmentality and the AIDS Pandemic* (New York: Columbia University Press, 2009); and whether this frame leads to better international health policy, see S. Elbe, *Security and Global Health* (Cambridge: Polity Press, 2010).

[211] D. P. Fidler, "Constitutional Outlines of Public Health's 'New World Order'," *Temple Law Review* 77, no. 247 (2004): 247–90.

more fairly, there is a need for theories of justice to define the obligations of institutions and actors.

Critical ethical issues confront us as we seek to develop a moral vision that addresses global health's most confounding problems. What are the moral consequences of global health? Is health a special global good, and if so, what are the moral implications for domestic and global actors and institutions? Why are global health inequalities, externalities, and cross-border problems a matter of justice—or are they? How do we measure global health inequalities? What ethical challenges do these global health issues pose? What is the moral justification for trying to reduce them?

Questions of justice across state boundaries have sparked penetrating academic and policy debate. How do those questions relate to global health—or do they? Do global health issues imply global egalitarianism or do more limited theoretical approaches, such as limited globalism or extended nationalism, provide a better approach for global health? Do global-level health justice duties exist? If so, how do we identify and define them? What duties and responsibilities attach to global and state actors, and to what degree? Does global health justice require global health government? What does reducing global health disparities require? Do states have special obligations for their citizens' health? If so, how do states weigh these special duties against general duties? Is national self-determination inviolate when governments fail their own citizens? May global institutions coerce national governments when they neglect their populations' health? What role, if any, do international and domestic law and human rights play in global and domestic health? Can we find a universal consensus on health? What distributive principles (equality, priority, sufficiency) apply to global health? How much priority do disadvantaged groups merit?

Despite well-known theories of global justice and more recent work in global health ethics, theorists have neglected to offer relevant theoretical insights into global health inequalities, externalities, or cross-border problems. This lack of a theoretical foundation for global health has resulted in skeptics and realists who question whether universal moral standards exist and if a normative framework is required to take action. Are there, or can there be, globally shared values and priorities in global health, and if so, which are central? Addressing such questions precedes understanding our obligations to shape the conditions for all to be healthy. Global and domestic institutions, groups, and individuals need a theoretical foundation on which to build a more just world.

This book offers a foundation, the provincial globalism/shared health governance (PG/SHG) line of reasoning, grounding it in capability theory. Ethical principles underlying this approach include the intrinsic value of health to well-being and equal respect for all human life; the importance of health for

51

individual and collective agency; assessment by measuring the shortfall from the health status of a reference group; and the need for a disproportionate effort to help disadvantaged groups. Global actors and institutions have responsibilities and roles, as do individuals. An essential first step in redressing wrongs, to the extent that wrongs exist, is exposing the wrong and "making explicit the values on which proposed action is based."[212] In the PG/SHG view, allowing individuals to die prematurely and suffer unnecessary morbidity when the global community could create the socioeconomic conditions necessary to support health is unjust. This deprivation-oriented view calls for identifying the most deprived within and between countries by disaggregating health outcomes. It also urges policy-makers to monitor progress and thereby supplement, rather than displace, the typical tracking of changes in average health. Global and national efforts could then focus on improving opportunities for health in disadvantaged groups. This view would not abandon attempts to improve average health or to improve the health of groups that reside in the middle of the ill-health spectrum. But in supporting universal health coverage (UHC), the PG/SHG view addresses conditions that undermine individuals' capabilities, including those particularly prevalent among disadvantaged groups, such as tuberculosis, malaria, and AIDS. UHC between and within countries depends on the moral values that underlie health policy at the state[213] and global level. This approach also stresses that alternative global and national structures and behavior must be voluntary and self-imposed.

Global health justice and ethics also raise a number of issues related to the allocation of moral responsibility in global health: Who is responsible, and thus accountable? For what are they responsible and accountable? Principles of allocation and the competing views that underlie them include important and divergent rationales. One idea uses causality for harm to determine responsibility for remediation. Justice and governance in this view would entail determining a harm, demonstrating its cause, and assigning moral responsibility for remediating it. The challenge of proving causation, however, makes assigning responsibilities difficult. A second rationale is connectedness to others and partiality: justice extends to the citizens of a given state who share a common identity, and state boundaries mark the limits of obligation. A third rationale rests on functions and capabilities. Allocation of responsibilities depends on required functions and the roles, abilities, and effectiveness of actors and institutions in alleviating global health inequalities, addressing

[212] M. Whitehead, G. Dahlgren, and L. Gilson, "Developing the Policy Response to Inequities in Health: A Global Perspective," in *Challenging Inequities in Health*, ed. T. Evans, M. Whitehead, and F. Diderichsen (New York: Oxford University Press, 2001), 308–23.
[213] U. Reinhardt and T. Cheng, "Sick around the World," *Frontline*, November 10, 2007.

externalities, and remedying cross-border problems. The PG/SHG perspective parcels out respective roles and responsibilities at the global, state, local, and individual levels based on functional requirements and needs, identifying actors and institutions, their obligations, and how they are held accountable. Institutions and actors perform core functions, functions required to protect and promote human's health capabilities, particularly central health capabilities, meeting health functioning and health agency needs. This view acknowledges concurrent general duties toward foreigners and special duties toward fellow nationals. It also recognizes that our impartiality toward fellow human beings and our partiality toward those with whom we share circumstances, such as statehood, are compatible rather than mutually antagonistic.

Even the idea of global justice is controversial. Indeed, some theories deny altogether any claims of justice in the global realm. Chapter three assesses major theoretical perspectives on global justice and examines their implications for the existence, scope, and assignment of global health justice duties. Chapter four then lays out the main analytical components of PG.

# Part II
# Global Health Justice

# 3

# Contrasting Theories of Global Justice

Does massive global inequality pose moral questions for the world community? The human experience differs sharply depending on where in the world one lives. While many in prosperous countries have adequate nutrition, housing, education, and health care, extraordinary hardship afflicts those in impoverished countries who lack the most basic of life's necessities. Where one is born—a morally arbitrary accident of birth—can condemn one to a brief and destitute existence, through no fault of one's own. Is rectifying this state of affairs a moral duty? Does that moral duty extend universally to all persons, or only to those within associative boundaries of communities or nations? How expansive is this duty—how much help must be given? Whose duty is it? Theories of global justice address these questions.

Global justice issues encompass, in addition to material and health deprivations, human rights and the performance of global institutions such as the World Bank, the International Monetary Fund (IMF), and the World Trade Organization (WTO). The focus here, however, is global distributive justice in health. Global justice theories fall into four main perspectives: realism, particularism, social contractarianism (society of states), and cosmopolitanism.

This grouping is not exhaustive or definitive; some theorists deny the idea of global justice altogether. These perspectives are examined because they have implications for the existence, scope, and assignment of global justice duties.

## 3.1 Realism

Realism as a framework is more descriptive than prescriptive—it deals with how the world actually works. Applied globally, realism takes two major forms, but in both forms anarchy reigns. No formal hierarchy organizes states and no overarching authority maintains order or enforces agreements. Increasing power for security and perhaps expansion motivate state action.

Thucydides,[1] Thomas Hobbes,[2] and twentieth-century theorists such as Hans Morgenthau[3] propounded classical realism, which they saw as rooted in human nature. Hobbes, for example, believed that sovereign states exist in a state of nature with one another, and human desire for gain, security, and glory drives conflicts.

In neorealism, Kenneth Waltz,[4] among others, emphasizes anarchy and the pursuit of security above all in the international system. States are the principal actors and promote their own national interests. States try to maintain or improve their own relative positions to ensure survival. A zero-sum element arises in international relations because states fear that gains of others will come at their expense. Neorealism sees no obligation to help other countries in need, unless by aiding another country a state furthers its own strategic interests. No international moral laws apply in either realism perspective. There is no global ethical standard and no global moral imperative.

Neoliberalism shares realism's basic premise—state actors pursuing self-interest in anarchy—but this view, from Robert Keohane and Joseph Nye,[5] allows greater cooperation among states to further their individual interests and thus diminishes the zero-sum element. Neoliberalism also gives international organizations a greater role than realism: it envisions a world with international coalitions. Though actors under neoliberalism can give aid, neither considerations of justice nor aid's effects on recipients motivate it, but rather each actor's own goals and objectives. Benefiting aid recipients is secondary.

Under realism and self-interest-maximizing rational actor perspectives, no players have a duty to mitigate the suffering of others. In the realist focus on relative advantage—to be richer or more powerful than others—international inequalities are built in; in neoliberalism, inequality is not considered problematic. The voluntary exchange of labor, services, and goods, including the distribution of foreign aid, is to be left to the free market (regulating to prevent violence, stealing, and cheating). Even when states offer aid, their self-interest can undercut its effectiveness and might even make it counterproductive: pathology in foreign aid is well known.[6] As noted in Part I, rich countries direct much foreign aid not where the need is greatest, but to former colonies,

---

[1] Thucydides, *History of the Peloponnesian War*, ed. M. I. Finley, trans. R. Warner (London: Penguin, 1972).

[2] T. Hobbes, *Leviathan* (Lawrence, KS: Digireads.com Publishing, 2009).

[3] H. J. Morgenthau, *Politics among Nations: The Struggle for Power and Peace*, 4th ed. (New York: Alfred A. Knopf, 1967).

[4] K. N. Waltz, *Theory of International Politics* (New York: Waveland Press, 1979).

[5] R. O. Keohane and J. S. Nye, *Power and Interdependence*, 4th ed. (London: Pearson, 2011); see also R. O. Keohane, *After Hegemony: Cooperation and Discord in the World Political Economy* (Princeton, NJ: Princeton University Press, 2005).

[6] A. Deaton, *The Great Escape: Health, Wealth, and the Origins of Inequality* (Princeton, NJ: Princeton University Press, 2013); J. E. Stiglitz, *Globalization and Its Discontents* (New York: W.W. Norton & Company, 2002).

strategic allies, or regions they seek to influence.[7] Politics often control aid, and inefficiencies run rampant. The realist approach dominates global health governance (GHG) today—in the competition among actors, the pursuit of donors' narrow agendas, and the self-interested motivations driving much of the health enterprise. Thus, many global health efforts fail to relieve suffering or to strengthen health systems.

## 3.2 Particularism: Communitarianism and Nationalism

The particularist view assigns rights and duties to persons bound together in affiliative communities. In particularism, one's fellow community members have priority claims on distribution. Some particularists refute entirely the possibility of justice standards or obligations beyond the community. Communitarianism and nationalism are two versions of this view.

Most people intuitively accept that they bear obligations to affiliates. Under communitarianism, group connections and relationships shape peoples' identities and envelop their lives. The society holds common values, which dictate moral judgments in that community. Michael Walzer proposes in *Spheres of Justice* that "[a] given society is just if its substantive life is lived in a certain way—that is, in a way faithful to the shared understandings of the members."[8] The society's values and priorities determine resource distribution. Each society constructs those shared principles as it evolves; morality reflects culture, history, and tradition. Alasdair MacIntyre believes that different "traditions of enquiry, with histories" will produce different conceptions of justice—"justices rather than justice."[9] There are no global moral standards, no global moral community, and thus no basis for global distributive justice. And so global health inequalities pose no moral problem and require no remedy.

David Miller argues that nationality consists of an active community defined by "shared belief," "mutual commitment," history, connection to a territory, and a "distinct public culture."[10] Miller and Jeff McMahan[11] base partiality in distributive justice on reciprocity between fellow nationals in cooperative national systems. Richard Dagger[12] applies partiality more

---

[7] E. Neumayer, "Self-Interest, Foreign Need, and Good Governance: Are Bilateral Investment Treaty Programs Similar to Aid Allocation?" *Foreign Policy Analysis* 2, no. 3 (2006): 245–67.

[8] M. Walzer, *Spheres of Justice: A Defense of Pluralism and Equality* (New York: Basic Books, 1983), 313.

[9] A. MacIntyre, *Whose Justice? Which Rationality?* (Notre Dame, IN: University of Notre Dame Press, 1988), 9.

[10] D. Miller, *On Nationality* (Oxford: Oxford University Press, 1995), 27.

[11] J. McMahan, "The Limits of National Partiality," in *The Morality of Nationalism*, ed. R. McKim and J. McMahan (New York: Oxford University Press, 1997).

[12] R. Dagger, *Civic Virtues: Rights, Citizenship, and Republican Liberalism* (New York: Oxford University Press, 1997).

specifically to a state's citizens, as opposed to nationals. Nationalists can allow for universal values, but Miller contends that fellow nationals, and not necessarily outsiders, have the primary duties derived from such values. Nations respect other nations' sovereignty, and self-determination and non-intervention are key principles. In humanitarian crises, one may help foreigners, but in general the obligation to fellow nationals is much greater. The state thus has normative significance on grounds of reciprocity (a single cooperative scheme in which duties of reciprocity[13] are only owed to fellow citizens), identity (identification with one's own country creates duties only owed fellow citizens), and/or coercion (the power, authority, and public mandate of the state enable it to promote justice, but only among its own citizens). These three elements give rise to special and exclusive duties to fellow citizens.

The particularist view respects collective self-determination and bases substantive notions of the good on community values, rather than abstractions that might carry biases of their own (especially Western liberal bias). But the darker side of particularism is that it permits gravely disparate conditions and treatment of persons, due to nothing more than morally arbitrary accidents of birth. Some communities accept practices such as caste discrimination, forced child marriage, widow burning, and slavery as just, and without some supracommunal moral values, those practices' victims have nowhere to turn.

Nationality's ethical significance, moreover, is open to challenge: some argue that nations are not in fact real communities in which members have direct relationships and engage in genuine reciprocal cooperation. Instead, nations are imagined communities whose members might cooperate as much with members of other nations as among themselves.[14] In the state, compatriots may be in a better position to fulfill duties for one another, but that is an instrumental attribute of national affiliation, and not morally significant in and of itself.[15] In truth, members of different nations often share values and find common cause in pursuing them, despite cultural variations.

Realist and particularist theories might have been more defensible in a world of self-sufficient states and communities, but globalization's increasing interconnection and interdependence mean that conditions elsewhere—disease outbreaks, for example, or economic or political crises—can severely impact one's own community or country. So quite aside from more universal moral claims, self-interest suggests working to remediate deprivations and inequality that can cause negative spillovers. In addition, supranational bodies

---

[13] For a view of reciprocity and mutual provision of collective goods see A. Sangiovanni, "Global Justice, Reciprocity, and the State," *Philosophy & Public Affairs* 35, no. 1 (2007): 3–39.

[14] S. Caney, "International Distributive Justice," *Political Studies* 49 (2001): 974–97.

[15] R. E. Goodin, "What is So Special about Our Fellow Countrymen?" *Ethics* 98, no. 4 (1988): 663–86.

(for example, WTO and IMF) and transnational actors like global corporations often encroach upon states' self-regulation,[16] though these bodies also reflect state interests. In today's world, an excessively narrow definition of self-interest is no longer realistic, and states cannot ignore conditions beyond their borders.

## 3.3 Social Contractarianism (Society of States)

John Rawls' *The Law of Peoples*[17] sets forth social contractarianism at the global level, extending his thought experiment about the original position, described in *A Theory of Justice*,[18] beyond the domestic context into the international realm. Rawls' actors are peoples. Each people shares common values and conceptions of justice, and a common government rules them. States represent their peoples. Peoples reach mutually acceptable principles of international justice—the law of peoples—from behind a veil of ignorance. This is the original position, in which participants know about the world and human affairs, but do not know the attributes and position of the people they represent. Because peoples are equally uninformed about their population, size, resources, and relative power—an attempt at impartiality—they will arguably set rules treating all contracting parties fairly. These rules are quite minimal: to respect freedom and independence, to follow treaties, to refrain from intervention and from war except for self-defense, to constrain military conduct, and to honor human rights. Rawls also specifically stipulates a "duty to assist other peoples living under unfavorable conditions that prevent their having a just or decent political and social regime."[19]

Thus, there is an international duty—as a principle of international justice—to come to the aid of those in need. Nonetheless, Rawls' international system permits inequality: it provides neither for global egalitarianism nor redistribution. It requires assistance for burdened societies only to the degree that actors can set up and maintain decent institutions. Rawls' conception of core human rights, including subsistence, suggests what this point might be. Where subsistence and decent, basic institutions obtain, international inequality is not a justice concern, though Simon Caney argues Rawls' framework would permit more egalitarian global redistribution than Rawls admits.[20] International distributive justice is not the focus of Rawls' law of peoples; the justice of rules governing international interactions is. The

---

[16] J. E. Stiglitz, *Making Globalization Work* (New York: W.W. Norton & Company, 2007).
[17] J. Rawls, *The Law of Peoples* (Cambridge, MA: Harvard University Press, 2001).
[18] J. Rawls, *A Theory of Justice* (Cambridge, MA: Harvard University Press, 1971).
[19] Rawls, *The Law of Peoples*, 37.
[20] Caney, "International Distributive Justice," 985.

international order it produces is just because free and equal actors set the governing rules under fair conditions.

The law of peoples sets forth a universalist conception of justice insofar as contracting parties have equal standing and the agreed-upon principles apply universally to all contracting parties. But this account is not fully universal, because Rawls imposes limits on the peoples who may participate as contracting parties. Only liberal or decent peoples may enter into the international social contract. Liberal peoples have constitutional and democratic governments, "common sympathies," and a moral commitment to justice and rightness.[21] Decent peoples, while not liberal and/or democratic, embrace core human rights and, through consultation, represent all persons in policymaking. Liberal and decent peoples reject aggressive foreign policies and for Rawls have equal status. But the social contract excludes benevolent absolutisms, outlaw states, and burdened societies. Benevolent absolutisms bar citizens from the political process. Outlaw states threaten international peace in their pursuit of power and domination, or abrogate their citizens' human rights. Liberal and decent peoples may wage war against outlaw states to defend themselves or to enforce human rights. Burdened societies, lacking social and economic resources, cannot establish liberal or decent institutions, and other peoples must help until these societies can order their own affairs. These states are excluded from the society of peoples.

Rawls did not intend for his principles of justice, especially his equality of opportunity principle, to apply at the global level. Still, in arguing for liberal and decent peoples to help burdened societies, Rawls' framework asserts global justice duties that the realist and some particularist perspectives lack.

Rawls' thought experiments and their resulting justice principles have methodological vulnerabilities. Thought experiments might produce varying outcomes depending on either the theorist or the participating parties. Liberal and decent peoples might agree to strikingly different principles than those to which non-liberal, non-decent peoples assent. Whether peoples would actually agree on Rawls' principles of international justice is unknowable, and the framework does not explain why or how actors would choose in hypothetical situations. Further, liberal and decent peoples, in Rawls' view, are those who agree with his justice principles. Peoples' agreement on honoring human rights rests on a vision of the good life, so what is needed is a justifiable theory of the good—what is good for humanity—not a thought experiment. Thus, outcomes ultimately depend on a substantive, not just procedural, theory of the good. That being the case, different principles of justice might emerge under a different theorist or with a different set of participants. Concern for

---

[21] Rawls, *The Law of Peoples* (Cambridge, MA: Harvard University Press, 1999), 23–5, citing J. S. Mill, *Considerations* (1862).

and inclusion of burdened societies as contracting parties, for example, might well yield global distributive justice principles. Stephen Macedo provides a moral defense for Rawls' "conditional accommodation of diversity among peoples"; peoples qualify for full respect when they are "genuinely collectively self-governing." Collective self-governance, on this view, has moral significance.[22]

By minimizing obligations, the law of peoples has a bias that largely ignores the real world's interdependence and hegemonies. Rules made under ideal situations might not ensure peoples' freedom and independence in today's global realities. Indeed, Rawls asserts that peoples themselves affect their successes and failures: "the causes of the wealth of a people and the forms it takes lie in their political culture and in the religious, philosophical, and moral traditions that support the basic structure of their political and social institutions, as well as in the industriousness and cooperative talents of its members, all supported by their political virtues."[23] This view ignores the deleterious political and economic impacts that rich, powerful countries and the transnational actors they arguably control inflict on developing countries.[24] Amartya Sen has critiqued the Rawlsian account of closed impartiality, which limits assessments of impartiality to the focal group for which principles of justice are determined. Sen argues, first, that it excludes individuals and groups who exist outside the focal group but who may nevertheless be impacted by policies of the closed group; second, that it may result in inconsistencies when decisions made by the focal group impact the future size and membership of that very group; and third, that it allows for procedural parochialism in that the biases, prejudices, and vested interests of the focal group are not questioned and challenged. Sen, following Adam Smith, argues rather for "open impartiality" with the help of impartial spectators, giving voice to others beyond the focal group.[25]

Other contractarian theorists argue for more extensive global redistribution, based on contracts that everyone on Earth would agree to behind a veil of ignorance in the global original position. For domestic society Rawls formulated the difference principle, which permits distributive inequalities when those inequalities benefit the worst off. But Rawls rejects its application in the international society of states. Charles Beitz first countered Rawls, noting that domestic societies in fact exist within a context of global economic

[22] S. Macedo, "What Self-Governing Peoples Owe to One Another: Universalism, Diversity, and the Law of Peoples," *Fordham Law Review* 72, no. 5 (2004): 1723.

[23] Rawls, *The Law of Peoples*, 108.

[24] C. R. Beitz, *Political Theory and International Relations*, rev. ed. (Princeton, NJ: Princeton University Press, 1999); T. W. Pogge, "An Egalitarian Law of Peoples," *Philosophy & Public Affairs* 23, no. 3 (1994): 195–224.

[25] A. Sen, *The Idea of Justice* (Cambridge, MA: Harvard University Press, 2009), 124–52.

cooperation, and thus the difference principle ought also to apply globally.[26] He later revised his argument to include everyone in the global original position and the global application of the difference principle because humans have an "effective sense of justice" and the ability to "form, revise, and pursue a conception of the good."[27] Thomas Pogge claims that to maintain well-ordered societies and avoid huge international inequalities peoples would choose more egalitarian distribution than Rawls suggests—especially because disadvantaged peoples have the global activities and institutions of rich peoples to thank for much of their disadvantage.[28] More fundamentally, individuals, and not simply peoples, would arguably favor a more egalitarian distribution to avoid severe poverty and "large discrepancies between their own socio-economic level and that prevailing in more affluent societies."[29] The application of Rawlsian domestic social justice would thus seem to apply globally as well as nationally. Brian Barry, drawing on both John Rawls and Thomas Scanlon,[30] proposes a global social contract that no person could reasonably reject, which would stipulate equal consideration unless it could justify partiality in terms acceptable to everyone.[31] These global applications of social contractarianism bear similarities to cosmopolitanism.

## 3.4 Cosmopolitanism and Utilitarianism

Cosmopolitanism's lineage dates to ancient Greece. Different theorists have differing views of global justice and its requirements, but common to all is the belief that all humans belong to the same community. Individuals are the object of universal moral standards, and all shoulder justice duties. This universalism contrasts with particularism's emphasis on attachments and obligations to one's own community or country. Cosmopolitanism weakens the significance of the state as the space in which justice pertains. It is about the scope of moral principles; it does not necessarily focus on prescribing distributive justice or democratic systems. Within cosmopolitanism, two strains, utilitarianism and human rights cosmopolitanism, are especially relevant for global distribution.

---

[26] Beitz, *Political Theory and International Relations*.

[27] C. R. Beitz, "Cosmopolitanism Ideals and National Sentiment," *Journal of Philosophy* 80, no. 10 (1983): 595.

[28] T. W. Pogge, "The Incoherence between Rawls's Theories of Justice," *Fordham Law Review* 72, no. 5 (2004): 1739–59.

[29] Ibid., 1752.

[30] T. M. Scanlon, "Contractualism and Utilitarianism," in *Utilitarianism and Beyond*, ed. A. Sen and B. Williams (Cambridge: Cambridge University Press, 1982): 103–29.

[31] B. Barry, "International Society from a Cosmopolitan Perspective," in *International Society: Diverse Ethical Perspectives*, ed. D. R. Mapel and T. Nardin (Princeton, NJ: Princeton University Press, 1998), 144–163.

### 3.4.1 *Utilitarianism*

The good in utilitarianism is welfare or utility, which takes on different meanings with different theorists. Jeremy Bentham[32] and John Stuart Mill,[33] for example, identify utility as pleasure or happiness; more generally, utility subjectively measures the satisfaction of one's preferences. All humans feel pain and pleasure, and their welfare and preferences can be compared and aggregated across individuals. Utilitarianism aims to maximize this aggregated utility. How utility is maximized is irrelevant, as long as it is maximized. Neither citizenship nor other special relationships have moral significance. Utilitarianism prescribes no specific duties or procedures; duties and rights derive not from theory but from empirical experience with maximizing utility.

In his 1972 article "Famine, Affluence, and Morality," Peter Singer, a utilitarian theorist on global distributive justice, endorses the utilitarian view that everyone "ought, morally, to be working full time to relieve great suffering of the sort that occurs as a result of famine or other disasters."[34] Suffering is bad and people have an obligation to prevent it, he argues, as long as doing so does not entail "sacrificing anything of comparable moral importance."[35] In other words, fulfilling this obligation should not cause an outcome comparable to the suffering one seeks to prevent. Proximity is irrelevant: the obligation applies as much to those in distant countries as to those next door. Rather than spending money on non-necessities (travel, movies, or jewelry, for example), Singer believes people should give wealth away to relieve poverty and starvation. Indeed, Singer calls for people to give until they reach the "level of marginal utility—that is, the level at which, by giving more, [one] would cause as much suffering to [oneself] or [one's] dependents as [one] would relieve by [one's] gift."[36] In Singer's example of helping Bengali refugees, people would give until their material circumstances are comparable to the refugees. Utilitarianism is not concerned with equality per se, but Singer's rigorous demand, taken to its logical conclusion, would affect a radical global redistribution of goods. On the other hand, Singer cautions against slowing the consumer economy excessively, since a shrunken economy will produce lower levels of aid and inferior results. Singer's normative claim of equal duties to all individuals exists irrespective of special relationships or geography. This individualist account outlines duties owed by individuals to other individuals, in contrast to institutional accounts, which outline duties owed by states to

---

[32] J. Bentham, *The Principles of Morals and Legislation* (Amherst, NY: Prometheus Books, 1988).
[33] J. S. Mill, *Utilitarianism*, 2nd ed., ed. G. Sher (Indianapolis, IN: Hackett, 2002).
[34] P. Singer, "Famine, Affluence, and Morality," *Philosophy and Public Affairs* 1, no. 3 (1972): 238.
[35] Ibid., 231.
[36] Ibid., 241.

other states, or those in which institutions discharge the individuals' duties to foreigners.

Singer's excessive demands raise objections. Most people do not feel the same obligation toward strangers half a world away that they feel toward those nearby. Most also distinguish between mandatory and optional duties and put humanitarian contributions in the latter category—itself a kind of discretionary expense. Optional duties are indeterminate and discretionary; it is up to the individual whether or not she fulfills them. Few expect this expense to materially reduce their own living circumstances. The claim of a duty to give to strangers to the point of marginal utility is too demanding for most to accept. Singer later proposed a sliding scale that would set contributions at 5 percent for those in the bottom half of the top 10 percent of earners, and at least 10 percent for those at the top. This sliding scale could extend beyond the top 10 percent as well.[37]

Beyond the excessive demands problem, the utility metric's subjectivity poses questions about interpersonal comparability, especially globally. One's perception of one's welfare can in fact be a misperception, as Amartya Sen and Martha Nussbaum point out. People suffering extended deprivation or discrimination (illiterate women in poor countries, for example) might have insufficient information to compare their situation with others, thus distorting their grasp of their welfare. Such perceptions may not accurately reflect one's objective quality of life and well-being. Sen offers the example of widows in India reporting significantly less ill health than widowers (2.5 percent of widows versus 48.5 percent of widowers), despite suffering truly deplorable health.[38] The standards by which these individuals and groups judge their utility or welfare are usually very different. Oppressed, impoverished widows expect little welfare, compared to more privileged widowers (to say nothing of citizens of rich developed countries). Utilitarian calculations based on such adaptive preferences have questionable value.[39] Sen further argues that, even when accurate, preferences or desires are not suitable indicators of well-being. Indeed, they can exacerbate social inequalities in health. Instead, the capability to achieve valuable functionings should be the main variable for evaluation.

Utilitarian principles and metrics can also disadvantage the elderly and those with disabilities, because the young and able-bodied are more able to convert resources to utility. People with less capacity to benefit from resources

---

[37] P. Singer, *The Life You Can Save: Acting Now to End World Poverty* (New York: Random House, 2009); P. Singer, *The Most Good You Can Do: How Effective Altruism is Changing Ideas about Living Ethically* (New Haven, CT: Yale University Press, 2015).

[38] A. Sen, *Commodities and Capabilities* (New Delhi: Oxford University Press, 1985), 53.

[39] M. C. Nussbaum, "Capabilities and Human Rights," *Fordham Law Review* 66, no. 2 (1997): 283.

may derive less utility per unit of resource, so allocating resources to them fails to maximize aggregate utility. The commensurability of everyone's burdens and utility is problematic both theoretically and empirically.

An additional objection is that utilitarianism does not impose any moral limits on steps to increase utility. A single metric measures all. Utility is thus directly comparable and exchangeable; all trade-offs are possible and permitted. Utilitarianism accords no special place to life or liberty. Collective interests can override individual interests. Individuals are expendable as means to ends; they are not ends in themselves. If sacrificing individuals would increase aggregate welfare, utilitarianism would permit it. Utilitarianism could thus defend forced sterilization to uphold population-control policies, for example.

A further objection acknowledges the difficulties in requiring every agent to give money to the point beyond which she is giving up something of equal value. This objection faults, first, the demand's unrealistic severity. But it also recognizes the difficulty of distributing burdens fairly so that all give an equal share to address problems such as poverty.[40]

Singer's approach also largely ignores the individual and collective agency of poor people in alleviating poverty and striving for the good life. This kind of charity or humanitarianism might be considered anti-development in that it treats poor individuals as passive beneficiaries or recipients rather than active agents of their own development, thus undermining their ability to determine their own values and vision.[41]

### 3.4.2 *Human Rights Cosmopolitanism*

Under a human rights cosmopolitanism view, all individuals have rights by virtue of being human. These include civil and political rights—freedom to travel, to worship, to express oneself, to participate in political life, for example—and a right to certain levels of economic resources. But though human rights theorists believe that all are entitled to basic resources, they do not necessarily require global equality. Levels of provision can range from relatively minimal subsistence that enables exercising and securing other rights, as Henry Shue[42] and Charles Jones[43] assert, to Hillel Steiner's strongly egalitarian argument for equal shares of natural resources.[44] Pogge falls

---

[40] L. B. Murphy, "The Demands of Beneficence," *Philosophy and Public Affairs* 22, no. 4 (1993): 267–92.

[41] For further discussion, see ch. 10 in D. Goulet, *The Cruel Choice: A New Concept in the Theory of Development* (New York: Atheneum, 1971).

[42] H. Shue, *Basic Rights: Subsistence, Affluence, and U.S. Foreign Policy*, 2nd ed. (Princeton, NJ: Princeton University Press, 1996).

[43] C. Jones, *Global Justice: Defending Cosmopolitanism* (Oxford: Oxford University Press, 1999).

[44] H. Steiner, *An Essay on Rights* (Oxford: Blackwell, 1994).

between these two, asserting a right to the resources required to access literacy, political participation, and other objects of human rights.[45]

For some cosmopolitan theorists like Beitz and Pogge, the basic global structure including the IMF, WTO, World Bank, and United Nations (UN) is enough to trigger global distributive justice principles, because the global structure has significant influence on individuals' lives and their life prospects. Whether new organizations and distributive schema are needed under this umbrella depends on the basic structure's adequacy. Some argue that the global institutional structure is woefully underdeveloped and does not affect individual lives the way the domestic structure does (for example, in the regulation of property and in coercion and law enforcement), certainly not enough to support claims of justice on a global scale.[46] If sovereignty is the permitting condition of justice, then global justice cannot be achieved absent a global sovereign.[47] Strict cosmopolitans will be skeptical of the "normative peculiarity of the state."[48] Still, the global importance and scope of cosmopolitan justice principles may not depend on whether there is a political, economic, or institutional correlation between the domestic and global realms.[49]

Pogge's cosmopolitan framework includes individualism (human beings as the unit of concern), universality (everyone included equally), and generality (all persons worldwide must treat every other person worldwide as a unit of concern). Global redistribution for Pogge rests on more than universal human entitlement. Through the global institutions they support, citizens of rich Western nations are causally responsible for misery among the poor. International trade rules privilege rich countries, a bias visible, for example, in agricultural subsidies and strong intellectual property (IP) protection for medicines. Conceptions of state sovereignty in international law and norms prop up corrupt rulers, exacerbating the suffering of the poor. Powerful countries design and operate these global institutions for their own enrichment, thus violating the negative duty to not uphold injustice. The hurt the current institutions inflict is avoidable; actors could design and operate institutions in ways more beneficial to the poor. Their complicity in an unjust order puts them under an obligation to redistribute resources globally and remedy the suffering of the poor.

Pogge thus allocates duties by causality, and ties individuals' and institutions' actions, directly and indirectly, to the suffering of the poor. However,

[45] T. Pogge, *World Poverty and Human Rights*, 2nd ed. (Cambridge: Polity Press, 2008).

[46] S. Freeman, *Rawls* (New York: Routledge, 2007), 442–54.

[47] T. Nagel, "The Problem of Global Justice," *Philosophy & Public Affairs* 33, no. 2 (2005): 113–47.

[48] M. Risse, "What to Say about the State," *Social Theory and Practice* 32, no. 4 (2006): 681.

[49] K. C. Tan, *Justice without Borders: Cosmopolitanism, Nationalism, and Patriotism* (Cambridge: Cambridge University Press, 2004).

establishing and proving causal connections, even co-contributions, can be difficult amid the complex and multidimensional factors involved in poverty, ill health, and other species of misery. Alan Patten disputes Pogge's strategy, arguing that a minimalist normative principle (the duty to avoid harming the poor) cannot support maximalist conclusions about obligations to the poor.[50] Norman Daniels critiques the international causality approach, arguing that it does not deal with inequalities caused by natural conditions or domestic problems. Daniels also claims that Pogge is unclear about how to measure harm to the human right to health.[51] Still, arguing for an alternative set of global arrangements to avoid harm to the poor is a welcome critique of the international order and its preponderant benefits for rich countries.

Beyond critiques of specific cosmopolitan theories, the cosmopolitan perspective as a whole faces some general objections. Cosmopolitanism overall sheds little light on justice requirements. It does not identify morally relevant attributes to be protected and promoted for all; it can coexist with both liberal and illiberal values. Thus, by itself, cosmopolitanism is insufficient as a basis for global public policy, global institutional reform, or global governance. The global community needs substantive notions of the good with specified goals and principles for achieving those goals, which cosmopolitanism cannot provide without other theoretical perspectives. Particularists committed to society-specific conceptions of justice have noted this weakness in cosmopolitanism: Walzer, for example, argues that drawing up a determinant universal set of human goods and values would yield a set that must "be conceived in terms so abstract that they would be of little use in thinking about particular distributions."[52] On the other hand, Kwame Anthony Appiah's conception of cosmopolitanism as "universality plus difference," although prioritizing universality, respects different cultures.[53] Appiah also makes the important point that a commitment to cosmopolitan ideals means more than financial obligations and contributions to charities; rather, solutions to specific problems that arise in specific situations is essential, and the state is the primary space for such resolutions. He also expresses concerns with strict application of act-consequentialism on a global scale in terms of denying individuals the ability to make personal choices leading to fulfilling lives. Seyla Benhabib's cosmopolitan vision seeks to reconcile the tension between the universal and particular through incorporation of universal cosmopolitan values such as

[50] A. Patten, "Should We Stop Thinking about Poverty in Terms of Helping the Poor?" *Ethics & International Affairs* 19, no. 1 (2005): 19–27.

[51] N. Daniels, *Just Health: Meeting Health Needs Fairly* (New York: Cambridge University Press, 2008), 333–56.

[52] Walzer, *Spheres of Justice*, 8.

[53] K. A. Appiah, *Cosmopolitanism: Ethics in a World of Strangers* (New York: W.W. Norton & Company, 2006), 151.

human rights into democratic practice at the state level.[54] The history of human rights provides a rich account of the evolution of this idea in its thickest and thinnest embodiments across the globe.[55]

## 3.5 Application of Global Justice Perspectives to Global Health

### 3.5.1 Global Health Justice: Largely Unheeded in Justice Theories

While there is growing interest in applying global justice perspectives to global health, relatively little work has done so systematically or addressed global health inequalities, externalities, and cross-border problems. The Hobbesian realist or normative skeptic view would take national self-interest as the primary concern among the international community. From this perspective, global health inequalities provide no moral motive for remedy. John Rawls and Thomas Nagel's accounts, favoring a society of states, would ground justice obligations in the state. In this view, global health inequalities have no moral standing; justice is owed solely to our fellow citizens. Justice is dependent upon enforceable laws, coercive institutions, and political solidarity, which occur at the state level, not the global.

Cosmopolitan approaches would vary from rigorous demands for global cooperation to a minimum adherence to the no-harm principle—prohibiting states, individuals, corporations, and the international community from causing harm, particularly extreme poverty, to others. In the case of health care and medical conditions, this brand of cosmopolitanism would argue from a causality perspective that we have a more compelling moral duty to alleviate medical conditions to which we have substantially contributed, such as poverty-related ill health. The question is: How are we causally related to medical conditions from which individuals suffer? Pogge argues that "foreigners' medical conditions in whose incidence we are materially involved have greater moral weight for us than compatriots' medical conditions in whose incidence we are not materially involved."[56] This view, however, depends on the ability to establish one person or group's material involvement in another person or group's ill health. Examining these links is also important in indirect relationships, as, for example, when individuals simply support institutions implicated in foreigners' medical conditions. Economic institutions that

---

[54] S. Benhabib, *Another Cosmopolitanism: Hospitality, Sovereignty, and Democratic Iterations* (New York: Oxford University Press, 2006).

[55] J. Winter and A. Prost, *René Cassin and Human Rights: From the Great War to the Universal Declaration* (Cambridge: Cambridge University Press, 2013).

[56] T. Pogge, "Responsibilities for Poverty-Related Ill Health," *Ethics & International Affairs* 16, no. 2 (2002): 72.

perpetuate poverty are an illustration: in this view, individuals supporting these institutions contribute materially to poverty-related medical conditions.

This approach raises challenging questions. What is the relative or weighted causality assigned to domestic and foreign persons and groups of persons? Under what circumstances is an individual or state more causally responsible for foreigners' medical conditions than for compatriots' medical conditions? For Pogge, citizens in developed countries such as the United States have a stronger moral obligation to help alleviate medical conditions of foreign victims than to support "most services provided under ordinary health programs (such as Medicare) for the benefit of their compatriots."[57] The claim that poverty is a significant cause of medical conditions and that international institutions are a chief cause of poverty is itself a critical causal pathway. Can we separate out persons who do not support certain institutions and assess whether their opposition defines their moral status differently, freeing them of obligations toward foreigners and compatriots? This perspective, with a focus on these indirect and direct pathways, has opened up a way of critically scrutinizing these relationships and their implications for global justice.

Social contract theorists like Rawls reject the cosmopolitan view. Rawls argues that developing countries' own local economic institutions, in which developed countries' citizens have little involvement, are mostly responsible for severe poverty in these countries—not international economic institutions. Of course, this claim ignores the effects of international economic institutions on local economic policies, development, and structures. Many dispute Rawls' claim, arguing that international organizations such as the IMF and the World Bank and powerful economies like those of the G8 in fact undercut developing countries' wealth and well-being. Pogge argues that international organizations, at the very least, share responsibility for poverty and poverty-related ill health in developing countries.

The major global justice perspectives do not specify substantive ends of justice, even those that call for an egalitarian distribution of resources. The possible exception is the utilitarian strain of cosmopolitanism, which seeks to maximize utility or welfare, but those concepts have their own significant drawbacks.

Nor do these global justice perspectives set specific requirements for pursuing justice or place limits on actions taken to achieve justice. Utilitarians would permit individual sacrifice for the greater good. Human rights cosmopolitan theorists who recognize universal moral status and human rights do set limits on the treatment of and impositions on individuals, in that human

---

[57] Ibid., 74.

rights must be observed. But specific requirements and limits must be derived by individual theorists from external considerations.

Global justice is distinct from global ethics. Pogge and Darrel Moellendorf assert that global justice addresses "moral entitlements and duties in relation to global and international institutional arrangements,"[58] whereas global ethics concerns the "moral responsibilities of individuals, governments, and other agents with respect to issues that have global dimensions, taking the global institutional background as given."[59] Thus a viable global health justice approach would both establish justice entitlements and associated duties and allocate ethical responsibilities to relevant actors to fulfill those duties.

Global health ethics is more directly relevant to current global health practice, since it seeks to guide actions in non-ideal global health situations. Because global health conceptions typically focus on vulnerable populations—due to poverty and the lack of education, social status, political control, and so on—the power disparity between wealthy, developed-world actors and the people of developing countries, and how to prevent harm and exploitation of the latter by the former, are driving concerns.

In other work on medical and public health ethics in the international realm, Onora O'Neill asserts that medical ethics has focused too narrowly on clinical medicine—often in developed countries only—and has neglected public health ethics. It has also failed to address obligations of state and non-state actors in addressing developing countries' health issues, especially the poorest countries. Medical ethics has been especially preoccupied with patient autonomy, and justice literature in political philosophy has been preoccupied with justice requirements within states rather than across borders.[60] While conceptualization of public health ethics is ongoing, this work, too, focuses domestically.[61]

International research ethics[62] has begun to widen its scope to broader questions of global health ethics and justice.[63] Henry Richardson, for example, recognizes the broader moral backdrop for relevant society-wide judgments of justice and the special relationships that exist within the medical research context. He focuses on ethical obligations of ancillary care in

---

[58] T. Pogge and D. Moellendorf, eds., *Global Responsibilities*, vol. 1 (St. Paul, MN: Paragon House, 2008), xxv.

[59] T. Pogge and K. Horton, eds., *Global Responsibilities*, vol. 2 (St. Paul, MN: Paragon House, 2008), xxv.

[60] O. O'Neill, "Public Health or Clinical Ethics: Thinking beyond Borders," *Ethics & International Affairs* 16, no. 2 (2002): 35–45.

[61] J. F. Childress, R. R. Faden, R. D. Gaare, L. O. Gostin, J. Kahn, R. J. Bonnie, et al., "Public Health Ethics: Mapping the Terrain," *Journal of Law, Medicine & Ethics*, 30, no. 2 (2002): 170–8.

[62] J. V. Lavery, C. Grady, E. R. Wahl, and E. Emanuel, eds., *Ethical Issues in International Biomedical Research: A Casebook* (New York: Oxford University Press, 2007).

[63] A. J. London, "Justice and the Human Development Approach to International Research," *Hastings Center Report* 35, no. 1 (2005): 24–37.

clinical trials and medical research, particularly in developing countries, but with relevance throughout the world.[64] Bridget Pratt and Adnan Hyder advance an ethical framework for the governance of transnational global health research with health equity at the core.[65]

Others focusing on responsibility and access to essential medicines argue that the strong emphasis on HIV/AIDS in global health policy reveals a need to probe more deeply into different principles for allocating responsibility for health. They suggest that applying theories of responsibility to global problems might be difficult.[66] Still others recommend specific responsibilities: one proposal involves an international tax on at least the seven major countries of the Organisation for Economic Co-operation and Development for distribution to worse-off states,[67] or a 1 percent gross domestic product transfer from rich to poor countries to target fundamental determinants of health and individual well-being.[68] Another reform advocates lowering drug prices by rewarding the development of new drugs "in proportion to [their] impact on the global disease burden."[69] Benatar and colleagues argue for mutual caring in global health ethics.[70] Others argue that data on health inequalities alone, especially individual inequalities, is not enough to help policy-makers address these inequalities; and they note that health inequality measures by the World Health Organization (WHO) and other agencies are not value-free.[71] An alternative view of inequality, as argued by Larry Temkin, supports an individualistic approach to inequality that "can account for the considered moral judgments of most egalitarians whether those judgments are absolute or relative in nature."[72]

Others assert that multiple perspectives can justify and support global health initiatives.[73] Daniels identifies viewpoints that can "break the stalemate between the statist and cosmopolitan views."[74] Lowry and Schüklenk

[64] H. S. Richardson, *Moral Entanglements* (New York: Oxford University Press, 2012).

[65] B. Pratt and A. A. Hyder, "Governance of Transnational Global Health Research Consortia and Health Equity," *The American Journal of Bioethics* 16, no. 10 (2016): 29–45.

[66] C. Barry and K. Raworth, "Access to Medicines and the Rhetoric of Responsibility," *Ethics & International Affairs* 16, no. 2 (2002): 57–70.

[67] G. Sreenivasan, "International Justice and Health: A Proposal," *Ethics & International Affairs* 16, no. 2 (2002): 81–90.

[68] G. Sreenivasan, "Health and Justice in our Non-Ideal World," *Politics, Philosophy & Economics* 6, no. 2 (2007): 218–36.

[69] T. Pogge, "Human Rights and Global Health: A Research Program," *Metaphilosophy* 36, no. 1/2 (2005): 182.

[70] S. R. Benatar, A. S. Daar, and P. A. Singer, "Global Health Ethics: The Rationale for Mutual Caring," *International Affairs* 79, no. 1 (2003): 107–38.

[71] Y. Asada and T. A. Hedemann, " A Problem with the Individual Approach in the WHO Health Inequality Measurement," *International Journal for Equity in Health* 1, no. 1 (2002): 1–5; D. M. Hausman, "What's Wrong with Health Inequalities?" *Journal of Political Philosophy* 15, no. 1 (2007): 46–66.

[72] L. S. Temkin, *Inequality* (New York: Oxford University Press, 1993), 306.

[73] M. Johri, R. Chung, A. Dawson, and T. Schrecker, "Global Health and National Borders: The Ethics of Foreign Aid in a Time of Financial Crisis," *Globalization and Health* 8 (2012).

[74] Daniels, *Just Health*, 337.

prefer a utilitarian approach to Pogge's emphasis on responsibility, because utilitarianism's "single-minded focus on preventable suffering" offers reasons why we should aid a country beset by economic mismanagement or natural disasters, even though these factors are not caused, directly or indirectly, by richer nations.[75]

The rise of globalization has focused significant philosophical attention on global justice. The UN has sought to formulate universal health norms in the Universal Declaration on Bioethics and Human Rights and a right to the "highest attainable standard of health" in the WHO Constitution. Yet these declarations fail to provide theoretical grounding for global ethical standards, for defining duties and allocating them to actors.


### 3.5.2 Health as a Human Right

More recently, some have examined global justice theories in the health context, comparing and assessing their implications for global health policies. The perspective most frequently used to ground health obligations is the human rights view. Human rights have several advantages as an approach. Theoretically, a rights approach imposes obligations on—rather than seeking discretionary charity from—individuals and states. It concerns equality, and depending on the human rights definition it can go beyond health care to cover social determinants of health. Specifically, the UN Economic and Social Council proposed a human rights approach in General Comment No. 14, on "substantive issues arising in the implementation of the International Covenant on Economic, Social and Cultural Rights."[76] Under a right-to-health approach, the responsibility for realizing this right falls primarily to the state.

Practically, human rights have gained political support and are well integrated into international law; every country is party to at least one international convention involving health-related rights.[77] Yet this approach has its weaknesses too. Although the right to health is legally binding in international law through the International Covenant on Economic, Social and Cultural Rights (ICESCR), specific obligations for this right are hard to determine, are conceptually problematic,[78] too individualistic,[79] and "few countries...utilise [the ICESCR's] norms as a framework for formulating health

[75] C. Lowry and U. Schüklenk, "Two Models in Global Health Ethics," *Public Health Ethics* 2, no. 3 (2009): 279.

[76] Committee on Economic, Social, and Cultural Rights, General Comment 14. E/C.12/2000/4, 22nd Session, Geneva, April 25–May 12, 2000.

[77] WHO, "Gender, Equity, and Human Rights," *Health and Human Rights Team*, 2017.

[78] G. Persad, "The Right to Health: From Maximization to Adequacy," *APA Newsletter: Philosophy and Medicine* 13, no. 1 (2013): 14–19.

[79] J. Tasioulas and E. Vayena, "The Place of Human Rights and the Common Good in Global Health Policy," *Theoretical Medicine and Bioethics* 37, no. 4 (2016): 365–82.

policy."[80] There might not be sufficient political and resource commitment to fulfill health-related human rights. Weak enforcement mechanisms in international human rights treaties permit states to sign on for appearance's sake without good faith intention to implement rights, though evidence shows that civil society has sometimes been able to harness these new human rights norms to pressure governments and improve human rights practices.[81] But given the constraints of global institutions and globalized markets, states may have less policy latitude to realize rights, and the international legal framework has difficulty regulating non-state actors.[82] Where resources are lacking, the progressive realization of a right to health is possible, but David Fidler argues that such an approach undermines "the establishment of a universal health baseline of basic public health services and information because the principle renders health standards relative to the availability of economic resources."[83]

More fundamentally, what social and economic rights entail and how to enforce them is inadequately understood,[84] and international human rights law generally is ambiguous, reflecting much compromise.[85] Further, Daniels argues that framing global health inequalities as an international human rights issue would not fully address the inequalities arising from different countries' rates of realization and unequal national resources.

Audrey Chapman notes that "[d]ifferences in the approach to health offered by the disciplines of medicine and public health contribute to the conceptual problems related to interpreting the right to health."[86] Medicine emphasizes individual health status and therefore stresses individual access to health care, shortchanging collective goods and public health systems by its bias toward the curative and clinical model of health. This bias favors medical responses instead of broader public health and health policy solutions.

Some base their legal global health perspective on a collective human right to development[87] more broadly, focusing more on the social determinants of

---

[80] A. Chapman and Sage Russell, eds., *Core Obligations: Building a Framework for Economic, Social and Cultural Rights* (Antwerp: Intersentia, 2002), 193.

[81] E. M. Hafner-Burton and K. Tsutsui, "Human Rights in a Globalizing World: The Paradox of Empty Promises," *American Journal of Sociology* 110, no. 5 (2005): 1373–411.

[82] A. R. Chapman, "Globalization, Human Rights, and the Social Determinants of Health," *Bioethics* 23, no. 2 (2009): 97–111.

[83] D. P. Fidler, "International Law and Global Public Health," *University of Kansas Law Review* 48 (1999): 46.

[84] L. O. Gostin, "The Human Right to Health: A Right to the 'Highest Attainable Standard of Health'," *Hastings Center Report* 31, no. 2 (2001): 29–30.

[85] E. De Kadt, "Some Basic Questions on Human Rights and Development," *World Development* 8, no. 2 (1980): 97–105.

[86] Chapman and Russell, eds., *Core Obligations*, 187.

[87] B. Mason Meier and A. M. Fox. "Development as Health: Employing the Collective Right to Development to Achieve the Goals of the Individual Right to Health," *Human Rights Quarterly* 30 (2008): 259–355.

health and health inequalities; when needed social, economic, and political conditions are not in place, human rights cannot be universal or enforceable. Because the international community already recognizes a right to development, this view can apply international human rights law to reform international governance for fairer trade and more egalitarian participation among developing countries. Here, too, the state is primarily responsible for fulfilling the right to development; the international community must cooperate where state capacities fall short.

An international regulatory system for the right to health is also lacking, as well as individuals' precarious international legal status to hold states accountable for failing to uphold this right,[88] so debates about it "have not advanced the right to health much as a matter of international law."[89] Domestically, litigation of right to health claims has had mixed results, ranging from decisions to provide high-cost treatments (and thus reducing funds available for public health) through the *tutela* system in Colombia,[90] to granting access to high-cost medications that distort the health budget in Brazil, Argentina, and Costa Rica, to the controversies surrounding the Soobramoney denial-of-care and nevirapine cases in South Africa and their health care and public health implications.[91] Right to health litigation through the judicial system runs counter to the role of democratic decision-making in establishing an adequate standard for health. Amy Gutmann argues for democratic deliberation in health and health care.[92]

Whatever its inadequacies, though, human rights as the "lingua franca of the international community" is a salient perspective for thinking about global justice and health beyond "moral parochialism."[93]

### 3.5.3 Global Health Justice and Ethics Issues

Rich and poor actors interface in many areas, including health resources availability and access and medical research conducted in developing countries. International trade and trade rules restrict the availability and affordability of

---

[88] A. Hendriks, "The Right to Health in National and International Jurisprudence," *European Journal of Health Law* 5, no. 4 (1998): 389–408.

[89] Fidler, "International Law and Global Public Health," 40.

[90] A. E. Yamin and O. Parra-Vera, "How Do Courts Set Health Policy? The Case of the Colombian Constitutional Court," *PLoS Medicine* 6, no. 2 (2009): 0147–0150.

[91] C. Ngwena, "The Recognition of Access to Health Care as a Human Right in South Africa: Is It Enough?" *Health and Human Rights* 5, no. 1 (2000): 27–44; G. J. Annas, "The Right to Health and the Nevirapine Case in South Africa," *New England Journal of Medicine* 348, no. 8 (2003): 750–4.

[92] A. Gutmann, "For and Against Equal Access to Health Care," *Milbank Memorial Fund Quarterly, Health and Society* 59, no. 4 (1981): 542–60. A. Gutmann and D. Thompson, *Why Deliberative Democracy* (Princeton, NJ: Princeton University Press, 2004).

[93] R. Baker, "Bioethics and Human Rights: A Historical Perspective," *Cambridge Quarterly of Healthcare Ethics* 10, no. 3 (2001): 250.

drugs in developing countries. Because developing countries are not profitable markets, pharmaceutical companies underinvest in research and development for diseases affecting those populations, generating a significant gap in research resources devoted to developing countries' health problems. IP laws increase prices on already patented drugs. Developing countries attempting to use or make generic versions often find themselves in battles against pharmaceutical companies and the countries in which they are incorporated, who fight these efforts with economic, political, and legal maneuvers. Corporate moral responsibility is, in additional to or in the absence of legal oversight, however, a route for a better understanding of the roles and responsibilities of pharmaceutical companies.[94]

Bulk purchasing of medicines, such as through the Global Drug Facility, can make drugs more affordable.[95] Under alternative proposals, patent holders could out-license to allow generic manufacturers to compete in poor countries while retaining patent rights in rich countries;[96] or manufacturers could reap rewards based on a drug's effects on the global disease burden; or a new global institution could reward justice-promoting innovation and authorize compulsory licenses on a country-by-country basis.[97] Others advocate reining in IP rights for essential drugs,[98] and propose that states use compulsory licensing in public health disasters, arguing from consequentialist[99] and Hobbesian positions.[100] Different principles can justify allocating scarce drugs, including the potential for best outcomes and priority for groups considered socially important (health workers and teachers, for example). In Daniels' framework, relevant stakeholders would consider these principles and justify or revise their position when deciding on an allocation scheme, through a fair, deliberate, and transparent process.[101] As an example, stakeholders might decide,

[94] M. Lane, "The Moral Dimension of Corporate Accountability," in *Global Responsibilities: Who Must Deliver on Human Rights?*, ed. A. Kuper (New York: Routledge Taylor & Francis Group, 2005), 229, 232–3, 239.

[95] WHO, "Prospectus: Global TB Drug Facility: A Global Mechanism to Ensure Uninterrupted Access to Quality TB Drugs for DOTS Implementation," *WHO*, 2001.

[96] M. A. Friedman, H. den Besten, and A. Attaran, "Out-Licensing: A Practical Approach for Improvement of Access to Medicines in Poor Countries," *The Lancet* 361, no. 9354 (2003): 341–4.

[97] A. Buchanan, T. Cole, and R. O. Keohane, "Justice in the Diffusion of Innovation," *Journal of Political Philosophy* 19, no. 3 (2011): 306–32.

[98] M. Risse, "Is there a Human Right to Essential Pharmaceuticals? The Global Common, the Intellectual Common, and the Possibility of Private Intellectual Property," in *Global Justice and Bioethics*, ed. J. Millum and E. J. Emanuel (New York: Oxford University Press, 2012).

[99] U. Schüklenk and R. A. Ashcroft, "Affordable Access to Essential Medication in Developing Countries: Conflicts between Ethical and Economic Imperatives," *Journal of Medicine and Philosophy* 27, no. 2 (2002): 179–95.

[100] R. E. Ashcroft, "Access to Essential Medicines: A Hobbesian Social Contract Approach," *Developing World Bioethics* 5, no. 2 (2005): 121–41.

[101] N. Daniels, "Fair Process in Patient Selection for Antiretroviral Treatment in WHO's Goal of 3 by 5," *The Lancet* 366, no. 9480 (2005): 169–71.

on consequentialist grounds, to shift resources from HIV/AIDS treatment to prevention, thereby saving more lives.[102]

An objection to the considerable focus on pharmaceuticals in the global health ethics literature is that it is not the most salient issue at the nexus of poverty and public health. Problems with making high-quality medicines and technologies available to individuals in poor countries require redress. Other issues relate to the pharmaceutical industry itself, ranging from innovation and drug discovery to marketing and prescription patterns.[103] But an excessive focus on pharmaceuticals within global health ethics arguably prevents focusing on more fundamental problems in health care, public health systems, and the social determinants of health.

Trade provisions also impact developing countries' health systems. The General Agreement on Trade in Services supports health services privatization and trade liberalization, which can produce high costs and more inequitable health and health access, and influences governments as they develop national health systems.[104] Additionally, developed countries recruit health workers from the developing world, causing brain drain in already resource-stressed health systems. Reversing brain drain may require training more physicians in and limiting recruitment by developed countries; some recommend locally relevant medical training to reduce Western demand and improve retention in developing nations.[105] Others draw on Pogge's causality and responsibility argument for a global justice approach to the brain drain problem: along with training more health workers in developed countries for deployment in the developing world, it would reverse structural adjustment policies that undercut health system investment and health worker retention in developing countries.[106]

An edited volume on global bioethics identifies several "selected problems in global justice and bioethics."[107] In clinical care, these include health tourism, organ trafficking, and access to medicines; in research, responsiveness, benefit sharing, standards of care, ancillary care, and post-trial access; in health policy, parallel health systems, IP, brain drain, international disease threats, and lifestyle exports; and in theory, cultural variation, priority setting,

---

[102] D. W. Brock and D. Wikler, "Ethical Challenges in Long-Term Funding for HIV/AIDS," *Health Affairs* 28, no. 6 (2009): 1666–76.

[103] M. Angell, *The Truth about the Drug Companies: How they Deceive Us and What To Do about It* (New York: Random House, 2004).

[104] K. Lee and M. Koivusalo, "Trade and Health: Is the Health Community Ready for Action?" *PLoS Medicine* 2, no. 1 (2005): 0012–0014.

[105] N. Eyal and S. A. Hurst, "Physician Brain Drain: Can Nothing Be Done?" *Public Health Ethics* 1, no. 2 (2008): 180–92.

[106] S. Taché and D. Schillinger, "Health Worker Migration: Time for the Global Justice Approach," *The American Journal of Bioethics* 9, no. 3 (2009): 12–14.

[107] J. Millum and E. J. Emanuel, "Introduction," in *Global Justice and Bioethics*, eds. Millum and Emanuel, 11.

the right to health, and ideal and non-ideal theory. That volume deals with several of these topics in various chapters: Jonathan Wolff writes on the right to health,[108] Gopal Sreenivasan on relating ideal to non-ideal theory,[109] Alan Wertheimer on researchers' obligations,[110] and Lisa Fuller on the role of international nongovernmental organizations (NGOs).[111] These burgeoning areas need considerably more work. A WHO report by lead authors Trygve Ottersen and Ole Norheim puts forward a strategy for countries to pursue fair progressive realization of universal health coverage (UHC),[112] whereas a global steering committee developing a global charter for UHC under the auspices of the Elders seeks to develop precepts to attain UHC that is financially sustainable and supports both economic growth and human development.[113] Moreover, a volume on ethics in global health focuses on topics such as cultural beliefs and attitudes regarding policies and practices affecting women's health, justice and HIV/AIDS, and international research ethics. The volume defends universal ethical principles in global health, despite international cultural differences.[114]

Profoundly complex, health involves not just medicine and health care but also, inter alia, poverty, education, and environment. The multiplicity of global actors exacerbates this complexity, as do international rules. These factors elude national, not to mention individual, control. Health-sphere actors—global, state, and non-state—need to understand their interests more comprehensively. A more fully developed moral framework and ethical guidelines are essential if health-sphere actors are to tackle global health problems effectively.

The provincial globalism (PG) account encompasses various components, theoretical and empirical, to build a theoretically grounded global health justice framework that in turn can guide implementation. PG applies the health capability paradigm as a theoretical foundation for the right to health and recasts the right to health as an ethical demand for health equity. Chapter 4 discusses PG in depth.

---

[108] J. Wolff, "Global Justice and Health: The Basis of the Global Health Duty," in *Global Justice and Bioethics*, ed. Millum and Emanuel, 78–101.

[109] G. Sreenivasan, "Non-Ideal Theory: A Taxonomy with Illustration," in *Global Justice and Bioethics*, ed. Millum and Emanuel, 135–53.

[110] A. Wertheimer, "The Obligations of Researchers amidst Injustice or Deprivation," in *Global Justice and Bioethics*, ed. Millum and Emanuel, 279–304.

[111] L. Fuller, "International NGO Health Programs in a Non-Ideal World: Imperialism, Respect, and Procedural Justice," in *Global Justice and Bioethics*, ed. Millum and Emanuel, 213–40.

[112] T. Ottersen, O. Norheim, B. Chitah, R. Cookson, N. Daniels, F. Defaye, et al., "Making Fair Choices on the Path to Universal Health Coverage," Final report of the WHO Consultative Group on Equity and Universal Health Coverage, 2014.

[113] E. Zedillo and the UHC Charter Steering Committee. The Elders and the Yale Center for Globalization, 2017; E. Zedillo, "Why is Universal Health Coverage Vital to Achieving the Health SDG?", *The Elders*, September 26, 2016.

[114] R. Macklin, *Ethics in Global Health: Research, Policy and Practice* (New York: Oxford University Press, 2012).

# 4

# An Alternative Account

## Provincial Globalism[1]

The world community clearly needs a moral orientation to assess various proposals for the global health architecture; it needs a moral compass to determine the best way forward. It needs a comprehensive theory of global health and a governance structure to effectuate it. Such a theory would enable analysis and evaluation of the current global health system; it would ground proposals, ethically and empirically, to reform global health and align the global system more closely with moral values.

What are the roles and responsibilities of global, national, and local communities as well as individuals in addressing health deprivations, cross-border problems, and global contagions? This chapter sets out the foundational components of a global health justice theory, arguing for universal ethical

---

[1] Provincial globalism (PG) has been developed over many years, manuscripts, and presentations, including, but not limited to, the following: J. P. Ruger, "Millennium Development Goals for Health: Building Human Capabilities," *Bulletin of the World Health Organization* 82, no. 12 (2004): 951–2 (part of Round Table Discussion section with Jeffrey Sachs, William Savedoff, Guy Carrin, David Sanders); J. P. Ruger, "Review of Peter Baldwin's *Disease and Democracy: The Industrialized World Faces AIDS*," *British Medical Journal* 331, no. 7522 (2005): 970; J. P. Ruger, "Democracy and Health," *Quarterly Journal of Medicine* 98, no. 4 (2005): 299–304; J. P. Ruger, "Ethics and Governance of Global Health Inequalities," *Journal of Epidemiology and Community Health* 60, no. 11 (2006): 998–1003; J. P. Ruger and H.-J. Kim, "Global Health Inequalities: An International Comparison," *Journal of Epidemiology and Community Health* 60, no. 11 (2006): 928–36; J. P. Ruger, "Review of Jeffrey Sachs' 'The End of Poverty: Economic Possibilities for Our Time'," *Global Public Health* 2, no. 2 (2007): 206–9; J. P. Ruger, "Global Health Justice," *Public Health Ethics* 2, no. 3 (2009): 261–75; J. P. Ruger, "Global Health Justice and Governance," *The American Journal of Bioethics* 12, no. 12 (2012): 35–54; J. P. Ruger, "Response to Letter to the Editor: Making Power Visible in Global Health Governance," *The American Journal of Bioethics* 12, no. 7 (2012): 65; J. P. Ruger, "Responses to Open Peer Commentaries on 'Global Health Justice and Governance'," *The American Journal of Bioethics* 12, no. 12 (2012): W6–W8; J. P. Ruger, "Global Health Justice," in *Leadership and Global Justice*, ed. D. Hicks and T. Williamson (New York: Palgrave Macmillan, 2012), 113–29; J. P. Ruger, "Good Medical Ethics, Justice and Provincial Globalism," *Journal of Medical Ethics* 41, no. 1 (2015): 103–6; M. DiStefano and J. P. Ruger, "Reflective Solidarity as to Provincial Globalism and Shared Health Governance," *Diametros* 46 (2015): 151–8.

norms (a general duty owed to all persons) with shared global and domestic responsibility (specific duties) for health. It offers a global minimalist view, provincial globalism (PG), as a mean between nationalism and cosmopolitanism, in which a provincial consensus accompanies a global consensus on health morality.

This global health justice theory aims to enhance justice and to address the injustice that affects states and global citizens. It involves a shift in focus from international relations, adversarial global politics, and mutual group interests to people's health capabilities. In contrast to the social contract tradition of reciprocity among self and nationally interested actors, this alternative approach grasps the needs, vulnerabilities, and insecurities of real people living in the world today. This theory moves beyond the cosmopolitan and nationalist stalemate that inhibits global health theory development.

This chapter examines the health claims due to all human beings by virtue of their humanity, and how such claims can be secured. In addition to justifying these entitlements and their guarantee, the focus is also on fostering appropriate public moral norms and ethical commitments to support the conditions in which all individuals have the ability to be healthy. Global health justice requires progressively securing for each person a threshold level of health capabilities. More specifically, this chapter examines the following analytical components: (1) the moral imperative to address global health inequalities, externalities, and cross-border problems; (2) concerns of measurement, evaluation, and prioritization; (3) respective duties and responsibilities of global and state actors and individuals themselves; and (4) comparisons and contrasts with other approaches.

In this view, global health justice involves a duty to address premature mortality and escapable morbidity and entails shared health governance (SHG) to reduce and prevent shortfall inequalities in these central health capabilities. This theory shapes the allocation of responsibility to the contours of health determinants. It does not confine our obligations to currently available technology and information, but rather supports investments in biomedical and health research to prevent and treat vexing health deprivations. It does not presuppose a relational view of justice, as is the case in social contract theory; rather it takes as its starting point the equal dignity, the state of being worthy of respect, and moral status of all persons, and then examines cooperative and institutional associations.

Several distinguishing features set this minimalist account apart. First, this approach offers a theory of the good rooted in capability theory, unlike social contractarian theories, which rely primarily on procedures to determine a theory of justice. Contracts for mutual advantage provide the contractarian's solutions to social issues. The PG view begins with the universal ethical duty to protect and promote human flourishing and central health capabilities and follows with an assessment of moral responsibility. But unlike purely consequentialist frameworks, this theory has a proceduralist component in the special place it gives health agency; by contrast, a utilitarian single-minded focus on maximizing aggregate welfare ignores human agency. Good health governance both expands people's health and does so in ways that engage and expand their agency. In PG, people should be the agents of their own health and the health of their loved ones, as opposed to being passive recipients or coerced by global and domestic health and public health policy. A person should decide for herself, rather than being forced to decide, based on reasons and goals she values; and she should be able to contribute to positive health changes for others in the world. When people participate in their own health and that of others they learn about the impacts of social and individual choices. These lessons in turn influence their health values.

Second, unlike certain contractarian frameworks that limit distributive duties to the state, this approach allocates responsibility both nationally and globally, but third, contrasting with certain cosmopolitan perspectives, it does not demand causal attribution to define moral responsibility, nor does it attenuate responsibility in descending governmental and personal levels.

Fourth, the PG view examines charity and humanitarian assistance. A significant objection to the charity approach is that it leaves individuals' interests and their fulfillment vulnerable to the discretion and arbitrary choices of others, who might limit their commitments because of costs, inconvenience, perceived risks, changed preferences, or simply indifference. Charity is also typically a backward-looking rather than forward-looking idea. Charity and humanitarian assistance are therefore weak and unsatisfactory responses to health needs; they provide no duty to foster equality for all. In PG, health needs and enhancing health capabilities serve as the basis of claims individuals have upon others in society. These are claims of justice effectuated by public institutions along with other actors and institutions through SHG. Shortfalls in or threats to health capabilities ground an assessment of the justice of global and domestic institutions, actors, and governance more broadly. These are claims of justice, not charity.

Fifth, this view advances an important role and responsibilities for the international community in remedying global health problems, unlike particularist perspectives. Sixth, this approach, however, goes beyond existing international justice and public health frameworks, setting forth health capabilities as a moral goal, prioritizing central health capabilities, and applying shortfall inequality for measurement and evaluation—all building blocks of a global health justice theory. PG focuses on institutions as well as individual and social behavior. It evaluates interactions among institutions, individuals, and society by their impact on human flourishing and human capabilities, in particular health capabilities. It is broadly consequentialist in its focus on need, ability, responsibility, and choice, but unlike utilitarian or strict cosmopolitan beneficence approaches like Singer's, PG includes agent-sensitive considerations in health agency.

Seventh, it then offers a theory for allocating global and domestic responsibilities to expand health capabilities and solve global health problems. PG is a theory of global justice, not solely international justice, although international justice with its focus on the state as the primary unit of justice fits within the broader PG focus on relations among individuals and groups. As an account of global justice that takes individuals as the central unit of moral concern, PG examines an array of institutions, behaviors, and situations, including states and their impact on individual and group health capabilities.

Eight, it theorizes a framework within which global and domestic actors can collaborate to achieve health equity goals. In PG, narrow self-interest, national interest, collective security, and humanitarian assistance are insufficient foundations for health justice. It recognizes that the interests of all persons should be given expression and consideration through global public reason. PG deploys the more robust concept of human flourishing to shape a world in which all have the capability to be healthy. PG critically expands beyond the closed partiality of particularist perspectives on international justice, which fail to address bias and vested interests within states and to assess critically the justice of structures and relationships across states and other groups. Through this more expansive framework, PG also considers the plural subjecthood of individuals and the multiple ways in which human beings are connected to one another both within and beyond national boundaries.

Finally, PG differs from other consequentialist and utilitarian theories and other variants of normative economics on some central assumptions. A key assumption of these other approaches is to judge policies and actions by their impacts on aggregate well-being. Well-being is then typically estimated by individual preference satisfaction, psychological states such as pain or pleasure, desire fulfillment, or revealed preference. From a PG perspective, these assessments are problematic because two individuals may be judged the same on these well-being assessments though their respective functionings are not equal. For example, one person is in bad health but she is so accustomed to it that she does not report pain and suffering. This adaptive preference problem means that individuals can be equal from a preference, hedonic, or utility perspective but highly unequal from a health functioning perspective. Other objections to the welfare as preference satisfaction accounts of consequentialism include concerns about induced or perverse preferences, unawareness, and addiction, all adding to the skepticism about hedonic theories of well-being. PG defines these inequalities in well-being, rather, in terms of capabilities, abilities to function in relevant ways that individuals have reason to value. From the PG perspective, inequalities in central health capabilities are fundamentally unjust. Inequalities in income or other resources are problematic, but what matters most is that all people everywhere have the ability to be healthy.

Achieving this goal requires differential rather than equal resources to convert into functionings. This view contrasts with resource-based theories of inequalities and justice; health capabilities, not resources, provide the metric for evaluating social progress both at the domestic and global level and form the objective basis for justice. All individuals have equal dignity, the state of being worthy of respect, and are owed equal respect, transcending national boundaries. But this universalism is tempered by a respect for self-determination within and by states and the exercise of health agency by individuals and collectives. PG envisions designing and managing domestic and global institutions according to the functions they serve, and how effectively and efficiently they effectuate justice.

The current global health architecture does not provide the institutional structure to fulfill needed general and specific duties. A shared institutional scheme, SHG envisions compulsory political institutions in place in the domestic space along with voluntary commitments in the domestic and global space to effectuate duties of justice. PG leaves room for and supports the norms of sovereignty and self-determination that govern international law, rather than conflicting with them.

## 4.1 Human Flourishing and Capabilities

PG builds on the health capability paradigm (HCP), which argues from an Aristotelian/capability perspective that health capabilities are the central focal variable for evaluating justice, equity, and efficiency in health policy. This view grounds the special moral importance of health capabilities. It posits that humans' ability to flourish, their capabilities, is the proper end of social and political activity. This obligation to human flourishing is universal, applying to all human lives, regardless of class, gender, race, ethnicity, community, nationality, or state citizenship. Human flourishing is a person's ability to live a good life as defined as a set of valuable beings and doings (for example, being in good health or being well educated). Core concepts are functionings and capability. Functionings are states of being and doing (such as being well nourished) and capability is the set of valuable functionings to which a person has effective access.

*Health and Social Justice* (2009) developed the HCP, focusing particularly on central health capabilities, social choice theory and its role in public policy for health, the demands of social justice, and the right to health at the domestic level. The HCP developed a line of reasoning that humans are owed the conditions for their flourishing, and that health capability—and central health capabilities expressly—are intrinsic and instrumental components of human flourishing. Health capabilities, and central health capabilities in particular, are basic capabilities, because they are essential components of human flourishing; without life itself, for example, other capabilities are not possible. Central health capabilities are not, however, the only component necessary for a flourishing life; they are not everything but fit within a larger set of capabilities. Rather than posit a right to health in the legal sense, the HCP advanced the argument for theorizing the right to health as an ethical demand for equity in health, with corresponding societal obligations for effectuating this claim. Humans have a claim to the fundamental conditions for maintaining and promoting their central health capabilities. This book extends these ideas to the global realm: in PG justice applies both domestically and globally. Global justice begins with human flourishing.

This account advances a general social obligation to enable all human lives to flourish, not just those within our family, community, or national borders. Flourishing is a morally central aim that all persons share. Flourishing encompasses capability, that which humans are able to do and be and what possibilities they have. Capability includes human agency, an essential good to be ensured and promoted. All people deserve the ability to direct their own lives and make their own choices. Agency is key to flourishing, because people flourish by shaping their own circumstances. Health agency encompasses decisions and choices about one's health. There is a set of central health capabilities intrinsic to our shared conception of human flourishing and also instrumentally important to other human capabilities. Social conditions should provide for actualizing central health capabilities.

The distinction between achievement and the freedom to achieve is important. Functionings are a person's achievements, what they are and do—their activities and states of being. Capability is the ability and freedom to achieve valued functionings. Capabilities include both actual and potential functionings. Examining capabilities, or individuals' abilities to function, even if they are not functioning at that level at a given time, reveals the deprivation and suffering many individuals experience worldwide, helping to provide answers to questions about which inequalities and threats matter and why. Examining functionings also reveals the range of activities and states of being possible for people. Staying or being healthy is but one type of functioning, within a broad range of functionings; being a concert violinist or an expert surfer, for example, could be at certain ends of the spectrum, and not achieved or achievable by every person. There are certain functionings that each individual is able to achieve; her capability set is the combination of functionings that she is able to achieve. The expansion or contraction of one's or a group's capability set vis-à-vis another individual's or group's is one way of making interpersonal and intergroup comparisons. Staying or becoming healthy is one essential constituent of well-being and individual flourishing.

Each particular functioning associates with a particular capability. Each functioning and capability may be expanded or contracted over time. Also, in particular dimensions such as health, comparisons can be made to another individual's functioning or capability. Both external and internal factors can contract or expand health capabilities; some relate to human diversity and variable capacities to convert resources into functionings, while others relate to the external environment and the extent to which an enabling health care or public health system (for example, availability of vaccines or clean water) affects the ability to be healthy.

Philip Pettit has analyzed the relationship between capability of functioning and freedom to function. He argues for the importance of functioning capability as opposed to functioning prospect as the main standard for evaluating societies and lives in the capability approach.[2] The difference between actual and potential functioning of the world's population is a key indicator in assessing injustices, which require redress.

In PG, the goal of global planning is a global and domestic distribution of conditions enabling people to function in important ways. Accounting for human heterogeneity is important for assessing justice from this perspective. Individuals have various internal and external characteristics that inform equality assessments; justice requires the global community to aid people in proportion to their degree of disadvantage, in line with Aristotle's principle of proportionality. Individuals are entitled to different allocations, depending on what they need to lead a flourishing life. Additionally, determinants of health capability operate differently in various societies, and assessing capability inequalities requires accounting for these differences. For example, inadequate infrastructure can complicate efforts to provide important treatment regimens such as antiretroviral therapies.

In PG, health capabilities and functionings are essential elements that individuals have reason to value. Across time and diverse cultures, certain health capabilities and functionings have emerged as valuable to individuals and societies. PG assesses individual and group advantage and disadvantage relative to a threshold level of these capabilities and functionings. PG focuses on them as critical for interpersonal and intergroup comparisons of well-being

---

[2] P. Pettit, "Symposium on Amartya Sen's Philosophy: 1 Capability and Freedom: A Defence of Sen," *Economics and Philosophy* 17, no. 1 (2001): 1–20.

and the evaluation of global public policy and governance. It sees global health deficits as shortfalls in capabilities and functionings that require remedy. The obligation to promote capabilities and functionings is not open-ended, however, as efficiency is also an important concern. Indeed, the measure of global success lies in the extent to which our global and domestic arrangements enable individuals to function best, given their natural circumstances, while doing so efficiently, using the fewest resources possible.

A Rawlsian focus on primary goods, by contrast, fails to consider adequately how the same bundle of goods affects different people. Resources are means to ends and do not in and of themselves constitute appropriate ends of social and political activity. Resources alone do not have intrinsic value; our search is for a set of global goals that goes beyond resources alone to include individuals' ability to function.

The state of being human itself confers moral status. The PG account proposes morally salient functionings that warrant respect and require protection and promotion. In focusing on the capability to achieve valuable functionings, this theory entitles individuals to differential allotments of goods and circumstances necessary to produce capabilities, while simultaneously respecting freedom and reason in enabling all to make choices. Meeting these needs is essential for human flourishing.

A primary human interest is leading a good life.[3] Some theorists believe that interests form the foundation for duties and rights. Joseph Raz's theory of rights holds others under a duty based on individuals' interests or well-being: "'X has a right' if and only if X can have rights, and, other things being equal, an aspect of X's well-being (his interest) is a sufficient reason for holding some other person(s) to be under a duty"; "[r]ights are grounds of duties in others."[4] Allen Buchanan cites "the connection between equal concern and respect for persons, human rights, and basic human interests," noting that "we show equal concern and respect for persons...by acknowledging that there are human rights."[5] Although these views help justify duties, fleshing out the content of such rights and duties requires a conception of well-being and quality of life: the deontological idea of equal respect needs a substantive theory of the good to explicate duty, obligation, and rights. The PG account roots these rights in human flourishing and capability, drawing on the HCP to ground the right to health. This grounding offers a foundation for protecting humans by requiring duty bearers to secure their interests through actions and inactions. It protects humans' interest in health, creating an inviolable trust

---

[3] W. Kymlicka, *Liberalism, Community, and Culture* (Oxford: Oxford University Press, 1989), 10–13.

[4] J. Raz, *The Morality of Freedom* (Oxford: Oxford University Press, 1988), 166,167.

[5] A. Buchanan, *Justice, Legitimacy, and Self-Determination: Moral Foundations for International Law* (Oxford: Oxford University Press, 2004), 90.

between a right holder and duty bearer. It thus provides a conceptual framework for potential solutions to today's injustices.

The PG account presupposes human flourishing as the common good and argues that promoting it serves everyone's interest. Health capabilities, as the object of justice, are a global societal good. The common good includes each individual's good and the good of others. Individuals should comprehend their good in relation to their community; individual health capability for all is a common good within and across societies even as individuals everywhere pursue their own vision of the good life. PG sees the common good of health capability as the goal of global and domestic health governance. The promotion of health capability confers legitimacy on institutions and actors, but only if it benefits all, not a majority or particular groups within global or domestic society.

In PG, individuals' health capability should not be sacrificed for the private interests of others by veto (will of the powerful) or as a result of the summation of private interests (will of all) but rather should be promoted and protected as a representation of shared common interests (general will). A genuine or authentic consensus on what is good from an impartial viewpoint contrasts with the promotion of partial private interests. The common good connects the community's health capability with its members' individual health capability, since the effective functioning of society is inseparable from individuals' functioning. PG's theory of SHG seeks to promote the common good to the advantage of all.

Some object that PG would suppress those who do not embrace its conception of the common good—health capability. But PG is rooted in both deductive and inductive reasoning, including evidence from the social and basic sciences and the humanities. This evidence shows that the health capability of all is a notion of the common good held by communities throughout history and across cultures, inclusive of all and shared by individuals in those societies. All individuals have the common interest of creating and maintaining the conditions for health capability to provide everyone with the opportunity to flourish. SHG is rooted in this evidence.

### 4.1.1 *Health Capabilities*

The ethical principles of human flourishing and capability justify taking health capabilities as global health policy's objective. Indeed, aspects of health capability are essential to all human flourishing, because without life itself, other human functionings are impossible. Although it recognizes the interrelatedness of health and other social ends, the PG approach emphasizes the importance of health for individual agency—the ability to live a life one values. All human lives have equal value. Deprivations in health capability are unjust; they reduce the capability for health functioning, diminish agency, and undermine flourishing. Policies to deny treatment to malaria patients, for example, or to deny antiretroviral drugs to HIV/AIDS patients are morally troubling not only because they deliver subliminal health care, reduce individuals' opportunity for employment, and cause suffering (as important as these problems are), but fundamentally because they undermine physical and mental functioning, even survival. Functional deprivations rob individuals of the freedom to be what they want to be.[6] This underlying principle applies to all persons wherever they live, whatever their specific relationships to others, whatever the communities to which they belong. The moral worth of an inaction or action is assessed by its effects on individuals' health capabilities.

This perspective views health as both intrinsically and instrumentally valuable; all individuals should have equal capability to achieve good health and to prevent premature mortality and avoid escapable morbidity. Health deprivations are inequalities in individuals' capability to function and direct threats to their well-being and agency. Such functional diminishments conflict with Aristotle's view that justice requires public policies to bring "people as close to good functioning as their natural circumstances permit."[7] If basic capabilities—crucially important functionings such as health, which are associated with basic needs[8]—are unavailable, most other human capabilities are also inaccessible. The "particular moral and political importance" of basic capabilities like health derives from their essential role in "fulfilling well-recognized, urgent claims."[9] Thus society should create the conditions for individuals to rise above a certain threshold level of health capability, health functioning, and health agency.

As a theory of global health justice, PG focuses efforts to evaluate and reform global health policies and practices. It is relevant for studying individual and group advantage and disadvantage, whether a given individual or group of individuals (in a particular country, for example) is better off or worse off. It is relevant for examining inequalities, externalities, and cross-border issues. It also reveals what must change. Taking health capability as the objective or focal variable, the next stage is to assess the instrumental effectiveness and cost-effectiveness of health capability's determinants and the public policies focused on improving them.

PG holds that health capabilities and, more specifically, central health capabilities are morally salient human interests and are also needed for the

<hr>

[6] A. Sen, *Commodities and Capabilities* (New Delhi: Oxford University Press, 1985).
[7] M. C. Nussbaum, "Nature, Function, and Capability: Aristotle on Political Distribution," in *Aristoteles' "Politik"*, ed., G. Patzig (Göttingen: Vandenhoeck & Ruprecht, 1990), 155.
[8] A. Sen, *Inequality Reexamined* (Cambridge, MA: Harvard University Press, 1992).
[9] A. Sen, "Capability and Well-Being," in *The Quality of Life*, ed. M. C. Nussbaum and A. Sen (Oxford: Oxford University Press, 1993), 40.

enjoyment of many other capabilities. Common intuition supports justifying health capabilities as both universally valued (accepted by and acceptable to all persons) and instrumentally needed to attain many other valuable functionings.

No other functionings are possible without life itself. Empirical evidence from the natural and social sciences shows the effects of disease on cognition and the ability to make decisions and engage in physical activities.[10] Some health conditions, such as schizophrenia and Alzheimer's disease, bar sufferers from free speech and political participation, exercising agency, and forming conceptions of the good.[11] Some disabilities bar participation in the life of some faith communities[12] and other organizations with inaccessible facilities. Musculoskeletal conditions can prevent working.[13] Disabilities and autism can prevent associating with others.[14] Morally relevant health needs and health agency needs demand provision because they are essential for human flourishing. Central health capabilities are a source of moral claims, at the core of our common humanity. Some question health's role as a necessary prerequisite to other rights;[15] others would argue that health is not an uncontroversial human interest.[16] PG views health capabilities as morally salient human interests due respect. Appeal to this universal feature of human life grounds general duties to all persons.

### 4.1.2 *Central Health Capabilities*

Distinguishing between central and non-central health capabilities helps extend this conceptualization to global health justice and allows prioritizing for policy and institutional purposes. Avoiding premature death and

[10] M. E. Soto, S. Andrieu, C. Arbus, M. Ceccaldi, P. Couratier, T. Dantoine, et al., "Rapid Cognitive Decline in Alzheimer's Disease: Consensus Paper," *Journal of Nutrition, Health, & Aging* 12, no. 10 (2008): 703–13; M. P. Dymek, P. Atchison, L. Harrell, and D. C. Marson, "Competency to Consent to Medical Treatment in Cognitively Impaired Patients with Parkinson's Disease," *Neurology* 56, no. 1 (2001): 17–24; A. J. Mitchell, J. Benito-León, J. M. González, and J. Rivera-Navarro, "Quality of Life and Its Assessment in Multiple Sclerosis: Integrating Physical and Psychological Components of Wellbeing," *The Lancet Neurology* 4, no. 9 (2005): 556–66.

[11] B. D. Kelly, "The Power Gap: Freedom, Power, and Mental Illness," *Social Science & Medicine* 63, no. 8 (2006): 2118–28.

[12] J. R. Cerhan and R. B. Wallace, "Predictors of Decline in Social Relationships in the Rural Elderly," *American Journal of Epidemiology* 137, no. 8 (1993): 870–80.

[13] A. D. Woolf and B. Pfleger, "Burden of Major Musculoskeletal Conditions," *Bulletin of the World Health Organization* 81, no. 9 (2003): 646–56.

[14] S. Kinne, D. L. Patrick, and D. L. Doyle, "Prevalence of Secondary Conditions among People with Disabilities," *American Journal of Public Health* 94, no. 3 (2004): 443–5; E. Ochs, T. Kremer-Sadlik, O. Solomon, and K. G. Sirota, "Inclusion as Social Practice: Views of Children with Autism," *Social Development* 10, no. 3 (2001): 399–419.

[15] S. Caney, *Justice Beyond Borders: A Global Political Theory* (New York: Oxford University Press, 2005).

[16] R. Dworkin, *Sovereign Virtue: The Theory and Practice of Equality* (Cambridge, MA: Harvard University Press, 2002).

preventable morbidity should claim priority in evaluating global health policies. Without these central health capabilities, other capabilities—developing abilities, using talents, and carrying out plans—are diminished if not entirely extinguished. Possessing these essential elements of health is a universal human objective. A set of health-related goods is key to ensuring central health capabilities. These include: individual health care services (prevention, diagnosis, treatment, and rehabilitation); public health and social support systems; adequate nutrition; and safe, sanitary living and working environments.

Once specified, one decides how to measure health capabilities and at what levels to provide them. Capability evaluation can measure either "*realized* functionings (what a person is actually able to do) or . . . the *capability set* of alternatives she has (her real opportunities)."[17] A person's capability set underlies the alternative combinations of functionings she can achieve. Capability itself is not directly observable; to evaluate global health policy, then, requires assessing realized functionings and agency. This approach also includes assessing a person's potential health achievement, which is especially relevant when considering preexisting illness and disability.

For measurement, the currency matters.[18] PG rejects the use of utilities, preferences, or desires, in and of themselves, as unreliable indicators of well-being, quality of life, human flourishing, or health. Capability to achieve valuable functionings should be the main variable for evaluation. This focus is key to a theory of justice and global health. Employing preferences or utilities to evaluate policy and systems does not necessarily produce equitable and effective allocations of responsibilities and resources to address health needs, health functionings, and health capabilities across the globe. Such preferences might not sufficiently correlate with objectively important health functionings.[19] In many developing countries, for example, preferences for maternal, prenatal, and infant health during and after pregnancy are very low and result in high rates of maternal and child mortality.[20] In these settings, distributions of health resources based on utilities or preferences would be different from those based on health capabilities.

PG is grounded in both deductive and inductive reasoning. Empirically, evidence of actual domestic agreements based on explicit consent to health

---

[17] A. Sen, *Development as Freedom* (New York: Alfred A. Knopf, 1999), 75.

[18] M. D. Adler and M. Fleurbaey, *Oxford Handbook of Well-Being and Public Policy* (New York: Oxford University Press, 2016).

[19] D. Hausman, "Valuing Health," *Philosophy & Public Affairs* 34, no. 3 (2006): 246–74.

[20] D. S. Manandhar, D. Osrin, B. P. Shrestha, N. Mesko, J. Morrison, K. M. Tumbahangphe, et al., "Effect of a Participatory Intervention with Women's Groups on Birth Outcomes in Nepal: Cluster-Randomised Controlled Trial," *The Lancet* 364, no. 9438 (2004): 970–9; A. Wade, D. Osrin, B. P. Shrestha, A. Sen, J. Morrison, K. M. Tumbahangphe, et al., "Behaviour Change in Perinatal Care Practices among Rural Women Exposed to a Women's Group Intervention in Nepal," *BMC Pregnancy and Childbirth* 6 (2006): 20.

guarantees provides valid and reliable substantiation of central health capabilities' normative force. By contrast, hypothetical contracts based on hypothetical consent behind a veil of ignorance in the original position provide no proof that such agreements have actually been reached or would be reached. The original position is a hypothetical scenario in which people are perfectly egoistic (completely self-interested, considering only their own interests and not those of others) and rational (they make no mistakes in calculating and weighing costs and benefits). PG is skeptical of the justification of such hypothetical contracts and theorizing that lack a basis in the real world where people live. Research demonstrates that individuals in these societies choose health guarantees through their political processes or social and political institutions and surrender some of their autonomy through regulation, oversight, spending, and tax payments to effectuate these entitlements. That these agreements are only motivated by rational self-interested agents on purely or primarily instrumental terms for mutual advantage is difficult to imagine given the broad attention to principles and entitlements in these systems. It is also hard to believe that the desire to be acceptable to or not rejected by others would motivate such agreements. Rather, the widespread evidence suggests that numerous societies over time and across the world have reached basic health entitlement agreements, which govern actions of social and political institutions in those societies and ground correlative obligations for individuals, groups, and institutions.[21]

A global consensus on such morally salient features of human life is voluntary under PG, because situations of power asymmetry, deceit, coercion, or other conditions of unfair advantage render consensus invalid. In PG, evidence of the fundamental interest in human health and its corroboration in agreements through time and across societies provides a reliable and valid grounding of humanity's general duty to achieve global health equity and domestic protections from health deprivation. All people have reason to want to be healthy.

### 4.1.3 Transpositionality: A Global View of Health Capabilities

PG requires a global view of health capabilities, under which the global health community strives for a coherent set of goals to enhance justice. Universal agreement on all goals is unnecessary, but achieving justice requires a consensus on a minimal set of objectives. Determining the scope and content of

---

[21] Seventy-five countries have "legislation mandating universal access to healthcare services," according to D. Stuckler, A. B. Feigl, S. Basu, and M. McKee. "The Political Economy of Universal Health Coverage," Background Paper for the Global Symposium on Health Systems Research in Montreux, Switzerland, 2010, 2. Moreover, an additional eighteen countries are estimated to have legislation mandating, but have not yet achieved, UHC. Thus a total of nearly a hundred countries are on their way to UHC.

health capabilities becomes a step toward delineating obligations of global, national, local, and individual actors. This section offers a view of health capabilities that could yield a consensus. PG does not rely on a purely hypothetical thought experiment for normative justification of health capabilities. Such thought experiments cannot provide a conception of global health justice that starts with a theory of the good, human flourishing, and intrinsically and instrumentally valued health capabilities. Global justice is not a contract for mutual advantage, but a means to human flourishing and health capabilities, to actualizing one's potential as a human being.

Health capabilities are the freedom to achieve health goals; health functionings are the achievement itself. There is feedback between the two. Health capabilities encompass both health functionings and health agency. Health functionings link causally to health capabilities; the ability to walk, for example, fosters a person's physical functioning. Impairments in functionings reduce health capabilities, affecting in turn a host of other capabilities.

Provision for health needs—physician care and medications, for example—supports health functionings, which in turn foster health capabilities. Thus, the degree to which we meet health needs is an objective indicator of how well we improve people's health capabilities. Medical necessity and medical appropriateness are useful criteria in specifying health needs.

The philosophical and medical literatures discuss at length how to define health and its most important dimensions. While no unanimous account of health exists, isolating certain central features of health in assessing political arrangements could be possible. Health, however, does not have one true meaning, but clearly entails social and cultural construction. Reaching any global consensus involves decisions among all the possible definitions. As Thomas Scanlon argues, though, there is merit in searching for a substantive account against which to assess activities, an account that can ground criticism of injustices and oppression.[22] Even communitarians like Michael Walzer acknowledge that while objectivity may not exist, the construction of meaning remains a genuine process, and criticism and discussion within a given culture can help shape real values.[23] A major objection to cultural relativism is, however, that in the absence of transpositional or transcultural moral principles, practices such as the oppression of women, female genital mutilation, child marriage, or slavery, for example, would persist, because a particular culture's standards allow them. Cultural relativists argue that no transcultural normative truth can be found, and efforts to determine cross-cultural justice principles are futile; no moral standards are universally applicable.

---

[22] T. M. Scanlon, *What We Owe to Each Other* (Cambridge, MA: Harvard University Press, 2000).
[23] M. Walzer, "Objectivity and Social Meaning," in *The Quality of Life*, ed. M. Nussbaum and A. Sen (Oxford: Oxford University Press, 1993), 165–85.

The concept of "positional objectivity"—that assessments of social affairs can be considered objective if the individuals making them share similar circumstances or positions—raises the possibility of a more objective view of health. A more constructed or transpositional view could develop from "synthesizing different views from distinct positions."[24] This more global point of view could then help assess health capabilities across communities. More subjective accounts of health—for example, health utilities or health preferences—might fail to reveal deprivations in health: positional assessments of health by individuals themselves, which can reflect medical ignorance and/or destructive social norms, can divert resources away from those with rightful medical needs. Transpositional or global points of view on crucially important functionings are necessary for health justice.

History provides evidence of health's value in diverse social and cultural contexts. The provision of health care services to all at no cost is over 3,000 years old. Evidence shows that physicians in ancient Egypt provided free care to all, and that a form of insurance, pension, and sick leave were available to workers during the building of the pyramids.[25] In thirteenth-century Egypt, many hospitals provided charitable health care to the public. The largest of these institutions, the Mansuri Hospital in Cairo, was large enough to treat 8,000 patients at once and provided free care to all regardless of gender, nationality, status, or wealth. "The hospital shall keep all patients, men and women until they are completely recovered. All costs are to be borne by the hospital whether the people come from afar or near, whether they are residents or foreigners, strong or weak, low or high, rich or poor, employed or unemployed, blind or sighted, physically or mentally ill, learned or illiterate. There are no conditions of consideration and payment; none is objected to or even indirectly hinted at for non-payment. The entire service is through the magnificence of Allah, the generous one."[26] This example suggests that from the earliest civilizations, societies eventually come to acknowledge health needs and to develop health systems to meet them among their citizens. These trends continued in the centuries BCE when the ancient Roman Aesculapium provided free care to the ill,[27] and in the Middle Ages, when in Europe

---

[24] A. Sen, "Positional Objectivity," *Philosophy & Public Affairs* 22, no. 2 (1993): 130.

[25] K. Kelly, *The History of Medicine: Early Civilizations: Prehistoric Times to 500 CE* (New York: Infobase Publishing, 2009).

[26] D. L'Orange and G. Dolowich, *Ancient Roots Many Branches: Energetics of Healing Across Cultures and Through Time* (Twin Lakes, WI: Lotus Press, 2002), 44. For further discussion of charitable hospitals during this period, see L. Chipman, *The World of Pharmacy and Pharmacists in Mamlūk Cairo* (Leiden: Koninklijke Brill NV, 2010), 137–43; A. Sabra, *Poverty and Charity in Medieval Islam: Mamluk Egypt, 1250–1517* (Cambridge: Cambridge University Press, 2000), 69–80.

[27] D. N. Robinson, "Medicine and Society: The Business of Healing, Then and Now," *American Medical Association Journal of Ethics* 11, no. 5 (2009): 399–401.

social insurance schemes in Germany and dispensaries in England[28] sought to pool risk to subsidize disability and life insurance and provide medicines to the poor, respectively. Then, in the nineteenth century, friendly societies in Europe[29] and community health initiatives in Asia[30] sought again to redistribute resources and pool risks. History provides ample examples of the interlinkages between morality and health and the role of cultural, political, economic, and psychological factors in shaping these connections.[31]

Furthermore, as societies and countries grow economically, they spend more public funds in both real and percentage terms on health.[32] As they develop, they tend to pass legislation and establish health systems to guarantee all citizens access to health care and financial protection from its costs. This trend appears even in some countries or regions with limited income. One study found no link between gross domestic product (GDP) and the achievement of universal health coverage (UHC); instead, political commitment and decisions about how best to design and manage health systems and their financing are integral.[33] In fact, countries "with low GDPs, such as Costa Rica, Cuba, Gambia, and Gabon, have attained impressive prepaid coverage compared with those with higher GDPs, such as China, India, and the USA."[34] Other studies have also stressed the importance of sustained political commitment and a health system design that incorporates a shift over time toward greater pooled spending,[35] as opposed to out-of-pocket payments.[36]

Critically, developing countries constitute the new wave in universal health reform, following the pattern set by many industrialized democracies and socialist countries in the post-World War II era.[37] While the twenty-five wealthiest nations (excluding the USA) already enjoy some form of UHC, middle-income countries like Brazil, Thailand, and Mexico have also achieved success, with low-income countries like the Philippines, Vietnam, Rwanda,

---

[28] M. M. Davis and A. R. Warner, *Dispensaries: Their Management and Development* (New York: Macmillan Company, 1918).

[29] P. H. J. H. Gosden, *The Friendly Societies in England* (Manchester: Manchester University Press, 1961).

[30] S. Ogawa, T. Hasegawa, G. Carrin, and K. Kawabata, "Scaling Up Community Health Insurance: Japan's Experience with the 19th Century Jyorei Scheme," *Health Policy and Planning* 18, no. 3 (2003): 270–8.

[31] A. Brandt and P. Rozin, eds., *Morality and Health* (New York: Routledge Press, 1997).

[32] O. Smith and S. N. Nguyen, *Getting Better: Improving Health System Outcomes in Europe and Central Asia* (Washington, DC: World Bank Publications, 2013).

[33] L. Garrett, A. M. R. Chowdhury, and A. Pablos-Méndez, "All for Universal Health Coverage," *The Lancet* 374, no. 9697 (2009): 1294–9.

[34] Ibid., 1296.

[35] P. Gottret, G. J. Schieber, and H. R. Waters, eds., *Good Practices in Health Financing: Lessons from Reforms in Low- and Middle-Income Countries* (Washington, DC: World Bank Publications, 2008).

[36] W. D. Savedoff, D. de Ferranti, A.L. Smith, and V. Fan, "Political and Economic Aspects of the Transition to Universal Health Coverage," *The Lancet* 380, no. 9845 (2012): 924–32.

[37] Y. Huang, "World Momentum Builds for Universal Health Coverage," in *The New Global Health Agenda Universal Health Coverage* (New York: Council on Foreign Relations, 2012), 1–5.

and Ghana not far behind.[38] A report by the World Bank adds Chile, Colombia, Costa Rica, Estonia, the Kyrgyz Republic, Sri Lanka, and Tunisia to the list of low- and middle-income countries that have embarked on a path toward UHC.[39] In Africa, Ghana, Rwanda, Kenya, Mali, and Nigeria have each "implemented national health insurance reforms designed to move towards universal health coverage."[40] Finally, traditional health and human rights "blind spots" like China, India, and South Africa have begun making strides toward UHC.[41] India hopes to achieve universal coverage by 2022 and has targeted reforms since 2008 toward the rural poor by implementing cashless and portable access to health care through its RSBY (Rashtriya Swasthya Bima Yojana; National Health Insurance Program) scheme. China expects to provide "safe, effective, convenient and affordable" care to all by 2020.[42] Neighboring South Korea and Taiwan[43] achieved UHC over several years of reforms to enhance equity and reduce risk.

That these reforms are taking place across income levels and in politically disparate countries at varying stages of development indicates that health is increasingly valued globally. UHC is not simply a goal of the wealthiest or most liberal nations; it occurs across diverse cultures and ethnicities, from Asia to Africa to Latin America, North America, and Europe. In short, history suggests that all societies eventually come to acknowledge common health needs and seek to meet them. The historical and cross-cultural record thus suggests a transpositional view.

Achieving global health justice requires finding a shared health standard to enable interpersonal comparisons of health capabilities, and establishing a coherent framework for setting global health goals. The challenge is to construct a conception of health that reflects the view from everywhere, which relates to but is different from the "view from nowhere."[44] This quest for a universal health morality is highly contentious, open to criticism both philosophically and politically. PG does not seek to establish a universal view of health. It is practical, not epistemological. It seeks to identify elements of

---

[38] J. Rodin and D. de Ferranti, "Universal Health Coverage: The Third Global Health Transition?" *The Lancet* 380, no. 9845 (2012): 861–2.

[39] Gottret, Schieber, and Waters, eds., *Good Practices in Health Financing*.

[40] G. Lagomarsino, A. Garabrant, R. Muga, and N. Otoo, "Moving towards Universal Health Coverage: Health Insurance Reforms in Nine Developing Countries in Africa and Asia," *The Lancet* 380, no. 9845 (2012): 933.

[41] Huang, "World Momentum Builds for Universal Health Coverage"; K. S. Reddy, V. Patel, P. Jha, V. K. Paul, A. K. S. Kuma, L. Dandona, and *The Lancet* India Group for Universal Healthcare, "Towards Achievement of Universal Health Care in India by 2020: A Call To Action," *The Lancet* 377, no. 9767 (2011): 760–8.

[42] Huang, "World Momentum Builds for Universal Health Coverage," 2.

[43] J.-F. R. Lu and C. Hsiao, "Does Universal Health Insurance Make Health Care Unaffordable? Lessons from Taiwan," *Health Affairs* 22, no. 3 (2003): 77–88; J.-F. R. Lu and T.-L. Chiang, "Evolution of Taiwan's Health Care System," *Health Economics, Policy and Law* 6, no. 1 (2011): 85–107.

[44] T. Nagel, *The View from Nowhere* (New York: Oxford University Press, 1986).

health from which to build a global consensus, grounded in a scientific world-view. PG starts with our common interest in human capability and humans' claims for basic capabilities—health capabilities among them—which allow them to live and act in the world, thus justifying the minimum health and health agency needs that are to be guaranteed. Rather than hypothetical choices, PG turns to actual choices, empirical data that show societies have chosen and continue to choose entitlements to health capabilities over time and across the world.

In 1948, the World Health Organization (WHO) defined health as "a state of complete physical, mental and social well-being, and not merely the absence of disease or infirmity."[45] Since then, health policy and medical scientists have added concepts to the WHO definition so that it approaches quality of life. PG takes a different approach to defining health, conceptualizing it in terms of freedom and an intrinsic and instrumental component of human flourishing. While this model of health is discussed extensively elsewhere,[46] briefly, health involves optimal functioning, a state of dynamic balance in which an individual's ability to cope with her circumstances of living is at an optimal level; anatomic, physiologic, and psychological integrity; the ability to perform personally valued roles and to deal with physical, biologic, psychologic, and social stress. It is freedom from the risk of avoidable disease and untimely death.

PG is a global minimalist view that privileges both universalism and localism (the provincial level). PG enables localities to have a universal minimalist health morality, recognizing morality's source and strength in particular societies and families, practices, and institutions. PG requires a common global moral currency for making comparisons and judgments across different societies, but this thin universalism can be found in an incompletely theorized agreement (ITA) bringing together recurring ideas on health morality among different societies. By contrast, some societies may disagree with cosmopolitans' view of justice; this raises an important objection since those societies will not properly discharge the cosmopolitan duty if they disagree with it. Global health justice is real-world justice and must be locally relevant.

### 4.1.4 Health Capability Components: Functionings, Agency, and Needs

Why should we be concerned, as a matter of justice, with health capabilities? Why not make the ethical perspective health or health functionings

---

[45] Preamble to the Constitution of the WHO as adopted by the International Health Conference, New York, June 19–22, 1946; signed July 22, 1946, by the representatives of sixty-one states (Official Records of the WHO 2: 100) and entered into force on April 7, 1948.

[46] J. P. Ruger, *Health and Social Justice* (Oxford: Oxford University Press, 2009).

alone? First, a health capabilities approach seeks opportunities for good health as the objective, as opposed to schemes that justify functioning or health care for equality of opportunity or some other societal objective such as utility. Being capable of functioning as a human being and health are ends in and of themselves. Second, a health capabilities focus distinguishes between achieving a given health outcome through coercion versus voluntary action. Just looking at health outcomes alone (for example, fertility rates), while a key component of this theory and helpful for practical policy purposes, will not in and of itself demonstrate the justice or injustice involved in achieving them—through coercive sterilization, pregnancy termination, or one-child policy laws, for example. Third, health capabilities appeal to theories of choice by revealing the choices and options individuals have at their disposal in achieving health outcomes. Fourth, this approach includes health agency, which illuminates an individual's or group's ability to pursue valuable health goals and to effectively bring about health. Finally, health capabilities, through health agency, incorporate a role for individual responsibility, crucial to any global health justice theory. Individual responsibility reveals the limits of social responsibility in the context of irresponsible choice and underlines the causal influence of individual choices on health outcomes, as lifestyle and behavior are health determinants.

The relationship between health functionings and health needs is key. Health needs map to health functionings, which in turn map to health capabilities. Health needs, through their relation to functioning, define what is required to improve individuals' health capabilities. For example, a person might suffer from malnutrition or diabetes or a broken leg. Improving her health capabilities requires meeting the needs those conditions present. Thus, how well we meet health needs is an objective measure of our success in improving health capabilities. The task, then, is to specify health needs as they relate to health functionings and health capabilities. Medical necessity and medical appropriateness are important concepts and help clarify health needs under the HCP. National systems are critical for meeting health needs. Operationalizing and implementing the HCP at the state level is a central component of the PG view.

Importantly, this analysis does not depend on reconciling normative and non-normative approaches to defining health. For the purposes of resource distribution and policy evaluation, relying on the distinction between health and disease and on scientific knowledge about human anatomy, physiology, and biochemistry can identify sufficient core criteria and areas of convergence. The HCP's basic model of health (see 4.1.3) provides a workable distinction between health-related needs and the goods and services that address those needs.

### 4.1.5 *Health Agency*

Health agency is a core value in PG; global health justice requires meeting health agency needs. That said, health agency is not strictly autonomy in one's health. Health agency is more positive and reflects the interdependency of individuals. PG recognizes that individual choices do not occur in a vacuum. Individual choices have personal and societal consequences, and social conditions shape our decisions and actions. Individuals merit assistance in meeting health agency needs; and they owe their global and domestic communities the responsible exercise of health agency. The privilege of individual health agency entails the obligation to make wise choices that do not harm others. Health agency at both the individual and the collective level is a critical end of global health justice and the primary means through which it will come about. Health agency is thus an essential objective of global and national health policy. Failing to meet health agency needs also leaves individuals and groups vulnerable to coercion and oppression. Individual and group health agency develop over time as a stable and consistent feature forming the foundation for health decisions and actions. The development of health agency, both individually and collectively, is centrally important in PG.

A reciprocal relationship links individual health agency to global health justice and governance. Global health justice requires both individual and group health agency; good domestic and global governance enables it through competent and accessible medical services, effective education programs, and other means. Conversely, individuals and groups deploy their health agency to serve global health justice and participate in governance—caring for themselves to achieve and maintain good health, using resources wisely, working collectively to influence their governments and build healthier communities, and advocating for clean environments, good sanitation, and other health determinants.

Promoting central health capabilities depends upon health agency development. The extent to which one's accomplishments result from one's own choices and values is an important aspect of health capability. Health functionings are more valuable—they manifest a more enhanced state of affairs—when one effectuates them through one's own choice, fulfilling one's own responsibilities. For example, efforts to control HIV and AIDS depend critically on the ability to acquire and effectively use knowledge about HIV/AIDS transmission, preventive measures, and health behaviors' costs and benefits. Controlling HIV/AIDS requires self-governance and management skills and the ability to link behavior and outcomes. It requires seeking treatment and adhering to it, and monitoring laboratory test results. These abilities and personal management skills together constitute health agency. Individual behaviors cause much ill health; individuals use their health agency to improve their health. Ill health poses many different challenges with various complexities and implications. Developing health agency—the ability to handle these practical issues—is essential if people are to resolve particular situations effectively. Health competency develops over time, from cradle to grave, by developing stable and consistent habits and decision-making ability. Clinical psychologists and public health practitioners can share their expertise about how people learn and apply these lessons, based on inner disposition and external conditions.

In PG, collective or group agency exists in addition to individual agency. Groups can be moral agents because they act and/or make decisions as an entity above and beyond the aggregation of individual decisions and actions. From a PG perspective, collective agency ranges from formal group decision-making and institutional structures (such as those defining corporations)[47] to more informal groups of individuals, such as families or ethnic groups, engaged in cooperative action that influences individual members.[48] Philip Pettit provides evidence for the existence of group agency in work that distinguishes between group reasoning and decisions made by aggregating individual choices in groups (by majority vote, for example).[49]

Acknowledging the importance of collective or group agency helps set the stage for identifying global moral norms and for allocating group and individual rights and responsibilities. Individual and collective agency are both important analytical components in PG; both individuals and groups are moral agents with duties and responsibilities. PG puts forth a substantive foundation for identifying and allocating group rights and responsibilities in global health justice. For example, groups within societies need collective health agency to demand the necessary conditions for health, and to shape and reshape health systems through political and civic engagement. Collective agency is necessary to create an effective and accountable public health and health care system, one that provides medically necessary, appropriate, and cost-effective care, and in turn further enhances health agency. But health agency also depends on health values, goals, and norms. Internalizing norms about the value of health and health-related goals and behaviors and about the morality of health at the provincial and global levels is fundamental. These norms include the agency of the disabled and provision for children and others who experience limitations in exercising agency.

[47] P. A. French, "The Corporation as a Moral Person," *American Philosophical Quarterly* 16, no. 3 (1979): 207–15.

[48] J. Feinberg, "Collective Responsibility," *Journal of Philosophy* 65, no. 21 (1968): 674–88. See especially the discussion of collective liability on p. 677.

[49] P. Pettit, *A Theory of Freedom: From the Psychology to the Politics of Agency* (New York: Oxford University Press, 2001), 104–24.

Health agency is a necessary though not sufficient component of health capability, which is a necessary although not sufficient component of human flourishing. Many if not all valuable health outcomes require health agency to be achieved. Health agency encompasses practical wisdom—a way of knowing how to secure positive health outcomes effectively and efficiently. Health agency is empowering to its holder. It needs to be developed and nurtured, becoming stable over time, while remaining open to ongoing revision through new knowledge and skills. The purpose of fostering health agency is to develop and support everyone's ability to make the right decision and do the right thing at any given time, thus obviating the need to micromanage individual decisions. Positive natural endowments and learned behaviors are encouraged, and negative natural endowments and learned behaviors discouraged, to develop the right health habits. A person who values, promotes, and protects her health and others' across all situations—not simply to maximize utility or adhere to duty or rules—has built that trait into her personhood and does not need external motivation. That said, the cultivation of health agency requires external factors, as noted in the health capability profile. Health agency is good in itself as its own reward, but it is also good for people and communities. It involves conscientiousness about the impact of our behavior on others' health and well-being; self-interest is compatible rather than in conflict with other-regarding behavior.

Health agency depends on a sense of justice at the individual and collective level. Stable and consistent health agency focuses on what matters for oneself and for others: the fair distribution of goods and services to promote and protect one's own and others' health. If each individual and group possesses this aspect of health agency, more sensible actions and decisions will reduce injustice. Social institutions and norms also support these qualities, manifesting principles of justice with which individuals and groups voluntarily comply. Minimally obligatory state measures should be taken to bring individuals and groups who do not yet exercise health agency into the fold, because both individuals and society benefit when people exercise positive health agency. While laws and other forms of external motivation are important and necessary to bring the unwilling on board, developing the inner qualities of health agency and supporting it with enabling conditions tilts our motivations from avoiding punishment toward becoming responsible individuals, both locally and globally. Taking or getting more than one's fair share or taking others' share of goods and services is an individual and group health agency failure and contravenes social justice. When positive health agency develops, individuals and groups will voluntarily create, support, and promote just social arrangements.

### 4.1.6 *Ethical Individualism*

In the PG framework, individual health functioning and health agency for all are both the ends and means of global health—that is, of a global enterprise comprising national health systems, social structures, global norms, actors, and institutions. Thus, while the universal ethical norm of health equity rests upon a normative framework of human flourishing, PG applies a more functionalist approach in allocating responsibility for achieving that equity. This approach begins with the health capability—health functioning and health agency—of every person worldwide as morally significant. It then works outward from this ethical individualism toward the enveloping necessary conditions, starting with the local and national environment. While PG depends upon individual freedom and presupposes voluntary action and individual intention, it also presupposes shared responsibility and the allocation of moral responsibility among both individuals and collectivities. Shared and institutional responsibility is a major component of the PG framework applied to problems of global health injustice.

It is important, then, to analyze health agency and health functioning in the context of health needs and health agency needs, and look at how structures at the individual, local, national, and global levels can meet those needs. The immediate and local nature of meeting needs (nurse and doctor providing prenatal care and delivery services in a clinic with necessary equipment and medicines, for example) requires beginning the systematic study of global health at the individual level and expanding outward. Telemedicine, foreign aid, management, and global governance notwithstanding, ultimately a local provider in a local facility with drugs and medical devices on hand will provide medical attention to the person in need of health services. Solving public health and health care problems requires a grasp of local realities. The near-eradication of malaria in Eritrea illustrates the effectiveness of local design and implementation.[50] No global health system will function optimally without national and local health systems to meet the needs of local populations. They are the cornerstone of global health architecture.

To support national and local health systems in meeting their populations' health needs and health agency needs, the global health system and global health policy perform two important tasks: (1) containing and eliminating externalities (pandemics, for example); and (2) supporting the development and sustainability of fully functional national and local health systems.

---

[50] For a discussion of the decentralization of Eritrea's malaria eradication efforts as the focus at local *zoba* and sub-*zoba* levels, see "Appendix 3: Four Success Stories: Malaria Control in Brazil, Eritrea, India, and Vietnam," in World Bank, *Rolling Back Malaria: The World Bank Global Strategy and Booster Program* (Washington, DC: World Bank Publications, 2005), 157–69.

Failures in these systems, such as inadequate financing and access to care, can have damaging effects both on global commons like disease surveillance systems and on local populations. From this perspective, externalities and inequalities are imbalances in the global health system and require correction to move the system to a more just equilibrium.

These systems are indispensable, because health capability depends not just on individual traits and strengths but also, critically, on societal-level factors and conditions essential to optimal health. But this understanding of socially dependent capabilities differs from analytical frameworks typically applied in the social determinants of health, epidemiological, or health economic literatures. These frameworks use group-level variables (neighborhood income, for example) that can yield atomistic fallacy (drawing group inferences from individual-level data) and ecological fallacy (drawing individual inferences from group-level data). PG understands that socially dependent capabilities reflect at the individual level the extent to which group-level factors are at play. Group-level factors may have varying effects on individuals, and require evaluation in light of these effects.

## 4.2 Global Distributive Justice

In PG, global distributive justice starts with a set of principles to be applied, progressively as needed, so that all individuals worldwide have the opportunity to be healthy, not simply the opportunity for more or equal resources. Social goods like norms, health agency development, and ethical engagement are less amenable to material distribution. This approach contrasts with other views. In Pogge's global resources dividend concept, for example, states and governments pay dividends on any resources they sell or use. The dividends raised then go to reduce poverty globally. Beitz applies Rawls' difference principle globally to address inequalities and maximize the state of the worst-off person or group of persons, in part because he sees the global and domestic systems of interdependence and cooperation as similar and thus amenable to these measures.[51] In other words, global interdependence puts all persons in relation to each other, thus justifying associative global duties. Robert Goodin offers an alternative approach, a duty to the vulnerable manifested in an international aid mandate.[52] As

[51] C. R. Beitz, *Political Theory and International Relations*, rev. ed. (Princeton, NJ: Princeton University Press, 1999).
[52] R. E. Goodin, *Protecting the Vulnerable: A Reanalysis of our Social Responsibilities* (Chicago: University of Chicago Press, 1985).

we have seen, Singer and like-minded cosmopolitan theorists call for radically redistributing resources from the wealthy to those who are suffering. Van Parijs has called for a mix of capitalism and universal income at the state level.[53]

Manifestos of various social movements, not necessarily supported by theorists, also call for global distributive justice measures: fairer trade policies, global commons and multinational corporation taxes (from the Commission on Global Governance), world debt cancellation among highly indebted poor countries, migration and immigration liberalization, and a Tobin tax on international money markets.[54]

In one sense, PG's principles for global health justice are thinner than these conceptualizations, but they are thicker in another. In the thin sense, though its global health justice principles recognize the importance of quality of life and overall freedom, they cannot realistically guarantee a minimum income to all. Such basic income proposals may be consistent with PG although they fit within a scheme of global justice more broadly.[55] Thus PG limits the focal variable for global health justice to central health capabilities. That said, these principles are more demanding or thicker than these other conceptualizations in their goals, aiming to raise all individuals' health to the highest average, and as efficiently as possible, even if realizing these goals occurs over time. This is considerably more ambitious than the rudimentary right to subsistence.[56] David Miller, a nationalist in global justice debates, supports an account of global justice principles, including basic human rights, non-exploitation of the vulnerable, and "the obligation to provide all political communities with the opportunity to achieve self-determination and social justice."[57] PG is also more rigorous than the minimum no-harm principles in some versions of cosmopolitanism.

---

[53] P. Van Parijs, *Real Freedom for All: What (If Anything) Can Justify Capitalism?* (Oxford: Clarendon Press, 1998).

[54] See, for example, the World Fair Trade Organization; for the work of the Commission on Global Governance, see *Our Global Neighborhood* (Oxford: Oxford University Press, 1995); for a short discussion of national debt relief, see IMF, "Debt Relief Under the Heavily Indebted Poor Countries (HIPC) Initiative," Washington, DC, September 2013; for a discussion of migration reform, see A. Pécoud and P. de Guchteneire, eds., *Migration without Borders: Essays on the Free Movement of People* (New York: Berghahn Books, 2007); for a discussion of the Tobin tax, see J. Weaver, R. Dodd, and J. Baker, eds., *Debating the Tobin Tax: New Rules for Global Finance* (Washington, DC: New Rules for Global Finance Coalition, 2003).

[55] P. Van Parijs and Y. Vanderborght, *Basic Income: A Radical Proposal for a Free Society and a Sane Economy* (Cambridge, MA: Harvard University Press, 2017).

[56] C. Jones, *Global Justice: Defending Cosmopolitanism* (Oxford: Oxford University Press, 1999); H. Shue, *Basic Rights: Subsistence, Affluence, and U.S. Foreign Policy*, 2nd ed. (Princeton, NJ: Princeton University Press, 1996).

[57] D. Miller, *Citizenship and National Identity* (Cambridge: Polity Press, 2000), 177.

### 4.2.1 *Principles and Measurement in Health Equity Theory*

#### 4.2.1.1 EQUALITY, PRIORITY, SUFFICIENCY

Some of PG's components are easier to measure and track empirically (for example, health functionings) than others (for example, health norms, health agency, and ethical engagement),[58] but measurement theory is key in PG. Theorists propose numerous principles to evaluate justice in different domains, including equality, priority, and sufficiency. PG applies the concept of shortfall equality to integrate these core elements.

One version of the equality principle justifies allocating resources to correct differences across groups and equalize them in certain outcomes, here health outcomes or access to health care. We can dispatch this view quickly, because guaranteeing equal health outcomes or equal amounts of health care is impossible. Moreover, a global health justice theory based on fulfilling health needs would call for differing amounts of health care, and more and different types of health care, according to medical need and medical appropriateness. Another objection to this equality standard is that equality under this principle is typically classified as attainment equality, which compares individuals according to absolute levels of achievement. But attainment equality ignores the reduced potential of some individuals or groups and thus limits society's obligation to consider potential achievement. In doing so, it "'level[s] down … all to the condition of the lowest achiever"[59] and prevents many individuals from realizing their full potential.

A second principle is prioritarian,[60] which justifies allocation of resources to the worst off first and foremost, above all others, seeking to aid the most deprived. Critics assert that it does not specify how to set the threshold against which to assess the worst off or others. And it too raises the leveling-down objection, because when resources are scarce, channeling them to the worst off can arguably diminish others' health and their access to health care.

The threshold view, a third approach, proposes a threshold of sufficiency, a minimally adequate health status, to guide international resource allocations.

#### 4.2.1.2 MEASURING GLOBAL HEALTH INEQUALITIES AND EXTERNALITIES BY SHORTFALL EQUALITY

The HCP and PG apply the concept of shortfall equality to integrate these core elements—equality, priority, and threshold. The field of welfare economics

---

[58] R. Kanbur, "Capability, Opportunity, Outcome—and Equality," Dyson Working Paper 16-05, http://publications.dyson.cornell.edu/research/researchpdf/wp/2016/Cornell-Dyson-wp1605.pdf (accessed November 27, 2017).

[59] Sen, *Inequality Reexamined*, 93.

[60] D. Parfit, "Equality or Priority?" in *The Ideal of Equality*, ed. M. Clayton and A. Williams (New York: Palgrave Macmillan, 2000): 81–126.

has used the shortfall equality construct, but its more recent application to health has been gaining support as well.[61] Using shortfall equality involves setting a norm or threshold against which to assess health equity; it considers the worse off and the need for proportional allocation, and it incorporates equality, but not full equality, of health outcomes or access to health care. The shortfall equality concept can assess health capabilities through the proxies of health functioning and health agency and can thus point toward more equitable conditions, especially where equalizing achievements among different people is difficult. This approach is especially promising in assessing the health capabilities of the disabled, because it recognizes differences in maximal potential and thus does not level down the achievement goals of the larger population. Shortfall equality therefore balances consideration of improvements for the worse off with improvements for all. Under PG, efforts to improve the health functioning and health agency of the worse off should not interfere with the health functioning and health agency of others. In fact, improving the health functioning and health agency of the worse off will ultimately improve the situation of all: the individual exercise of health agency benefits both individuals and communities by enabling the voluntary creation, support, and promotion of just social arrangements for all. Shortfall equality complements a conceptualization of health emphasizing optimal functioning.

At the global or country level, measuring shortfall equality—comparing the actual achievement of a given health policy or health system with the possible maximum—can show quantitatively how much a society has realized its health potential and how much remains unrealized. The country is typically the unit of analysis, though the method can also compare groups within countries. This process focuses primarily on estimating what should be possible and how to allocate resources to achieve those possibilities. The United Nations (UN) used a shortfall equality method to compare life expectancies across countries,[62] and researchers have employed it to evaluate global health inequalities empirically.[63] One study used the World Bank's World Development Indicators database to examine cross-national differences in under-5 mortality and adult mortality. The study applied clustering techniques to stratify national populations into better-off, mid-level, and worse-off groups and examined the risk factors for inequality—illiteracy, urbanization, pollution,

---

[61] See Sen, *Inequality Reexamined*, 89, for a short discussion of shortfall use in the development of welfare economics; while for applications to health see Ruger, "Ethics and Governance of Global Health Inequalities," 998–1003.

[62] UNDP, "Defining and Measuring Human Development," in *Human Development Report 1990* (New York: Oxford University Press, 1900), 9–11.

[63] Ruger and Kim, "Global Health Inequalities," 928–36.

economic performance, natural resources, and many more. The better-off stratum served as the reference group against which to measure shortfalls.

In global health, this construct points the way toward public policies that bring each individual's health functioning up to a norm level (within the limits of that person's circumstances), but do not lower the general population's health functioning beneath the norm. Priority thus goes to individuals whose health status falls below their potential status, to deprivations below the shortfall equality norm. Those with the greatest deficit should receive the highest priority. Policies can address deprivations above the norm when greater resources permit the scope of justice to expand (an expansion amply possible in many industrialized countries today). However, because improving one person's functioning or agency should not come at the expense of another's, PG differs from modes of consequentialism that would sacrifice individuals in efforts to achieve a preferred outcome.

The obligation to promote capabilities and functionings is not open-ended, however, as efficiency is also an important concern. PG includes a theory of efficiency, relying on cost-management measures that identify the goal and examine costs and efficiency, and applying analytical tools to minimize costs. Collective and individual responsibilities delineate respective roles for goal attainment.

## 4.3 Joint Commitments: Plural Subjecthood[64]

PG employs plural subject theory (PST)[65] to conceptualize different subjecthoods that individuals everywhere experience, which lead us to make ethical commitments and assume obligations. PG is related to but distinct from the conventional concept of solidarity. There are numerous definitions of solidarity. But as Wilde notes, "The paradox at the heart of solidarity has long been evident. On the one hand it has connotations of unity and universality, emphasizing responsibility for others and the feeling of togetherness. On the other hand it exhibits itself most forcefully in antagonism to other groups, often in ways which eschew the possibility of compromise."[66] Solidarity tends to have an either–or, us-versus-them mentality, unproductive in contexts where multiple identities, relationships, affiliations, and motivations for cooperation exist. Houtepen and ter Meulen observe the move from "voluntary solidarity in reciprocal arrangements" to "organised and enforced

---

[64] This section stems from J. P. Ruger, "Shared Health Governance," *The American Journal of Bioethics* 11, no. 7 (2011): 32–45.

[65] M. Gilbert, *Living Together* (Lanham, MD: Rowman & Littlefield, 1996).

[66] L. Wilde, "The Concept of Solidarity: Emerging from the Theoretical Shadows?" *British Journal of Politics & International Relations* 9, no. 1 (2007): 173.

solidarity" or "contractual solidarity" in the modern European welfare state.[67] As to health, despite comparisons between solidarity and justice, only limited discussions explore health, health care obligations, and health actions required by solidarity, domestic or global.

Jodi Dean's conception of "reflective solidarity"[68] is more promising and a useful corrective to conventional solidarity. Conventional solidarity arises around shared interests and concerns, shaped by common traditions and values. Some Western nations' UHC systems rest on conventional solidarity. But as Dean explains, when a community based on conventional solidarity brings outsiders into its circle, it seeks to convert these outsiders to its own worldview. If they do not succeed, these communities separate themselves from those they cannot convert and discourage and repress the differences in those they do convert. Conventional solidarity thus evinces indifference toward the other. A divide persists between us and them. Reflective solidarity, by contrast, considers "the other . . . a member despite, indeed because of, her difference."[69] Reflective solidarity collapses the divide between us and them by acknowledging that community members "are always insiders and out-siders . . . [and] are always situated in a variety of differing groups all of which play a role in the development of our individual identities."[70] Reflective solidarity is more consistent with PG/SHG and PST.

Plural subjecthood represents our affiliations and obligations as nuances along the spectrum from the individual to the collective, both domestically and globally. PST sees human beings as both individuals and members of multiple domestic and global communities. Within this plural subjecthood, a distinction exists between one's own individual objectives and one's object-ives (and attendant obligations) as a group member, though these are related. These subjecthoods precede health; but in the health context, individuals are subjects in at least three domains: (1) ourselves and our own endeavors individually and locally; (2) our state; and (3) our world. At the individual level, PG provides, and indeed requires, a high degree of individual expression and agency, both in pursuing one's own health and in advocating for stron-ger, more equitable systems; it also stresses the responsibility of individuals in making wise choices. In our national subjecthood, we have special justice obligations to compatriots deriving from our shared commitments to health equity goals and the special intrinsic meaning that such relationships give our lives. We take on roles and responsibilities to meet these goals and to support

---

[67] R. Houtepen and R. ter Meulen, "New Types of Solidarity in the European Welfare State," *Health Care Analysis* 8, no. 4 (2000): 329.

[68] J. Dean, *Solidarity of Strangers: Feminism after Identity Politics* (Berkeley, CA: University of California Press, 1996).

[69] Ibid., 30.

[70] Ibid., 34.

the shared political and social institutions required to ensure these goals. Of course, individuals also have special duties to members of their own families or communities, and these relationships have special meaning in their lives, but we are focused here on the compatibility of domestic and global associations and responsibilities.

PG thus accepts our partiality for compatriots as one of the many relationships and associations humans experience and value. But PG reaches beyond this affiliation and allows us to balance our partiality toward compatriots (our domestic subjecthood) with our partiality toward foreigners (our global subjecthood). Each one of us is a global subject: each of us is inextricably embedded in the human race on this Earth. Each of us is playing a role, however unwittingly, in the development of a healthy or unhealthy society. Even if we do not understand or acknowledge our global subjecthood, it already exists. PG envisions an educational process to strengthen this understanding, a necessary step if we are to achieve justice.

One's sense of global subjecthood might not be as strong in attachment or identity as local and national associations, but even so our commitment to global health equity could be very strong—a commitment that requires assuming roles and responsibilities incorporating both moral motivations simultaneously. Thus, these moral motivations need not be incompatible. This compelling commitment—to live in a world where all have the ability to be healthy—can provide motivation for people to act, to accept progressive taxation, to mobilize politically, to sacrifice some privilege on behalf of the suffering. But extending the commitment beyond capability to flourishing for all people across the globe asks more, and in a world where jobs are uncertain, wages and salaries stagnant, and competing concerns demand our attention (terrorism, for example, or catastrophic climate change), some might think it asks too much. Nevertheless, health capability, combined with other capabilities, will lead to flourishing, and flourishing is the proper goal of societal arrangements. PG can aid our understanding of appropriate relations among us all and define our duties to one another. Duties at the global level differ in extent and complexity from state and local duties: not all actors are responsible for discharging all of them.

PG applies PST to health, suggesting a common subjecthood around coproducing a healthy society. Mutual understanding of common problems and joint commitments to solving them are fundamental to this common subjecthood. This view is consistent with moral psychology and social psychology literatures, which see attachments, identities, and commitments to principles as motivation for people's actions,[71] but it brings these three motivations

---

[71] Attachment theory seeks to describe the dynamics of interpersonal relationships. See P. R. Shaver and M. Mikulincer, "Attachment Theory and Research: Core Concepts, Basic Principles, Conceptual Bridges," in *Social Psychology: Handbook of Basic Principles*, ed.

together in the concept of plural subjecthood. Attachments, which primarily involve very close relationships, arguably exert more force at the individual level and less at the state and global level; there the greater motivating force could be identities and moral values. If attachments do operate at the state level, then they can motivate there as well. When we identify with compatriots and fellow human beings and commit to common goals, we also commit to solving common problems, like health protection and promotion. The common good of health equity at the national level and the enforcement nature of state institutions both ground duties of justice between compatriots and offer explanations for a stronger duty toward compatriots as compared to non-compatriots.

Under this view, special relationships and geographic proximity are morally relevant criteria for balancing general duties or universal concerns with special duties derived from specific associations and the sharing of specific commitments. Prioritizing among these duties is not only morally acceptable but morally required. Indeed, failing to discharge special duties, such as those toward fellow citizens, is morally unacceptable. Discharging our general duties toward foreigners involves influencing our own political leaders to support just and effective governments in our own and other countries to help them fulfill their duties toward their own populations. Wealthy governments can be morally responsible for leading to or failing to prevent or address global health deprivations. This collective identity is important for trust and willingness to sacrifice. It helps us grasp the larger picture and rise above self and group private interests.

PG enables coexistence of our different subjecthoods and our commitments to shared conceptions of the common good, the good of each individual including the good of others, within the bounds of both global and domestic communities. Joint commitments with others in which individuals are informed about the interests of others promote the common good to everyone's advantage, not just that of the elite, the well connected, the majority, or aggregated private interests. Based on the common good, PG and its accompanying SHG theory apply rules to all based on the interests shared by all. These rules form the basis for public decision-making. Thus, PG supports the integration of impartial global equity with domestic partiality. This global minimalist view proposes that the goals of health justice be set globally, for all persons on the planet, but that these objectives be applied within the state with acceptable partiality toward co-nationals in meeting

A. W. Kruglanski and E. T. Higgins, 2nd ed. (New York: Guilford, 2007), 650–78; for a discussion of identity-based motivation, see D. Oyserman, "Social Identity and Self-Regulation," in *Social Psychology*, ed. Kruglanski and Higgins, 432–54, and D. Oyserman, S. A. Fryberg, and N. Yoder, "Identity-Based Motivation and Health," *Journal of Personality and Social Psychology* 93, no. 6 (2007): 1011–27.

them. Common objections to cosmopolitan duties of assistance focus on the impracticality of providing the same level of assistance to foreigners and co-nationals and on the ineffectiveness of direct wealth redistribution to poor countries due to governance inefficiencies in those countries. But the plurality of affiliations among human beings across borders requires a model that extends beyond the political boundaries of the state even as it recognizes the importance of the affiliations of compatriots in a vision of justice and health.

## 4.4 Relativism versus Universalism

Despite the global dimensions of health justice values and principles, borders and states have moral significance in more than one way. The world's sovereign-state system with its principle of self-determination requires respect for the collective agency of peoples and mutual respect among states. Citizens' ability to cooperate to achieve shared goals is an important aspect of human agency. People should be able to participate politically, and their actions should result in meaningful collective achievements. On the other hand, countries and cultures often embrace destructive public norms and engage in morally wrong, even heinous, practices like slavery, widow burning, or genocide.[72] Other destructive norms stigmatize sufferers of diseases like HIV/ AIDS and interfere with treatment. Health capability requires positive norms—evidence-based health information, respect for women, and human dignity. Cultural relativism fails to provide normative criteria for condemning immoral social practices within particular cultures, and many cultures themselves reject cultural relativism, viewing their values and traditions as absolutes.[73] But critics of moral universalism charge that it suppresses cultural diversity and ignores the role of moral contestation within cultures. Cosmopolitans have trouble justifying special obligations, such as those within the family, due to their perceived lack of universality.[74] The global justice debate has been one of seemingly irreconcilable opposites: cosmopolitanism on the one hand and nationalism and state sovereignty on the other.

More recent scholarship in global justice seeks to reconcile these extreme positions but has encountered resistance. Samuel Black argues that a "distributive theory, that ascribes rights and claims on the basis of certain universal attributes of persons, cannot at the same time restrict the grounds for those

---

[72] A. Gewirth, "Is Cultural Pluralism Relevant to Moral Knowledge?" *Social Philosophy and Policy* 11, no. 1 (1994): 22–43.

[73] M. C. Nussbaum, *Women and Human Development: The Capabilities Approach* (Cambridge: Cambridge University Press, 2000).

[74] P. T. Lenard and M. Moore, "Cosmopolitanism and Making Room (or Not) for Special Duties," *The Monist* 94, no. 4 (2011): 615–27.

claims to a person's membership or status within a given society" (the "fallacy of *restricted universalism*").[75] His point is well taken, but it ignores the position of analysis: Does one take the duty bearer's perspective or the entitlement bearer's, or both? Taking the entitlement bearer's perspective first and the duty bearer's second, the stages are to identify an overarching goal first and then to allocate duty bearers to achieve this goal, even if it means that not every duty bearer would personally support the entitlement. For example, when a global commitment to central health capabilities obtains, an individual who practices widow burning must refrain from it since he has a duty to respect each individual's capability to avoid premature mortality. Global relationships and systems of cooperation differ from national ones, and we need discrete but related cooperative systems to address overarching human needs. But though the domestic and global realms of cooperation do not correspond in political, economic, institutional, and pragmatic ways, this lack of correspondence does not threaten the global importance and scope of universal justice principles.[76]

PG is a middle-ground view with a gradualist approach to collective responsibility. Allocating responsibilities in PG defines mutual accountability, legitimacy, and recourse when actors abrogate their obligations. PG acknowledges the close connections between personal identity and cultural community deriving from nationalism[77] or even local affiliations. But social and personal identity involve more than just national identity. Group affiliations (for example, gender, race, ethnicity, class, caste, occupation, religion, sport, or other avocations) define persons as well; indeed, the social ties that can constitute identity seem limitless. There is no reason why political identities cannot be established to support global health justice.

Though some object that nationalism can be dangerous, as national biases can lead to conflict among nations,[78] PG recognizes that states are ethical communities (welfare states, for example, deliver benefits to citizens); attachments to fellow citizens have ethical significance and belonging to a shared institutional order—state membership, for example—creates obligations.[79] Some argue that associational relations affect justice duties in the economic

[75] S. Black, "Individualism at an Impasse," *Canadian Journal of Philosophy* 21, no. 3 (1991): 357.

[76] On cosmopolitan justice and global egalitarianism, see generally, K. C. Tan, *Justice without Borders: Cosmopolitanism, Nationalism, and Patriotism* (Cambridge: Cambridge University Press, 2004); G. Brock, "Liberal Nationalism versus Cosmopolitanism: Locating the Disputes," *Public Affairs Quarterly* 16, no. 4 (2002): 307–27.

[77] On liberal nationalism, see generally, Y. Tamir, *Liberal Nationalism* (Princeton, NJ: Princeton University Press, 1993), especially the right to culture and the right to self-determination.

[78] For a critique of liberal nationalism see generally, J. Mayerfield, "The Myth of Benign Group Identity: A Critique of Liberal Nationalism," *Polity* 30, no. 4 (1998): 555–78.

[79] See, for example, D. Miller, "The Ethical Significance of Nationality," *Ethics* 98, no. 4 (1998): 647–62; on the right to culture and the right to (national) self-determination, see Tamir, *Liberal Nationalism*; for arguments concerning the state as a political community, see M. Walzer, "The

and political realm (for example, prioritizing the welfare and protection of compatriots over those of others).[80] These points overlap with the nationalism and political obligations literature.[81] Liberal nationalism[82] or moderate nationalism tends to view the nation as a community that seeks self-direction and self-determination toward common goals; shares commitments, culture, language, and historical continuity; and encourages sympathetic attachment to others' interests along with fellow feeling, trust, reciprocity, solidarity, and willingness to redistribute resources. Such characteristics, it is argued, make social justice more attainable.

These nationalism-based claims fit within the provincial globalist framework; they can ground obligations to fellow citizens. Canada's universal health care, for example, has a collectivist basis and is central to Canadian citizenship, serving a unifying purpose in a multicultural state.[83]

## 4.5 Fulfilling Global Health Justice Requirements: Principles for Allocating and Prioritizing Responsibilities

Who then is responsible for realizing health equity at the global level? What duties and responsibilities do global and state actors and institutions have? A backward-looking perspective attributes responsibility based on the party or parties who, by commission or omission, caused or contributed to global health injustice—and could have foreseen the resulting harm. A forward-looking perspective, by contrast, analyzes the party or parties who should or are able to address current or obviate future global health injustices due to their roles, resources, and capabilities.

### 4.5.1 *Causality, Remediation, and Partiality*

To determine which actors have particular moral obligations, one could start with the principles of causation or remediation. Causality, as discussed, has been used to attribute responsibility in global justice theory, arguing, for example, that wealthy countries and corporations distort the terms of

Moral Standing of States: A Response to Four Critics," *Philosophy & Public Affairs* 9, no. 3 (1980): 209–29.

[80] Miller, "The Ethical Significance of Nationality."

[81] J. Horton, "In Defence of Associative Political Obligations: Part One," *Political Studies* 54, no. 3 (2006): 427–43; J. Horton, "In Defence of Associative Political Obligations: Part Two," *Political Studies* 55, no. 1 (2007): 1–19; D. Miller, *On Nationality* (Oxford: Oxford University Press, 1995); Tamir, *Liberal Nationalism*.

[82] Tamir, *Liberal Nationalism*.

[83] C. J. Redden, *Health Care, Entitlement, and Citizenship* (Toronto: University of Toronto Press, 2002).

international cooperation, thus creating an unfair multilateral system of institutions that undercuts developing countries and creates global injustices through development policies or other practices. The long-term cumulative effects of such policies and practices have been deleterious to developing countries and their citizens. Responsibility for resultant global injustice on this argument is attributed to these wealthy states and their citizens. To the extent that poverty in many countries results from exploitation by wealthier nations and the international system due to either historical factors like colonialism or contemporary policies and practices, obligations for compensation arise. But causation requires a very high burden of proof, and achieving clarity about respective roles and responsibilities is difficult. The causal chain of events leading to a harm includes all those situated in it, going as far back in history as is necessary to assess attribution. Assessment of the responsibility of bystanders, those who witness or may even benefit from a harm to others,[84] is also a question, one which could expand further the scope of responsibility and the individuals and collectivities within that scope. In assessing causation, intention is a factor: liability involves an individual or collectivity having foreseen yet failed to avoid a harm, and guilt or culpability involves an individual or collectivity as the main actor or abettor to harm. Therefore, charging an actor with global health injustices is arguably not possible.

One could also start with the principles of partiality and connectedness, on the grounds that moral principles should apply to our actions and obligations toward compatriots (fellow citizens) because we are in special relation to them. But different appeals to this principle yield different positions, from the broadly cosmopolitan to the social contractarian, nationalist, or communitarian perspectives. Arguments from partiality and connectedness are intuitively appealing, but they prove inadequate in a global health justice theory focused on human flourishing, which takes each individual person as the moral unit of analysis. In global health, the world is the moral community. Taking human flourishing as foundational for our moral obligations, we assess responsibility for the human flourishing of foreigners.

### 4.5.2 *Functions and Capabilities*

In PG, responsibility allocation begins with a universal ethical principle of health equity and a general obligation, through SHG, for global and state actors to realize health capabilities and thus to address global health inequalities and threats. PG then proposes a framework of analytical components needed to resolve current health inequalities and obviate future ones, contain

---

[84] For a helpful thought experiment see, generally, J. Rachels, "Active and Passive Euthanasia," *New England Journal of Medicine* 292 (1975): 78–80.

the threat of externalities, and address cross-border issues going forward. Responsibilities at the global, state, local, and individual levels are assessed and allocated. Key concepts for responsibility allocation are functions, capabilities, effectiveness, and efficiency; a forward orientation; and holding responsible state and non-state actors who (a) serve key functions and (b) have the capability to address past, present, and future global health problems. Responding to claims of global health justice against state and non-state actors may be more effective and efficient, even if such institutions and actors are not the only ones causally linked to global health injustices.

Principles for allocating responsibilities encompass voluntary commitments and functional requirements and needs. Individuals and groups at global, state, and local levels make voluntary commitments to share resources and relinquish some autonomy to address health problems through collective action; institutions and agents accept functional roles in addressing health issues. Global health injustices are the result of social decisions and institutions—global, state, and local—that place individuals in contexts without the conditions necessary for health. The failure to provide health care goods and services for safe motherhood, for example, does not result from the lack of such goods and services worldwide but the persistence of environments where people cannot readily and affordably access them.

Creating the conditions for health capability requires collective action reflecting positive interdependence and shared responsibilities, not tit-for-tat reciprocity or an anarchic state of nature. Thus, this framework begins with a general duty to promote central health capabilities globally and follows with specific duties to one's own fellow citizens, rooted in a commitment to health agency for all and a functional allocation of responsibilities. Because specific duties follow from general duties, a provincial consensus on these obligations accompanies a general global consensus; otherwise, parties responsible for the specific duty (for example, states) will not fully embrace and fulfill it. Voluntary commitment is important because specific duties cannot be imposed on individuals and groups who do not willingly enter into those relationships. Realizing provincial and global consensus can take us to a new global health equilibrium, one that recognizes the compatibility, rather than the discordance, of particular demands with the ideals of universality.[85]

Though the evolution and legitimacy of the post-modern state is certainly open to question, still it remains the functional unit of international relations. Our analysis of global health either accepts it or seeks its dissolution. This project takes the former path, placing an obligation on states to prevent

---

[85] P. Dumouchel and R. Gotoh, eds., *Social Bonds as Freedom: Revisiting the Dichotomy of the Universal and the Particular* (Oxford: Berghahn Books, 2015).

and reduce shortfall inequalities in their populations' central health capabilities. National health systems are structures for self-determination and collective action. Global actors also have responsibilities under this general duty, but these essential global health functions reach beyond what individual states can accomplish. Global health inequalities reflect broader social, political, and economic environments at both the global and state levels. Nor will market mechanisms alone reduce health inequalities, externalities, and cross-border problems. Government, policy, individual, and social commitments are essential.

Preventing and reducing global health disparities and containing externalities require organization and action around four key functions: (1) redistribution of resources within and among societies; (2) related legislation and policy (progressive taxation, equitable and efficient risk pooling, redistributive expenditure patterns, subsidies, and cash transfers); (3) public regulation and oversight; and (4) creation and distribution of public goods.

These key functions occur at both the global and state level, but the state has the primary responsibility. The sovereign state has particular legitimacy in taking on this role—perhaps the only current legitimacy—given its central function in raising and redistributing revenue and creating and implementing policies and laws; we have no global government. The state is the institution most capable of responding to claims of health justice. State policies and laws promoting central health capabilities gain legitimacy through the joint political project of democratic self-governance and the state's authority as the functional structure to which individuals cede some autonomy and resources to pursue common goals. The state is the principal channel through which individuals and groups realize their duties of justice and health. The state thus carries out this vital function and provides the best chance of effectuating our duties at the domestic level. The state may in turn discharge its duties to substate entities such as provinces, states, localities (villages and cities), and so on. Indeed, empirically, there are many examples of countries' use of both state and substate actors and institutions to discharge collective duties for population health. Moreover, regional federations such as the European Union have begun to experiment with the region as the primary locus of cooperation, and it is precisely such experimentation that has illuminated regional and global problems that require global moral standards for alleviation. Failing to meet the collective responsibility to create conditions for individuals to be healthy violates a moral duty; whether these omissions and commissions also violate a legal duty under international human rights law depends on the extent to which that body of law imposes legal culpability or liability in such cases.

Some argue that we owe more to compatriots than non-compatriots because compatriots share "in the creation of laws and policies that [they and other compatriots] are forced to obey."[86] Others focus on the value of encompassing groups and justify leaving decisions regarding self-government to such groups.[87] Still others see the state as a unit of cooperation, regulation, allocation, transfer of wealth, and group membership; a unit that must be self-sufficient and whose way of ordering society we must, as Rawls notes, tolerate and respect under liberalism. Regardless of the specific argument, justification lies in the political process, including public dialogue and the give-and-take among political parties and interest groups. PG likewise accepts that societies need to agree upon health equity ideals if public action is to follow. Policy measures will require ethical commitments evolving from the inculcation of fundamental health equity norms, values, and social roles.

Thus, while from a moral universalist perspective individuals' fundamental moral claims and duties might bind a global government to guarantee their fulfillment, PG does not take this tack. Rather, it allocates duties and responsibilities for universal health claims to the state and other domestic and global actors and institutions, who are obligated to address health needs, functionings, and agency through global and domestic cooperation. While individuals and voluntary associations such as nongovernmental organizations (NGOs) and civil society have roles and responsibilities in this cooperative venture, such informal operations are insufficient for health entitlement guarantees. In this regard, PG differs from utilitarian cosmopolitanism, which focuses primarily on every individual's duties toward all other individuals on the planet and de-emphasizes institutional responsibility. Such utilitarian cosmopolitanism reflects a narrow moral psychology and a simplistic understanding of the good. This view puts an overwhelming and impossible-to-implement responsibility for securing individual entitlements primarily on all individuals with the ability to help, leaving them with little or no prerogative to do anything of private value for themselves or their loved ones. Moreover, leaving the securing of universal health claims up to what amounts to the voluntary aid of others, either individually or through groups, opens the system to unfairness and favoritism and makes individuals in need dependent upon the discretionary preferences of others.

### 4.5.3 Ethical Commitments, Public Norms

Without ethical commitments, organizing socially and redistributing resources is not possible; these efforts are to be voluntary and rest on moral

[86] R. W. Miller, "Moral Closeness and World Community," in *The Ethics of Assistance: Morality and the Distant Needy*, ed. D. K. Chatterjee (Cambridge: Cambridge University Press, 2004), 105.

[87] A. Margalit and J. Raz, "National Self-Determination," *The Journal of Philosophy* 87, no. 9 (1990): 439–61.

grounds. To achieve health equity, better-off individuals sacrifice some of their resources and autonomy to help others whose need is greater, although no one should have to sacrifice her own central health capabilities for the sake of others. The inculcation of this norm and others through intentional education programs is an essential task in the quest for global health equity. The public at large, elected representatives, and other government officials accept and embrace the moral claim of health equity for all. Once individuals internalize these norms, they freely accept them and create obligations to obey them. Other-regarding or prosocial altruistic behavior is motivated by considering and promoting the interests of others as well as advancing one's own interest. It contrasts with egoistical or narrow self-interested behavior motivated by a return favor, benefit or reward, reciprocity, or reputational advantage. Prosocial behavior arises from internalized public moral norms. Individuals who willingly cede some prerogatives through collective action can work toward the goals inherent in their ethical commitments. Motivational pluralism is acceptable under a PG view, however, the objective health interests of others and oneself should combine in forming the primary motive. The same reasoning applies to states as to individuals and groups. For example, tit for tat or exchanging favors in global health may help one state—the United States, for example—realize its own interests in global health diplomacy (for example, through global AIDS programs),[88] but such efforts may undermine the legitimacy and functioning of international organizations (and be deceptively portrayed as civic-minded). Social norms and conventions serve as coordination mechanisms for human actions,[89] and global and domestic health is no exception. Social norms can also impact individuals' preferences, a more robust way of understanding human behavior in social contexts.[90]

PG allocates respective roles and responsibilities to individuals and groups based on functions and needs, and levels moral criticism at those who fail to live up to these objectives. PG treads a line in the global justice debate between agent-centered prerogatives and extreme act-consequentialism. PG preserves agent-centered prerogatives, recognizing that extreme act-consequentialism as applied to fairly benign and normal personal activities (such as going to a movie with one's family rather than donating the ticket money) is overly demanding and likely not necessary to effectuate global health equity if good governance obtains. PG does espouse act-consequentialism in the

---

[88] A. Ingram, "HIV/AIDS, Security and the Geopolitics of US–Nigerian Relations," *Review of International Political Economy* 14, no. 3 (2007): 510–34.

[89] C. Bicchieri, *The Grammar of Society: The Nature and Dynamics of Social Norms* (Cambridge: Cambridge University Press, 2006).

[90] G. A. Akerlof and R. E. Kranton, *Identity Economics: How Our Identities Shape Our Work, Wages, and Well-Being* (Princeton, NJ: Princeton University Press, 2010).

sense that it supports individuals taking actions that help generate the best consequences. However, what those actions are is open to debate in the global justice literature. On one end of the spectrum, strict act-consequentialists such as Peter Singer argue that failing to act in ways that produce the best consequences to combat poverty is morally wrong.[91] For example, failing to donate money to the point where the donor's condition equals the recipient's violates one's moral duty. Singer's is an admirable moral stance, but it might not produce the most effective outcomes. Under PG, individuals and groups act with the best consequences as the moral target, but achieving global health equity requires an overall plan, greater coordination, and allocation of roles and responsibilities for actions and institutions. Contributing money to charities is helpful, but in and of itself is not sufficient for global health equity.

PG thus preserves agent-centered prerogatives, but applies act-consequentialism in that all agents should take actions to achieve global health equity. Promoting and protecting one's own health and being mindful of others' should be complementary goals. While certain areas of life should be free from moral interventions, health is not one of them. The stakes are too high to ignore act-consequentialist duties. But unlike act-consequentialism, PG accepts that an action can be right even if it does not maximize the good for the largest number of people. The morally salient qualities of an action's consequences are individuals' capabilities, functionings, and agency. Nor does PG endorse act-consequentialism's aggregative method—seeking the greatest good (for example, utility) for the greatest number—in assessing states of affairs. Rather, PG assesses the moral value of a state of affairs by comparing the actual state with the highest possible state through shortfall equality calculations. Ethical commitments in PG are therefore commitments to achieve states of affairs that prevent and reduce shortfall inequalities in central health capabilities. Given those ethical commitments, individuals, states, and global entities provide reasonable help to the person whose human flourishing and health fall below the feasible threshold. PG's commitments tie the assessment of individuals', groups', and institutions' actions to the consequences they produce in functioning and agency as opposed to procedures or rules alone. Leaving open the evaluation of counterfactual states of affairs—what could have occurred with an alternative option—holds institutions and actors to a more dynamic and comparative standard than the status quo, which accepts a set of actors and institutions as legitimate because a social contract created it.

PG has some affinities with rule-consequentialism in that one of the theory's goals is to construct principles of action, rules, and institutions that lead to

---

[91] P. Singer, *The Life You Can Save* (New York: Random House, 2009).

the best consequences. The PG framework goes further, stipulating the set of principles and rules that have the best chance of producing optimal consequences.

### 4.5.4 *Institutions and Actors: Global and State Obligations*

Today's global and national institutions and programs make up an often dysfunctional system that fails to achieve needed health results. As we have seen, profound inequalities obtain both within and among countries. From a consequentialist perspective, the current system has resulted in less good— less health equity—than the counterfactual alternative (PG). PG's principles for allocating responsibilities and duties are forward-looking. Sustainability is key: it seeks a new global health equilibrium which not only remedies current health inequities, externalities, and cross-border issues but also structures institutions, actors, systems, and commitments to address health threats in the years ahead. Health capability is the core principle, but second-stage principles of voluntary commitments and functional requirements and needs are essential for allocating responsibilities among global health's innumerable institutions and actors. The primary duty falls to states. The limits of state obligations then reveal extra-national or international obligations. These limits also reveal needs for institutions to bring together state and international players, NGOs, communities, businesses, foundations, families, and individuals to correct and prevent global health injustice. And individuals themselves, through personal and collective health agency, assume their own obligations for preventing and managing disease, maintaining and improving health.

#### 4.5.4.1 RESPONSIBILITY ALONG A MULTILEVEL GOVERNANCE CONTINUUM

Thus, PG, which takes the entitlement bearer's perspective first and then the duty bearer's, determines the health capabilities to which individuals are entitled and then allocates duties along a continuum from the global to the domestic spheres. Domestic commitments, through national and subnational governments, align with global, universal commitments. In this multilevel governance system, functions, needs, and voluntary commitments define roles and responsibilities for all actors. A multilevel system is demonstrably the best approach for achieving universal global health objectives; this is because various institutions and actors perform core functions, functions required to protect and promote humans' health capabilities, particularly central health capabilities, and meet health functioning needs and health agency needs. No one (or set of) institution(s) or actor(s) on its own is able to perform these core functions and meet these fundamental needs. As such, PG/SHG parcels out respective roles and responsibilities at the global, state, local, and individual levels based on functional requirements and needs, identifying actors and institutions, their obligations, and how they are held accountable. One example is the successful polio eradication effort in Latin America and the Caribbean. Those campaigns involved actors all along the continuum: international entities such as WHO, United Nations International Children's Emergency Fund, and Rotary International; regional organizations such as the Inter-American Development Bank and Pan American Health Organization; foreign national agencies such as United States Agency for International Development, Centers for Disease Control and Prevention (CDC), and the Canadian Public Health Association; and state structures such as ministries of health and other sectoral ministries.

All participants in this health cooperation give to and receive from the system. In health cooperation, individuals and groups accept and adhere to individual- and group-level rules and standards to accomplish effective and efficient health production. Health is the product of institutions and actors performing core functions and responsibly fulfilling key roles. This condition both accords with and differs from the reciprocity-oriented motivation of a system of cooperation based on mutual advantage. "[W]hen a number of persons engage in a mutually advantageous cooperative venture according to rules, and thus restrict their liberty in ways necessary to yield advantages for all, those who have submitted to these restrictions have a right to a similar acquiescence on the part of those who have benefited from their submission," Rawls writes, "We are not to gain from the cooperative efforts of others without doing our fair share."[92]

The difference lies in PG/SHG's organizational structure, which employs systems thinking and envisions joint production through shared roles and responsibilities shaped by core functions and meeting fundamental needs. States in a mutual-advantage approach do not always act as a system of cooperation; in some cases, their decisions derive from the aggregation of preferences or the strongest preferences (which can be manipulated by wealth). Health cooperation through the state requires an underlying social cooperation theory, rather than simply an assumption that cooperation will naturally happen in a liberal or democratic society.

The state has a key role too in building an overarching framework within which private actors, including individuals, accept and fulfill their responsibilities. In the Latin American polio eradication efforts, health ministries chaired national interagency committees, which coordinated government sectors and other national and international organizations to prepare and

---

[92] J. Rawls, *A Theory of Justice* (Cambridge, MA: Harvard University Press, 1971), 112.

approve national plans and budgets, organize resources and technical inputs, and raise funds.[93] The social organization benefits the health capabilities of all, especially the most vulnerable, rather than just the wealthy, formally employed, or well connected; such favoritism would be unjust. Domestic societies cooperate to create the common good, and in this cooperation individuals and groups shoulder their fair share of the burden. These duties include avoiding irresponsible choices that undermine the distribution of benefits to others (for example, free-riding, or overuse of resources, which depletes resources available to others) or directly or indirectly harm or fail to protect or promote others' health capabilities.

The state's primary role notwithstanding, global and regional actors also have key, though secondary, obligations in the multilevel system. This secondary position might seem incongruous in our globalized world, where diseases cross borders and international issues overtake us. But the local nature of health service provision, disease prevention, and health promotion programs means that states and subnational entities best fulfill health system functions. National government efforts have achieved notable health successes, such as Thailand's "100 percent condom program" for HIV prevention, Sri Lanka's maternal mortality reduction, and Chile's Hib immunization program.[94] But while states are the primary locus for health cooperation, global cooperation is still necessary to produce valuable collective and public goods, such as disease surveillance and global standards. Individuals, groups, and states do their share of the work to create such goods, which then become available to everyone.

### 4.5.4.2 GLOBAL OBLIGATIONS

Global players should promote health, focusing on all determinants of health. Global health functions are actions to promote global public health goods— measures that benefit all countries but lie beyond the reach of national governments and independent groups. They include setting norms and standards; providing professional management; transferring financial resources; building technical and scientific research capacity, surveillance, and reporting; and leadership. These functions depend on global health actors playing varying roles, fulfilling their duties to remedy inequities in health, and deploying their affluence, power, and social, economic, and political opportunities to this end. Though global actors are secondary to states in the health realm, they express the international community's will to rectify global market failures,

---

[93] R. W. Sutter and C. Maher, "Mass Vaccination Campaigns for Polio Eradication: An Essential Strategy for Success," *Current Topics in Microbiology and Immunology* 304 (2006): 195–220.

[94] R. Levine and What Works Working Group, *Millions Saved: Proven Successes in Global Health* (Washington, DC: Center for Global Development, 2004).

create public goods, and address equity concerns. While no global institutions have the authority and power of global government, the global health architecture can be developed and reformed to manage global health better and expand justice.

Global actors and institutions should foster equitable growth in developing countries, global financial stability, global public goods, country participation in global fora, debt relief and development assistance, fair trade and open markets for developed countries, and technical assistance for developing countries.

Duties in five health-related functional categories, in particular, fall to global health institutions: (1) generating and sharing knowledge; (2) empowering developing-country players in national and global fora; (3) facilitating health system development; (4) reducing overlap and redundancies; and (5) creating global public goods. In the knowledge and information category, global institutions can help spur new technologies; transfer, adapt, and apply existing knowledge; set standards; and support expanded information and research capacity. To empower developing-country actors, global health institutions can help reform state and local institutions; encourage political engagement; support public administration; and help states involve stakeholders in decision-making. In health system development, global institutions can provide technical assistance in equitable, efficient health financing; professional medical and public health training; facilities management; development of regulatory agencies; and standardized diagnostic categories. Global health organizations can mobilize resources for health systems development and specific disease areas, and offer global advocacy. Global public health goods include global health advocacy, bioethical and human rights agreements, disease and risk surveillance and knowledge, investment in critical health problems, and promoting norms and standards.

The UN established WHO specifically to advance global health. Its Constitution defines its work, identifying three core functional categories: (1) setting norms, including international conventions and agreements, regulations, and non-binding standards and recommendations; (2) direction and coordination, including its health-for-all, poverty, and health programs; the fight against disease; and access to essential medicines; and (3) research and technical cooperation.[95] The promotion of international ethics and human rights through international legal instruments and WHO's leadership in measures like the Framework Convention on Tobacco Control and the International Health Regulations are examples of key WHO functions. WHO amply illustrates some core responsibilities of global health agents.

---

[95] G. L. Burci and C. H. Vignes, *World Health Organization* (The Hague: Kluwer Law International, 2004).

### 4.5.4.3 RESPONSIBILITIES OF THE STATE

Meeting health needs and health agency needs requires legitimate and functioning local and national health systems. The sovereign state has central roles in raising and redistributing revenue and enacting and implementing policy—functions no existing global structures perform. These roles position the state uniquely to meet health needs and health agency needs. Individuals cede some resources and autonomy to the state to pursue common goals. The normative significance of the state is related to its power and authority to manage society, correct health injustices, and bring about greater health justice. No international institution has this kind of authority or enforcement power. To be sure, the contemporary distribution of state sovereignty in international relations can be contested. Nor is the existing set of state boundaries either undisputed or immutable. Multiple examples today—the Kurds and Catalonians, for example—demonstrate the yearnings of peoples for their own countries. But these yearnings themselves underscore the state's moral and political significance in contemporary international relations. This shared political unit—the state—is important for moral, functional, and empirical reasons.

States are primarily responsible for addressing health inequalities and externalities. They have the chief obligation for fostering health capabilities, because they are best positioned to provide systems and services—health care and public health—and to shape the social determinants of health, those economic, political, and social factors without which health capability is not possible. These determinants include clean air and water, adequate sanitation, employment, and safe, functioning communities. National health systems finance and ensure the quality of health-related goods and services. They ensure the availability of these goods and services when health needs and health agency needs arise. When confronted with serious symptoms or conditions (prenatal complications, shortness of breath, loss of consciousness, pain, bleeding, or fever, for example), every individual is to be able to obtain care. Regulation and stewardship of the health system are critical and include public health surveillance systems, similar to the US CDC, which feed into WHO's global surveillance system. In all these ways states foster health agency and thus reduce the shortfall between potential and actual health. And in these ways, more broadly, states bring about the health equity that justice demands.

Providing medically necessary and medically appropriate health care and public health services for all is a matter of justice. Neither democracy nor advanced development guarantees health justice; the United States, with all its wealth, has not achieved it. The equity at the heart of PG comes about through strong domestic systems effectively addressing health needs. These countries are then in a position to share information, expertise, and resources with countries where inequalities persist.

When national governments fail to meet health needs, justice summons the global community to work for health equity even while respecting countries' self-determination. Self-determination is much more than freedom from intervention by foreign powers. A self-determining country inspires ownership and engagement among its citizens, who willingly work for its progress and development, for justice and equality.

Rawls, in the interest of tolerance, declined to examine tyrannical and dictatorial societies, but the PG approach sets higher standards. It aspires to self-actualized societies in which governments and peoples commit fully to ensuring central health capabilities for all. The global community provides assistance and oversight when incompetent states fail to deliver effective public health and health care systems. PG does not encourage the use of force, coercion, or sanctions, because such measures often cause more harm than good, especially among the populations suffering most. The Iraq sanctions are a case in point. But the power of social movements and their influence in changing norms and governance through the value formation process is an important area for further study. Movements for racial justice, women's rights, and environmental protection, among many others, prove that values and norms can change in dramatic ways, with far-reaching effects.

## 4.6 Finding Consensus among Plurality: Incompletely Theorized Agreements

In a multifarious global community, a broad diversity of actors, values, and viewpoints makes achieving consensus on health morality challenging. But PG employs ITAs to go beyond this plurality. There is considerable diversity in religious and moral conceptions across the world and within any given society. Agreement on fundamental principles of health morality is feasible through an incompletely theorized—an uncoerced—agreement. As we have seen, humankind has evinced a consistent commitment to health provision across time and cultures. A consensus can emerge within the health domain where conditions are ripe for convergence on fundamental moral norms, drawing on intuitively appealing ideals and empirically grounded entitlements. Where universal agreement—assent by every person on the planet—is not possible, ITAs can help find consensus even among differing conceptions of the right and the good. The ITA method for social choice can produce agreement on the substance of global health equity and on global and domestic policies to bring it to pass. It can bring people together on a specific issue—maintaining central health capabilities like mobility, for example, or providing UHC—even absent agreement on a larger philosophical theory of equality, or on a health plan's concrete details.

Different societies can themselves use ITAs to hone their own more precise definitions of central health capabilities—what avoiding premature death and preventable morbidity looks like on the ground in given countries. But PG envisions a global consensus on the fundamental conceptions. This consensus permits identifying global health equity indicators and then applying shortfall equality to measure health equity, our progress toward it, and our failures in achieving it.

The failure to reach a provincial-global consensus on health morality continues to challenge the global health community. Perhaps the pursuit of subjective self-interest—an unwillingness to participate in internal, bilateral, or multilateral health actions, or participation with ulterior motives—trumps collective health interests. Another explanation, from behavioral ethics, suggests that failures in moral reasoning result from "[i]nconsistency, factual mistakes, selfishness, manipulation, dogma, laziness, pride and an unwillingness to admit that one is wrong, complacency, and wishful thinking."[96] Human and public reasoning are fallible, and the willingness to act on moral principles is unreliable. Failures, then, can reflect errors in moral judgment rather than profound moral disagreements. Thus, they do not necessarily reveal deep irreconcilable disagreement on health morality, but rather a failure to fully converge on basic norms and ethical prescriptions for global and domestic health.[97]

The solutions to such behavioral ethics problems at the individual and domestic level include: full information, free choice, transparency, equality, and public debates that expose biases and narrow, selfish interests. As one scholar notes, there exist "values that can be justified to all persons *when those persons' reasoning is not distorted by self-interest, factual mistakes, complacency, and so on.*"[98] Human beings are capable of making reliable moral judgments when they respect and value the interests of all equally through a universal moral standpoint—a transpositional point of view. Such a view rests on general principles undistorted by self-interest; it does not privilege powerful groups. Empathetic understanding yields fairer moral judgments. One study, for example, examined a group deliberative setting in which participants discussed people who are uninsured or vulnerable to losing insurance. Factual information revealed how the lack of insurance affected not just the uninsured, but insured people, businesses, and communities. As a result of the discussion, participants were more willing to contribute some of their health care dollars to cover the uninsured, especially children.[99] Another approach is

---

[96] Caney, *Justice Beyond Borders*, 48.

[97] Ibid. Some argue that moral disagreement supports the falsity of moral universalism. Caney offers arguments against this position on pp. 45–50.

[98] Ibid., 49.

[99] S. D. Goold, S. A. Green, A. K. Biddle, E. Benavides, and M. Danis, "Will Insured Citizens Give Up Benefit Coverage to Include the Uninsured?" *Journal of General Internal Medicine* 19, no. 8 (2004): 868–74.

to employ a community engagement and education methodology and continually revise it to protect moral arguments from distortion and bias, even in the context of public debate.

Information about people's health capabilities fosters concern among both decision-makers and the public about individuals' real lives; it also enhances their individual and collective health agency. This more inclusive discourse at the global and domestic levels, both formal and informal, better enables social and political processes to respond to individuals' needs. Open collection and distribution of such information is important for global and domestic public reasoning and is the responsibility of both domestic and global institutions.

In PG, the adoption of a transpositional point of view—a universal moral standpoint—and an ITA on a core health conception are important for justifying general principles of health morality.

## 4.7 Global Health Citizenship

PG aspires to global health citizenship, in which all people know that wherever they are and wherever they travel they will find what they need to protect their health and prevent disease and injury. Global health citizenship does not mean political status[100] under a global political authority or legal status under a global legal authority. Global health citizenship means global standards of right conduct—the promotion of central health capabilities—toward all people with respect to health. Global health citizenship is not national health citizenship, with its associated entitlements. The latter entails legal rights and duties through membership in a state. France, for example, grants its citizens rights and expects them to fulfill certain duties, such as paying taxes. Clearly states are to be able to meet the health needs of their own citizens as well as those of persons who may reside or travel to that state on a temporary basis. Global health citizenship does not entail this reciprocity because there is no global government to which to belong. Nonetheless, moral rights and duties and the expectation of reciprocity with other individuals, groups, and states is an important aspect of global health citizenship. While this goal is not currently within reach, and is not resourced with a plan of global redistribution, it is an important aspiration for this global health theory.

---

[100] J. Winter, *Dreams of Peace and Freedom: Utopian Moments in the Twentieth Century* (New Haven, CT: Yale University Press, 2008).

## 4.8 Provincial Globalism versus Other Frameworks

PG presents some sharp contrasts with other theoretical frameworks. The PG view occupies the middle ground between nationalism and cosmopolitanism. In general, the contractarian or utilitarian views see contracts to achieve mutual advantage—states of affairs that maximize the aggregation of individual welfare—as approaches to global justice. However, PG does not address global justice in terms of narrow self-interest, national interest, collective security, or humanitarian assistance because these have all proved to be insufficient foundations for health justice. Rather, it endorses the more robust concept of human flourishing and the commitment to creating a world where all people have the ability to be healthy. Unlike general cosmopolitan theory, PG does not attenuate duties and obligations attached to the state, local communities, and fellow citizens. In addition to the distinctions already discussed, we can compare and contrast PG with other views on several important analytical components.

### 4.8.1 *Motivation*

PG embodies forward-looking aims: to create conditions to prevent and manage epidemics and other threats, to rectify arbitrary disparities in health and prevent future ones, and to pursue human flourishing, health capabilities, and health equity.

By contrast, cosmopolitanism, though it aims for global equity, does not specify what equity entails, and allows for utilitarian and rights-based interpretations. Communitarianism does not specify motivation beyond whatever a given community values and chooses to pursue; nor does nationalism, for which national identity is central to moral motivation and defines objects of moral concern. In the realist or *Homo economicus* view, motivation is narrow self- or national interest; for utilitarians, it is to maximize aggregate welfare. And Rawls' law of peoples framework seeks to achieve a peaceful international order of liberal and decent peoples, which constrains state aggression, observes human rights, and channels aid to burdened countries. None of these frameworks can adequately pursue the goals and values PG deems crucial.

### 4.8.2 *Objectivity versus Subjectivity*

PG advances a positionally objective or transpositional interest in health. Health is both intrinsically valued for its own sake and manifestly necessary for human flourishing and other central human interests like education.

Cosmopolitanism's emphasis on universality and generality implies values applicable to all individuals everywhere. Under the cosmopolitan umbrella, the international human rights perspective sees many human rights as objective, but conceptions of human rights can vary in breadth. For communitarians and nationalists, human rights can be either objective or subjective, according to the community's or the nation's values. In realism, actors pursue subjective self-interest, which is self-defined, though generally seen as power or economic gain. Utilitarians seek welfare and utility, but do not define them objectively. For Rawls, goals are objective: peace, and human rights including subsistence, personal property, security, equality before the law, protection against genocide, some freedom of conscience, freedom from enslavement, and freedom to emigrate. But aside from minimal subsistence, these are primarily civil and political rights, not economic or social rights.

### 4.8.3 *Methodology*

In PG, justice entails both substantive ends and procedural means. PG delineates duties and relationships with a view to end results—health capabilities and health equity—in contrast to approaches that define justice only procedurally. The principles of justice focus on the relevant actors and duties. PG is justified and grounded in both deductive and inductive reasoning. Central health capabilities, as an essential human interest, are what any person needs and rationally desires. Central health capabilities are also what societies over time and across cultures accept and agree to secure for their populations. PG thus has a greater claim to validity and reliability as a normative framework than approaches that fail to ground their claims in an objective foundation. PG claims about what human flourishing requires—central health capabilities—are grounded both in scientific facts and in people's interests, rational desires, and abilities. This normative theory creates and develops universal principles to judge and guide right actions in particular situations. Individual and collective health agency and practical wisdom (knowing how to obtain positive health outcomes effectively and efficiently) aid this effort.

Methodologically, as a universalist global health justice theory, PG does not derive solely from a Rawlsian thought experiment under a veil of ignorance, from a reflective equilibrium that achieves coherence among conflicting beliefs by deliberative reasoning, from a social contract for mutual advantage, from arguments in discourse ethics,[101] or from deontological principles of equal moral status and respect, although the latter are important. Rather,

---

[101] J. Habermas, "Discourse Ethics: Notes on a Program of Philosophical Justification," in J. Habermas, *Moral Consciousness and Communicative Action*, trans. C. Lenhardt and S. W. Nicholsen (Cambridge: Polity Press, 1990).

PG's theory of the good employs transpositionality, validity, and reliability as methodological resources. PG seeks to determine objectively justifiable normative principles.

Cosmopolitans, on the other hand, pursue no specific substantive end; principles of justice derive from the equal moral status of individuals and obligations binding on all. Cosmopolitans do recognize the equal moral status of marginalized, weak, and vulnerable people and rule out mere mutually advantageous cooperation among powerful or resourced parties. International human rights approaches define justice by human rights and equality in enjoying those rights; principles of justice derive from the equal moral status of individuals and direct attention to the subjects of human rights violations. But states have primary responsibility, and the substantive content of rights and duties is inadequately specified.

In communitarianism and nationalism, community or national values define justice, and duties and rights derive not from end goals but from membership in the community or nation. For realists, justice is simply not a concern. Utilitarians define justice in terms of maximized welfare or utility, but do not specify what these elements entail. Nor do they specify procedures, duties, or actors; how utility is maximized is unimportant. And Rawls sees international justice as fairness: liberal and decent societies determine principles of justice at an international original position. Rawls is concerned with procedural fairness, not substantive equity, and offers no objective theory of the good. Mutual advantage, which self-interested parties would want to ensure for themselves when deciding under a veil of ignorance, motivates cooperation, not substantive ends.

A sharp contrast with contractarian approaches is illustrative. Different types of contract theory apply for the domestic and global realms. There are individual-centered and peoples-centered approaches. Rawls puts forth procedures for the domestic and international realm; in the latter, for example, he outlines a peoples-centered approach whereby the contracting parties are liberal and decent peoples. Principles of international justice under this approach are principles to which liberal and decent peoples agree. In Rawls' idea, other kinds of peoples are not party to the contract.[102] Rawls' assumption that the contract would include elements of human rights is tautological given that the liberal and decent peoples privy to the contract would accept human rights and those peoples who do not accept human rights are excluded

---

[102] For critiques of Rawls' methods, see: A. Buchanan, "Rawls's Law of Peoples: Rules for a Vanished Westphalian World," *Ethics* 110, no. 4 (2000): 697–721; S. Caney, "Survey Article: Cosmopolitanism and the Law of Peoples," *Journal of Political Philosophy* 10, no. 1 (2002): 95–123; A. Kuper, "Rawlsian Global Justice: Beyond the Law of Peoples to a Cosmopolitan Law of Persons," *Political Theory* 28, no. 5 (2000): 640–74; K. C. Tan, *Toleration, Diversity, and Global Justice* (University Park, PA: Pennsylvania State University Press, 2000).

from the contract.[103] Rawls' theory has been criticized for, among other things, not considering the "significant political and economic interdependencies that exist"[104] among nations.

David Gauthier and other contractarian scholars argue that principles are moral if rational agents accept them.[105] James Nickel asserts prudential and moral reasons for human rights and the conversion of "prudential choice into rational choice within the moral point of view."[106] Jürgen Habermas argues for discourse ethics: methodologically, a set of principles or values is justified if it represents agreement reached through discourse under ideal speech situations.[107]

Despite the plausibility of all of these methodologies, such approaches ultimately need a theory of the good to provide criteria for judging states of affairs that we sense to be unjust; this need for substantive assessment is where theories of well-being and quality of life provide relevant information. Narrow or strict consequentialist reasoning is inadequate, however, in that it does not take into account the means by which outcomes or consequences occur, which also have moral meaning.

In PG's view of justice, what we owe others stems from our common humanity and from the centrality of health capability as a fundamental human interest. It is a transpositional view, based on reasoning and historical, comparative, and empirical evidence of health's moral salience as a core human interest. This evidence (see 4.1.3) suggests common, culturally invariant health needs that societies eventually acknowledge and seek to meet among their citizens. PG evaluates and understands justice claims through

---

[103] C. R. Beitz, "Rawls's Law of Peoples," *Ethics* 110, no. 4 (2000): 669–96; S. Caney, "Cosmopolitan Justice and Equalizing Opportunities," *Metaphilosophy* 32, no. 1/2 (2001): 113–34.

[104] T. W. Pogge, "An Egalitarian Law of Peoples," *Philosophy & Public Affairs* 23, no. 3 (1994): 196.

[105] D. Gauthier, *Morals by Agreement* (Oxford: Oxford University Press, 1986).

[106] J. W. Nickel, *Making Sense of Human Rights: Philosophical Reflections on the Universal Declaration of Human Rights* (Berkeley, CA: University of California Press, 1987), 91. For useful critiques of the justice-as-mutual advantage methodology, especially issues of inequality in power and self-interest, see B. Barry, *Theories of Justice: A Treatise on Social Justice*, vol. 1 (Berkeley, CA: University of California Press, 1989).

[107] Habermas, "Discourse Ethics." Scholars advancing deontological arguments include Nagel, who argues that individuals have equal moral status, which is non-aggregative and cannot be "redistributed or increased in quantity" (T. Nagel, "Personal Rights and Public Space," *Philosophy & Public Affairs* 24, no. 2 (1995): 85), corresponding with the inviolability of persons emphasized also in R. Nozick, *Anarchy, State, and Utopia* (New York: Basic Books, 1974). Critics of this view note that equal moral status does not constitute rights of any kind; it is too indeterminate in that it does not tell us what morally relevant characteristics of individuals merit respect. It doesn't consider outcomes or consequences. Deontologists would counter that equal respect grounds rights, including human rights, through free choice or autonomy. This assertion does not answer the question, however, of which freedoms to secure, or what personal characteristics require respect. Respect for persons or equal moral status, which is at the center of deontological theory, is not enough for a theory of justice, which needs an account of the morally relevant characteristics of individuals that require protecting and promoting. Caney, *Justice Beyond Borders*; J. Griffin, *Well-Being: Its Meaning, Measurement, and Moral Purpose* (Oxford: Oxford University Press, 1986).

social, historical, and cultural considerations, based in empirical research. Traditional theories of political philosophy, particularly political liberalism and variations of social contract theory, are not empirically based. PG's theory of justice does not rely on hypothetical methods and mock classifications. PG produces and justifies moral principles for social and global justice assessments, principles that reasonable human beings will accept and have accepted through real agreements, which may or may not be incompletely theorized. Rather than a hypothetical device, such as an original position in which parties are behind a veil of ignorance, in PG reasonable human beings will agree and have agreed to such principles of justice because they have intrinsic moral value to them based on moral and scientific facts.

A tension exists between objective interests—in health, for example—and subjective self-interest or preferences. John Stuart Mill and numerous libertarians and neoclassical economists agree that people are best placed to determine their own interests, that they are more motivated to protect their own interests than others are, and that individuals should be responsible for their own interests.[108] Some behavioral economists, with empirical evidence to support their claims, disagree, arguing that people do not always know their interests or do not always have the ability to pursue them, due to heuristic errors, preference reversals, a lack of self-control, and so on. Therefore paternalism, restraints on individual liberty for one's own good, is acceptable in some situations because it helps individuals make choices that are in their best interests.[109]

The PG methodology also recognizes objections to universality that question objectivity,[110] a transcommunal ground or standpoint, independent vindication, and individuals' independence from context (even under a veil of ignorance) or tradition.[111] By comparison to the Rawlsian reflective equilibrium or Habermasian discourse ethics projects, this approach identifies as universally necessary certain health goods, needs, and capabilities derived from human knowledge, science, research, and experience (including moral experience). The PG approach is thus not a metaphysical notion; rather it works from human experience and knowledge. It seeks to measure the value of health for and in our individual and social and political experience. It connects political philosophy and the natural and social sciences.

Critics have challenged political philosophy for lacking a canon of methodologies for determining the correct view or assessing errors in views

---

[108] J. S. Mill, *On Liberty* (Mineola, NY: Dover, 2002).

[109] R. H. Thaler and C. R. Sunstein, "Libertarian Paternalism," *American Economic Review* 93, no. 2 (2003): 175–9.

[110] R. Rorty, *Objectivity, Relativism, and Truth: Philosophical Papers* (Cambridge: Cambridge University Press, 1991).

[111] A. MacIntyre, *Whose Justice? Which Rationality?* (Notre Dame, IN: University of Notre Dame Press, 1988).

(reflective equilibrium and rational reconstruction[112] are exceptions). In PG's theory of the good, validity and reliability serve as criteria for justification and for assessing health values and principles. Validity connotes the extent to which the method—for example, the method to determine the universality of health—produces broadly applicable results; reliability connotes the extent to which the method turns up the same or similar results time after time. PG advances that public and moral reasoning normatively justifies health's value, and empirical reasoning (empirical evidence from history, cross-cultural comparisons, basic, natural, and social sciences) demonstrates health's universal value and importance. The combined methodology strives for validity and reliability, as compared to other methods—hypothetical agreement approaches, for example.

We observe in the real world how individuals and societies value health and how health is important to other types of functioning. Do these observations align with our theory of health assets' value? This methodology seeks to capture this alignment.

### 4.8.4 *Unit of Analysis/Ontology*

PG views the individual as the central moral unit of justice; individuals' health functioning and health agency have moral significance. The state is an instrumental actor in achieving individual health capabilities, channeling individual agency and resources toward common health goals. The state is also a unit of analysis with particular duties and agency in the form of national self-determination. In this multilevel system, international actors are secondary to the state.

Likewise, both the cosmopolitan and the international human rights frameworks see the individual as the central moral unit of justice. But in communitarianism, the community is the central moral unit. Community membership creates special obligations among community members, and individual members of a community have duties to each other. The rights and duties of communities are paramount. Nationalists take the same approach, making the nation the central moral unit and national citizenship the basis of special obligations. National self-determination is justifiable and defensible, but states also respect the self-determination and sovereignty of other states. In realism, the individual as *Homo economicus* is the central moral unit, though states become units of analysis in the context of international relations. For utilitarians, the unit of analysis ranges from individuals to larger entities. Finally, Rawls sees societies or peoples as the relevant units. In his framework,

---

[112] J. Habermas, *Legitimation Crisis*, trans. T. McCarthy (Boston, MA: Beacon, 1975); J. Habermas, *Communication and the Evolution of Society*, trans. T. McCarthy (Boston, MA: Beacon, 1979).

societies respect self-determination and do not intervene in other societies except in cases of gross human rights violations and to provide assistance to burdened societies.

In PG, moral principles apply to all. Onora O'Neill points out that "[t]he most elementary thought of universalists is formal: there are certain ethical principles or standards which hold for all."[113] Scope denotes *"who* falls within the domain of universal principles"—the applicable domain.[114] In understanding universalism, a useful distinction involves: (1) "universalist content," duties that apply to and are binding on all; and (2) "universal justifiability," an understanding of duties that "each person, simply by virtue of being rational, has good reason to accept."[115] Some gradualism appears on two fronts. In justification, on one end principles are justifiable to everyone; on the other, they are justifiable only to a chosen few. For agreement, the spectrum extends from agreement by every individual to agreement of a majority to agreement by some. Rawls, alternatively, does not apply egalitarian liberal principles globally and thus does not support an egalitarian liberal cosmopolitanism. Pogge's definition of cosmopolitanism includes three elements: (1) individualism, humans as the unit of concern; (2) universality, everyone included equally; and (3) generality, all persons worldwide must treat all other individuals worldwide as the unit of concern.[116]

In content, PG principles include procedures and substance. These principles are both universalist and cosmopolitan. They are universalist in content, in that values and principles apply to and bind all. They are universalist to a lesser extent in justifiability: the public reasons for accepting them are reasonable, people should accept them, and empirical evidence suggests people across the globe would and do accept them as public moral norms about health justice. For PG, the overlapping consensus should occur at all levels, from global, to state, to local, to the individual, but it need not require unanimity. The exact balance or tipping point for consensus (majority or supermajority) would need to be worked out.

Universality has been a sticking point in human rights, which some might argue are universal in content without being universal in justification. Although universalists might agree to human rights and agree that they can be claimed by all, not all people acknowledge them.

PG is cosmopolitan in that it both pertains to all human beings on the planet and applies in both the global and domestic spheres. However, the PG approach allows proportionality in responsibility, such that responsibilities to

---

[113] O. O'Neill, *Towards Justice and Virtue: A Constructive Account of Practical Reasoning* (Cambridge: Cambridge University Press, 1996), 11.

[114] Ibid., 4.

[115] C. Larmore, *The Morals of Modernity* (Cambridge: Cambridge University Press, 1996), 57.

[116] T. W. Pogge, "Cosmopolitanism and Sovereignty," *Ethics* 103, no. 1 (1992): 48–75.

foreigners may not always be the same as those to one's own family and fellow citizens. Building on PST, individuals can have a range of duties, general and specific, the latter of which reflect specific kinds of relationships with varying content and weight.

### 4.8.5 *Shared versus Individual Responsibility*

Responsibility is both individual and shared within PG. The combined efforts of individuals, localities, states, and the global community coproduce health interdependently. They accomplish this coproduction through personal health habits, medical care by health professionals, the public health system, clean environments, safe foods and medicines, health systems, surveillance, and the control of national and international disease outbreaks. Health production is a scheme of social cooperation, which creates benefits and compels action. Population and individual health is the result of cooperation of all, including the wealthy and the poor. The better off are obligated to contribute to health production for all others, including the worse off. Health production requires reciprocity and fair treatment for all, though health equity, not reciprocity per se (or enforceability or coercion), is the normative justification. Reciprocity itself is not the foundational idea for health justice; mutual benefit is but one of multiple motivations embedded in our plural subjecthood, and reciprocity is owed as a matter of mutual health needs, not as tit for tat or mutual advantage. PG employs reciprocity as a way of ensuring social cooperation and the distribution of social goods, norms, and circumstances to coproduce a healthy society.

Libertarian, utilitarian, and even desert-based arguments of justice are not appropriate for health since it is a scheme of social cooperation: individuals and groups within the scheme have the needed conditions and make responsible choices for the scheme to succeed.[117] In this way PG emphasizes that shared responsibility, both individual and social, is central to domestic and

---

[117] Luck egalitarianism views inequalities based on luck (circumstances for which a person does not have control or did not create) as unjust; justice therefore requires neutralizing, nullifying, or compensating for such bad or brute luck. In contrast, inequalities based on responsible choice or option luck, even if imprudent, are just. On questions of luck and justice see, generally, E. S. Anderson, "What is the Point of Equality?" *Ethics* 109, no. 2 (1999): 287–337; R. J. Arneson, "Luck Egalitarianism Interpreted and Defended," *Philosophical Topics* 32 (2004): 1–20; G. A. Cohen, "On the Currency of Egalitarian Justice," *Ethics* 99, no. 4 (1989): 906–44; R. Dworkin, "Equality, Luck and Hierarchy," *Philosophy & Public Affairs* 31, no. 2 (2003): 190–8. There is also the question of whether the causes of inequality both within and among states is the result of bad luck (for example, poor natural resources or geographical location), bad choices (for example, the institutional structures of each state), or both. There is the additional question of how the background global institutional structure is linked to inequalities within and between nations. While a backward-looking assessment of the justness of inequalities is interesting, PG focuses on societal obligations for creating the conditions for optimal choice based on shared responsibility.

global justice and requires creating the conditions for optimal health choices for all persons. In PG, the benefits that individuals receive in the coproduction of population and individual health depend upon and result from others' cooperation in the system; and those individuals, like all others, have an obligation not only to distribute benefits and burdens of the system fairly, but also to contribute and cooperate with others to create benefits and reduce burdens.

Cosmopolitanism, too, asserts individual and shared responsibility, in that individuals have responsibilities to provide humanitarian assistance (Singer) and/or refrain from upholding unjust institutions (Pogge). But practical efforts toward global equity would require involvement of states and global entities. The international human rights approach assigns responsibility to the state since individuals cannot provide most human rights; the state ensures most civil, political, social, and economic rights. In communitarianism, community members have responsibility, but only to other community members; and likewise in nationalism, citizens have responsibilities only to fellow citizens. Realists place responsibility on the state; there is no meaningful shared responsibility. Actors act unilaterally, and cooperation results from a convergence of individual interests. Utilitarians argue that individuals and larger entities are to maximize the overall good—the greatest good for the greatest number—but there might be no agreed-upon definition of happiness or coordination to pursue it, making responsibility allocation difficult. Rawls believes that societies are responsible for maintaining their own liberality and decency; together they share responsibility for containing aggressive states, helping burdened societies, and intervening in societies that violate human rights.

### 4.8.6 *Scope of Responsibility*

PG recognizes individuals as plural subjects who identify and belong to families, and to local, state, and global communities. It puts forth a general duty to foreigners and a specific duty to fellow citizens in the pursuit of health capability for all. The force of these duties varies according to the collective, becoming weaker as attachments attenuate.

Cosmopolitanism, by contrast, is universalist in scope, making no distinction between compatriots and foreigners; indeed, cosmopolitans can assign us a greater duty to help foreigners if we have contributed in direct or indirect ways to their suffering. In the international human rights view, all human beings are entitled to human rights; the perspective embraces both universality, in that principles apply equally to all persons, and generality, in that human beings are the ultimate concern for everyone. Communitarianism asserts a duty only toward members of one's own community; in this view,

137

there is no conception of global moral standards or global justice. Similarly, nationalism asserts a duty to one's fellow citizens; the nation might engage in multilateral and global efforts, but out of self-interest and choice, not moral obligation. Realism offers no global ethical standards and no justification for global justice. Utilitarianism is universalist in scope, with players maximizing their own utility and societies maximizing utility for the greatest possible number. For Rawls, societies have domestic duties and limited duties toward other societies. A set of common external rules binds states; illiberal or outlaw states lie beyond the bounds of toleration and outside the scope of responsibility for liberal and decent peoples.

### 4.8.7 *Distribution*

PG seeks to create conditions for individuals to achieve certain levels of health functioning and health agency; it seeks also to prevent and remedy shortfalls in health capability with a focus on all those below or at risk of being below the established threshold, giving priority to the worse off where progressive realization is necessary.

In cosmopolitanism, everyone on Earth has equal moral standing and should receive equal treatment, perhaps even equal attainment. Global interdependence and the arbitrary distribution of world resources may justify worldwide redistribution of goods or resources. Cosmopolitanism poses the danger of leveling down, reducing the attainment of many by an indiscriminately egalitarian distribution of scarce resources. For international human rights advocates, distribution depends on whether human rights are defined minimally or maximally. Human rights can be civil, political, and/or socioeconomic, and the degree of distribution would depend on the rights stipulated—subsistence,[118] for example, versus a set of rights that would also include child support and education.[119]

Communitarians confine principles of distributive justice to the community; nationalists confine them to the nation, where fellow nationals participate in the state as a system of cooperation. Realists acknowledge the possibility of cooperation with others, but only to increase one's own benefits. Utilitarianism does not specify what should be distributed or how, though it would in principle endorse redistribution across borders to increase aggregate welfare. In the Rawlsian scheme, liberal and decent peoples assist societies too socially or economically burdened to maintain a just political and social

---

[118] Shue, *Basic Rights*.
[119] D. Held, *Democracy and the Global Order: From the Modern State to Cosmopolitan Governance* (Stanford, CA: Stanford University Press, 1995).

regime. Economic sanctions or military intervention are permissible if a society violates human rights and puts itself outside the limits of tolerance.

### 4.8.8 Limits of Responsibility

PG focuses on health agency; health outcomes will depend partly on individual characteristics, choice, and behavior, putting equality of attainment beyond reach. PG will not sacrifice any person's central health capabilities to improve another's health capability, even if that other person's health capability falls below the norm or threshold.

Utilitarian cosmopolitanism argues that aid to the needy should not come at the cost of something of comparable moral significance, though some argue for an obligation to intervene in the case of humanitarian need. The international human rights approach does not specify limits of responsibility or address the dilemma in which extending aid compromises one's own rights. It does, however, permit intervention in cases of genocide, ethnic cleansing, war crimes, and crimes against humanity. Communitarianism does not necessarily protect individual autonomy and rights against claims of community interest. It opposes intervention into other states' affairs as contrary to communal integrity, but provides exceptions for aiding communitarian self-determination within a larger community, for secession, counter-intervention, and in humanitarian crises (for example, massacre or enslavement).[120] Still, the decision to intervene may weigh lives of fellow nationals against lives of foreigners.[121] Individual autonomy and rights are not necessarily protected against claims of national interest (liberal nationalism would protect them, however). Citizens unable to reciprocate contributions could potentially be limited rights.

For realists, the distribution of benefits derives from power and influence, not from need. States have no duty to intervene, though they might choose to do so to protect or advance their political, economic, or geostrategic interests. Utilitarians determine distribution by its overall consequences; collective interests—that is, welfare or utility—can override individual interests. The weak and vulnerable do not necessarily receive special consideration. Rawls imposes no further requirements for distribution among societies beyond aid for burdened societies. He is unconcerned with international equality per se, and does not extend his domestic distributive justice into the international realm. He rejects utilitarian principles and does not expect peoples to sacrifice themselves to attain greater aggregate global welfare.

---

[120] Walzer, "The Moral Standing of States," 209–29.
[121] Caney, *Justice Beyond Borders*.

### 4.8.9 *Legitimacy*

PG bases substantive legitimacy on health as a fundamental human interest, intrinsically valuable and necessary for the enjoyment and pursuit of other goals and endeavors. In this framework, procedural legitimacy derives from individuals' freedom and ability to participate in decision-making, and from public deliberation yielding shared understandings and commitments about injustice and its redress. Overall, legitimacy rests on the equal moral standing of all individuals and respect for their human capabilities.

For communitarians, legitimacy comes from community values and goals and from the commitment involved in community membership.[122] Nationalism, similarly, bases legitimacy on attachment to a particular territory, with distinct public culture, shared belief and history, and mutual commitment.[123] Under realism, legitimacy derives from libertarian ideals of non-interference, free will to pursue one's own or the state's own interests, with consequences for oneself. Power and expedience drive the system. Utilitarianism bases legitimacy on consequences for the aggregate. There is no emphasis on individual agency or autonomy, and how utility is maximized is unimportant as long as it is maximized. For Rawls, the legitimacy of relations between societies derives from fair conditions under which societies of equal moral standing determine principles of justice and consent to them. The legitimacy of societies comes from their standing as decent or liberal.

### 4.8.10 *Implementation*

PG sets a substantive moral goal—health capability—for all. The program to achieve this moral goal includes a theory of priority, valuing central capabilities over non-central ones and giving special consideration to the worst off. It includes shortfall inequality as a theory of measurement and evaluation. It includes a theory of efficiency, relying on cost estimation and efficiency evaluation and applying analytical tools to minimize costs and achieve equity goals as efficiently as possible. Collective and individual responsibilities delineate respective roles for goal attainment.

Cosmopolitanism, on the other hand, does not specify goals. There is no explicit theory of measurement, though distribution matters. It does not specify a theory of efficiency. Under international human rights, the goal is a stipulated set of human rights. Civil and political rights have priority over social and economic rights. Communitarianism specifies no substantive moral goal, no theory of measurement and evaluation, and no theory of

---

[122] M. J. Sandel, *Liberalism and the Limits of Justice* (Cambridge: Cambridge University Press, 1982).
[123] Miller, *On Nationality*, 188.

efficiency. Its theory of priority rests on community membership. Nationalism is much the same, with a theory of priority only for one's fellow nationals. For realism, the only goal is achieving one's maximum self-interest. Priority goes to self- or national interest. It offers no theory of measurement, though power is often measured in economic and military terms, nor does it offer a theory of efficiency, except perhaps for maximizing one's own interests within a budget constraint. Utilitarianism's goal is maximizing utility or welfare through aggregation. It embraces efficiency as it seeks to maximize aggregate utility with the fewest possible resources. Rawls, by contrast, sets substantive goals of peace and core human rights. His framework prioritizes domestic duties to maintain a decent or liberal society and limits duties to other societies. It would measure the attainment of core human rights—subsistence, for example. It does not, however, specify a theory of efficiency.

# Part III
# Global Health Governance

# 5

# Divergent Perspectives in Global Health Governance

What type of global health system would move our world toward health justice? How can we take what we have learned about global health justice and apply it to health governance? What should global health governance (GHG) look like? Provincial globalism (PG) as a global health justice theory joins with the theory of shared health governance (SHG) to address these questions. SHG is a governance theory, based on a genuine commitment among global health actors to achieve health justice as opposed to pursuing narrow self, group, or state interest alone.

SHG provides the theoretical underpinnings absent from today's global health enterprise. Neither international relations and law nor public health and health policy nor bioethics and medical ethics as academic disciplines have focused on providing a theory of international or global health based in moral and political theory. The current theoretical framings of health—as an issue of security and foreign policy, or of human security, or as a human right or global public good—neglect theoretical norms for GHG. International health diplomacy, over its 150-year history, has unfolded without the necessary theoretical foundation to govern state and non-state health actions.

The need remains acute for a theory grounding global health in moral principles and developing moral commitments for GHG. The political will and practical policy action required to achieve reforms must have their roots in consistent principles; otherwise, those reforms will be vulnerable to recurrent failure. Redistribution of resources is essential to remedy health inequalities, but without ethical commitments it is not possible. Values, ideas, and norms have critical roles to play in GHG. Principles and a shared ethic of health equity will guide national and global actors as they design and redesign institutions and programs.

The world needs a new way forward. SHG elucidates standards of global and domestic responsibility and accountability for health equity. It proposes a common conceptual and policy framework based on a set of distinct but complementary responsibilities for governments, nongovernmental organizations (NGOs), the private sector, and individuals themselves. SHG provides the needed focal point drawing different actors' expectations together, and a foundation upon which to build in the future. In the SHG framework, the state has duties to create conditions in which all individuals have the opportunity to be healthy and to prevent and reduce the shortfall between actual and potential health within their countries. Global actors have a duty to help shape conditions in which countries can flourish and promote the health of their populations.

The GHG literature frames health variously as a matter of security and foreign policy, human rights, or a global public good.[1] These frames are not mutually exclusive, but do have distinct implications. And the divergence among these perspectives has forestalled the development of a consensus vision for global health.[2] Global health policy will differ according to the frame applied.

## 5.1 Health as Security and Foreign Policy

Framing health as a security issue stresses the defense of borders against infectious diseases and bioweapons. Non-communicable diseases (NCDs) and social determinants of health receive little attention within this framing.[3] Disease surveillance and outbreak control are chief policy issues, though HIV's impact in high-prevalence countries has raised concerns about regional stability and security.[4] Developed (mostly Western) states drive action, seeking to protect their trading interests and their borders from contamination.[5] Those infectious diseases geographically concentrated away from developed countries go largely neglected because they pose no imminent threat in the developed world.[6] Critics charge the World Health Organization's (WHO) International Health Regulations (IHR) and Global Outbreak Alert and Response Network with bias

[1] R. Labonté, "Global Health in Public Policy: Finding the Right Frame?" *Critical Public Health* 18, no. 4 (2008): 467–82.

[2] B. Bennett, I. G. Cohen, S. E. Davies, L. O. Gostin, P. S. Hill, A. Mankad, and A. L. Phelan, "Future-Proofing Global Health: Governance of Priorities," *Global Public Health* is published online, but not in print yet (2017): 1–9.

[3] C. McInnes and K. Lee, "Health, Security and Foreign Policy," *Review of International Studies* 32 (2006): 5–23.

[4] L. Garrett, *HIV and National Security: Where are the Links?* (New York: Council on Foreign Relations, 2005).

[5] N. Howard-Jones, "Origins of International Health Work," *British Medical Journal* 1, no. 4661 (1950): 1032–7.

[6] B. Liese, M. Rosenberg, and A. Schratz, "Neglected Tropical Diseases 1: Programmes, Partnerships, and Governance for Elimination and Control of Neglected Tropical Diseases," *The Lancet* 375, no. 9708 (2010): 67–76.

toward the West.[7] For example, bioterror agents as defined by the US Centers for Disease Control and Prevention, not diseases causing the most fatalities in the past decade, dominate the revised IHR's definition of public health emergencies of international concern.[8] If developing states perceive themselves to be ignored or ill-served by the IHR, their confidence in WHO's authority might erode and their cooperation diminish. Yet the world needs their cooperation: the ability and willingness of poorer states to detect and verify outbreaks is critical in effective surveillance and response. The 2007 Speaker case, in which a man believed to be infected with extensively drug-resistant TB was permitted to travel by plane and car across several international borders before being quarantined, illustrates the need for all states, not just Western nations, to develop standardized procedures for addressing infectious diseases. But the counter-incentives are powerful—some developing countries are reluctant to reveal disease outbreaks associated with underdevelopment, fearing diminished trade and tourism and reputational damage.[9] Wealthy nations might also react to outbreak reports by stockpiling drugs, potentially diminishing access in poorer countries.[10]

Some, rejecting the humanitarian concerns of public health, assert that health matters only as a security or foreign policy issue under neorealist and neoliberal foreign policy approaches.[11] Framing health in terms of security or foreign policy enhances state sovereignty and the state's role in international health. China is an oft-cited example. China integrates health into foreign policy, and thus more actively engages in international health. But a realist agenda behind this engagement both guides and impedes China's role.[12] A security approach may emphasize intelligence and military entities, shifting global health response away from participating civil society actors and undermining concerns for civil liberties and democratic participation. On the other hand, a security frame increases attention and resources for health on both

[7] S. E. Davies and J. R. Youde, *The Politics of Surveillance and Response to Disease Outbreaks: The New Frontier for States and Non-State Actors* (Farnham: Ashgate Publishing, 2015).

[8] A. Kelle, "Securitization of International Public Health: Implications for Global Health Governance and the Biological Weapons Prohibition Regime," *Global Governance* 13, no. 2 (2007): 217–35.

[9] A. L. Taylor, "Controlling the Global Spread of Infectious Diseases: Toward a Reinforced Role for the International Health Regulations," *Houston Law Review* 33 (1997): 1327–62.

[10] *PLoS Medicine* Editors, "How is WHO Responding to Global Public Health Threats?" *PLoS Medicine* 4, no. 5 (2007): 0777–8.

[11] C. McInnes, "Health and Security Studies," in *Health, Foreign Policy and Security: Towards a Conceptual Framework for Research and Policy*, ed. A. Ingram (London: Nuffield Trust and Nuffield Health and Social Services Fund, 2004), 43–58.

[12] Y. Huang, "Pursuing Health as Foreign Policy: The Case of China," *Indiana Journal of Global Legal Studies* 17, no. 1 (2010): 105–46; J. D. Reader, "The Case against China: Establishing International Liability for China's Response to the 2002–2003 SARS Epidemic," *Columbia Journal of Asian Law* 19, no. 2 (2006): 519–71.

domestic and international levels.[13] It might also rebalance the emphasis between health and foreign policy. For example, seven countries now avowedly view foreign policy through a health lens, assessing policies at least partly by their health impacts; infectious diseases remain the focus, but this perspective no longer judges health policy just by its foreign policy implications.[14]

Viewing health as a security and foreign policy concern absolves the management or mismanagement of globalization through free market economics and neoliberalism from critique. This approach is based on the notion that a country's economic failure is caused by internal and domestic factors alone, and international and foreign states are not causally linked to countries' economic performance. This explanation neglects evidence about the influence of international institutions such as the World Bank, the International Monetary Fund (IMF), or the World Trade Organization (WTO) on developing countries. Joseph Stiglitz has criticized international institutions extensively for coercing policy decisions and imposing financing conditions on developing countries to those countries' detriment. Health framed as security or foreign policy puts health at risk through the application of neoliberal policies such as market liberalization, privatization, and fiscal austerity.[15] In international relations, including international health discussions, wealthy and more powerful countries are in a better position to achieve their foreign policy and security objectives. Even if developing countries achieve some gains, the playing field for implementing health objectives is tilted toward better-resourced developed countries.

## 5.2 Health as Human Security

Some advocates have proposed framing health as a human security issue. The human security approach seeks freedom from fear and want. It is people-centered rather than state-centered. It encompasses economic, food, health, environmental, personal, cultural, and political security.[16] These advocates see health, universally valued and essential to the other components, as central to human security.[17] They focus on issues the traditional security

---

[13] S. Elbe, "Should HIV/AIDS be Securitized? The Ethical Dilemmas of Linking HIV/AIDS and Security," *International Studies Quarterly* 50, no. 1 (2006): 119–44.

[14] Ministers of Foreign Affairs of Brazil, France, Indonesia, Norway, Senegal, South Africa, and Thailand, "Oslo Ministerial Declaration—Global Health: A Pressing Foreign Policy Issue of Our Time," *The Lancet* 369, no. 9570 (2007): 1373–8.

[15] J. Stiglitz, *Globalization and Its Discontents* (New York: W. W. Norton, 2002).

[16] UNDP, "Chapter 2: New Dimensions of Human Security," in *Human Development Report 1994*, ed. B. Ross-Larson, A. Strong, K. Bieler, J. Peabody, E. Hanlon, D. Sinmao, et al. (New York: Oxford University Press, 1994): 22–46.

[17] P. Gutlove, *Summary Report on the Consultation on Health and Human Security* (Cambridge, MA: Institute for Resource and Security Studies, 2002).

framing neglects, including NCDs and social and economic determinants of health. Human security, some argue, can help us understand changes generating novel or escalated threats, and analyze "what security is provided and for whom."[18] Some argue that GHG should address "the structural causes of human fear and want as fundamental sources of insecurity."[19] HIV is a high human security priority among proponents of this view.[20] Advocates have defined and operationalized human security in various ways,[21] but they lack clear agreement on what it entails, and critics charge them with vagueness and excessive expansiveness.[22] Health security is a related concept, but users and agencies define it inconsistently too, undermining its usefulness as a basis of cooperation.[23]

## 5.3 Health as a Human Right

International human rights law has increasingly promoted the pursuit of global health.[24] When health is a human right, then health provision is no longer a discretionary charitable activity but a global human entitlement. This conception adds legal muscle to appeals to help the poor.[25] Promoting health as a human right accords with advancing other human rights—civil, political, social, and economic.[26] Although scholars have yet to evaluate empirically and comprehensively the impact of a human rights frame on health, observers expect these rights to enhance health.[27]

---

[18] S. Maclean, "Microbes, Mad Cows and Militaries: Exploring the Links between Health and Security," *Security Dialogue* 39, no. 5 (2008): 475.

[19] Ibid., 478.

[20] L. Chen and V. Narasimhan, "Human Security and Global Health," *Journal of Human Development* 4, no. 2 (2003): 181–90.

[21] G. King and C. J. L. Murray, "Rethinking Human Security," *Political Science Quarterly* 116, no. 4 (2002): 585–610; F. O. Hampson, J. Daudelin, J. B. Hay, T. Martin, and H. Reid, *Madness in the Multitude: Human Security and World Disorder* (Don Mills, ON: Oxford University Press, 2002).

[22] R. Paris, "Human Security: Paradigm Shift or Hot Air?" *International Security* 26, no. 2 (2001): 87–102.

[23] W. Aldis, "Health Security as a Public Health Concept: A Critical Analysis," *Health Policy and Planning* 23, no. 6 (2008): 369–75.

[24] P. C. Kuszler, "Global Health and the Human Rights Imperative," *Asian Journal of WTO & International Health Law and Policy* 2, no. 1 (2007): 99–123.

[25] WHO, *25 Questions and Answers on Health & Human Rights* (Geneva: WHO, 2002).

[26] The Writing Group for the Consortium for Health and Human Rights, "Health and Human Rights: A Call to Action on the 50th Anniversary of the Universal Declaration of Human Rights," *Journal of the American Medical Association* 280, no. 5 (1998): 462–4; P. Farmer, *Pathologies of Power: Health, Human Rights, and the New War on the Poor* (Berkeley, CA: University of California Press, 2003).

[27] L. Gable, "The Proliferation of Human Rights in Global Health Governance," *Journal of Law, Medicine & Ethics* 35, no. 4 (2007): 534–44; M. M. Kavanagh, "The Right to Health: Institutional Effects of Constitutional Provisions on Health Outcomes," *Studies in Comparative International Development* 51, no. 3 (2016): 328–64.

The movement between traditional security and foreign policy approaches and the human rights perspective in global health has generated much discussion. The IHR and other international health instruments adopt principles from both frameworks.[28] In India and some other countries, an expanding conception of rights is building popular demand for services and sharpening state accountability.[29]

The human rights and health movement has grown since the WHO Constitution's Preamble in 1946, the 1966 International Covenant on Economic, Social, and Cultural Rights, the 1978 Declaration of Alma Ata, and General Comment 14 on the Right to the Highest Attainable Standard of Health in 2000, but its potential remains undeveloped. The rhetorical force of individuals' rights-based claims has not been matched by effective institutional backing in monitoring and evaluating the progressive realization of these rights. WHO has limited, if any, formal authority to hold states accountable. Moreover, WHO itself is subject to considerable influence by powerful state and non-state actors who manipulate it for their own ends. A realistic understanding of these interests and power dynamics is necessary to seek solutions to these failures. The Western orientation and definition of rights—and in particular the United States' dominant influence—have also contributed to the right to health's failure in global politics. As one scholar writes, the United States "far more than in other liberal democracies, is characterized by hyper-individualism, exaggerated absoluteness, and silence with respect to personal, civic, and collective responsibilities."[30]

Furthermore, the health and human rights approach does not clearly define respective roles and responsibilities in effectuating a right to health. It does not prioritize which medically effective health care services to offer and which to exclude,[31] or order them in relation to other rights. It does not offer a collaborative approach to share fairly the benefits and burdens of coproducing health. The HIV/AIDS community has used the right to health and human rights more broadly in effectively gaining more resources and access to treatment for this population.[32] This favorable treatment, a vertical approach, does not, however, constitute successful effectuation of the right to health for

[28] M. G. Baker and D. P. Fidler, "Global Public Health Surveillance under New International Health Regulations," *Emerging Infectious Diseases* 12, no. 7 (2006): 1058–65.

[29] K. Misra, "Politico-Moral Transactions in Indian AIDS Service: Confidentiality, Rights and New Modalities of Governance," *Anthropological Quarterly* 79, no. 1 (2006): 33–74.

[30] A. R. Chapman, "Reintegrating Rights and Responsibilities", in *International Rights and Responsibilities for the Future*, ed. K. W. Hunter and T. C. Mack (Westport, CT: Praeger, 1996), 3–28; 3.

[31] G. Sreenivasan, "A Human Right to Health? Some Inconclusive Skepticism," *Proceedings of the Aristotelian Society* 86, no. 1 (2012): 239–65.

[32] J. Wolff, *The Human Right to Health* (New York: W. W. Norton & Company, 2012).

whole populations. The right to health is an individual right, which has focused on individual access to health care instead of disease prevention and collective health promotion. And the movement has failed to win broad recognition of the right to health as a fundamental human right.

## 5.4 Health as a Global Public Good

Framing health as a global public good places it beyond the jurisdiction of any one country and acknowledges its interest to two or more countries or their populations.[33] Public goods are non-excludable—no one can be barred from consuming them. They are also non-rival—one person's consumption of such goods does not preclude consumption by another. Communicable disease control, disease eradication, disease surveillance, the generation and dissemination of research and best practices, and health-related rules and standards are examples of global public goods in health.[34] But this approach also poses problems. The non-excludable nature of public goods means little commercial incentive exists for their production. National governments may provide public goods nationally, but no global government exists to provide or pay for global public goods. The global public good perspective, then, must focus on how to ensure collective action—production of global health goods—at the international level.[35] Proponents emphasize mutual benefit among countries rich and poor, rather than aid from the rich to the poor. But the health interests of the rich and poor are often different, and the rich are more able to act on their own interests, so this strategy raises justice and equity concerns.

A public goods frame stems from economics. Negative and positive externalities or spillovers transcending national boundaries motivate powerful and affluent actors and states to cooperate internationally for the benefit of all. However, many public health issues—orphan or tropical diseases, for example, or lack of access to proven and cost-effective medicines in some parts of the world—will not receive the focus morality requires. Such incentives will not solve these social problems absent clear threats to one's own national or self-interest. The overall concept fails to offer a prioritization of

---

[33] D. T. Jamison, J. Frenk, and F. Knaul, "International Collective Action in Health: Objectives, Functions, and Rationale," *The Lancet* 351, no. 9101 (1998): 514–17; I. Kaul, P. Conceição, K. Le Goulven, and R. U. Mendoza, eds., *Providing Global Public Goods: Managing Globalization* (New York: Oxford University Press, 2003).

[34] I. Kaul and M. Faust, "Global Public Goods and Health: Taking the Agenda Forward," *Bulletin of the World Health Organization* 79, no. 9 (2001): 869–74; D. Woodward, N. Drager, R. Beaglehole, and D. Lipson, "Globalization, Global Public Goods, and Health," in *Trade in Health Services: Global, Regional, and Country Perspectives*, ed. N. Drager and C. Vieira (Washington, DC: Pan American Health Organization, 2002): 3–11.

[35] R. D. Smith, "Global Public Goods and Health," *Bulletin of the World Health Organization* 81, no. 7 (2003): 475.

global health issues,[36] or guidance on how to implement remedies.[37] A broad consensus accepts, however, that provision of global public goods needs to begin at the national level.[38]

## 5.5 Rational Actor Model of Global Health Governance

GHG today operates on a rational actor model in which agents on the global health stage are rational decision-makers. They are individuals (health ministers, for example); NGOs; multilateral public institutions (WHO, World Bank); public–private partnerships (Gavi, for example); and states and their component parts. Actors are both state and non-state and have their own distinct goals and objectives. They analyze the costs and benefits of various available options and act accordingly. Broadly speaking, the rational actor model encompasses a continuum from the purely self-interest-maximizing position at one extreme to a more nuanced approach that takes others' interests into account when making one's own calculations. Thus, in today's rational actor world, different actors can have conflicting goals and priorities: some embrace humanitarian goals and support the creation of global public goods, while others operate solely out of their own narrow interests.

The latter, in particular, become involved in the global health pursuits that fulfill their own aims, regardless of the overall impact on global and domestic society. In the environment they shape, power imbalances are rife, and powerful players can dominate multilateral institutions, effectively steering policy and resource allocations for their own purposes. These dysfunctions sift down through the whole global health enterprise. International organizations have their own agendas, which might accord with or diverge from those of states. Even NGOs, with their altruistic flavor, reflect their own interests in their operations. The health aid and technical assistance they provide serve their own political, economic, and strategic purposes, whether nationally, organizationally, or both.

State and non-state actors seek the most favorable conditions to pursue their own interests, conditions that will effectively limit any constraints on their independence. Both state and non-state actors prefer a competitive, fragmented, uncoordinated approach because that paradigm creates better

---

[36] L. C. Chen, T. G. Evans, and R. A. Cash, "Health as a Global Public Good," in *Global Public Goods: International Cooperation in the 21st Century*, ed. I. Kaul, I. Grunberg, and M. Stern (New York: Oxford University Press, 1999), 284–304.

[37] R. Smith, D. Woodward, A. Acharya, R. Beaglehole, and N. Drager, "Communicable Disease Control: A 'Global Public Good' Perspective," *Health Policy and Planning* 19, no. 5 (2004): 271–8.

[38] I. Kaul, I. Grunberg, and M. Stern, "Global Public Goods: Concepts, Policies and Strategies," in *Global Public Goods*, ed. Kaul, Grunberg, and Stern, 465.

conditions for such actors to pursue and achieve their own ends. Actors mount significant resistance to reform, though all purport to favor it. Indeed, there is deception in the self-interest-maximizing rational actor model that shrouds narrow, selfish agendas in a rhetorical façade of common purpose such as the Millennium Development Goals (MDGs).

International health negotiations and policies unfold asymmetrically and disproportionately to favor wealthier and more powerful actors' interests. International institutions and developed countries have powerful sway over developing countries and actors with less power and fewer resources, leaving the latter open to coercion in international health financing and technical assistance. In a rational actor model, international health treaties, such as the proposed Framework Convention on Global Health, lack feasibility because nations that are net losers—in control over foreign policy or the allocation of burdens and benefits—will not sign on. International treaties require state consent. An international health treaty will only be ratified if all parties, especially powerful states, benefit in their narrowly construed self-interest; poor and less powerful states may be slightly or moderately better off than without the treaty, but these treaties will not achieve the kind of global optimum that provides sustainable benefits to all. This kind of treaty reflects a consensus dictated by asymmetries in power and resources: wealthy nations impose their terms on poor countries. Poor countries simply lack the bargaining power to exert significant influence on global organizations and their interests, and basic needs can be sacrificed to further the narrow interests of the more powerful. This kind of treaty agreement is superficial and does not represent authentic cooperation and a genuinely shared consensus. Other problems vex these international agreements, including effort duplication; a lack of feasibility; having a questionable impact, resulting in negative consequences;[39] and lacking reasonable prospects of yielding net positive effects.[40] Treaties in other areas, such as global environmental governance, have proved ineffectual due to problems in follow-through, leadership, national interest asymmetries, and powerful private interests.

Even where humanitarian concerns are clearly and admirably at play, the problem of mixed motivations remains. Often selfish interests are also at work, and actors disguise them behind humanitarian motives. Thus, humanitarianism itself can serve the ends of wealthy and powerful interests.

To remedy the rational actor model's deep structural imbalances, the PG/SHG framework proposes impartial concern for the fundamental health interest of all

---

[39] S. J. Hoffman and J. A. Røttingen, "Dark Sides of the Proposed Framework Convention on Global Health's Many Virtues: A Systematic Review and Critical Analysis," *Health and Human Rights* 15, no. 1 (2013): 117–34.

[40] S. J. Hoffman, J. A. Røttingen, and J. Frenk, "Assessing Proposals for New Global Health Treaties: An Analytic Framework," *American Journal of Public Health* 105, no. 8 (2015): 1523–30.

people everywhere. Impartial concern can be articulated through an overarching charter such as a Global Health Constitution (GHC). It also proposes terms of cooperation that all state and non-state parties must accept, and it stipulates the goal of achieving a global optimum. It pursues a deep view of the common good. Failing to modify the global health architecture in these ways will generate more and greater health deficits, many of which could be irreversible.

Today's global health landscape features record numbers of public and private actors and funding sources. Along with WHO and World Bank, Gates Foundation, the United States President's Emergency Plan for AIDS Relief, the Global Fund to Fight AIDS, Tuberculosis, and Malaria (Global Fund), and corporations (for example, pharmaceutical companies) have all swelled the ranks of global health's major actors. The Global Fund provides 20 percent of all international funding for HIV/AIDS, 50 percent of all malaria funding, and 65 percent of all TB funding.[41] With its selective aid for narrow disease control programs in particular countries, the Global Fund is the quintessential contemporary initiative. It focuses on monitoring and evaluating intermediate indicators rather than health systems development—even though systems are essential building blocks for sustainable health. Systems development, however, does not grab headlines.

One study identified several key challenges to health development within this environment. Overlapping mandates, competition, duplication of health activities, shifting power structures, and poor coordination all vex development efforts.[42] Most technical assistance and funding conform to donors' values rather than those of recipient countries.[43] And because donors often evaluate development by their own criteria, such development can elude critical scrutiny of its effectiveness in health and disease control. The World Bank estimated in 2006 that half of health aid failed to reach intended clinics and hospitals in sub-Saharan Africa.[44] Another study found that confusing priorities and policies at the global and country level undermined children's immunization programs and delayed new vaccine delivery; this study urged correcting overlap among WHO, World Bank, Gates Foundation's Children's Vaccine Program, and other organizations.[45]

---

[41] Global Fund to Fight AIDS, Tuberculosis, and Malaria, *Global Fund Results Report 2017* (Geneva: The Global Fund, 2017).

[42] G. Walt and K. Buse, "Global Cooperation in International Public Health," in *International Public Health: Diseases, Programs, Systems and Policies*, ed. M. H. Merson, R. E. Black, and A. J. Mills (Sudbury, MA: Jones and Bartlett Publishers, 2006): 649–76.

[43] For a discussion of the "stovepiping" effect, see L. Garrett, "The Challenge of Global Health," *Foreign Affairs* 86, no. 1 (2007): 14–38.

[44] Ibid., 22.

[45] A. Brooks, F. T. Cutts, J. Justice, and G. Walt, *Policy Study of Factors Influencing the Adoption of New and Underutilized Vaccines in Developing Countries* (Washington, DC: USAID, 1999).

Donor demands often control how developing countries manage projects. These demands can conflict with the recipient country's needs and abilities. By creating their own parallel systems and by adding vertical programs to an already weak primary health care system, donors in Ghana, Zambia, and Kenya have actually undermined their own stated goals of building an integrated reproductive health service delivery system.[46] Much donor funding fails to address weak in-country institutional capacity because it focuses on specific diseases and programs.

Recipient countries illustrate the difficulties. The Organisation for Economic Co-operation and Development (OECD), studying eleven recipient countries in 2003, identified recipient countries' five heaviest burdens as donor-driven priorities and systems, difficulties with donor procedures, uncoordinated donor practices, excessive demands on time, and delays in disbursements.[47] Another study in Global Fund beneficiary nations Mozambique, Tanzania, Uganda, and Zambia found that incorporating additional resources and meeting donor requirements was challenging for all four countries. The need to learn the management of a new financial mechanism and to juggle proliferating activities among multiple donors overwhelmed them.[48]

Self-interest maximization produces suboptimal results in global health policy. Eight counterproductive elements emerge from a review of the literature: (1) political and social power; (2) donor ideology and preference; (3) turf protection; (4) inter-NGO competition; (5) profits; (6) geopolitical interests; (7) recipient manipulation of aid; and (8) mutual dependence on ineffective aid (see Table 5.1 for examples). The empirical evidence points to these problems' intransigence and strong resistance to GHG reforms that would lead to genuine coproduction and cooperation, as set out in SHG's more socially rational, integrated, and standardized approach.

A theoretically grounded normative approach to GHG is needed. Without a normative framework to undergird global health relations, actors will continue to strive for power and self-preservation as under a self-interest-maximizing model. Narrow interests will defeat justice considerations in an environment where power rather than justice is the currency of international relations. Unrestrained self-interest is leading to chaos and anarchy in GHG. Equilibrium in current GHG is a matter of balance of power rather than adherence to global health justice principles.

---

[46] S. H. Mayhew, G. Walt, L. Lush, and J. Cleland, "Donor Agencies' Involvement in Reproductive Health: Saying One Thing and Doing Another?" *International Journal of Health Services* 35, no. 3 (2005): 579–601. See especially pp. 592–4.

[47] OECD, *Harmonising Donor Practices for Effective Aid Delivery* (Paris: OECD, 2003).

[48] R. Brugha, M. Donoghue, M. Starling, P. Ndubani, F. Ssengooba, B. Fernandes, et al., "The Global Fund: Managing Great Expectations," *The Lancet* 364, no. 9428 (2004): 95–100.

**Table 5.1.** Examples of Self-Interest Maximization and Suboptimal Results in Global Health

| Interest being Maximized | Examples |
| --- | --- |
| **Political and Social Power** | • Focus on health in foreign policy agenda dominated by infectious diseases and bioterror—on how West is affected by health risks from the developing world, rather than on promotion of global public health.[49] |
| | • Governments in low-income countries often direct disproportionate resources to politically important urban and elite populations, e.g., in Ghana in 1994, richest fifth of population received 33% of public spending in health, while poorest fifth received 12%.[50] |
| | • Birth control arbitrarily dispensed by community-based distributors wishing to develop prestige and respect.[51] |
| **Donor Ideology and Preference** | • IMF's neoliberal economic approach called for fiscal austerity and imposed public spending ceilings, which almost blocked Ugandan government from accepting $52 million from the Global Fund.[52] |
| | • Some faith-based organizations stress abstinence and faithfulness but marginalize or exclude condoms from HIV/AIDS prevention campaigns; HIV and those infected are often stigmatized.[53] |
| | • Uncoordinated focus on specific diseases leads to lopsided health funding and neglect of overall health system development.[54] |
| **Turf Protection** | • Attempts to streamline United Nations (UN) system thwarted by disagreements on how to redefine duplicating and overlapping functions.[55] |
| | • Botswana physicians hindered scale-up of antiretroviral therapy by resisting use of phlebotomists to ease medical staff shortage.[56] |
| | • Honduran town receiving UN World Food Program (WFP) aid wished to participate in a project run by NGO Cooperative for Assistance and Relief Everywhere (CARE); WFP threatened to leave if town accepted CARE assistance.[57] |

[49] McInnes and Lee, "Health, Security and Foreign Policy."

[50] C. Blouin, "Economic Dimensions and Impact Assessment of GATS to Promote and Protect Health," in *International Trade in Health Services and the GATS: Current Issues and Debates*, ed. C. Blouin, N. Drager, and R. Smith (Washington, DC: World Bank, 2006), 169–202.

[51] A. Kaler and S. Watkins, "Disobedient Distributors: Street-Level Bureaucrats and Would-Be Patrons in Community-Based Family Planning Programs in Rural Kenya," *Studies in Family Planning* 32, no. 3 (2001): 254–69.

[52] Global Health Watch, *Global Health Watch 2005–2006: An Alternative World Health Report* (London: Zed Books, 2005).

[53] S. Woldehanna, K. Ringheim, C. Murphy, J. Gibson, B. Odyniec, C. Clérismé, et al., *Faith in Action: Examining the Role of Faith-Based Organizations in Addressing HIV/AIDS* (Washington, DC: Global Health Council, 2005).

[54] G. Walt, N. Spicer, and K. Buse, "Mapping the Global Health Architecture," in *Making Sense of Global Health Governance: A Policy Perspective*, ed. K. Buse, W. Hein, and N. Drager (Basingstoke: Palgrave Macmillan, 2009), 47–71.

[55] Ibid.; J. Frenk, J. Sepúlveda, O. Gómez-Dantés, M. J. McGuinness, and F. Knaul, "The Future of World Health: The New World Order and International Health," *British Medical Journal* 314 (1997): 1404–7.

[56] A. Swidler, "Syncretism and Subversion in AIDS Governance: How Locals Cope with Global Demands," *International Affairs* 82, no. 2 (2006): 269–84.

[57] J. T. Jackson, *The Globalizers: Development Work in Action* (Baltimore, MD: Johns Hopkins University Press, 2005).

| | |
|---|---|
| **Inter-NGO Competition** | • To remain competitive for funding, NGOs sometimes withhold information about ineffective programs, undertake projects in areas for which they have little expertise, and tolerate recipient misbehavior; NGOs offered Kyrgyzstani politicians bribes to maintain good relations.[58] |
| | • To satisfy donor demands for accountability and ensure continued funding, aid recipients deal with duplicate paperwork and onerous monitoring requirements at the expense of substantive work;[59] Tanzania in 2001–2 had 1,000 donor meetings a year and 2,400 donor reports each quarter.[60] |
| **Profits** | • 10/90 gap; lack of drug R&D for tropical diseases.[61] |
| | • Price of Pentamidine, a previously cheap treatment for sleeping sickness, rose 500% after it was discovered to be effective for AIDS-related *pneumocystis carinii* pneumonia; the drug disappeared from the markets of poor African and Southeast Asian countries.[62] |
| | • Tobacco industry lobbies government and UN agencies (e.g., Food and Agriculture Organization) to resist WHO's tobacco control programs;[63] tobacco companies in many developing countries also use marketing strategies banned in many developed countries.[64] |
| | • Corruption and theft in public sector medical supply chain.[65] |
| **Geopolitical Interests** | • Rich countries direct aid to strategic allies, former colonies, or regions they wish to influence, rather than giving aid based on need; the poorest countries receive just 40 cents of every dollar sent overseas.[66,67] |
| | • A 2007 UN resolution addressing Myanmar's failure to respond to its HIV epidemic was vetoed by China, which considered Myanmar a long-term strategic ally and which did not desire the introduction of US influence into the region.[68] |
| **Recipient Manipulation of Aid** | • Ethiopian government denied food aid to rebel-controlled territories during the 1983–5 famine.[69] |

*(continued)*

---

[58] A. Cooley and J. Ron, "The NGO Scramble: Organizational Insecurity and the Political Economy of Transnational Action," *International Security* 27, no. 1 (2002): 5–39.

[59] A. J. Bebbington, "Donor–NGO Relations and Representations of Livelihood in Nongovernmental Aid Chains," *World Development* 33, no. 6 (2005): 937–50.

[60] I. Kickbusch, "Action on Global Health: Addressing Global Health Governance Challenges," *Public Health* 119, no. 11 (2005): 969–73.

[61] B. Pécoul, P. Chirac, P. Trouiller, and J. Pinel, "Access to Essential Drugs in Poor Countries: A Lost Battle?" *Journal of the American Medical Association* 281, no. 4 (1999): 361–7.

[62] C. Thomas, "Trade Policy and the Politics of Access to Drugs," *Third World Quarterly* 23, no. 2 (2002): 251–64.

[63] K. Buse and C. Naylor, "Commercial Health Governance," in *Making Sense of Global Health Governance: A Policy Perspective*, ed. Buse, Hein, and Drager, 187–208.

[64] R. Beaglehole and D. Yach, "Globalisation and the Prevention and Control of Non-Communicable Disease: The Neglected Chronic Diseases of Adults," *The Lancet* 362 (2003): 903–8.

[65] M. Lewis, "Governance and Corruption in Public Health Care Systems," Working Paper No. 78, Center for Global Development, Washington, DC, 2006.

[66] A. Shah, "Foreign Aid for Development Assistance," *Global Issues*, April 25, 2010, http://www.globalissues.org/article/35/us-and-foreign-aid-assistance (accessed November 28, 2017).

[67] T. Deen, "Development: Three Decades of Missed Aid Targets," *Inter Press Service News Agency*, April 18, 2005, http://www.ipsnews.net/2005/04/development-three-decades-of-missed-aid-targets/ (accessed November 28, 2017).

[68] Huang, "Pursuing Health as Foreign Policy."

[69] O. Barrow, "International Responses to Famine in Ethiopia 1983–85," in *The Charitable Impulse: NGOs and Development in East and North-East Africa*, ed. O. Barrow and M. Jennings (West Hartford, CT: Kumarian Press, 2001), 63–80.

**Table 5.1.** Continued

| Interest being Maximized | Examples |
|---|---|
| | • Filipino government, dealing with insurgency during the WHO Malaria Eradication Program, stopped malaria spraying on at least one important island to allow the spread of the disease among the insurgent population.[70] |
| **Mutual Dependence on Ineffective Aid** | • Madagascar continued to receive aid despite poor performance in meeting goals, due to mutual dependence of donors and recipient. Donors depended on continuing need for aid as a reason to pursue interests such as maintaining/expanding spheres of influence and containing terrorism. NGOs benefited from persisting justification for their existence, Malagasy elites received material benefits, while the government derived legitimacy from attracting aid and dealing with donors.[71] |
| | • NGOs in Honduras opted for uncoordinated chaos rather than be told that their project might not be needed; Honduran government opted for allowing chaos to persist rather than have funding cut off, and did not enforce coordinated plan.[72] |

For a global health regime to be effective, it must be fair to all, because effectiveness requires universal participation. Indeed, achieving global health justice is in the interests of all nations, because it will serve the health interests that all people prize—a different kind of interest from those of powerful countries and organizations. These health interests have a claim to moral validity that narrower interests lack. Accepting the shared goal of global health justice will, to the extent that it is realized, benefit nations by benefiting their citizens and equipping them to do and to be more.

## 5.6 Missing: A Moral Basis in Global Justice for Global Health Governance

The particular framing of health determines which GHG issues are relevant. For example, inequity in health may be more important in a human rights frame than in a national security and foreign policy frame, in which the trade–health link may take on greater significance. Overall, despite successes in global health, the literature shows that GHG continues to suffer from decades-old problems. The system lacks a general theory grounded in global justice. SHG offers an alternative conceptual and operational framework.

---

[70] J. Siddiqi, *World Health and World Politics: The World Health Organization and the UN System* (Columbus: University of South Carolina Press, 1995).

[71] N. Horning, "Strong Support for Weak Performance: Donor Competition in Madagascar," *African Affairs* 107, no. 428 (2008): 405–31.

[72] Jackson, *The Globalizers*.

SHG recognizes as a backdrop the mismanagement of globalization, neo-liberal policies, and practices, and the asymmetric global health system favoring wealthier and more powerful actors. SHG evaluates the justice of the global health system by its impact on global health equity and the fair distribution of the system's benefits and burdens. In SHG, a general duty to global health equity undergirds the global health system. It reforms institutions. Different global, national, and local actors integrate values in a shared vision of health and health provision. This consensus propels program design, implementation, evaluation, and coordination. SHG can square with different framings of health, even potentially bringing the frames together if the shared vision has sufficient strength. SHG also promotes health agency, integrating affected but marginalized groups in national and global health programs. This participation is key to addressing aid recipients' needs effectively. It is also essential for reining in powerful industry and national interests and the influence they wield on global health and international law instruments. The global community must recognize health as a claim.

# 6

# Global Health Governance as Shared Health Governance[1]

## 6.1 Advancing Ideals of Global Health Justice

Global health governance (GHG) can be seen as the set of standards, institutions, rules, norms, and regulations voluntarily accepted by non-state and state actors.[2] Both state and non-state actors are important instruments in achieving global health justice. GHG has two overarching responsibilities: to ensure that all have the ability to be healthy, and to allocate fairly both the benefits and burdens of cooperation. Good governance, as opposed to government, will advance these justice ideals. We must examine the existing global health architecture to determine whether it is just and serves the core health interests of all the world's people.

The health capability framework focuses both consequentially on health outcomes and deontologically on health agency—good GHG promotes both. Shared values and an overlapping consensus tapping into these core values motivate actors. But when health is a security issue, as in realism and neorealism, the chief concerns are infectious diseases, bioweapons, and geopolitical security. And while the liberal and neoliberal views might consider health a

[1] This chapter stems from the following: J. P. Ruger, "Global Health Governance as Shared Health Governance," *Journal of Epidemiology & Community Health* 66, no. 7 (2012): 653–61; C. Wachira and J. P. Ruger, "National Poverty Reduction Strategies and HIV/AIDS Governance in Malawi: A Preliminary Study of Shared Health Governance," *Social Science & Medicine* 72, no. 12 (2011): 1956–64; J. P. Ruger, "Global Health Justice and Governance," *American Journal of Bioethics* 12, no. 12 (2012): 35–54.

[2] For example, global governance encompasses states, international organizations, NGOs, foundations, private corporations, various forms of networks and coalitions, partnerships, rules, laws, norms, regimes, political entrepreneurs, and ad hoc arrangements and conferences. See M. P. Karns, K. A. Mingst, and K. W. Stiles, *International Organizations: The Politics and Processes of Global Governance*, 3rd ed. (Boulder, CO: Lynne Rienner Publishers, 2015); global governance can be seen as: (1) an analytical concept; or (2) a political program/agenda with a normative perspective. See K. Dingwerth and P. Pattberg, "Global Governance as a Perspective on World Politics," *Global Governance* 12, no. 2 (2006): 185–203.

global public good—the World Health Organization (WHO), for example, is a product of post-World War II liberal values, and furnishes global public goods like the coordination of disease surveillance and outbreak control[3]—such values emphasize negative rights or civil and political liberties above positive rights or social and economic freedoms, for which health is fundamental. Even though the United Nations (UN) system, including WHO, practices a one-state and one-vote decision-making procedure, poor and vulnerable actors have a disadvantage in bargaining power as compared to wealthy and powerful actors. WHO's financing and budget structure mean that it acts primarily according to state and wealthy non-state contributor interests. Greater equality can come from powerful actors voluntarily constraining their own narrow interests to promote and protect the fundamental interests of others, including the vulnerable. This requires a normative shift from power and influence to global health justice and equity in defining global health goals.

## 6.2 Normative Theory and Global Health Governance

### 6.2.1 The Role of Values, Ideas, and Norms

Values, ideas, and norms are fundamental to GHG, but scholars have largely neglected to build a theoretical framework incorporating them. Global health problems must be analyzed within a normative framework because without a powerful normative commitment to improving health and achieving health equity, the world's most menacing health issues will persist. A normative framework can serve as a mechanism for measuring actors' commitment to health. Are they making sacrifices and effectuating programs that transcend self-interest and narrow notions of individual rationality? Norms are internalized, taken as a given. Systematic study of public moral norms, their degree of internalization, and the level of social consensus around them is thus important to GHG and to resolving the world's health threats.

International relations theory[4] demonstrates that ideas shape international policy in multiple ways. First, they provide a road map "that increase[s] actors' clarity about goals or ends-means relationships."[5] Principled ideas or beliefs in the form of values can impact global political action profoundly. The Eastern

---

[3] J. Mohan Rao, "Equity in a Global Public Goods Framework," in *Global Public Goods: International Cooperation in the 21st Century*, ed. I. Kaul, I. Grunberg, and M. A. Stern (New York: Oxford University Press, 1999), 66–88.

[4] J. Goldstein and R. O. Keohane, eds., *Ideas and Foreign Policy: Beliefs, Institutions, and Political Change* (Ithaca, NY: Cornell University Press, 1993).

[5] J. Goldstein and R. O. Keohane, "Ideas and Foreign Policy: An Analytical Framework," in *Ideas and Foreign Policy*, ed. Goldstein and Keohane, 3.

Europeans who put their lives on the line for freedom in 1989 are an example.[6] In the health arena, the tragedy of malnourished and dying babies across the developing world exposed the infant formula scandal, sparked the decades-long Nestlé boycott, and mobilized the World Health Assembly (WHA) in 1981 to pass an international (though non-binding) code banning formula promotion and advertising. Principled belief is essential to shift the global health discussion from power interests to moral concerns.

Second, ideas help coordinate behavior to solve shared problems. "[I]deas affect strategic interactions, helping or hindering joint efforts to attain 'more efficient' outcomes."[7] They serve as "focal points that define cooperative solutions or act as coalitional glue," thus helping groups come together.[8] "[I]deas focus expectations and strategies," especially in the absence of "objective" criteria.[9] "[G]iven that most agreements are likely to be incomplete," Garrett and Weingast note, "...shared beliefs about the spirit of agreements are essential" to maintain cooperation.[10]

Third, ideas acquire force as rules and institutionalized norms: "[o]nce institutionalized,...ideas continue to guide action,"[11] leading to "reinforcing organizational and normative structures."[12] A change in European normative thinking about self-determination, for example, can help explain European shifts toward decolonization.[13] Epistemic communities—networks of experts—can deploy both social scientific and normative knowledge[14] to help instill ideas in the public mind.

Fourth, ideas reinforce basic values of justice, equality, and fairness, shaping actors' commitments and benefiting those actors' reputations and leadership globally. To the extent that strong moral principles and leadership lead to stronger political and even economic capital, such ideas are influential in forming and sustaining international cooperation. Investments in global public health motivated only by narrow economic considerations fall well short of the investments that are morally required. A broader conception of global goods, reaching beyond the global public goods approach and its economic motivations, will encompass moral motivations and incorporate others' values and interests in personal and collective decision-making. Some have tied these ideas

---

[6] Ibid.

[7] Ibid., 12.

[8] Ibid.

[9] Ibid., 18.

[10] G. Garrett and B. R. Weingast, "Ideas, Interests, and Institutions: Constructing the European Community's Internal Market," in *Ideas and Foreign Policy*, ed. Goldstein and Keohane, 176.

[11] Goldstein and Keohane, "Ideas and Foreign Policy," 5.

[12] Ibid., 13.

[13] R. H. Jackson, "The Weight of Ideas in Decolonization: Normative Change in International Relations," in *Ideas and Foreign Policy*, ed. Goldstein and Keohane, 111–38.

[14] P. M. Haas, "Introduction: Epistemic Communities and International Policy Coordination," *International Organization* 46, no. 1 (1992): 1–35.

to analyses of power in international relations, arguing that smart power entails acting as an "agent for good" by "providing things people and governments in all quarters of the world want but cannot attain in the absence of American leadership."[15] Others, however, critique this smart-power approach as still too closely aligned with neoliberal international politics, still grounded in enlightened national self-interest, still ultimately reflecting the preferences of one global power and its ideological imperialism. Others suggest that morality, along with self-interest, can guide international action on health.[16]

Evidence demonstrates that generating a shared commitment to an ideal can spur actors to fulfill their rightful roles. The US environmental movement that sprang to life in the 1960s, for example, exposed the extent of environmental degradation, enlisted ever-growing numbers of adherents, and rapidly succeeded in pushing Congress to take responsibility, resulting in the 1970 Clean Air Act, the 1972 Clean Water Act, and the 1973 Endangered Species Act.

### 6.2.2 Common Goals and Common Commitments: The Social Agreement Model

Shared goals serve everyone's interest objectively and reflect a shared conception. Health equity is right and just because it helps all people and their communities to flourish and resolves the myriad practical problems that inequity creates. Solving collective issues—reducing infant mortality, for example—requires promoting the health of individuals and populations simultaneously. The common good is the basis for the health equity norm. In shared health governance (SHG), as plural subjects we seek the common good in various domains of our subjecthood and enter into commitments to achieve it. This kind of norm-inspired collective action has succeeded in some cases despite the dominant rational actor model, and exemplifies good global health cooperation. Examples include Africa's Onchocerciasis Control Programme (OCP) and the Task Force for Child Survival and Development, HIV/AIDS control in Brazil, and WHO's Global Influenza Surveillance Network. Each example embodies four core provincial globalism (PG)/SHG elements: partnerships defined by a shared goal; coordination and cooperation through the delineation of complementary expertise; clear responsibilities and obligations leading to accountability in pursuing goals; and donors' willingness to let others lead and develop agency.

The OCP and the Merck ivermectin donation program administered by the Task Force for Child Survival and Development are widely considered

---

[15] R. L. Armitage and J. S. Nye, Jr., *CSIS Commission on Smart Power: A Smarter, More Secure America* (Washington, DC: Center for Strategic and International Studies, 2007), 5.

[16] R. Batniji and P. H. Wise, "The Morality of Saved Lives," *The American Journal of Bioethics* 12, no. 12 (2012): 1–2.

exemplary. The 1974 OCP covered West Africa and was a collaboration between the World Bank, WHO, the United Nations Development Programme, and the Food and Agriculture Organization. The 1995 African Programme for Onchocerciasis Control expanded the effort to central and eastern Africa, and extended participation to twenty-seven donor nations, more than thirty non-governmental organizations (NGOs), and more than 80,000 rural communities. Both programs used ivermectin donated by Merck. The programs halted parasite transmission in eleven West African countries and made 25 million arable hectares safe for resettlement.[17] What explains these successes? These programs encompassed a shared goal to control onchocerciasis; willing actors allowing for regional coordination and cooperation; clearly delineated roles, obligations, and mutual accountability; and health agency built through community involvement and grassroots empowerment.

In Brazil, an egalitarian ethos underlies the health care system, with the state responsible for health care. Health policy planning involves civil society, and the government funds health advocacy groups. Many view the Brazilian effort to combat HIV/AIDS as a model to be emulated; between 1996 and 2002, Brazil halved AIDS mortality.[18] The World Bank funded part of this Brazilian undertaking, making loans despite the divergence of Brazilian health policies from World Bank positions and thus suggesting a "respect for different values and social choices."[19] A shared goal of HIV/AIDS prevention and control, clear recognition and accountability for the state's obligation to provide health care, civil society involvement leading to enhanced health agency, and country ownership of health policies all played roles in this success.

Some 142 National Influenza Centres in 115 countries have worked together in WHO's global influenza surveillance program, begun in 1948. This partnership applies internationally accepted norms to strengthen national case detection systems and labs; it further analyzes virus isolates from national labs in four WHO influenza collaborating centers, and then it puts these data to work in the annual vaccine design process. The program effectively handled the 1997 influenza A virus subtype H5N1 outbreak in Hong Kong: a collaborating Dutch lab rapidly identified the virus strain, and WHO centers in the USA mobilized and coordinated an investigating team.[20] It developed and distributed scientific studies, public information, and diagnostic test kits quickly,

---

[17] R. Levine and the What Works Working Group, "Controlling Onchocerciasis in Sub-Saharan Africa," in R. Levine and What Works Working Group, *Millions Saved: Proven Successes in Global Health* (Washington, DC: Center for Global Development, 2004), 57–64.

[18] S. Okie, "Fighting HIV: Lessons from Brazil," *New England Journal of Medicine* 354, no. 19 (2006): 1977–81.

[19] R. Araújo de Mattos, V. Terto Júnior, and R. Parker, "World Bank Strategies and the Response to AIDS in Brazil," *Divulgação em Saúde para Debate* 27 (2003): 215–27.

[20] D. L. Heymann and G. R. Rodier, "Global Surveillance of Communicable Diseases," *Emerging Infectious Diseases* 4, no. 3 (1998): 362–5.

yielding a "timely, ordered, and effective response."[21] A shared goal of outbreak surveillance and control; mutual obligation and accountability to detect and report outbreaks; and coordination and cooperation to provide a global public health good were key factors in this success.

Additional successes, exhibiting similar key SHG attributes, include campaigns to eradicate polio, guinea worm, and lymphatic filariasis. These efforts bring together numerous international and national actors, corporate and non-profit entities such as WHO, United Nations Children's Fund (UNICEF), the US Centers for Disease Control and Prevention (CDC), the Carter Center, the Gates Foundation, DuPont, and Merck.[22] A drive by national governments, WHO, UNICEF, the American Red Cross, and the CDC has also greatly reduced global measles mortality since 2000.[23]

### 6.2.3 Committing to Global Health Equity

SHG takes health justice as the end goal of political activity in global health, requiring a principled commitment to health equity to enhance health capabilities—a common interest of all people and nations. One cannot separate out efforts to coproduce global health specifically for one individual or one nation. No doubt, some individuals and nations will benefit more from a global health system, particularly those with graver health threats and sicker populations. Nevertheless, the ill health of another person or population does pose greater risks to one's own health and the health of nations, both through the spread of infectious agents and through significant burdens on society as a whole imposed by non-communicable diseases like heart disease, cancer, and diabetes. Thus, while SHG finds its motivation in principled moral norms embodying justice and equity, it satisfies rational self-interest as well.

While today's global health community may proclaim health equity as a goal, it has neither committed fully to global health justice principles nor set up an effective system to realize them. Thus, no genuine conviction supports health equity in this context. Nor, arguably, did the Millennium Development Goals, a product of the current global health architecture. The current global health architecture represents a rational actor model of cooperation behind a façade of global health ethics. In today's global health regime, wealthy and

---

[21] Ibid., 365.

[22] Levine et al., *Millions Saved*; D. Molyneux, "Lymphatic Filariasis (Elephantiasis) Elimination: A Public Health Success and Development Opportunity," *Filaria Journal* 2, no. 13 (2003); R. Voelker, "Global Partners Take Two Steps Closer to Eradication of Guinea Worm Disease," *Journal of the American Medical Association* 305, no. 16 (2011): 1642.

[23] W. J. Moss and D. E. Griffin, "Global Measles Elimination," *Nature Reviews Microbiology* 4 (2006): 900–8; WHO, "Global Elimination of Measles: Report by the Secretariat," EB125/4, Provisional Agenda Item 5.1, Geneva, April 16, 2009.

influential actors define and deploy security frames to justify bilateral and multilateral measures that preserve their power and prominence.

SHG insulates health and disease control from the narrow interests of powerful countries and wealthy NGOs. It does not deny self or national interest but seeks through ethical commitments to align it with shared goals. A combination of interests and norms of fairness has been found to ground commitments to global cooperation in other areas, such as global climate change.[24] SHG also contrasts sharply with the realist and neorealist emphasis on national survival, independence, geopolitical interests, and relative economic and military power.[25] Nor does SHG rely on mutual advantage, absolute gains, or convergence of interests, unlike liberal and neoliberal perspectives. It offers an overarching substantive goal, unlike transnationalism, whose less specific foci may or may not include goals of equity or social justice, and constructivism.[26] Wealthier countries have general duties to choose global health policies that help people in developing countries with health needs. Global health goals are shared goals to which responsible people and nations throughout the world will hold themselves and others accountable.

Reductions in global health inequalities and reducing shortfalls from target standards both involve using available solutions to avert global health harms. Measures to accomplish these goals require significant economic support from developed countries and must avoid imposing economic losses with significant human costs on developing countries. Given the moral considerations of need, equity, capabilities, and responsibility, wealthier countries should provide financial assistance to poor countries initially, and thereafter developing countries should contribute as they have the means to prevent and reduce global health inequalities. Developed countries' citizens should not have to sacrifice their own health needs, which have moral significance, for the sake of others. Global burden sharing depends on countries' funding capacity to meet their own health needs and to assist other countries in meeting their citizens' health needs.

[24] M. M. Bechtel, F. Genovese, and K. F. Scheve, "Interests, Norms and Support for the Provision of Global Public Goods: The Case of Climate Co-operation," *British Journal of Political Science*, 2017: 1–2.

[25] See, for example, J. M. Grieco, "Anarchy and the Limits of Cooperation: A Realist Critique of the Newest Liberal Institutionalism," *International Organization* 42, no. 3 (1988): 485–507.

[26] TNCs, for example, would likely have profits as a goal, whereas global civil society may turn its attention to equity or social justice. See R. O'Brien, "Global Civil Society and Global Governance," in *Contending Perspectives on Global Governance: Coherence, Contestation, and World Order*, ed. A. D. Ba and M. J. Hoffmann (New York: Routledge, 2005), 213–230. See also M. J. Hoffmann, "What's Global about Global Governance? A Constructivist Account," in *Contending Perspectives on Global Governance*, ed. Ba and Hoffmann, 110–128. But global civil society doesn't necessarily seek the global common good or represent a global equity ethos either; such groups can be as interest based as states. Global civil society and state and other actors can complement each other.

Norms of health equity are universal. They apply to and protect all people. They exist independent of legal enactment or recognition by domestic governments. They constitute international standards for assessment and critique and provide the basis for global governance, domestic government, and individual and interpersonal behavior. They become binding when internalized by individuals and groups and enacted through policy and legislation at the domestic level. Public moral norm internalization at the policy level involves legislation setting broadly accepted expectations for individual and group behavior. National policy action can also take the form of judicial decisions. Globally, treaties, conventions, and covenants can establish international law and strengthen domestic law. Norm internalization at the individual and group level can provide direction for individual and group behavior. The norm of global health equity serves as the moral foundation for domestic and global health policy.

As a normative theory of governance, SHG can be compared and contrasted to other perspectives in international relations theory, namely, realism and neorealism; liberalism, neoliberalism, and regime theory; transnationalism; constructivism; the English School; and world government. While this set of schools of thought is not exhaustive, the sections that follow will juxtapose SHG in relation to them on important analytical components of the theory.

### 6.2.4 Global Governance Is Not Global Government

Unlike realist or neorealist approaches that stress instrumental value in international relations, SHG incorporates both instrumental and intrinsic value. It exhibits some cosmopolitan affinities, but much cosmopolitanism calls for world government. Charles Beitz distinguishes between moral and institutional cosmopolitanism. In the former, cosmopolitan moral ideals undergird institutions in international relations; the latter vests authority in some sort of supranational agency, a world government or associated regional bodies, for example.[27] As a theory of GHG, SHG does not require a world government.

Both government and governance seek to solve shared problems by establishing collective rules and policies. The literature offers five common criteria for evaluating governments and governance—legitimacy, effectiveness, efficiency, equity, and accountability. These criteria apply to both government and governance, but in different ways. The primary difference is government's coercive power to compel compliance. Justification for using the state's power to command and control individual citizens comes from

---

[27] C. R. Beitz, "Cosmopolitan Liberalism and the States System," in *Political Restructuring in Europe: Ethical Perspectives*, ed. C. Brown (London: Routledge, 1994), 119–32.

numerous scholars, but perhaps most famously from Thomas Hobbes, who advocated coercive power to avoid a state of nature. "Hereby it is manifest, that during the time men live without a common power to keep them all in awe, they are in that condition which is called War; and such a war, as is of every man, against every man," Hobbes wrote.[28] The government's tool kit has expanded greatly since Hobbes, but generally includes regulation, legislation, oversight, and enforcement.

No coercive legal system exists at the global level. World government would involve a centralized common political authority or unified global state. The world state would transcend a state of nature among nations and is seen by its advocates as a better way to solve global collective action problems like climate change. But those objecting to a world state argue that a sovereign institutional cosmopolitanism is undesirable, impractical, and susceptible to tyranny, with no bounds and no exit, despite the lack of enforcement of many treaties and democratic deficits in the UN system. Because there is no world state there is no global government to enforce rights or duties. Governance has no such strong enforcement powers and depends instead on shared norms. For norms to be effective, people must internalize them and comply voluntarily.

Both governance and government must come together in a mutually reinforcing, multilevel system if we are to create a world where all can be healthy. A Global Health Constitution (GHC), Global Institute for Health and Medicine (GIHM), and a master plan for global health could combine in an effective governance structure to ensure legitimacy, effectiveness, efficiency, equity, and accountability. Effectiveness, equity, and efficiency as consequentialist-oriented frameworks might apply similarly at both global and domestic levels; legitimacy and accountability will differ for global, state, subnational, and non-state actors, and standards for them must be part of a GHG theory.

This restructuring requires a strong role and responsibility for the state but does not require world government. Weiss, for example, distinguishes between governance as a set of "values, norms, practices, and institutions," and government, which is associated with "political authority, institutions, and effective control."[29] A government has powers of enforcement, taxation, and policy development that governance lacks, but no world government exists and one is unlikely to emerge any time soon. In its absence, global governance practices and institutions (both formal and informal) can help bring state and non-state actors together to construct and sustain a just health system.

---

[28] T. Hobbes, *Leviathan* (Lawrence, KS: Digireads.com, 2009), 56.
[29] T. G. Weiss, "What Happened to the Idea of World Government," *International Studies Quarterly* 53, no. 2 (2009): 257.

## 6.3 Governing for the Common Good[30]

In SHG, the proper object of GHG is the common good, ensuring that all people have the opportunity to flourish. A well-organized global society that promotes the common good is to everyone's advantage. Enabling people to flourish includes enabling their ability to be healthy. Thus, we must assess health governance by its effectiveness in enhancing health capabilities.

This view contrasts sharply with current GHG. Current asymmetries in bargaining power, information, expertise, and representation taint the shape and practices of WHO and other global organizations, even though these institutions purportedly embody norms of consensus, fairness, and equality. Current GHG results from a series of consent-based decisions in international relations, but such consent is hollow and invalid because poor and vulnerable actors, lacking bargaining power and influence, must accept the terms and conditions of more powerful parties. These conditions have not ameliorated persistent deprivation and destitution for people all over the world, in poor and rich countries alike.

Currently, the main GHG functions are security, commerce, preparedness and response, and human rights, most of them reflecting powerful actors' interests. These "constitutional outlines"[31] are the structure and substance of global public health, arising out of anarchy and chaos in international relations. Such structures reflect the will of a select set of actors, not the general will of all. An important contribution to addressing health globally is the proposed Framework Convention on Global Health (FCGH) as set out in Lawrence Gostin's book, *Global Health Law*.[32] The FCGH is an international treaty, requiring state consent, based on the current system of international law. States, however, only agree to treaties that serve their own perceived interests. Like the problems of climate justice, states are unlikely to sign an international agreement that goes against these perceived interests or in which they could be net losers—better off without the treaty than with it. Remedying these problems and overcoming the need for actual direct consent, which GHG does not currently achieve, requires identifying what is ethically justifiable. These judgments motivate individuals to accept and adhere to rules and norms. Reforming current GHG requires an alternative constitutional framework, grounded in shared common interests and what is good for all.

---

[30] This section stems from J. P. Ruger, "Governing for the Common Good," *Health Care Analysis* 23, no. 4 (2015): 341–51.

[31] D. P. Fidler, "Constitutional Outlines of Public Health's 'New World Order'," *Temple Law Review* 77, no. 247 (2004): 247–89.

[32] L. O. Gostin, *Global Health Law* (Cambridge, MA: Harvard University Press, 2014).

Recognizing that the common good involves the flourishing of all individuals is an important first step in achieving health capabilities for all. The individual's capacity for well-being links inextricably to the effective functioning of society; an organized, functioning community that promotes the common good is basic to individual well-being. Despite GHG's current state, which would suggest otherwise, cooperation is not an anomaly, but a hardwired characteristic of human beings and other species. Cooperation, working together for common benefit, evolved in humans because societies that did not cooperate did not survive.[33]

Empirical evidence demonstrates that cooperation requires fairness.[34] Unfair situations generate negative responses. Inequalities in power, for example, inhibit trust and undermine cooperation, whereas constraints on power, such as monitoring and sanctions, facilitate trust. Monitoring, transparency, and sanctions thus serve as ways to check and balance among actors and institutions and address failure to meet agreed commitments. Averting inequities advances cooperation. Rules and codes of conduct provide principles to guide collaboration. A GHC and GIHM could foster such cooperation, although they do not have the political power to direct state governments. These structures embody the interests of all, not a chosen few, and provide rules based on the common good. With no world government, voluntary compliance with these norms is the best hope for the global community's well-being. Good governance requires regularly evaluating whether international actors and institutions are promoting the common good; a GHC and GIHM provide the means to do so.

### 6.3.1 Seeking the Common Good

A focus on the common good contrasts with other goals of governance. Other objectives might include a neoliberal emphasis on free markets, or a utilitarian focus on maximal societal utility, welfare, or happiness. Another objective is the good for the majority or the supermajority. These neoliberal, utilitarian, and majority-based groundings rest on a summation of private individual and group preferences or utilities. Some might argue that these methods themselves constitute notions of the common good, but in fact they do not; such objectives represent aggregations of private interests and fail to incorporate the general will.[35] The general will, the common good, should guide global health politics, rather than aggregated partial interests.

---

[33] M. Tomasello, A. P. Melis, C. Tennie, E. Wyman, and E. Herrmann, "Two Key Steps in the Evolution of Human Cooperation: The Interdependence Hypothesis," *Current Anthropology* 53, no. 6 (2012): 673–92.

[34] S. F. Brosnan and F. B. M. de Waal, "Evolution of Responses to (Un)fairness," *Science* 346, no. 6207 (2014): 314–21.

[35] J.-J. Rousseau, *The Social Contract*, trans. M. Cranston (London: Penguin Books, 1968).

### 6.3.2 *The Common Good as Human Flourishing and Health Capabilities*

The common good unites individual and societal well-being. Individual well-being cannot be understood as separate from a well-organized society that promotes the common good. Enabling individuals to flourish, to do and be what they want to do and be, is one such idea of the common good. Human flourishing and health capability on this view form the very bedrock of the common good. It includes everyone, a radical inclusion that offers every person the opportunity to flourish. Such governance is acceptable to everyone since it applies to everyone and rests on a shared conception of the common good.

Current GHG does not support human flourishing or the common good. PG offers a conception of the common good, articulating justice norms to govern global health. It offers a prospect for continuous well-being for all, requiring ongoing evaluation of global actors and their performance in promoting the shared health interests of all. Equal respect and inclusion require that institutions be justifiable under global health principles that seek to make everyone better off, offering terms of cooperation that reflect the health capability interests of all, rather than serving powerful actors' narrow self-interest. SHG's mechanisms would redress current wrongs: the GHC would identify health failures and assign responsibilities for addressing them, and the GIHM would supply the reliable scientific information and analysis necessary to overcome these intransigent obstacles to human flourishing.

### 6.3.3 *Cooperation*

Because no global government with coercive powers exists, voluntary compliance with global health justice and governance norms is the most likely route to well-being in the global community. But why would actors cooperate? Why would they work together toward collective goals rather than continue to pursue narrow national and self interest? Even if actors did cooperate, why wouldn't they do so only in instrumental terms, viewing other actors as potential sources of costs or benefits as under a rational actor model?

Extensive evidence helps answer these questions. Mechanisms for shared outcomes have fostered evolving cooperation among unrelated persons. Evidence demonstrates reciprocal altruism and mutual cooperation in humans.[36,37] Evidence also shows social motivations for effective cooperation—attitudes, shared identities, common values, trust in the character and

[36] L. A. Dugatkin, *Cooperation among Animals: An Evolutionary Perspective* (New York: Oxford University Press, 1997).

[37] P. M. Kappeler and C. P. van Schaik, *Cooperation in Primates and Humans: Mechanisms and Evolution* (Berlin: Springer, 2006).

motivation of others, joint commitments, fair procedures, fair exercise of authority and decision-making, legitimacy, emotional connections—rather than narrow instrumental self-interest alone.[38] Humans are social beings and cannot be understood apart from their domestic and global context. Prosocial behavior by groups and individuals facilitates cooperation.

Scholarship on socially and morally motivated cooperation in communities, organizations, and societies has a long history. Cooperation appeals to common identities, shared values, virtues, and a sense of obligation, because values are basic to successful governance. People must willingly cooperate with public institutions if governance is to be effective, especially where behavior is outside authorities' abilities to incentivize or sanction with credible rewards and punishments. Scholars contrast two approaches to motivation: an instrumental approach in which government authorities apply rewards and punishments for desired and undesired behavior, and a social motivation approach, socializing people into groups and supporting ties. Social motivations include identities, values, and attitudes. They motivate people to cooperate based on their own internal aspirations and their links to social groups.[39] Empirical cross-cultural studies in management, regulation, and governance demonstrate that social motivation is as effective, if not more so, than instrumental motivation, because the type of behavior increasingly necessary for collective activity is cooperation rather than compliance alone.[40] Compliance requires significant resources to monitor populations and punish violators. In the health arena, moreover, the social goal is the production of a healthy society with healthy individuals. People must act voluntarily to promote the health of their communities, their families, and themselves, cooperation that legalistic rewards and punishments alone do not effectively motivate.

This globalized world has joined us all together in unprecedented ways, creating a similarly unprecedented level of interdependence; from this interdependence arise new levels of shared responsibility for one another. The GHC would establish cooperation and partnerships and articulate elements of successful global collaboration and specific roles, responsibilities, and functions of global, national, subnational, and individual actors, providing guidance for interaction between governmental and nongovernmental actors and among different levels of government. It would create duties of cooperation and collaboration as obligations of states, non-state entities, and individuals.

---

[38] T. R. Tyler, *Why People Cooperate: The Role of Social Motivations* (Princeton, NJ: Princeton University Press, 2010).
[39] Tomasello, "Two Key Steps in the Evolution of Human Cooperation."
[40] Tyler, *Why People Cooperate.*

### 6.3.3.1 AUTHENTIC COOPERATION

Authentic cooperation is essential to achieving global health justice. The production of health equity globally and domestically requires interdependent parties to finance, organize, and deliver health care and public health; to aggregate and share knowledge; and to develop and oversee expert providers.[41] It involves determining the ethical responsibilities, both individual and collective, of the different actors involved in global health equity. Determining responsibilities involves coordination to prevent and reduce shortfall inequalities in health capabilities. In this task individuals and groups embrace and fulfill varying roles and responsibilities. Functions, needs, and voluntary commitments determine these roles and responsibilities. Voluntary assumption of duties—by individuals and also professional groups like medical associations—enhances autonomy and may also increase effectiveness.[42] The constructive public moral norms drawing institutions and individuals into this enterprise incorporate national and self interest and create expectations for compliance. This interdependent coproduction of the conditions for all to be healthy is challenging, but not impossible when an overarching framework and motivated actors provide the right resources and abilities.

The powerful ethical commitment to universal and equitable health care among Germans illustrates the possibilities. This commitment has produced a social right, which voters and major political parties expect the federal government to honor. Under the policies evolving from this commitment, the federal government, responding to citizens' convictions, sets the parameters and broad health policy goals in framework legislation and delegates implementation to physician associations and sickness funds. These latter groups decide on specific policies through collective bargaining. This multilevel, multifaceted collaboration, with responsibilities distributed according to functions across the health care landscape, produces the German health care system.[43]

---

[41] This coincides with realists' normative claim that states have a duty to pursue national interests and have special duties and obligations to their own citizens first and foremost. Moreover, there is no incentive for states to meet the needs of foreigners or foreign nations, and they only do it if their voters/citizens/constituents want them to. For a discussion of normative realism (and other varieties), see F. R. Tesón, "International Abductions, Low-Intensity Conflicts and State Sovereignty: A Moral Inquiry," *Columbia Journal of Transnational Law* 31, no. 3 (1994): 551–86, especially pp. 559–60. If interests—national or individual—are viewed more objectively rather than defined by the narrow self-interest of much thinking in rational choice, such duties and obligations would fit within the overarching PG and SHG framework.

[42] E. Kirchler, E. Hoelzl, and I. Wahl, "Enforced versus Voluntary Tax Compliance: The 'Slippery Slope' Framework," *Journal of Economic Psychology* 29, no. 2 (2008): 210–25.

[43] C. Altenstetter and R. Busse, "Health Care Reform in Germany: Patchwork Change within Established Governance Structures," *Journal of Health Politics, Policy and Law* 30, nos. 1/2 (2005): 121–42; T. Bärnighausen and R. Sauerborn, "One Hundred and Eighteen Years of the German Health Insurance System: Are there any Lessons for Middle- and Low-Income Countries?" *Social Science & Medicine* 54, no. 10 (2002): 1559–87.

Joint commitments through plural subjecthood are one way of proceeding at the global level, as individuals, groups, and states accept shared responsibility for health by jointly committing to the global health enterprise. Under SHG our commitments to citizens of other countries need not displace our commitments to our fellow citizens. Indeed, the commitment to our own citizens helps justify fulfilling their claims and those of non-citizens to just treatment globally.

Mexico extends this cooperation beyond national borders. The Secretariat of Health of Mexico seeks health improvement for global citizens as well as Mexicans. It develops partnerships with other countries, multilateral institutions, and NGOs. The US–Mexico Border Diabetes Prevention and Control Project, for example, was a collaboration between the Secretariat of Health of Mexico, CDC, Division of Diabetes Translation, the US and Mexico Border State Diabetes Control Programs, the US–Mexico Border Health Association, the Pan American Health Organization, Paso del Norte Health Foundation, the California Endowment, Project Concern International, the Border Health Foundation, and the El Paso Diabetes Association.

This example and others spotlight the interface between global and national health policy. The Mexican Secretariat of Health embodies key SHG principles. It illustrates the possibilities for states to manage up and across and coordinate global health work. In enhancing populations' individual and collective health agency, SHG fosters managing up and across; it locates legitimacy and accountability with the state, where primary responsibility rests, and it provides for managing down. In this example, Mexico's approach allows citizens, through representation, to share in health governance and promote the goals and objectives of the global health community, while maintaining their own sovereignty and agency. Multicountry partnerships can also manage up and across, as numerous emerging countries illustrate. Table 6.1 compares SHG components with those of the current global health regime.

Public moral norm internalization and ethical commitments bind systems together and hold different actors accountable, and are thus essential to authentic global health coordination. Realism and neorealism, by contrast, focus on competition among self-interested states concerned primarily with their own security[44] and their relative economic and military power. Realism and neorealism offer weaker states little protection against powerful states and the imposition of their will.

Like SHG, liberalism and neoliberalism emphasize interdependence as motivation to cooperate for absolute gains, but SHG's emphasis on respective roles and responsibilities and ethical commitments requires actors' full

[44] J. J. Mearsheimer, "The False Promise of International Institutions," *International Security* 19, no. 3 (1994): 5–49.

**Table 6.1.** Shared Health Governance vs. Current Global Health Regime

|  | Shared Health Governance | Current Global Health Regime |
|---|---|---|
| **Values and Goals** | • Joint commitments and mutual obligation align common good and individual and national interest | • Pursuit of self and national interests and priorities |
|  | • Consensus among global, national, and subnational actors on goals and measurable outcomes | • Actors have different, often competing, values and interests<br>• Lack of agreement on strategies, goals, and outcomes |
|  | • Full knowledge and mutual understanding of objectives and means | • Ideology driven rather than problem driven |
| **Coordination** | • Actors are willing to be coordinated with or without communication or centralization | • Actors often do not coordinate and are often not willing to be coordinated |
| **Evaluation** | • Agreement on indicators for evaluation of common purpose | • Lack of agreement on outcomes and indicators for evaluation |
| **Accountability** | • MCA | • Limited accountability (esp. in bilateral aid, NGO implementation) |
| **Agency/Participation** | • Enhancement of individual and group health agency, special efforts to include marginalized and vulnerable groups; focus on enabling environments | • Intended beneficiaries often excluded from policy planning and program design; lack of knowledge and skills |
| **Efficiency** | • Cost management and efficiency are integral | • Competition between actors and lack of participation by intended beneficiaries lead to funding inefficiencies and cost escalation |
| **Legitimacy** | • Legitimacy through appeal to moral and public reason, the common good, accountability, inclusive participation of stakeholders, respect for self-determination | • Legitimacy of actors and initiatives not always clear, inadequate representation of stakeholder interests, lack of effectiveness |
| **Level of Analysis** | • Local and national actors as foci to perform work of GHG with global and national duties and institutions as guides | • Top-down, country-driven efforts and reforms moderately successful (e.g. PRSP); specific countries and local-level collaboration programs highly successful (e.g., smallpox, OCP, etc.) |

engagement in cooperation around core functions and needs. While liberalism and neoliberalism may allow space for principled beliefs, global health equity is not necessarily one of them; these beliefs have tended toward classic liberal values such as international peace, open trade, and democracy.[45]

Realist, neorealist, liberal, and neoliberal regime theoretical frameworks clearly fall short in the value they assign to global health equity. History

---

[45] D. Green, "Liberal Imperialism as Global-Governance Perspective," in *Contending Perspectives on Global Governance*, ed. Ba and Hoffmann.

suggests that cooperation in these approaches does not always yield good or positive outcomes, to say nothing of failing to promote health justice.[46] Actors and their partners benefit from cooperation on self-interested projects, but harm to others can result. Cooperating on non-self-interested projects can work in many contexts, if national and international actors genuinely commit to global cooperation. GHG must be restructured to support and implement these goals more effectively.

### 6.3.4 Determining Responsibilities: Functions and Needs

Functions and needs determine SHG's allocations of responsibilities. Functions are both technical (providing information on outbreak surveillance, for example) and political. Given its authority and powers, the state is best situated to develop and sustain just and functional health systems. The state can serve as a structure for both self-determination and collective action in health. The support and legitimacy of local and national health systems are essential to meeting health needs and health agency needs, in part because of the immediate and local nature of those needs. No legitimate body exists to perform the sovereign state's central functions in revenue raising, redistribution, policy legislation, and implementation on a global scale. But on the national level, individuals cede the state some resources and autonomy to pursue common goals.

SHG thus comports with aspects of the functionalist school in international relations,[47] which locates authority with functions rather than territory[48] (though with a complementary notion of supraterritorial authority). However, unlike functionalism, SHG sees the state as the lead actor in realizing the health capability paradigm. The state serves a key function in meeting health justice objectives, but supranational and subnational entities with specific functions tied to particular needs also have important roles to play in global health policy.

In the 2003 severe acute respiratory syndrome (SARS) outbreak, for example, WHO coordinated scientific and medical entities in numerous countries for different components of the response. Research centers, NGOs, and epidemiology programs from Australia, Thailand, and France, among others, collaborated on field investigations. Research institutes in high-research-capacity

---

[46] The WTO Agreement on TRIPS, for example, represented cooperation between WTO member states that also had the effect of limiting access to essential medicines in some developing nations, thus harming many individuals in need. See Cecilia Oh, "TRIPS and Pharmaceuticals: A Case of Corporate Profits over Public Health," *Third World Network* (August/September 2000). Available at: http://www.twn.my/title/twr120a.htm (accessed December 12, 2017).

[47] D. Mitrany, *The Functional Theory of Politics* (New York: St. Martin's Press, 1975).

[48] J. A. Scholte, *Globalization: A Critical Introduction* (New York: Palgrave, 2000).

countries including Canada, China, France, Germany, Hong Kong, Japan, Netherlands, Singapore, the United Kingdom, and the United States collaborated on laboratory identification of the SARS virus.[49] Hospitals in China, Canada, Singapore, Slovenia, and Ireland worked together on clinical response. As in this response, SHG allocates duties and obligations to global, state, local, and individual actors based on functional ability and a balanced understanding of the components needed to solve global health problems.

Both functional and legitimacy considerations give states primary responsibility. The scope of national obligations then defines global obligations, so these global duties do not impinge on states' rights to govern themselves. In privileging the state, through which voting citizens can shape their own affairs, this model respects both individual and collective health agency and self-determination. While some states demonstrably fail to allow agency and self-determination, the state remains the world's principal means of effective self-government.

In specifying global duties, however, SHG differs from realist and neorealist foreign policy objectives, which tend, even in global health, to give way to geopolitical and economic interests when states are the only relevant actors, acting on their own behalf. Liberal and neoliberal frameworks also give states responsibility; states create and maintain structures to reduce the costs of cooperation and joint action, providing information and enhancing transparency among states.[50] But since states influence institutions, the balance of power among states is an important input, and stronger states can dominate. Transnationalism gives a greater role to global civil society organizations (CSOs) and transnational corporations (TNCs). Constructivism permits nonstate actors to serve as norm entrepreneurs or form transnational advocacy networks to work toward norm convergence; however, the state-based international system still sets boundaries around these actors' influence.[51]

SHG envisions a better alignment between global and domestic health objectives through a GHC and a GIHM.

SHG also resolves the diffusion of responsibility whereby even though conditions such as global health inequities require moral action, no group takes a leadership role and individual and collective accountability evaporates. PG creates a collective duty to reduce inequities and an imperative to determine responsibilities for cooperation and coordination. In GHG's current

[49] WHO, "The Operational Response to SARS", "*WHO*, April 16, 2003; WHO, "Update 31: Coronavirus Never before Seen in Humans is the Cause of SARS," *WHO*, April 16, 2003. Available at: http://www.who.int/csr/sarsarchive/2003_04_16/en/ (accessed January 11, 2018).

[50] R. O. Keohane and L. L. Martin, "The Promise of Institutionalist Theory," *International Security* 20, no. 1 (1995): 39–51.

[51] M. Finnemore and K. Sikkink, "International Norm Dynamics and Political Change," *International Organization* 52, no. 4 (1998): 887–917.

pluralism and fragmentation, as more actors enter the global health space and the distance between various actions and consequences increases, moral responsibilities are unclear, moral agency is attenuated, and moral action by any individual or group is increasingly suppressed. The disorganization of current global health actors also blurs links between actor and action and thus thwarts evaluation and moral criticism of actors. A lack of centralized information also hinders evaluating the outcomes of any individual or group as they attend to their own fragmented segment. Failure to act collectively often results in invisible suffering, enabling the diffusion of responsibility. Moreover, even well-intentioned efforts to fill the void of moral action—ad hoc donations to charity for programs around specific diseases, for example— underestimate the gravity of health inequity and the solutions required to realize global health justice. Indeed, such efforts can actually undercut the imperative for collective action. In the absence of responsibility allocation, no one is truly responsible. SHG employs transparently collected data to evaluate the respective contributions of all actors.

## 6.3.5 Inequity Aversion

Just as prosocial behavior by groups and individuals facilitates cooperation, anti-social behavior—unfairness, inequities, a lack of trust, selfish attitudes and behaviors, and short-term self-interest maximization—undermines it. Experiment after experiment has found negative reactions to unequal outcomes in games that violate proportionality in effort and gain and treat joint contributions to a particular undertaking inequitably.[52,53] Negative reactions include emotional responses (for example, anger and moral disgust), rejection of outcomes, and refusal to cooperate, as shown in ultimatum game and impunity game experiments in many countries.[54,55] Humans have evolved with a sense of justice and fairness, which facilitates cooperation, social reciprocity, conflict resolution, and shared endeavors. Research suggests that aversion to inequity is widespread in cooperative species under many conditions (including refusing immediately advantageous outcomes) and that it has evolutionary benefits. Humans experience both "first-order inequity aversion" (rejecting unfavorable unequal outcomes so as not to be taken

---

[52] Brosnan and de Waal, "Evolution of Responses to (Un)fairness."

[53] E. Fehr and K. M. Schmidt, "A Theory of Fairness, Competition, and Cooperation," *Quarterly Journal of Economics* 114, no. 3 (1999): 817–68.

[54] J. Henrich, R. Boyd, S. Boyles, C. Camerer, E. Fehr, and H. Gintis, eds., *Foundations of Human Sociality: Economic Experiments and Ethnographic Evidence from Fifteen Small Scale Societies* (Oxford: Oxford University Press, 2004).

[55] T. Yamagishi, Y. Horita, H. Takagishi, M. Shinada, S. Tanida, and K. S. Cook, "The Private Rejection of Unfair Offers and Emotional Commitment," *Proceedings of the National Academy of Sciences of the United States of America* 106, no. 28 (May 15, 2009): 11520–3.

advantage of) and "second-order inequity aversion" (rejecting favorable unequal outcomes).[56] Indeed, demonstrating second-order inequity aversion can help obviate first-order inequity aversion, by developing a cooperative reputation and equalizing outcomes.[57] "The pressure for increased cooperation combined with advanced cognitive abilities and emotional control," Brosnan and de Waal observe, "allowed humans to evolve a complete sense of fairness."[58]

A central feature of this sense of fairness is the moral norm of impartiality. Outcomes are judged against a standard which applies to all individuals, not a partial or chosen few. While humans differ by culture and circumstance, their common humanity provides the basis for core standards and ideals. Neither the current GHG scheme overall nor its major actors are impartial. Its constitutional outlines favor wealthy and influential actors, and it fails to equalize conditions for all. In this self-interest-maximizing model, individuals and actors with power are overcompensated, and few trust their motivations. The system lacks legitimacy, fair exercise of authority, and balanced decision-making. People do not trust WHO, because powerful leaders have coopted it. People have lost faith in the thirty-plus international health and human rights treaties and conventions, which have not accomplished their purpose. Today's GHG has failed to address unconscionable health inequities and gross imbalances in decision-making power.

GHG needs impartial institutions that engender trust and legitimacy, embedding shared values and agreed-upon policies and practices. Only this kind of institution can inspire acceptance and adherence. SHG's GHC and the GIHM are such institutions.

The GHC process can eliminate the undue influence of powerful countries, corporations, and NGOs by delineating relations among multiple actors. Informed by authoritative standards, the GHC would specify responsibilities to share global health burdens equitably. Equity will be a central focus of the GIHM: as an independent entity separated from politics, the GIHM would be able to give the objective scientific advice so desperately needed to implement more cost-effective global health policies and enhance equity.

These institutions and their shared mandate will tap deeply into the sense of fairness and justice that empirical research has confirmed in people around the world, across time and cultures. And because in their impartiality and reliability they inspire trust and confidence, they will motivate ownership among all actors and a commitment to the common good they embody.

---

[56] Brosnan and de Waal, "Evolution of Responses to (Un)fairness."

[57] D. Semmann, H.-J. Krambeck, and M. Milinski, "Strategic Investment in Reputation," *Behavioral Ecology and Sociobiology* 56, no. 3 (2004): 248–52.

[58] Brosnan and de Waal, "Evolution of Responses to (Un)fairness," 1251776-1.

### 6.3.6 Building Social Motivation in Global Health

Research demonstrates that social motivation is built in five key areas: attitudes, values, motive-based trust, identity, and procedural justice.[59] Attitudes are internal inclinations, beliefs, and feelings. Empirical studies suggest attitudes shape people's behavior and their willingness to cooperate as much as if not more than narrow self interest alone. In global and domestic health, people need to have positive feelings and beliefs about promoting their own health and the health of others and the institutions and groups tasked with these responsibilities. If this motivation is intrinsic, fulfilling, and rewarded, it will influence behavior even absent external incentives or punishment, reducing the need for external motivation measures.[60] Commitment and positive emotion associated with a group, institution, or organization and its activities increases one's motivation toward certain behaviors. When one derives satisfaction or meaning from working with others in one's community, country, or beyond, then such internal motivations can foster health promotion and disease prevention behaviors. Positive attitudes toward an institution such as a GHC would motivate people to act for the principles and goals of that institution and feel personally fulfilled when it succeeds.

Values, especially ethics, are another key feature of social motivation and behavior. Research on social motivation and cooperation has identified two sets of values that are particularly important: legitimacy and moral values. Legitimacy in this literature is defined as "the property that a rule or an authority has when others feel obligated to voluntarily defer to that rule or authority.... [A] legitimate authority is one that is regarded by people as entitled to have its decision and rules accepted and followed by others."[61] A legitimate institution instills in people a sense that it, rather than their own narrow self interest, is entitled to determine right behavior. A GHC could have this kind of standing. Existing groups, organizations, and institutions in global health lack legitimacy; they exercise their authority for the gain of particular individuals, groups, and nations, and people do not feel obligated to obey their decisions or directives. A GHC, by contrast, would serve to benefit all. Its authority would flow from this universal commitment. Such legitimacy necessarily precedes cooperation and compliance. One approach to motivating people to cooperate with the GHC would be to tap into their

---

[59] Tyler, *Why People Cooperate*.

[60] E. L. Deci and R. M. Ryan, "The Empirical Exploration of Intrinsic Motivational Processes," *Advances in Experimental Social Psychology* 13 (1980): 39–80.

[61] W. Skogan and K. Frydl, eds., *Fairness and Effectiveness in Policing: The Evidence* (Washington, DC: National Academies Press, 2004), 297, citing R. M. Merelman, "Learning and Legitimacy," *American Political Science Review* 60 (1966): 548–61.

ethical values about legitimacy and the obligation to cooperate. The GHC also must embed fair procedures to further enhance its legitimacy.

Research has also demonstrated that people are more likely to cooperate with organizations whose moral values are consistent with their own—a concept known as moral value congruence.[62] People act in accordance with their own values and are motivated to support institutions with similar moral principles. Motivating people to cooperate thus involves institutionalizing their values. Such values are self-regulatory. In the international context there are individuals' values and the values of states. As noted, inequity aversion is a moral value that humans share. A GHC would clearly articulate moral standards for global health. People will conform their conduct to a GHC's code of conduct if it accords with their own values. Current GHG violates people's moral values about health and justice. Global citizens cannot accept a system in which so many organizations spend so much money and yet so many people are left deeply deprived and destitute. The 2014 Ebola and 2016 Zika epidemics are cases in point: while the initial outbreaks might have been difficult to predict, policies consistent with a PG/SHG perspective could have prevented much of the suffering and loss of life that followed. The reaction to the epidemics was widespread skepticism about global and domestic institutions and effectiveness.

But why embrace the conception of global health set out in PG and the health capability paradigm? First, this framework's moral principles are consistent with what empirical research shows is important to people and to states—health and social guarantees of population health protection and promotion. These commitments to individual and population health, widespread across time and cultures, have strong empirical validity and reliability. This conception reflects a transpositionally objective perspective.

PG/SHG and institutions such as a GHC also provide a fertile understanding of health equity that can ground the construction and effectuation of global health justice and governance. This second reason relates to John Rawls' reflective equilibrium methodology: any candidate conception must demonstrate that it supports plausible decisions and policies.[63] Are the policies this conception supports reasonable? The provisions of PG and SHG are more comprehensive, socially rational, and compelling than current arrangements. The competing theoretical approaches, whether social contractarian, utilitarian, brute luck egalitarian, neoliberal, or others, fail to address many of the difficult dilemmas that global health presents. PG supports reasonable proposals, which would move our world a long way toward a more just global society.

---

[62] E. A. Amos and B. L. Weathington, "An Analysis of the Relation between Employee-Organization Value Congruence and Employee Attitudes," *Journal of Psychology: Interdisciplinary and Applied* 142, no. 6 (2008): 615–31.

[63] J. Rawls, *A Theory of Justice* (Cambridge, MA: Harvard University Press, 1971).

Finally, motive-based trust fosters cooperation. Research demonstrates that people are more likely to cooperate with trustworthy institutions and people, whose motivations are benign and concerned with the well-being of others.[64] Genuine trust depends on a person or institution's character and competence. Societal institutions and authorities are supposed to act as agents of society; failing to do so undermines trust and confidence. This loss of trust afflicts global health, whose institutions often demonstrably fail to help the people they are meant to serve. Nor do people believe that group decision-making about global health policies and practices reflects justice norms. An erosion of confidence in and willingness to cooperate with such institutions inevitably results. People want to be treated fairly based on justice principles, not just instrumental concerns of material gains and losses, even if the latter produces outcomes more favorable to themselves. Social motivations lead to benefits for all because they rest on the connections and commonalities we all share.

### 6.3.7 Greater Coherence and Clarity in Global Health

These new institutions provide an explicit, coherent system to reduce inefficiencies, especially duplication and waste, in an approach involving comprehensive national obligations and normative guidance of individuals. Since the GIHM will do much of the work in analyzing and formulating policy and the GHC delineates responsibility for implementation, international organizations—multilateral institutions or NGOs—will be less prone to manipulation by powerful states and distortion by their own bureaucratic interests. The PG framework, with a constitution and an unimpeachable scientific body, can construct a new global health enterprise and promote the common good.

## 6.4 Legitimacy and Accountability in SHG

### 6.4.1 Legitimacy

Is a global health system based on PG and SHG the best route to creating a global health enterprise? How does the PG/SHG framework address the question of international legitimacy? In numerous views, understanding and assessing legitimacy focuses predominantly on domestic institutions. These include national governments, whose right to rule encompasses moral reasons for obeying rules and laws coupled with powers of coercion and enforcement to compel compliance. One major concept of legitimacy is consent-based social contract theories in which populations consent to the rules and actions

---

[64] R. M. Kramer and T. R. Tyler, *Trust in Organizations: Frontiers of Theory and Research* (Thousand Oaks, CA: Sage Publications, Inc., 1996).

of political institutions that derive their political authority from that consent. Other sources of legitimacy are public reason and public participation in the development of laws and rules affecting the public, proceduralist or process focused. Associative obligations, for example among fellow citizens, also ground legitimacy and political authority.

Other concepts of legitimacy rest on notions of fair play—the idea that one must contribute one's fair share to the collective enterprise to provide collective goods—and of duties of beneficence and justice—that we discharge our duty to help others by supporting institutions that serve this purpose. So multiple sources of domestic legitimacy and political authority exist, but whether these sources pertain to international relations is unclear.

In the absence of world government, global political authority, in the sense of issuing laws and claiming compliance, does not exist. While international and multilateral institutions do issue rules and claim authority for them, they lack coercive power and cannot assert the same authority as domestic institutions.[65] Thus even though international institutions such as World Bank, International Monetary Fund (IMF), UN, WHO, and other multilateral and international institutions do create international laws and policies, they lack the political authority of national governments. What then is the basis for global institutions asserting legitimate authority? Can global institutions even claim legitimacy? And what do we make of powerful states that can shape and constrain policy options bilaterally and multilaterally through global institutions, thus controlling citizens of other states, often at the expense of domestic democratic control?

SHG reconceptualizes legitimacy—political authority for global health institutions—along multiple lines, incorporating a general duty to protect and promote health equity; cooperation and coordination to address global health issues fairly; an equitable distribution and acceptance of responsibility for particular functions to achieve global health equity; participation; and the duty to support and hold global health institutions accountable for effectiveness and efficiency in achieving global health equity. These ideas, working synergistically, provide sources of legitimacy for global health institutions' normative authority. SHG grounds legitimacy in an appeal to public reason, goals, and objectives. It derives from acceptance of and adherence to rules and norms, and effectiveness and efficiency in achieving global health equity. Legitimacy is also based on accountability, independent review of performance and outcomes, and empirical evidence of effectiveness, efficiency, and accountability.

In the current global landscape, international instruments' legitimacy rests on state consent—that is, ratification—of international agreements. Under

---

[65] A. Buchanan and R. O. Keohane, "The Legitimacy of Global Governance Institutions," *Ethics & International Affairs* 20, no. 4 (2006): 405–37.

realism and neorealism, international legitimacy is irrelevant in a system based on power and self-interest, though state sovereignty is an exception. Liberals and neoliberals base legitimacy on consent, or voluntary membership and participation; legitimacy also rests on goals—for example, mutual gain or international peace. Procedural legitimacy comes from adherence to institutional rules and reciprocity among members. Regime theorists also base legitimacy on consent, voluntary membership, and participation, as well as goals. For transnationalists, legitimacy rests on persuasion and justificatory discourse; it is based on expertise, output, and possibly procedures for issue-specific networks. Legitimacy can also derive from actors giving voice to global civil society. Constructivism bases legitimacy on what is appropriate or valid, or justificatory discourse. The English School bases it on accepted rules, norms, and conceptions of propriety. Legitimacy is not specified under the world government framework; it might rest on output or effectiveness and/or on justificatory discourse.[66]

The state-centered consent model asserts that state consent or the consent of well-ordered peoples confers international legitimacy. This concept derives from the social contract idea of consent but rises to the international level, where states and their governments' consent provide the normative authority and legitimacy for global rules and agreements. But Buchanan and Keohane criticize standards of legitimacy they call "state consent, consent by democratic states, and global democracy."[67] In their view neither peoples' nor states' consent is necessary or sufficient to provide the basis for global political authority and legitimacy. Rather, protection of individual rights by institutions claiming normative authority and legitimacy are the focus. They propose a six-part standard for legitimacy in global governance institutions. These legitimacy requirements are minimalist, upholding basic human rights and the rule of law in a minimally democratic environment. Buchanan and Keohane decline, however, to set a "principled specification of the division of institutional labor for pursuing global justice."[68] Their notion of "minimal moral acceptability" sees global governance institutions as legitimate if they do not violate uncontroversial human rights, even if they fail to promote them.[69]

This minimal moral responsibility is insufficient in the PG/SHG approach. Institutions that fail to promote human rights cannot claim normative global authority and legitimacy. Disagreement and uncertainty are no excuse for dithering in the face of unacceptable health consequences, ineffectiveness, and inefficiency. We must not fail to act; addressing health inequalities and

---

[66] K. D. Wolf, "The New Raison d'État as a Problem for Democracy in World Society," *European Journal of International Relations* 5, no. 3 (1999): 333–63.

[67] Buchanan and Keohane, "The Legitimacy of Global Governance Institutions," 412.

[68] Ibid., 418.

[69] Ibid., 419.

threats is a moral imperative. Incomplete theorization and partial agreements can provide greater clarity, even incrementally, amid wide disagreement. The PG and SHG framework lays the foundation for legitimacy assessment. It addresses a gap in normative theories of political authority in global health and contrasts sharply with a rational actor approach based in the realist and neorealist literature on international relations, in which narrow national and self interests prevail. Evaluating global health institutions through a PG/SHG lens demonstrates that rational actor institutions lack full legitimacy.

Ad hoc assessments of particular institutions' legitimacy are certainly helpful. But global health's diffused authority and proliferating actors require an overall assessment of the global health system's legitimacy and the roles and responsibilities of various players. An assessment of WHO's legitimacy, for example, will vary depending on the context in which it is viewed, whether within the global health institutions regime (including Global Fund, World Bank, Gates Foundation, and others), under a global standard of health justice, or in isolation without system-wide global health benchmarks. Viewed narrowly, WHO appears to lack legitimacy and effectiveness, but a more comprehensive perspective might recognize that we have placed unrealistic expectations on this organization, especially in an increasingly fragmented health landscape.

In SHG, global health institutions are necessary both to solve global coordination and cooperation problems unsolvable at the state level, and to assert global values of justice, equality, and fairness. Establishing legitimacy begins with an appeal to public reason about global health goals and objectives based on justice principles. Without this prerequisite step and a degree of agreement, global health has no benchmark against which to measure the performance of institutions and actors. Is this global health system valid? What criteria justify it? How accountable is it?

International norms and laws can provide some standards of legitimacy—the UN Charter, the World Bank's Articles of Agreement, and WHO's Constitution, for example. Many cases, however, require new, broader standards. The PG/SHG framework addresses this need, identifying and clarifying standards of global health responsibility and accountability in the GHC, with its specifications of principles for global health policy and governance, general and specific duties, roles, and obligations. The GHC can also provide epistemic reliability for the global health community, laying out the coordination and cooperation functions of different global and domestic actors and institutions. WHO's purpose, like those of the UN and the World Bank, has evolved over the years; it can no longer "act as the directing and co-ordinating authority on international health work."[70] Ultimately, we must ask: Whose interests does

---

[70] Constitution of the World Health Organization, Chapter II, Article 2.

the global health system serve? Do those interests justify the use and delegation of power and authority in the system?

Global health requires global governance, and thus needs different standards of legitimacy than national health structures. Does the global health
system respect self-determination, self-governance, and voluntary participation by states and non-state actors in GHG? Does it effectively achieve shared
goals and cost-effectiveness in the quest for global health equity? Is it accountable to those whom it is meant to serve? The headlong rush into more new
NGOs and multilateral institutions expresses, at least in part, a loss of faith in
core international health organizations (WHO, UNICEF, World Bank, and
Joint United Nations Program on HIV/AIDS). These organizations proved
sluggish and insufficiently responsive to new global health challenges and
new collaboration possibilities and thus undercut their own effectiveness and
efficiency.[71] Often they have also failed to police themselves well: allegations
of Global Fund corruption threaten its legitimacy and long-term stability.[72]

The system's legitimacy will derive further from independent, external
review and the evidence it produces about effectiveness, efficiency, and
accountability. Mutual collective accountability (MCA) will measure accountability by key indicators. These indicators together also help address problems.
Issues might arise from differences in measurement or missing information;
the World Bank and WHO, for example, measure impact by different indicators, and transparency can be a problem with other actors. A Global Fund
grant's impact, for example, depends for success on the Ministry of Health and
partner donors, so joint assessment illuminates these evaluations. Finally, by
stressing goal alignment, MCA and independent review help clarify roles and
responsibilities, overarching objectives, and duty allocation for achieving
health goals.

Domestically, legitimacy derives from a normative framework at the domestic level, such as the health capability paradigm, government legislation,
regulations, and laws (universal health insurance, for example). De jure
authority, moral power, or the normative political authority to claim obedi-
ence to laws and rules is necessary. States have de facto authority to issue rules
and expect compliance because as sovereign states they have the necessary
political power. Moral support for states' laws and rules justifies or legitimizes
domestic institutions. The health capability paradigm and SHG line of reasoning proposes multiple principles grounding normative authority domestically.
Domestic institutions are necessary to exemplify justice, fairness, and equality

[71] K. Buse and G. Walt, "Global Public–Private Partnerships: Part I—A New Development in
Health?" *Bulletin of the World Health Organization* 78, no. 4 (2000): 549–61.

[72] V. Hausman, P. Yadav, D. Ballou-Aares, and B. Herbert, "Global Fund: Reform Needed to
Regain Credibility," *Financial Times*, November 30, 2011.

and to solve national coordination and cooperation problems through collective action. These problems are beyond the free market to solve on its own and require public sector collective action grounded in both de jure and de facto authority. New modes of governance and a new conceptualization of institutions' legitimacy are necessary at the domestic level as well as the global one. International health law (International Health Regulations (IHR), for example) can also help assess domestic health regulation and laws.

Under international law more generally, states have the right of self-determination and freedom from intervention. They also have the ability to make treaties and thus to exercise authority in the international community. Realists typically acknowledge this external legitimacy by recognizing control of territory; territorial control confers sovereignty upon that state. Despite this generally accepted view of international relations, the normative basis for domestic legitimacy and policies is open to scrutiny. In the PG/SHG framework, states must meet agreed-upon standards of justice, and such standards guide global health policy. This justice-based account stipulates the expected health justice threshold in each state. It has ramifications both for achieving a global consensus on public moral norms and creating a more just world.

### 6.4.2 *Mutual Collective Accountability*

Two forms of accountability—democratic and legal—stand out in the literature. Grant and Keohane structure the discussion differently and identify "'participation' and 'delegation' models of accountability" in world politics.[73] For them, accountability implies "that some actors have the right to hold other actors to a set of standards, to judge whether they have fulfilled their responsibilities in light of these standards, and to impose sanctions if they determine that these responsibilities have not been met."[74] They argue that democratic states and multilateral organizations are "the only types of organization in world politics consistently subjected to delegated as well as participatory accountability," and that multilateral organizations are "in general more accountable than NGOs, firms, transgovernmental networks, and non-democratic states—not less accountable."[75] But in health, the line between delegation and participation is often unclear, because officials entrusted with powers (a developing country's health minister, for example) are often both "instrumental agents of the public" and "authorities with discretion."[76]

---

[73] R. W. Grant and R. O. Keohane, "Accountability and Abuses of Power in World Politics," *American Political Science Review* 99, no. 1 (2005): 29.
[74] Ibid.
[75] Ibid., 40.
[76] Ibid., 31.

Further, "[a]ccountability mechanisms . . . always operate after the fact: exposing actions to view, judging and sanctioning them."[77]

MCA is a third approach. Under MCA, both democratically accountable states and unaccountable and undemocratic global health institutions (World Bank and Global Fund, for example), would fall under accountability standards that stretch across the global health enterprise, holding all actors to joint requirements. SHG incorporates MCA as an appropriate framework in a multilevel and multi-actor enterprise with shared responsibility for global health problems.

Under MCA, all actors working on a health issue identify common goals and assign responsibilities for achieving them. Without this prerequisite, holding actors to any objectives is difficult and arguably unreasonable. It is especially important in global health to address issues of attribution as different from contribution. If attribution is impossible or difficult to separate from contribution, then ex post evaluation and sanctions for subpar execution will be impossible or difficult at best and may be open to criticism, ultimately undermining the accountability framework. In global health activities in which multiple actors are working on the same problem, empirically teasing out the separate attribution of any given actor (for example, World Bank) can be problematic.

MCA extends both within and across institutions. For example, a World Bank health economist is accountable to the World Bank for fulfilling her duties; the health economist and the World Bank are accountable to, for example, the Global Fund for accomplishing goals and adhering to agreed-upon standards and procedures.

The initiative among Southern Cone countries to control the spreading insect vector for Chagas disease is a good MCA example. Each country's effort depends for success on that of its neighbor; the shared responsibility that bordering countries acknowledged urged them forward in their own campaigns.[78] The US Institute of Medicine (IOM), among others, is now calling for shared responsibility to address HIV/AIDS in Africa.[79]

MCA thus ties ex ante (not just the ex ante threat of a sanction, but ex ante standard setting) and ex post assessments more closely together. It emphasizes ex ante measures particularly, given governance systems today and a future in which decreasing numbers of formal sanctioning instruments may be available. Explicit joint commitments push actors to fulfill their obligations and conform to standards of conduct. Accomplishing these objectives will support better health policy decisions and more effective and efficient use of resources.

---

[77] Ibid., 30.
[78] Levine et al., *Millions Saved*.
[79] T. C. Quinn and D. Serwadda, "The Future of HIV/AIDS in Africa: A Shared Responsibility," *The Lancet* 377, no. 9772 (2011): 1133–4.

Agreeing on the means of assessing joint work is fundamental to MCA. Agreement on desired outcomes and principle indicators for their evaluation is essential. Global, national, and subnational actors, especially key vulnerable groups most affected by policy decisions, must all participate. These principles are effective. Successful HIV/AIDS efforts, for example, have incorporated "broad social mobilisation, accompanied by clear deliverables."[80] In Senegal, the government and medical experts together set up an HIV/AIDS program; the prevention campaign involved civil society and targeted marginalized groups such as sex workers and migrants for education. The result is a low and stable HIV infection rate compared to other West African countries.[81]

Wise resource use is another key MCA component. Organizations must account for financial resources and submit to audit. Global health assistance must be organized efficiently. Better accountability for resources means that more resources are available to achieve goals.

As deployed in SHG, MCA distributes power and accountability according to a delineation of duties, for example through the GHC. With no world health government and no global democratic and legal accountability, MCA—applying checks and balances, peer review, and systematic assessment of performance—is important to this global health theory.

At the state level, democratic and legal accountability do exist, both through government and courts and through global governance. The citizens of a given country can and should share in governance; they can and should exercise their rightful agency in global health policy-making, whether through direct representation at the country level or indirectly through national representation at the global level. The Framework Convention on Tobacco Control (FCTC), the first binding treaty under WHO, illustrates this participatory governance.

Accountability under realism and neorealism, by contrast, is limited and inequitable. States answer only to themselves, and powerful states answer virtually to no one. States pursue their own interests through diplomacy, threats, and use of force. Weak states, on the other hand, must constantly answer to powerful nations. Neither state- nor civil-society-based accountability alone is adequate for a workable global health theory. Liberalism and neoliberalism provide for cooperation and adherence through institutions and rules of conduct, but, absent world government and a world court, no real mechanism exists for authoritative interpretation when states fail to fulfill their duties.

[80] D. Moran, "HIV/AIDS, Governance and Development: The Public Administration Factor," *Public Administration and Development* 24, no. 1 (2004): 13.

[81] N. Meda, I. Ndoye, S. M'Boup, A. Wade, S. Ndiaye, C. Niang, et al., "Low and Stable HIV Infection Rates in Senegal: Natural Course of the Epidemic or Evidence for Success of Prevention?" *AIDS* 13, no. 11 (1999): 1397–405.

International institutions often privilege those who set the rules because of their economic or political strength. For example, despite WHO's strong multilateral Constitution and orientation, its democratic decision-making body, the WHA, essentially has little or no voice in specific programs supported by donor states with extra-budgetary funding; roughly 75 percent of WHO funding falls into this non-democratic extra-budgetary category. The neoliberal institutionalist approach lacks a common ethos.

Nor do transnationalists (for example, transgovernmental networks) or constructivists grapple adequately with accountability. In transnationalism, global civil society and TNCs apply pressure for or against particular institutions, policies, or practices (the World Trade Organization (WTO), for example, or dams in developing countries). But the accountability of CSOs—how and to whom they are accountable—is not always clear. Constructivists seek through persuasion to shape states' interests, but they propose no specific measures such as checks and balances, world government, balance of power, or institutional rules.[82]

The hybrid PG/SHG governance-cum-government system may seem unwieldy, but for ethical and empirical reasons the global health architecture must integrate governance at the global, national, and subnational levels with national and subnational governments. Of necessity, the system assesses the five major criteria—legitimacy, effectiveness, efficiency, equity, and accountability—differently for governance and government. Current global health law looks to standardized procedures to increase accountability, on the view that deviations can be easily identified. But the accountability of parties depends on specifics of the international law in question.

What happens when actors fail to perform? In the realist view, states are accountable to themselves, and powerful states are not accountable to others; powerful states could, however, hold weaker states accountable through pressure or coercion. Under liberalism, institutions have rules that states are expected to follow, but might not always have a mechanism for authoritative interpretation when states disagree. States may be accountable to each other through peer pressure or decentralized enforcement. In regime theory, too, regimes have rules members are expected to obey, and members may be accountable to each other through peer pressure or decentralized enforcement.[83] Under transnationalism, the accountability of global civil society actors is unclear. TNCs are accountable to shareholders; state components answer to the state but may also develop allegiances to their networks. Constructivism does not specify a means of accountability. States may feel

---

[82] Hoffmann, "What's Global about Global Governance?"

[83] A.-M. Slaughter, "The Accountability of Government Networks," *Indiana Journal of Global Legal Studies* 8, no. 2 (2001): 347–67.

some kind of social responsibility to other states with which they cooperate, but this obligation would depend on what states make of anarchy; it could differ depending on the results of socialization, because, for example, it is possible to be socialized into being realists. Neither does the English School specify accountability. States may feel some kind of social accountability to other states based on accepted assumptions and norms of propriety, and great powers may hold secondary states to account. Accountability under world government is not clear and would depend on the form the world government takes.

SHG, by contrast, uses MCA based on a clear assignment of duties through shared goals and prior agreement on measurements for evaluation.

### 6.4.2.1 MUTUAL COLLECTIVE ACCOUNTABILITY IN SHG: EVIDENCE FROM MALAWI

The SHG framework necessitates reliable mechanisms to ensure that actors fulfill their duties. Unlike the competing interests and contrasting goals of the rational actor model, SHG entails agreement among different actors on values and goals. The framework expects accountability for resource use, implementation, and results, and the means to guarantee it. Global health policy must also specify health agency-enhancing processes. Individuals and groups have a moral claim to be the agents of their own health. Because primary responsibilities rest with the state, accountability mechanisms start there.

Carefully selected indicators can assess these elements empirically. These indicators include: (1) goal alignment; (2) adequacy of human and financial resources; (3) mutual understanding of key outcomes and the pertinent data and indicators measuring those outcomes; (4) constructive engagement of relevant global, national, and subnational groups and institutions; (5) genuine efforts to involve groups that policy decisions affect (for example, the poor, women, youth, persons with disabilities, and the elderly); and (6) effectiveness and efficiency. Research that examined the Malawi Poverty Reduction Strategy Papers (PRSP) process through the SHG lens in 2007 used a survey focused on these indicators. (Chapter 9 discusses quantitative research examining the effectiveness of a World Bank-sponsored maternal and child health project in Indonesia.)

The IMF and the World Bank initiated the PRSP process in 1999, recognizing that impoverished countries must claim ownership of development efforts. The intention was a participatory process involving domestic stakeholders and international actors, including donors and global agencies. The PRSP process rested on five key principles: results oriented, focusing on outcomes benefiting the poor; partnership based, engaging and coordinating multiple actors; comprehensive, recognizing the multidimensional nature of poverty; country driven, involving broad-based civil participation and national ownership; and a long-term perspective, seeking sustainable results over time.[84]

These principles accord well with SHG. SHG's MCA supports PRSP's orientation to results and partnerships. The consensus SHG seeks among global, national, and subnational actors on objectives and means is consistent with the five PRSP principles. And SHG's emphasis on health agency enhancement—the participation of affected individuals and groups and the development of health knowledge and skills—accords with the PRSP commitment to broad-based participation, national ownership, and long-term results.

The measures SHG identifies to assess health performance can thus evaluate performance under PRSP principles. The SHG indicators of adequate resource levels and program effectiveness and efficiency can measure PRSP results. SHG's measures of goal alignment and agreement on key outcomes and indicators can assess partnerships, national ownership, and participation under PRSP. And gauging the meaningful inclusion of population groups, especially the vulnerable, can also serve to evaluate how well the PRSP process achieved broad-based participation and national ownership.

In 2000, the IMF and the World Bank connected debt relief for Malawi to the development of a PRSP and progress in combating HIV/AIDS, thus leveraging the PRSP process to improve HIV/AIDS programming in this country. The 2007 study sought to learn if the PRSP process fostered key SHG elements—as measured by selected indicators.

The results were mixed. Survey respondents, who included government and NGO representatives involved in both the PRSP process and its efforts to combat HIV/AIDS, believed that PRSP resulted in greater efficiency and improved accountability for the resources used in the HIV/AIDS response. They believed goal alignment between their agencies and the state's National HIV/AIDS Strategic Framework was good. They praised the president and the formation of the Malawi National AIDS Commission, a widely respected semi-autonomous public trust. They noted a substantial and rapid scale-up in anti-retroviral therapy. But they said resources were insufficient, and information about how to participate effectively in PRSP development was inadequate. Key stakeholders—persons living with HIV/AIDS, rural women, and even parliamentarians—believed the PRSP process excluded them. Many respondents did not think they could actively press for and obtain resources; they did not view the PRSP process as influential in budget allocations. SHG indicators revealed both the accomplishments and the gaps in PRSP performance.

[84] IMF, "Factsheet: Poverty Reduction Strategy in IMF-supported Programs," *IMF*, 14 March 2016. Available at: https://www.imf.org/external/np/exr/facts/prsp.htm (accessed January 11, 2018).

# 6.5 Global Health Constitution[85]

Because there is no world health government with global authority and enforcement powers, a global health system requires multiple actors performing disparate functions to formulate effective global health policy and solve global health problems. Thus, SHG's units of analysis are many: individuals; local, state, and non-state agencies; and global actors and institutions. A GHC—an overarching governance structure to coordinate independent yet interdependent actors—would delineate actors, including national and subnational governments, global and international institutions, and individuals, and define their duties and obligations in general terms. MCA demarcates more specific relations among actors. WHO's SARS response illustrates this kind of coordination; the laboratory network collaborated to sequence the SARS virus DNA in six days and developed diagnostic tests.[86] A GHC would set a global standard for health cooperation that does not simply reflect the interests and goals of wealthier developed nations. Global health justice requires a uniform set of standards to constrain the dominance of powerful states and non-state actors.

A GHC, unlike a treaty,[87] brings individuals and non-state actors into the GHG realm, enabling relations among institutions and people. The GHC can thus reduce or eliminate the influence of rich and powerful countries in its creation, implementation, and enforcement. An international treaty, by contrast, requires both the signatures of participating nations' heads of state and the ratification of signatory nations' domestic law-making bodies to have the force of law within those countries. Within countries a number of obstacles to domestic ratification exist, including powerful private and corporate interests and limited domestic understanding of and support for global health action. Even if ratification occurs there is no guarantee of enforcement at the domestic level. With a GHC, authoritative standards and principles would inform its framework and procedures, its obligations would be clear, and evasive or irresponsible behavior readily identifiable. SHG enables greater global accountability through checks and balances among global actors, peer review, and continual scientific feedback, along with compliance and enforcement at the country level. It does not require ratification through domestic law-making bodies, however, and incompletely theorized agreements on core dimensions of health morality globally and provincially provide stability.

---

[85] This section stems from J. P. Ruger, "A Global Health Constitution for Global Health Governance," *Proceedings of the Annual Meeting (American Society of International Law)* 107 (2013): 267–70, and Ruger, "Global Health Governance as Shared Health Governance."

[86] B. Brett Finlay, R. H. See, and R. C. Brunham, "Rapid Response Research to Emerging Infectious Diseases: Lessons from SARS," *Nature Reviews Microbiology* 2 (2004): 602–7.

[87] L. O. Gostin, "A Framework Convention on Global Health: Health for All, Justice for All," *Journal of the American Medical Association* 307, no. 19 (2012): 2087–92.

The current global system, including WHO, cannot adequately deal with global health's persistent problems. Effective governance demands new solutions and a framework for solving global health problems. A GHC can provide such a framework, offering principles and objectives, specifying functions, establishing checks and balances among global health actors, and integrating global health work. Without such a structure, the global health community will continue flying blind and will suffer the consequences of coerced consensus and corruption. The GHC acts as a self-restraining guide for global decision-making, bypassing the need for direct consent by state representatives and representing the health interests of all global citizens. A process of public discourse focused on humans' health needs further strengthens the GHC with morally justifiable decisions. The Constitution along with other global institutions sets the rules for the global health order's basic institutional structure. The global health architecture must be designed to achieve global health equity. The GHC is needed to obtain foundational justice requirements. Charity alone cannot secure the rights of people to health opportunities.

Constitutions, which need not be legal (that is, not legally enforceable by court action), offer common principles and common ground. They coordinate actors and actions; assign duties and delegate functions; bring coherence, clarity, and legitimacy to formerly chaotic conditions; and generate and limit authority.

They also help establish boundaries between government and governance. In the absence of global government with authority and enforcement powers, solving the world's health problems and shaping effective health policy will require new approaches to coordinate independent yet interdependent actors. A GHC can provide such a structure.

A GHC can serve many useful purposes. First, this document sets out underlying moral principles for global health. These principles could serve eventually as a legal framework. By offering moral principles, a constitution can integrate issues into a single set of fundamental standards or codes of conduct to guide behavior. It codifies core values, thus institutionalizing a moral responsibility that all persons have toward each other and that institutions have toward individuals; and creates duties of cooperation for all parties—individuals and larger entities. Its principles are moral and scientific in their basis and ground global health obligations.

Second, these principles and standards can serve as common ground, a unifying reference for state and non-state actors as they devise their own policies and laws to reflect GHG concepts. It can thus bring coherence to negotiations and agreements. Even within states, a GHC can serve this function among different branches of government. PG avers a provincial-global continuum of consensus in which actors voluntarily accept principles and procedures for global health. A GHC embodies a universal consensus on moral norms to foster their implementation and administration worldwide. Today, numerous health treaties, agreements, and institutions lack the support of various states and non-state entities, exacerbating the global health landscape's inconsistencies and chaos.

Third, a GHC brings together diverse and disconnected health principles and norms. International health law and policy are mostly ad hoc, incremental, and disease specific. But the world needs harmonized global norms with universal acceptance. The GHC meets the need for a global framework for the entire field of health, not just specific diseases, conditions, or risk factors (tobacco, for example).

Fourth, unlike a treaty among states, a GHC brings all actors into the fold—states, individuals, multilateral groups, NGOs, and private sector players. The reciprocity and mutual material advantage that motivate treaties mean that these legal instruments cannot support comprehensive shared commitments in health and human flourishing. Various arrangements have widely accepted principles and objectives, but they do not state holistically either general or specific obligations for all actors in a cooperative plan based on shared responsibility. Unlike state-based treaties concerning specific issues, the GHC will benefit all people and the global community as a whole.

Fifth, a GHC, informed by authoritative standards, would identify all actors and their responsibilities in a single document, providing an equitable sharing of burdens to address global health issues.

Sixth, a GHC provides a roadmap for meeting health needs and health agency needs, achieving global health equity through global and national cooperation. By fostering efficiency in governance, a GHC can maximize human and material resources; as a comprehensive and authoritative standard, it can expedite future negotiations and organizations. It would not control or restrict the formation of new organizations or their purposes, but it could provide much-needed coordination and coherence.

Seventh, a GHC can ground multilateral and bilateral negotiations and global and domestic health policy and law, thus minimizing conflict and aiding in its resolution.

Global health equity will not result when independent actors work in silos. Only a unifying governance structure such as a GHC can bring about the global collaboration needed to address health issues. Actions and inactions of global and national entities are interdependent and can be mutually reinforcing. The starting point is a genuine consensus on a global health morality and assignable roles and responsibilities in achieving these moral goals. An overarching instrument such as a GHC incorporates and articulates this consensus. Otherwise politics as usual, and a swirl of competing preferences, interests, and power relations, will continue to thwart the achievement of global health justice.

## 6.6 Global Institute of Health and Medicine

### 6.6.1 *Independent and Unbiased Expertise*

Global health requires a high level of scientific and technical collaboration; authoritative scientific bodies must use technical expertise to provide reliable scientific information and analysis. Rigorous science must undergird any rational plan for global health. WHO does not serve this function, nor does any other bilateral, multilateral, or academic organization on its own or in collaboration. A primary task in GHG is establishing an independent organization that engages internal and external scientists and other experts to provide the substantive, objective, and authoritative scientific basis for global health policy.

A GIHM, akin to the US NAS/IOM at the national level, could perform this core function. But a theory that stresses both health outcomes and health agency needs to ensure individual and collective agency through a joint scientific and deliberative approach, so the GIHM, even as a scientific institution, would give voice to many key stakeholders, not just scientists, in the decision-making process. This deliberative approach, however, must bar political influence and serve instead a true consensus to foster central health capabilities for all. A scientifically rigorous global health policy is necessary to undergird any rational plan for global health.

The GIHM would develop and maintain a network of technical and scientific experts across the globe, thus providing a set of experiments and perspectives from national and subnational level institutions. Expertise in health, medicine, and related disciplines would serve as criteria for selection in the network. A networked approach would also obviate the imposition of a top-down technocracy. GIHM study committees would engage participants, based on expertise and credentials, in particular study areas. A rigorous vetting process would protect the committee appointment process against any financial, professional, or personal conflicts of interest. While WHO has a number of technical working groups that generally advise on various global health topics, they do not exercise this level of scrutiny around conflicts of interest and bias. GIHM committees would give scientific advice to inform strategic programmatic choices for global health.

The GIHM could quickly draw on a network of experts for specific expertise in any given GIHM study. While the United States has a NAS/IOM and a Board on Global Health with the mission of advising the US government and providing valuable scientific expertise on a number of global health issues, their purpose is not to offer specific strategic and programmatic advice for the global health system. It is not the NAS/IOM's primary role to influence international health policy. The GIHM is its global equivalent, designed to offer this same kind of expertise for GHG. The GIHM's role will be advisory: it will not make policy but will provide the scientific evidence essential to crafting sound policy.

As an entity independent of politics, the GIHM would be able to provide the objective advice so desperately needed to develop and implement more equitable and cost-effective global health policies. GIHM policies and procedures ensuring against bias, conflicts of interest, and self-dealing will provide greater credibility and legitimacy to GHG and policy.

The GIHM would put the necessary scientists and technical experts to work on the most pressing issues and the most important global health policies. It would also establish a network of National Academies of Science and scientific institutions in countries around the world, and a web of experts in fields pertinent to global health and various geographic areas.

As an independent organization, the GIHM would also provide advice to WHO and even directly to the WHA as relevant. The GIHM could provide authoritative and independent advice to state and local governments, too, as well as foundations and other private nongovernmental entities, but its focus would be on global health issues. Separating these scientific functions from political ones protects knowledge, science, and their use from politicization. External peer review, which the GIHM would employ, would add an additional layer of scrutiny.

At the moment, the global public has little confidence in the integrity and reliability of current information sources; and academic institutions alone, while more credible, serve the interests of their own constituents. The GIHM would be legitimate and independent, and serve no one person, party, or nation. Rather, it would seek the truth in science through rigorous, objective scientific inquiry. Global health needs an authoritative voice free of political, national, corporate, organizational, and donor interests.

### 6.6.2 *Master Plan for Global Health*

WHO has a vague and unrealistic objective of the "highest possible level of health,"[88] but no master plan or vision for health. Nor does WHO have sufficient concrete plans and procedures for coordinating other actors. The lack of sufficiently specific objectives diminishes accountability at WHO and for other actors, and the capacity to coordinate these actors. In WHO's health objective, the criteria for success shifts depending on the audience—primarily states under the current WHO system. WHO's Constitution does not require WHO to develop a master plan, but global health needs one. The GHC would provide for a master plan and involve other global health actors in developing it to ensure participation. The GIHM would offer specific criteria, outcomes, and measures, and support global health coordination.

---

[88] Constitution of the World Health Organization, Chapter I, Article 1.

A comprehensive global health plan covering both public and private sectors is critical in establishing both global health strategy and action plans. This master plan will follow a comprehensive analysis assessing global health and providing an evidence base for global health programming. Under the GIHM's direction, these analyses will be objective and based on valid and reliable data. Features of a global health plan include key goals, timelines for achieving goals, monitoring, and evaluation.

Developing a global health master plan will be a major task. The plan will make explicit commitments for specific health policies (for example, support for universal health coverage at the national level) to achieve global health equity. These commitments will be evidence based, objective, and explicit. The plan must clearly identify those responsible for objectives based on functional requirements and capabilities. The GIHM will work toward establishing clear guidelines and protocols for all actors in discharging their duties and achieving the plan's goals. Evading responsibilities will not be an option; monitoring and evaluating these actors' performance is part of the global health strategy. Reflecting the commitment to achieve provincial-global consensus on health equity, the global health plan aligns with national health plans in explicitly committing to health equity. Different countries will take varying paths to this objective, but each prioritizes health equity.

With an alternative normative framework in place, and the establishment of a GHC and a GIHM, the role of international and multilateral organizations becomes both more and less substantial. As organizing system components, these new institutions embody an ordered system to reduce inefficiencies, especially duplication and waste. The system's comprehensive national obligations and normative guidance of individuals combine for a global minimalist approach. Again, the polio eradication campaigns illustrate health effort organization on a reduced scale. Regional and national interagency coordinating committees tackled inefficient competition and duplication among multilevel actors, and evidence-based guidance came from a technical advisory group. Additionally, since the GIHM will help analyze and formulate policy and the GHC allocates responsibilities, powerful states will no longer manipulate international organizations, nor will actors' own bureaucratic interests distort their work. Other international regimes, for example in the environment, have similarly argued for new institutional mechanisms and reforms for better global governance.[89,90]

[89] D. C. Esty and M. H. Ivanova, eds., *Global Environmental Governance: Options & Opportunities* (New Haven, CT: Yale School of Forestry and Environmental Studies, 2002).

[90] A. Hurrell and B. Kingsbury, eds.. *The International Politics of the Environment: Actors, Interests, and Institutions* (New York: Oxford University Press, 1992).

This framework offers an explicit system in which a genuine consensus and commitments, clear objectives, and an evidence-based approach constrain the powerful interests that prevent more equitable distribution of the gains from cooperation. Other approaches simply tinker with a broken system, continuing to emphasize cooperation for mutual benefit and absolute gains too often distributed according to power and strategic interests of some, rather than global health equity. The GHG framework, with a constitution and an unimpeachable scientific body, digs deeper to construct a new global health enterprise that benefits all.

## 6.7 Deploying Evidence-Based Standards and Best Practices

SHG provides for states to manage down through conduct of their internal affairs and manage up and across to coordinate global health efforts. The global consensus on standardized national procedures to prevent and control contagions like extensively drug-resistant TB illustrate this management approach. SHG acknowledges the complexities inherent in multiple governance layers and does not rule out international treaties and conventions, but it does stress the central importance of evidence-based standards, guidelines, and best practices in global consensus and governance.

SHG focuses sharply on greater uniformity in addressing health issues—in preventing disease, ensuring health, and eradicating unacceptable health deprivations. But even with common standards, health systems can achieve these goals in different ways. With shared standards, better learning, imaginative and diverse talent, and rigorous effort applied to creating optimal health societies and systems, SHG strives to harmonize the key components of a health society across systems. Still, the system will find different expression in different cultures and communities. For example, a health capability perspective repudiates destructive practices (such as fallacious norms about AIDS and its spread/prevention in Africa), but different countries will apply evidence-based knowledge differently to promote health.

Managing up, down, and across contrasts with liberal and neoliberal approaches, which emphasize contractual mechanisms such as UN Conventions and membership in multilateral bodies. Through these mechanisms states give up some autonomy for mutual benefit. SHG acknowledges the role of explicit consent through international treaties, but it probes more deeply to discover consensus on ethically and empirically justified global health principles. It uses this consensus to shape the public moral norms necessary for an ethical global health system. Through the GIHM and its national counterparts, actors can seek, agree to, and implement evidence-based guidelines and practices. SHG contrasts as well with realism and neorealism, because policy substance, rather than power politics, drives action.

## 6.8 From GHG to SHG: A Dynamic Progression of Development and Change over Time

Transforming GHG can be seen as a dynamic progression, which first requires a larger role for GHG institutions and other actors to serve key functions until states are able to shoulder greater responsibilities. The eventual goal is a global health architecture in which state governments and global health institutions work in synchrony as parts of a multifaceted system, fully capable of meeting current and future health needs and agile in adjusting to changing conditions.

International health governance and GHG as structured today have vacillated from an early realist pursuit of national interest, to the purported human rights/right to health approach of the mid-twentieth century, back to a realist national security orientation today. This progression offers only the appearance of a shift.

Under realism, temporal progression depends on conditions. Hegemonic stability might have a cyclical aspect in that hegemons rise and fall;[91] and the balance of power can change if resource distribution changes or if one state conquers another. Liberalism and neoliberalism do not specify a temporal progression: systems under this approach are not obviously dynamic, though some may envision progress toward greater international respect for liberal values like peace and order. Nor does regime theory, although path dependence—the shaping of future conditions by the influence of prior events—is relevant. Transnationalists do not specify temporal progression, either, although they acknowledge that greater technological connectivity changes the potential for global civil society. Constructivists expect ideas about appropriate values, relevant actors, problems, and solutions to change over time, but not necessarily in a teleological or goal-oriented fashion. The English School does not specify a temporal progression. The world government paradigm aims to achieve a world state and thus envisions progression toward greater mutual recognition among states and greater collective security, from a Hobbesian system of states to a world government.

SHG is dynamic, addressing current and future challenges. Its progressive realization involves three primary stages.

---

[91] G. Arrighi, "Hegemony Unravelling: 1," *New Left Review* 32 (2005): 23–80; G. Arrighi, "Hegemony Unravelling: 2," *New Left Review* 33 (2005): 83–116.

### 6.8.1 *Stage One: Global Health Institutions Play Substantial Roles in Key Functions*

In this initial stage, global health institutions support states as they strive to fulfill specific health duties to ensure their citizens' health capability. When states are unjust or lack capacity to carry out health duties, the global community helps them fulfill their duties and, within the boundaries of those societies' self-determination and self-governance, strives for health equity. The global system provides aid and oversight, but eschews coercion in favor of incentives, persuasion, and other forms of architecture. The financial and technical support required is largely already in place, and the scale up and reallocation needed are acceptable investments. Public opinion supporting global health efforts is high in many domestic and international settings, though public understanding must evolve further. Rectifying asymmetries of affluence and vulnerability is essential.

Where tasks exceed national capacity, global health institutions take responsibility. They can coordinate efforts to limit and prevent externalities like disease outbreaks; support national and local health systems; create and share global public goods, norms, and standards; address cross-border issues; and continue to strengthen consensus on global health goals and actions.

### 6.8.2 *Stage Two: Global Health Institutions' Roles Diminish as States Assume More Functions*

Steps taken in stage one strengthen states for stage two, when they begin to meet their own populations' health needs, reduce health inequities, and address externalities. Their capacity for disease surveillance and control at the domestic level grows. States distribute resources, take responsibility for oversight and regulation, and provide health goods and services, based on a consensus about health. States embrace equity through the political process and internalize it in national health systems. Global health institutions continue to undertake tasks beyond state capabilities, coordinating global efforts to limit and prevent disease outbreaks; bolstering health systems; creating and sharing global public goods, norms, and standards; addressing cross-border issues; and supporting ongoing consensus building on global health priorities and actions.

### 6.8.3 *Stage Three: Achieving Equilibrium*

In this stage, which entails both the process of achieving balance and the accomplished balanced state, sufficiently developed and sophisticated national health systems, in coordination with global health institutions, can respond to external health shocks through internal regulation and adjustment. Assigned global health functions define local health institutions' and actors' specific duties. The system holds global health actors and institutions responsible for effectively and efficiently meeting obligations. When global institutions fail to perform, global health actors and states collaborate in creating a new consensus and/or new multilateral mechanisms to manage persistent or new challenges. A consensus-building process integrates global health actors to achieve a more comprehensive global health system capable of handling shifting realities and greater complexity. Within this system, high principles and a shared ethic of health equity will guide national and global actors in an ongoing process as they design and redesign institutions and programs.

## 6.9 Shared Health Governance versus Other Frameworks

SHG presents some sharp contrasts with other theoretical frameworks. In addition to the distinctions already discussed, we can compare and contrast SHG with other views on several important analytical components.

### 6.9.1 *Motivation*

Current international and global health law and policy seek to monitor and respond to international outbreaks of infectious diseases; regulate health-related issues such as food safety, access to medicine, and tobacco; provide standardized codes of conduct; and make available financial and technical resources and information exchange among state signatories. Limited dispute resolution and enforcement mechanisms are also available (for example, WTO Trade-Related Aspects of Intellectual Property Rights (TRIPS) agreement). The motivation is pragmatic.

In the realist and neorealist perspectives, the international system is formally anarchic, with no overarching authority over states, no explicit system, and no external rules governing states. Power, influence, and interests motivate action. Realpolitik holds sway; power is omnipresent. There is no morality at the international level, and no global moral norms bind states. In constructivism, state identity and interests emerge intersubjectively through social interaction with other states. This view is compatible with multiple framings of health. In the English School view, states have basic common interests (for example, avoiding unrestrained violence); maintaining some kind of international order is a motivation. States are concerned with self-interest, but are also attentive to obligations, standing, and propriety.[92] This perspective, too, is compatible with multiple framings of health.

In liberalism and neoliberalism, the motivation is to maximize absolute gains, through cooperation and mutual advantage facilitated by institutions. This view allows for pursuit of principled beliefs and classic liberal values such as international peace through open trade, arms control, and the creation of international institutions.[93] There are shared values, but these approaches do not specify the degree to which values are shared and by whom. Health may be treated as a global public good (with mutual benefits for rich and poor states) or as a human right in pursuit of liberal values.

Regime theory seeks to solve specific international problems, especially those of a scientific or technical nature (environmental degradation, for example). Actors pursue self-interest or long-term enlightened self-interest; rules result from rational calculations.[94] Regime theory is also compatible with multiple framings of health. The transnationalist/global civil society approach does not specify motivation; global civil society, with NGOs as a primary component, may wish to pursue equity or social justice;[95] TNCs may pursue profits and favorable regulations. This perspective can advocate goals transcending state borders, which may tend to be more principled than those based on self-interest, except for those of TNCs. This framework is compatible with the treatment of health as global public good and a human right.

Motivation in the world government paradigm is to ensure global compliance; to harness resources; to shape policy scope, reach, and coherence; to enable equal recognition among states; and to fully collectivize security.[96] This perspective is compatible with multiple framings of health, especially health as public good, though health as an individual good is less clear.

In SHG, the motivation is an overarching common goal that aligns with self-interest. Actors across levels share a joint ethical commitment to internalized public moral norms of health equity and the promotion of health capabilities. Shared goals rest on shared values developed through an overlapping consensus that taps into core beliefs. SHG denies neither power politics nor the pursuit of self or national interests. But it embodies a system crafted around a set of goals, in which a genuine consensus and commitments, clear objectives, and an evidence-based approach place checks and balances on the

[92] T. Evans and P. Wilson, "Regime Theory and the English School of International Relations: A Comparison," *Millennium: Journal of International Studies* 21, no. 3 (1992): 329–51.

[93] R. O. Keohane, *After Hegemony: Cooperation and Discord in the World Political Economy* (Princeton, NJ: Princeton University Press, 1984).

[94] Evans and Wilson, "Regime Theory"; S. D. Krasner, ed., *International Regimes* (Ithaca, NY: Cornell University Press, 1983).

[95] O'Brien, "Global Civil Society and Global Governance."

[96] A. Wendt, "Why a World State is Inevitable," *European Journal of International Relations* 9, no. 4 (2003): 491–542.

powerful actors and interests that threaten more equitable distribution of the gains from cooperation. SHG thus contrasts with liberal and neoliberal perspectives, with their emphasis on cooperation through institutions for mutual advantage and absolute gains whose distribution powerful states and strategic interests might well determine.[97] SHG also emphasizes creating and maintaining an explicit system with clear lines of responsibility and accountability, distinct from the topical or issue area focus of transnational and regime theories.[98]

### 6.9.2 Locus or Levels of Responsibility

In the current global architecture, state parties are responsible for complying with international health laws, with WHO involvement where applicable (for example, in the case of the IHR). To fulfill international obligations, national and subnational authorities must carry out relevant duties: the WHO's FCTC, for example, refers to other jurisdictional levels.

Under realism, states have responsibility to maximize their own utility and further their own self-interest; the international system requires self-help. For the liberal and neoliberal, states have primary responsibility and shape institutions. Power plays a role; more powerful states are likely to receive greater gains. Institutions facilitate state action and cooperation by improving transparency, reducing transaction costs, and providing technical support. Non-state actors such as NGOs may participate in institutional efforts (for example, with WHO and the FCTC). In regime theory, responsibility rests on states that are members of specific regimes. Non-state domestic and transnational actors may influence state negotiations in forming and maintaining regimes. Transnationalists believe that states remain important actors, though global civil society and TNCs act to influence state behavior and shape institutional rules. Transnational cooperation among state components on a given issue may also affect state behavior. For constructivists, sovereign states are central units of the system, but other actors can have various duties (for example, as norm entrepreneurs—those who work to change norms). States are the locus of responsibility for the English School, too; great powers have particular rights and obligations in maintaining order in international society.[99] In the world government approach, states remain major actors in national, regional, and

---

[97] H. Milner, "International Theories of Cooperation among Nations: Strengths and Weaknesses," Review of *Cooperation among Nations*, by Joseph Grieco and *Saving the Mediterranean*, by Peter Haas, *World Politics* 44, no. 3 (1992): 466–96.

[98] A.-M. Slaughter, "The Real New World Order," *Foreign Affairs* 76, no. 5 (1997): 183–97; O. R. Young, "Regime Theory and the Quest for Global Governance," in *Contending Perspectives on Global Governance*, ed. Ba and Hoffmann, 88–109.

[99] Evans and Wilson, "Regime Theory."

global affairs if the world body is a federation. The world body coordinates and enforces state actions.

SHG takes a more balanced view. It allocates duties and obligations to global, state, and local entities and to individuals, based on functions and needs, to solve global health problems. States have primary responsibility due to functionality and legitimacy; the scope and limit of national obligations defines international obligations. Individuals, too, have responsibility via health agency. This approach balances and respects individual agency and national self-determination.

In this way, SHG shares some features with the subsidiarity principle in European Union (EU) law. This principle provides guidance where the EU and member states share legislative competence. Its spirit is a useful guide on areas of national insufficiency and comparative efficiency. On national insufficiency the subsidiarity principle contends that if member states (at the central, regional, or local level) on their own are unable to achieve a proposed objective sufficiently, the EU shall have the authority to act. Similarly, if the EU is better able to achieve a given objective then it shall have the authority to act. With its emphasis on functions and needs, SHG is concerned with allocating roles and responsibilities to those actors best able to achieve health policy objectives. In SHG, global actors have the duty to assist countries in achieving objectives, so if states are not able to achieve the proposed objective on their own, the global community will help. However, some proposed actions with global scope—global disease surveillance, for example—are better achieved at the global level. This cooperative division of labor in SHG provides a general guide, not a specific rule or blueprint for action.

### 6.9.3 Implementation

Currently, WHO member states negotiate international health laws and regulations, like the IHR and the FCTC, under WHO auspices. Nongovernmental entities work to shape negotiations by influencing member states. National and subnational authorities and actors carry out relevant duties to fulfill the state's international obligations (for example, reporting disease incidence, isolation, and quarantine). Monitoring, evaluation, and enforcement depend on specifics of international law; domestic actors, domestic and international NGOs, or other state parties may carry them out (for example, the WTO provides for dispute resolution and enforcement among state parties).

In the realist view, states pursue interests through diplomacy, a balance of power, deterrence (or threat of force), and the use of force. States, especially powerful ones, shape international institutions, often with the avowed purpose of pursuing an objective, and use them to protect or further their own interests. Powerful states may choose to take on regulatory and security duties if they are consistent with their interests—for example, supporting the international monetary system, responding to and punishing illegal warfare, and generally maintaining order (hegemonic stability theory). Under the liberalism and neoliberalism framework, institutions supply rules of conduct, coordinate members, and facilitate the generation and sharing of ideas and knowledge. Powerful states are more able to shape institutions. States may enter into contracts where they agree to cede some degree of sovereignty or autonomy for gain (for example, WTO membership). States may also enter into conventions in which they agree to constrain or direct domestic policies in certain ways (for example, the UN Convention on the Elimination of All Forms of Discrimination against Women).

Regime theory is much the same, but regimes may take various forms. Some are integrated and comprehensive, like the WTO for trade. Others, regime complexes, can be fragmented and more loosely structured. These regime complexes bring together related regimes covering various aspects of an issue (regulation and assessment, for example) and involve an array of domestic, bilateral, and multilateral actors and instruments.[100] They can deal with large, complicated issues involving diverse components and interests (climate change, for example). Regime complexes offer flexibility but may be less coherent than integrated approaches. Under transnationalism, global and civil society actors and/or TNCs may propose new norms and mobilize political support or opposition to states and institutions (anti-WTO protests, for example). Global civil society actors may monitor and evaluate behavior and performance of states and international organizations, as in Global Health Watch's *Alternative World Health Report*. State component parts may also engage in transnational cooperation through professional, issue-specific networks that may or may not involve other types of actors.

The constructivist approach uses persuasive communication to share and influence states' understanding of their interests. Norms have power if states are convinced of their validity and rightness. Power is still an issue, but it does not determine everything. In the English School, social rules, conventions, practices, and conventional assumptions make up the institutions that allow states to distinguish appropriate from inappropriate behavior.[101] Formal institutions such as the North Atlantic Treaty Organization and the WTO are important, but only insofar as they contribute to the more fundamental set of institutions such as international law, diplomacy, and balance of powers.[102]

[100] R. O. Keohane and D. G. Victor, "The Regime Complex for Climate Change," *Perspectives on Politics* 9, no. 1 (2011): 7–23.

[101] H. Suganami, "The Structure of Institutionalism: An Anatomy of British Mainstream International Relations," *International Relations* 7, no. 5 (1983): 2363–81.

[102] Evans and Wilson, "Regime Theory."

The world government view envisions a world body to ensure compliance, harness resources, and facilitate global problem solving.

Under SHG, actors with assigned duties check and balance one another. Citizens share in governance and exercise sovereignty and agency through participation and representation. Citizens are empowered to mobilize for the good of all, as when citizen scientists monitor progress toward the Sustainable Development Goals and hold governments accountable.[103] Assessments that one's actions are negligible is an insufficient basis for inaction on global commons problems, such as climate change[104] or global health. States manage down through regulation and administration of internal affairs; they manage up and across globally to coordinate efforts in global health. Global actors and institutions step in where the scope of national obligation or capacity ends.

### 6.9.4 Units of Analysis

Today, in our current chaotic international and global health system, states are the primary units of analysis, as parties to legal regimes such as WHO's IHR and the FCTC. WHO has authority to make and adopt treaties and binding regulations, and international health law has implications for international, regional, national, and local actors.

Other frameworks also see states as the unit of analysis. This focus is true for realism and neorealism; for constructivism, in which states are members of a society of states; and for the English School, which sees states as members of a self-conscious, self-regulating society of states.[105] Liberal and neoliberal approaches take a broader view; states, non-state entities, and institutions or regimes (formal and informal procedures, norms, conventions) are all units of analysis. Under the liberal and neoliberal umbrella, regime theory focuses, not surprisingly, on regimes—"principles, norms, rules, and decision-making procedures around which actor expectations converge in a given issue-area"[106]— and actors participating in regimes (primarily states, but these can also include non-state domestic and transnational actors). Transnationalist and global civil society perspectives analyze non-state, transborder actors such as CSOs and TNCs as well as state components dealing with transborder and/or global issues.

---

[103] A. Hsu, O. Malik, L. Johnson, and D. C. Esty, "Development: Mobilize Citizens to Track Sustainability," *Nature* 508, no. 7494 (2014): 33–5.

[104] M. Lane, "Uncertainty, Action and Politics: The Problem of Negligibility," in *Nature, Action and the Future: Political Thought and the Environment*, ed. K. Forrester and S. Smith (Cambridge: Cambridge University Press, 2018, 157–179).

[105] B. Buzan, "From International System to International Society: Structural Realism and Regime Theory Meet the English School," *International Organization* 47, no. 3 (1993): 327–52.

[106] S. D. Krasner, "Structural Causes and Regime Consequences: Regimes as Intervening Variables," *International Regimes*, ed. Krasner, 1.

The world government approach analyzes the world government body; if the world government is a federation, then states are also relevant units.

SHG contrasts with realist, neorealist, and even some constructivist world government and society of states models, which either take unitary states as the primary actors and posit anarchy as the reality or seek federated world government or a society of states as the objective.[107] SHG understands that all players—individual, local, state, non-state, and global actors and institutions—are proper and necessary units of analysis in health efforts. Though SHG envisions global governance structures, it does not go as far as some transnationalists in privileging transnational actors (whether global civil society, TNCs, or the like) as primary actors, and has more in common with liberal and neoliberal traditions that also emphasize states, non-state entities, institutions, and regimes (both formal and informal) in international relations.[108]

### 6.9.5 Organizational Principle

Under current global health law and its state-centered system, international laws may be bilateral or multilateral, with the most prominent examples made through WHO, as an international institution. Legal regimes organize around issue areas, such as infectious diseases, tobacco control, or food safety.

Most theoretical frameworks view the international system as anarchic. In the realist approach, the anarchic international system has no overarching authority over states. States may organize among themselves based on power and interests. Liberalism, too, sees the international system as anarchic, though it believes states can create order and undertake major cooperative endeavors through institutions for mutual benefit and absolute gains. The distribution of gains, however, might not be equal; power remains a consideration. Under regime theory, growing international interdependence makes traditional self-help less effective and regime formation to deal with increasingly complex problems desirable. These regimes organize around issue areas like the environment or labor;[109] states form regimes to coordinate policy in the absence of a global political structure.[110] In transnationalism, too, actors are likely to organize around issue areas. Constructivists see states forming a

---

[107] See, for example, Grieco, "Anarchy and the Limits of Cooperation"; A. Wendt, "Anarchy is What States Make of It: The Social Construction of Power Politics," *International Organization* 46, no. 2 (1992): 391–425.

[108] For a transnational/globalized perspective, see J. N. Rosenau, *Distant Proximities: Dynamics Beyond Globalization* (Princeton, NJ: Princeton University Press, 2003). For the neoliberal perspective especially, see R. O. Keohane and Joseph S. Nye, Jr., *Power and Interdependence* (Boston, MA: Little, Brown & Co., 1977).

[109] Young, "Regime Theory and the Quest for Global Governance."

[110] For a discussion of spontaneous and negotiated regimes, see O. R. Young, "Regime Dynamics: The Rise and Fall of International Regimes," *International Organization* 36, no. 2 (1982): 277–97.

society with norms, but do not specify the content of those norms. Depending on socialization and how states come to perceive their identities and interests, a range of organizational possibilities may exist. In the English School view, institutions such as war, great powers, balance of power, diplomacy, and international law maintain order. The organizing principle for the world government paradigm varies according to the theorist; some, for example, retain states but establish a global parliament and interconnected global legal system.[111]

SHG, in contrast, offers an explicit, coherent system for organizing health efforts and reducing inefficiency. It calls for minimalist global involvement, comprehensive national obligations, and normative guidance of all actors. It prescribes a GHC to allocate duties and obligations to actors based on function, need, role, and effectiveness.

### 6.9.6 Compliance and Enforcement

Because its multilevel global health system relies on both government and governance, SHG envisions various modes of compliance and enforcement. The overarching principle is voluntary compliance rising from common values, shared norms, and both substantive and procedural legitimacy. This voluntary compliance is more sustainable as power relations shift. A global command-and-control system does not exist now and is not likely in the foreseeable future. Nor is centralized power in all likelihood justified, necessary, or effective. The distribution of power occurs and continues through checks and balances. The global system needs to centralize only enough to fashion a global health strategy to benefit all.

SHG privileges self-determination and health agency, both intrinsically and because voluntary compliance is arguably as effective as coercion, if not more so. Thai sex workers, for example, once instructed in the importance of condom use, came to resist demands for unprotected sex, even when clients offered higher pay.[112] Both countries and individuals follow principles and rules they grasp and accept more willingly than those they do not.[113]

Under SHG, countries voluntarily provide universal health coverage through legislation that guarantees quality health care regardless of ability to pay. No organization or individual can or should force another country to provide this benefit for its people. PG recognizes the need for global and national consensus on the morality of health, not a top-down world government compelling

---

[111] D. Held, *Democracy and the Global Order: From the Modern State to Cosmopolitan Governance* (Stanford, CA: Stanford University Press, 1995), 279.

[112] Levine et al., *Millions Saved.*

[113] Kirchler, Hoelzl, and Wahl, "Enforced versus Voluntary Tax Compliance."

compliance through coercive powers. The legitimacy and effectiveness of a genuine consensus on health morality drives SHG's emphasis on voluntary compliance. Within states, the role of compliance and enforcement can expand as government joins governance as a tool for health equity. Governments will use various measures to gain compliance. But the role of governance, with its greater reliance on norms, is fundamental.

A multilevel structure of governance at the global level and both government and governance within states thus effect compliance with global health policy in SHG. National and local health authorities, for example, must educate people about health risks and gain their compliance with health measures, such as travel restrictions or vaccination programs. Under SHG, the global community may intervene within states only if such intervention respects self-determination and self-governance and the state or a component part requests help, when they cannot fulfill their health duties. Persuasion, criticism, condemnation, mediation, and incentives are among the non-interventionist ways to address violations of global health justice principles. In place of realism and neorealism's coercion, SHG applies persuasion, value change, and the inculcation of norms. Dynamic game theoretical approaches show us that reputation matters in working toward mutually desirable outcomes; compliance is self-enforcing as states try to avoid reputational damage, which could hamper participation in future collaborations.

In today's world, compliance with international health laws is mixed, due to inadequate national capacity, a reluctance to report diseases, problematic surveillance systems, domestic barriers to implementation, and poor protection measures. WHO has no enforcement powers; health-related WTO laws may be enforced through WTO provisions. Under some circumstances, domestic courts may enforce international law. Compliance with international law generally may stem from a recognition of its substantive and/or procedural legitimacy, or from the internalization of international rules into the domestic legal system.

Realism and neorealism allow both voluntary and involuntary compliance. Any agreements must be self-enforcing and can become unstable if the balance of power changes. Powerful states may enforce compliance through coercion, but are themselves unlikely to pay a price for non-compliance. Weak states may be forced to comply with preferences of more powerful states. Liberalism and neoliberalism specify chiefly voluntary compliance. Agreements should be self-enforcing, since they rest on mutual benefit, and compliance may cease if the agreement stops yielding benefits. States may comply to avoid reputational costs.

Regime theory also envisions chiefly voluntary compliance; mutually beneficial agreements should be self-enforcing. Depending on the specifics of regime rules, non-compliance may incur different costs. Soft enforcement occurs through self-help and/or an international tribunal (for example, WTO proceedings), or through international peer pressure, as in the acceptance of rules and norms as a condition of legitimate regime membership. Coercive enforcement by regimes is generally not practicable. For transnationalists, states and entities may respond to and adopt transnational actors' positions with sufficient persuasion or pressure. Global civil society is not necessarily directly subject to global policies, so compliance might not be applicable; organizations and individuals engaging in transnational activities are, however, subject to applicable national and international laws. Actors may also comply to avoid reputational costs.

Constructivism does not specify compliance or enforcement mechanisms, which depend on the results of socialization. Compliance could be norm driven or habitual if norms are taken for granted. The English School specifies voluntary compliance with accepted norms to further common interests (for example, the mutual recognition of sovereignty). Soft enforcement occurs through diplomatic measures or peer pressure; ostracism from international society is a possible sanction. Enforcement by great powers is possible, but this view sees intervention as potentially destabilizing for international order and security. The world government framework does not specify enforcement and compliance measures, but the world body would have coercive power over states under a federation.

SHG relies on persuasion, education, and social movements to shape positive moral norms. Fully inculcated, these shared values and norms yield voluntary compliance and substantive and procedural legitimacy, though states have coercive resources to enforce appropriate compliance at the domestic level. This voluntary approach to cooperation and compliance should be stable in times of power shifts.

### 6.9.7 Intervention

Humanitarian intervention can take the form of military or non-military intervention. While *jus ad bellum* or just war theory involves a set of moral principles related to the justifiability of military force, a parallel set of principles relates to the justifiability of humanitarian military and non-military intervention. The *jus ad bellum* criteria of just cause, right intention, proportionality, and reasonable expectation of success apply to any interventions that infringe upon state sovereignty. The doctrine of state sovereignty prohibits intervention in any other state's affairs because states are considered equal independent entities with the right to self-determination and territorial integrity. External agencies impinging on state sovereignty are typically intergovernmental bodies like the UN, a coalition of states, a regional body, or in some cases another state. *Jus ad bellum* requires proportionality (that the response is proportional to the circumstances and humanitarian need), reasonable likelihood of success, and avoiding double effect, that harmful outcomes not be the intent of humanitarian military intervention. While humanitarian military intervention is a violation of state sovereignty and international law and convention, even when it seeks to prevent or rectify human rights violations, it is sometimes viewed as an exception to the prohibition against military aggression in international relations.

Though humanitarian military intervention can address abuses of power, it also challenges state sovereignty. How then do we justify humanitarian interventions? What conditions warrant intervention? Some argue, for example, that intervention to address genocide does not violate sovereignty, essentially because neither self-determination nor sovereignty obtains in these situations.[114] Others argue that a general duty to assist victims of injustice vindicates intervention.[115]

Non-military humanitarian intervention can take the form of sanctions, economic boycotts, or stipulations about or withholding development assistance. These interventions are considered coercive and typically must adhere to the principles of military intervention *jus ad bellum* sets out. Notable cases of sanctions and boycotts include those against South Africa during the Apartheid era, against Iran after its invasion of Iraq, and structural adjustment regimes imposed on many developing countries by the World Bank and IMF.

International health law today does not provide for military intervention, but WHO can publicize outbreak information and/or declare a public health emergency of international concern, with input from but not necessarily the agreement of the state where the outbreak originated.[116] SHG does not envision the creation of an international health court, akin to the International Criminal Court, which would be a step toward implementing cosmopolitan law. Indeed SHG is skeptical of the effectiveness of both international and domestic courts in the absence of strong global and domestic health policy.

Under realism, states intervene if it serves their political and geostrategic interests, but this approach does not provide for purely humanitarian intervention. Realist and moral considerations for international relations make clear that humanitarian intervention violates the principle of state sovereignty and is impermissible. Classical liberals may intervene to promote democracy and liberal values, including some human rights;[117] neoliberals may intervene

---

[114] M. Walzer, *Just and Unjust Wars: A Moral Argument with Historical Illustrations* (New York: Basic Books, 1977).
[115] F. Tesón, *Humanitarian Intervention: An Inquiry into Law and Morality* (Dobbs Ferry, NY: Transnational Publishers, 2005).
[116] WHO, International Health Regulations (2005), Articles 10, 12.
[117] M. W. Doyle, "The Ethics of Multilateral Intervention," *Theoria: A Journal of Social and Political Theory* 53, no. 109 (2006): 28–48.

to serve economic and trade interests or due to international norms.[118] Under regime theory, the extent of intervention depends on the regime but the international human rights regime permits intervention in case of genocide, ethnic cleansing, war crimes, and crimes against humanity; the UN Security Council must authorize such intervention. Transnationalists and global civil society theorists do not offer a universal position regarding intervention; in this view, certain global civil society actors—humanitarian NGOs, think tanks, media, intellectuals—contribute to changing international norms regarding humanitarian intervention.[119] For constructivists, humanitarian intervention can occur in a normative context that expands ideas of who counts as human, spurring protection against human rights abuses in other countries.[120] Two strains in the English School have divergent views of intervention: pluralists oppose humanitarian intervention as a violation of sovereignty and because they fear instability in state society; solidarists may allow intervention to "strengthen the legitimacy of international society by deepening its commitment to justice."[121] World government theories would give the world body power to intervene to enforce human rights standards worldwide, much like domestic law enforcement.

SHG resists coercion and respects self-determination. While SHG includes a general duty to protect and promote global health equity and specific duties to assist those experiencing health injustice, it does not necessarily yield a duty to intervene. The use of military force and foreign military interference in states' domestic affairs poses significant costs and harms not just in physical terms but also in terms of regional destabilization and financial and reputational damage, undermining the receiving state's capacity to exercise governance and self-determination. The total financial costs of intervention to all parties could be so substantial that the money would be more effective if spent directly on functions necessary for global health equity. Military intervention can be substantially disruptive and thus the costs, harms, and benefits should be weighed against those of alternative forms of assistance and intervention.

While most arguments for humanitarian military intervention have concerned serious violations of human rights such as massacre, whether intervention actually rectifies such injustices is unclear. The human interests at

---

[118] M. Finnemore, "Constructing Norms of Humanitarian Intervention," in *The Culture of National Security: Norms and Identity in World Politics*, ed. P. J. Katzenstein (New York: Columbia University Press, 1996), 153–85.

[119] M. Kaldor, "A Decade of Humanitarian Intervention: The Role of Global Civil Society," in *Global Civil Society 2001*, ed. H. Anheier, M. Glasius, and M. Kaldor (London: LSE Global Governance, 2001).

[120] Finnemore, "Constructing Norms of Humanitarian Intervention."

[121] N. J. Wheeler, *Saving Strangers: Humanitarian Intervention in International Society* (Oxford: Oxford University Press, 2000), 11.

stake in health injustice are substantial, especially the greatest shortfalls from the threshold level of central health capabilities, but financial and technical assistance will likely yield greater benefits and smaller costs. Thus, the expected value of this assistance is greater than that of humanitarian military intervention. Rather than stopping or harming an offender, interventions should embody a systematic approach to public health and health care. Such constructive efforts are more proportional to public health and health care system conditions and the health needs of suffering populations.

To be justifiable under a PG/SHG approach, policies for attaining health goals must have a reasonable likelihood of success and be based in social scientific research and policy practice. In PG/SHG, likelihood of success is evidence based. Ad hoc military intervention is likely not the most effective or cost-effective action. Nor are non-military interventions—for example, coercive structural adjustments—necessarily effective. Despite efforts to end world poverty and focus on the economic interests of the poor in targeted states, the World Bank and IMF have not been successful with their coercive adjustments imposed on particular state governments. SHG thus only allows the global community to intervene in state affairs at a state's invitation, without violating self-determination and self-governance, when the state is unwilling or unable to carry out its health duties.

SHG also focuses on local populations' own perceptions of their needs, discerned through individual and collective health agency. A participatory approach more fully illuminates the conditions, assumptions, and constraints underlying injustice. Intervention in SHG respects and enhances health agency; SHG thus conceptualizes intervention differently. In SHG, a person's effective freedom to achieve goals that she values, her ability to decide for herself rather than having someone else force a decision upon her (as with coercive interventions), forms the basis for engagement. Individuals and groups will base their decisions on reasons and the pursuit of particular goals; granting all a role in creating and accomplishing solutions recasts intervention.

Strengthening health agency makes people agents of their own development as opposed to passively receiving development assistance. When people deliberate about health policies and problems, they learn about the impact of political choices on themselves and others. Involving people in identifying health problems and creating solutions is important for both intrinsic and instrumental reasons. When interventions are participatory and promote health and health agency, they also foster joint intentions and commitments among plural subjects throughout the world. This approach in turn creates greater possibilities for MCA in global and domestic health policy and practice. And it illuminates further deficits in GHG legitimacy and accountability, in turn moving the system beyond a rational actor paradigm to SHG.

## 6.10 Conclusion

Without doubt, this project will encounter skepticism. Many will question the possibility of a common consensus and globally shared values.[122] Many will doubt that such a paradigm shift is possible. Some will question the likelihood of displacing power politics and vested interests with ethical principles and moral norms, yet the potential of persuasion, both direct and indirect, is regarded as a promising and undertheorized area of international relations, particularly in relation to power.[123]

Realist and traditional international relations perspectives have, to be sure, substantial force. We must expose them for what they are: global realpolitik, devoid of moral content. The PG/SHG approach, by contrast, proposes a comprehensive plan for global health justice, reshaping major institutions and ordering them according to justice principles. But the shift in global health's normative structure and politics must be broad enough and deep enough to prevent a retreat to the unjust system dominating global health politics today.

The world sorely needs to disentangle global health from geopolitical and military interests. The importance of this goal further justifies an intentionally constrained global health theory that does not try to do too much. The PG/SHG approach does not try to specify all necessary conditions for a just world order. Theories of global justice and policy have earned ample criticism for this sort of expansiveness. Nor does SHG entail (1) a "single integrated legal instrument"; (2) "nested regimes" or "regime complexes"; or (3) "highly fragmented arrangements."[124] Various analyses in health law, both global and domestic, indicate that legal instruments have lacked effectiveness and that an international legal treaty would fall short. But GHG's proliferating players and fragmentation—fostered by independent decisions among both state and non-state actors and WHO on various health issues (AIDS, TB, malaria, SARS, avian flu, and others)—can no longer provide the coordination so essential to health governance. The redirection of global health resources from WHO and other core health institutions to proliferating actors in disparate issue areas is unlikely to change. A constitutional structure with clear principles and allocations of responsibility along functional lines is arguably more constructive. Such an approach allows

---

[122] R. Foot, "Introduction," in *Order and Justice in International Relations*, ed. R. Foot, J. L. Gaddis, and A. Hurrell (Oxford: Oxford University Press, 2003), 1–23; A. Hurrell, "Order and Justice in International Relations: What is at Stake?" in *Order and Justice in International Relations*, ed. Foot, Gaddis, and Hurrell, 24–48.

[123] R. O. Keohane and S. Krasner, "Subversive Realist," in *Back to Basics: State Power in a Contemporary World*, ed. M. Finnemore and J. Goldstein (New York: Oxford University Press, 2013), 28–52.

[124] Keohane and Victor, "The Regime Complex for Climate Change," 7.

both for independent effort and for greater accountability in the shared global health production enterprise.

The complex interactions between global and domestic health and the extent of globalization, by which individuals, goods, and services cross national borders at an unprecedented rate and volume, necessitate attention to the ways that different societies shape (or fail to shape) health systems, domestic and global. PG seeks a common moral purpose and a genuine consensus on global health justice claims. Power is real, and it matters in global health politics, but the imposition of powerful states' interests on the world is a far cry from a consensus. Consensus means norm creation, internalization, and revision within and across societies. SHG proposes shared institutions, policies, and practices undergirded by global and domestic consensus, striving for global health justice. It provides a normative basis, sorely lacking in global health law. How can the law best serve health justice? Chapter 7 turns to that discussion.

# 7

# International and Global Health Law[1]

## 7.1 Normative Foundations of Global Health Law

International health law and global health law comprise a rather new field of academic study. Most broadly, this field encompasses all international legal arrangements pertinent to public health—international environmental law, humanitarian and human rights law, trade and labor law, laws relating to arms control, and so on.[2] More narrowly, it incorporates only international legal systems targeting health threats. The two most prominent examples are the International Health Regulations (IHR), focused on infectious diseases, and the World Health Organization's (WHO's) Framework Convention on Tobacco Control (FCTC), concerned with chronic diseases.

Though they are often conflated, an important distinction divides international health law from global health law. The former is a more traditional framework of rules governing relations among states. The evolving system of global health law, on the other hand, sees the world as a community, not just a collection of disconnected countries. This structure includes individuals and nongovernmental organizations (NGOs) as well as states, especially where health problems are truly global in scope. Globalization has dramatically heightened the necessity of worldwide health cooperation.

International health law dates to the mid-nineteenth century, when it developed to control infectious diseases. It has evolved over time to encompass many norms and standards and to occupy an important place in foreign

---

[1] This chapter stems from J. P. Ruger, "Aristotelian Justice and Health Policy: Capability and Incompletely Theorized Agreements," PhD dissertation, Harvard University, 1998; J. P. Ruger, "Health and Development," *The Lancet* 362, no. 9385 (2003): 678; J. P. Ruger, "Normative Foundations of Global Health Law," *Georgetown Law Journal* 96, no. 2 (2008): 423–43; J. P. Ruger, "Global Tobacco Control: An Integrated Approach to Global Health Policy," *Development* 48, no. 2 (2005): 65–9.

[2] D. P. Fidler, *International Law and Public Health: Materials on and Analysis of Global Health Jurisprudence* (Ardsley, NY: Transnational Publishers, 2000).

policy.[3] But the absence of normative theory has deprived the field of both a basis for justice and a common understanding of the ethics and governance of global health threats. Research ignored normative issues and the importance of global health justice in addressing them. In particular, research neglected the importance of moral norms in guiding international and domestic health law.

The provincial globalism (PG)/shared health governance (SHG) approach reaches beyond international health law to offer a normative global health law theory. It sees human flourishing as global society's end goal and proposes an ethical demand for health equity as the criterion for evaluating global health law. Realizing this ethical goal will likely require legal instruments, but, more fundamentally, it will require public moral norms. Additionally, this theory requires evaluating global health law in the contexts of international relations and global public policy; both global and state levels should link law and policy. We cannot study global health law's moral underpinnings separately from other global and domestic tools to reach global health equity.

International treaties, conventions, and recommendations will not solve global health disparities and externalities. Effective solutions require domestic health policy, law, and institutional reforms creating sustainable health systems, including universal health coverage and infrastructure for public health and health care. Thus, the success and future of global heath law depend as much on domestic health policy and law as they do on international law itself.

### 7.1.1 Recognizing Threats, Seeking Justice

#### 7.1.1.1 INTERNATIONAL HEALTH RELATIONS

International health relations as an academic field does not exist. Health has been peripheral and largely ignored in the history of international relations theory.[4] Health-related international relations grew out of a Westphalian sovereign-state approach to infectious diseases. It came to encompass multiple standards in subsequent decades; it now includes bilateral and multilateral collaborative efforts to prevent external threats to national health and economic security,[5] as well as an elaborate and expanding regime to secure and expand human rights.

---

[3] D. P. Fidler, "Caught between Paradise and Power: Public Health, Pathogenic Threats, and the Axis of Illness," *McGeorge Law Review* 35, no. 1 (2004): 45–104.

[4] See R. O. Keohane and J. S. Nye, Jr., *Power and Interdependence* (Boston, MA: Little, Brown & Co., 1977).

[5] D. P. Fidler, "The Globalization of Public Health: The First 100 Years of International Health Diplomacy," *Bulletin of the World Health Organization* 79, no. 9 (2001): 842–9. Fidler describes the history of international health law and diplomacy, which—although it dates back to European quarantine practices in the fourteenth century—really began in the mid-nineteenth century.

Historically, as we have seen, the world's imperial powers drove health diplomacy, working to protect their populations and commerce from infectious agents. From the mid-nineteenth century until 1948, numerous international arrangements arose to address public health issues, particularly treaties dealing with contagions, opium and alcohol, occupational hazards, and cross-border pollution. The first International Sanitary Conference met in 1851 to discuss Europe's quarantine requirements. The first International Sanitary Convention, in 1892, was adopted to contain infectious diseases like cholera. The next eleven years saw repeated revisions of this convention, until a permanent international health bureau was created in 1903.[6] International efforts in the early twentieth century targeted narcotics control, ranging from the 1909 International Opium Commission meeting to alcohol trade treaties.[7]

The United Nations Economic and Social Council convened an international conference in 1946 to discuss creating a single United Nations (UN) health agency. By 1948 the world body had created WHO and ratified its Constitution; the first World Health Assembly (WHA) convened that year in June.[8] WHO's creation signified a new health diplomacy era marked by norms and standards. This era aspired to "Health for All," and the right to health was an animating ideal. But these efforts were more rhetoric than substance, often masking hidden self and national interests and a failure of political will globally and domestically.[9] Now, seventy years later, "Health for All" remains only an aspiration. Though appeals to human rights and the right to health have dominated the discourse, the human rights movement and the right to health especially have encountered considerable skepticism. Concerns include uncertain compliance with international human rights law and whether human rights instruments can in fact influence state behavior and non-state actors.[10] No normative theory emerged.

Normative global justice views more broadly provide some help,[11] though they have not focused on international health law. In the natural law tradition, Hugo Grotius grounded justice in human dignity and natural law.[12,13]

---

[6] WHO, "Origin and Development of Health Cooperation," *WHO,* http://www.who.int/global_health_histories/background/en/ (accessed December 12, 2017).

[7] Fidler, "The Globalization of Public Health."

[8] WHO, *Working for Health: An Introduction to the World Health Organization* (Geneva: World Health Organization, 2007).

[9] For various perspectives on self-interest and other motivations in general, see J. J. Mansbridge, ed., *Beyond Self-Interest* (Chicago: University of Chicago Press, 1990).

[10] O. A. Hathaway, "Do Human Rights Treaties Make a Difference?" *Yale Law Journal* 111, no. 8 (2002): 1935–2042.

[11] A. Buchanan, *Justice, Legitimacy, and Self-Determination: Moral Foundations for International Law* (Oxford: Oxford University Press, 2004).

[12] H. Grotius, *De Jure Belli Ac Pacis Libri,* ed. J. Brown Scott and trans. F. W. Kelsey (1646; Oxford: Clarendon Press, 1927).

[13] F. R. Teson, *A Philosophy of International Law* (New York: Westview, 1998), 73–98.

These principles have carried considerable weight in both global justice and international law.[14] Buchanan, for example, argues that justice as a goal of international law is to be understood as respect for basic human rights and as a safeguard to ensure access to institutions of justice that protect basic rights.[15] Immanuel Kant's approach to international relations builds on moral grounds.[16] However, both the natural law tradition and the Kantian approach are largely inattentive to international health law's role in delivering health justice.

Moral norms for global health governance are absent from these frameworks. For 150 years, international health diplomacy[17] has unfolded without the needed moral foundation to guide and govern state and non-state health actions. Except for WHO, international health relations and international law doctrine have consistently expressed a realist or positivist worldview. In this view, the strategic interactions of self interested states constitute international health relations; no overarching moral order guides and limits state actions, and moral theorizing about international relations and international law is meaningless.[18] Legal nihilists argue that international law itself is illegitimate law, rejecting it as a legitimate legal system, due both to its lack of enforcement mechanisms for its rules and to the only modest authority it provides the courts.[19] Legal positivists insist that non-textual international law has no place in moral inquiry; legal positivism takes law as affirmatively enacted or written and looks to texts, treaties, and statutes as the law, whereas natural law scholars and practitioners look to moral or natural reasoning to determine what law is.

But a larger moral order should exist, encompassing principles to govern behavior among states, within states, and among non-state actors. SHG posits a higher moral purpose for international health relations and proposes an alternative focus on and for global health law. Global health law needs theories of global health justice elucidating principles, policies, and tools to confront global inequalities and threats and to frame collective action.

---

[14] Martha Nussbaum has developed a theory of central human capabilities that relates to the Grotian view in that these capabilities are universal—without each, one cannot live a life "worthy of human dignity." See M. C. Nussbaum, *Frontiers of Justice: Disability, Nationality, Species Membership* (Cambridge, MA: Harvard University Press, 2007): 78.

[15] Buchanan, *Justice, Legitimacy, and Self-Determination*, 118–90.

[16] See M. W. Doyle, "Kant, Liberal Legacies, and Foreign Affairs," *Philosophy & Public Affairs* 12, no. 3 (1983): 205–35; M. W. Doyle, "Kant, Liberal Legacies, and Foreign Affairs, Part 2," *Philosophy & Public Affairs* 12, no. 4 (1983): 323–53.

[17] T. E. Novotny, I. Kickbusch, and M. Told, *21st Century Global Health Diplomacy* (Hackensack, NJ: World Scientific Press, 2013).

[18] For a discussion of the role of theory in explaining international law, see K. N. Waltz, *Theory of International Politics* (New York: McGraw-Hill, 1979).

[19] See H. L. A. Hart, *The Concept of Law* (Oxford: Oxford University Press, 1961), 124–37.

## 7.1.1.2 GLOBAL HEALTH EQUITY AS MORAL PURPOSE

As we have argued, central health capabilities pose an urgent moral claim; global health inequalities and global threats to human health demand redress in global society and its member states. But what does global health equity mean for global health law? PG/SHG recognizes that different people have different health circumstances, so it argues not for complete health equality but for ensuring capabilities for good health. Equal outcomes are not the goal. Global health equity, then, means that all people are equally able to realize their health potential. The health capability paradigm uses shortfall rather than attainment to assess equality: it sets global thresholds of health—life expectancy, for example, or maternal mortality—against which to measure health performance gaps.[20] It thus focuses more on an attainable level of health and how to deploy resources to reach it than on current health system accomplishments. This approach allows quantitative assessment of the extent to which a given country or community has realized its health potential and how far it has to go, by comparing a health system's actual achievement to the stated norm. Health equity means reducing the threat of, and ultimately eliminating, shortfall inequalities in central health capabilities worldwide.

To achieve this goal, a normative theory of global health law must specify obligations for global and domestic institutions.[21] Global inequalities in mortality and morbidity reflect broader social, political, and economic environments. Research suggests that market mechanisms alone cannot reduce the health threats posed by inequalities and externalities: government, law, and policy are centrally important. Nor can the health sector alone accomplish these goals. Broad-based social organization and collective action can diminish health disparities and negative externalities.

Achieving global health equity requires the key functions of redistribution of resources, related legislation and policy, public regulation and oversight, and creation of public goods. Progressive taxation, broad risk pooling, redistributive expenditure policies, and subsidies will be essential redistributive measures. Financing health care through health insurance, providing public health care services when markets fail to deliver, and public health information, surveillance, and services are key legislation and policy functions. In other sectors, policy measures include promoting economic opportunities and addressing poverty and unemployment; improving education, especially for women; expanding participation in trade through institutional reforms; lowering social barriers so all can develop skills and build up assets; and

---

[20] For an empirical cross-national study of global health inequalities from a shortfall perspective, see J. P. Ruger and H.-J. Kim, "Global Health Inequalities: An International Comparison," *Journal of Epidemiology & Community Health* 60, no. 11 (2006): 928–36.

[21] For the argument that most political theory and political philosophy do not include institutional analysis, see Buchanan, *Justice, Legitimacy, and Self-Determination.*

safeguarding against catastrophic financial risk. Health care services, health insurance, health providers, pharmaceutical companies, and medical devices all require adequate public regulation and oversight. Other essential functions are clean air and pollution control, toxic substance regulation, sanitation, occupational safety, housing and building code regulation, and risk management. In the public goods category, health equity requires accurate and effective disease surveillance, swift control of outbreaks, and competent public health systems, for example.

Where does responsibility for these varied functions lie? Individual states have obligations including building systems for equitable and affordable health care; public health; surveillance; and food, drug, and consumer safety. The state must also regulate and oversee these systems. Though their role is secondary, global actors and institutions still embody the global community's will to address injustice—to correct market failures, create public goods, and support countries in developing and flourishing as healthy societies. And indeed all actors, state and global agencies, institutions, NGOs, communities, businesses, foundations, families, and individuals bear responsibility in this enterprise.

Strong, internalized public moral norms will be critical. Without ethical commitments, for example, it is not possible to organize and redistribute resources.[22] Redistribution must be voluntary; otherwise, the effort will be coercive and thus morally unacceptable. Individuals must willingly relinquish some resources if those resources are to be redistributed; they must relinquish some autonomy to effective public regulation. These norms motivate them to help those whose human flourishing and health are threatened. States and global entities, as instruments of the people's will, can and should do the same.

### 7.1.2 Global Health Law's Role in Achieving Health Equity

International health law and global health law can serve as tools to prevent the spread of disease and to ensure that all global citizens reach or exceed a central health capabilities threshold. International health laws have been written and enacted, though most have targeted cross-border pathogen control rather than global health inequalities.

---

[22] Elsewhere, I argue for widespread internalization of the public moral norm of willingness to pay taxes for others' health insurance to achieve domestic health care reform on universal health insurance in the United States. See J. P. Ruger, "Health, Health Care, and Incompletely Theorized Agreements: A Normative Theory of Health Policy Decision Making," *Journal of Health Politics, Policy and Law* 32, no. 1 (2007): 51–87.

### 7.1.2.1 INTERNATIONAL LAWS

Both bilaterally and multilaterally, global actors have written international health laws. International health law has also emerged through constitutions and institutions, in particular WHO. The IHR are among the most important international health laws, although other international legal regimes have also been influential in health.[23] WHO's WHA enacted the IHR in 1951, revising them in 1969 and 2005. The IHR's stated purpose is "to ensure maximum security against the international spread of disease with minimum interference with world traffic."[24] As the only international communicable diseases agreement binding on WHO's 196 member states, the IHR provide a standardized code for infectious disease control.

WHO's Constitution empowers it to adopt treaties and enact binding regulations. Under the Constitution's Article 19, the WHA has the "authority to adopt conventions or agreements with respect to any matter within the competence of the Organization."[25] Thus WHO has a legal role in international health law.

Article 21 empowers the WHA to pass legally binding rules in five public health domains: sanitary and quarantine regulations; nomenclatures on diseases, causes of death, and public health practices; international standards for diagnostic procedures; standards for "safety, purity and potency of biological, pharmaceutical and similar products moving in international commerce"; and advertising and labeling of internationally traded biological, pharmaceutical, and similar products. Member states, however, may reject or submit reservations to any regulations under Article 22. Though WHO has had these legal powers since 1948, until the FCTC in 2003 it had not proposed a convention or treaty and had adopted only one set of regulations, the original and then revised IHR.

### 7.1.2.2 THE GLOBAL HEALTH LAW IMPERATIVE

The urgency behind the 2005 IHR revisions and the international agreement on them revealed the pressing need for global health law in controlling contagions.[26] Infectious diseases like severe acute respiratory syndrome

---

[23] Examples of such regimes include Trade-Related Aspects of International Property Rights (TRIPS) regulation in international trade law and Sanitary and Phytosanitary (SPS) regulation in international food safety law.

[24] D. P. Fidler, "Revision of the World Health Organization's International Health Regulations," *American Society of International Law Insights* 8, no. 8 (April 2004). Available at: https://www.asil.org/insights/volume/8/issue/8/revision-world-health-organizations-international-health-regulations (accessed December 12, 2017).

[25] Constitution of the World Health Organization, Chapter V, Article 19.

[26] M. G. Baker and D. P. Fidler, "Global Public Health Surveillance under New International Health Regulations," *Emerging Infectious Diseases* 12, no. 7 (2006): 1058–65.

(SARS), avian flu, West Nile virus, Ebola, and Zika can quickly become public health emergencies requiring global action.

The revised IHR seek "to prevent, protect against, control and provide a public health response to the international spread of disease in ways that are commensurate with and restricted to public health risks, and which avoid unnecessary interference with international traffic and trade."[27] They include human rights principles and are consistent with international human rights law.[28] The new IHR expand the number of covered diseases from just cholera, plague, and yellow fever to all infectious illnesses; they also cover non-communicable diseases (NCDs) caused by chemical or radiological agents and releases of biological, chemical, or radiological substances.[29] They direct states to "develop, strengthen and maintain" surveillance and response capacities,[30] though they provide no funding or technical resources for this purpose. They require states to notify WHO of any potential international health emergency they find within their borders; WHO can determine whether the event is of international concern and make non-binding recommendations for state action.[31] WHO may also respond to data from unofficial and nongovernmental sources, such as its Global Outbreak Alert and Response Network, provided the state involved verifies the information. The SARS and avian flu episodes made the value of unofficial sources clear. No new enforcement mechanism for addressing compliance failure appears in the revised IHR, however.

NCDs also cause death and suffering worldwide, and international legal regimes have emerged to address them as well. Because tobacco consumption is a prime culprit in many NCDs, WHO's FCTC promotes national action on tobacco control.[32] Numerous international factors involved in tobacco use—trade liberalization, direct foreign investment, global marketing and advertising, and international sales of contraband and counterfeit cigarettes[33]—made a global tobacco control treaty necessary.

Under the FCTC, countries must combat tobacco use through both supply and demand tools. On the demand side, the treaty specifies price, tax, and non-price measures, including protection from secondhand smoke; regulation of tobacco products' contents, packaging, and labeling; regulation of

---

[27] WHO, International Health Regulations (2005), Article 2.

[28] P. Alston and R. Goodman, *International Human Rights* (New York: Oxford University Press, 2012).

[29] D. P. Fidler and L. O. Gostin, "The New International Health Regulations: An Historic Development for International Law and Public Health," *Journal of Law, Medicine & Ethics* 34, no. 1 (2006): 85–94.

[30] WHO, International Health Regulations, Articles 5, 13.

[31] Ibid., Articles 6, 12, 15–16.

[32] R. Roemer, A. Taylor, and J. Lariviere, "Origins of the WHO Framework Convention on Tobacco Control," *American Journal of Public Health* 95, no. 6 (2005): 936–8.

[33] A. L. Taylor and D. W. Bettcher, "WHO Framework Convention on Tobacco Control: A Global 'Good' for Public Health," *Bulletin of the World Health Organization* 78, no. 7 (2000): 920–9.

disclosures concerning tobacco products; and provision for education, training, communication, public awareness, and smoking cessation efforts.[34] On the supply side, it targets illicit trade and sales to minors. The treaty also requires clean indoor air controls.

In all, 168 nations have pledged their commitment to FCTC goals.[35] For ratifying member states, it is legally binding. It directs each party to the treaty to "develop, implement, periodically update and review comprehensive multisectoral national tobacco control strategies, plans and programmes in accordance with this Convention and the protocols to which it is a Party."[36] Under Article 5.2, each party shall, "in accordance with its capabilities: (a) establish or reinforce and finance a national coordinating mechanism or focal points for tobacco control; and (b) adopt and implement effective legislative, executive, administrative, and/or other measures and cooperate, as appropriate, with other Parties in developing appropriate policies for preventing and reducing tobacco consumption, nicotine addiction and exposure to tobacco smoke."[37]

The FCTC aspires to be an instrument of international cooperation and national tobacco control. Can it work?

### 7.1.2.3  GLOBAL HEALTH LAW: IS IT EFFECTIVE?

The developing body of international health law illuminates the impact of various international health instruments—agreements, conventions, treaties, and organizations. Do these instruments lead to real on-the-ground results? Do they promote health, prevent disease, and reduce health inequalities?

One study of the IHR concluded that they had largely failed to achieve their chief objective, primarily because of failures in their surveillance system and a lack of measures to prevent the spread of contagious diseases like tuberculosis, malaria, and HIV/AIDS. Other IHR failures have stemmed from inadequate national surveillance systems, local barriers to reporting, and states' reluctance to report outbreaks for fear of reputational damage and reduced trade and tourism. Further undercutting compliance, WHO has no IHR enforcement powers, despite non-binding recommendations and a dispute resolution procedure for addressing notification failures. Critics have noted that the dispute settlement process is non-mandatory and therefore unlikely to improve compliance.[38] Furthermore, states are permitted to settle disputes by any "peaceful

---

[34] WHO Framework Convention on Tobacco Control (2003), Articles 6–14.

[35] For a full list of parties to the WHO FCTC, see http://www.who.int/fctc/signatories_parties/en/ (accessed November 30, 2017).

[36] Framework Convention on Tobacco Control, Article 5.

[37] Ibid.

[38] K. Wilson, J. S. Brownstein, and D. P. Fidler, "Strengthening the International Health Regulations: Lessons from the H1N1 Pandemic," *Health Policy and Planning* 25, no. 6 (2010): 505–9.

means of their own choice";[39] this permission does nothing to incentivize or compel new, more cooperative behavior among states aimed at improving surveillance and control of the international spread of disease.

That WHO member states ignore both legally binding rules and non-binding WHO recommendations is clear in the IHR's history. It has been argued that the numerous international treaties leading up to the IHR—and the IHR themselves—created rules of customary international law to be carried out by states based on perceived obligations under these treaties. Perceived obligations include the duty to report infectious disease outbreaks and the duty not to apply excessive measures when another state experiences an outbreak.[40] Only forty-one of 212 countries and territories—about 20 percent—implemented WHO policy on HIV/AIDS education for schoolchildren, and only 102 of 212 adopted WHO's Directly Observed Treatment Short Course policy for tuberculosis treatment.[41] The record of state compliance with WHO recommendations is mixed at best.

While there is noted progress, FCTC critics wonder whether it will help control tobacco use, suggesting that member states are failing to change their practices to achieve FCTC goals.[42] Will countries prohibit cigarette advertising? Will they ban tobacco sales to minors? Will they end smoking in public places?

Many view international health law as ineffective from multiple viewpoints—legally, because states fail to follow stipulated legal rules; behaviorally, because signatories have not changed their behavior despite treaty obligations; and in a practical sense, because treaties simply have not accomplished their objectives.[43]

The IHR, the FCTC, and similar instruments fall far short of the goals they seek to achieve. In the absence of a comprehensive global health framework

---

[39] WHO, International Health Regulations (2005), Article 56.

[40] For a discussion of this line of argument and its implications for customary international law rules and state responsibility, see D. P. Fidler, *International Law and Infectious Diseases* (Oxford: Oxford Monographs in International Law, 2000), 81–2, 99–104.

[41] WHO, *Report on Infectious Diseases: Removing Obstacles to Healthy Development* (Geneva: WHO, 1999), 31.

[42] For a discussion of how the countries least able to implement the FCTC are those most in need of its reforms, see P. Cairney and H. M. Mamudu, *The WHO Framework Convention for Tobacco Control (FCTC): What Would Have to Change to Ensure Effective Policy Implementation?* (Stirling: University of Stirling, 2013). For a discussion of how the FCTC has not adequately controlled tobacco supply, see N. Freudenberg, *Lethal but Legal: Corporations, Consumption, and Protecting Public Health* (Oxford: Oxford University Press, 2014), 169–71.

[43] For more on the different meanings of effectiveness in international law, see, generally, R. B. Mitchell, "Compliance Theory: A Synthesis," *Review of European Community & International Environmental Law* 2, no. 4 (1993): 327–34; D. G. Victor, K. Raustiala, and E. B. Skolnikoff, eds., *The Implementation and Effectiveness of International Environmental Commitments: Theory and Practice* (Cambridge, MA: MIT Press, 1998); O, R. Young, "The Effectiveness of International Institutions: Hard Cases and Critical Variables," in *Governance Without Government: Order and Change in World Politics*, ed. J. N. Rosenau and E.-O. Czempiel (Cambridge: Cambridge University Press, 1992): 160–95.

like SHG and without the inculcation of positive norms, states will continue to resist those provisions that they perceive to be disadvantageous or too burdensome. Without moral norms, little motive for compliance exists. The PG/SHG paradigm provides these norms and moves beyond the limits of international health law to a global health law approach. Even so, because SHG does not encompass enforcement at the global level, it does not control state-level activities, where the largest part of health governance occurs. This freedom of states to act as they choose is precisely the reason norms are so important.

### 7.1.2.4 WHAT CONDITIONS DOES GLOBAL HEALTH LAW REQUIRE TO BE EFFECTIVE?

International law scholars have long studied whether treaties and agreements work, as well as the conditions that can make them effective. Both theoretical and empirical international law literature can help assess global health law's effectiveness. A key issue is the role of enforcement mechanisms, such as military force or sanctions. Are they needed?

The enforcement model of states' behavior sees states as rational actors maximizing utility. In this view they will obey treaties or not according to pragmatic cost-benefit calculations.[44] Treaty regimes must therefore include costly enforcement provisions to force compliance. In contrast, a managerial model argues that parties to treaties intend to comply but fail not out of willful defiance but rather because they lack capacity or a clear understanding of objectives.[45] Building capacity, providing technical and economic help, and identifying and overcoming barriers are, under this model, the most promising path to enhancing treaties' effectiveness—not coercion and punishment.

States do not implement international law primarily because of sanctions and threats, despite views to the contrary. Many factors come into play. Treaty compliance can result from reciprocity, a mutually beneficial bargain between states; transparency, by which obvious violations may damage a state's reputation, thus creating a dynamic for treaty compliance legitimacy, a good-faith commitment to adherence; social learning, in which treaties can help states better understand their own interests; mobilization, whereby treaties engender public support for their goals; and internalization, the incorporation of treaty provisions into states' legal systems and bureaucracies.[46]

---

[44] J. L. Goldsmith and E. A. Posner, *The Limits of International Law* (Oxford: Oxford University Press, 2005), 83–106.

[45] A. Chayes and A. H. Chayes, *The New Sovereignty: Compliance with International Regulatory Agreements* (Cambridge, MA: Harvard University Press, 1995).

[46] D. Bodansky, "Technical Briefing Series: What Makes International Agreements Effective? Some Pointers for the WHO Framework Convention on Tobacco Control," *Framework Convention on Tobacco Control Technical Briefing Series* (Seattle: University of Washington, 1999); M. Finnemore and K. Sikkink, "International Norm Dynamics and Political Change," *International Organization* 52, no. 4 (1998): 887–917.

Effective elements in past international agreements inspired several key FCTC features. Some of them are: clear, specific, and readily verifiable rules (packaging and labeling requirements for cigarettes, for example, and advertising restrictions for tobacco); funding aid for states lacking capacity to comply; and regular meetings among signatories for information sharing and continuing negotiation. These features could enhance the FCTC's effectiveness.[47]

The FCTC and the IHR are two of international health law's most promising tools. As such, they can help shape a social learning process by which states come to understand their own interests in combating global health inequalities and externalities. Both also illustrate the overarching governance mechanisms so useful in implementation (through technical and financial assistance) and compliance. Both treaties emphasize transparency and thus could prompt compliance among potential violators unwilling to risk reputational damage. And both treaties could become internalized in member states' domestic systems.

By embedding global health laws in its normative framework, SHG could make them more effective, more likely to be observed in the world's nations. SHG's norms embody the attributes that make laws and policies effective: fairness, impartiality, a broad inclusiveness, a rootedness in shared values of justice and equity, a grounding in the common good. Undergirded by the PG/SHG paradigm, the IHR and the FCTC could make a greater difference than they do today.

### 7.1.3 *Health Law and Policy, Global and Domestic*

#### 7.1.3.1 THE RELATIONSHIP BETWEEN GLOBAL AND DOMESTIC HEALTH LAW

The relationship between global and domestic health law is important to studying global health law's normative foundations. In international law, this relationship can develop through three different channels. The first downloads (or internalizes or domesticates) international law into domestic law; an example is the human rights norm against "disappearances" or state-sponsored kidnappings. The second channel uploads legal concepts into international law and then downloads them into domestic systems, like the guarantee of a fair trial. In the third channel, law is borrowed or horizontally transplanted from one country to another;[48] the right to privacy is an example.

The transnational legal process is one model in which international and domestic law interact; in it, countries and domestic and transnational private

---

[47] Bodansky, "What Makes International Agreements Effective?"

[48] H. H. Koh, "Is there a 'New' New Haven School of International Law?" *Yale Journal of International Law* 32, no. 2 (2007): 559–73.

actors engage in cycles of interaction, interpretation, and internalization.[49] Actors identify favored global norms, which internalization agents then incorporate into domestic legal systems. These agents can be states themselves, transnational norm entrepreneurs, governmental norm sponsors, transnational issue networks, and interpretive communities.[50] While norm internalization is central to transnational legal process theory, the moral or ethical content of the norms is not; the model is primarily procedural.[51] Moreover, critics charge that it contravenes domestic self-determination and self-rule and thus democratic principles.[52]

Another model for the international/domestic law nexus anticipates that the future of international law is domestic; the function of international law thus becomes enhancing domestic institutions' capacity and effectiveness.[53] Anne-Marie Slaughter has proposed that a new world order based on a web of government linkages (among courts, regulatory agencies, ministries, and legislatures across national borders and between national and multinational institutions) would achieve more than either the current state-based arrangements or a top-down world government.[54] In any event, we cannot study law as a public health tool in isolation from the roles of domestic and global policy.

None of these models fully meets the requirements of SHG. Transnationalism raises issues of democracy and self-determination. The networked approach might slight the essential and primary role of states. The "future-is-domestic" view downplays the role for global institutions.

The task ahead is threefold. The first is to achieve a global consensus on a health equity standard. The second is to persuade domestic actors voluntarily to accept and internalize this health equity norm and to construct their own domestic systems to achieve it with the help of global institutions. The third is to create and integrate important global institutions—the Global Health Constitution (GHC) and Global Institute of Health and Medicine (GIHM).

### 7.1.3.2 DEVELOPING GLOBAL HEALTH LAW AND POLICY

The health challenges confronting us globally and nationally necessitate a new global health cooperation paradigm. Old international health law theory and practice have failed to address many global health problems or their

---

[49] H. H. Koh, "Transnational Legal Process," *Nebraska Law Review* 75 (1996): 181–207.

[50] T. Risse and K. Sikkink, "The Socialization of International Human Rights Norms into Domestic Practices: Introduction," in *The Power of Human Rights: International Norms and Domestic Change*, ed. T. Risse, S. C. Ropp, and K. Sikkink (Cambridge: Cambridge University Press, 1999), 1–38.

[51] M. E. O'Connell, "New International Legal Process," *American Journal of International Law* 93, no. 2 (1999): 334–51.

[52] A. Chander, "Globalization and Distrust," *Yale Law Journal* 114, no. 6 (2005): 1193–236.

[53] A.-M. Slaughter and W. Burke-White, "The Future of International Law is Domestic (or, The European Way of Law)," *Harvard International Law Journal* 47, no. 2 (2006): 327–52.

[54] A.-M. Slaughter, *A New World Order* (Princeton, NJ: Princeton University Press, 2004), 166–215.

domestic roots. Global health law founded on normative health equity principles must supersede international health law, with its roots in interstate legal systems. It requires an alternative construct that can extend to and shape domestic health policies and law and use national actors and instruments to achieve globally shared goals.

Integrated legal and policy instruments working together are necessary to produce tangible results against global health inequalities and threats. Finding the best combination of legal and policy structures—to control epidemics, for example, and to create standards regulating international transactions involving health—will require empirical research. The revised IHR should help, but public and private funding for overseas development assistance are essential, as is technical assistance for capacity building in countries with inadequate health systems. Confronting and solving global health problems must encompass global health policy, institutions, and decision-makers, along with the law, to mobilize and allocate resources and provide needed technical aid.

Global health equity depends on global law and policy that can strengthen domestic institutions, laws, and policies so that they can in turn manage health issues within their countries; global health law ties inextricably into domestic health law and policy going forward. Successfully shaping and internalizing public moral norms as a foundation for health institutions, policies, and laws will also depend on global law and policy.

### 7.1.3.3 CORNERSTONE: DOMESTIC HEALTH LAW AND POLICY

National and subnational governments have primary moral and legal responsibility for addressing global health inequalities and threats. The state needs an integrated theoretical framework for health ethics, policy, and law, combining substantive criteria and procedural mechanisms to steer reform and allocate scarce resources, and to create an institutional framework for equitable, high-quality, and affordable health care and public health. It will also ensure other health-related determinants necessary for individuals to develop the agency required to convert health resources into health functioning. Weak and failing states often obstruct progress with unreliable institutions and inadequate resources, abilities, and technical capacities. In such cases, the global health community must step in. The World Bank's role is important for providing financial and technical assistance to develop sustainable national health systems. This project will also involve transnational nongovernmental and governmental networks, as these vertical and horizontal networks linking actors around the world can be powerful agents of change and action.

### 7.1.3.4 THE USE OF INTERNATIONAL LAW

International health law does not operate in a vacuum. The links among health, human rights, environmental law, labor law, and trade are increasingly clear.

232

International treaty law becomes ever more important as a mechanism of international collective action.[55] Some argue for governing health through international law.[56] They see WHO, with its legal authority, institutional mandate, and public health expertise, as uniquely positioned to write international health law and public health treaties. But WHO largely abstained from using its international law-making powers[57] until the 2003 FCTC, which, along with litigation and courts, holds the tobacco industry liable.[58] And another project, the 2004 Global Strategy on Diet, Physical Activity and Health, was neither binding on parties nor norm setting; it seemed to retreat from law-making to a technical and administrative support role.[59] It gave states chief responsibility and did not provide for enforcement or policy interpretation. Some scholars have advocated for a larger WHO role in international law—for example, to lead effective health law development,[60] to help countries draft and negotiate trade laws,[61] and to catalyze health law codification.[62] Reader proposes an "ex post facto liability regime" that would call countries to account for deliberately suppressing disease outbreak information. It would improve IHR compliance, strengthen global health norms, and urge governments to prioritize GHG. He charges that China's behavior during the SARS outbreak was tantamount to an "abuse of rights" in international law.[63]

But while international law and agreements can support health efforts, they can also undercut them. As we have seen, existing laws and pacts—trade-related instruments in particular—sometimes work against health. Intellectual property obstacles to drug access and disputes over countries' efforts to ban harmful imports like tobacco and lamb mutton flaps hinder public health progress. Power and wealth influence law-making, and results can favor affluent countries and corporations. Industries and the powerful countries where

[55] A. L. Taylor, "Governing the Globalization of Public Health," *Journal of Law, Medicine & Ethics* 32, no. 3 (2004): 500–8.

[56] L. O. Gostin and D. Sridhar, "Global Health and the Law," *New England Journal of Medicine* 370, no. 18 (2014): 1732–40.

[57] L. O. Gostin, "Meeting the Survival Needs of the World's Least Healthy People: A Proposed Model for Global Health Governance," *Journal of the American Medical Association* 298, no. 2 (2007): 225–8; J. D. Reader, "The Case against China: Establishing International Liability for China's Response to the 2002–2003 SARS Epidemic," *Columbia Journal of Asian Law* 19, no. 2 (2006): 519–71.

[58] H. Wipfli, D. W. Bettcher, C. Subramaniam, and A. L. Taylor, "Confronting the Tobacco Epidemic: Emerging Mechanisms of Global Governance," in *International Co-operation in Health*, ed. M. McKee, P. Garner, and R. Stott (Oxford: Oxford University Press, 2001), 127–50.

[59] E. Lee, "The World Health Organization's Global Strategy on Diet, Physical Activity, and Health: Turning Strategy into Action," *Food and Drug Law Journal* 60, no. 4 (2005): 569–601.

[60] Taylor, "Governing the Globalization of Public Health."

[61] C. Thomas, "Trade Policy and the Politics of Access to Drugs," *Third World Quarterly* 23, no. 2 (2002): 251–64.

[62] A. L. Taylor, "Global Governance, International Health Law and WHO: Looking Towards the Future," *Bulletin of the World Health Organization* 80, no. 12 (2002): 975–80.

[63] Reader, "The Case against China," 523.

they are based, for example, can shape agreements like the Codex Alimentarius, which regulates food trade.[64]

But the weakness of international law overall is the fundamental problem. This deficiency is serious in the health sphere, where WHO lacks enforcement capacity. Without an international system with convincing enforcement powers, international law cannot promise to be effective. WHO member states often fail to comply with either binding rules or non-binding recommendations.

### 7.1.3.5 TAKING TO THE COURTS: JUDICIALIZING THE RIGHT TO HEALTH

The search for legal remedies has opened a new front in the battle against health inequalities. Known as the judicialization of the right to health, this strategy deploys legal action against states that fail to provide promised health services. In the USA and similar older judicial systems, courts have proved reluctant to enforce positive social rights like education and health, but plaintiffs in other nations where the government pledges universal health care have had more success in securing their rights through the courts.

Citizens in dozens of countries have filed thousands of cases seeking the right to health services under the law, and courts are ruling in their favor. The "law" in these cases can be international treaties or national constitutional provisions. The 1948 Universal Declaration of Human Rights, for example, states that "[e]veryone has the right to a standard of living adequate for the health and well-being of himself and of his family, including... medical care and necessary social services."[65] The 1946 WHO Constitution similarly asserts that "[t]he enjoyment of the highest attainable standard of health is one of the fundamental rights of every human being."[66] Other cases appeal to national constitutions and charters. The South African Constitution specifies that "[e]veryone has the right to have access to... health care services, including reproductive health care... [and] [t]he state must take reasonable legislative and other measures, within its available resources, to achieve the progressive realisation of each of these rights."[67] Canada's Charter of Rights and Freedoms guarantees all persons the "right to life, liberty and security of the person and the right not to be deprived thereof except in accordance with the principles of fundamental justice."[68] A Canadian court used this clause to find a right to decent health care.

Several decades ago, courts seemed reluctant to enforce health care access. But the tide turned as the twentieth century ended. In Colombia, for example,

---

[64] Lee, "The World Health Organization's Global Strategy."
[65] UN, The Universal Declaration of Human Rights, Article 25.
[66] Constitution of the World Health Organization, Preamble.
[67] Constitution of the Republic of South Africa (1996), Section 27.
[68] "Canadian Charter of Rights and Freedoms," The Constitution Act (1982), Section 7.

where health coverage increased from 24 percent before 1993 to more than 80 percent in 2007[69] and a Constitutional Court was established in 1991, dissatisfied patients took to the court in droves, using a new legal action called a "tutela" to file more than 328,000 claims related to the right to health between 1999 and 2005. They won more than 80 percent of these cases.[70] By 2008, however, critics were taking an increasingly jaundiced view of this process. "Through the tutelas, justices have granted coverage of interventions that may be compelling for the individual but not be cost-effective for society," wrote Leonardo Cubillos, director of the Management of Health Care Demand in the Colombian Ministry of Social Protection.[71] "The legal system may not have expertise or perspective to judge these complex decisions on resource rationing."[72] The same year the Constitutional Court ordered the government to effectuate universal coverage.[73] The political process continues to play out there.

Brazil, Argentina, Chile, Costa Rica, Peru, and Uruguay have also seen expanding judicialization of health.[74] And in South Africa, a government decision to limit the availability of nevirapine for HIV-positive pregnant women to just two hospitals in each province prompted a case on behalf of the thousands of women denied access at other public clinics. This decision had massive implications for maternal and infant health. The court, citing the South African Constitution, ruled against the government.[75]

Judicial review can have beneficial effects for health. It can correct process failures, force deliberation, and correct discrimination and unequal treatment. Some view law as necessary for the realization of social rights, for example.[76] But the judicialization phenomenon has drawbacks as well. Enforcing positive rights through the courts has unusual and significant impacts on national budgets. The courts lack authority to raise taxes equitably. Courts also adjudicate one case at a time, thus administering uneven justice and often skewing the setting of national priorities. Other governmental branches might ignore court rulings, undermining judicial authority in consequence. Judges are unelected and thus less democratically legitimate or accountable. And judges

---

[69] U. Giedion and M. Villar Uribe, "Colombia's Universal Health Insurance System," *Health Affairs* 28, no. 3 (2009): 853–63.

[70] A. Ely Yamin and O. Parra-Vera, "How Do Courts Set Health Policy? The Case of the Colombian Constitutional Court," *PLoS Medicine* 6, no. 2 (2009): 147–50.

[71] T. C. Tsai, "Second Chance for Health Reform in Colombia," *The Lancet* 375, no. 9709 (2010): 110.

[72] Ibid.

[73] Ibid.

[74] R. Iunes, L. Cubillos-Turriago, and M.-L. Escobar, "Universal Health Coverage and Litigation in Latin America," *En Breve* 178 (2012): 1–4.

[75] K. Cullinan, "Court Orders South Africa to Treat Pregnant HIV-Positive Women with Nevirapine," *Bulletin of the World Health Organization* 80, no. 4 (2002): 335.

[76] K. L. Scheppele, "Amartya Sen's Vision for Human Rights—and Why He Needs the Law," *Proceedings of the Annual Meeting (American Society of International Law)* 105 (2011): 12–22.

are generalists, not policy experts with an in-depth grasp of health issues. Sunstein is leery of this trend: "There is a big difference," he observes, "between what a decent society should provide and what a good constitution should guarantee."[77]

SHG does not incur these negative consequences. SHG sees health not as a legal right to be enforced in the courts but as a moral imperative carried out through a common commitment to public moral norms.

## 7.2 Where Global, National, and Subnational Health Law Intersect: Control of Extensively Drug-Resistant Tuberculosis[78]

### 7.2.1 XDR-TB: Analyzing Root Causes in the Speaker Case

In 2007, Andrew Speaker allegedly defied public health officials' directives and carried multi-drug-resistant TB (MDR-TB) (originally feared to be the even more virulent extensively drug-resistant TB (XDR-TB)) on multiple transnational flights between the USA, Europe, and Canada. His case raises key questions about the appropriate roles for international, federal, state, and local governments and law, along with those of health care personnel and individuals themselves, in addressing global infectious agents.

A root cause analysis (RCA) of the Speaker case yields important lessons about current system inadequacies and the potential benefits of SHG. RCA allows a comprehensive view of the profoundly complex global health apparatus, breaking complicated problems into increasingly defined components, making probing analysis from one dimension to the next possible. Central RCA methodological features are recursive questioning to identify a problem's causal factors and finding effective solutions to prevent recurrence.[79] RCA follows four main steps—problem definition, data collection, identification of possible causal factors, and recommendation of potential solutions. The Speaker incident was an international public health fiasco; its root causes appear at numerous levels and involve aspects of the law, ethics, governance, and drug-resistant TB itself.

---

[77] C. Sunstein, "Against Positive Rights", *East European Constitutional Review* 2 (1993): 36.

[78] This section stems from J. P. Ruger, "Control of Extensively Drug-Resistant Tuberculosis (XDR-TB): A Root Cause Analysis," *Global Health Governance* 3, no. 2 (2010): 1–20.

[79] NASA, "Root Cause Analysis Overview," Memo from Office of Safety & Mission Assurance (2003); J. Reason, *Human Error* (Cambridge: Cambridge University Press, 1990); T. L. Rzepnicki and P. R. Johnson, "Examining Decision Errors in Child Protection: A New Application of Root Cause Analysis," *Children and Youth Services Review* 27, no. 4 (2005): 393–407; H. Wald and K. G. Shojania, "Chapter 5: Root Cause Analysis," Report prepared for Agency for Healthcare Research and Quality, 2001.

## 7.2.2 What Were the Root Causes?

### 7.2.2.1 THE VIRULENCE OF XDR-TB

XDR-TB is a rare organism. The infection kills most victims—thus the Centers for Disease Control and Prevention's (CDC's) isolation order. Successful XDR-TB treatment depends on finding the right cocktail of four or more drugs, a difficult challenge.[80] Poor profit prospects have led pharmaceutical companies to neglect research and development into improved drugs or a vaccine.[81] International health officials thus have only twentieth-century treatment options for twenty-first-century strains of a virulent disease capable of infecting the world in hours.

US courts have stated that the Constitution requires "clear, cogent and convincing evidence" to justify involuntary isolation.[82] Speaker felt well; he was asymptomatic and smear-negative for acid-fast bacilli. Thus the medical evidence of the tuberculosis bacteria was thin. He apparently did not infect others, suggesting that the transmission potential was negligible. But it was not zero; roughly 17 percent of all TB cases result from exposure to smear-negative individuals.[83]

Soon enough—after he left the country—Speaker's test results did indicate active and thus contagious TB. Why no local, state, or federal process operated to generate discussion and deliberation of preliminary results while awaiting convincing medical advice is an important question. This case also illustrates how failing to address XDR-TB in one locale can balloon into a global problem.

### 7.2.2.2 US PUBLIC HEALTH LAW

Numerous laws provide effective public health strategies to treat and contain XDR-TB and other infectious diseases. US public health law has historically assigned primary public health responsibility to local and state governments.[84] State governments' enforcement powers enable them to implement laws and regulations to secure their citizens' health, safety, and welfare.[85] State-level legal authority covers disease reporting and TB treatment. Nationally, the

---

[80] J. Furin, "The Clinical Management of Drug-Resistant Tuberculosis," *Current Opinion in Pulmonary Medicine* 13, no. 3 (2007): 212–17.

[81] M. Spigelman and S. Gillespie, "Tuberculosis Drug Development Pipeline: Progress and Hope," *The Lancet* 367, no. 9514 (2006): 945–7.

[82] *Green v. Edwards*, 263 S.E. 2nd 661 (1980); G. J. Annas, "Control of Tuberculosis: The Law and the Public's Health," *New England Journal of Medicine* 328, no. 8 (1993): 585–8.

[83] CDC, "Public Health Investigation Seeks People Who May Have Been Exposed to Extensively Drug Resistant Tuberculosis (XDR TB) Infected Person," Press Release, May 29, 2007.

[84] G. J. Annas, "Bioterrorism, Public Health, and Civil Liberties," *New England Journal of Medicine* 346, no. 17 (2002): 1337–42.

[85] Ibid.; K. R. Wing, *The Law and the Public's Health*, 5th ed. (Chicago: Health Administration Press, 1999).

United States Code gives the Surgeon General, acting with the Secretary of Health and Human Services (HHS), responsibility to prevent "the introduction, transmission, and spread of communicable diseases from foreign countries into the United States and within the United States and its territories/possessions."[86] The CDC's quarantine authority derives from this provision.

The CDC sought to isolate Speaker in successive stages. The agency first contacted Speaker in Rome, right after identifying his illness as XDR-TB. Speaker immediately fled Rome and, violating the CDC directive, flew commercially from Prague to Montreal. From there he traveled by car to the USA.[87] Dr. Martin Cetron, director of CDC's Division of Global Migration and Quarantine, then directed Speaker to a New York City isolation facility for evaluation.[88] Speaker voluntarily drove himself to the facility, where medical officials evaluated him and then turned him over to state and local authorities in Fulton County, Georgia, where he lived.

### 7.2.2.3 INTERNATIONAL HEALTH LAW INSTRUMENTS: WHO INTERNATIONAL HEALTH REGULATIONS

Just two years earlier, WHO's IHR revisions sought to establish a global framework for containing infections. The IHR focuses particularly on reporting and responding to diseases with important international implications. The new IHR pertained to the Speaker case in numerous ways, including requirements for reporting to WHO, information sharing and consultation with pertinent parties at home and abroad, and developing effective national capacities to detect and respond to contagion threats. In several of these categories, the system broke down.

The CDC said it notified US state and local health departments, foreign Ministries of Health, the airline industry, and WHO, and followed up with potentially exposed individuals. Officials in Canada, Greece, and Italy, however, claimed they did not receive CDC notification in time to act, and Italian officials actually assert that they contacted the USA about Speaker, not vice versa. Such a progression of events would violate IHR requirements.[89] The Committee on Homeland Security issued a report confirming CDC's delay in notifying WHO.[90]

---

[86] CDC, "Questions and Answers on the Executive Order Adding Potentially Pandemic Influenza Viruses to the List of Quarantinable Diseases," *CDC* (2007). Available at: https://www.cdc.gov/ncezid/dgmq/ 2014 (accessed December 12, 2017).

[87] V. Valentine, "A Timeline of Andrew Speaker's Infection," *NPR*, June 6, 2007.

[88] CDC, "Public Health Investigation."

[89] J. Schwartz, "Tangle of Conflicting Accounts in TB Patient's Odyssey," *New York Times* (June 2, 2007).

[90] United States House of Representatives Committee on Homeland Security Majority Staff, "The 2007 XDR-TB Incident: A Breakdown at the Intersection of Homeland Security and Public Health," Report presented September 2007, p. 3.

The CDC sought to adhere to IHR provisions for individual travelers. But Speaker failed to heed the CDC's recommendations, spotlighting potential gaps around individual compliance and the CDC's powerlessness to keep travelers at home.

Under the IHR, WHO can declare a public health emergency of international concern and intervene. The IHR's decision instrument indicates that the Speaker case would probably have been judged as such, possibly compelling the USA to act.

US federal and state public health powers are broad and strong enough to fulfill IHR requirements for maintaining adequate capacity to detect and address public health risks. Indeed, one would expect the American public health infrastructure to be among the world's most effective for tuberculosis surveillance and treatment. Yet the state-level public health system in Georgia emerges as a root cause because in not providing adequate surveillance, reporting, intervention, and personnel training, it failed to deal with this infection promptly and prevent the ensuing international debacle.

Finally, and distinct from the IHR, WHO guidelines dictate that persons carrying either XDR-TB or MDR-TB "must not travel by public air transportation" until evidence confirms that they are not contagious. However, Fulton County officials failed to apply WHO no-fly restrictions, instead relying on Speaker to voluntarily restrict his travel.

### 7.2.2.4 THE CIVIL RIGHTS–QUARANTINE NEXUS

The practice of quarantine emerged in the fourteenth century, when ships—likely carrying plague victims—were required to stand offshore at Venetian ports for a month or more to stave off contagion. In America, yellow fever and other disease outbreaks prompted Congress to pass federal quarantine legislation in 1878, augmenting state and local quarantine regulations already in effect. Early in the twentieth century the federal government assumed most state and local quarantine administration, and in 1921 nationalized the system.[91] The 1944 Public Health Service Act emphatically asserted federal quarantine authority, assigning "responsibility for preventing the introduction, transmission, and spread of communicable diseases from foreign countries into the United States" to the US Public Health Service.[92] The CDC acquired quarantine power in 1967.

The CDC expanded its tool kit with surveillance to monitor epidemics abroad and inspection systems to oversee international traffic. Its Division of Global Migration and Quarantine has the power to "detain, medically

[91] CDC, "History of Quarantine," *CDC* (2014). Available at: https://www.cdc.gov/quarantine/historyquarantine.html (accessed December 12, 2017).
[92] Ibid.

examine, or conditionally release individuals and wildlife suspected of carrying a communicable disease."[93] In the Speaker case, however, clear and convincing evidence that he had active TB was lacking, and he traveled abroad before the degree of contagion was established or effectively communicated. The confusion and lack of clarity were a root cause of this case's mishandling.

A counterfactual case can illuminate this episode. In the counterfactual, even absent clear and convincing medical evidence of active TB, the menace the disease poses and the threat of international contagion would warrant protective measures through a formal process: the public's health would trump Speaker's free choice. Speaker should have willingly stayed home. There should have been an established process to persuade him to act wisely and forgo travel and, failing that, to restrain his travel. But no such procedure was available to either Fulton County or Georgia state officials.

Both state and local authorities lacked the power to act. The government's only available recourse was to obtain a court detention order if Speaker ignored medical advice—in other words, if he traveled internationally, at which point a court order is too late. Legal and regulatory structures created a catch-22 situation, in which neither government authorities nor the Fulton County doctor had any effective recourse.[94]

### 7.2.2.5 THE LIMITS OF VOLUNTARY COMPLIANCE

Julie Gerberding, then CDC director, stated that by traveling the patient violated a "covenant of trust"—an implicit understanding that infected patients, out of consideration and decency, will willingly obey medical advice and avoid harming others. Gerberding noted that willing compliance is the first line of tuberculosis defense: typically, she said, "we do not issue isolation orders under our quarantine statute, because . . . we have a high success record using voluntary means of information and advice."[95] But voluntary measures failed here.

### 7.2.3 Solving Global Health Problems: Ethics, Policy, and Law

The Speaker case illustrates vividly the interplay among international, national, subnational, county, and individual actors. The primary role of containing communicable diseases globally rests with international health law, particularly the revised IHR. US public health law grants authority to the federal government

---

[93] Ibid.

[94] United States House of Representatives Committee on Homeland Security Majority Staff, "The 2007 XDR-TB Incident," 8.

[95] CDC, "Public Health Investigation Seeks People Who May Have Been Exposed to Extensively Drug Resistant Tuberculosis (XDR TB) Infected Person," Press briefing, May 29, 2007.

(HHS and the CDC) to issue federal isolation orders; the federal government has residual authority under the US Constitution's Commerce Clause to control the spread of disease between states and from foreign countries.[96] State and local jurisdictions are responsible for isolation and quarantine more locally. And at the individual level, every person must act ethically and weigh the costs and benefits of his actions for himself and his fellow citizens. Accepting and internalizing public norms of ethical conduct, to respect the health of all individuals, is a responsibility that falls to us all.

Local and state public health officials proved themselves ineffective in evaluating the case's full dimensions, communicating the facts and their implications to Speaker, and eliciting his voluntary compliance. As for Speaker, no legal orders prevented his travel and he broke no laws, but his decisions suggest that he might have placed his self-interest and personal desires above others' health. On the other hand, perhaps he lacked the information about his infection necessary to make an informed decision about rejecting the covenant of public trust.

This case also revealed failings in the US Department of Homeland Security and US Customs and Border Protection; these agencies have authority to retain "ill persons" at the US border,[97] but they allowed Speaker to cross from Canada even though the Treasury Enforcement Communications System had flagged him for detention.[98]

Barring a national/global police state monitoring every person's health status and whereabouts, health law and policy must require individuals and their health care providers to protect public health and reduce the threat to others. This case emphasizes the importance of genuine ethical commitments at all levels to contain contagions, as in SHG.

The first links in this case's long chain of events reveal its root causes. System corrections should thus occur at the local level; they should fortify the covenant of trust and redesign regulations. Voluntary compliance is central, but patients must fully understand the costs (both forcible quarantine and legal liability for illness in exposed persons) and benefits of their behavior; the regulatory structure must communicate effectively. Additionally, voluntary compliance necessarily occurs within relationships among patients, health providers, and local health officials. As this case shows, uncertainty and indecisiveness among local health providers and government officials who are also parties to the covenant of trust can produce miscommunications, patient mismanagement, and misunderstanding. Further, a regulatory framework

---

[96] Annas, "Bioterrorism, Public Health, and Civil Liberties," 1337.

[97] HHS and DHS, "Memorandum of Understanding between the Department of Health and Human Services and the Department of Homeland Security," October 2005.

[98] United States House of Representatives Committee on Homeland Security Majority Staff, "The 2007 XDR-TB Incident."

explicitly permitting legal action following a breach of trust must undergird voluntary compliance.

A single integrated framework encompassing both self-regulation and governmental and legal oversight is a critical need. We must transform the regulatory structure. We must also engage the public and educate them about the costs, risks, and benefits of health behaviors, because the public must fully and effectively possess this information if we are to win their voluntary compliance. Otherwise, the consequences can be dire: Speaker chose an unwise and potentially dangerous course. Had he known that state, federal, and international authorities could find him and detain him, that travelers near him could sue him, and that his reputation would suffer such harm, he would surely not have fled the USA and eluded authorities in several countries—even absent definitive identification of his TB.

Today's global realities require a uniform international standard for policies to protect parties from miscommunication, misinformation, misrepresentation, or misunderstanding. Health providers and local health officials should meet with patients and review fully the implications of their infection and their behavior for themselves and for others. A defined question-and-answer period should follow to confirm that patients fully understand these personal and social implications and to help them internalize it. Together they should discuss and agree to the full course of medical treatment, prevention and recovery, and a plan for voluntary compliance. An agreed-upon strategy should provide for continual updates, progress review, and additional decision-making. Parties should agree also to a plan for reintegration following voluntary compliance and isolation, and on ways to update it as needed. Officials must clearly explain their legal authority and the potential for sanctions if the patient does not heed medical advice and isolation. Advocates should be available to help patients through the process.

Local authorities must follow these guidelines; if they do not, national authorities should have the power to step in. In the USA, the CDC's Division of Global Migration and Quarantine is the appropriate agency for federal oversight. This division and its counterparts in other countries could either use existing structures or create new offices to review and oversee local- and state-level cases. Sharing information and findings at the international level should be part of the process. These national offices should also create processes for handling cases that the local level cannot manage, by establishing a country-level protocol as a backup. National oversight is also necessary to set procedures for imposing isolation or quarantine involuntarily. Additional protocols for medical and patient management, for pursuing legal action when needed, and for better coordination with international authorities are all necessary as well.

The informed consent process used in clinical ethics could help shape voluntary compliance procedures, but these procedures should reflect the effects of voluntary decisions on society as well as the individual. Informed consent models could provide elements such as disclosure standards, written and signed consent forms, and legal processes such as medical malpractice remedies. Clear, standardized requirements and a signed consent by the individuals and health and governmental officials involved are important.

The gap between voluntary compliance and full-force quarantine demands new standardized rules and processes. Such a procedure might diminish governments' reluctance to impose isolation by creating more convincing justifications for them. Because local variations could undermine the global system's legitimacy, global standards for rules and procedures in local case management could also be necessary. Deploying psychologists and ethicists to build trust on all sides could help shape an effective system. Unintended consequences are always a danger, and thoughtful, systematic study of rules and procedures is important.

Enhancing voluntary compliance and undergirding it with legal authority for involuntary isolation would transform the control of cross-border contagions. The Speaker case shows the central importance of greater oversight and standardized procedures early in disease detection and at the local level. Local and national regulations will be more enforceable than global standards; they are also closer to the ground-level sources of disease, though global standards could prove necessary. Corrective actions early and locally—tighter, more effective rules at the levels of patient, health provider, and local public health authority—could dramatically reduce contagions both within and among countries. Local authorities had too much latitude in the Speaker case. Improvements in local systems to stop epidemics at their origins are critical to containing epidemics going forward.

Reflecting on the Speaker case's root causes reveals, by sharp contrast to the current regime, the benefits of the PG/SHG approach. The root causes behind the Speaker fiasco were in fact the lack of many necessary elements—clear and convincing evidence of Speaker's infection; a standardized procedure to convince him not to travel or, failing that, to prevent him from traveling; adherence to the covenant of trust; internalized norms; coordination among local, state, and various federal agencies; and a cogent design for regulations, rules, and procedures within a framework that permits legal action following a breach of trust.

Under SHG, these missing pieces would be in place. The GHC would define roles and responsibilities for local, subnational, national, and global actors. The GIHM would provide the needed scientific knowledge to craft effective policies and inform both domestic and global systems. Internalized norms would lead parties to honor the covenant of trust. Actors would expend resources efficiently under clearly defined procedures.

The current domestic and global health structure collaborated in a serious health capability failure; it undermined Speaker's health functioning and health agency and that of his fellow air passengers. It resulted as well in a massive waste of resources. We can do much better. Part IV turns to an examination of global heath institutions and how they serve—and fail to serve—health justice.

# Part IV
# The International Order and Global Institutions

From the creation of the United Nations (UN) and World Health Organization (WHO) until late in the twentieth century, few major international actors had the political or financial power to shape global agendas. WHO, the Rockefeller Foundation, the United Nations Children's Fund, and, more recently, the World Bank, dominated global health's research, policy, and investment priorities.

A new global health framework is evolving in our increasingly globalized world. Many new organizations of various kinds are taking the stage alongside earlier actors. Some are financial investors; others have mixed finance, policy, and operations functions.

Whereas health debates previously took place in cloistered health departments and WHO, they now occur regularly at G8 and other multilateral meetings. The UN Security Council has focused on HIV/AIDS. The World Economic Forum has addressed HIV/AIDS and considered health issues ranging from vaccines to obesity to tobacco control. The private and non-profit sectors, too, have emerged as relatively new actors in global health: the Global Fund to Fight AIDS, Tuberculosis and Malaria (Global Fund), the Bill & Melinda Gates Foundation, and pharmaceutical companies (for example, Merck, Pfizer, Novartis, and GlaxoSmithKline) have all assumed more prominent roles. Over fifty private–public partnerships (PPPs) are tackling infectious diseases or micronutrient deficiencies. Some have vast resources: Gavi, the Global Alliance for Vaccines and Immunization, has a billion-dollar budget. Non-governmental organizations (NGOs)—Médecins Sans Frontières, Oxfam, and the Cooperative for Assistance and Relief Everywhere, for example—engage in disaster and health emergency relief and help shape policy on issues like access to essential medicines.

These new funds, initiatives, and actors have produced real global health benefits. But this proliferation of actors has also splintered international health agencies and produced an increasingly fragmented, uncoordinated, ad hoc, and diffuse global health enterprise. These conditions, in turn, have opened a yawning gap in leadership and revealed a need for an overarching convening and coordinating function.

The principles of provincial globalism (PG) and shared health governance (SHG) challenge the current global health architecture and its multiplying component institutions. Do these global health actors promote human flourishing? Do they treat the individual as the central moral unit of justice? Do they foster health capabilities? Have they fully inculcated within themselves public moral norms of health equity? Are they explicitly committed to global health equity? Do they work intentionally and effectively to achieve it? Do they foster health agency, encouraging individuals to take responsibility for their own health through the choices they make? Do they create conditions to prevent and manage epidemics and other threats to health capabilities? Do they contribute to the resolution of cross-border issues? Do they help countries develop, flourish, and promote health?

Other questions arise at a more practical level: Whose interests do global health institutions serve? Perhaps the principal beneficiaries are the suffering and the underserved; but perhaps instead they are wealthy nations and powerful industries. Do those interests justify the current use and delegation of power and authority? Perhaps current power distributions serve the cause of justice; or possibly, in some cases, they simply entrench disparities and worsen health problems. Are they accountable? Do global health institutions respect self-determination, self-governance, and voluntary participation by states and non-state actors in global health governance? Or do they often ride roughshod over national sovereignty and individual autonomy? Do these institutions succeed in achieving both health equity goals and efficiency?

As we have seen, carefully selected empirical indicators can help us answer many of these questions. These indicators measure: (1) goal alignment among actors and levels of government; (2) adequate levels of resources, both human and financial; (3) consensus on key outcomes, principle indicators for evaluating those outcomes, and the data that measure them; (4) meaningful participation of key global, national, and subnational groups and institutions; (5) efforts to engage vulnerable groups most affected by policy decisions—the poor, women, youth, racial and ethnic minorities, persons with disabilities, and the elderly; and (6) effective, efficient resource use for priority areas.

How do existing global institutions stand up to scrutiny using the PG/SHG framework and criteria? The chapters that follow will employ these criteria as a standard to assess WHO and other UN agencies and programs; the World Bank; the G8 and G20; NGOs; PPPs; and the health-focused work of emerging economies.

# 8

# WHO and Other United Nations Agencies

## 8.1 The World Health Organization

### 8.1.1 *Introduction*[1]

The establishment in 1948 of the World Health Organization (WHO) marked a new international health diplomacy era characterized by norms and standards. "Health for All" became the hope, and a right to health was a guiding ideal. Until the 1990s, international health was the domain of states and multilateral organizations with state members. WHO was prominent, coordinating worldwide efforts such as smallpox eradication, handling international reporting, and managing disease outbreaks through the International Health Regulations (IHR). Still today, the world community sees WHO as the leading global health governor and expects it to solve global governance problems. In the current multilateral environment, WHO maintains its unique coordinating function, deriving from its Constitution. It is the only agency with authority to develop and implement international law and health norms and standards and facilitate ongoing discussion among member states on priorities. The benefits of cooperative supranational action are numerous.

But today's WHO is a weakened institution, riddled with budgetary problems and power politics. Its reputation, effectiveness, and legitimacy have diminished greatly. WHO's failings in handling the 2014 West African Ebola outbreak demonstrated that it lacks an emergency operations culture and the capacity to prevent and contain pandemics. Despite its early successes, it lacks coordination capacity, authority, accountability, fairness, a master global health plan, and reliable compliance mechanisms. WHO's vision of "Health

[1] Sections 8.1.1–8.1.3 stem from the following: J. P. Ruger and D. Yach, "The Global Role of the World Health Organization," *Global Health Governance* 2, no. 2 (2009): 1–11; J. P. Ruger and D. Yach, "Global Functions at the World Health Organization," *British Medical Journal* 330, no. 7500 (2005): 1099–100.

for All" remains unfulfilled.[2] Proposals abound to strengthen WHO, to use its treaty powers more effectively, and to give it enforcement powers—all in the absence of a real alternative. On a theoretical level, WHO lacks a substantive justice-oriented conception of international institutional legitimacy.

While WHO reforms will improve its operational capabilities, the global health governance (GHG) system itself needs a new vision, based on a substantive conception of justice and legitimacy, and broader restructuring to serve GHG functions effectively and efficiently. Even former WHO Director-General Margaret Chan observed that "[t]he level of WHO engagement should not be governed by the size of a health problem. Instead, it should be governed by the extent to which WHO can have an impact on the problem. Others may be positioned to do a better job."[3] The basis of international institutional legitimacy creates a faulty foundation for WHO, and structural problems in WHO and its constitution undermine its governance role. WHO has neither the ability nor the moral authority to serve all health functions and act as the normative force in global health. Provincial globalism (PG) and shared health governance (SHG) present a comprehensive alternative view of international institutional legitimacy and global justice, which reworks the terms of international cooperation and the structure of international institutions. This in turn affects the configuration and norms of GHG. It offers an ethical perspective for evaluating WHO and guiding GHG reforms for a more effective WHO role.

### 8.1.2 Trends in WHO Leadership: Recent Directors-General and their Varying Priorities

Gro Harlem Brundtland was elected as WHO director-general in 1998 on the strength of her skills and experience as Norway's Minister of the Environment and later prime minister. Greater differentiation from the regions and health ministries and an emphasis on WHO's core global functions marked her leadership. She used the WHO platform to launch initiatives like the Commission on Macroeconomics and Health led by Jeffrey Sachs, the Framework Convention on Tobacco Control (FCTC), and health systems assessment; to strengthen the Codex Alimentarius Commission and WHO-World Bank collaboration; to revise the IHR; to support the creation of the Global Alliance for Vaccines and Immunization (now Gavi) and the Global Fund; and to foster more international health coordination among the G8.

When Brundtland left WHO, she had moved health more to the center of the development agenda. International treaties and norms embodied GHG.

---

[2] R. Narayan and C. Schuftan, "People's Health Movement," in *Health Systems Policy, Finance, and Organization*, ed. G. Carrin, K. Buse, H. K. Heggenhougen, and S. R. Quah (San Diego, CA: Academic Press), 123.

[3] Dr. Margaret Chan addressing WHO Executive Board at its 128th session on January 17, 2011.

WHO emphasized global surveillance and systems of epidemic alert and response to transnational health threats like severe acute respiratory syndrome (SARS) by building and maintaining a strong base of technical expertise.

Jong-Wook Lee succeeded Brundtland in 2003. His work on TB and vaccines at WHO during the two decades prior to his appointment as director-general shaped his leadership. His close advisors were frustrated by slow progress in delivering effective AIDS and TB drugs to patients. Reflecting those frustrations, his solutions shifted staff to countries, made WHO more operational on drug distribution, and built up country offices. WHO's "3 by 5" initiative exemplified Lee's approach: it was a commendable effort to treat 3 million HIV/AIDS sufferers in developing countries by 2005, aiming to establish universal access to antiretroviral therapy. The program represented a shift away from WHO's broad-based direction. The 3 by 5 initiative embodied a narrower focus on specific diseases, on treatment over health determinants and health promotion strategies, and on country-level operational work.

Margaret Chan, director-general between 2007 and 2017, built on her past experience in communicable disease surveillance and response to enhance training for public health professionals and foster collaborations locally and internationally. She focused WHO's efforts accordingly, emphasizing its strength in managing global outbreaks such as avian flu and SARS, yet WHO failed miserably in managing the 2014 Ebola outbreak, while the Zika virus, while no longer an international emergency, remains a serious public health threat. She also prioritized equity to guide health development, particularly in disadvantaged and vulnerable regions.

The current WHO Director-General, Tedros Adhanom Ghebreyesus, commenced his tenure in July 2017 with a focus on five priorities for WHO: health emergencies; universal health coverage; health impacts of climate and environmental change; women's, children's, and adolescents' health; and a transformed WHO.

### 8.1.3 Core Functions

WHO's Constitution divides WHO's core functions into three broad domains: (1) normative functions—international conventions and agreements, regulations, and non-binding standards and recommendations; (2) directing and coordinating functions, including its "Health for All," poverty and health, and essential medicine activities and specific disease programs; and (3) research and technical cooperation functions,[4] including disease eradication and emergencies. Examples of WHO functions are the 2001 World Health Day, making

[4] G. L. Burci and C.-H. Vignes, *World Health Organization* (London: Kluwer Law International, 2004).

mental health a global priority; the promotion of international human rights through international legal instruments; and leadership in developing such global norms and standards as the International Code of Marketing of Breast-Milk Substitutes, the FCTC, and the IHR.

More specifically, WHO's key roles fall into multiple categories. Within normative functions, WHO is responsible for norms and standards, encompassing the proposal, negotiation, and ratification of conventions, regulations, agreements, standards, and recommendations in international health matters. This category also includes developing, establishing, promoting, and ensuring compliance with international standards related to travel; to reciprocity in treatment among nations; and to food, biological, pharmaceutical, and similar products. A second category in this domain concerns surveillance and outbreak response, especially tracking the spread of pathogens and extremely resistant infectious agents that tax national public health surveillance systems.

Under the directing and coordinating functions domain, WHO has functions in empowerment and agency enhancement, including reforming state and local institutions to enhance democratic governance; fostering political will; helping to improve public administration; encouraging greater participation in national and international fora; expanding citizen participation in decision-making; improving public health communication and education; and, overall, enhancing individual and collective health agency. Advocacy is a second category in this domain. A third is global coordination, agenda setting, and consensus building, and bringing together donors and program activities into a coherent whole to reduce redundancies.

Under research and technical cooperation, WHO's functions fall into four categories.

The first is knowledge generation and dissemination, as well as research and development (R&D). It includes the creation of new technologies; the transfer, adaptation, and application of existing knowledge; knowledge and information management; and the development of research and information capacity. The second category covers technical assistance and policy advice, and encompasses help in designing and implementing equitable and efficient health system financing; training medical and public health professionals; health facilities management; equipping regulatory agencies; and standardizing diagnostic categories. Both of these categories have a normative element as well, since they involve identifying and promoting best practices in health care and delivery.

Also under the research and technical cooperation domain is health system development and sustainability—supporting nations in creating, regulating, and stewarding equitable and affordable health care and public health systems. The last category is evaluation and monitoring.

Within these categories, WHO's Constitution specifies functions including epidemiological and statistical services, control and eradication of disease, and establishing international nomenclatures and classifications of diseases and causes of death as essential to a world health information system. WHO has assumed vital roles in these areas and has provided technical assistance to countries developing their own information systems. In fulfilling these roles, WHO combines political, legislative, and executive functions all in one institution. WHO's Constitution specifies its political and legislative functions; the World Health Assembly (WHA) effectuates them (Chapter V, Articles 10–23). The Executive Board (Chapter VI, Articles 24–9) and the Secretariat (Chapter VII, Articles 30–7) fulfill executive roles.

Recent trends, however, suggest shifting priorities. Emerging entities in academia[5] and the US government are stepping in to fill the void WHO leaves, testifying to this shift. The US Centers for Disease Control and Prevention (CDC), for example, has expanded its global health surveillance role, strengthening national public health and information systems, developing an integrated disease-detection strategy, and formulating an information-sharing code of conduct for itself and others.[6] Moreover, the Global Health Security Agenda, an effort by nations, civil society, and international organizations, offers promise for facilitating regional and global cooperation for a world that is secure and safe from communicable disease threats. While these entities promise more resources and expertise for global information systems, many governments depend on WHO to standardize methods, integrate information systems, and ensure the accuracy of health statistics.

Examining WHO's extensive portfolio reveals responsibilities ranging from the global to the local, from the strategic to the operational, from health systems to specific diseases. Over the past several decades, as WHO has prioritized varying categories of work, analysts have critiqued its operational effectiveness.[7] In the mid-1990s Fiona Godlee scrutinized WHO's management, effectiveness, policy choices, headquarter–regional negotiations and power struggles, and weak operational and training capacity in a series of *British Medical Journal* articles.[8] At about the same time, WHO commissioned a self-study that analyzed the effectiveness of its core functions and recommended

[5] C. J. L. Murray, A. D. Lopez. and S. Wibulpolprasert, "Monitoring Global Health: Time for New Solutions," *British Medical Journal* 329, no. 7474 (2004): 1096–100.

[6] US CDC, "GDD Conference Group Reports," Presented at Consultation on Global Disease Detection (GDD), Miami, December 8–9, 2004.

[7] G. Walt, "WHO under Stress: Implications for Health Policy," *Health Policy* 24, no. 2 (1993): 125–44.

[8] F. Godlee, "WHO in Retreat: Is It Losing Its Influence?" *British Medical Journal* 309, no. 6967 (1994): 1491–5; F. Godlee, "WHO in Crisis," *British Medical Journal* 309, no. 6966 (1994): 1424–8; F. Godlee, "WHO Fellowships: What Do They Achieve?" *British Medical Journal* 310, no. 6972 (1995): 110–12.

reforms to strengthen especially its technical capacity and its global health and coordinating roles.[9] In 1996–7, WHO's Executive Board, after six special constitutional review meetings, recommended re-emphasizing coordination, health policy development, norms and standards, health for all advocacy, and advice and technical cooperation.[10]

In the late 1990s, international health scholars and practitioners held a retreat on "Enhancing the Performance of International Health Institutions" in Pocantico, New York, to consider whether the international institutional health structure could meet health needs effectively in the twenty-first-century context of global health interdependence. The Pocantico report concluded, "the importance of WHO was seen primarily for its global normative functions which need to be strengthened and updated," that "the emphasis on technical assistance has often come at the expense of the normative role," that "WHO should be the 'normative conscience' for world health," and that "WHO should assume leadership in achieving more coherence and equity in the system."[11] An article by Jamison, Frenk, and Knaul stressed this view as well,[12] distinguishing between WHO's core functions, including global normative work, and supplementary functions, including technical cooperation. The demand for both kinds of programs has grown, but because most new global health actors address primarily operational functions, the need for WHO's core global functions is even greater.

But a decade and a half into the twenty-first century, WHO proved to be disastrously unprepared for the 2014 West African Ebola pandemic, a failure that resulted in various examinations within and external to WHO to assess its future role in GHG. An Independent Panel on the Global Response to Ebola, convened by the Harvard Global Health Institute (HGHI) and the London School of Hygiene & Tropical Medicine, published a report in *The Lancet* in November 2015. Though they faulted numerous actors, citing "deep inadequacies in the national and international institutions responsible for protecting the public," they reserved their harshest criticism for WHO, noting in particular the five-month delay in declaring Ebola a "public health emergency of international concern." Ashish Jha, HGHI director, told the *Harvard Gazette* that WHO's delay was an "egregious failure." Ebola, the report said, "exposed

---

[9] WHO, *Report of the Executive Board Working Group on the WHO Response to Global Change*, WHO (Geneva: WHO, 1993).

[10] WHO, "Review of the Constitution and Regional Arrangements of the World Health Organization: Report of the Special Group," EB101/7, Presented at Executive Board 101st Session, November 14, 1997.

[11] *Pocantico Retreat: Enhancing the Performance of International Health Institutions*, 1–3 February (Cambridge, MA: Harvard Center for Population and Development Studies, 1996).

[12] D. Jamison, J. Frenk, and F. Knaul, "International Collective Action in Health: Objectives, Functions, and Rationale," *The Lancet* 351, no. 9101 (1998): 514–7.

WHO as unable to meet its responsibility for responding to such situations and alerting the global community.... [D]ecisive, time-bound governance reforms will be needed to rebuild trust in WHO in view of its failings during the Ebola epidemic."[13]

Then, in 2016, the mosquito-borne Zika virus exploded across Latin America and once again challenged WHO's competencies. Though the illness itself is typically mild and its victims are often asymptomatic, the outbreak in some locales coincided with alarming increases in severe birth defects and the incidence of the debilitating Guillain-Barré syndrome. Again, observers were left wondering why WHO wasn't acting. "Despite internal reforms" following the Ebola failures, "WHO [was] still not taking a leadership role in the Zika pandemic."[14] Shortly afterward, WHO did in fact declare Zika an emergency of international concern.

### 8.1.3.1 EXAMINING THE SOCIAL DETERMINANTS OF HEALTH

WHO's Commission on Social Determinants of Health (CSDH),[15] led by Michael Marmot, gathered practitioners and academics to review current knowledge on health's social determinants, prompt public debate, and promote policies to reduce health inequalities within countries and internationally.[16] The commission's work thus served two key WHO roles—as agenda setter, by giving social determinants like housing, sanitation, and education priority for global collaboration and national action; and as knowledge generator, in reviewing, synthesizing, and disseminating public health and social scientific information. The CSDH's final report in 2008 listed recommendations for reducing global health inequalities. Only time will tell whether its recommendations are effective, but WHO clearly asserted its global role in convening this body and focusing on producing public goods for global health improvement. This work also informed WHO's Medium-Term Strategic Plan. Of the thirteen strategic goals, the seventh was "To address the underlying social and economic determinants of health through policies and programs that enhance health equity and integrate pro-poor, gender-responsive, and human rights-based approaches."[17]

---

[13] S. Moon, D. Sridhar, M. A. Pate, A. K. Jha, C. Clinton, S. Delaunay, et al., "Will Ebola Change the Game? Ten Essential Reforms before the Next Pandemic. The Report of the Harvard-LSHTM Independent Panel on the Global Response to Ebola," *The Lancet* 386, no. 10009 (2015): 2204–21.

[14] D. R. Lucey and L. O. Gostin, "The Emerging Zika Pandemic: Enhancing Preparedness," *Journal of the American Medical Association* 315, no. 9 (2016): 865–6.

[15] J.-W. Lee, "Public Health is a Social Issue," *The Lancet* 365, no. 9464 (2005): 1005–6.

[16] M. Marmot, "Social Determinants of Health Inequalities," *The Lancet* 365, no. 9464 (2005): 1099–104.

[17] WHO, Proposed Programme Budget 2002–2003.

## 8.1.4 *International Institutional Legitimacy*[18]

International institutional legitimacy,[19] the basis for an international institution's right to rule or exercise power, is important for understanding WHO's role in GHG. WHO was established by a United Nations (UN) treaty, an example of a social contract conception of legitimacy whereby consenting states contract to follow institutional rules. One problem with this approach for WHO is that it cannot demand recognition by those not party to the contract, including, for example, a whole host of global health initiatives such as the Global Fund, the Gates Foundation, and Gavi.

A second concern with the agreement-by-states approach for WHO legitimacy is that it fails to ground WHO accountability to individual persons or substate groups; transferred legitimacy through states is not sufficient. WHO thus has no legitimacy to enact policies for the world's population, only for states. Even John Rawls' application of social contract theory to peoples rather than states would not offer legitimacy to WHO for individual persons.

Another approach to international institutional legitimacy is procedural; legitimate international institutions visibly articulate and enforce the rule of law. The authority of procedures for international institutions rests on four key values: self-determination, fairness, epistemic reliability, and stability. WHO embodies self-determination and equal participation through the state consent and WHA processes. To the extent that the WHA instantiates a fair process, by which all states are represented equally (and recognizing that not all states are themselves democratic and legitimate), this process confers legitimacy on its results, although it does not ensure just or good outcomes. From an epistemic viewpoint, the legitimacy of democratic processes, such as the WHA, stems from their reliability and stability compared with other alternatives (for example, one state's authority overriding others) and general assent to it as a peaceful way to make decisions among states. The stability basis for international institutional legitimacy is vulnerable, however, to power relations that underlie such processes. Noted international realist Henry Kissinger wrote, "an order whose structure is accepted by all major powers is 'legitimate',"[20] underscoring that legitimacy is attained only when powerful actors support institutional rules.

Though based on both social contract and procedural models of legitimacy, WHO procedures and contracts nevertheless lack a moral foundation,

---

[18] This section stems from: J. P. Ruger, "International Institutional Legitimacy and the World Health Organization," *Journal of Epidemiology and Community Health* 68, no. 8 (2014): 697–700.

[19] For a discussion of international institutional legitimacy in the context of global justice, see J. Rocheleau, "International Institutional Legitimacy," in *Encyclopedia of Global Justice*, ed. D. K. Chatterjee (Heidelberg: Springer, 2011), 562–4.

[20] H. Kissinger, *A World Restored: The Politics of Conservatism in a Revolutionary Era* (London: Victor Gollancz, 1977), 145.

reinforcing de facto asymmetries and manipulations of power. A substantive model of legitimacy, by contrast, confers legitimacy on institutions that are just or promote justice. In PG/SHG, WHO and other international institutions are legitimate if they adhere to principles of justice and health. This perspective commences with a theory of global health justice and the long-term target of global health equity, and determines international institutions' legitimacy by their effectiveness in achieving these goals. A conception of morality is a condition for governance. Critics object that this model conflates legitimacy and justice,[21] but without a moral foundation undergirding social contracts and procedures, power politics prevails and bias is unrestrained.

Despite extensive UN-endowed powers, particularly to serve as the coordinating and directing authority in international health, WHO faces a conundrum: its basis and structure (and its failure to fulfill its mission) undermine its claim to compliance.

### 8.1.5 WHO Failures in Global Health Governance

#### 8.1.5.1 COORDINATION

Though WHO has a mandate to coordinate efforts in global health (Chapter II, Article 2, a, b), it has not been able to fulfill this charge effectively in a context of autonomous states and many new non-state actors. Some note that WHO instruments make no provision for involving nongovernmental organizations (NGOs) beyond consultation and cooperation. On a related front, others charge that WHO has failed to adapt to the new GHG landscape.[22]

While the world looks to WHO as the global coordinating health agency, WHO's Constitution impedes efforts to engage with other organizations, requiring a two-thirds majority to approve many WHO relations with other actors (Chapter XVI, Articles 69, 70, 72). Should WHO amend its Constitution and grant an explicit place for non-state actors? Former Director-General Chan, reflecting on the complexity of the global health system, believed it was not WHO's role to coordinate all of it. "WHO can no longer aim to direct and coordinate all of the activities and policies in multiple sectors that influence public health,"[23] she said. National autonomy and proliferating non-state actors have thwarted WHO's attempts to fulfill this charge.

[21] A. Buchanan and R. O. Keohane, "The Legitimacy of Global Governance Institutions," *Ethics and International Affairs* 20, no. 4 (2006): 405–37.

[22] J. C. Chow, "Is the WHO Becoming Irrelevant?" *Foreign Policy*, December 9, 2010.

[23] I. Kickbusch, W. Hein, and G. Silberschmidt, "Addressing Global Health Governance Challenges through a New Mechanism: The Proposal for a Committee C of the World Health Assembly," *Journal of Law, Medicine & Ethics* 38, no. 3 (2010): 550–63.

Nor does WHO have power to require coordination.[24] Without a credible compliance mechanism, WHO is often ignored and rendered irrelevant by other global health actors. Numerous new global health projects have emerged as alternatives to WHO, arguably providing greater benefits and revealing WHO's weaknesses. But amending the Constitution to give WHO enforcement powers is highly unlikely; member countries demonstrate deep skepticism about WHO management. They routinely circumvent the official budget and the WHA through extra-budgetary financing. Many find WHO's governance structure and bureaucracy bloated and inefficient.

Indeed, some donors arguably reject coordination: the assistance they provide serves their own political, economic, and strategic purposes, whether nationally or organizationally or both. For others, fundamental disagreement on objectives and/or strategy undercuts any impulse for collaboration or overarching authority. Only fundamental changes in underlying motivations and ethical commitments can alter these actors' engagement.

WHO's own lack of legitimacy, transparency, and accountability also challenge its coordinating role among global health actors. Reform proposals[25,26,27] tackle these problems, but basic questions remain about WHO's essential functions and priorities.

### 8.1.5.2 OVERLAPPING FUNCTIONS

Due to the overlapping functions its Constitution stipulates, an admixture of political, legislative, and executive functions plagues WHO. In addition to the overlap among the WHA, the Executive Board, and the Secretariat, problematic functional overlaps also appear in its roles as advisor, evaluator, and advocate on projects. WHO has missed opportunities to amend its Constitution and thus has not adapted to new conditions over time.

### 8.1.5.3 THE UN-CONSTITUTION

Nor does WHO's Constitution function according to the typical constitutional model, which provides for legislative, executive, and judicial powers but also limits these powers. Some interpretations of constitutionalism argue that this capacity to constrain its own power is a key source of an institution's

---

[24] L. Eaton, "WHO Lacks Teeth on International Issues, Says Professor," *British Medical Journal* 327, no. 7423 (2003): 1070.

[25] For recommendations to incorporate NGOs in decision-making beyond consultation and cooperation, bring the private sector organizations under the technical wing, and include them as voting members, see Chow, "Is WHO Becoming Irrelevant?"

[26] On a Committee C as part of the WHA for non-state actors, see Kickbusch, Hein, and Silberschmidt, "Addressing Global Health Governance."

[27] For positions for non-state actors on the executive board, giving more voice and representation to key stakeholders, including philanthropies, private sector, and civil society, see D. Sridhar and L. Gostin, "Reforming the World Health Organization," *Journal of the American Medical Association* 305, no. 15 (2011):1585–6.

legitimacy. WHO's failures to articulate and implement such constraints, along with its lack of specific authority to fulfill its proper roles, further undermine its legitimacy, leadership, and effectiveness. Nor does WHO set forth clear responsibilities for state governments, other organizations, or individuals themselves. These failures are less attributable to WHO, more to the overall system of GHG. WHO was simply not designed to deal with current global health complexities.

### 8.1.5.4 WHO AND MEMBER STATES' AUTONOMY

Respect for national sovereignty is a foundational principle in WHO and the UN system overall. But to solve GHG problems we must move away from the current mutual-advantage model of international relations and its social contract-based view of international institutional legitimacy. Politics and influence pervade even the selection of regional officers and directorships at WHO. At the highest level, Japan's 1988 trade sanctions threat against small states that failed to support the unpopular Hiroshi Nakajima as director-general tainted that appointment. States must broaden their understanding and recognize that they serve their own people best when they integrate their national autonomy and parochial interests into a larger global vision of human flourishing.

### 8.1.5.5 WHO'S FAILURES IN ACCOUNTABILITY, TRANSPARENCY, AND JUSTICE

WHO came under sharp criticism in 2009 for procedural opacity and bowing to commercial interests in the H1N1 outbreak.[28] Some experts advising WHO had financial links to pharmaceutical companies producing antivirals and vaccines. Further, the emergency committee advising Dr. Chan on the timing for declaring a pandemic (with financial implications for pharma companies) did not deliberate publicly.[29] Many impartial experts concluded that WHO declared the H1N1 pandemic without adequate scientific justification. "WHO insists," claimed a report to the Council of Europe's Parliamentary Assembly, "on maintaining the pandemic at level 6 against all evidence." That year, pharmaceutical companies earned between $7 billion and $10 billion from the H1N1 vaccine business.[30]

WHO's helplessness in coordinating global actors creates other governance problems. Individual actors remain accountable for programs or projects under their direct control, but many global heath efforts involve numerous

[28] P. Flynn, "The Handling of the H1N1 Pandemic: More Transparency Needed," Report of the Social Health and Family Affairs Committee, Parliamentary Assembly, Council of Europe, 2010.

[29] D. Cohen and P. Carter, "WHO and the Pandemic Flu 'Conspiracies'," *British Medical Journal* 340 (2010): c2912.

[30] Flynn, "The Handling of H1N1 Pandemic," 2.

actors, and the absence of coordination blurs lines of responsibility. Account-ability failures often follow. Expecting better WHO accountability is a vain hope, given its institutional shortcomings. Mutual collective accountability offers one solution to these issues.

As a one-state-one-vote body, the WHA is more democratic and egalitarian than other international organizations. Still, WHO governance remains unfair and unbalanced. Influential countries and organizations shape WHO affairs through extra-budgetary funding[31] for purposes they choose, thus bypassing the WHA and WHO's budget.[32] WHO has aligned with powerful countries' interests: it focused on malaria eradication from 1949 to 1956 because Western nations wanted to expand overseas markets and undermine the USSR and communism. Unwritten rules have influenced the appointment of senior officials, requiring five of six assistant directors-general to come from the USA, former USSR, France, China, and the United Kingdom.[33] Power interests among countries and international actors and key actors' ideological commit-ments have shaped WHO's work and prevented it from taking a normatively and scientifically grounded approach. For example, when US-based pharma firms opposed WHO's essential drug program in 1985, the USA withheld WHO funding.[34] WHO legitimacy suffers from this kind of corrosive manipulation.

Though WHO has on occasion produced notable health successes, it remains bound by a global framework of self-interest maximization that yields inadequate global health results. This approach fails to bring about what is most needed—health equity.

### 8.1.5.6 WHO FUNDING: SHORTCHANGING HEALTH PROJECTS

A failure of coordination also results in funding problems. Without compre-hensive coordination of projects and funding through a global health policy master plan, health efforts must rely on unorganized, short-term funding from multiple organizations. In the past actual WHO extra-budgetary funding accounted for about 75 percent of the total. These extra-budgetary contribu-tions do not necessarily align with WHO's program priorities. They thus deprive the organization of sufficient funds to execute its core functions—technical collaboration, policy advice and dialogue, norms and standards

---

[31] For reforms which promote phasing out such spending measures rather than amending the WHO Constitution, see M. Reeves and S. Brundage, *Leveraging the World Health Organization's Core Strengths* (Washington, DC: Center for Strategic & International Studies, 2011).

[32] G. Walt, "Globalisation of International Health," *The Lancet* 351, no. 9100 (1998): 434–7.

[33] J. W. Peabody, "An Organizational Analysis of the World Health Organization: Narrowing the Gap between Promise and Performance," *Social Science & Medicine* 40, no. 6 (1995): 731–42.

[34] T. M. Brown, M. Cueto, and E. Fee, "The World Health Organization and the Transition from 'International' to 'Global' Public Health," *American Journal of Public Health* 96, no. 1 (2006): 62–72.

setting, knowledge generation and dissemination, and convening—all of which are vital to WHO's impact and, more broadly, to global public health.

This situation is unpredictable and unsustainable.[35] It diminishes WHO's accountability, transparency, and fairness, politicizing the institution and compromising its legitimacy in international health relations. The distortion in funding cedes WHO control to wealthy and influential donors and undermines the WHA's rightful authority. Most member countries are too poor to make significant extra-budgetary donations, giving them little say over WHO's donor-earmarked projects, many of which do not serve recipient countries' needs. The proliferation of global health actors and donors is in part a response to these distortions.

Many also believe WHO is highly inefficient and internally politicized. Human resource issues, regionalization, and internal decision-making squabbles expose these problems. Gaps exist between stated objectives and results on the ground. Why would independently resourced global health actors submit to WHO coordination? Collective financing, a multiyear framework agreement with donors, and a contingency fund for public health emergencies are potential reforms that could help, but WHO financing issues have their roots in deeper problems and the overarching need for a new GHG paradigm.

### 8.1.5.7 SCIENTIFIC CREDIBILITY: DECOUPLING SCIENCE FROM POLITICS

In spite of its besetting ills, WHO can perform many essential global health functions. The world needs a scientifically credible executive agency to shape and implement policies to improve world health. Separating the executive functions of WHO from the WHA and its associated legislative and political officials would maintain representative democracy in the WHA, divorce politics from implementation, peel away overlapping functions, and reestablish WHO's scientific integrity.

A system of checks and balances eludes WHO and the larger global health system. WHO has not asserted functional independence in either the scientific or coordination realms. WHO must redesign its components and procedures to shake off its powerful member states' influence. These countries will only agree, however, if they turn from narrow national interests and fully embrace a global health equity norm.

### 8.1.5.8 WHO'S PERFORMANCE THROUGH THE SHARED HEALTH GOVERNANCE LENS

WHO's problems reveal the depths of its failure to meet SHG standards. As we have seen, the influence of wealthy and powerful actors—states, corporations,

---

[35] WHO, "The Future of Financing for WHO: Report by the Director-General," EB128/21, Presented at WHO Executive Board 128th Session, December 15, 2010.

NGOs—means that their interests prevail, and so the system fails to align goals among actors and governments. These same interests monopolize resources, diverting and reducing funds available for essential work; and often actors simply renege on their financial obligations to WHO, which, without enforcement mechanisms, is left to struggle with inadequate funding. The extent to which partisan actors have co-opted scientific decision-making, and the haphazard approach inherent in the multiplicity of actors, makes mutual understanding of key outcomes and principle indicators nearly impossible. Though governments, agencies, and organizations might operate with the best philanthropic intentions, they often fail to involve various stakeholders. Vulnerable groups in particular are frequently left aside in the programs of these powerful entities. WHO lacks the capacity and power to change these patterns.

WHO's performance thus fails under the scrutiny of the PG/SHG framework. We cannot rely on WHO alone to promote human flourishing. Without a broader vision and structure, we will not achieve global health equity, diminish worldwide contagions, or resolve cross-border issues.

### 8.1.6 *The Future for WHO*

All is not lost with WHO; the world continues to look to this institution to coordinate and advance the global health agenda. Strong WHO leadership in the past has helped open critical global health pathways. WHO has pressed health's importance in trade debates, human rights contexts, public–private partnerships (PPPs), and treaty revisions and reinterpretations: the Agreement on Trade-Related Aspects of International Property Rights process is a notable example.

WHO's leadership is visible in its work on FCTC implementation and protocol development,[36] the Codex Alimentarius Commission, revision and implementation of the IHR, analysis of trade settlements' impact on health, and efforts to move the Global Strategy on Diet, Physical Activity and Health into implementation. In this role, WHO has brought together technical experts in law, economics, trade, and other relevant fields.

Three further illustrations show the continuing need for WHO. One major issue is trade in medicines. The Medical Research and Development Treaty, first proposed in 2005, urges signatory countries to invest in medical innovation. Much like the Kyoto Protocol for greenhouse gas emissions, it provides for trading investment credits with other countries.[37] This pact helps resolve

---

[36] D. Yach, "Injecting Greater Urgency into Global Tobacco Control," *Tobacco Control* 14, no. 3 (2005): 145–8.

[37] A. Jack, "WHO Members Urged to Sign Kyoto-Style Medical Treaty," *Financial Times*, February 25, 2005.

global issues, such as finding treatments for developing countries' neglected diseases, while also providing intellectual property (IP) protection to incentivize R&D. WHO would play a central role in writing the treaty, building consensus, and member state ratification and implementation. Action on this treaty stalled, but the need for it remains. No international organization besides WHO has the normative or technical capacity to steward these efforts.

A second example involves WHO's role in coordinating the international activities of various organizations. Here the health field can learn from international biotechnology law-making (in which, for example, overlapping jurisdictions have adopted conflicting IP standards) and the environmental arena, where the absence of an overarching authority has meant "counterproductive and inconsistent results."[38] WHO could promote more integrated and collective decision-making and thus fill a void in current global health leadership.

In a third governance role, WHO could continue to update infectious disease control regulations, such as the IHR.[39] Most observers agree that improving global health in the twenty-first century will require coordination and cooperation among states, using both legal and non-legal mechanisms. This consensus envisions a role for WHO as a convener and coordinator for codifying future health laws.[40]

The real issue is less WHO's problems and more today's GHG requirements. The global health enterprise needs an institution arching over WHO's Constitution: a Global Health Constitution (GHC). It must specify WHO functions and articulate the roles and duties of other entities.

### 8.1.7 Global Tobacco Control: A Case Study in Integrated Global Health Policy[41]

#### 8.1.7.1 THE FRAMEWORK CONVENTION ON TOBACCO CONTROL

Though beset with structural and political problems, WHO has nevertheless scored important global health successes, for example, the FCTC—the "first

---

[38] A. L. Taylor, "Global Governance, International Health Law and WHO: Looking Towards the Future," *Bulletin of the World Health Organization* 80, no. 12 (2002): 975–80; P. Birnie and A. Boyle, *International Law and the Environment* (Oxford: Oxford University Press, 2002).

[39] L. O. Gostin, "International Infectious Disease Law: Revision of the World Health Organization's International Health Regulations," *Journal of the American Medical Association* 291, no. 21 (2004): 2623–7.

[40] A. Taylor, D. Bettcher, S. Fluss, K. DeLand, and D. Yach, "International Health Law Instruments: An Overview," in *Oxford Textbook of Public Health: The Scope of Public Health*, ed. R. Detels, R. Beaglehole, M. A. Lansang, and M. Gulliford (Oxford: Oxford University Press, 2002), 359–86.

[41] This section stems from the following: J. P. Ruger, "Global Tobacco Control: An Integrated Approach to Global Health Policy," *Development* 48, no. 2 (2005): 65–9; J. P. Ruger, "Combating HIV/AIDS in Developing Countries," *British Medical Journal* 329, no. 7458 (2004): 121–2;

international treaty negotiated under the auspices of WHO."[42] The WHA's 192 members unanimously adopted this historic document in May 2003 to reduce tobacco-related disease and death worldwide. The FCTC seeks to lower the demand for tobacco through advertising, price, and tax policies, and to reduce supply by prohibiting smuggling and sales to and by minors. The FCTC exemplifies an expanding trend in development policy toward broad, integrated, and multifaceted approaches.[43,44,45,46] It relies on partnerships to exploit institutional advantages and eliminate redundancies. The FCTC marks a policy shift toward addressing health needs on multiple fronts and integrating public policies into overall health improvement strategies. It is consistent with the health capability paradigm: it measures development by the expansion of individual freedom rather than by gross national product or personal income. Instead of judging health policy by spending or defined benefits, important as these are, it understands policy's purpose as the expansion of individuals' opportunities for good health.

### 8.1.7.2 A BROADER PUBLIC HEALTH APPROACH

A multidimensional, integrated approach to health improvement rejects a narrow view of health and its determinants. We know that many important health determinants lie beyond the boundaries of the health care sector.[47] Thus, health care, critical as it is, cannot alone ensure good health or prevent illness resulting from, for example, tobacco use or HIV/AIDS. Multifaceted strategies have produced better results than narrower approaches for reining in tobacco use in numerous countries.[48] Bans on advertising, promotion, and sales to children; mandatory health warnings; smoke-free environments; higher taxes on tobacco products; and investment in health education, smoking prevention, and cessation programs have all been successful. Under the

J. P. Ruger, "Millennium Development Goals for Health: Building Human Capabilities," *Bulletin of the World Health Organization* 82, no. 12 (2004): 951–2; J. P. Ruger, "Health and Development," *The Lancet* 362, no. 9385 (2003): 678; J. P. Ruger, "Ethics of the Social Determinants of Health," *The Lancet* 364, no. 9439 (2004): 1092–7.

[42] WHO, "About the WHO Framework Convention on Tobacco Control," *FCTC* (2017). Available at: http://www.who.int/fctc/en/ (accessed December 12, 2017).

[43] J. E. Stiglitz, "An Agenda for Development in the Twenty-First Century," in *Annual World Bank Conference on Development Economics 1997*, ed. B. Pleskovic and J. E. Stiglitz (Washington, DC: World Bank, 1998), 17–33.

[44] A. Sen, *Development as Freedom* (New York: Knopf, 1999).

[45] J. D. Wolfensohn, *A Proposal for a Comprehensive Development Framework* (Washington, DC: World Bank, 1999).

[46] D. Rodrik, *The New Global Economy and Developing Countries: Making Openness Work* (Washington, DC: Overseas Development Council, 1999).

[47] M. Marmot, M. Bobak, and G. Davey Smith, "Explanations for Social Inequalities in Health," in *Society and Health*, ed. B. C. Amick, III., S. Levine, A. R. Tarlov, and D. C. Chapman (New York: Oxford University Press, 1995), 172–211.

[48] F. J. Chaloupka, "Curbing the Epidemic: Governments and the Economics of Tobacco Control," *Tobacco Control* 8, no. 2 (1999): 196–201.

FCTC, for example, ministries of health and associations like physician groups joined forces with ministries of finance, economic planning, taxation, labor, industry, and education, and with citizen groups and private-sector actors, to coordinate tobacco-control efforts. Such efforts helped achieve multisectoral support for the framework.[49]

### 8.1.7.3 DEVELOPMENT AND HEALTH

Integrated public policy goes well beyond disease-specific interventions to encompass a country's overall development strategies. For example, disadvantaged individuals have higher rates of smoking initiation and addiction, in both developed and developing countries. Poverty, in particular, correlates with smoking.[50] Adolescent smoking also correlates with socioeconomic status, and the impact of poverty and social disadvantage makes escaping tobacco addiction, which sometimes goes back generations, difficult for young people. Conversely, positive influences, such as cultural disapproval of smoking, expectations that one will not smoke, and smoke-free workplaces,[51] strengthen prevention and cessation strategies. In addition, empowering political, civil, and job opportunities[52] foster tobacco abstinence and cessation; these freedoms enhance personal agency, enabling greater self-control and promoting healthier life strategies.

Integrated policy thus has horizontal and vertical dimensions. The horizontal dimension encompasses policies across projects that target specific diseases, bringing together complementary interventions to prevent disease and improve health. The vertical dimension aligns varied domains of public policy. Improving education and employment prospects, for example, can improve health. Horizontal integration can enhance vertical integration, and vice versa.

A third kind of integration links organizations with disease-specific missions to those with broader development goals in coordinated strategies. Government agencies can ban workplace smoking, for example, and employers and insurers can provide cessation programs. The shift toward PPPs illustrates this approach, but closer integration between specific disease prevention efforts and broader development activities, as in the FCTC, is key.

Important as it is, integrated public policy is no panacea. For example, smoking reductions through workplace bans and higher taxes may be slow

[49] D. Yach, H. Wipfli, R. Hammond, and S. Glantz, "Globalization and Tobacco," in *Globalization and Health*, ed. I. Kawachi and S. Wamala (New York: Oxford University Press, 2007), 39–67.

[50] K. E. Warner, "The Economics of Tobacco: Myths and Realities," *Tobacco Control* 9, no. 1 (2000): 78–89.

[51] M. J. Jarvis, "ABC of Smoking Cessation: Why People Smoke," *British Medical Journal* 328, no. 7434 (2004): 277–9.

[52] M. E. Northridge, "Building Coalitions for Tobacco Control and Prevention in the 21st Century," *American Journal of Public Health* 94, no. 2 (2004): 178–80.

to materialize. Coordinating many different strategies might prove challenging. Implementing strategies sequentially is also time intensive, and because it weaves policies together, evaluating them for systematic review and revision can be difficult.

In the FCTC, development policy shifted toward integration and multiplicity, creating possibilities for novel global tobacco control efforts. The World Bank's development agenda at the time articulated a deeper grasp of poverty and its multidimensional causes and more comprehensive development. Comprehensive development focused on individuals in client countries, balancing strengths of the market with those of institutions. In the lead-up to the FCTC, WHO collaborated with the World Bank on global tobacco control, especially in macroeconomic analysis and establishing an evidence base for the most effective tobacco-control strategies. Two Bank reports in particular, *Curbing the Epidemic* and *Tobacco Control in Developing Countries*, examined research results on tobacco control efforts and their impact. The Bank also analyzed household expenditure surveys in Bulgaria, Tajikistan, and Egypt to assess household spending on tobacco products.

### 8.1.7.4 THE ESSENTIAL ROLE OF SUSTAINABLE SYSTEMS

Many development scholars recognize that development requires varied elements, ranging from functional, supervised financial systems to a sustainable environment, and they have offered models encompassing this view. Amartya Sen's development paradigm,[53] for example, views development as the expansion of individual freedoms, including freedom from avoidable diseases (for example, those caused by tobacco use). This paradigm addresses basic capabilities like health on multiple fronts and would integrate public policies into a comprehensive package of development strategies. This integration requires various institutions with complementary roles. More than fifty years of theory and experience suggest, for example, that macroeconomic stability, liberalization, and privatization—key components of the Washington Consensus—may still count, but development is complex and needs more than the Washington Consensus provides. Promoting prosperity, reducing poverty, and expanding human freedom require many elements, including economic growth and stability, a strong private sector, investment in people and physical assets, a sustainable environment, and fair institutions and policies.

The FCTC embodies a paradigmatic shift in thinking about global tobacco control that parallels a change in global development policy toward a broad, integrated, and multifaceted framework. These shifts, evolving steadily over several decades, rest on empirical evidence and theoretical foundations about

---

[53] Sen, *Development as Freedom*.

human well-being, including health and the conditions that improving health and well-being requires. While these efforts have not yet fully borne fruit, the need for a multifaceted, integrated approach to health improvement and development is becoming ever clearer.

### 8.1.8 *Conclusion*

Restoring confidence in WHO's competence will require reassessing its role and responsibilities vis-à-vis other global health actors. A GHC could help in this task. WHO should focus on areas where it serves a unique role or has a comparative advantage, such as disease surveillance, control, and elimination; technical collaboration; convening; and norms and standards setting. A clear mandate tailored to WHO's strengths enables greater efficiency and accountability, which in turn can renew member countries' support and their willingness to make predictable, sustainable, and flexible contributions adequate to fund WHO's budget.

Sustaining collective WHO financing requires shared commitment and contributors' confidence that their funds will be managed effectively to benefit all countries, rich and poor. WHO must achieve greater efficiency and transparency, better program monitoring and evaluation, and an advisory role for countries in its work, through a reform process that is forward thinking, methodical, harmonized, inclusive, and transparent. These governance improvement measures could be presented as conditions for increased contributions to the regular budget.

Dr. Tedros Adhanom Ghebreyesus is the new director-general of WHO. He served as Minister of Foreign Affairs, Ethiopia, from 2012 to 2016 and as Minister of Health, Ethiopia, from 2005 to 2012. He has also served as chair of the Board of the Global Fund; as chair of the Roll Back Malaria Partnership Board; and as co-chair of the Board of the Partnership for Maternal, Newborn, and Child Health. The world awaits his WHO leadership.

## 8.2 Other UN Agencies: UNICEF, UNAIDS, UNFPA

UNICEF, the United Nations Children's Fund, was established in 1946 to meet an immediate crisis: in World War II's aftermath, countless European children faced famine and disease. UNICEF formed to provide them with food, clothing, and health care. In 1953, it became a permanent branch of the UN. Its work has evolved into five broad focus areas, of which three—Child Survival and Development, HIV/AIDS and Children, and Child Protection—explicitly target health and survival. Basic Education and Gender Equality and Policy Advocacy and Partnerships, the other two focus areas, relate to health as well.

UNICEF has staff in some 190 countries,[54] and has functions in at least seven of the same categories as WHO's duties, including technical assistance and policy advice, empowerment and agency enhancement, advocacy, coordination/agenda setting/consensus building, setting and promoting norms and standards, health system development and sustainability, and promoting growth in the macrosocial environment.

Over the years UNICEF has done invaluable work and fulfilled an essential global health role. But the program has come under sharp criticism for, among other things, its opposition to foreign adoptions,[55] promoting a policy that keeps children in home country orphanages in respect for their cultural heritage. Critics charge that this approach unnecessarily consigns millions of infants and children to lives of desperate deprivation in poor conditions. It is possible that UNICEF also has insufficiently addressed high and in some countries increasing child mortality rates. In numerous countries, mortality among children has proved resistant to intervention efforts, and observers believe UNICEF must bear some of the responsibility for this failure.[56]

UNAIDS—the Joint United Nations' Program on HIV/AIDS—launched in 1996 to combat HIV/AIDS and currently comprises numerous UN agencies and other actors. Its mission includes preventing transmission, caring for and supporting HIV/AIDS sufferers, helping protect people and communities from the virus, and averting a severe pandemic. Global efforts against HIV/AIDS have achieved some significant successes. A 2013 UNAIDS report documented notable progress on AIDS in Africa, noting that the number of people receiving antiretroviral treatment there increased from less than 1 million in 2005 to 7.1 million in 2013.[57] According to the report, both AIDS-related deaths and the numbers of new HIV infections have been decreasing. But UNAIDS is just one of a growing number of actors in the global HIV/AIDS battle, fighting alongside and sometimes competing with the US President's Emergency Plan for AIDS Relief, Gavi, and other actors.

The United Nations Population Fund (UNFPA: originally the UN Fund for Population Activities) formed in 1969 to promote the right of every person to enjoy a life of equal opportunity and health. UNFPA seeks to promote "a world where every pregnancy is wanted, every childbirth is safe and every young

---

[54] UNICEF, "Information by Country and Programme," *UNICEF* (2017). Available at: https://www.unicef.org/where-we-work (accessed December 12, 2017).

[55] E. Bartholet, "International Adoption," in *Children and Youth in Adoption, Orphanages, and Foster Care*, ed. L. Askeland (Westport, CT: Greenwood Press, 2006).

[56] R. Horton, "UNICEF Leadership 2005–2015: A Call for Strategic Change," *The Lancet* 364, no. 9451 (2004): 2071–4.

[57] UNAIDS, "Special Report: How Africa Turned AIDS Around," African Union Summit, Geneva, May 2013.

person's potential is fulfilled."[58] Its goals include universal access to reproductive health services, universal primary education, reducing maternal and infant mortality, increasing life expectancy, and decreasing HIV infection rates.

As with WHO, the performance of these UN agencies often falls short under SHG scrutiny. UNICEF adoption policies, for example, sometimes conflict with those of national governments, preventing goal alignment among actors and levels of government. A proliferation of global actors, in the HIV/AIDS arena, for example, entails competition for finite resources. A multiplicity of actors also typically yields multiple and diffuse approaches to common problems, making mutual understanding of outcomes and indicators difficult. The continuing proliferation of these actors reduces the possibilities for engaging other global, national, and subnational groups and institutions in a coordinated way, or for achieving effective, efficient resource use for priority areas. Finally, while each of these agencies undoubtedly seeks to engage the vulnerable groups within its mandate, the reality often fails to meet the aspiration.

## 8.3 The Millennium Development Goals

In 2000, the 189 UN member states, along with more than a score of international organizations, adopted eight international development goals: (1) eradicating extreme poverty and hunger; (2) achieving universal primary education; (3) promoting gender equality and empowering women; (4) reducing child mortality; (5) improving maternal health; (6) combating HIV/AIDS, malaria, and other diseases; (7) ensuring environmental sustainability; and (8) developing a global partnership for development—all by 2015.

Unquestionably, these goals spoke to critical needs and urgent moral imperatives. And the UN and its many Millennium Development Goals (MDG) collaborators around the world achieved some striking successes. In his foreword to *The Millennium Development Goals Report 2013*, then Secretary-General Ban Ki-moon noted, "Significant and substantial progress has been made in meeting many of the targets—including halving [both] the number of people living in extreme poverty and the proportion of people without sustainable access to improved sources of drinking water."[59] Indeed, the potable water target was met five years ahead of schedule. Since 1990, the child mortality rate has dropped by 41 percent; 14,000 fewer children are dying each day.[60]

---

[58] UNFPA, "About UNFPA," *UNFPA*. Available at: http://www.unfpa.org/about-us (accessed December 12, 2017).
[59] UN, *The Millennium Development Goals Report 2013* (New York: UN, 2013), 3.
[60] Ibid., 24.

Regrettably, however, these statistics tell only parts of a larger story, as the *Report* itself readily acknowledges. Taking child mortality as just one example, the *Report* states, "6.9 million children under age five died in 2011—mostly from preventable diseases. In sub-Saharan Africa, one in nine children die[s] before age five, more than 16 times the average for developed regions."[61] Eastern Asia and Northern Africa were "the only regions that have met the target so far."[62] And gaps were growing: "As under-five mortality rates fall in richer developing regions, the majority of child deaths are occurring in the poorest ones—sub-Saharan Africa and Southern Asia. In 2011, these two regions accounted for 5.7 million of the 6.9 million deaths in children under five worldwide. This represents 83 per cent of the global total in 2011, up from 69 per cent in 1990."[63] Ban himself observed that "the achievement of the MDGs has been uneven among and within countries."[64]

The global financial crisis, beginning in 2008, unquestionably thwarted MDG progress, yet there are much deeper systemic problems underlying these failures.[65] A fundamental barrier was the lack of adequate data systems. For example, while MDG monitoring drew "global attention to the problem of child mortality, established targets for its reduction, and informed policy-makers about the impact of their actions," the *Report* notes that many developing countries lacked "complete vital registration systems, the best source of monitoring data...."[66] These data gaps confounded many MDG efforts.

Much more broadly, achieving the health-related MDGs required ramping up government health care spending, investing in human and physical capital, and allocating resources within the health sector to medically appropriate and medically necessary care and specific populations and geographical areas. Significant efficiency and health care quality improvements were also critical. Low-tech, inexpensive solutions are available to prevent death and disease—antibiotics, immunizations, basic hygiene and health care, health knowledge, bed nets, prenatal and obstetric care, and nutrition. The problem is not a lack of interventions; it is access. The challenge of universal coverage and access to technology is a problem not of medicine or public health but of collective action. Achieving the health-related MDGs, then, requires more than scaling-up health investments, important as they are; transformed values and societal structures are also essential. National and

---

[61] Ibid., 24.
[62] Ibid., 25.
[63] Ibid., 25.
[64] Ibid., 3.
[65] M. R. Reich, K. Takemi, M. J. Roberts, and W. C. Hsiao, "Global Action on Health Systems: A Proposal for the Toyako G8 Summit," *The Lancet* 371, no. 9615 (2008): 865–9.
[66] UN, *The Millennium Development Goals Report 2013*, 26.

local leaders, accountable to their electorates, must make a genuine commitment if progress is to be made toward health for all.

Although the MDGs and the succeeding Sustainable Development Goals offer a basis for cooperation, they both arose out of the current global health architecture. Today's global heath governance is power and interest driven, consistent with a pervasive realist and neorealist model, operating behind a façade of global health justice and ethics. The current global health establishment failed both to set up an effective system to achieve the MDGs and to commit fully to global health justice principles.

# 9

# The World Bank and Other Organizations

## 9.1 Development Assistance for Health: An Alternative Approach

As we saw in Part I, current development assistance for health (DAH) framings support widely varying donor motivations for foreign aid, and while both beneficence and non-maleficence underlie some aid, neither value is a system requirement, nor necessarily leads to global justice. Nor does the promotion of economic development or welfare, as traditionally defined, necessarily promote global justice. While initiatives like the Paris Declaration and Accra Agenda for Action have placed additional conditions on foreign aid, standard motivations persist within an underlying neoliberal development paradigm. Criticisms of the DAH system and proposed solutions are outlined in Table 9.1.

The provincial globalism (PG) and shared health governance (SHG) line of reasoning offers an alternative DAH approach and a strong critique of the current development paradigm. SHG rejects welfare, understood as satisfaction, desire fulfillment, or happiness, as a basis for judging social arrangements. The welfare concept is not unimportant: in two societies with equal socioeconomic development, the one where people are happy would be better than the one where people are unhappy. But policy assessment and interpersonal comparisons should not depend on people's subjective assessments of their well-being.

A SHG approach also rejects frameworks that rely on individual or social contracts that purport to respect individual and group autonomy because these parties accept agreements believed to be mutually beneficial and resulting from fair terms of cooperation. There are reasons to be skeptical of this social contract view because individuals and groups are often not in fact free to negotiate effectively: the social, political, and economic circumstances underlying these agreements lead less privileged groups, paradoxically, to accept contracts undercutting their interests and yielding lower well-being than a broader view of global justice would provide.

Additionally, as we have seen, empirical research demonstrates that donors are not solely altruistic, but often have self-serving objectives for providing

**Table 9.1.** DAH Criticisms and Proposed Solutions

| Criticisms | Solutions |
| --- | --- |
| *DAH undermines the ability of recipient countries to finance sustainable health systems* | *Financing* |
| • Current total DAH levels are considered inadequate<br>• The volatility of overall health financing exacerbates uncertainty for recipients<br>• DAH may actually crowd out domestic health financing<br>• Donor-driven development is still the dominant paradigm | • International taxes (for example, airline ticket levy, billionaire and sin taxes, financial transaction taxes)<br>• Financial mechanisms (for example, Advance Market Commitments, International Finance Facility for Immunization, Debt2Health)<br>• Products in the private sector (Product Red, product labeling for purchase) |
| *The influences driving DAH decision-making and priority setting are unclear* | *Coordination and accountability mechanisms* |
| • Lack of coordination among an increasingly fragmented set of DAH actors creates and exacerbates inefficiencies in health administration, delivery, and processes in recipient countries | • Sector-wide approaches<br>• "One" or "Unified" initiatives ("Three Ones" for HIV/AIDS, One United Nations)<br>• The Paris Declaration on Aid Effectiveness and the Accra Agenda for Action<br>• IHP+<br>• PRSPs |
| *The legitimacy and accountability of the DAH system questionable* | • Health 8<br>• Health 4+ for MCH |
| • DAH lacks effective accountability mechanisms to ensure that both donors and recipients are accountable, not just for use of funds and their impact, but for overall DAH system<br>• There is no clearly recognized global normative framework for DAH<br>• Recipients are not adequately included in decision-making processes<br>• Actors are not held accountable for performance and results | *UN commissions and international laws and treaties*<br>• UN Commission on Information and Accountability for Women's and Children's Health<br>• FCTC<br>• Framework Convention on Global Health<br>• Framework Convention on Obesity<br>• Global Social Protection Fund<br>• International convention on R&D (proposed)<br>• International convention on alcohol (proposed)<br>• International Health Regulations |

aid. These multiple objectives often mean that aid privileges donor interests, not recipient country health needs. Donors can unduly influence recipient country health sectors and policies because they have more financial and technical resources, capacity, and diplomatic prowess. Donor countries influence recipient country policies in ways that diverge from or disregard altogether the needs and preferences of recipient countries' governments and people.[1] The social contract framing thus fails to provide a just basis for development assistance.

---

[1] K. Buse, "Keeping a Tight Grip on the Reins: Donor Control over Aid Coordination and Management in Bangladesh," *Health Policy and Planning* 14, no. 3 (1999): 219–28; R. Hayman, "From Rome to Accra via Kigali: 'Aid Effectiveness' in Rwanda," *Development Policy Review* 27, no. 5

PG/SHG also rejects the neoliberal idea that development equals economic growth, measurable by gross national product (GNP). The economic growth view rises from neoclassical economic theory, which focuses on maximizing economic welfare, free markets, property rights, and employing economic efficiency as a guiding principle. The SHG approach by contrast focuses on people and expanding their capabilities, with equity as a guiding principle. Economic growth is important if it is people centered and creates opportunities for individuals to do and be what they value. In SHG, therefore, DAH requires a normative basis for evaluating individual well-being, social arrangements and structures, and for the design of institutions and policies.

A normative evaluative framework for public and private development policies assesses DAH in terms of global justice. A framework to guide international development assistance must abandon the recipient/beneficiary dichotomy and replace it with equal respect for the capabilities of all. Development policies and practices should strengthen health outcomes and health agency. They should empower people as agents of change in their own countries rather than merely aid recipients and political pawns.

In this SHG view, donors recognize a positive duty to the flourishing of all people globally. This duty calls donors to prevent and reduce shortfall health inequalities among all global citizens. Donors also have an obligation to assist developing countries in discharging their duty to prevent and reduce shortfall health inequalities among their own populations. Recipient countries have a duty to use aid effectively and efficiently for their populations' health and flourishing. This duty includes creating and maintaining institutions and policies and allocating resources so that people can flourish and have opportunities to be healthy. These institutions focus on addressing populations' health functioning and health agency.

Because this global justice approach is universal in scope, duties apply to all global citizens, populations within and foreign to a donor country. But while this program's scope is broader than the current disjointed project-by-project approach, it does have limits. The limits of donors' obligations lie at the point where giving more would risk their own populations' central health capabilities, which are equally valuable morally as the central health capabilities of non-citizens.

To discharge this duty, donors must deploy normative and empirical analysis to ensure effective aid. Ineffective aid not only does little good but also takes money away from more effective uses of those resources. The SHG framework attends closely to opportunity costs—the real societal costs of given resources, or the resources' value in their alternative or next best use.

(2009): 581–99; B. Woll, "Donor Harmonisation and Government Ownership: Multi-Donor Budget Support in Ghana," *The European Journal of Development Research* 20, no. 1 (2008): 74–87.

Since ideal market conditions rarely apply to health care and public health programs—considerable market failures and distortions exist—SHG requires evaluations of these DAH costs.

The normative and empirical evaluation of foreign aid is a critical component of SHG's DAH framework. Because the DAH system is pluralistic and fragmented, the global justice project further requires cooperation, coordination, and complementarity toward the end goal of developing and maintaining conditions for all to be healthy. The DAH system is ethical when it collaborates with domestic systems to address potential or current shortfalls in health capabilities that undermine health functioning and health agency. These criteria require a DAH system that contributes to health equity directly and indirectly, building the capacity of domestic systems to enable all to be healthy.

In SHG, the DAH system fulfills its duty when it serves to create and maintain governance structures ensuring human flourishing, health functioning and health agency. This approach specifies terms for permissibly discharging this duty. These terms govern both DAH processes and outcomes. Since this duty is owed equally and all have an equal claim to it, the DAH paradigm must abandon the hierarchical donor/recipient dichotomy and embrace equal partnerships defined by roles and responsibilities. Rather than competing interests and contrasting goals, SHG requires congruence on DAH values and goals among global, national, and subnational communities.

SHG recasts DAH's evaluation. It requires full knowledge and mutual understanding of objectives, as well as agreement on indicators for evaluating health efforts. Global health policy should reflect: (1) a consensus among global, national, and subnational actors on common goals and measurable outcomes; (2) mutual collective accountability (for example, for resource use, implementation, and results); and (3) health agency-enhancing processes. Cost management and efficiency are essential. Processes must be in place to ensure deliberation among various participants about how DAH will meet health functioning needs and health agency needs. The indicators developed to assess these principles empirically and a summary of the SHG framework for DAH appear in Table 9.2.

Through this framework, actors and groups at the global and domestic level are able to work collectively to amplify their efforts. This structure is being tested empirically in the developing world.[2] We must abandon the current DAH paradigm in favor of a model that examines global justice issues thoroughly and acts upon them in the development process. This view guides

---

[2] C. Wachira and J. P. Ruger, "National Poverty Reduction Strategies and HIV/AIDS Governance in Malawi: A Preliminary Study of Shared Health Governance," *Social Science & Medicine* 72, no. 12 (2011): 1956–64.

**Table 9.2.** Shared Health Governance Framework for DAH

| Principles | **Mutual Collective Accountability** for resource use, implementation, and results | **Consensus**, knowledge, and mutual understanding among global, national, and subnational actors of objectives and means | **Health Agency Enhancement** participation of affected individuals and groups; knowledge and skills development |
|---|---|---|---|
| Measures | • Adequate resource levels <br> • Effectiveness and efficiency | • Goal alignment <br> • Agreement on key outcomes and indicators for evaluation | • Meaningful inclusion and participation of groups, especially the vulnerable |
| SHG Components | Values and goals | • Joint commitments and mutual obligation, aligning common good and self-interest <br> • Consensus among global, national, and subnational actors and measurable outcomes <br> • Full knowledge and mutual understanding of objectives and means | |
| | Coordination | • Actors are willing to be coordinated with or without communication or centralization | |
| | Evaluation | • Agreement on indicators for evaluation of common purpose | |
| | Accountability | • Mutual collective accountability | |
| | Agency/ participation | • Enhancement of individual and group health agency, special efforts to include marginalized and vulnerable groups; focus on enabling environments | |
| | Efficiency | • Cost management and efficiency are integral | |
| | Legitimacy | • Legitimacy through appeal to public reason, general duty to protect and promote health equity, cooperation and coordination to address global health issues fairly, equitable distribution and acceptance of responsibility for particular functions to achieve global health equity, inclusive participation of stakeholders and accountability | |
| | Level of analysis | • Local and national actors as foci to perform the work of GHG with global and national duties and institutions as a guide | |
| Indicators | • Goal alignment <br> • Adequate resource levels <br> • Agreement on key outcomes and indicators for evaluating those outcomes <br> • Meaningful inclusion and participation of groups and institutions <br> • Special efforts to ensure participation of vulnerable groups <br> • Effectiveness and efficiency measures | | |

deliberations of donors and recipients at all levels as they consider whether resources are sustainable and appropriate; whether expenditures are focused on key priorities in the right way; how shifting health needs ought to be addressed; which groups should be making these decisions and how; and who should expend and receive these funds.

The literature on economic growth and welfare in development aid and on income transfers in global redistributive justice focuses too narrowly. SHG's approach to DAH provides an alternative approach. While economic success and the redistribution of income from developed to developing countries is important, it is imperative to direct additional resources to enlarging individuals' opportunities to be healthy. The emphasis must expand beyond financial transfers of foreign aid to building and maintaining basic structures ensuring these fundamental interests. The dual focus on health agency and health functioning is central, providing a more equitable foundation for collaboration among equal partners sharing health governance. The moral obligation to health equity precedes any DAH project. The current system is ineffective, inefficient, and inadequate for expanding health capabilities and social opportunities for individuals worldwide.

The public sector comprises governments who give aid bilaterally or multilaterally, including the G8 and G20. Private entities include nongovernmental organizations (NGOs) and civil society organizations (CSOs). There are also public–private partnerships (PPPs). The largest multilateral agency for development assistance remains the World Bank Group, which, through the International Development Association (IDA) and International Bank for Reconstruction and Development (IBRD), provides billions annually. IDA provides zero or very low interest long-term loans to the lowest income countries, and IBRD offers below-market interest rates and medium-term loans to other developing countries. Given its size and influence, the World Bank deserves critical scrutiny in terms of global health justice and governance.

## 9.2 The World Bank[3]

### 9.2.1 *The Changing Role of the World Bank in Global Health*

#### 9.2.1.1 INTRODUCTION

The World Bank opened its doors in Washington, DC, in 1946. The Bretton Woods Conference in July 1944 created IBRD along with its sister institution, the International Monetary Fund (IMF). The IBRD's name specified its dual roles, though its chief function was to rebuild Europe after World War II. Unlike other specialized United Nations (UN) agencies, however, the Bank went to private financial markets for funds and received regular contributions from the world's richest countries.[4] It used these monies to provide

---

[3] This section stems from the following: J. P. Ruger, "The Changing Role of the World Bank in Global Health," *American Journal of Public Health* 95, no. 1 (2005): 60–70; J. P. Ruger, "What Will the New World Bank Head Do for Global Health?" *The Lancet* 365, no. 9474 (2005): 1837–40; J. P. Ruger, "Ruger Responds: The Changing Role of the World Bank in Global Health," *American Journal of Public Health* 95, no. 7 (2005): 1092; J. P. Ruger, "Global Health Governance and the World Bank," *The Lancet* 370, no. 9597 (2007): 1471–4; J. P. Ruger, "Joy Phumaphi: Leader in Human Development at the World Bank," *The Lancet* 370, no. 9597 (2007): 1477; J. P. Ruger, "The World Bank and Global Health: Time for a Renewed Focus on Health Policy," *Journal of Epidemiology and Community Health* 68, no. 1 (2014): 1–2.

[4] World Bank, "Getting to Know the World Bank," *The World Bank* (July 26, 2012).

interest-bearing and interest-free loans, credits, grants, and technical assistance to war-ravaged nations and to those developing countries too strapped to borrow money in international markets. These activities continue, making the Bank the "world's premier economic multilateral" institution.[5]

Over seventy years, the Bank's development priorities and philosophy—along with its global role—have changed, from rebuilding Europe to relieving poverty in the developing world. Development perspectives have changed significantly. New thinking and evidence have reshaped both development views and the Bank's practices and decisions. The Bank's view of well-being, living standards, and poverty has become more sophisticated. With accumulating evidence about ways to reduce poverty and foster development, the Bank has a broader, though still evolving, grasp of effective development approaches.

### 9.2.1.2 BRETTON WOODS: ESTABLISHING THE WORLD BANK

The Mount Washington Hotel in Bretton Woods, New Hampshire, was the setting, in July 1944, for delegates from forty-four national governments to meet to adopt the Articles of Agreement for the World Bank and the IMF and thus establish them in international law.[6] The new Bank was the first "multilateral development bank," a unique public sector institution created in the postwar era's spirit of intergovernmental cooperation. (The IMF was created to stabilize the international monetary system and monitor world currencies.) The Bank's board of executive directors first met on May 7, 1946.[7] A new era of multilateralism had dawned.

### 9.2.1.3 THE TURN TO DEVELOPMENT

On May 9, 1947, the Bank made its first loan—$250 million to France for postwar reconstruction. Within three months, it had approved loans to the Netherlands ($195 million), Denmark ($40 million), and Luxembourg ($12 million).[8] These first loans were for reconstruction as distinct from project-specific loans, and propelled the new Bank into international capital markets. The international community soon realized, however, that European and Japanese reconstruction would require much more than limited piecemeal loans. The Marshall Plan was developed in June 1947 to meet this larger need.

---

[5] D. Kapur, J. P. Lewis, and R. Webb, *The World Bank: Its First Half Century*, vol. 1: *History* (Washington, DC: Brookings Institution, 1997), 2.

[6] World Bank, "World Bank Group Historical Chronology 1944–1949," *World Bank Group Archives,* January 2001.

[7] World Bank, "Pages from World Bank History: The Bank's 57th Birthday Retrospective," June 20, 2003.

[8] World Bank, "Pages from World Bank History: The Bank's First Development Loans," May 30, 2003; World Bank, "World Bank Group Historical Chronology 1944–1949."

Thus freed from responsibility for reconstruction, the Bank's directors focused on development.

In these postwar years, the Bank concentrated chiefly on significant investments in physical capital and heavy infrastructure. More than 80 percent of its loans to less-developed countries between 1948 and 1961 funded power and transportation projects. Most of the remaining commitments funded other forms of economic overheads—industry and telecommunications, for example—with a small fraction going to agriculture and irrigation.[9] During this time the Bank gave 280 loans totaling $5.1 billion to fifty-six countries, primarily for economic development.[10] Education, health, and other social sectors received no funding.[11]

This economic development-driven investment philosophy prevailed for some twenty years, reflecting the conviction that public works projects, financial stability, and a robust private sector were the best route to development.[12] These projects were also simply considered more appropriate recipients of Bank financing.[13] The World Bank steered clear of sanitation, education, and health investments, both because of the prevailing development paradigm and because of the Bank's financial-institution ethos; as one Bank history puts it, "by the early 1950s the Bank's operations and development thinking had been set into a banker's mold."[14] This mold privileged investments producing measurable and direct monetary returns. As Edward Mason and Robert Asher explain in their book, *The World Bank since Bretton Woods*:

> The contribution of social overhead projects to increased production...is less measurable and direct than that of power plants.... Financing them, moreover, might open the door to vastly increased demands for loans and raise hackles anew in Wall Street about the "soundness" of the Bank's management. It therefore seemed prudent to the management...to consider as unsuitable in normal circumstances World Bank financing of projects for eliminating malaria, reducing illiteracy, building vocational schools, or establishing clinics.[15]

Even when staff advocated ardently for social programs, the Bank declined. In Nicaragua, for example, none of the World Bank's eleven loans between 1951 and 1960 covered water, sanitation, health, or education,[16] despite urgent recommendations from its 1952 Survey Mission to that country.

---

[9] Kapur, Lewis, and Webb, *The World Bank,* 85–6, 109–10.

[10] Ibid.

[11] Ibid., 82; World Bank, "The Bank's First Development Loans."

[12] E. S. Mason and R. E. Asher, *The World Bank since Bretton Woods* (Washington, DC: Brookings Institution, 1973).

[13] L. Currie, *The Role of Economic Advisors in Developing Countries* (Seattle, WA: Greenwood Press, 1981).

[14] Kapur, Lewis, and Webb, *The World Bank,* 85.

[15] Mason and Asher, *The World Bank since Bretton Woods,* 151–2.

[16] Kapur, Lewis, and Webb, *The World Bank.*

The Bank had both academic and financial reasons for its chosen course. Contemporaneous academic development theory stressed a trickle-down approach, arguing that economic growth through industrialization and urbanization[17] was the most effective anti-poverty tool in developing countries and that investments in social services would not work. Devesh Kapur, John P. Lewis, and Richard Walsh wrote, "Such measures would be temporary palliatives, at the expense of savings and productive investment; direct and immediate attacks on mass poverty would only squander limited national resources."[18] Sociologists and economists argued that urbanization was an inevitable component of development,[19] income inequality was inevitably linked to economic growth,[20] and growth, not distribution, should be the focus of development.[21]

Social and human resources investments also ran counter to the World Bank's financial interests. Robert Cavanaugh, the Bank's chief fundraiser and a link between the New York stock market—the Bank's principal funding source—and the Bank's lending instruments during this time, stated in 1961:

> If we got into the social field . . . then the bond market would definitely feel that we were not acting prudently from a financial standpoint. . . . If you start financing schools and hospitals and water works, and so forth, these things don't normally and directly increase the ability of a country to repay a borrowing.[22]

### 9.2.1.4 HEALTH, NUTRITION, AND POPULATION PROGRAMS GAIN A CHAMPION

On April 1, 1968, Robert S. McNamara took the Bank's helm. During his thirteen-year tenure, he moved poverty reduction to center stage and transformed the Bank. A forceful agent of change, he worked tirelessly to redefine the Bank as a true development agency rather than a financial institution.[23]

A shift in academic thinking and research about development coincided with McNamara's arrival and strengthened his hand. Theorists began to question orthodox growth-focused views of development in the 1950s.[24] Studies showed that physical capital played a smaller role in economic growth than

---

[17] J. Morris, *The Road to Huddersfield: A Journey to Five Continents* (New York: Pantheon, 1963).

[18] Kapur, Lewis, and Webb, *The World Bank*, 115.

[19] G. D. H. Cole, *Introduction to Economic History, 1750–1950* (London: Macmillan, 1952).

[20] S. Kuznets, "Economic Growth and Income Inequality," *American Economic Review* 45, no. 1 (1955): 1–28.

[21] W. Arthur Lewis, *The Theory of Economic Growth* (London: Allen & Unwin, 1955).

[22] R. W. Cavanaugh, interviewed by R. W. Oliver of the Brookings Institution, World Bank Oral History Program, July 25, 1961, pp. 63–4, quoted in Kapur, Lewis, and Webb, *The World Bank*, 119–20.

[23] Kapur, Lewis, and Webb, *The World Bank*.

[24] Lewis, *The Theory of Economic Growth*.

previously thought and that a residual factor seemed to exist in macroeconomic statistical models.[25] Scholars came to believe that this residual factor was investment in education, innovation, entrepreneurship, and, later, health.[26] Human capital and human development conceptions—investments in people—also gained a following.[27] This basic needs approach reshaped the way academics and policy-makers saw development[28] (and laid the foundation for the US Agency for International Development (USAID) program).

These insights resonated for McNamara. Internal Bank research and reports from the field testified that developing countries were riddled with extreme poverty. Hundreds of millions lacked health clinics, primary and secondary schools, and safe drinking water. This underdevelopment obstructed productivity, economic growth, and poverty reduction efforts. That this poverty resulted, in part, from insufficient investments in health and education had become increasingly clear.

McNamara saw population control as the first step toward poverty relief. The Bank's turn toward social sector lending thus began with population control efforts. Other development agencies at the time, particularly the Ford Foundation and USAID, were emphasizing population control. By 1970, McNamara had created the Bank's Population Projects Department; and population control continued to be a major focus in his speeches and dialogue with governments.

McNamara also began advocating Bank support of health and nutrition programs. A 1975 *Health Sector Policy Paper* was among the Bank's first efforts to generate health policy knowledge, and in 1974 the Bank launched the Onchocerciasis Control Program (OCP), to eliminate river blindness and enhance country and regional control of the disease,[29] one of its most successful programs. The Bank had not significantly addressed health issues until then, so its decision to tackle river blindness was a landmark step. The OCP propelled the Bank into the health sector; the Bank established a health department in 1979 as well as a policy to consider both stand-alone health projects and health components in other projects for funding.[30] These health-focused efforts

---

[25] M. Abramovitz, *Resource and Output Trends in the United States since 1870*, Occasional Paper 52 (New York: National Bureau of Economic Research, 1956).

[26] S. Enke, *Economics for Development* (London: Dennis Dobson, 1963).

[27] T. W. Shultz, "Investment in Human Capital," *American Economic Review* 51, no. 1 (1961): 1–17, 11.

[28] P. Streeten, "The Distinctive Features of a Basic Needs Approach to Development," Basic Needs Paper 2, World Bank Policy Planning and Program Review Department, Washington, DC, August 10, 1977.

[29] World Bank, "Pages from World Bank History: The Fight against Riverblindness," March 14, 2003.

[30] Kapur, Lewis, and Webb, *The World Bank*, 345.

reflected growing recognition within academic and policy-making circles that poverty reduction required a basic needs approach.[31]

The basic needs approach laid the foundation for health, nutrition, and population (HNP) expansion at the Bank. The Bank created the Population, Health, and Nutrition Department in 1979 and began allowing stand-alone health loans, thus translating development theory and research into action and marking a turning point in the Bank's engagement in health. The Bank's *World Development Report, 1980* officially and publicly recognized this shift. It proposed that better health and nutrition would likely accelerate economic growth and urged greater emphasis on social sector lending.[32]

In 1987, the Bank, World Health Organization (WHO), and the United Nations Population Fund (UNFPA) co-sponsored a safe motherhood conference in Nairobi, Kenya,[33] launching the Bank's Safe Motherhood Initiative. This project, the Bank's first global effort in maternal health, committed the organization to family planning and maternal and child health (MCH). The Bank joined forces with the same agencies and the United Nations Children's Fund (UNICEF) for a second safe motherhood conference in 1989 in Niamey, Niger. A Bank report titled *Sub-Saharan Africa: From Crisis to Sustainable Growth*, followed in November 1989 and urged doubling human resource development expenditures.[34] Momentum gathered for investments in family planning and child and maternal health. The Bank emphasized governments' role in reducing fertility and mortality in its *World Development Report, 1984: Population and Development*,[35] sparking criticism, and its family-planning projects drew it into abortion politics in Latin America and elsewhere.[36]

Early HNP activities also included a 1981 loan to Tunisia for expanding basic health services, the 1987 study *Financing Health Services in Developing Countries: An Agenda for Reform*, and the Bank's groundbreaking *World Development Report, 1993: Investing in Health*.[37] The 1987 report particularly stressed the importance of improved health sector financing. The 1993 report, the first devoted entirely to health, sought to make the health investment case to the broader development community and gave the Bank greater exposure and legitimacy in the health sector; it identified international health systems

---

[31] P. Streeten with S. J. Burki, M. Ul Haq, N. Hicks, and F. Stewart, *First Things First: Meeting Basic Human Needs in Developing Countries* (Oxford: Oxford University Press, 1981).

[32] World Bank, *World Development Report, 1980* (New York: Oxford University Press, 1980).

[33] World Bank, "World Bank Group Historical Chronology: 1980–1989" (Washington, DC: World Bank Group Library & Archives of Development, 2013).

[34] Ibid.

[35] World Bank, *World Development Report, 1984: Population and Development* (New York: Oxford University Press, 1984).

[36] World Bank, "World Bank Group Historical Chronology: 1990–1999" (Washington, DC: World Bank Group Library & Archives of Development, 2013).

[37] World Bank, *World Development Report 1993: Investing in Health* (New York: Oxford University Press, 1993).

problems—inefficient use of funds and human resources, inequitable heath care access, and rising costs in particular.

### 9.2.1.5 EXPANDING GLOBAL HEALTH WORK AT THE WORLD BANK

Since 1993, the Bank has expanded operational research and analysis, including its Special Programme of Research, Development and Research Training in Human Reproduction, WHO/ United Nations Development Program (UNDP)/ UNICEF/World Bank Special Programme for Research and Training in Tropical Diseases, and the Micronutrient Initiative. It has also fostered more country-specific research and analysis in HNP issues, primarily through Bank loans and credits, resulting in external HNP research funding in the developing world.[38] The Bank has also conducted training and seminars on HNP topics for developing countries' policy-makers.

But the Bank's main advantage in global health is its power to mobilize financial resources. The most striking change in its global health role has been its expanded HNP funding through loans, credits, and grants. The Bank has also changed the types of HNP activities it supports, transitioning from basic health services toward broader policy reforms.[39] And it has recognized the importance of interagency cooperation for improving development aid's effectiveness and strengthened its collaborations with other international organizations. In Brazil, Uganda, and Ghana, for example, it partnered with other donors in its sector-wide programs. These programs enlist multiple donors to fund an entire sector, develop comprehensive policies, and pursue shared policy objectives, but they have stirred controversy as well.

The Bank has provided WHO with technical assistance to improve the design, supervision, and evaluation of Bank-supported projects, and WHO and the Bank have worked together to broaden international understanding of HNP issues. Through the Framework Convention on Tobacco Control (FCTC), for example, the two institutions worked to establish the evidence base for effective methods to curb tobacco use. But the Bank must further strengthen its partnerships with client countries, civil society, stakeholders, and other agencies.

### 9.2.1.6 CRITICISMS OF THE WORLD BANK

The World Bank and its policies are among the most hotly debated and highly criticized in the global development community. With regard to health sector policies, key concerns have involved user fees, structural adjustment, the use of disability-adjusted life years (DALYs) to measure overall disease burden, and privatization.

---

[38] HDN, *Health, Nutrition, & Population* (Washington, DC: World Bank Group, 1997), 11.
[39] Ibid., 15.

In its 1987 report on financing, the Bank highlighted user fees as an instrument for mobilizing resources. However, empirical evidence demonstrates that user fees reduce the demand for necessary as well as unnecessary care and that they disproportionately affect poor and sick people. Evidence also suggests that such fees have not been overwhelmingly successful in raising revenue or enhancing efficiency. In its 1997 sector strategy, the Bank claimed that it does not support user fees; however, it maintained that such fees are one tool for mobilizing resources. Critics prefer renouncing user fees entirely, a policy the Bank has yet to pursue.

In the 1980s and 1990s, the Bank pressured countries to adopt structural adjustment programs for their economies and to follow many prescriptions of the Washington Consensus by opening markets (trade liberalization), reducing government expenditures (in some cases for health), and privatizing state-owned enterprises. Critics argue that such programs reduce health care spending and have deleterious health effects.[40] UNICEF estimated that adjustment policies may have been associated with 500,000 deaths of young children in a twelve-month period,[41] though a 1998 study of the effect of structural adjustment operations on health expenditures and outcomes and the Bank's own research[42,43] found no negative impact. Still, much concern remains about such programs' effectiveness and negative impact, and the Bank has moved away from endorsing them. Another critique argues that the Bank's role in the global HIV/AIDS agenda has been significant and problematic. The Bank's Multi-Country AIDS Program, it has been argued, led to several negative long-term disease-specific and institutional outcomes.[44] The Bank also was criticized for introducing DALYs to global health assessments. Critics argue that DALYs lack a sound theoretical framework and are inequitable because they value years saved for the able-bodied more than for the disabled, the middle-aged more than the young or old, and the currently ill more than those who will be ill tomorrow.

Critics also have been concerned about the World Bank's support for privatization in general and privatizing the health sector specifically.[45] Research has demonstrated that a strong government is necessary to address market

---

[40] M. Rao, ed., *Disinvesting in Health: The World Bank's Prescriptions for Health* (Thousand Oaks, CA: Sage Publications, 1999).

[41] UNICEF, *The State of the World's Children* (New York: Oxford University Press, 1989), 1, 16–17.

[42] World Bank, *Adjustment Lending: Policies for Sustainable Growth* (Washington, DC: World Bank, 1990), 11.

[43] J. van der Gaag and T. Barham, "Health and Health Expenditures in Adjusting and Non-Adjusting Countries," *Social Science & Medicine* 46, no. 8 (1998): 995–1009.

[44] S. Harman, *The World Bank and HIV/AIDS: Setting a Global Agenda* (Cambridge: Routledge, 2008).

[45] M. Turshen, *Privatizing Health Services in Africa* (New Brunswick, NJ: Rutgers University Press, 1999).

failures in financing, consuming, and providing both personal and public health services. Insurance market failures, credit shortages, information asymmetries, and insufficiencies in particular can prevent people from realizing the economic benefits of risk pooling.[46] The Bank now admits that open markets and economic management are insufficient, that good governance and strong institutions are critical for eradicating poverty. But in the health sector specifically, critics argue the Bank needs to be clearer about the trade-offs between public and private financing and delivery of health services.[47] Moreover, an evaluation conducted by an Independent Evaluation Group of the World Bank Group found that Bank-generated data on poverty reduction projects and programs has not been effectively fed back to analyze data, diagnose problem areas, and formulate and revise strategy for successful implementation.[48] Such feedback loops and processes are important for impactful Bank performance. In the late 1990s, the Bank's *Voices of the Poor* study shared detailed interviews of impoverished people in developing countries,[49] graphically revealing the multidimensional experiences and determinants of poverty. For the poor, development requires not just higher incomes, but security and empowerment; education, jobs, health, and nutrition; a clean and sustainable environment; a well-functioning judicial and legal system; civil and political liberties; and a rich cultural life. This evidence accords with seventy years of development experience and theory.

The World Bank's role in global health has evolved dramatically since Bretton Woods. These changes in philosophy, mission, leadership, practice, and research have made HNP priorities at the World Bank and in the wider development community.

### 9.2.2 *The World Bank's Role in Global Health Governance*

Now, more than a decade and a half into the twenty-first century, the World Bank needs to clarify its role further and assert its leadership in health at both the global and country levels. Can the Bank impact an increasingly diffuse and complex global health enterprise with its unprecedented numbers of

---

[46] J. P. Ruger, D. T. Jamison, and D. E. Bloom, "Health and the Economy," in *International Public Health: Disease, Programs, Systems, and Policies*, ed. M. Merson, R. Black, and A. Mills (Gaithersburg, MD: Aspen Publishers, 2001), 617–66; J. P. Ruger, "Catastrophic Health Expenditure," *The Lancet* 362, no. 9388 (2003): 996–7.

[47] A. Wagstaff, "Economics, Health and Development: Some Ethical Dilemmas Facing the World Bank and the International Community," *Journal of Medical Ethics* 27, no. 4 (2000): 262–7.

[48] S. Fardoust, R. Kanbur, X. Luo, and M. Sundberg, "An Evaluation of the Feedback Loops in the Poverty Focus of World Bank Operations," *Evaluation and Program Planning* 67 (2018): 10–18.

[49] D. Narayan, R. Patel, K. Schafft, A. Rademacher, and S. Koch-Schulte, *Voices of the Poor: Can Anyone Hear Us?* (New York: Oxford University Press, 2000); D. Narayan, R. Chambers, M. K. Shah, and P. Petesch, *Voices of the Poor: Crying Out for Change* (New York: Oxford University Press, 2000).

organizations, initiatives, and foundations? How can the Bank help reshape and strengthen global health governance (GHG)?

### 9.2.2.1  TODAY'S GLOBAL HEALTH LANDSCAPE

An in-depth look at today's vastly expanded global health architecture suggests an exciting environment but also raises concerns. Consultants in donor countries, not recipient countries or individuals from these countries, receive much of the Bank's funding, for example. Though aid has grown overall, much of it has gone to debt relief. Much of it also funds other types of humanitarian assistance, focuses on specific diseases, or advances foreign policy objectives as bilateral aid to specific countries. Results are often mixed: poorer countries rely more on external assistance; aid frequently does not support health systems or other government priorities; and efforts are unpredictable, short- or medium-term, and unsynchronized among donors. And despite global health partnership initiatives, including the International Health Partnership (IHP+), health governance is still fragmented, incoherent, and driven by donor preferences.

### 9.2.2.2  RETHINKING THE BANK'S HEALTH STRATEGY

This complex climate has made the World Bank rethink its global health role. As a first step, several years ago the Bank conducted a strategic planning process culminating in a more results-oriented HNP strategy. The strategy targeted the Bank's work to areas where it holds a comparative advantage and emphasizes discernment in engagement with partners. This strategic process helped the Bank identify eight areas of strength where it could generate knowledge, offer policy and technical advice, and provide funding. These areas included intersectoral country assistance; health system strengthening; health financing and financial protection; economics; financial sustainability in the health sector; sound macroeconomic and fiscal policy; regulatory frameworks for the health sector; and good governance, accountability, and transparency in the health sector.

The planning process identified several key elements for strengthening health systems: financing, a regulatory framework for private–public collaboration, governance, insurance, logistics, provider payment and incentive mechanisms, information, well-trained personnel, basic infrastructure, and supplies. This approach also stressed a collaborative division of labor among global actors and extricated the Bank from functions like technical aspects of disease control, human resource training in health, and internal organization of clinics and hospital services, leaving them to WHO, UNICEF, the UNFPA, and other agencies.

This strategy appears sensible and parsimonious. It promised neither too much nor too little and built on the Bank's health systems expertise. It also leveraged the Bank's unique development strengths. The Bank focuses on generating and disseminating knowledge and best practices through technical assistance and policy advice. These features set the World Bank apart from commercial banks, other aid sources, and even some development banks.

For the Bank to have on-the-ground effects and achieve positive health sector results, however, it must focus much more on the political economy of health in developing countries; on gaining a better understanding of policy reforms; on how different governments implement policies; and on how actions for policy change take place.

### 9.2.2.3 POLITICAL ECONOMY OF HEALTH: A BROADER APPROACH

Many factors underlie the unprecedented levels of development funding prosperous countries are providing to developing countries, including the humanitarian impulse to help those in need. Humanitarianism is unquestionably an improvement over the seeming indifference of earlier years, but it has also yielded today's proliferating and uncoordinated initiatives focused on specific diseases. By concentrating on vertical programs in specific locations, it has widened the gap between functioning and failing health systems and failed to address weaknesses in public health and health care infrastructure.

An approach focusing on the political economy of health examines the social production of health and disease, especially political and economic determinants at the national and global level. In this framework, political and economic institutions and policies either exacerbate inequalities in health or reduce them through reform. It studies structural barriers and interventions that either impede or foster the potential for good health. It embeds a crucial compass—an analysis of the flow, distribution, and regulation of financial, human, and physical capital within societies, as well as the benefits and costs of health-related policies and programs. Its reforms focus on resources and power, their distribution and management in the economy, and the government's oversight role. These reforms target both incremental and large-scale public efforts to effect change in and beyond the health sector. Equity is central.

The Bank can help countries strengthen health systems through a political economy of health approach in at least three crucial areas—(1) growing their economies and economic equity; (2) establishing good public and health governance; and (3) reforming health policies.

### 9.2.2.3.1 *Building a Strong Economy*

Effective health systems require sufficient resources—financial, human, and physical—which are more likely to be found in robust economies. As countries' economies grow stronger, they can raise more revenue through formal sector employment, increased tax revenue from earnings, and improved tax administration. These changes are critical if low-income countries are to mobilize resources to improve public health and health care long term.

Among all the global institutions involved in health, the Bank is uniquely positioned to help countries to grow their economies and foster equity. The Bank's work in private sector development has grown, including a 2005 *World Development Report* devoted entirely to investment climates in developing countries. It focused on improving countries' business environments through foreign direct investment, corporate governance, business regulations, improving small and medium enterprises, and corporate social responsibility. But the Bank must pay close attention to its economic policy advice and lending and their equity effects.

Additionally, debt relief for poor countries frees economies from crushing burdens and helps them grow. It can bolster the health sector, as savings in debt service payments can go instead toward health care and social services. In many struggling countries, debt service payments exceed health sector investments. Where debt has been written off—in Benin, Senegal, and Mozambique, for example—health spending has increased. But though heavily indebted poor countries' (HIPC) assistance and grant aid might promise increased health sector investments, trends shifting Bank investments toward infrastructure can come at the expense of human development.

### 9.2.2.3.2 Health Requires Good Governance

Good governance and effective political and economic institutions throughout the public sector are fundamental to health and population well-being. The Bank has claimed an apolitical stance and has not publicly embraced democratic development as part of its core mission. Since its major restructuring in 1997, however, governance issues have become a focus. Indeed, an entire public governance sector has been established to promote the development of accountable and efficient public sector institutions. Are elections free and open? Can citizens express themselves freely, associate with whom they wish, and hold governments accountable for results? Does the country enjoy political stability, free from domestic violence, civil strife, war, and terrorism? Are public services adequate and effective? Does the civil service function well? What is the process for policy formulation and implementation? Does government regulate the economy and the private sector effectively? Has it legitimately institutionalized rules of law? Do police and the courts enforce them? Can the country rein in corruption and prevent powerful elites from pursuing illicit personal gain? Winning foreign assistance and allocating it wisely require strong governance, particularly good public management and transparency.

The Bank might, for example, establish performance standards for effective parliaments or legislatures, multiparty competition, representation, and voting systems. Or it might impose political conditions on aid. These conditions could range from public sector effectiveness to the establishment of democratic institutions (for example, voting, legislative bodies, multiparty elections, free press, and constitutionalism). Making aid conditional on democratic reforms could, however, be a double-edged sword. In addition to the coercive nature of such demands, they could also result in lower lending and inhibit overall development.

The Bank has been studying and monitoring these and other indicators of governance. But though the Bank has a key role in helping states achieve good governance, the motivation and action must come from the countries themselves. Because top-down approaches are demonstrably unsustainable over time, the Bank's role should be advisory, supportive, financial, and facilitative, not directive.

And to avoid the perception of hypocrisy, a democracy-driven agenda would necessarily entail a third component: democratizing the World Bank itself. Critics have long protested against the Bank's governance structure for its unequal distribution of executive board votes, opaque decision-making processes, and lack of board accountability to elected officials and legislative bodies in the countries the Bank aims to serve.

Will a democracy and governance agenda improve health? Although studies on the relation between political institutions and health are limited, researchers believe democracy can have a positive impact on health. One theory is that democratic principles—regular elections, universal suffrage, representation, multiparty competition, civil liberties—generally produce competition for popular support among elites who are vying to maintain or win elected office. Competition for votes increases political participation and can lead to universal health insurance and access as in the British National Health Service or the Canadian Health Insurance system. Authoritarian regimes, by contrast, suppress political competition and tend to have an interest in preventing human development because improved health, education, and economic security mobilize citizens to demand greater sociopolitical participation and more resources. Thus, democracy itself could have a positive influence on health. Cuba's public health and health care system is, however, a notable counterexample; it is a country achieving formidable health outcomes within a communist political regime.

Within the health sector, principles of good governance improve health. Anti-corruption measures, for example, can highlight health sector dysfunction. Financial accountability can reveal mismanagement in health sector investments. Reforming the fiscal, political, and administrative framework for subnational governments can improve health sector performance and civic engagement in these local units. Finally, reforming tax policy and administration are critical, as they pay for and regulate health insurance and health services. Without them, the health sector is unsustainable.

Improving political and economic institutions will help countries effect needed structural-level health system changes. The public sector budget should have a permanent provision for health expenditures. Individuals, companies, governments, or a combination of all three should fund health insurance. Countries should also be able to pool risk effectively: health insurance risk pooling requires both government policies and programs and strong regulatory oversight.

For equity reasons, progressive financing is necessary to provide universal health insurance coverage. WHO's Commission on Macroeconomics and Health estimated that countries could provide a basic benefits package that would effectuate the Millennium Development Goals (MDGs) for as little as $34 per person per year. And while financing through international donations can be a good short- or medium-term means of jumpstarting a country's health system development, in the long term countries must be able to purchase health care goods and services cost-effectively themselves, whether through public sector provision or from the private and non-profit sectors.

Sustainable health systems require these structural-level changes. The Bank has a role in providing technical assistance to governments for policy reform and policy-making. In particular, the Bank could help government officials develop strong leadership skills and ensure that factors such as equity, efficiency, and sustainability are in place.

### 9.2.2.3.3 Changing Minds, Reforming Policy

In a political economy of health approach, health equity is fundamental to improving overall population health. This approach commits to social justice and recognizes that a country's health policies are choices made by governing authorities. Successful policy reforms at the state level depend on several important principles, and the Bank, uniquely among global health institutions, can advance these principles as it advises and aids countries during their reform processes.

### 9.2.2.3.3.1 Reforming Health Systems

Health-policy design and implementation require an evidence base—knowledge about what does and does not work. The Bank creates and disseminates these public goods, but countries need to build their own research capacity, and the Bank can help. Any country undertaking health system reforms should start with gathering existing evidence from its own historical experience and from lessons learned elsewhere. The Bank can expedite this process with policy analysis, research synthesis, and its clearinghouse capabilities, and take countries step by step through other countries' experiences. In Mexico, for example, sound evidence helped the public understand that health care costs were impoverishing citizens. Evidence illustrating out-of-pocket expenditures and poverty brought on by catastrophic illness increased public awareness and raised interest in financial protection and health care access. Planners can effectively strengthen the case for reform by deploying sound and convincing evidence.

Getting health on the policy agenda is, of course, basic to reform. Other important steps to successful policy reform include working out health reform's budgetary implications to ensure adequate spending levels, improving government accountability, and reducing corruption. The Bank can help on all these fronts.

The World Bank has been working to develop health systems for some time now, focusing especially on issues such as health financing, insurance, services and delivery, human resources for health, pharmaceuticals, hospital and clinic management, and public–private health sector reform. Several years ago, however, the Bank lost momentum on these fronts, most notably to WHO, whose Commission on Macroeconomics and Health, led by economist Jeffrey Sachs, took the lead in studying and recommending health system and reform measures to meet the MDGs. The Bank also lost substantial legitimacy through its strong and unpopular stance on health system privatization. The Bank's work failed to discern whether and when public versus private functions are the most equitable and efficient in the health sector. By contrast, WHO's commission report and other studies recognized the important role of public sector financing in partnership with private service delivery in meeting developing countries' essential health needs.

### 9.2.2.3.3.2 Generating Political Will

Global actors have successfully generated political will for health systems reform, and health financing increased at the international level as a result, but strengthening health systems ultimately requires domestic commitments. Individuals, groups, and national leaders need to coalesce around health system reform, particularly universal health coverage, make it a priority, and work tirelessly to achieve it. Few reforms succeed absent this thrust for change. Generating political will is often a lengthy and laborious process, involving numerous political and institutional elements—political parties, personal politics, legislative policy-making strategies, re-election incentives, financial incentives, civil society and interest groups, and political leadership. Timing in the political realm—taking advantage of windows of opportunity—is critical.

Reforms in developing countries must confront, too, the severe, seemingly intractable inequality pervading these economies. And they must address the need for strong health-related institutions—medical, nursing, and public-health schools; think tanks; institutes; government agencies; and advocates for vulnerable groups. The Bank can help generate political will and foster reforms.

### 9.2.2.3.3.3 Advancing Norms and Values

Values and norms are crucial for marshaling support for reform. Though seemingly abstract and intangible, principles form an essential conceptual framework that undergirds practical issues—illness and raising the financial resources to pay for health care, for example. Planners can integrate disparate values in a coherent basis for reform. The indispensable norm for health system reform and universal health coverage, however, is citizens' willingness to pay higher taxes to fund others' health care. This policy reality requires a commitment to equity, and the ability to look beyond one's own personal situation to achieve collective benefits at the national level. Large-scale social movements and changes in collective values raise awareness of injustices and inefficiencies, such as extensive health inequities and inaccessibly high health care prices, and in turn can foster new social and economic trends. Challenging established norms could be the key in many countries to inspiring public consensus on legislative action, ensuring health equity for all.

The World Bank can contribute to value construction and coalition building for collective action. Consider Brazil's response to HIV/AIDS, which was built on Brazilian values of solidarity and human dignity. In 1994, the World Bank, developing its first AIDS prevention and control loan, elicited participation from Brazilian AIDS activists. Through nearly a decade, the development, approval, and implementation of Bank projects strengthened the work of the National AIDS Program and the activist community. Bank projects helped support the Ministry of Health for NGO activities, leading to a proliferation of NGOs, advocacy activities, and greater financial commitments to combat HIV/AIDS at the national level. Indeed, the Bank has significantly sharpened its HIV/AIDS focus over the past several years, making it one of the world's largest actors in the HIV/AIDS fight.

### 9.2.2.3.4 RENEWING THE WORLD BANK'S FOCUS ON HEALTH POLICY

Jim Yong Kim, a global health expert, succeeded Robert Zoellick as president of the World Bank in 2012. In 2013, Timothy Evans, a long-time champion of global health equity, moved to the Bank as director of HNP. These changes in leadership spotlight global health's ascendance in development work.

In today's ever more pluralistic and chaotic global health landscape, the Bank and its current leaders must focus sharply on global health impact. Its leadership must develop and follow a clear plan that builds on its unique role in health and development policy, leveraging this role and maximizing the health equity opportunities globalization offers.

Achieving on-the-ground results in the health sector will require the Bank to focus on health policy and developing countries' health systems, consistent with its strategic plan. Sustainability is essential: the Bank's goal should be to strengthen countries and eliminate their need for aid. All this is possible: consider South Korea, Japan, and Singapore, which graduated from needing development assistance, establishing their health systems as they built their economies. They have achieved major health policy successes, most notably universal health insurance coverage for their populations.

Most organizations and initiatives in the current global health context focus narrowly on specific diseases or conditions (Global Fund and the US President's Emergency Plan for AIDS Relief (PEPFAR), for example) or practices (for example, the Tobacco Free Initiative). The Bank's approach, by contrast, is holistic and multisectoral. With this broader perspective and its prodigious resources and capabilities, the Bank can be an important global institution for health policy and health systems in developing countries, especially in some key areas.

First, the Bank can help develop the necessary evidence base and analytical capacity for health reform and implementation. Its financial and technical assistance can significantly augment country-led efforts in health financing, for example, which requires pooling risk across populations through insurance and government regulation of insurance and reinsurance markets. In developing financing policies, countries need to know what has worked and what has failed, at home and elsewhere. The Bank serves as knowledge bank, generating and disseminating this information and helping countries build their own policy development capacities. The Bank staff worked with Moroccan Ministry of Health officials, for example, to assist in developing, passing, and implementing an expansion of health insurance to formal sector employees and poor Moroccans. The Bank and the Moroccan government jointly sponsored a symposium on health sector financing, covered by the Moroccan press and media outlets. Through an open dialogue this symposium increased public awareness and likely support of proposals to address key health policy issues. Likewise, in Rwanda, World Bank financial and technical assistance helped expand health insurance significantly between 2003 and 2008, and supported Rwandan social protection efforts, including health insurance. These efforts resulted in increases in facility-based births between 2006 and 2009, and reductions in child mortality.

Second, the Bank could bring global shifts in attitudes toward health financing and the importance of health to the domestic level. In the recent past global health financing has doubled and the political will for improving health has grown. Agendas at the UN General Assembly and the annual G8 summit, among other global gatherings, have highlighted health. But in many countries, domestic financing has lagged well behind global funding, and evidence suggests that greater development aid for health actually reduces domestic health expenditures. One study found that for every $1 in international health aid to governments, public domestic health spending decreased by \$0.43 to \$1.14.[50] This trend is counterproductive. The Bank can help strengthen country-level budgetary planning to reverse this funding displacement. The Bank also has the financial and political capabilities to help countries set agendas and summon political will for health action. In Brazil, where Bank loans supported the prevention components of the National AIDS Program, its efforts helped encourage the active participation of CSOs, a key element in Brazilian HIV/AIDS efforts.[51]

Third, the Bank can help foster good health sector governance. Implementing policy and programs is a national and subnational role, but the Bank can support them. The Bank's encouragement for identified governance indicators—voice and accountability, respect for the rule of law, government effectiveness, regulatory quality, corruption control, and political stability and order[52]—can help countries strengthen their health sectors. The Bank can counsel governments on such accountability and transparency measures as clear goals, time frames, evaluations, indicators, and benchmarks, as well as fair, transparent, inclusive, and participatory processes.

Top-down, donor-driven development is both unjust and ineffective, as the Bank learned from past mistakes. It must not lose sight of these lessons. Its Poverty Reduction Strategy Papers (PRSP) and Country Assistance Strategies, both of which started with a country's vision for its own development, have sought to serve countries in achieving their own goals.

In its HNP strategy, the Bank narrowed its focus to its particular strengths and comparative advantages. A few caveats aside, the Bank has a promising strategy and has promulgated a renewed vision for the future. Will the Bank succeed in turning this vision into reality? The answer will hinge on whether the Bank effectively governs its health sector portfolio, improving program quality and effectiveness. It also depends on whether developing countries continue to see the Bank as an effective health partner. Most importantly, the Bank must enhance its role in providing policy advice and technical assistance. Doing so will help countries not only build health systems, but also grow past their need for Bank assistance. After all, the Bank's ultimate goal should be to close its own doors—to create a world of strong, prosperous nations where all can flourish and sectors function effectively and sustainably, without Bank help.

---

[50] C. Lu, M. T. Schneider, P. Gubbins, K. Leach-Kemon, D. Jamison, and C. J. L. Murray, "Public Financing of Health in Developing Countries: A Cross-National Systematic Analysis," *The Lancet* 375, no 9723 (2010): 1375–87.

[51] R. Parker, "Building the Foundations for the Response to HIV/AIDS in Brazil: The Development of HIV/AIDS Policy, 1982–1996," *Divulgação em Saúde para Debate* 27 (2003): 143–83.

[52] World Bank, "Governance and Anti-Corruption," *IEG* (Washington, DC: World Bank, 2006).

Sections 9.2.3 and 9.2.4 present results of studies of Bank programs and investments in health.

### 9.2.3 World Bank Investments in Health: A Case Study of the Bank's Maternal and Child Health Intervention among Indonesia's Poor[53]

#### 9.2.3.1 BACKGROUND AND SIGNIFICANCE

Indonesia is the world's largest archipelagic state and has the world's largest Muslim population. Of the time of this study, relevant data indicated significant health, economics and social issues. Twelve percent of Indonesia's population fell below the Indonesian poverty line, with income of less than $0.55 per person per day.[54] The nation had high rates of child and maternal mortality. About 80 percent of Indonesia's maternal deaths and complications,[55] and half of its infant and child deaths,[56] were avoidable. Maternal and child mortality were among the top causes of the global disease burden.[57] Poverty substantially impacts MCH; in particular, it undermines birth outcomes for mother and child and physical well-being for children under 5.[58] Poverty also diminishes educational achievement, and the level of female education impacts MCH substantially.[59,60] Even small improvements in maternal education levels can lower child mortality.[61]

The Indonesian government had stressed development policy to improve conditions for its poor since the 1970s.[62] A poverty reduction strategy specified high-quality data collection to measure policy effectiveness through

---

[53] This section stems from J. L. Baird, S. Ma, and J. P. Ruger, "Effects of the World Bank's Maternal and Child Health Intervention on Indonesia's Poor: Evaluating the Safe Motherhood Project," *Social Science & Medicine* 72, no. 12 (2011): 1948–55.

[54] Kepala Badan Pusat Statistik, *Key Indicators of Indonesia, Special Edition 2007* (Jakarta: Kepala Badan Pusat Statistik, 2007).

[55] M. Mathai, "Reviewing Maternal Deaths and Complications to Make Pregnancy and Childbirth Safer," *Regional Health Forum WHO South-East Asia Region* 9, no. 1 (2005): 27–9.

[56] WHO Department of Reproductive Health and Research (RHR), *Beyond the Numbers: Reviewing Maternal Health and Complications to Make Pregnancy Safer* (Geneva: WHO, 2004).

[57] A. Lopez, C. Mathers, M. Ezzati, D. Jamison, and C. Murray, *Global Burden of Disease and Risk Factors* (Washington, DC: World Bank, 2006).

[58] A. Case and C. Paxson, "Children's Health and Social Mobility," *Future of Children* 16, no. 2 (2006): 151–73.

[59] D. E. Bender and M. F. McCann, "The Influence of Maternal Intergenerational Education on Health Behaviors of Women in Peri-Urban Bolivia," *Social Science & Medicine* 50, no. 9 (2000): 1189–96.

[60] A. Deaton, "Health, Inequality, and Economic Development," *Journal of Economic Literature* 41, no. 1 (2003): 113–58.

[61] A. Basu and R. Stephenson, "Low Levels of Maternal Education and the Proximate Determinants of Childhood Mortality: A Little Learning is Not a Dangerous Thing," *Social Science & Medicine* 60 (2005): 2011–23.

[62] Pusat Data Kesehatan (Indonesia), *Indonesia, Evaluating the Strategies for Health for All by the Year 2000: Common Framework, Third Evaluation CFE/3* (Jakarta: Centre for Health Data, Ministry of Health, Republic of Indonesia, 1997).

exacting quantitative assessment.[63] Over these years, the government worked on improving the country's infrastructure and agriculture, as well as reducing urban poverty.[64] It targeted World Bank lending to human development, including HNP. From 1988, Indonesia prioritized safe motherhood programs and invested major resources in them.[65]

### 9.2.3.2 EVALUATING THE SAFE MOTHERHOOD PROJECT

The Safe Motherhood Project (SMP) was one piece of a larger Indonesian effort in maternal and child health, through which the government pledged to upgrade its institutional structure and capacity and improve women's and children's health.[66] The project sought to improve the services of midwives and other health care providers, especially in poor villages, by addressing their training quality, technical and counseling capacity, and sustainability, with an emphasis on governance and stewardship. SMP emphasized enhancing family planning, awareness, and reproductive health among a target population of child-bearing-age women, families with newborn children, and adolescents. The Indonesian government also sought financial and technical help from other international agencies, including UNICEF, with its focus on health and protection for children and mothers. The SMP was distinct from the Bank's Health Project 5 (HP5), a broader initiative to expand use, distribution, and efficiency of health personnel among rural and low-income urban residents. HP5 stressed institutional change in the health sector, particularly greater decentralization and coordination, and improved training, regulation, and oversight. Together, HP5 and SMP emphasized strengthening Indonesia's financial and human capital for health improvement.

An empirical study covering the years 1990–2005—one of the first to examine the impact of a Bank intervention in the field of MCH—yielded instructive data for evaluating the SMP. Overall, in both SMP and non-SMP provinces, clinically relevant changes did occur. For example, the rate of deliveries involving trained personnel increased by 52–68 percent, infant mortality fell by 25–33 percent, and under-5 mortality dropped by 8–14 percent in both study groups. However, except for the under-5 mortality rate, the study showed that outcomes in provinces with SMP were not statistically

---

[63] P. Surbakti, *Indonesia's National Socio-Economic Survey: A Continual Data Source for Analysis on Welfare Development* (Jakarta: The Central Bureau of Statistics, 1995).

[64] R. Weaving, ed., "Enhancing the Quality of Life in Urban Indonesia," OED précis, no. 106, World Bank Operations and Evaluation Department, Washington, DC, 1996.

[65] J. Shiffman, "Generating Political Will for Safe Motherhood in Indonesia," *Social Science & Medicine* 56, no. 6 (2003): 1197–207.

[66] World Bank Population and Human Resources Division, "Project Appraisal Document on a Proposed Loan in the Amount of US$42.5 Million to the Republic of Indonesia for a Safe Motherhood Project: A Partnership and Family Approach," World Bank Report No. 16624-IND, Washington, DC, June 3, 1997.

significantly different from those without this intervention. It's possible that the study's design and time frame precluded it from observing statistically significant independent differences in key indicators.

This research project studied the SMP's impact on several primary and secondary outcomes. The SMP sought to raise the percentage of deliveries using trained personnel and the use of MCH care services. A secondary outcome tied to this increased use was a reduced infant mortality rate. Over the longer term, the SMP aimed to increase women's demand more broadly for all motherhood health services, with a secondary effect of decreasing under-5 mortality rates. The research showed that the SMP had no statistically significant benefit for either the percentage of deliveries involving trained personnel or infant mortality rates, though it did show a statistically significant positive effect on under-5 mortality rates. As noted, however, comparable positive changes occurred in both primary outcomes for both groups.

The study showed that improvements in these outcomes were associated primarily with education, employment status, and membership in UNICEF's Maternal and Child Survival Program, Development and Protection Project. In all provinces, the pupil–teacher ratio improved over time, indicating improved education quality. This ratio improvement was associated with greater reproductive health services use and reduced infant and under-5 mortality rates. Rising female education levels, occurring in all provinces, contributed to lower under-5 mortality. These associations accorded with other research.[67,68,69] The study's results thus highlight education's significance, especially its quality and inclusion of girls and women, in health outcomes for women and children. The primacy of female education as a necessary foundation for maternal and child health development programs is important.

The study's approach in evaluating the SMP intervention in the context of other development projects—namely UNICEF's MCS project and the HP5—demonstrate the complexity in assessing SMP's independent effect outside other development projects.

In some key ways, the Bank's SMP in Indonesia manifests core SHG principles. In prioritizing women and children's health, it sought to improve rates of infant and under-5 mortality—that is, to reduce Indonesia's shortfall inequality in these indicators. While research showed that it did not statistically significantly improve infant mortality, it did lower the rate of under-5 mortality, thus addressing a central health capability. Though extraneous

[67] K. Beegle, E. Frankenberg, and D. Thomas, "Bargaining Power within Couples and Use of Prenatal and Delivery Care in Indonesia," *Studies in Family Planning* 32, no. 2 (2001): 130–46.

[68] P. Gertler and J. Molyneaux, "How Economic Development and Family Planning Programs Combined to Reduce Indonesian Fertility," *Demography* 31, no. 1 (1994): 33–63.

[69] C. Morrisson, *Education and Health Expenditure, and Development: The Cases of Indonesia and Peru* (Paris: OECD Development Centre, 2002).

variables—other agencies' concurrent SMPs and domestic policies and programs targeting MCH—make definitive conclusions about the project's impact difficult, the Bank's long-term commitment to safe motherhood in Indonesia is noteworthy and expresses a commitment to health justice and equity.

### 9.2.4 PRSP and HIV/AIDS in Malawi: A Case Study of Accountability and Assessment in the World Bank and International Monetary Fund's Poverty Reduction Strategy Papers[70]

#### 9.2.4.1 BACKGROUND AND SIGNIFICANCE

Both the public health and development communities understand the importance of integrating HIV/AIDS and poverty policies. One approach has been to integrate poverty reduction efforts, such as the World Bank's PRSP process, with national HIV/AIDS initiatives.

With a per capita GNP of roughly $342.6 in 2014, Malawi ranks among the world's poorest countries.[71] This southern African country has one of the world's lowest life expectancies primarily because of HIV/AIDS, just 47 years in 1990, though it was 54 in 2012.[72] National adult HIV prevalence rates ranged from 11.8 percent in 2004,[73] to 14.1 percent in 2005,[74] to 11.9 percent in 2007.[75] Malawi was thus a prime target for an effort to combat HIV/AIDS and poverty together.[76] Malawi's poverty also qualified it for external debt relief under the HIPC Initiative, the World Bank and IMF's program to relieve debt and lend money at low interest to poor countries that commit in return to specified economic and governance reforms.

#### 9.2.4.2 CONCEPTUALIZING AND MEASURING GOVERNANCE

In December 2000, the IMF and World Bank granted Malawi US$643 million in HIPC debt relief. Conditions included: (1) preparing and implementing a full one-year PRSP by 2003 and (2) "making progress in implementing the National AIDS strategy, in particular [a] fully staffed, functional and

---

[70] This section stems from C. Wachira and J. P. Ruger, "National Poverty Reduction Strategies and HIV/AIDS Governance in Malawi: A Preliminary Study of Shared Health Governance," *Social Science & Medicine* 72, no. 12 (2011): 1956–64.

[71] See http://data.un.org/CountryProfile.aspx?crName=MALAWI (accessed December 4, 2017); IMF, World Economic Outlook Database, http://www.imf.org/external/pubs/ft/weo/2013/01/weodata/index.aspx (accessed December 4, 2017).

[72] See http://www.unicef.org/infobycountry/malawi_statistics.html (accessed December 4, 2017).

[73] National Statistical Office (Malawi) and ORC Macro, *Malawi Demographic and Health Survey 2004* (Calverton, MD: NSO and ORC Macro, 2005).

[74] UNICEF, "HIV/AIDS: Malawi," *UNICEF* (2013).

[75] UNICEF, "Factsheets: Malawi," *UNICEF* (2013).

[76] UNICEF, "Malawi: Decision Point Document," *UNICEF* (2013).

autonomous National AIDS Control Secretariat, and implement[ing] an effective Behavior Change Communication Strategy, among others."[77] Thus, the Malawian government's commitment to addressing HIV/AIDS countrywide was part of the quid pro quo for debt relief. This strategy leveraged the PRSP process to strengthen HIV/AIDS programming. Servicing debt drains resources, so debt relief can free up funds to increase government health spending. In Malawi, for example, an average $52 million reduction in annual debt services obligations (2000–9) represented roughly 38 percent of 1998 social sector spending.[78] The Malawi Decision Point Document for the Enhanced HIPC Initiative specified that the Malawi government had to meet certain benchmarks to receive 100 percent debt service relief.

Governments in low-income countries prepared PRSPs together with domestic stakeholders, related institutions, and external development partners. The method had five core principles—the plan was to be country driven, result oriented, comprehensive, partnership oriented, and long term. The PRSP process' broad-based engagement was both normatively superior to less participatory approaches and possibly more effective in designing and carrying out development projects. Development officials expected more committed national ownership, improved public program governance, and increased funding from the PRSP process.[79] The Malawian government, with particular support from the UNDP, proposed to allocate 30 percent of debt relief savings to HIV/AIDS prevention and mitigation.[80]

In Malawi, PRSP became a principal development planning instrument, bringing together activities and policies in a "coherent framework for poverty reduction."[81] The strategy encompassed "four strategic pillars": sustainable pro-poor economic growth, human capital development, improvements in quality of life for the most vulnerable, and good governance.[82] The PRSP process identified HIV/AIDS as a core problem in all four priority areas, threatening previous development gains and undermining poverty reduction efforts.[83] Malawi's PRSP process thus stressed resourcing Malawi's National

---

[77] African Development Fund, "Malawi–HIPC Approval Document: Decision Point under the Enhanced Framework," *African Development Fund* 2001, 2.

[78] J.-P. Tan, A. Soucat, and A. Mingat, *Enhancing Human Development in the HIPC/PRSP Context: Progress in the Africa Region during 2000*, Africa Region Human Development Working Paper Series (Washington, DC: World Bank, 2001).

[79] African Forum and Network on Debt and Development (AFRODAD), "Prospects for Poverty Reduction in Malawi: A Critical Analysis of the Poverty Reduction Strategy Paper (PRSP) Process and Outcomes," AFRODAD PRSP Series Malawi Report, April 2003.

[80] Factsheets: Malawi.

[81] E. Bwalya, L. Rakner, L. Svåsand, A. Tostensen, and M. Tsoka, *Poverty Reduction Strategy Processes in Malawi and Zambia* (*CMI Reports R 2004: 8*) (Bergen: Chr. Michelsen Institute, 2004).

[82] Government of Malawi (GoM), "Malawi Poverty Reduction Strategy Paper: Final Draft," April 2002.

[83] Ibid.

HIV/AIDS Strategic Framework (NSF) adequately and implementing the HIV/AIDS action plan. The PRSP included an HIV/AIDS Thematic Working Group that addressed five key issues: reducing HIV/AIDS prevalence rates; reducing HIV transmission through awareness, education, and distribution of condoms; increasing access to appropriate drugs; improving the lives of those living with HIV/AIDS; and mainstreaming HIV/AIDS issues.[84] The PRSP process sought more money for the NSF and for strengthening governance and participation, both considered critical for implementing the national AIDS strategy.

In accordance with the Thematic Working Group focus, the NSF had three main goals: (1) lower HIV and AIDS incidence; (2) improve quality of life for HIV-infected individuals; and (3) mitigate the economic and social consequences of AIDS.[85] The first goal targeted youth, perceived to be among the most vulnerable; here the NSF focused on preventing HIV infection among schoolchildren.[86] The NSF was to be participatory, especially engaging individuals and groups representing people living with HIV and AIDS (PLWHA). It also formed the National AIDS Commission (NAC) in 2001 to develop an expanded multisector HIV/AIDS response. The National HIV and AIDS Policy, launched in 2003, emphasized consultation with civil society groups, NGOs, and PLWHA, to identify guiding principles for HIV/AIDS prevention and treatment programs.[87]

### 9.2.4.3 SHARED HEALTH GOVERNANCE: HOW DID MALAWI'S PRSP PROCESS PERFORM?

It is illuminating to view the Malawian PRSP process and its impact on HIV/AIDS through the SHG lens. The Joint United Nations Programme on HIV/AIDS (UNAIDS) identified two key challenges in Malawi—accountability and better engagement of civil society in policy discussions.[88] The Malawian PRSP was the subject of a 2007 study in which researchers asked respondents directly about the effectiveness and efficiency of HIV/AIDS resource use. This study developed and tested various SHG indicators empirically, including: (1) goal alignment; (2) agreement on key outcomes and on the principle indicators and statistics for evaluating them; (3) adequate financial and human resources; (4) effective and efficient deployment of resources to priority needs; (5) meaningful inclusion and involvement of key global, national, and subnational actors; and (6) special efforts to identify and engage vulnerable groups most affected by policy decisions (the poor, women, youths,

---

[84] GoM, "Malawi Poverty Reduction Strategy Paper: HIV/AIDS," July 17, 2002.

[85] GoM, "Malawi Poverty Reduction Strategy Paper: Final Draft."

[86] Ibid.

[87] UNAIDS, "Malawi," (n.d.) http://www.unaids.org/en/regionscountries/countries/malawi/ (accessed April 10, 2014).

[88] Ibid.

persons with disabilities, and the elderly). A survey examined these dimensions. The project collected data from budget allocations; health, social, and economic indicators; and face-to-face interviews with people engaged in the PRSP and NSF processes, representing both government agencies and NGOs.

### 9.2.4.4 PRSP: MIXED REVIEWS FROM RESPONDENTS

This study raised important questions at the health–development nexus. The Malawi government needed to attract resources and coordinate all actors' contributions, while maintaining accountability and making room for criticism. Did the increased involvement of international actors help or hinder these functions? Did the PRSP process foster SHG for HIV/AIDS in Malawi's NSF?

The results were mixed. Respondents were positive about PRSP and NSF governance efforts. They believed that PRSP implementation did bring greater efficiency and improved accountability for resources. They found good goal alignment between their organization or government department and the NSF before and after the PRSP process. They believed their organizational HIV/AIDS Action Plans supported and/or complemented the NSF. But their perceptions of resourcing, information access, and inclusion were less positive. More than two-thirds believed the process did not provide adequate resources to implement their Action Plans successfully; nearly half thought they had not received sufficient information to participate constructively in the national plan's development.

Many stakeholders—from PLWHA to rural women to parliamentarians— felt excluded from the process. Parliamentarians lacked the opportunity to review, debate, and make decisions on the proposed budgets. PLWHA advocates said they were excluded from important initial deliberations. Many thought that PLWHAs were brought into the process too late, especially in view of the pervasive HIV/AIDS challenge across the poverty reduction agenda, and some PLWHAs believed they were simply rubber-stamping a program that did not meet their needs. Respondents from women's organizations also expressed concerns, citing inadequate and mismatched representation. As primary caregivers, women bear a disproportionate share of the AIDS burden. Further, though the vast majority of births occur in rural areas and rural women are essential to Malawi's agro-based economy, the majority of PRSP participants, especially in important decisions, were urban dwellers. Other research projects have similarly found that programs often fail to provide needed and long-term funding to help those most directly affected—villagers, for example—due to a lack of input.[89]

---

[89] A. Swindler and S. C. Watkins, "'Teach a Man to Fish': The Sustainability Doctrine and Its Social Consequences," *World Development* 37, no. 7 (2009): 1182–96.

Survey participants believed that the convergence of stakeholders' HIV/AIDS Action Plans with the NSF helped scale up antiretroviral therapy (ART). The Christian Health Association of Malawi, the second largest health care provider after the government, included HIV/AIDS testing, counseling, treatment, and prevention in its services and thus certainly increased the number of people helped. But excluding key stakeholders arguably impacted NSF policy outcomes. The PRSP's marginalization of rural women might well have undermined prevention of mother-to-child transmission (PMTCT) efforts. The setting in which nevirapine can be administered to newborn infants and birthing women is especially important for PMTCT effectiveness. Considering birthing conditions is thus essential when evaluating program effectiveness. Respondents explained that home births are typically a more rural phenomenon, occurring in remote areas that PMTCT efforts didn't reach. Thus the low success rate of Malawi's PMTCT programs. Thailand and Cambodia, by contrast, improved the quality of rural health care by deploying trained health volunteers. Had Malawi's PRSP process included rural women adequately, it might have improved results.

Despite these drawbacks, survey participants believed that PRSP implementation affected favorable outcomes. Two-thirds of the respondents found post-PRSP public expenditures for HIV/AIDS programming to be more effective and efficient, with faster proposal review and more expeditious release of funds for approved proposals. Many attributed these improvements to commitments and political will in the Office of the President and Cabinet and to the formation of the semi-autonomous Malawi NAC. The NAC was established as a public trust, with responsibility for coordinating the national HIV/AIDS response.[90] Though the NAC operated under the Minister of Health, its Trust Deed authorized it to appoint its own staff and manage its own affairs independently.

Assessments of NSF goals and objectives were mixed. Though 64 percent of respondents thought the program had met the overall NSF goals, 34 percent—many of them in the NAC and key implementing organizations—disagreed. The effort failed to meet principal NSF prevention goals, including increasing the use of voluntary confidential counseling and testing (VCCT), ensuring greater involvement of PLWHA, and effectively scaling up PMTCT activities. In 2005, only about 6 percent of eligible women received nevirapine at childbirth (up from 1 percent in 2002). On the other hand, the number of clients tested in HIV centers increased about twelvefold from 2001 to 2005. Between 2003 and 2006 the number of public and private ART facilities rose fifteenfold, the number of new ART patients quadrupled, the total number of

---

[90] NAC, *Strategic Management Plan 2003–2008* (Lilongwe: Government of Malawi, June 2003).

ART patients increased over 2,800 percent and the number of patients alive on ART rose by about 600 percent. Respondents credited NAC and key policy guidance from the president and cabinet with the rapid ART scale-up under NSF. Respondents also praised the convergence of stakeholders' HIV/AIDS action plans with the NSF, although the data suggest this alignment obtained pre-PRSP as well, so whether the PRSP measurably increased it is unknown. Still, the preparation for the PRSP, which coincided with the pre-PRSP period in the study, could have been significant.

Most respondents valued the rapid ART scale-up highly, but wondered if this achievement overshadowed key prevention strategies—testing, condom use, and education. They expressed particular concern about the lack of prevention strategies geared toward youth and students; the varying prevalence rates among levels of education are concerning. University of Malawi study findings highlighted the critical need for effective prevention strategies among youth aged 15 to 24, who are particularly vulnerable to and marginalized by HIV infection and suffer the highest prevalence rates.[91] However, HIV prevalence measures do continue to reflect rates of infection that occurred pre-PRSP.

Some respondents recalled that condoms and prevention literature were available in discreet university bathroom locations in the 1990s, but by the time of the survey few if any HIV/AIDS prevention programs targeted students. Whether PEPFAR impacted these prevention strategies is unclear, but the disappearance of condoms and prevention materials is suggestive and parallels trends in Zambia, for example.[92] Also among prevention measures, low VCCT use rates elicited concern. In 2004, only about 17 percent of all Malawians knew their serostatus.[93] Logistical issues—inconvenient hours, locations, and cost—inhibit VCCT in Malawi and elsewhere in Africa; free, mobile, rapid, and anonymous testing services can help.[94] Other observed barriers included a paucity of information, cultural beliefs, unequal gender relations, and general misconceptions, especially within high-risk groups.[95] Stigma and discrimination also impede testing and prevention.

[91] Integrated Regional Information Networks (IRIN), "Youth and HIV/AIDS—The Most Vulnerable Face the Toughest Challenges," February 2007.

[92] V. Kreha, "Zambia," November 30, 2006, http://www.publicintegrity.org/2006/11/30/6390/zambia (accessed April 10, 2014).

[93] N. Angotti, A. Bula, L. Gaydosh, E. Kimchi, R. Thornton, and S. Yeatman, "Increasing the Acceptability of HIV Counseling and Testing with Three C's: Convenience, Confidentiality and Credibility," *Social Science & Medicine* 68, no. 12 (2009): 2263–70.

[94] S. Morin, G. Khumalo-Sakutukwa, E. Charlebois, J. Routh, K. Fritz, T. Lane, et al., "Removing Barriers to Knowing HIV Status: Same-Day Mobile HIV Testing in Zimbabwe," *Journal of Acquired Immune Deficiency Syndromes* 41, no. 2 (2006): 218–24.

[95] A. Kaler, "AIDS-Talk in Everyday Life: The Presence of HIV/AIDS in Men's Informal Conversation in Southern Malawi," *Social Science & Medicine* 59, no. 2 (2004): 285–97.

Achieving NSF goals and objectives depended on sufficient, fair, and timely funding for NSF activities. Only 38 percent thought PRSP implementation had increased resources for their HIV/AIDS action plans. Indeed, several respondents from implementing organizations came to believe that they had not sufficiently understood the PRSP process and that these organizations had thus missed out on critical financing for NSF-consistent HIV/AIDS interventions.

Respondents believed that accountability had improved under the Malawi PRSP process and commended the Office of the President and Cabinet and the NAC for improved stewardship of resources. NAC evaluated grant proposals and scrutinized results for each recipient; it used its findings to make follow-on funding decisions and course corrections to ensure effective and efficient spending. These corrections occurred swiftly, according to respondents. The Malawi Economic Justice Network and other CSOs involved in the PRSP process helped hold the government, NAC, and implementing agencies accountable.

This inquiry concluded that Malawi's PRSP and HIV/AIDS process applied roughly half of SHG's governance principles and achieved between a third and a half of the targeted outcomes. In particular, the study showed: (1) goal alignment between organizations and NSF was good before and after the PRSP process, suggesting that the PRSP process was supportive but not determinative; (2) participants judged resources insufficient for implementing NSF-related action plans, implying that the PRSP process did not raise HIV allocations sufficiently (and might have been limited by, for example, IMF ceilings on public sector spending); (3) the PRSP process excluded some stakeholders, possibly impacting HIV policy and strategy; and (4) respondents attributed more effective and efficient HIV public expenditure post-PRSP to the NAC, as well as greater political commitment and increased civil society involvement.

The 2007 Malawi study underscored the need to involve stakeholders in the PRSP process. Planning, budgeting for, and implementing HIV/AIDS prevention and treatment strategies should engage relevant stakeholders, especially those most vulnerable and marginalized. This engagement is fundamental to SHG. Lessons from the Malawi PRSP process can be invaluable for countries testing and evaluating mechanisms of accountability, participation, and efficient resource allocation. Malawi's experiences can show how to strengthen SHG and how to produce more effective and sustainable outcomes worldwide.

## 9.3 The G8, G20, and WTO

As Chapter 2 noted, other multilateral institutions are taking on larger roles in GHG. In some cases, they bring real strengths to the table. The G8, distinguished by a small membership, public–private collaborations,[96] task orientation, common values, and a degree of intragroup accountability, is arguably more effective than other global institutions.[97] Its structural flexibility can be an asset, too: unburdened by the regulations governing WHO's interactions with NGOs and the private sector, the G8 can sidestep global health bureaucracies.[98] Highly visible, it can spotlight global problems, and its access to financial and human resources helps it raise funds for specific activities. The Global Fund, for example, formed under G8 auspices. Others suggest that the G20, an expanded version of the G8, has more to offer: an intergovernment group based on national governments accountable to their populations, the G20 represents more than 60 percent of the world's population. It brings together primarily finance ministers with substantial funding authority, and is a "broadly representative leaders-level grouping."[99]

Both these bodies have acknowledged GHG roles—in financing, advocacy, surveillance and outbreak response, health system development, and efforts to develop the macrosocial environment. But examining them through the SHG lens reveals serious problems with G8 and G20 health performance. The freedom from constraints that makes them flexible also means they needn't seek either broad-based goal alignment with other actors and levels of government or agreement on key outcomes and indicators. They can act independently of other global, national, and subnational actors. Representing the world's powerful economies and their interests, these bodies can and do operate with those interests in view. What those interests are in specific cases will determine whether the G8 and G20 engage vulnerable populations in their health programs—or not. The G8's inaction on tobacco[100] and its inadequate efforts toward redistribution[101] reveal the influence of powerful interests on G8 policy and practice. The G20, for its part, made little mention if any of the poverty and suffering resulting from the 2008 world financial

[96] J. Orbinski, "AIDS, Médicins Sans Frontières, and Access to Essential Medicines," in *Civil Society in the Information Age*, ed. P. I. Hajnal (Aldershot: Ashgate, 2002), 127–37.

[97] J. Kirton, N. Roudev, and L. Sunderland, "Making G8 Leaders Deliver: An Analysis of Compliance and Health Commitments, 1996–2006," *Bulletin of the World Health Organization* 85, no. 3 (2007): 192–9; Orbinski, "AIDS, Médicins Sans Frontières."

[98] M. Reich and K. Takemi, "G8 and Strengthening of Health Systems: Follow-Up to the Toyako Summit," *The Lancet* 373, no. 9662 (2009): 508–15.

[99] C. Bradford, "Reaching the Millennium Development Goals," in *Governing Global Health: Challenge, Response, Innovation*, ed. A. Cooper, J. Kirton, and T. Schrecker (Aldershot: Ashgate, 2007), 79–86.

[100] R. Labonte, T. Schrecker, D. Sanders, and W. Meeus, *Fatal Indifference: The G8, Africa and Global Health* (South Africa: University of Cape Town Press & Canada: International Development Research Centre, 2004).

[101] R. Labonte and T. Schrecker, "Committed to Health for All? How the G7/G8 Rate," *Social Science & Medicine* 59, no. 8 (2004): 1661–76.

meltdown in their 2009 summit, and some see the G20 as unlikely to deliver fundamental reforms.[102]

The WTO has GHG functions in setting norms and standards and in developing the macrosocial environment. But its effects on health can be negative: its trade regime, serving powerful industry interests, raises issues about access to drugs and health services, and about major risk factors such as tobacco, food safety, and unhealthy diets and their role in non-communicable diseases. With the power to enforce compliance with its rules and to limit sovereign choice in public health policies, the WTO's impact on GHG runs counter to the SHG vision: to craft shared goals among all actors and levels of government, to elicit meaningful participation of disparate actors, and to represent the poor, women, youths, the disabled, and the elderly in decision-making.

## 9.4 Civil Society: Nongovernmental or Civil Society Organizations and Public–Private Partnerships

NGOs have distinct advantages over governments in the global health landscape. Their organizational flexibility, cost-effectiveness, and access to communities, especially in remote and difficult areas, can make them more nimble in providing services.[103] Many proven successes in global health have grown out of work by and with NGOs. The Task Force for Child Survival, Bangladesh Rural Advancement Committee, Carter Center, Helen Keller International, and the International Trachoma Initiative are but a few examples. Most PEPFAR funding goes to NGOs instead of governments. CSO participation can also enhance democracy, giving voice to and empowering aid recipients, particularly those with few resources, by helping them understand issues and engage in negotiations. These organizations deserve credit for making drug access a high-profile issue during the WTO Doha Round,[104] and for influencing the FCTC negotiations.[105] Many routinely call for broader inclusion of NGOs and civil society.

Regrettably, however, experience has revealed NGOs' own pathologies. NGOs compete amongst themselves for donor money, turf, and attention, damaging program design, implementation, and interorganization coordination.[106]

---

[102] A. Guise, D. Woodward, P. Lee, R. Vogli, T. Tillman, and D. McCoy, "Engaging the Health Community in Global Economic Reform," *The Lancet* 373, no. 9668 (2009): 987–9.

[103] C. Doyle and P. Patel, "Civil Society Organisations and Global Health Initiatives: Problems of Legitimacy," *Social Science & Medicine* 66, no. 9 (2008): 1928–38.

[104] E. 't Hoen, "TRIPS, Pharmaceutical Patents, and Access to Essential Medicines: A Long Way from Seattle to Doha," *Chicago Journal of International Law* 3, no. 1 (2002): 27–46.

[105] G. Jacob, "Without Reservation," *Chicago Journal of International Law* 5, no. 1 (2004): 287–302.

[106] A. Cooley and J. Ron, "The NGO Scramble: Organizational Insecurity and the Political Economy of Transnational Action," *International Security* 27, no. 1 (2002): 5–39; M. Shamsul Haque, "Governance Based on Partnership with NGOs: Implications for Development

Ideology can undercut NGO effectiveness: religious beliefs, for example, some-times obstruct condom use and promotion.[107] Nor are NGOs funded just by civil society, but also by states and corporations whose interests shape their initia-tives.[108] Observers have realized that although NGOs often purport to represent the public interest, these actors are not elected, and their controlling interests—whom they represent or to whom they are accountable—are often shrouded in mystery. Reliance on NGO/CSO service delivery also bypasses and can under-mine elected governments; higher NGO salaries can cause health-worker brain drain and thus damage public sector organizations. Some observers question altogether the broader notion of a global civil society.[109] These concerns dem-onstrate that CSOs cannot be assumed to serve the goals of SHG.

PPPs constitute another group of actors on the global health stage. Their functions include knowledge generation and dissemination, empowerment and agency enhancement. Many believe PPPs can bring together civil society, the public sector and private sector to correct market failures. PPPs offer advantages including managerial skills, extensive financial and in-kind resources, innovation, and efficiency.[110] They may also be inevitable in some settings: in drug research and development (R&D), for example, the private sector "own[s] the ball."[111] The singularly successful PPPs, such as Merck's ivermectin donation and Pfizer's trachoma programs, tend to be pharmaceutical. Studies have found that these public health partnerships do typically help control disease at a lower cost,[112] and target the most menacing diseases and the poorest countries relatively well.[113]

The Global Fund is perhaps the most prominent PPP in the health arena today. Established by the G8 in 2001, the Global Fund quickly became a dominant multilateral health funder. According to its website, it delivers 82 percent of international funding for TB, 50 percent for malaria, and 21 percent

Empowerment in Rural Bangladesh," *International Review of Administrative Sciences* 70, no. 2 (2004): 271–90; A. Bebbington, "Donor–NGO Relations and Representations of Livelihood in Nongovernmental Aid Chains," *World Development* 33, no. 6 (2005): 937–50.

[107] S. Woldehanna, K. Ringheim, C. Murphy, J. Gibson, B. Odyniec, C. Clérismé, et al., *Faith in Action: Examining the Role of Faith-Based Organizations in Addressing HIV/AIDS* (Washington, DC: Global Health Council, 2005).

[108] R. Lencucha, R. Labonté, and M. Rouse, "Beyond Idealism and Realism: Canadian NGO/Government Relations during the Negotiation of the FCTC," *Journal of Public Health Policy* 31, no.1 (2010): 74–87.

[109] Doyle and Patel, "Civil Society Organisations."

[110] K. Buse and G. Walt, "Global Public–Private Partnerships: Part II: What are the Health Issues for Global Governance?" *Bulletin of the World Health Organization* 78, no. 5 (2000): 699–709.

[111] K. Buse and G. Walt, "Global Public–Private Partnerships: Part I: A New Development in Health?" *Bulletin of the World Health Organization* 78, no. 4 (2000): 549–61.

[112] Bill and Melinda Gates Foundation, *Developing Successful Global Health Alliances* (Seattle, WA: Gates Foundation, 2002).

[113] K. Caines, K. Buse, C. Carlson, R.-M. de Loor, N. Druce, C. Grace, et al., *Assessing the Impact of Global Health Partnerships* (London: DFID Health Resource Centre, 2004).

for AIDS. It makes direct investments in more than 150 countries. Strictly a funding agency, the Global Fund channels contributions from donor nations, the private sector, and civil society groups like the Bill and Melinda Gates Foundation. It also receives and deploys expert technical assistance from WHO, UNAIDS, the UNDP, other PPPs, and the World Bank (the Global Fund's trustee). In the years since the Global Fund's founding, the world has made significant progress against HIV/AIDS, tuberculosis, and malaria in many places, and the Global Fund can claim at least partial credit.

Gavi (formerly the Global Alliance for Vaccines and Immunizations) is another major PPP. With the mission of "saving children's lives and protecting people's health by increasing access to immunisation in poor countries," Gavi brings together the major actors in global immunization—key UN agencies, leaders of the vaccine industry, representatives of bilateral aid agencies and major foundations—to expand vaccination among the world's poorest children. Since its inception in 2000, Gavi has helped immunize 640 million children, and it has prevented 9 million future deaths through ten vaccines: measles, pneumococcal disease, pentavalent, meningitis A, Japanese encephalitis, human papillomavirus (HPV), measles-rubella, measles second dose, rubella, rotavirus, and yellow fever. These are laudable results.

Still, reservations abound about PPPs. Some assert that in PPPs the public sector bears the risks while the private sector reaps the rewards, and that PPPs are fundamentally corporate public relations and market expansion ploys.[114] Both Oxfam and Médicins Sans Frontières, for example, have criticized Gavi for including pharma executives on its board of directors, where they might skew decisions about vaccine selection to benefit their firms. Because PPPs include specific companies and industries, these partnerships tend to concentrate on technical approaches and vertical programs with their attendant problems. Nor are they necessarily pro-poor: PPP programs can exclude large populations in impoverished countries or nations with questionable governments or bad infrastructure. PPPs often elude accountability, lacking procedures to hold them responsible.[115] Recent years have seen allegations of corruption against the Global Fund, particularly about the way some countries expend its monies. Northern participants tend to control PPPs, with under-representation from the South,[116] though that imbalance has begun to

---

[114] E. Ollila, "Global Health Priorities: Priorities of the Wealthy?" *Global Health* 1 (2005): 6; J. Lister, "Can Global Health Be Good Business?" *Tropical Medicine and International Health* 11, no. 3 (2006): 255–7.

[115] J. A. Alexander, M. E. Comfort, and B. J. Weiner, "Governance in Public–Private Community Health Partnerships: A Survey of the Community Care Network Demonstration Sites," *Nonprofit Management and Leadership* 8, no. 4 (1998): 311–32.

[116] K. Buse and A. Harmer, "Power to the Partners?: The Politics of Public–Private Health Partnerships," *Development* 47, no. 2 (2004): 49–56.

change.[117] PPPs may also have a corrosive effect on governments and multilateral organizations, diminishing the public sector's normative focus. Similarly, they can undermine the values of international organizations and thus their moral authority to set norms and standards.[118]

Thus, PPPs often fail to meet SHG criteria. Powerful industry interests often determine goals, rather than a deliberative process bringing actors and levels of government together. Though PPPs can marshal impressive resources, the organization typically determines key outcomes and principle indicators for evaluating those outcomes without necessarily including other involved parties. Key global, national, and subnational groups and institutions might or might not participate. They are not under obligation to engage vulnerable groups most affected by policy decisions. While PPPs can perform invaluable functions, they fall short of meeting SHG criteria.

[117] S. Bartsch, "The South in Global Health Governance: Perspectives on Global Public–Private Partnerships," Paper presented at the International Studies Association (ISA) Annual Convention, San Diego, California, March 21–25, 2006.
[118] K. Buse and A. Waxman, "Public–Private Health Partnerships: A Strategy for WHO," *Bulletin of the World Health Organization* 79, no. 8 (2001): 748–54.

# 10

# Emerging Countries[1]

## 10.1 Introduction

With a growing presence on the world stage, the BRICS nations—Brazil, Russia, India, China, and South Africa—are expanding their influence and impact worldwide. Global health scholarship has not given the BRICS the attention they merit, particularly in the aggregate. But these countries can address global health issues as they build their own health systems and help developing countries improve their populations' health, taking a unique place in the global health system. As components of the global health architecture, the BRICS are growing in significance, separately as nations and collectively as a center of gravity. They are assuming multiplying roles in global health, including funding, knowledge generation and dissemination, technical assistance and policy advice, empowerment and agency enhancement, advocacy, surveillance and outbreak response, and health system development. In June 2009, they gathered for their first-ever summit in Yekaterinburg, Russia, emerging as a policy consultation and coordination group.[2]

Though growth in these economies has slowed (Brazil, for example, was in recession in 2016, and political turmoil), collectively these countries have much to offer in the quest to improve global health.

## 10.2 What BRICS Can Contribute to Global Health

### 10.2.1 Financial Assistance

With their growing material resources, these emerging BRICS nations are expanding financial assistance to developing countries, where they invest in

---

[1] This chapter stems from: J. P. Ruger and N. Y. Ng, "Emerging and Transitioning Countries' Role in Global Health," *Saint Louis University Journal of Health Law & Policy* 3, no. 2 (2010): 253–89.

[2] T. Halpin, "Brazil, Russia, India and China Form Bloc to Challenge US Global Dominance," *The Times*, June 17, 2009, p. 33.

health care, public health, and disease-specific programs.[3] India, for example, has underwritten HIV/AIDS programs in several African countries.[4] Indian pharmaceutical firms have built plants in Africa and Latin America, helping make antiretroviral drugs (ARV) affordable and creating jobs and economic development in the bargain.

The BRICS nations have transitioned to donor status in development assistance. All five BRICS countries have supported the Global Fund. As of 2005, India rose to fifteenth among World Food Programme donors, and in 2004 lent more than $400 million in hard currency to Brazil, Burundi, and Indonesia, under International Monetary Fund (IMF) auspices.[5] Russia has given aid to numerous countries, including Cuba, Iran, Chechnya, Kyrgyzstan, Iraq, China, Lebanon, Palestine, Afghanistan, Serbia, and Iceland, though the bulk of this aid has focused on economic or geopolitical issues and does not support public health.[6] China has granted aid to African countries through debt write-offs, preferential loans, buyer's credit, investment, training, and infrastructure construction.[7] For Central Asian nations suffering in the global economic recession, former Chinese President Hu Jintao pledged $10 billion of credit support.[8] Observers have noted, "China's health sector is overwhelmingly internally focused,"[9] but China does send some medical financial aid to Africa.[10] Though most Russian and Chinese foreign aid is not now health focused, these emerging countries are clearly positioned to give health-related assistance if health assumes more importance in their foreign policy agenda.

India's foreign aid also tends to target the economy and trade. As a donor, India typically shows up in another country "only when it is also an investor, trade partner or political ally, or can become one."[11] India has, for years, provided economic and military aid in South Asia: it has funded nearly 60 percent

---

[3] Q. Han, L. Chen, T. Evans, and R. Horton, "China and Global Health," *The Lancet* 372, no. 9648 (2008): 1439–41; C. Schläger, *New Powers for Global Change? Challenges for International Development Cooperation: The Case of Brasil* (Berlin: Friedrich Ebert Stiftung, 2007).

[4] J. S. Morrison and J. Kates, "The G-8, Russia's Presidency, and HIV/AIDS in Eurasia," CSIS Task Force Report on HIV/AIDS in collaboration with the Kaiser Family Foundation, Washington, DC, June 2006.

[5] D. Chanana, "India as an Emerging Donor," *Economic and Political Weekly* 44, no. 12 (2009): 11, 12.

[6] "Russia's Aid to Quake-Hit China Totaled $14 Million," *RIA Novosti*, July 16, 2008; "Russia May Continue Giving Aid to Palestine—Foreign Ministry," *RIA Novosti*, May 8, 2006; "Russia Offers Afghanistan Aid in Establishing Political System" *RIA Novosti*, June 15, 2009; "Russia Proposes Aid to Lebanon to Rebuild Infrastructure," *RIA Novosti*, September 7, 2006; "Third Plane with Russian Humanitarian Aid Lands in Serbia," *RIA Novosti*, April 8, 2008.

[7] "Chinese Aid Flows into Africa," *VOA News*, May 8, 2007.

[8] G. Faulconbridge, "Developing World Leaders Show New Power at Summits," *Reuters*, June 15, 2009.

[9] Han et al., "China and Global Health," 1439.

[10] Ibid.

[11] M. Jobelius, "New Powers for Global Change? Challenges for the International Development Cooperation: The Case of India," Friedrich Ebert Stiftung (FES) Briefing Paper 5 (Berlin: FES, 2007).

of Bhutan's budget, and supports Afghanistan, Nepal, and Myanmar with aid and loans.[12] India has also branched out to Africa, in part to compete with China. In 2009, India doubled the amount of available loans for Africa to $5.2 billion; Africa has become one of the largest recipients of Indian development aid.[13] The health sector benefits: some of India's financial assistance goes toward health needs such as HIV/AIDS.[14]

Brazil focuses its foreign financial assistance more prominently on health. In 2007, Brazil spent an estimated $120 million globally on HIV/AIDS relief programs, the rehabilitation of former combatants, and non-health projects like agricultural development and vocational training.[15] Paraguay, East Timor, Haiti, Mozambique, Angola, and Guinea-Bissau receive the largest part of Brazil's aid.[16] Brazil also supports infrastructure development: it built a pharmaceutical laboratory for the production of ARVs in Mozambique, for example.[17]

### 10.2.2 Medical Goods and Services

BRICS can also help developing nations with necessary medical goods and services, by direct exports and by modeling successful domestic generic drug enterprises. Brazil's homegrown generic drug industry has supported the government in providing free ARV medications to all who need them.[18] India and China manufacture ingredients for drug production, and both have substantial generic drug industries, supplying medications, including ARVs, domestically and internationally.[19] Brazil's generics industry buys ingredients from India and China to manufacture ARVs for its own population.[20] India especially supplies ARVs to countries that lack manufacturing capacity.[21] It is also branching out into pharmaceutical research and development (R&D) and the manufacture of other complex medications, such as cancer treatments.[22]

Emerging nations export other medical goods as well. India's Aravind Eye Care System, for example, makes intraocular lenses for cataract surgery at its

---

[12] Chanana, "India as an Emerging Donor," 11.
[13] Ibid., 12.
[14] Morrison and Kates, "The G-8, Russia's Presidency, and HIV/AIDS."
[15] Schläger, *New Powers for Global Change?*
[16] J. Soares, Jr., "Brazil as a South–South Cooperation Partner," in *It's Time for Brazil in Singapore*, ed. T. Rosito (Berlin: Friedrich-Ebert-Stiftung, 2008), 50, 51–2.
[17] E. J. Gómez, "Brazil's Blessing in Disguise," *Foreign Policy*, July 22, 2009.
[18] J. Cohen, "Ten Years After," *Science* 313, no. 5786 (2006): 484–7.
[19] C. Grace, *The Effect of Changing Intellectual Property on Pharmaceutical Industry Prospects in India and China: Considerations for Access to Medicines* (London: DFID Health Systems Resource Centre, 2004).
[20] Cohen, "Ten Years After," 484, 487.
[21] Grace, *The Effect of Changing Intellectual Property*, 14–15.
[22] S. Chaturvedi, "Emerging Indian Entrepreneurship in Biotechnology and National Innovation System: Exploring Linkages and Prospects," *International Journal of Technology and Globalisation* 5, no. 1/2 (2010): 76–92.

own Aurolab plant.[23] Making lenses permitted Aravind to cut lens costs from $200 to less than $10, and Aurolab lenses now go to more than one hundred countries, exported through nongovernmental organization (NGO) partners and distribution centers. Today they make up 10 percent of the global market.[24]

BRICS also increasingly export human resources, a short-term way to bridge health system gaps and deal with developing countries' brain-drain problem. Russia has actively helped staff some African HIV programs,[25] and has sent doctors and supplies to Haiti and Chile after devastating earthquakes.[26] China runs training programs for personnel to treat malaria, HIV/AIDS, and other diseases as part of its diplomatic engagement with Africa.[27] Since 1964, China has "cumulatively sent over 15,000 doctors to more than forty-seven African countries and treated approximately 180 million African patients."[28] The recipient countries pay these teams' costs, but for the poorest nations China covers travel costs as well as medical supplies.[29]

Even countries lacking the BRICS' economic prowess can help poorer nations. Cuba exports medical aid.[30] Cuba has dispatched doctors to disaster areas like Haiti after Hurricane Mitch in 1998 and Pakistan after the 2005 earthquake. Remote and underserved areas in countries like Honduras, Belize,[31] and Equatorial Guinea have all benefited from the work of Cuban doctors.[32] The Cuban government also provides free cataract surgery in Cuba to patients from Latin America and the Caribbean.[33] Perhaps most famously, Cuba provides free medical education to Latin American, Caribbean, and African students, on condition that they return to their home countries to work once they become doctors. Cuba has deployed this diplomatic strategy effectively, developing positive relationships around the world despite US efforts to isolate the country. Cuba's medical aid efforts also bolster its trade. Venezuela sends subsidized oil to Cuba in exchange for the 20,000 Cuban medical personnel working there.[34] Cuba thus illustrates diplomatic and

---

[23] A. Bhandari, S. Dratler, K. Raube, and R. D. Thulasiraj, "Specialty Care Systems: A Pioneering Vision for Global Health," *Health Affairs* 27, no. 4 (2008): 964–76.

[24] Ibid.

[25] Morrison and Kates, "The G-8, Russia's Presidency, and HIV/AIDS," 4.

[26] "Russian Humanitarian Aid Arrives in Quake-Hit Chile," *RIA Novosti*, March 5, 2010, http://en.rian.ru/russia/20100305/158097559.html (accessed April 10, 2014); "Russia to Send Two More Aid Planes to Quake-Hit Haiti," *RIA Novosti*, January 31, 2010, http://en.ria.ru/russia/20100131/157730407.html (accessed April 10, 2014).

[27] D. Thompson, "China's Soft Power in Africa: From the 'Beijing Consensus' to Health Diplomacy," *China Brief* 5, no. 21 (2005): 1–4.

[28] Ibid.

[29] Ibid.

[30] H. Calvo Ospina, "Cuba Exports Health," *Le Monde Diplomatique*, English edition, August 2006.

[31] M. Voss, "Cuba Pushes Its 'Medical Diplomacy'," *BBC News*, May 20, 2009.

[32] M. Lloyd, "A Medical School in Cuba Trains Doctors for Poor Countries," *Chronicle of Higher Education*, July 20, 2001, A35.

[33] Voss, "Cuba Pushes Its 'Medical Diplomacy'."

[34] Ibid.

economic reasons for emerging countries to provide medical supplies and services to developing countries.

Beyond doctors and medical training, education for scientists and researchers is another way emerging nations reach out globally. Brazilian universities and institutions train scientists from elsewhere in South America, and Nigeria, Kenya, and Mali provide education for many African scientists.[35] Malaysia, Thailand, and the Philippines train Asian and African researchers, especially in epidemiology.[36]

## 10.2.3 Technical Assistance

Technical assistance is a third area in which emerging nations are helping internationally. Brazil and seven other middle-income countries, for example, created a network for sharing technology and best practices in pharmaceutical manufacturing.[37] The Brazil +7 initiative, an alliance among these countries, the United Nations Children's Fund, and the Joint United Nations Programme on HIV/AIDS, seeks to increase access to antiretroviral medicine, particularly those that prevent mother-to-child transmission.[38] This initiative has expanded treatment programs in those countries.

China and India offer technical assistance as well. Indeed, they may prove to be especially effective partners. China "ranked fourth internationally in 2005 for patents granted and publications in indexed journals."[39] India is globally known for its human resources and advanced medical expertise, and Morrison and Kates credit it with "great initiative and commitment" in researching and developing HIV vaccines and microbicides.[40] To expand these efforts, India created the Global Political Advocacy Initiative to bolster support for accelerated R&D in preventive HIV vaccines. Nor is technical assistance limited to medications. India's PanAfrican E-Network project emphasizes tele-education and telemedicine, and it aims to build capacity for medical professionals dealing with pandemics through its Africa-India Framework for Cooperation.[41]

---

[35] T. C. Nchinda, "Research Capacity Strengthening in the South," *Social Science & Medicine* 54, no. 11 (2002): 1699–711.

[36] Ibid.

[37] S. Okie, "Fighting HIV: Lessons from Brazil," *New England Journal of Medicine* 354 (2006): 1977–81. Brazil, Argentina, China, Cuba, Nigeria, Russia, Ukraine, and Thailand are working together to "improve each country's capacity to manufacture medicines, condoms, and laboratory reagents needed to fight AIDS...," 1981.

[38] The other countries are São Tomé and Príncipe, Bolivia, Paraguay, Cape Verde, Guinea-Bissau, East Timor, and Nicaragua.

[39] Z. Chen, "Biomedical Science and Technology in China," *The Lancet* 372, no. 9648 (2008): 1441–3, 1442.

[40] Morrison and Kates, "The G-8, Russia's Presidency, and HIV/AIDS," 20.

[41] T. Deen, "China, India Lead South–South Cooperation," *Inter Press Service (IPS) News Agency*, November 24, 2009.

Egypt's Fund for Technical Cooperation with Africa organizes and funds projects that, for example, send engineers to train medical equipment maintenance workers in Cameroon.[42] Egypt also provides technical assistance to Central Asian, Middle Eastern, and North African countries.[43]

South–South cooperation occurs among emerging countries. Mozambique received a health information system developed in South Africa; the neighboring countries share similarities in health system structure. The "physical proximity and feeling of shared interests ease[d] the cooperation between the original developers and the adapters," according to Kaasbøll and Nhampossa.[44]

Emerging countries are also partnering with each other to provide technical assistance to developing countries. Egypt and Turkey work together in health, agriculture, and security training for Africans.[45] Argentina works with the World Health Organization's (WHO's) Pan American Health Organization (PAHO) to help with polio eradication among Nigerian children and capacity building for organ transplants in Paraguay.[46]

### 10.2.4 *Improving Access to Medicines and Intellectual Property*

Another critical issue involves intellectual property (IP) and access to patented medicines. Here too emerging countries have begun playing a key role, acting in concert to negotiate IP regulations and gain access to essential drugs. Many believe that BRICS nations—or countries anchoring other blocs—could bargain for a more favorable reading of IP protections within the World Trade Organization (WTO) and elsewhere, thus accessing essential medicines both for their own populations and others in developing countries. Such collective strategies are already in play. In 2005, for example, Brazil helped forge an agreement among eleven Latin American governments and twenty-six drug companies to bring down the cost of HIV/AIDS drugs.[47]

Quite aside from political alliances, BRICS' actions and successes in reducing IP barriers can change global actors' norms and behaviors. In 2001, pressed by pharmaceutical firms, the USA planned to challenge Brazil and its drug patent

[42] "Egypt," INSouth.org.

[43] INSouth.org, "Egypt,"—Egyptian Fund for Technical Cooperation with Commonwealth and Trilateral Cooperation on South–South Basis with Islamic Development Bank.

[44] J. Kaasbøll and J. L. Nhampossa, "Transfer of Public Sector Information Systems between Developing Countries: South–South Cooperation," Paper presented at the International Federation for Information Processing Working Group 9.4 Conference on Social Implications of Computers in Developing Countries, Bangalore, India, May 29–31, 2002, p. 12.

[45] INSouth.org, "Egypt,"—Trilateral Cooperation on South–South Basis with Islamic Development Bank and Trilateral Cooperation on South–South Basis with Turkey.

[46] PAHO/WHO Argentina, "South–South Cooperation: Triangular Cooperation Experience between the Government of the Argentine Republic and the Pan-American Health Organization/ World Health Organization," *PAHO/WHO*, 2009.

[47] Okie, "Fighting HIV," 1981.

laws through the WTO. Through diplomatic and public relations campaigns, Brazil rallied global attention to its "fight for life" and successfully lobbied the Bush administration, which relented in the face of international pressure and a "potential public relations disaster."[48] In another instance, thirty-nine pharmaceutical companies, trying to block import of generic ARVs to South Africa, sued the government there,[49] but negative international opinion persuaded them to drop the suit.[50] BRICS countries have the resources to respond assertively to threatened IP-related trade sanctions and lawsuits; China, now a major economic power, can certainly play hardball and threaten countersanctions.[51]

These actions can redound to other developing countries' benefit. The Brazilian and South African confrontations helped raise public awareness and also revealed a broad normative consensus about essential drug access for developing countries. Pharmaceutical companies realized that IP actions could have terrible public relations consequences. If nothing else, these lessons could make them unlikely to sue another developing country.[52] These problems might also lead drug companies to donate or discount drugs to poor countries, thus increasing access, in hopes of garnering positive publicity.[53]

Some emerging countries are going farther in the quest for increased drug access. Under the Agreement on Trade-Related Aspects of Intellectual Property Rights, a WTO agreement on IP rights, governments may allow producers to make a patented product through compulsory licenses if the producer cannot obtain "reasonable commercial terms" from the right holder, or in a case of "national emergency."[54] Countries have threatened compulsory licensing as a negotiating tool to get deeper drug discounts from pharma firms.[55] Brazil, which relies on inexpensive ARVs, made numerous threats to license local producers, but only issued its first such license in 2007, for Merck's efavirenz.[56] Thailand granted compulsory licenses for two ARVs, efavirenz and lopinavir/

---

[48] R. Wadia, "Brazil's AIDS Policy Earns Global Plaudits," *CNN.com*, August 16, 2001.

[49] R. C. Bird and D. R. Cahoy, "The Emerging BRICS Economies: Lessons from Intellectual Property Negotiation and Enforcement," *Northwestern Journal of Technology and Intellectual Property* 5, no 3 (2007): 400–25, 407.

[50] O. Quist-Arcton, "South Africa: Drugs' Giants Drop Case Against South Africa," *ALLAfrica.com*, April 19, 2001.

[51] Bird and Cahoy, "The Emerging BRICS Economies," 410–11.

[52] G. Mutume, "Health and 'Intellectual Property': Poor Nations and Drug Firms Tussle over WTO Patent Provisions," *Africa Recovery* 15 (June 2001): 14–5.

[53] See, generally, Pharmaceutical Research and Manufacturers of America (PhRMA), "Global Partnerships: Humanitarian Programs of the Pharmaceutical Industry in Developing Nations," *PhRMA*, 2003.

[54] Mutume, "Health and 'Intellectual Property'," 14.

[55] Ibid., 15—Brazil persuaded Merck to reduce the prices of two HIV/AIDS drugs by threatening to permit compulsory licensing if it refused to make the drugs more accessible.

[56] K. Alcorn, "Brazil Issues Compulsory License on Efavirenz," *AIDSMAP.COM*, May 7, 2007; R. Amaral, "Brazil Bypasses Patent on Merck AIDS Drug," *Reuters*, May 4, 2007.

ritonavir, and has repeatedly renewed them.[57] In part, this Thai action seeks to forestall ballooning HIV/AIDS program costs as the virus develops resistance to generic first-line drugs and expensive patented second-line drugs become necessary. Some observers also think that Thailand's patent seizures are a step toward developing its generic drug industry into a regional hub.[58] But countries like Bolivia and Brazil have voiced support, and others, like the Philippines, are considering similar steps. Patent seizures in middle-income countries are described as "a massive political movement against intellectual property" that "seeks to make medicine into public, not private, goods."[59]

Recently, these various thrusts from emerging nations appear to be eliciting a new industry response, at least from one drug company. In 2016, the British pharma giant GlaxoSmithKline (GSK) announced a tiered approach to patent protection to help make essential drugs more accessible. In "least-developed" and "low-income" countries, GSK will not patent its medicines, enabling generics companies to manufacture and sell them at low cost. In "lower-middle-income" countries, GSK will apply for patents but will grant licenses to produce generics for ten years. In "high-income," "upper-middle-income," and G20 countries, the firm will not make any patent concessions. How much this policy will accomplish remains to be seen, but growing assertiveness among emerging nations could well effect meaningful change over time.

### 10.2.5 *Institutional Frameworks for Health*

Institutional frameworks for health care and public health sectors encompass the regulation of medical equipment, medicines, facilities, and worksites; oversight of personnel training, licensing, and accreditation; provision of hospitals, clinics, and health-related facilities; generation and dissemination of health-related knowledge and information; and the establishment of sustainable, equitable, and affordable health insurance systems. The BRICS countries clearly have not mastered these functions—they lack facilities and supplies, and notorious failures have marred their reputations in food and drug safety regulation. China's safety breaches—melamine in milk powders and pet food, antifreeze chemicals in toothpaste, and tainted heparin—are well known.[60] Indian investigations have exposed repeated instances of inaccurate dosage/duration in drug prescriptions and sometimes the lack of

---

[57] American University Washington College of Law, "Compulsory Licensing Controversy in Thailand," Program on Information Justice and Intellectual Property; E. Silverman, "Thailand Extends Compulsory Licenses on AIDS Meds," *PHARMALOT.COM*, August 4, 2010.

[58] G. Wehrfritz, "Thailand's New Drug War," *Newsweek*, April 8, 2007, http://www.newsweek.com/id/35843 (accessed April 9, 2014).

[59] Ibid.

[60] G. Fairclough and L. Chao, "Chinese Formula Maker Hid Toxic Danger for Weeks," *The Wall Street Journal*, September 18, 2008.

such information altogether.[61] Nevertheless, emerging countries offer some encouraging models for other countries to emulate.

India's Aravind Eye Care System[62] is an exemplary institutional health care framework. Aravind provides a particularly inspiring specialty care model. This "focused factory" model concentrates on a particular medical condition, disease area, medication, or procedure, and depends on standardized methods, management goals, core competencies, and an efficient and specialized human capital base. Four major features underlie this model's success: "(1)... management systems that emphasize standardization and continuous improvement; (2) the ability to attract and train a specialized workforce; (3) access to low-cost technology; and (4)... patient volume."

As of 2017 the Aravind Eye Care System had twelve hospitals, performed over 460,000 surgeries and laser procedures and treated 4.7 million outpatients annually. An Aravind surgeon operates on one patient as staff prepare the next patient on an adjacent table. The surgeon simply swings his or her surgical microscope over to the next patient when the first operation is finished. Surgeons can concentrate on surgery; paramedical staff complete tasks such as preparing patients and instruments. These standardized procedures and specialized staff contribute to care quality and make high-volume patient treatment possible. Each Aravind surgeon performs, on average, about 2,000 cataract surgeries per year, compared to the Indian national average of 250.

Aravind's financing system is progressive; paying patients subsidize the poor, who receive low-cost or free care. The system's Aurolab manufactures intraocular lenses in India, significantly lowering costs and expanding India's exports. Aravind also established the Lions Aravind Institute of Community Ophthalmology, which investigates and develops system-wide improvements in efficiency, effectiveness, and planning for all eye hospitals in India. India's Cataract Blindness Control Program, an internationally recognized public health success, used Aurolab lenses and followed the Aravind model. Aravind has worked with eye hospitals in Bangladesh, Tanzania, China, and elsewhere. The He Eye Care System in China, for example, has emulated Aravind since 2001.

Other examples of Indian specialty care include the LifeSpring Hospital System, a joint Acumen Fund and Hindustan Latex venture in reproductive and pediatric care for low-income urban mothers and their children; the Scojo Foundation, training community women to identify vision problems and sell inexpensive eye glasses; Jaipur Foot, prosthetic limbs locally made for local

---

[61] R. Sharma and B. Khajuria, "Letter to Editor: Prescribing Practices of Doctors in Rural and Urban India," *Journal of Clinical and Diagnostic Research* 3 (2009): 1480–2.

[62] The following information about the Aravind Eye Care System comes from Bhandari et al., "Specialty Care Systems," 964–70.

conditions; and the Medicine Shoppe, a major chain that operates health care clinics with attached pharmacies in low-income areas, offering low-cost care and generic drugs. Aravind and similar approaches model systems development for other countries, though applying these systems to other contexts and more complex areas of health could be difficult.[63]

The China Information System for Disease Control and Prevention (CISDCP) may set an example for infectious disease reporting and monitoring. CISDCP is "the world's largest internet-based disease reporting system," launched after the 2003 severe acute respiratory syndrome (SARS) outbreak.[64] With this system, hospitals and clinics can report case-based disease information immediately via the Internet, identifying outbreak locations and patients' cluster characteristics (age, sex, occupation). In 2008, CISDCP added cellular phone reporting.[65] Globalism's increasingly dangerous threat of communicable diseases makes strong national disease reporting systems ever more critical, and combining a functional national system with an integrated global system is essential to public health in the twenty-first century.

Emerging countries are taking more active steps to develop and reinforce their health sectors' institutional framework. For example, Brazil, China, Cuba, India, Indonesia, South Korea, Russia, South Africa, and Thailand established a Developing Country Vaccine Regulators' Network in 2004, under WHO auspices. Its purpose is to strengthen regulatory capacity: it exchanges information and expertise, encourages discussion, and shares procedures and policies to evaluate clinical trial proposals and data, with a goal of generating guidelines and recommendations. Other developing countries may request and receive its help.

## 10.2.6 *Sharing Lessons Learned*

Emerging countries' public health and health care systems have both positive and negative lessons to share. Their accomplishments can serve as role models and their mistakes as cautionary tales for health policy-making in the developing world. The positive models illustrate the key significance of an egalitarian ethos and government investment in health and social programs. Brazil, which has achieved successes in its public health programs and health system development, exhibits a commitment to universality and equality. Numerous

---

[63] Ibid., 972–4.

[64] L. Wang, Y. Wang, S. Jin, Z. Wu, D. P. Chin, J. P. Koplan, and M. E. Wilson, "Emergence and Control of Infectious Diseases in China," *The Lancet* 372, no. 9649 (2008): 1598–605, 1603.

[65] C. Yang, J. Yang, X. Luo, and P. Gong, "Use of Mobile Phones in an Emergency Reporting System for Infectious Disease Surveillance after the Sichuan Earthquake in China," *Bulletin of the World Health Organization* 87 (2009): 619–23.

system components show this commitment. Brazil's 1988 National Constitution, for example, establishes health care as a "right of everyone and the duty of the state."[66] The Unified Health System decides government health priorities, planning programs, and resource allocation with the participation of state and local health councils and consumer representation. The government funds civil society health advocacy groups, including those working with sex workers and intravenous drug users.[67] As early as the 1940s, the Brazilian government, with United States' help, began outreach to Amazonian populations.[68] This program, which the Brazilian Ministry of Health eventually absorbed, addressed many health issues, from water and sanitation systems to control of infectious diseases like malaria and Chagas. Observers believe it has "many lessons for the planners of health and disease control projects in tropical, low-income countries."[69]

Kerala, a state in India, has long been an exemplary model for India and Third World countries in providing primary health care. Though Kerala is poor, with a per capita income of just 1 percent of the world's highest-income countries, it has achieved striking health successes—low infant mortality rates and high life expectancy—with modest health care investments. An egalitarian ethos pervades the system in Kerala, which has accomplished a "relatively fair distribution of wealth and resources across nearly the entire population,"[70] along with high female literacy and strong political backing for social spending.[71] Among Kerala's other social investments are a public distribution system for subsidized essential foods, land reforms benefiting the poor and landless, and a strong transportation and communication infrastructure.

Other countries, either emerging or recently developed, offer models for health policy reforms. Morocco and Mexico, for example, have been expanding health insurance coverage, and South Korea attained universal insurance. In 2005, Morocco enacted two reforms, one to expand the payroll-based mandatory insurance for public and formal private sector employees, and the other to provide services for the poor through a public fund.[72] Despite competing concerns among various stakeholders (medical professionals

---

[66] K. Rochel de Camargo, "Celebrating the 20th Anniversary of Ulysses Guimarães' Rebirth of Brazilian Democracy and the Creation of Brazil's National Health Care System," *American Journal of Public Health* 99, no. 1 (2009): 30–1.

[67] Okie, "Fighting HIV," 1980.

[68] A. L. Mayberry and T. D. Baker, "Letter to Editor, Lessons from a Special Service for Public Health, Brazil," *Emerging Infectious Diseases* 15, no. 10 (2009): 1693.

[69] Ibid.

[70] K. R. Thankappan, "Some Health Implications of Globalization in Kerala, India," *Bulletin of the World Health Organization* 79, no. 9 (2001): 892–3, 892.

[71] "State Wise Social Sector Spending as Percentage of Total Expenditure," *InfoChangeIndia.org*, describing the growing percentage of social sector spending between 2001 and 2004.

[72] J. P. Ruger and D. Kress, "Health Financing and Insurance Reform in Morocco," *Health Affairs* 26, no. 4 (2007): 1009–16.

worried about compensation and insurers uncertain about reform's effects), these stakeholders reached substantial agreement around the need for greater solidarity and equity in access to quality care, and also for more resources and government oversight. A fifteen-year debate involving politicians, health care providers, employers, trade unions, insurers, national social security funds, international organizations and donors, NGOs, and the public achieved this consensus, illustrating the importance of broad participation by affected parties.

The 2003 Mexican reform aimed to correct its health system's segmentation. With its Popular Health Insurance scheme (PHI), it supplemented two older schemes that covered private sector workers, government workers, and their families; the PHI offered subsidized, publicly provided health insurance to the 50 million the earlier programs had left behind.[73] Mexico attained universal coverage in 2012. Solidarity has been a key emphasis: the federal government contributed an equal amount for each family across all three insurance schemes, thus fostering solidarity across the population regardless of work status. Another egalitarian funding component involves the federal government and "co-responsible contributor[s]"—that is, state governments; the federal contribution is not fixed, but is "increased for poorer states at the expense of those that are wealthier."[74]

South Korea, now fully developed, illustrates one path to universal national health insurance. Like China, South Korea developed rapidly. It achieved universal health insurance in just twelve years, 1977–89, through government-mandated coverage expansions. These expansions first involved large firms with more than 500 employees, then the public sectors and smaller firms, and finally, remaining residents.[75] Until 1996, South Korea was able to fund its national health insurance without deficits. The 1997 Asian financial crisis contributed to later funding problems, but the government is responsible for most of the more recent shortfalls due to various regulatory shortcomings. Despite these difficulties in supply-side market regulation, South Korea shows that nations can achieve universal health coverage as they develop their economies, and within a relatively short time.

In contrast, the experiences of China, Russia, and India (beyond Kerala) are cautionary tales warning against excessive and insufficiently regulated privatization and decentralization. They reveal the continuing importance of state stewardship in national health systems.

[73] F. M. Knaul and J. Frenk, "Health Insurance in Mexico: Achieving Universal Coverage through Structural Reform," *Health Affairs* 24, no. 6 (2005): 1467–76.

[74] Ibid., 1470, 1471.

[75] J.-C. Lee, "Health Care Reform in South Korea: Success or Failure?" *American Journal of Public Health* 93, no. 1 (2003): 48.

India's public health system has "stagnated even as incomes have grown."[76] Declining government spending and limited insurance coverage have contributed to poor performance.[77] The push for economic growth and India's IMF-mandated structural adjustment in the 1990s led to lower allocations for health and social sectors.[78] Health insurance has covered only about 15 percent of the population. The system has imposed user fees at public health facilities. Out-of-pocket payments exceeded 10 percent of income for all Indians except the richest urban quintile in 2004 and threatened to drive poorer households below the poverty line. Lucrative private sector work lures many Keralite health professionals away from the public sector, especially rural primary care clinics.[79] 2017 health reforms seek key policy initiatives.

In China, economic reforms since 1978 "destroy[ed] the nation's public health system," leaving many uninsured and vulnerable to health-related financial risks.[80] Before 1979, China provided nearly universal coverage through the rural Cooperative Medical Scheme (CMS) and, in urban areas, the Government Insurance Scheme (GIS) and Labor Insurance Scheme (LIS). Reforming the rural economy in 1979, the government established the Household Responsibility System, replacing the communes that financed CMS. The disintegration of that insurance plan left 90 percent of peasants uninsured. GIS and LIS gave way to a city-based social health insurance scheme that covered only formal sector workers and excluded their dependents, migrants, and informal sector workers. The move from a centrally planned economy to a market-based one shrank the state sector and reduced government revenue. Health spending sank among budget priorities, and government outlays plummeted from approximately 30 percent of total health spending to around 15 percent.[81] In 2009 China launched a health initiative to reverse this downward spiral and achieve essential health services coverage for 90 percent of the population by 2010, with a goal of universal coverage by 2020.[82]

Russia presents probably the most dramatic example of a wholesale public health system collapse. Since the Soviet Union's demise, Russia has taken what some call the "Great Leap Downward": it has suffered reversals in health

---

[76] "China and India: Reform Goes Global," *Health Affairs* 27, no. 4 (2008): 920.

[77] W. Yip and A. Mahal, "The Health Care Systems of China and India: Performance and Future Challenges," *Health Affairs* 27, no. 4 (2008): 921–32; See also Thankappan, "Some Health Implications."

[78] S. Srinivasan and M. Sukumar, *Liberalization and HIV in Kerala* (Geneva: United Nations Research Institute for Social Development, 2006).

[79] C. R. Sonam, "Kerala's Crisis," Boloji.com, February 3, 2007. Available at: http://www.boloji.com/analysis2/0182.htm (accessed December 12, 2017).

[80] "China and India: Reform Goes Global," 920.

[81] Yip and Mahal, "The Health Care Systems of China and India," 926.

[82] Y. Guo, K. Shibuya, G. Cheng, K. Rao, L. Lee, and S. Tang, "Tracking China's Health Reform," *The Lancet* 375, no. 9720 (2010): 1056–8.

achievements, especially in cardiovascular diseases and drug- and alcohol-related injuries and poisoning.[83] Between 1990 and 1994, diphtheria rose fiftyfold, and tuberculosis prevalence doubled between 1991 and 1998.[84] In just three years, from 2002 to 2005, Russia's government spending on the health care system dropped from 6.2 percent of gross domestic product (GDP) to 3 percent.[85] Russia accounted for about 70 percent of all HIV cases in Eastern Europe and Central Asia, with one of the world's most virulent HIV epidemics, yet only 6 percent to 15 percent of patients had access to antiretroviral treatment.[86] Russia's exemplary program to prevent mother-to-child transmission is one bright spot in an otherwise dismal picture.[87]

Incentives are important in health programs' design and performance, and inattention to economic realities can produce perverse incentives and outcomes. For example, South Africa's Disability Grant was intended to ensure that HIV/AIDS patients could afford adequate nutrition and transportation to clinics.[88] Eligibility is temporary and contingent on the recipient's CD4 count, which measures HIV/AIDS progression. The Disability Grant has been the "only form of social security available to working-age adults in South Africa."[89] Because jobs have been scarce in a country with an unemployment rate hovering around 28 percent, the Disability Grant frequently supported whole families, rather than merely supplementing HIV/AIDS treatment. Some observers believe that patients defaulted on treatment to keep their eligibility, though recent research does not confirm this suspicion.

These examples from India, China, Russia, and South Africa show that countries do not develop or maintain health systems in a vacuum. Other social and economic challenges and government policies play central roles. These lessons from emerging nations present compelling arguments for a comprehensive, multisector approach to health system development and health policy-making.

[83] N. Eberstadt and A. Shah, "Russia's Great Leap Downward," *Journal of International Security Affairs* 17 (2009): 73, 79–80.

[84] A. R. Constantian, "Russia's Public Health: National Security Issue for the United States?" *Military Medicine* 170, no. 4 (2005): 285–6.

[85] T. L. Koehlmoos, "The Russian Healthcare System," Lecture presented at George Mason University, June 2007, detailing the organization and operation of the Russian health care system.

[86] Morrison and Kates, "The G-8, Russia's Presidency, and HIV/AIDS," 10, 13.

[87] The Associated Press, "Russia is Urged to Switch Its Approach to Curbing Spread of HIV," *The New York Times*, October 28, 2009.

[88] A. S. Venkataramani, B. Maughan-Brown, N. Nattrass, and J. P. Ruger, "Social Grants, Welfare, and the Incentive to Trade-Off Health for Income among Individuals on HAART in South Africa," *AIDS and Behavior* 14, no. 6 (2010): 1393–400.

[89] "Disability Grants – You Can Choose to Be Sick or Hungry," *IRIN*, September 14, 2006.

## 10.2.7 *Building Stronger Economies, Reducing Poverty*

As their economies and their regional and international clout grow, BRICS can also help developing countries come to grips with health's economic determinants, by supporting economic expansion and the reduction of poverty. A growing economy can produce initial investments and ongoing spending both for health systems and for other health determinants—sanitation, clean air and water, safe communities, education.

Regional trade agreements (RTAs) can open markets to underdeveloped countries. These preferential trade agreements free up trade among members by reducing tariffs and restrictions; some might impose a common external tariff on non-members, or pursue even deeper economic integration, such as common currencies.[90] The BRICS countries participate in numerous RTAs. Brazil belongs to Mercosur, which includes as full or associate members[91] Argentina, Paraguay, Uruguay, Venezuela (suspended since December 2016), Bolivia, Chile, Colombia, Ecuador, Guyana, Suriname, and Peru. A free trade zone and a customs union, Mercosur is working toward a common currency. Since 2000, Russia has been part of the Eurasian Economic Community (EAEC; since 2015, the Eurasian Economic Union), along with Belarus, Kazakhstan, Kyrgyzstan, Uzbekistan, and Tajikistan; Armenia, Moldova, and the Ukraine are observers, with the right to attend and speak at public meetings but no vote.[92] Goals include the free trade of goods, encouraging investments, a common energy market, and a common customs regulation system. China and India have free trade agreements with the Association of Southeast Asian Nations (ASEAN), opening up their markets to Brunei, Myanmar, Cambodia, Indonesia, Laos, Malaysia, the Philippines, Singapore, Thailand, and Vietnam.[93] India also has a preferential trade agreement with Mercosur.[94]

Lower tariffs mean cheaper goods for consumers in these regional blocs. Average tariff rates on Chinese goods sold in ASEAN countries and ASEAN goods sold in China have dropped to almost zero.[95] Additionally, these

---

[90] See explanation of the relationship between RTAs and the WTO in I. Virág-Neumann, "Regional Trade Agreements and the WTO," *7th International Conference on Management, Enterprise, and Benchmarking* (2009): 381–90.

[91] C. Felter and D. Renwick, "Mercosur: South America's Fractious Trade Bloc," *Council on Foreign Relations*, December 26, 2017, https://www.cfr.org/backgrounder/mercosur-south-americas-fractious-trade-bloc (accessed March 13, 2018).

[92] EAEC, "About EurAsEC," http://www.evrazes.com/ (accessed December 12, 2017).

[93] J. Wong and S. Chan, "China–ASEAN Free Trade Agreement: Shaping Future Economic Relations," *Asian Survey* 43, no. 3 (2003): 507–8, see 508 n.3—explaining the potential for a free trade agreement to open up trade between China and East Asia; T. Sinha, "India–ASEAN Free Trade Agreement: A Survey of Literature," part of *Institute of Peace and Conflict Studies (IPCS) Special Report* series (New Delhi: IPCS, 2009); "India–ASEAN Free Trade Agreement to Come into Force in January 2010," *SIFY.COM*, November 23, 2009.

[94] "Preferential Trade Agreement between Mercosur and the Republic of India," *World Intellectual Property Organization*, January 25, 2004.

[95] S. Coates, "ASEAN–China Open Free Trade Area," *Sydney Morning Herald*, December 30, 2009.

agreements open up new markets for export, benefiting domestic businesses. RTAs are not simple instruments, however, and they too can have unintended consequences. They might, for example, encourage costlier imports from member countries rather than less expensive goods from non-members, and thus harm consumers.[96] Whether industries and sectors in the smaller trading partners' economies can stand up to competition from the BRICS economies, especially China, is another concern.[97]

Yet RTAs, designed well, can also bolster development. The Southern African Customs Union (SACU), part of a free trade arrangement anchored by South Africa, explicitly supports development.[98] This customs union brings together South Africa, Botswana, Lesotho, Namibia, and Swaziland in a free trade zone, with a common external tariff and a common excise tariff for the group. South Africa is custodian of the Revenue Fund, where all common customs revenue goes.[99] Botswana, Lesotho, Namibia, and Swaziland receive these revenues per a revenue-sharing formula; South Africa retains the residuals. SACU earmarks some of the revenue for development. These allocations are in inverse proportion to each nation's per capita GDP and thus redistribute resources.

Economic assistance takes additional forms. China, for example, committed aid worth billions of dollars for ASEAN nations to build China–ASEAN cooperation. The aid package includes investments in infrastructure, energy, information, and communications; preferential loans; scholarships; and rice for the emergency East Asia rice reserve.[100] In 2007, China committed about $5 billion in investments and another $5 billion in loans and credits to Africa, free of any political quid pro quos.[101] In 2005, Russia, as a G8 member, was part of a $40 billion debt forgiveness package for eighteen of the world's poorest countries.[102] Debt relief, as we have seen, frees budgets of debt service burdens and, along with development assistance, can support health and social spending. It was thought of as an important element in achieving the Millennium Development Goals for health.

---

[96] A. J. Yeats, "Does Mercosur's Trade Performance Raise Concerns about the Effects of Regional Trade Arrangements?" *World Bank Economic Review* 12, no. 1 (1998): 1–28, see 1, 2, 26—explaining that discriminatory trade barriers could deny access to higher-quality lower-priced goods for consumers in Mercosur.

[97] "The China–ASEAN Free Trade Agreement: Ajar for Business," *The Economist*, January 7, 2010, 44.

[98] SACU, "About SACU," explaining the history and present status of the Southern African Customs Union. Available at: http://www.sacu.int (accessed December 12, 2017).

[99] Department of International Relations and Cooperation of South Africa, "Southern African Customs Union (SACU): History and Present Status," 2004.

[100] Xinhua News Agency, "China Rolls Out Assistance Blueprint for ASEAN," *China View*, April 12, 2009.

[101] "Chinese Aid Flows into Africa."

[102] "G8 Agree to Cancel $40B in Debt Owed by 18 of World's Poorest Countries," *Medical News Today*, June 14, 2005.

Economic assistance is not necessarily monetary. By organizing and coordinating the G20, Brazil helped developing countries participate effectively in WTO agricultural negotiations. Brazil's technical experts from government and the private sector played a significant role in overcoming disparate and conflicting positions among G20 members and generating technically consistent proposals. As a result, the G20 won recognition as a major new actor in agricultural negotiations.[103] When such efforts strengthen developing countries' trading positions, they confer economic benefits.

### 10.2.8 Emerging Countries' Role in Global Health Governance

BRICS have a role as well in global health governance, with its multiplicity of actors and agendas. Their emergence as newer global actors with the political and financial might to impact health agendas adds to global health's pluralism and might worsen its fragmentation and disorder. But emerging countries can also serve as a counterbalance to more powerful countries. Joint statements from the first BRICS summit called for, among other things, opening up international financial institutions to greater representation of emerging and developing economies and comprehensive United Nations reform to grant India and Brazil greater status.[104] The Shanghai Cooperation Organisation (SCO), a regional forum led by Russia and China for security and economic cooperation among central Asian states, had met just before this first BRIC summit. "A common thread" at the SCO and BRICS summits was the "discussion of a new world order less dependent on the United States."[105]

The BRICS combine in other ways too. The India, Brazil, and South Africa Dialogue Forum (IBSA), for example, formed in 2003 to coordinate joint actions and pursue common interests within the WTO and other international organizations.[106] They planned to have consistent political consultations, share information, and coordinate positions. Some of the issues IBSA has tackled include pharmaceutical patents, public health, and government subsidies. Thus these nations mobilize their collective clout to win concessions on matters of concern to them. Economic, diplomatic, and institutional

---

[103] P. da Motta Veiga, "Brazil and the G20 Group of Developing Countries," in *Managing the Challenges of WTO Participation: 45 Case Studies*, ed. P. Gallagher, P. Low, and A. L. Stoler (Cambridge: Cambridge University Press/World Trade Organization, 2005), 109–15, quote at 109—arguing that Brazil helped form the G-20 to help developing countries bargain jointly.

[104] President of Russia Official Web Portal, "Joint Statement of the BRIC Countries' Leaders," January 16, 2009, http://en.kremlin.ru/supplement/209 (accessed April 10, 2014).

[105] Faulconbridge, "Developing World Leaders."

[106] G. Lechini, "Middle Powers: IBSA and the New South–South Cooperation," *NACLA Report on the Americas* 40, no. 5 (2007): 28–32.

tools combine in this soft balancing technique to challenge major powers. It may signal the shape of negotiations to come.

### 10.2.9 *Health as a Foreign Policy Concern*

Increasingly, foreign policy is focusing on health issues as globalization's vast and complex international trade and travel can quickly turn local health problems into global threats. Health has a profound impact on economies, too: healthy populations produce more, typically have more disposable income, and thus foster greater economic growth.[107] For countries with massive health challenges—sub-Saharan African nations, for example—foreign policies dealing with drug access and health program resources may be quite literally a matter of survival.

Health's status rises in international relations when it becomes a national economic and security interest. More attention and resources follow, as health expenditures become investments in economic productivity, national security, and future cost savings. It is an appeal to enlightened self-interest. The policy implications are that inadequate funds, inefficiencies, and bad governance, political decisions and power distributions, explain the global disease burden.

But this argument fails to acknowledge the fundamental international disparity in economic and political power and its real effects. For example, pharmaceutical R&D—which occurs chiefly in advanced industrialized countries—has ignored developing countries' tropical diseases because these countries are too poor to make such ventures profitable.[108] Between 1975 and 1997, 1,223 new chemical entities came to market; only 1 percent treated tropical diseases, and only 0.3 percent came directly from pharmaceutical—as opposed to military or veterinary—R&D.[109] The best governance and most efficient policy implementation will not help a low-income country with disease burdens if the necessary drugs do not exist.

The national interest/rational actor approach to health stands in contrast to shared health governance (SHG) and its consensus on health morality. The rational actor approach does not view health as a special social good. It places no responsibility on countries to promote health, either among its own

[107] Editorial, "The Self-Interest Case for US Global Health Cooperation," *The Lancet* 349, no. 9058 (1997): 1037—arguing that economic "greed" is a reason for the Institute of Medicine's Board on International Health to expand American efforts to improve global health.

[108] B. Pécoul, P. Chirac, P. Trouiller, and J. Pinel, "Access to Essential Drugs in Poor Countries: A Lost Battle?" *Journal of the American Medical Association* 281, no. 4 (1999): 361–7, quotes at 361, 363—for example, chloramphenicol is a simple and low cost treatment for bacterial meningitis, of which there were over 100,000 cases in Nigeria in 1996, but the drug was not available in sufficient quantities.

[109] Ibid., 364—citing P. Trouiller, B. Pecoul, and P. Chirac, "Analysis of Drug Development Patterns of Six Tropical Diseases Between 1975 and 1997," Paper presented at the Eighth International Congress on Infectious Diseases, Boston, May 15–18, 1998.

citizens or others. When health descends to national self interest, countries manage it politically, not medically, and not necessarily with an evidence-based approach. G8 countries, founders of the Global Fund, largely ignored tobacco, a chief cause of chronic illness and a deadly public health menace. Health can appear on the foreign policy agenda, but only as a relatively low priority. When health challenges powerful economic interests—such as the tobacco and pharmaceutical industries—it is likely to lose.

BRICS can offer many useful illustrations for a global health framework privileging health as a special social good, separate from other social goods like economic growth and trade. BRICS experiences show that nations need not—and should not—prioritize economic growth to the detriment of health. Rather, nations can and should take an inclusive approach, setting priorities and allocating resources in consultation with affected parties, and giving extra help to the most disadvantaged. Effective ethical health governance is already at work in the egalitarianism of the Brazilian, Keralite, and Mexican public health systems, the strong civic engagement of Brazil's HIV/AIDS program, and the deliberative process and consensus achieved in Moroccan health reform.

As emerging countries achieve increasing power in international affairs, they can lead by example, showcasing their successes. They can thus help take SHG to the global level. With more economic and political prowess, these countries can seek the developing world's collective agency more forcefully, winning due consideration for the needs and interests of recipient states in global and international health action. And these countries can claim a larger place in international organizations, working to coordinate policies across sectors—such as trade and health—to improve health outcomes.

BRICS are becoming economic and political forces, but they also bring the developing world's concerns and claims to the foreign policy table. BRICS and other countries have launched the Foreign Policy and Global Health Initiative (FPGH) to promote the integration of health issues in foreign policy. Participants are Brazil, France, Indonesia, Norway, Senegal, South Africa, and Thailand. The FPGH is a step toward "a more sustainable relationship between foreign policy and health."[110]

### 10.2.10 *Emerging Nations' Performance through the Shared Health Governance Lens*

In numerous ways, BRICS are putting important SHG elements into play. Brazil's Family Health Program models a constructive approach to ensure

---

[110] M. Chan, J. Gahr Støre, and B. Koucher, "Foreign Policy and Global Public Health: Working Together Towards Common Goals," *Bulletin of the World Health Organization* 86, no. 7 (2008): 498.

meaningful participation among all pertinent parties, engaging churches, NGOs, schools, and other community members in regular meetings at its clinics to understand community needs. In extending its coverage to the poor and populations in remote reaches of the Amazon basin, it engages vulnerable groups in health decisions. South Korea, in its emergent years, developed universal health insurance through fifteen years of national debate among politicians, providers, employers, trade unions, insurers, national social security funds, international organizations and donors, NGOs, and the public. Emerging countries are also bringing many more actors into the IP debate, mobilizing governments and generic medicine manufacturers against Big Pharma's hegemony in the provision of needed medicines. In doing so, they expand access to critical drugs and lower the costs of treatment.

BRICS are expanding resource levels significantly as they become donor nations both to poorer countries and to global health agencies, providing funding, technical assistance, and medical goods and services to nations in Africa and elsewhere. Projects like India's Aravind Eye Care System model progressive financing at its best, subsidizing free or low-cost care for the poor through revenue from wealthier patients. Aravind is also a stellar example of effective, efficient resource use, performing successful cataract surgeries, for example, at about eight times India's average national rate.

BRICS also work toward mutual understanding of outcomes and indicators: an example is the Developing Country Vaccine Regulators' Network, set up along with other emerging countries, which generates guidelines to evaluate clinical trial proposals and data. In these and many other ways, the BRICS nations are showing the way toward SHG.

## 10.3 Some Caveats

### 10.3.1 Still Emerging and Transitioning

Thus emerging countries—especially BRICS—have growing potential to help transform global health. But obstacles remain. The global recession since 2008 slowed BRICS' economic growth dramatically. Then, even as many economies have improved, albeit slowly, in the years since, various factors—plummeting oil prices, sanctions against Russia, shifts in investment patterns back toward developed nations—have revealed considerable fragility in the BRICS. Nor have their public health and health care systems overall necessarily kept pace with economic advancements they have achieved.

These countries face numerous health challenges. Brazil's HIV/AIDS program is a noteworthy public health success, but even there insufficient resources leave gaps.[111] Russia's health outcomes have deteriorated under the post-Soviet public health system decentralization, while at the same time alcohol and substance abuse are rising rapidly. Both alcohol and substance abuse create risks of tuberculosis, hepatitis, HIV/AIDS and other sexually transmitted diseases, mental health disorders, and injuries from auto accidents. Russia's HIV epidemic has been increasing. India's HIV/AIDS prevalence rate is relatively low but its vast population means that India has the world's third largest number of people living with HIV/AIDS.[112] Its maternal mortality rate is extremely high.

China's HIV/AIDS response needs greater physical and human resources. China has been the world's largest producer and consumer of tobacco and has over 320 million smokers—about a third of all smokers worldwide. Officials expect tobacco-related deaths to reach 3 million annually in 2050; over two-thirds of these deaths have been from chronic obstructive pulmonary disease, lung cancer, and tuberculosis.[113] South Africa's HIV/AIDS struggle continues. The country has had an antiretroviral treatment program globally, but also "the biggest and most high profile HIV epidemic in the world."[114] Its programs to prevent mother-to-child transmission are inadequate: its 2008 guidelines were criticized as below WHO standards.[115]

### 10.3.2 A Continuing Need: Help from the Global Community

BRICS face continuing and serious health problems, and their health systems are still developing. They still need assistance from the global health community, especially in public health surveillance, control of infectious agents, and health system development. The SARS case uncovered gaps in China's public health surveillance system as officials tried to cover up the outbreak to protect economic interests, the Chinese Communist Party's image, and social stability.[116]

---

[111] Cohen, "Ten Years After," 485—discussing increases in costs and fears about the long-term sustainability of the program.

[112] "HIV and AIDS in India," *AVERT.org* (2017). Available at: https://www.avert.org/professionals/hiv-around-world/asia-pacific/india (accessed December 12, 2017).

[113] H. Zhang and B. Cai, "The Impact of Tobacco on Lung Health in China," *Respirology* 8, no. 1 (2003): 17–21.

[114] "HIV and AIDS in South Africa," *AVERT.org* (2018). Available at: http://www.avert.org/aidssouthafrica.htm (accessed April 10, 2014).

[115] Ibid.

[116] Y. Huang, "The SARS Epidemic and Its Aftermath in China: A Political Perspective," in *Learning from SARS: Preparing for the Next Disease Outbreak*, ed. S. Knobler, A. Mahmoud, S. Lemon, A. Mack, L. Sivitz, and K. Oberholtzer (Washington, DC: National Academies Press, 2004), 116–36—explaining that "the overwhelmingly important issue for China is stability, without which nothing can be achieved," 119; J. P. Ruger, "Democracy and Health," *Quarterly Journal of Medicine* 98, no. 4 (2005): 299–304.

As the SARS outbreak demonstrated, disease surveillance, reporting, and monitoring in emerging countries still require global institutions' resources and technical oversight. Global public opinion and normative pressure could also help expand media access and foster a more open and transparent response. Indeed, the international reaction to its SARS response clearly showed China—and any other country that was paying attention—that an opaque and inadequate response could cause more economic and reputational damage than the outbreak itself. Its 2009 H1N1 response was accordingly much more aggressive and open to view.[117]

International aid is also needed for health system development in emerging countries. The BRICS nations have health systems that are at best insufficiently resourced and at worst, in Russia's case, near collapse. Help to repair and develop these systems is essential. They all face daunting challenges, including HIV/AIDS. The World Bank, the Global Fund, the Gates Foundation, and other global donors already help finance BRICS HIV/AIDS programs; nevertheless, the need persists.

HIV/AIDS impacts other health system components. Unsafe practices in China, resulting in mass infections of Chinese blood and plasma donors and recipients, showed the critical need for making blood collection and blood supply safe and secure.[118] Quality control procedures for drug and health products must become more rigorous. Almost 44 percent of Chinese condoms failed when tested. Active drug ingredients manufactured in India and China are not always dependable. Financial and technical assistance from the global health community would help address these issues. Efforts to protect human rights in HIV/AIDS programs could benefit from international norms and pressure.

Developing countries increasingly battle non-communicable diseases (NCDs) as their economies develop and their populations take up the lifestyle patterns of industrialized nations. Heart disease, cancer, diabetes, obesity, and other NCDs cause a significant proportion of global deaths and close to half of the global disease burden.[119] A significant majority of those deaths occur in low- and middle-income countries. East Africa, for example, has the world's

---

[117] Y. Huang, "The H1N1 Virus: Varied Local Responses to a Global Spread," *YaleGlobal Online*, September 1, 2009, proclaiming that, despite its "lackadaisical" and "secretive" approach during the SARS crisis, at the time of the H1N1 threats, China enacted stringent quarantine measures as if they were a "silver bullet for all infectious diseases."

[118] "HIV and AIDS in China" *AVERT.org* (2017). Available at: https://www.avert.org/professionals/hiv-around-world/asia-pacific/china (accessed December 12, 2017)—explaining that since the mid-1990s, the safety of China's blood supply has been improved by shuttering illegal blood collection agencies and disallowing the most hazardous practices.

[119] E. Lee, "The World Health Organization's Global Strategy on Diet, Physical Activity, and Health: Turning Strategy into Action," *Food and Drug Law Journal* 60, no. 4 (2005): 569, 571.

highest cervical cancer incidence and mortality rates.[120] Poor diet choices and inactivity are much to blame, as are environmental hazards, as well as limited access to vaccination and screening programs. Efforts to control and reverse these health threats must address globalized food trade; agricultural policy; regulations on marketing, labeling, and ingredients; and environmental degradation. BRICS, like all developing nations, need support as they address this emerging global health danger.

Emerging countries also need the global community's help in meeting the bioterrorism threat. Preventing, detecting, and countering bioterrorism is very difficult; those with basic biology and engineering training can make biological weapons cheaply from internet recipes. Deadly pathogens sit in barely guarded repositories. Of prominent concern are locations like Vector, the former Soviet Union's major bioweapons facility. Until the early 1990s, this previously well-guarded, well-equipped compound housed the only other stock of smallpox virus outside the US Centers for Disease Control and Prevention in Atlanta; it also housed hemorrhagic fever viruses like Ebola and Crimean-Congo. Less than a decade after the fall of the Soviet Union, Vector was "half-empty" and patrolled by "a handful of guards who had not been paid for months."[121] But steps are possible to limit the risks. Russia—and other countries with dangerous pathogens stockpiled—must ramp up protection and monitoring, and the global community should provide financial and technical help. It should also draft and implement a more coordinated global anti-bioterrorism strategy.

## 10.4 Conclusion

Emerging countries—especially BRICS—are in an interesting and useful position. Their emerging economies and health systems link them closely to the developing world's concerns, while their growing economic and political influence draws them into the company of industrialized countries and gives them a more powerful voice in global affairs. Their emergence as global health actors may call more attention to developing countries' needs and perspectives. If this new center of geopolitical gravity can constrain the hegemonic forces of powerful nations and industries, then perhaps previously

---

[120] N. G. Campos, J. J. Kim, P. E. Castle, J. D. Ortendahl, M. O'Shea, M. Diaz, and S. J. Goldie, "Health and Economic Impact of HPV 16/18 Vaccination and Cervical Cancer Screening in Eastern Africa," *International Journal of Cancer* 130, no. 11 (2012): 2672–84.

[121] D. A. Henderson, "Bioterrorism as a Public Health Threat," *Emerging Infectious Diseases* 4, no. 3 (1998): 488.

excluded stakeholders can take their place at the table and help build a new global health architecture.

On this large and densely populated global health stage, all states—industrialized countries, the BRICS, and developing nations alike—must play lead roles. States are responsible for shaping functioning health systems. They have the authority to tax, to legislate, and to enforce the law. Much of the work of fashioning a just global health society must take place at the national level. We now turn to states and their key roles in fostering health justice.

Part V
# States: Actors, Institutions, and Policies

# 11

# Fulfilling Global Health Justice Requirements

## Realizing the Health Capability Paradigm

### 11.1 Where Primary Responsibility Falls: States

Individual states have primary obligations to prevent and address health inequalities and externalities and to realize the health capability paradigm (HCP),[1] a principled reference point for health justice assessment. States are in the best position to prevent and reduce the shortfall between potential and actual health and to develop health agency, to foster individuals' health capabilities. States have primary responsibility for creating equitable and affordable health care and public health structures. They do so by creating equal access to quality health-related goods and services and to proximate and controllable determinants, including nutritious and safe food, potable water, clean air, sanitation, adequate living conditions, and health literacy. Regulation and stewardship of the health system are critical and include public

---

[1] The HCP was developed over many years, manuscripts, and presentations, including, but not limited to, the following: J. P. Ruger, "Aristotelian Justice and Health Policy: Capability and Incompletely Theorized Agreements," PhD dissertation, Harvard University, 1998; J. P. Ruger, "Health and Social Justice," *The Lancet* 364, no. 9439 (2004): 1075–80; J. P. Ruger, "Social Justice and Health Policy: Aristotle, Capability and Incompletely Theorized Agreements," Paper presented at Health Policy Doctoral Seminar Series, Harvard University, Boston, MA, November 25, 1997; J. P. Ruger, "Health, Capability, and Justice: Toward a New Paradigm of Health Ethics, Policy and Law," *Cornell Journal of Law and Public Policy* 15, no. 2 (2006): 101–87; J. P. Ruger, "Toward a Theory of a Right to Health: Capability and Incompletely Theorized Agreements," *Yale Journal of Law & the Humanities* 18, no. 2 (2006): 273–326; J. P. Ruger, "Rethinking Equal Access: Agency, Quality, and Norms," *Global Public Health* 2, no. 1 (2007): 78–96; J. P. Ruger, "Health, Health Care, and Incompletely Theorized Agreements: A Normative Theory of Health Policy Decision Making," *Journal of Health Politics, Policy and Law* 32, no. 1 (2007): 51–87; J. P. Ruger, "The Moral Foundations of Health Insurance," *Quarterly Journal of Medicine* 100, no. 1 (2007): 53–7; J. P. Ruger, "Ethics in American Health 1: Ethical Approaches to Health Policy," *American Journal of Public Health* 98, no. 10 (2008): 1751–6; J. P. Ruger, "Ethics in American Health 2: An Ethical Framework for Health System Reform," *American Journal of Public Health* 98, no. 10 (2008): 1756–63; J. P. Ruger, *Health and Social Justice* (Oxford: Oxford University Press, 2009).

health surveillance systems, similar to the US Centers for Disease Control and Prevention, which feed into the World Health Organization's (WHO's) global surveillance system. National and subnational public health and health care systems are ultimately responsible for the financing, accessibility, and quality of health-related goods and services. Such systems must ensure their populations can seek and obtain goods and services when health needs arise; every individual must be able to obtain care. Ensuring that medically necessary and medically appropriate health care and public health goods and services are available to all is the job of justice.

The provincial globalism (PG)/shared health governance (SHG) frameworks aspire to a goal of self-actualized societies imbued with a commitment to social justice, where governments and peoples promote the central health capabilities of all. The global community provides help and guidance when states fail to deliver, though this approach eschews coercive tactics. Rather, PG/SHG deploys public information and education programs to swell support for these commitments. An important area for further study are social movements, which in other areas—civil rights and the environment, for example—have wrought change.

An important component of the HCP is the recognition that health capabilities are part of a set of capabilities, dimensions of human flourishing we have reason to value. What social justice requires within any given society involves assessing how well that society promotes a core set of capabilities, health capabilities among them. The goal of policy is social arrangements that best promote these capabilities. The governance that best provides this core capabilities set for all is one that is shared, guided by equal inclusion of all in the duties and responsibilities involved in achieving the common good.

The HCP is both a moral guide and a multifaceted, integrated approach to expanding central health capabilities. Each capability helps to advance a person's general capability. This plural and integrative approach recognizes the intrinsic interconnections between health capabilities and other capabilities and obviates any need to peg the value of education, employment, political and civil rights, the environment, and other social determinants to health alone. Resources and protections in essential domains of human existence are justified in their own right, not simply as determinants of health.

Various countries only partially approach the health capability ideal, but, as a standard, the HCP can provide the basis for measuring progress in social and political arrangements in countries across the globe. It guides governmental and nongovernmental institutions in assessing how just they are. Securing health capability renders health charity unnecessary and builds a stronger foundation for securing health capabilities globally than humanitarianism does. Sections 11.2 and 11.3 summarize HCP's core principles for society and present a working model of health capability, specific guidance in HCP assessment for national public health and health care systems, and a form of shared governance, including government and nongovernmental institutions, to advance individuals' health capabilities. These sections sketch the types of institutions and policies the HCP will support and indicators for assessing progress towards greater health justice. Section 11.4 presents empirical results of studies, examining the relationship among health capabilities and other types of capabilities, demonstrating the importance of understanding their interconnections in fostering human flourishing.

## 11.2 Principles of the Health Capability Paradigm

The HCP line of reasoning is grounded in the idea that humans' flourishing, their capabilities, is the proper goal of social and political activity. Human flourishing is a person's ability to live a good life as defined as a set of valuable beings and doings. Functionings are states of being and doing and capability is the set of valuable functionings to which a person has effective access. Humans are owed the conditions for their flourishing and health capability, and central health capabilities are intrinsic and instrumental components of human flourishing. Health capabilities, and central health capabilities in particular, are basic capabilities, because they are essential components of human flourishing; without life itself, for example, other capabilities are not possible. Humans have a claim to the fundamental conditions for maintaining and promoting their central health capabilities. Central health capabilities are not, however, the only component necessary for a flourishing life; they are not everything but fit within a larger set of capabilities.

The HCP rests on several core principles.

(1) Health is properly the objective of health policy rooted both indirectly from the Aristotelian philosophical foundation of human flourishing and directly from Aristotle's conception that health is the end of medicine.[2]

(2) Health care and other resources are not ends in themselves. Their value is primarily instrumental, as a means to the end of good health.

(3) Justice in health policy should be assessed in terms of health capabilities (health functioning and health agency), rather than health achievements alone, and equality in health policy should be measured by shortfall equality—a comparison of the shortfalls of actual achievement from the optimal average or threshold level.

---

[2] Health capabilities are seen as a "distinguished capability comparison," in A. Sen, *Development as Freedom* (Oxford: Oxford University Press, 1999), 82.

(4) Justice in health policy requires allocating differential resources and circumstances to different people in order to advance shortfall equality—to attempt to obtain similar levels of shortfalls in actual achievement from optimal average or threshold levels—for all. Differential resources and circumstances are required to achieve this objective due to the heterogeneity in internal and external human characteristics.

(5) Some health capabilities are more central than others. These are the capabilities to avoid premature death and escapable morbidity. These capabilities have a higher priority than others. The selection and valuation of other non-central health capabilities should occur through a public process of deliberative decision-making or market mechanisms. There is substantial agreement on the extreme urgency of central health capabilities and associated health needs. They are consistent with what medicine and health policy prioritize at a practical level.

(6) The selection and weighting of health capabilities can occur through an iterative process of dominance partial ordering. A complete ordering of health capabilities is not necessary. Instead, justice requires ensuring that certain fundamental and crucially important capabilities and functionings—the central health capabilities—reach certain levels before addressing the inequalities in non-central health capabilities.

(7) The selection and weighting of non-central health capabilities can follow at a subsequent stage—sequentially and iteratively—through a public process of extending partial orderings. The market can also help prioritize these non-central capabilities.

(8) For health policy evaluation, observable data measure health functionings to get a partial view of persons' abilities to achieve and maintain health. Health capabilities map onto the definition and operationalization of health and can be defined narrowly or broadly, ranging from the most fundamental capabilities of avoiding premature death and escapable morbidity to more complex functionings such as the capability to take part in community life and to engage in various forms of social interaction. For health policy evaluation purposes, the specifications of health capabilities, health functionings, and health needs follows the definition of health noted in *Health and Social Justice*.

(9) Indicators for central health capabilities include, for a few examples, life expectancy; mortality; prevalence of disease, disability, dysfunction, deformity, malnutrition; and genetic mapping. These indicators derive from the empiricism of both health care and public health and accord with the scientific definition of health. We must look to

science, education, research, and practice for guidance in specifying these indicators.

(10) Inequalities in health functionings and health agency reveal inequalities in respective capabilities and thus provide the basis for assessing health capability inequalities.

(11) Equality in health policy should be measured in terms of shortfall equality and not equality in health outcomes. Just health policy requires allocating resources and circumstances to prevent and reduce shortfall inequalities. The theory supports the use of shortfall equality rather than attainment equality because the latter requires equal absolute levels of achievement (equal health outcomes), which are impossible to achieve, while the former targets respective potentials—attempting to reduce the shortfall from an optimal average level or threshold of health outcomes. Implementing this principle requires establishing goals and guaranteeing health-related goods and services to prevent and reduce shortfalls.

(12) Severity, choice, and temporal considerations are important in assessing the moral significance of health capability inequalities. Inequalities in health capabilities are unjust if they represent a shortfall from the optimal standard and can be prevented, avoided, or ameliorated. The larger the shortfall (greater severity), the more unjust such inequalities are. Individual choice must be examined as well to understand more precisely whether health functioning and health agency inequalities exist as a matter of constrained or unconstrained effective (option) freedom (choice). The current inability to diagnose, treat, or prevent certain health conditions does not render the inequalities they create just, because the assertion of such inequalities' injustice can have significant influence in the development of medical technologies and alternative treatments that will at some future point make these conditions preventable and treatable and thus address these inequalities. Likewise, health conditions caused or exacerbated by genetics require our moral attention through interventions to prevent and reduce shortfall inequalities in the health capabilities of current and future generations.

(13) Efficiency in health policy requires achieving this goal at the highest attainable level of quality, but with the fewest resources possible. Health policy must incorporate efficiency as a core goal. Cost estimation and minimization should guide resource allocation.

(14) The HCP prioritizes reducing shortfall inequalities in central health capabilities above non-central health capabilities up to the point at which all individuals have reached the optimal average or threshold

level. Redistribution, however, takes place only to the point at which another person's central health capabilities would be threatened. No individual should be required to sacrifice her central health capabilities for another's sake. The threshold level for evaluating shortfall equality is an optimal or maximal absolute average level, not a decent minimum, absolute minimum, or basic minimum. Moreover, while group differences are important for policy and public health purposes, assessing individual disadvantage is the most morally relevant criterion of justice.

## 11.3 Health Capability: Conceptualization and Operationalization[3]

Health capability, unlike other theoretical approaches, integrates health outcomes and health agency. Why is it so difficult for some populations or individuals to translate health resources into health outcomes? Why have health literacy efforts been only moderately successful? Why do some people have such difficulty adhering to specific treatment regimens? How do cultural norms about health behaviors support or undermine health? Conceptually, health capability enables us to understand the conditions that facilitate and barriers that impede health and the ability to make health choices. It offers an evaluatory framework of the aim and achievements of social policies and change.

In the HCP, the health goals of a just society are to ensure all individuals have the ability to be healthy. The health capability approach seeks to discover what individuals are actually able to be and do in an optimal environment (health capability) versus their current environment (health achievement). Assessing and understanding the gap between capability and achievement will strengthen our efforts to foster health capability.

The HCP contrasts with the narrow focus of disease diagnosis and epidemiology, which does not necessarily account for individuals' ability to navigate the health system and the broader environment to access needed health care and public health services. Nor does that narrow focus help us understand adequately other constraints individuals face in their ability to be healthy. Additionally, these approaches are more positivist than normative in their orientation.

The HCP recognizes that both individual level interventions to improve health functioning and health agency and policies to improve the broader social and physical environment can reduce health capability gaps for individuals and

---

[3] This section stems from J. P. Ruger, "Health Capability: Conceptualization and Operationalization," *American Journal of Public Health* 100, no. 1 (2010): 41–9, and J. P. Ruger, "Ruger Responds—Health Capability: Conceptualization and Operationalization," *American Journal of Public Health* 100, no. 10 (2010): 1824.

populations. The health capability profile that follows can analyze the impact of individual interventions and policies by measuring categories of individual health functioning, health agency, and the more general societal factors enhancing or diminishing health capability. Work to refine and develop valid and reliable components of such a profile will continue.

Although grounded in capability theory, this conceptualization of health capability creates a space at the intersection of a number of disciplines, including public health, health policy, medicine, health psychology, decision theory, behavioral economics, theories of addiction and positive psychology, social epidemiology,[4] and broader social scientific theory. Yet the health capability construct goes beyond this interdisciplinary nexus; it is distinctive and unique in numerous aspects from the contributions of these other disciplines.

Health capability comprises both health functioning and health agency. Health agency is individuals' ability to achieve health goals they value and act as agents of their own health and that of others; health agency achievement encompasses one's realized actions compared with potential actions. Health functioning is the outcome of actions to maintain or improve health. It is comprehensive, inclusive of mental and physical health functioning and more. Health is constitutive of but different from well-being or quality of life, connected and integrated with other dimensions of human flourishing. By respecting both the health consequences individuals face and their health agency, health capability seeks to strike a delicate balance between paternalism (interfering with individual choices on the grounds of improving conditions for persons or populations or protecting them from harm) and autonomy (freedom to live one's life according to one's own reasons and motivations).

Health capability allows the assessment of a wider range of factors, beyond the distribution of resources or liberties, to include conditions affecting individuals' freedoms and abilities: self-management, decision-making, skills, knowledge, competence, and social norms and relations, as well as resource distribution structures. This approach seeks to enable individuals to exercise personal responsibility for their health through health agency.

### 11.3.1 *A Conceptual Model of Health Capability*

Health capability includes, but is broader than, health functioning and health itself; it is the ability to be healthy. A working model of health capability involves numerous different theoretical constructs at the individual and societal level, because the external environment can enhance or detract from an individual's health capability. Though individual health capabilities involve

---

[4] L. F. Berkman and I. Kawachi, eds., *Social Epidemiology* (New York: Oxford University Press, 2000).

broader societal factors, in this paradigm the individual is the unit of analysis for evaluating health policy and institutions. As a result, it is necessary to conceptualize, operationalize, and gather information on health capability from the individual standpoint.

The HCP addresses the ecological fallacy by attempting to understand and measure the impact of irreducibly social goods—that is, goods such as democracy provided for entire groups of people rather than for individuals—on the individual, rather than judging them as good or bad from a social perspective and attributing that value at the individual level. This conceptualization provides a framework to evaluate the extent to which external factors such as social goods and structures enhance or impede one's health functioning and health agency.

The constructs of health agency and health functioning provide the guiding principles for further definitions of health capability. Table 11.1 lists broad health capability elements both internal and external to the individual. At the societal level, one's health capability depends on contextual influences: social norms; social networks and social capital related to health outcomes; decisional authority and freedom in familial and social contexts; group influences; material circumstances; economic, political, and social security; access to and availability of health-related goods and services; and the extent to which the public health and health care systems create an environment in which individuals can improve their health.

Internal factors include health status and health functioning; the abilities to acquire accurate health-related knowledge and resources and to use both to prevent morbidity's onset and exacerbation; the ability to link potential benefits and harms of behaviors and interventions to health outcomes; health-seeking skills, beliefs, and self-efficacy; the value one places on health and the health goals one sets; self-management to achieve health outcomes; the ability to make balanced decisions; motivation to achieve desirable health outcomes; and positive expectations about achieving outcomes. Health capability is a set of lifelong abilities that is always changing and adapting to new situations, and often involves managing multiple contexts and conditions (HIV/AIDS and tuberculosis, for example) simultaneously. There is frequently a cumulative and dynamic effect, as when technology, monitoring, knowledge, treatments, service delivery systems, and their contexts change over the years.

Health capability entails taking responsibility for acquiring the information, knowledge, and skills necessary for good health. Capability is the ability to perform with the potential for achieving desired ends. Capability also differs from human or natural endowments.[5] It recognizes and incorporates

---

[5] T. W. Pogge, "Can the Capability Approach Be Justified?" *Philosophical Topics* 30, no. 2 (2002): 167–228.

**Table 11.1.** Internal and External Health Capability Components

| I. Internal Factors | II. External Factors |
| --- | --- |
| A. Health status and health functioning | A. Social norms |

A. Health status and health functioning

1. Measures of self-reported health functioning (e.g., SF-36 health status questionnaire, mental functioning, and physical functioning)
2. Measures of health conditions (e.g., biomedical markers, biomedical diagnoses, disease (e.g., HIV/AIDS, tuberculosis, diabetes, depression, and other mental health conditions), risk factors (e.g., smoking, exercise, diet, drug abuse or dependence, safe sex practices, obesity, interpersonal violence))

B. Health knowledge

1. Knowledge of one's own health and health conditions (e.g., does the person with HIV, tuberculosis, or diabetes know one has it and know how to manage the disease?)
2. General knowledge of health and disease, preventive measures to protect health, and risk factors for poor health (e.g., nutrition and diet, transmission of disease, protection (from STDs), sanitation (handwashing and waste disposal and storage), immunization (to protect against onset of disease), pregnancy, and childbirth)
3. Knowledge of costs and benefits of health behaviors, lifestyles, and exposures
4. Knowledge of how to acquire health information and knowledge (e.g., modes of information gathering (provider, Internet, journals and books, special interest groups))

C. Health-seeking skills and beliefs, self-efficacy

1. Beliefs about one's ability to achieve health outcomes, even under adverse circumstances
2. Ability to acquire skills (e.g., monitoring glucose levels, use of condoms) and apply them under changing circumstances to work toward positive health outcomes
3. Confidence in ability to perform or abstain from health behaviors and actions

D. Health values and goals

1. Value of health
2. Value of health-related goals (e.g., cholesterol levels)
3. Value of lifestyle choices and behaviors (e.g., moderate vs. excessive drinking)
4. One's ability to recognize and counter damaging social norms

A. Social norms

1. Extent to which health norms are scientifically valid and evidence based
2. Extent to which health behaviors and health-seeking skills are viewed favorably (e.g., cultures of abstinence from alcohol, drugs, and sexual activity) or unfavorably (e.g., cultures of alcohol abuse, obesity within family)
3. Extent to which a health behavior is adopted by a majority or minority of a population in the culture (e.g., whether circumcision is widely accepted and practiced) and by whom
4. Extent to which discrimination or anti-discrimination is the dominant norm in the provision of health care and public health services, influencing disparities in access
5. Norms about decisional latitude or power in familial and social contexts
6. Society's ability to recognize and counter damaging social norms

B. Social networks and social capital for achieving positive health outcomes

1. Emotional or instrumental support from friends and family (e.g., loving and caring family and friends who help with specific tasks or needs, such as watching children, picking up children from school)
2. Existence of available networks of social groups
3. Extent to which social networks may negatively impact health (e.g., bullies and their complicit accomplices, the "old boys" network, the "in crowd")

C. Group membership influences

1. Church, union, community membership to supplement or counterbalance social norms and social assistance in other social contexts

D. Material circumstances

1. Economic: income and employment status
2. Neighborhood and community (e.g., safety, noise, environmental pollutants, neighborhood facilities and resources)
3. Safe water and good sanitation
4. Housing
5. Food security
6. Extent to which immediate environment is toxin or disease free (e.g., toxic air, soil, water, inundated with malaria-infected mosquitoes)

*(continued)*

**Table 11.1.** Continued

| I. Internal Factors | II. External Factors |
|---|---|
| E. Self-governance and management and perceived self-governance and management to achieve health outcomes | E. Economic, political, and social security |

E. Self-governance and management and perceived self-governance and management to achieve health outcomes

1. Self-management and self-regulation skills and expectations
2. Ability to manage personal and professional situations: ability to handle external pressures (e.g., children, work, household and extended family responsibilities, finances, marital and personal relationships)
3. Ability to make the connection between cause and effect with regards to personal behavior and health outcomes
4. Ability to draw on networks of social groups

F. Effective health decision-making

1. Ability to effectively use both knowledge and resources to prevent onset or exacerbation of disease or prevent death
2. Ability to weigh the short-term and long-term costs and benefits of health behaviors and actions (e.g., smoking)
3. Ability to identify health problems (e.g., employ guidelines of prevention, recognize signs and symptoms) and pursue effective prevention and treatment
4. Ability to make healthy choices under various environmental constraints (e.g., abstain from unpotable water, use sunscreen and bed nets)

G. Intrinsic motivation to achieve desirable health outcomes

1. Extent to which motivation for current or future behavior maintenance or change is internally (e.g., personal responsibility, personal assessment) or externally (e.g., mandates, rewards, requirements, peer pressure) motivated

H. Positive expectations about achieving health outcomes

1. Optimistic or pessimistic viewpoint on personal life and health prospects

E. Economic, political, and social security

1. Extent to which individuals and groups feel secure or insecure in their immediate and broader macrosocial environment (e.g., broader changes in the national and subnational economic and political systems generating job, financial, or political insecurity and pessimistic outlook, violence and criminal activity)

F. Utilization and access to health services sought and obtained health services when care was thought needed

1. Serious symptoms of poor health conditions (e.g., shortness of breath, frequent or severe headaches, chest pain, lump in breast, fever, back or neck pain, loss of consciousness)
2. Morbid symptoms of poor health conditions (e.g., sadness, hopelessness, anxiety, pain in knee or hip, fatigue or extreme tiredness, difficulty hearing, fall or other major injury)
3. Perception of the need to see a health provider when experiencing a serious or morbid health symptom
4. Ability to obtain health services when there is a perceived need
5. Presence of barriers (e.g., geographic, financial, linguistic) to access and utilization of high-quality goods and services

G. Enabling public health and health care systems

1. Extent to which health care and public health system environment interacts with individual to build and enable health agency (e.g., a health coach for diabetes management)
2. Extent to which health care and public health system environment protects health and safety of public (e.g., contaminated blood supply, food safety and contamination, drug regulation)
3. Health care and public health system quality, effectiveness, and accountability

*Notes*: SF-36 = 36-item short form health survey; STDs = sexually transmitted diseases.

societal factors in its definition because to model health capability accurately, we must consider both individual and societal factors to discover interactive influences. The overlapping circles in Figure 11.1 represent the way individual and societal factors interact to affect health capability.

This model differs from causal, sometimes reductionist models in health policy and the medical sciences, in that it encompasses multiple relationships among factors. Its overlapping circles allow for a more nuanced, sequentially interactive, iterative, and multidimensional understanding. It is unlike linear models, which are limited to one-to-one associations between variables, even with interactive terms and even when one controls for a number of variables. Similarly, reductionist models examine simple relationships first and then sum the principal subcomponents; the aggregated form of these models, however, can be difficult to interpret and misleading. By accounting for both internal and contextual influences at the individual level, the health capability model is a more flexible analytical approach that reveals the complexities in the influence of irreducibly social goods on the individual.

This type of model is fruitful for longitudinal, intersectoral, and multisectoral policy and institutional analysis and design over time. It allows for heterogeneous relations among individual level variables (for example, income and education). It attempts to understand the direct impact of external factors by conceptualizing health capability as opposed to just health. It therefore integrates external factors into the individual level rather than trying to draw inferences about individual health based only on group or macro level characteristics (for example, income).

### 11.3.2 Health Capability Profile

To assess health capability at the individual level, one must identify how well individuals can act as agents of their own health. This exploration encompasses subjective health psychology elements such as self-control,[6] self-efficacy,[7] and motivation to achieve desirable health outcomes,[8] but those measures do not account for the societal level conditions on which individual health capabilities depend.

---

[6] S. C. Thompson and S. Spacapan, "Perceptions of Control in Vulnerable Populations," *Journal of Social Issues* 47, no. 4 (1991): 1–21; K. A. Wallston, "Perceived Control and Health," *Current Psychological Research & Reviews* 6, no. 1 (1987): 5–25.

[7] A. Bandura, "Self-Efficacy: Toward a Unifying Theory of Behavioral Change," *Psychological Review* 84, no. 2 (1977): 191–215.

[8] W. R. Miller and S. Rollnick, *Motivational Interviewing: Preparing People to Change Addictive Behaviors* (New York: Guilford Press, 1991); J. O. Prochaska and C. C. DiClemente, "Stages and Processes of Self-Change of Smoking: Toward an Integrative Model of Change," *Journal of Consulting and Clinical Psychology* 51, no. 3 (1983): 390–5.

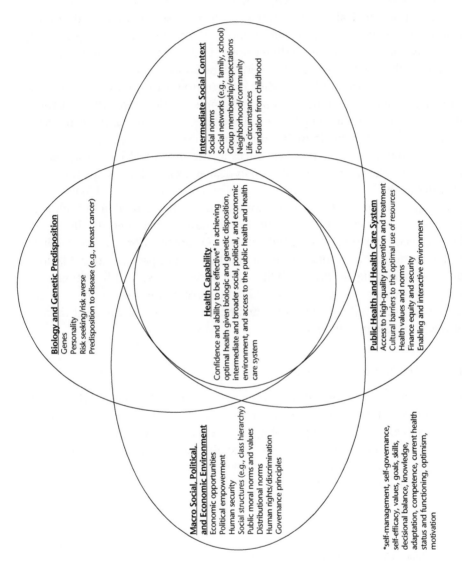

**Biology and Genetic Predisposition**
Genes
Personality
Risk seeking/risk averse
Predisposition to disease (e.g., breast cancer)

**Intermediate Social Context**
Social norms
Social networks (e.g., family, school)
Group membership/expectations
Neighborhood/community
Life circumstances
Foundation from childhood

**Health Capability**
Confidence and ability to be effective* in achieving optimal health given biologic and genetic disposition, intermediate and broader social, political, and economic environment, and access to the public health and health care system

**Macro Social, Political, and Economic Environment**
Economic opportunities
Political empowerment
Human security
Social structures (e.g., class hierarchy)
Public moral norms and values
Distributional norms
Human rights/discrimination
Governance principles

**Public Health and Health Care System**
Access to high-quality prevention and treatment
Cultural barriers to the optimal use of resources
Health values and norms
Finance equity and security
Enabling and interactive environment

*self-management, self-governance, self-efficacy, values, goals, skills, decisional balance, knowledge, adaptation, competence, current health status and functioning, optimism, motivation

**Figure 11.1.** Conceptual Model of Health Capability

Importantly, however, this notion of societally dependent capabilities differs from multilevel analytical frameworks typically employed in the epidemiological, health, economic, or social determinants of health literatures. These approaches use group level variables (for example, neighborhood income) that can lead to inferential fallacies, such as atomistic fallacy, which draws inferences about groups based on individual level data, and ecological fallacy, which draws inferences about individuals based on group level data. Rather, socially dependent capabilities aim to incorporate at the individual level the influence of group level factors on individual health capabilities. In this paradigm, group level factors may have individually variable effects, and require evaluation of their direct effect in impairing or enhancing individuals' ability to be healthy. Figure 11.1 illustrates how both individual and group level factors combine to influence individual health capability.

Developing a health capability profile leads to methods for addressing health capability deprivations. The sketch in Table 11.1 is an attempt to help investigators select concepts and domains for a health capability classification and map out the components of a working health capability profile. This profile will clarify the distinction between health functioning and health agency and create a framework for operationalizing health capability. At this point, there is no weighting scheme for combining these domains into a single summary measure, number, or index; the profile offers a range of useful indicators.

Different applications will require different measures. At the individual level, each person will integrate multiple domains of health capability, such as the ability to obtain accurate health-related knowledge and health-related resources; the ability to link knowledge of potential benefits and harms of behaviors and interventions to health outcomes; and health-seeking skills, beliefs, and self-efficacy. At the population level, it could be enough to examine discrete health capability domains to identify deprivations for policy action. A battery of scores[9] with entire scales and subscales from the survey is more likely to be useful at this stage than an overall score, which may take the form of a health capability index. Some policy questions might, however, require combining health capability domains, which, in turn, might require weighting. The profile could later be turned into a health capability index; determining weights and aggregating data across domains would become necessary.

### 11.3.3 *Operationalization and Survey Development*

Determination of individuals' various health capabilities under the profile indicates a baseline survey. A series of questions measuring several key profile

---

[9] A. L. Stewart, S. Greenfield, R. D. Hays, K. Wells, W. H. Rogers, S. D. Berry, et al., "Functional Status and Well-Being of Patients With Chronic Conditions: Results From the Medical Outcomes Study," *Journal of the American Medical Association* 262, no. 7 (1989): 907–13.

constructs to assess an individual's perspective about her ability to be healthy are in the testing stage. Once refined, this instrument will help identify the best possible circumstances for health. Understanding both the major dimensions of health capability and the reliability and validity of specific scales to measure these dimensions will require further study,[10] as will the potential usefulness of these surveys for policy evaluations and population-scale health assessments.

Study among specific populations will be especially important, both of individuals' conditions and the socioeconomic barriers to health functioning and health agency. These early efforts will conceivably create momentum for conceptualizing and measuring health capability for public policy, public health, and health care assessment.

Lessons learned from medical outcomes assessment and other performance-based measures[11] can inform health capability assessment efforts. These assessment approaches have stressed obtaining the patient's viewpoint to monitor the quality of medical outcomes.[12] Methodological advances made self-administered questionnaires easier to complete and more useful.[13] Like other self-reports, this exercise will attempt to assess conditions from the individual's viewpoint. However, the profile also incorporates objective data from individuals and others (for example, glucose and cholesterol levels), while biotechnologies such as microfluidic diagnostics promise more rapid, low-cost collection of biomedical data.

### 11.3.4 *Applications, Assessment, and Intervention Design*

The purpose is to conceptualize, in an ethically justifiable way, society's collective obligations in the health realm and then to operationalize a means for fulfilling them. This project involves normative and positivist

[10] J. E. Ware, Jr., "Standards for Validating Health Measures: Definition and Content," *Journal of Chronic Diseases* 40, no. 6 (1987): 473–80.

[11] M. Bergner, R. A. Bobbitt, W. B. Carter, and B. S. Gibson, "The Sickness Impact Profile: Development and Final Revision of a Health Status Measure," *Medical Care* 19, no. 8 (1981): 787–805; R. M. Kaplan and J. P. Anderson, "A General Health Policy Model: Update and Applications," *Health Services Research* 23, no. 2 (1988): 203–35; R. M. Rosser, "A Health Index and Output Measure," in *Quality of Life Assessment: Key Issues in the 1990s*, ed. S. R. Walker and R. M. Rosser (Dordrecht: Kluwer Academic Publishers, 1993): 151–78; A. L. Stewart and J. E. Ware, Jr., eds., *Measuring Functioning and Well-Being: The Medical Outcomes Study Approach* (Durham, NC: Duke University Press, 1992).

[12] A. R. Tarlov, J. E. Ware Jr., S. Greenfield, E. C. Nelson, E. Perrin, and M. Zubkoff, "The Medical Outcomes Study: An Application of Methods for Monitoring the Results of Medical Care," *Journal of the American Medical Association* 262, no. 7 (1989): 925–30.

[13] J. E. Ware, "Measuring Patients' Views: The Optimum Outcome Measure," *British Medical Journal* 306, no. 6890 (1993): 1429–30.

implications beyond the primarily positivist orientation of epidemiology or the primarily normative orientation of ethical theory.

The framework offered in Table 11.1 and Figure 11.1 provides a conceptual basis for intervention design and policy formulation under the HCP. As a comprehensive population health capability assessment model, it offers a way for countries, subnational governments, and local entities to improve health policies and public health practices and achieve improved health capability for their populations so that health systems are both fair and cost-effective. There are a number of possible applications of this approach.

At the individual level, the profile can be helpful both for assessing an individual's level of health functioning and health agency, and shaping interventions and environments. The profile can also help evaluate an intervention's effectiveness and can help individuals understand their own health capabilities. Intrinsic motivation, an individual level component, is significant to the HCP because it affects health behaviors. Of particular concern is how much individuals are subject to societal influences in making their decisions. Research has demonstrated that although extrinsic motivation achieves outcomes in the short run, these effects often attenuate over time, absent external reinforcement.[14] But external constraints on decisional power (for example, social norms that deny women authority at home and elsewhere) undermine intrinsic motivation to improve health.

Further, the health capability profile could help medical and public health researchers and practitioners evaluate the costs and effectiveness of medical interventions and behavioral approaches[15] that might foster health capability. Earlier experience with two behavioral interventions, motivational interviewing[16] and motivational enhancement therapy,[17] suggests, for example, that although these interventions have typically focused solely on the individual level, they might be useful in combination with broader economic and societal changes rooted in public policy. Unlike motivational interviewing and

---

[14] E. L. Deci, R. Koestner, and R. M. Ryan, "A Meta-Analytic Review of Experiments Examining the Effects of Extrinsic Rewards on Intrinsic Motivation," *Psychological Bulletin* 125, no. 6 (1999): 627–68.

[15] K. M. Carroll and L. S. Onken, "Behavioral Therapies for Drug Abuse," *American Journal of Psychiatry* 162, no. 8 (2005): 1452–60; W. R. Miller and S. Rollnick, *Motivational Interviewing: Preparing People for Change*, 2nd ed. (New York: Guilford Press, 2002).

[16] J. P. Ruger, M. C. Weinstein, S. K. Hammond, M. H. Kearney, and K. M. Emmons, "Cost-Effectiveness of Motivational Interviewing for Smoking Cessation and Relapse Prevention among Low-Income Pregnant Women: A Randomized Controlled Trial," *Value in Health* 11, no. 2 (2008): 191–8; J. P. Ruger, K. M. Emmons, M. H. Kearney, and M. C. Weinstein, "Measuring the Costs of Outreach Motivational Interviewing for Smoking Cessation and Relapse Prevention among Low-Income Pregnant Women," *BMC Pregnancy and Childbirth* 9, no. 1 (2009): 46–56.

[17] D. Mortimer and L. Segal, "Economic Evaluation of Interventions for Problem Drinking and Alcohol Dependence: Do within-Family External Effects Make a Difference?" *Alcohol & Alcoholism* 41, no. 1 (2006): 92–8.

motivational enhancement therapy, however, health capability focuses on fostering health agency early as an empowering motivation and developing it over the long term. The HCP focuses on developing traits along the positive psychology spectrum (for example, positive emotion and engagement and positive relationships).

More specifically, health capability might help researchers and practitioners develop an alternative behavioral-social intervention archetype, especially the augmentation of individual level approaches with broader structural interventions. The ability to understand socially constructed or socially dependent health capabilities offers hope for a more nuanced approach to shaping social structures and their impact on individual health functioning and health agency.

More broadly, the profile could help providers and policy makers assess individuals' social needs and current barriers to addressing these needs. The profile might also inform policy development through legislation and regulation by illuminating the ways the social environment facilitates or obstructs health capability and the need to design and implement processes for improving individuals' health capability profiles. In research, the profile can provide an overarching framework for interdisciplinary scholarship nationally and internationally—beyond narrow foci on mortality, morbidity, or even health functioning—on health capability and the societal factors affecting it. Indeed, the HCP is already providing an empirical method for evaluating public policy around the world, and has demonstrated its usefulness in, for example, India,[18] Indonesia, Malawi, South Korea, the United States, and Vietnam.

Health capability is a complex concept. Intervention development, then, must draw on multiple scientific disciplines. Strategies that integrate aspects of the behavioral and social sciences are especially promising. Components of potential integrated programs include, as just one example, behavioral interventions grounded in motivation theory and positive psychology and economic policies grounded in the economic theory of addiction and recovery. Combining approaches would be advantageous.

This framework offers a model for further discussion, refinement, and development in addressing individuals' health capability deprivations. This profile is under development.

---

[18] C. H. Feldman, G. L. Darmstadt, V. Kumar, and J. P. Ruger, "Women's Political Participation and Health: A Health Capability Study in Rural India," *Journal of Health Politics, Policy and Law* 40, no. 1 (2014): 101–64.

## 11.4 Resources for Health Capability: Financial Protection and the Need for Universal Insurance[19]

### 11.4.1 *The Growing Call for Scrutiny*

A greater focus on the role of health systems in health, development, and economic growth has led health policy research and analysis, domestic and global, to scrutinize health financing, insurance, and financial protection. Two World Health Reports (2000 and 2010)[20] called for evaluating health system performance in terms of health financing, and WHO's 64th World Health Assembly (WHA) reiterated the need for sustainable health financing and universal coverage worldwide.[21] With this increased focus has come closer examination of conventional frameworks and measures of financial protection in health both from academic and policy circles.[22]

Consensus had developed among academic and policy analysts on two primary metrics for financial protection: catastrophic and impoverishing spending. Both methods use as a measure the percentage of out-of-pocket (OOP) health spending in households' overall spending. They differ in the way medical spending is deemed problematic: catastrophic spending occurs above a threshold percentage, while impoverishing spending pushes a household below the poverty line. Both metrics are helpful indicators of the absolute and relative level of household OOP health care spending and have been employed in multiple studies worldwide.[23]

But the consensus has given way, and critiques of the conventional approach now run wide and deep. Critics include those who are most invested and who have employed these methodologies,[24] and those who argue

---

[19] This section stems from J. P. Ruger, "An Alternative Framework for Analyzing Financial Protection in Health," *PLoS Medicine* 9, no. 8 (2012): e1001294, and Ruger, "The Moral Foundations of Health Insurance."

[20] WHO, *The World Health Report 2000: Health Systems: Improving Performance* (Geneva: World Health Organization, 2000); WHO, *The World Health Report 2010: Health Systems Financing: The Path to Universal Coverage* (Geneva: World Health Organization, 2010).

[21] WHA, "Sustainable Health Financing Structures and Universal Coverage," WHA64.9, May 24, 2011.

[22] A. Wagstaff, *Measuring Financial Protection in Health* (Washington, DC: The World Bank, 2008).

[23] J. Habicht, K. Xu, A. Couffinhal, and J. Kutzin, "Detecting Changes in Financial Protection: Creating Evidence for Policy in Estonia," *Health Policy and Planning* 21, no. 6 (2006): 421–31; S. Limwattananon, V. Tangcharoensathien, and P. Prakongsai, "Catastrophic and Poverty Impacts of Health Payments: Results from National Household Surveys in Thailand," *Bulletin of the World Health Organization* 85, no. 8 (2007): 600–6; Y. Liu, K. Rao, and W. C. Hsiao, "Medical Expenditure and Rural Impoverishment in China," *Journal of Health, Population, and Nutrition* 21, no. 3 (2003): 216–22; K. Xu, D. B. Evans, K. Kawabata, R. Zeramdini, J. Klavus, and C. J. L. Murray, "Household Catastrophic Health Expenditure: A Multicountry Analysis," *The Lancet* 362, no. 9378 (2003): 111–7.

[24] E. van Doorslaer, O. O'Donnell, R. P. Rannan-Eliya, A. Somanathan, S. R. Adhikari, C. C. Garg, et al., "Catastrophic Payments for Health Care in Asia," *Health Economics* 16, no. 11 (2007): 1159–84.

that estimates of household health expenditures themselves are subject to considerable variability depending on survey design.[25]

### 11.4.2 *Critiques: Financial Protection Too Narrow*

A 2011 article[26] underscored numerous criticisms of the two conventional financial protection indicators. Concerns include the failure to capture the following: cost barriers to access;[27] differences in health care utilization by ability to pay;[28] protection inadequacies for poor individuals;[29] measures of illness vulnerability, such as the number of chronic conditions;[30] degrees of financial protection and coverage (underinsurance);[31] informal treatment payments;[32] debt or credit financing of health care expenditures;[33] and reduced consumption of other household necessities (for example, food, education, or utilities). Also neglected are the indirect costs of illness (income loss due to poor health, for example) and strategies of coping with these indirect costs, which themselves are costs in current or future consumption or savings. Conventional methods are likely to underestimate adverse consequences of inadequate financial protection in health.

Most damaging of the critiques is the charge that the current approach, by its inadequate representation of risk protection and of costs, can potentially mislead policy makers who, by relying on these conventional measures, might advance misinformed policy prescriptions.[34]

Health researchers need a multidimensional financial protection profile that offers a more holistic view of health spending, one that goes beyond the level

---

[25] C. Lu, B. Chin, G. Li, and C. J. L. Murray, "Limitations of Methods for Measuring Out-of-Pocket and Catastrophic Private Health Expenditures," *Bulletin of the World Health Organization* 87, no. 3 (2009): 238–44.

[26] R. Moreno-Serra, C. Millett, and P. C. Smith, "Towards Improved Measurement of Financial Protection in Health," *PLoS Medicine* 8, no. 9 (2011): e1001087.

[27] Commonwealth Fund, "Commonwealth Fund International Health Policy Survey," 2010; J. P. Ruger, "Catastrophic Health Expenditure," *The Lancet* 362, no. 9388 (2003): 996–7; C. Schoen, R. Osborn, D. Squires, M. M. Doty, R. Pierson, and S. Applebaum, "How Health Insurance Design Affects Access to Care and Costs, by Income, in Eleven Countries," *Health Affairs* 29, no. 12 (2010): 2323–34.

[28] J. P. Ruger, C. J. Richter, and L. M. Lewis, "Association between Insurance Status and Admission Rate for Patients Evaluated in the Emergency Department," *Academic Emergency Medicine* 10, no. 11 (2003): 1285–8.

[29] A. S. Preker, G. Carrin, D. Dror, M. Jakab, W. C. Hsiao, and D. Arhin-Tenkorang, "Rich–Poor Differences in Health Care Financing," in *Health Financing for Poor People: Resource Mobilization and Risk Sharing*, ed. A. S. Preker and G. Carrin (Washington, DC: World Bank, 2004), 3–52.

[30] J. P. Ruger and H.-J. Kim, "Out-of-Pocket Healthcare Spending by the Poor and Chronically Ill in the Republic of Korea," *American Journal of Public Health* 97, no. 5 (2007): 804–11.

[31] Ruger, Richter, and Lewis, "Association between Insurance Status and Admission Rate."

[32] Ruger and Kim, "Out-of-Pocket Healthcare Spending."

[33] W. Van Damme, B. Meessen, I. Por, and K. Kober, "Catastrophic Health Expenditure," *The Lancet* 362, no. 9388 (2003): 996.

[34] Moreno-Serra, Millett, and Smith, "Towards Improved Measurement of Financial Protection in Health."

of spending to cover aspects directly related to health care, such as health care access and insurance utilization, and examines broader impacts on current and longer term household consumption. This multidimensional approach will help policy makers understand the larger context of household health spending and adjust health and social policy to mitigate damaging effects.

### 11.4.3 *Theoretical Foundations of Health Insurance and Financial Protection*

Developing a framework for analyzing health insurance and financial protection requires a grasp of underlying theoretical foundations. Health insurance creates important conditions for human flourishing by, first, keeping people healthy, and second, protecting ill individuals and their households from insecurity and harmful deprivations in other essential goods (for example, food, basic education, utilities). Conventional measures of financial protection address neither of these important ethical goals adequately. A lack of access to insurance provided financial protection increases vulnerability, undermines well-being, and hinders human flourishing.

Individuals and households without health insurance must forgo necessary health care, use informal risk-sharing arrangements, self-insure, drain savings, diversify assets, borrow, sell assets, and more, all of which diminish current capabilities and future prospects. These funding methods, along with interrupted insurance, user fees, user charges, co-payments, deductibles, and waiting periods, fail to provide sufficient protection and deprive users of high-quality, medically necessary, and medically appropriate care. Unmet health needs can lead to further health declines, illness-related direct and indirect costs, and even irreversible disability and death. Access to and financing of health care have inescapable equity implications.

Analyzing financial protection from these theoretical foundations provides a broader and more complete picture of relevant factors. It also exposes the harmful health and financial consequences of inadequate health insurance and financial protection, and the distribution of those consequences.

### 11.4.4 *A Multidimensional Approach*

This approach maps out an alternative, multidimensional method to assess, quantitatively, important elements and their interrelations in the household context. The approach deploys a comprehensive household survey to collect data about health care needs (for example, measured as episodes of illness in the past twelve months) and their links with dimensions of financial protection and well-being. These dimensions include health insurance's direct, health care-related effects and its social impact beyond health. Dimensions of direct effects include: (1) access to health care, at what level, what type (outpatient, inpatient, self-treatment, or no treatment), and in what facility; (2) total costs of illness (direct, indirect, and other); and (3) health insurance utilization. Dimensions of social impact include: (4) coping strategies (for example, spending income or savings, relying on relatives or friends, borrowing); and (5) household resource reallocation from categories such as food, transportation, education, housing, utilities, farming or business equipment, construction, and interest on loans.

The financial and health implications of health needs are interrelated. For example, OOP health spending can significantly burden households, as found in South Korea.[35] Coping strategies, while helpful in stabilizing certain situations in the very short term, can damage household economic and health security over time. Decreased food consumption and stress caused by economic burdens can undercut health, and poor health weakens one's ability to work, diminishing one's capacity to repay loans—especially loans with high interest rates—and to afford other expenses such as education and work equipment. Understanding these interrelations is vital to enabling and maintaining the broader conditions for human flourishing.

## 11.4.5 *Financial Protection Profile*[36]

A financial protection profile offers a more accurate picture of how individuals and households of different poverty and income levels fare across numerous dimensions when confronting a health need.

### 11.4.5.1 TOTAL COSTS OF ILLNESS

When health needs arise, households cope with multiple financial challenges, in addition to direct payments to health facilities. The total costs of treatment (inpatient or outpatient) include not only direct medical costs, but also, depending on the culture and setting, indirect costs such as gifts, unofficial payments, transportation, costs of caretakers, food costs, and lost income from missed work. Conventional financial protection measures underestimate these costs.

---

[35] Ruger and Kim, "Out-of-Pocket Healthcare Spending."
[36] This section stems from the following: K. Thuy Nguyen, O. T. Hai Khuat, S. Ma, D. Cuong Pham, G. T. Hong Khuat, and J. P. Ruger, "Coping with Health Care Expenses among Poor Households: Evidence from a Rural Commune in Vietnam," *Social Science & Medicine* 74, no. 5 (2012): 724–33; K. Thuy Nguyen, O. T. Hai Khuat, S. Ma, D. Cuong Pham, G. T. Hong Khuat, and J. P. Ruger, "Impact of Health Insurance on Health Care Treatment and Cost in Vietnam: A Health Capability Approach to Financial Protection," *American Journal of Public Health* 102, no. 8 (2012): 1450–61; K. Thuy Nguyen, O. T. Hai Khuat, S. Ma, D. Cuong Pham, G. T. Hong Khuat, and J. P. Ruger, "Effect of Health Expenses on Household Capabilities and Resource Allocation in a Rural Commune in Vietnam," *PLoS One* 7, no. 10 (2012): e47423.

## 11.4.5.2 COPING STRATEGIES

A financial protection profile can assess a "catastrophic" or "impoverishing" situation based on the health and economic consequences for a household, broadly conceived. For example, catastrophic payments force households to reduce consumption necessary for general well-being and economic security or to rely on loans. Such health financing measures or coping strategies are often used to finance health care and to maintain economic viability following a costly health shock. Coping strategies help deal with direct treatment costs as well as the indirect costs of health care and medicines, but these strategies themselves also incur costs. Understanding the full catastrophic or impoverishing impact requires examining the aggregate impact of all these costs, not just those for treatment.

A study of 706 Vietnamese households found the five most common coping strategies to fund inpatient and outpatient treatments were using (1) income or (2) savings, (3) borrowing from relatives or friends, (4) taking out loans, and (5) reducing food consumption. For example, loans were more likely to fund extremely high-cost inpatient treatments for households of all poverty levels. Borrowing for outpatient treatments was more common among the poor and near-poor than the non-poor. Not only were loans frequent, but many households had to take out further loans to repay their original borrowing. A higher proportion of the poor (44 percent) than the non-poor or near-poor (24 percent) had to borrow to repay loans for inpatient treatment. The likelihood of reducing food consumption to pay for extremely high-cost treatments was higher than for low-cost treatments. For both inpatient and outpatient treatments, the poor were more likely than the non-poor to reduce food.

## 11.4.5.3 TREATMENT BY INSURANCE STATUS

Health insurance status is more nuanced, with gradations of coverage, than the conventional insured and uninsured categorization. First, individuals can fall into at least three health insurance categories: (1) insured; (2) uninsured; and (3) insured but unable or unwilling to use coverage. In other situations, individuals may be: (1) insured; (2) uninsured; and (3) underinsured. Second, insurance status may vary by each episode of treatment, rather than for each individual or household.

In the Vietnamese households study, for example, the poor and near-poor were less likely to be insured than the non-poor, who also constituted the greatest proportion of the insured who used insurance (50 percent of non-poor, compared to 31 percent of poor and 20 percent of near-poor). The poor accounted for the greatest proportion of those who were insured but did not use insurance (50 percent compared to 23 percent for near-poor and 27 percent for non-poor). The insured experienced fewer days of missed work and school due to illness than the uninsured (nine days versus twenty-five days for the uninsured for inpatient treatment).

---

**Box 11.1**  IMPACT OF HEALTH EXPENSES ON HOUSEHOLD CAPABILITIES AND RESOURCE ALLOCATION

---

Vietnam's Doi Moi economic reforms in the 1980s legalized free market enterprise in health care, establishing private facilities and a user fee system at public facilities and dramatically increasing OOP payments.[37] A study of catastrophic health expenditures in eighty-nine countries ranked Vietnam at the top.[38]

In a vulnerable population like the rural Hanoi commune of Dai Dong, where over half of the households live at or below the international poverty standard of $1.25/day per capita,[39] even small reductions in consumption can be problematic because they reduce individuals' nutrition, employment opportunities, and educational attainment. A 2008 study in Dai Dong sought to identify which consumptions decrease the most due to health care expenses, quantify this decrease, and learn how health expenses may affect a household's overall flourishing. This study surveyed 706 households comprising 2,697 people, with a response rate of near 100 percent. The survey examined demographics, income sources, household expenditures, and episodes of illness, categorized in three levels from fewest to most numerous.

The results showed the conspicuous disadvantages of poorer households. Within the lowest income quartile 1, households with inpatient and higher-level outpatient treatments reduced food consumption, which can exacerbate existing illness, threaten future health, and create more health costs. It can also decrease productivity in school and work, and compromise functionings such as earnings. When faced with inpatient treatment, higher-income quartiles did not experience the same food reductions as the poorest quartile. However, even quartile 3 and quartile 4 households with more treatment episodes did decrease food consumption.

Households in quartiles 1 and 2 with at least one inpatient treatment reduced education expenditure compared to households without treatment. When confronted with outpatient treatment, all quartiles decreased spending on education, increasingly as levels of treatment rose in quartiles 1, 2, and 4. Forced to decrease education, households lose the skills, qualifications, and resources to pursue occupations and achieve economic stability, an important capability.

All quartiles with inpatient treatment reduced production means, showing households might be forced to decrease spending on routine farming expenses. While single inpatient treatments cause sudden financial shocks, findings suggest that aggregated outpatient visits have a greater effect than inpatient treatment: quartile 4 households reduced food consumption for level 3 outpatient but not for inpatient treatment. Aggregated outpatient visits (due to prolonged episodes of illness, chronic disease, or multiple sick household members) can accumulate to force households to reduce other expenditures.

Health costs constitute a much greater percentage of the poorest households' expenditures. While higher-income households can reduce purchases of expendable items to pay health costs, lower-income households cannot. Instead, they reduce more essential consumptions (food, education, and production means) that impact basic capabilities. Higher-income quartiles also decrease spending in some of these areas, indicating they are not immune to detrimental health cost effects on basic capabilities, though their decreases were less. Health treatment costs demonstrably undermine basic capabilities by forcing households to decrease essential consumption.

---

[37] A. Chaudhuri and K. Roy, "Changes in Out-of-Pocket Payments for Healthcare in Vietnam and Its Impact on Equity in Payments, 1992–2002," *Health Policy* 88, no. 1 (2008): 38–48.

[38] K. Xu, D. B. Evans, G. Carrin, A. M. Aguilar-Rivera, P. Musgrove, and T. Evans., "Protecting Households from Catastrophic Health Spending," *Health Affairs* 26, no. 4 (2007): 972–83.

[39] S. Chen and M. Ravallion, "The Developing World is Poorer than We Thought, But No Less Successful in the Fight against Poverty," *Quarterly Journal of Economics* 125 (2010): 1577–1625.

11.4.5.4 HOUSEHOLD CONSUMPTION PATTERNS

Health expenses impact household capabilities and resource allocation. In the study of Vietnamese households (Box 11.1), compared to households without inpatient treatment, households with inpatient treatment reduced consumption of food, education, and production means, and the most significant decrease occurred in the lowest income quartile of the population. Higher income quartiles showed decreases in different categories of consumption, such as durable goods. Consumption of food, education, and construction decreased for households with the most episodes of outpatient treatment, compared to households with the fewest episodes; the lowest income quartile reported the greatest food reduction. No income quartile with inpatient or high outpatient treatment costs was exempt from decreases in consumption.

11.4.5.5 CONCLUSION

In response to health expenses, households (especially the poor) may reduce essential consumption—further diminishing their economic resources—and fall into downward debt spirals. Conventional, single-measure indicators of financial protection do not capture the full breadth of health costs, nor do they illuminate how costs affect health care access and utilization. Constructing a multidimensional financial protection profile has its challenges, however. It is necessarily more data intensive. Although some of the relevant data may be available through regularly conducted national household surveys, researchers will need to collect original data. The problems of recall error and bias affect retrospectively collected data, but survey design can mitigate them. A multidimensional profile is worth the extra effort, as it can give a more comprehensive view of illness costs, coping strategies, treatment by insurance status, and household consumption patterns. It presents more fully the impact of health costs, highlighting the urgent need for financial protection and offering better guidance to policy makers.

After examining theories of cooperation and models of governance, the final chapter lays out SHG's core premises for effecting these and other needed reforms in states worldwide.

# 12

# Shared Health Governance at the Domestic Level

*Health and Social Justice*[1] advances a series of goals for domestic societies. It envisions societies in which all people can realize central health capabilities. While no society can guarantee good health, societies can, if they will, create the conditions—effective institutions, social systems, and practices—to support all members as they seek to achieve these central health capabilities.

This book continues this journey by considering who is responsible for various aspects of these social objectives and how societies might make this vision a global reality. Societies differ significantly in the way in which they make decisions and take actions regarding health and health care. Some see governments as primarily responsible, setting up centralized national health systems. Others emphasize personal responsibility, relying heavily on the free market and individual choice, as in the United States and many developing countries. Scholarly discourse maps these trends, ranging from collective to individual responsibility, but the focus has tended to be more general than health care specific. In health care particularly, research efforts tend to be ad hoc, judging the ethical behavior of individuals and particular institutions like managed care organizations, for-profit hospitals, or the medical profession.[2]

This narrow approach diverts attention from the harder problem, mapping the interdependent and shifting roles of different actors in fostering health at both individual and societal levels. Individual and population health require shared responsibility, individual and collective. Social cooperation is essential. Economic cooperation theory offers both non-cooperative game theory (NCGT) and more cooperative game theory (CGT) approaches, but, in both, narrow self-interest is a chief motivation. Some have sought to merge the

---

[1] J. P. Ruger, *Health and Social Justice* (Oxford: Oxford University Press, 2009).
[2] A. Buchanan, *Justice and Health Care: Selected Essays* (New York: Oxford University Press, 2009); D. Wikler, "Personal and Social Responsibility for Health," *Ethics & International Affairs* 16, no. 2 (2002): 47–55.

study of game theory with that of ethics. Such efforts, however, have focused primarily on formalizing social contract theory and demonstrating the rationality of acting morally in accord with particular principles agreed upon through bargaining or negotiation.[3] The underlying premise here is still primarily narrow self-interest. Few applications of economic game and social contract theories to health and health care exist, and few focus on distributing societal responsibility and benefits for the wider common good and individual good simultaneously. A growing body of research, on the other hand, "eschews a narrow conception of rationality" altogether.[4]

This book takes a broad view of health governance. To create conditions in which all have the ability to be healthy, the shared health governance (SHG) model sets out allocations of responsibility, resources, and sovereignty to national and state governments and institutions, nongovernmental organizations (NGOs), the private sector, communities, families, and individuals themselves. In this view of health governance, ethical commitments are fundamental, in conjunction with institutions and policies. SHG focuses on the alignment between the common good and individual interest: it seeks societal conditions to achieve common and individual goods concurrently.

SHG is a more normatively compelling and potentially effective approach to governing health domestically than existing alternatives. It maintains that as a society we are all responsible for doing our fair share to seek health justice. Because health production at the individual and population levels demands resources and public environments that are beyond any one individual or group's ability to provide, it necessitates shared resources that are distributed fairly and efficiently. Because generating and distributing resources fairly and efficiently require the attention of us all—individuals, groups, and institutions— we are all responsible for steering such efforts. While the government may assume the role of redistribution, regulation, and oversight, we are all responsible for governing ourselves to use scarce resources wisely. Health and health care decision-making calls for input from both experts (for example, medical professionals) and laypersons (for example, patients). Thus, SHG involves shared sovereignty—inclusive decision-making and shared authority. But the corollary to this privilege is the obligation to make wise health decisions and take responsible health actions both for oneself and for society. Mutual collective accountability is the coin of the realm in the SHG framework. Thus, consensus on values, goals, and objectives is important among government, health providers, groups, and individuals.

SHG recognizes that while regulations and laws are of great consequence to social cooperation, alone they are not enough; although monitoring is

---

[3] D. Gauthier, *Morals by Agreement* (Oxford: Oxford University Press, 1986).
[4] S. D. Levitt and J. A. List, "*Homo Economicus* Evolves," *Science* 319, no. 5865 (2008): 909.

important, no government agency can micromanage and police everyone in every situation. Thus, SHG relies on public moral norms and their correlative social sanctions as both motivation and authoritative standard for action. Internalized public moral norms convey society's shared values and goals and are important to making SHG a reality.

## 12.1 Theories of Cooperation

Although an exhaustive review of the social cooperation literature is beyond this book's scope, most economic theories of cooperation, whether non-cooperative or cooperative, rest on the premise of *Homo economicus*, that cooperation or lack thereof involves strategic interactions among self-interested and rational individuals (seeking, for example, individual utility or payoff maximization). The distinctions between these theories and SHG are significant.

SHG contrasts notably, for example, with NCGT. NCGT says little about values (except maximizing one's own utility). Second, in NCGT each player makes her own decision, so there is no mutuality or shared deliberation. Third, classic NCGT games involve two players, so coalition building and group inclusion are absent, although group games have similar results.[5] Fourth, under certain circumstances people have an incentive to cheat or defect from cooperation in one-time interactions or in instances when they can elude punishment, potentially leading to a "sequence of successively higher order punishments."[6]

SHG also differs from CGT. The bargaining and division of benefits under CGT derive at least in part from layers of power and marginal contribution, meaning that CGT is unlikely to meet SHG's goals of shared sovereignty or shared resources. For example, the distribution of gains from cooperation under CGT could exclude weak, vulnerable, or marginalized groups. Nor does CGT emphasize public moral norms; a CGT bargain holds if it serves the parties' self-interest, not if it achieves an overarching societal objective. Finally, the CGT model presupposes conflict among players over the division of benefits, reflecting a lack of congruence on values and goals (except the goal of maximizing one's own utility or gains). SHG aligns more closely with cooperation models, including other regarding preferences and social norms[7] leading to cooperation. Additional work on cooperation theory and empirical social science research, particularly evolutionary game theory, biology, and

---

[5] S. Bowles and H. Gintis, "Cooperation," in *The New Palgrave Dictionary of Economics*, 2nd ed., ed. S. N. Durlauf and L. E. Blume (New York: Palgrave Macmillan, 2008), 1–10.

[6] D. Fudenberg and E. Maskin, "The Folk Theorem in Repeated Games with Discounting or with Incomplete Information," *Econometrica* 54, no. 3 (1986): 538.

[7] E. Ullman-Margalit, *The Emergence of Norms* (Oxford: Oxford University Press, 1977).

behavioral economics, testifies empirically to morality's role in solving recurring social problems, consistent with SHG.

A third general category of cooperation theory stems from the social contract theory tradition. Social contractarianism is a major model and relates to CGT and bargaining theory. Because it shares many features with CGT, its contrasts with SHG are similar. In *Morals by Agreement*, however, David Gauthier discusses a version of CGT called "constrained maximization." This version introduces an element of normative constraint on straightforward self-interest maximization that may be conducive to larger social interests. Moreover, the element of conditioning oneself to restrain self-interest for the sake of keeping an agreement is appealing, although likely difficult to implement in practice.

Social contractualism is another idea stemming from this tradition. Contractualism actually shares some SHG elements. Like SHG, it requires individuals and groups to consider others in their moral calculations, and that persons promote others' interests. Thomas Scanlon's contractualism,[8] in particular, rejects self-interest maximization with its emphasis on narrow individual rational agency. Scanlon places a more stringent criterion on how we live with others: the fact that a principle negatively affects oneself is insufficient reason for rejecting it. Individuals must rather ask how that principle affects others. By focusing primarily on individuals as they relate to each other, however, such approaches do not provide adequate analysis of aggregate or societal concerns. Moreover, SHG recognizes that there may be some actions that do impose greater burdens on others (for example, requiring others to pay more for health insurance so the agent at hand has coverage); these actions are justified as long as the sacrifice of others does not interfere with their own central health capabilities. Shared sovereignty, shared responsibility, and shared resources are the focus of SHG.

Another category of social cooperation is utilitarianism. Utilitarianism demands impartiality such that everyone's utility is counted equally in the aggregation scheme (although some have introduced equity weights to modify this requirement).[9] Utilitarianism thus does not give weak and vulnerable groups special consideration. Yet, there is a concern for vulnerable populations when expanding programs such as universal health coverage.[10] Moreover, the goal of maximizing overall utility does not address the distribution of utility. Average utilitarianism might mitigate this concern, but does not really

---

[8] T. M. Scanlon, *What We Owe to Each Other* (Cambridge, MA: Harvard University Press, 1998).

[9] J. Broome, *Weighing Goods: Equality, Uncertainty and Time* (Oxford: Blackwell, 1991); H. Sidgwick, *The Methods of Ethics* (New York: Cambridge University Press, 2012).

[10] N. Groce, "Questioning Progress towards Universal Health Coverage for the Most Vulnerable," *The Lancet Global Health* 5, no. 8 (2017): e740–1.

solve the problem of addressing those with the greatest needs. Utilitarianism, unlike SHG, lacks emphasis on individual agency or autonomy; collective interest may override individual interest.

## 12.2 Self-Interest Maximization and Suboptimal Outcomes in Health and Health Care

Self-interest maximization is at the heart of most theories of cooperation. But from the perspective of social cooperation in health and health care, narrow self-interest maximization alone produces suboptimal results. Health worker absenteeism, nepotistic hiring, medical supply theft, and corrupt procurement are significant problems in countries such as Uganda, Bosnia, the Dominican Republic, Argentina, and Venezuela, just to name a few.[11] Professional turf protection ploys sometimes exacerbate staffing imbalances, as higher-level professionals resist the delegation of tasks to subordinates. Botswanan doctors, for example, opposed blood drawing by phlebotomists despite staff shortages, thus hindering the scale-up of antiretroviral therapy.[12] Corruption is pervasive in global and domestic pharmaceutical industries and contributes to suboptimal health.[13] Numerous structural factors contribute to these practices, and they undermine health efforts and waste scarce public health resources. These instances represent self-interest run amok.

In the USA, examples abound of self-interest maximization among doctors, drug and medical device businesses, insurance companies, the tobacco industry, and patients, without concern for negative effects. Geyman compiled an extensive list.[14] Some doctors receive kickbacks from referrals, refer patients to medical facilities in which they have financial stakes, recommend and perform unnecessary procedures, and collect payments and gifts from hospitals and medical suppliers. Such practices demonstrate a broken physician–patient relationship, one that is devoid of the respect dutifully owed patients as persons.[15] In-depth studies of communities with high health care costs confirm many of these trends.[16] Even doctors' choice of specialties is affected by material concerns, as they avoid lower paying but crucial fields like family

---

[11] M. Lewis, "Governance and Corruption in Public Health Care Systems," Working Paper No. 78, Center for Global Development, January 2006.

[12] A. Swidler, "Syncretism and Subversion in AIDS Governance: How Locals Cope with Global Demands," *International Affairs* 82, no. 2 (2006): 269–84.

[13] J. C. Kohler, T. K. Mackey, and N. Ovtcharenko, "Why the MDGs Need Good Governance in Pharmaceutical Systems to Promote Global Health," *BMC Public Health* 14 (2014): 63.

[14] J. Geyman, *The Corrosion of Medicine: Can the Profession Reclaim its Moral Legacy?* (Monroe, ME: Common Courage Press, 2008).

[15] D. P. Sulmasy, *The Rebirth of the Clinic* (Washington, DC: Georgetown University Press, 2006).

[16] A. Gawande, "The Cost Conundrum," *The New Yorker*, June 1, 2009, http://www.newyorker.com/magazine/2009/06/01/the-cost-conundrum (accessed November 9, 2014).

medicine, internal medicine, and pediatrics. In prior years about 10 percent of American medical students choose one of these fields for residency training;[17] meanwhile, 70 percent of UK and 50 percent of Canadian doctors have been in primary care.[18] A weak primary care base renders the US system excessively specialized and inefficient.[19]

For-profit entities have boosted profits by various means. An illuminating historical analysis of the tobacco industry, for example, exposed tobacco companies' use of corporate power to conceal the health consequences of smoking, creating and prolonging a manmade epidemic of monumental proportions.[20] With the threat of obesity as a major global public health problem, critics have raised concerns that the food industry has been employing similar tactics to those of the tobacco industry.[21] In another example, one for-profit hospital chain was found to have inflated operating room charges by more than 800 percent and collected blood test fees more than seventeen times those of public hospitals.[22] Diagnostic, screening, and imaging centers often have arrangements in which they charge discounted prices to doctors— for example, $850 per MRI while doctors receive $2,300 from insurers for each MRI.[23] Such practices both inflate costs and use services needlessly. Some medical suppliers market and sell defective or unapproved medical devices. One supplier made and sold defective heart valves that caused 500 deaths. It paid civil penalties to avoid criminal charges, but then lobbied to ban future lawsuits against manufacturers of such devices.[24] Another company introduced a heart device (Prizm 2 DR) that malfunctioned in more than 33 percent of patients over a nineteen-month period, and failed to report to the US Food and Drug Administration (FDA) the resulting fifty-seven emergency surgeries and twelve deaths.[25]

The FDA itself is not immune to these concerns. In the past, half of the FDA's budget for reviewing marketing applications has come from the

---

[17] P. A. Pugno, G. T. Schmittling, G. T. Fetter, Jr., and N. B. Kahn, Jr., "Results of the 2005 National Resident Matching Program: Family Medicine," *Family Medicine* 37, no. 8 (2005): 555–64.

[18] B. Starfield, "Is Primary Care Essential?" *The Lancet* 344, no. 8930 (1994): 1129–33.

[19] Geyman, *The Corrosion of Medicine*.

[20] A. Brandt, *The Cigarette Century* (New York: Basic Books, 2009).

[21] K. D. Brownell and K. E. Warner, "The Perils of Ignoring History: Big Tobacco Played Dirty and Millions Died. How Similar is Big Food?" *Milbank Quarterly* 87, no. 1 (March 2009): 259–94.

[22] D. Benda, "Surgery Charges High at RMC: Hospital Ranked Fifth in U.S. for Operating Room Markups," *Record Searchlight*, May 17, 2003; L. Lagnado, "California Hospitals Open Books, Showing Huge Price Differences," *Wall Street Journal*, December 27, 2004.

[23] D. Armstrong, "Prosecutors Investigate Medical Scan Deals at Florida Center," *Wall Street Journal*, July 28, 2005.

[24] G. Palast, *The Best Democracy Money Can Buy* (New York: Plume, 2003).

[25] S. Finz, "Guilty Plea in Medical Fraud: 12 Patients Die / Bay Area Branch of Guidant Fined $92 Million over Malfunctions," *San Francisco Chronicle*, June 13, 2003; B. Meier, "F.D.A. Says Flaws in Heart Devices Pose High Risks," *New York Times*, July 2, 2005.

drug industry.[26] Ten of thirty-two members of the FDA advisory committee deliberating Vioxx and Bextra withdrawal had conflicts of interest with drug companies.[27] A 2004 article noted that of thirteen drugs removed from the market since 1997, at least seven had been approved despite FDA safety reviewers' objections.[28] Even the research and academic community can be compromised by industry ties. For example, a 2000 *New England Journal of Medicine* article omitted some risks of Vioxx; all thirteen authors were connected with the Vioxx maker Merck, through employment or other financial relationships.[29]

Both providers and patients have committed Medicaid and Medicare fraud. Providers have billed for services not rendered, double-billed to both Medicaid/Medicare and to patients' private insurance, upcoded, and used unauthorized service suppliers but billed at authorized supplier rates, among other tactics. Patients have loaned Medicaid/Medicare ID cards to others, deliberately received duplicate or excessive services and/or supplies, and sold Medicaid/Medicare supplies to others.[30] The Medicare and Medicaid programs have failed to meet the moral test of health equity in America,[31] despite a long and arduous decades-old journey of American health care reform that is ongoing.[32]

These examples do not necessarily represent universal behavior but serve to highlight the underlying importance of pursuing shared and individual goals simultaneously. SHG does not deny or eliminate self interest as a human motivation altogether; rather, it recognizes it, aligns individual interest with shared goals, and creates conditions (including incentives) to deploy it as a positive force for health care and health.

## 12.3  Models of Governance

One of the most widely employed approaches to rein in self-interest maximization in any field, including health and health care, is regulation and oversight, governmental and nongovernmental. Two major types of governance are top-down hierarchies and decentralized civic participation. In health,

---

[26] D. Willman, "How a New Policy Led to Seven Deadly Drugs," *Los Angeles Times*, December 20, 2000.

[27] G. Harris and A. Berenson, "10 Voters on Panel Backing Pain Pills had Industry Ties," *The New York Times*, February 25, 2005.

[28] A. Mundy, "Risk Management," *Harper's Magazine*, September 2004.

[29] C. Bombardier, L. Laine, A. Reicin, D. Shapiro, R. Burgos-Vargas, B. Davis, et al., "Comparison of Upper Gastrointestinal Toxicity of Rofecoxib and Naproxen in Patients with Rheumatoid Arthritis," *New England Journal of Medicine* 343 (2000): 1520–8.

[30] L. Morris, "Combating Fraud in Health Care: An Essential Component of Any Cost Containment Strategy," *Health Affairs* 28, no. 5 (2009): 1351–6.

[31] A. Cohen, D. Colby, K. Wailoo, and J. Zelizer, *Medicare and Medicaid at 50: America's Entitlement Programs in the Age of Affordable Care* (New York: Oxford University Press, 2015).

[32] P. Starr, *Remedy and Reaction* (New Haven, CT: Yale University Press, 2013).

top-down, centralized, hierarchical governance means state-directed health system control. For example, the Soviet Union's (USSR) federal Health Ministry in Moscow controlled medical education and training, health care facilities, personnel, and finances throughout the USSR, setting total health expenditures and allocating resources through annual and five-year plans. Regional and local health authorities operated under ministry budgets and rules, with little flexibility to address local needs.[33] Another version of the top-down approach is the New Managerialist/New Public Management model. Process oriented and target driven, this model aims to reduce health service inefficiencies, close gaps, and reduce overlaps in services, with the goal of moving individuals to less expensive parts of the system.[34]

Both the centralized Soviet model and New Managerialism reflect the ideologies and goals of the center rather than local need. To different degrees, these hierarchical models contrast with SHG. Where the center dictates policies and procedures, there is little mutual collective accountability, little involvement of individuals and the community, and little effort to achieve the consensus the SHG approach seeks. These approaches share resources, but often in arbitrary and unproductive ways.

Two other examples of hierarchical governance models have been examined within the evolving European Union (EU) food safety regulation context. One is technocratic governance, in which technical experts dominate and make decisions. Politicians (non-experts) rubberstamp those policies, because they lack the knowledge and training to understand complicated scientific and technological issues. Public participation is unnecessary in the "production of the scientific expertise."[35] Decisionist governance takes the opposite approach, giving priority to political decision-makers over scientific experts in the interest of clear accountability. Both these hierarchical models also run counter to SHG. While SHG respects scientific information and expertise, it differs from the technocratic model in understanding that political legitimacy involves normative reasoning and public deliberation. Political decisions are not purely scientific.[36] And even scientific experts can disagree.[37] The decisionist approach recognizes the political nature of policy decisions, but strict separation between policy-making and scientific expertise raises

[33] D. Rowland and A. V. Telyukov, "Soviet Health Care from Two Perspectives," *Health Affairs* 10, no. 3 (1991): 71–86.

[34] K. Rummery, "Healthy Partnership, Healthy Citizens? An International Review of Partnerships in Health and Social Care and Patient/User Outcomes," *Social Science & Medicine* 69, no. 12 (2009): 1802.

[35] R. Fischer, "European Governance Still Technocratic? New Modes of Governance for Food Safety Regulation in the European Union," *European Integration Online Papers* 12 (2008): 5.

[36] A. Gutmann and D. Thompson, "Deliberative Democracy Beyond Process," *Journal of Political Philosophy* 10, no. 2 (2002): 153–74.

[37] Fischer, "European Governance Still Technocratic?"

serious validity questions. SHG holds a middle view, recognizing the essential roles of both proceduralism for public engagement and epistemic values and standards for evaluating deliberative outcomes.

Decentralized, civic participation governance models are numerous. For example, another EU food safety regulation model is reflexive governance, which acknowledges that "facts are uncertain, values in dispute, stakes high and decisions urgent."[38] Reflexive governance seeks permanent, open lines of communication among experts, politicians, and the public, and attempts to democratize science by "control[ling] the scientists in the expert committees" and presenting the views of laypersons.[39] This is contrary to the central role SHG gives to science. It also reflects an overly optimistic view of civil society, NGOs, and laypersons as key decision-makers, ignoring laypersons' potential for injecting inefficiency, irrationality, and incoherence into health policy decision-making. The classic interest group representation model is a version of civic participation, but one that brings out some undesirable features in governance: interest-group competition in rule-making; rule-making based on log-rolling between agency and stakeholders; the treatment of agency officials as insiders and other stakeholders as outsiders; adversarial relationships among stakeholders; and government serving primarily as a "neutral and reactive arbiter among stakeholders."[40]

New localism and local state entrepreneurialism also place heavy emphasis on civic participation. Citizens are asked to get involved in "every government directive."[41] But these approaches may not empower citizens as much as expected. Constant citizen consultation can result in fatigue and disengagement. Citizens are pressed to work with government and the private sector, while entrenched inequalities in power and influence continue; professionalizing citizen participation means that some citizens may acquire more power than others. Participation as a governmental scheme may be a means of co-opting important citizens and legitimizing domination, instead of a strategy of empowerment. While new localism shares SHG's focus on individual agency, SHG relies significantly more on the give and take between the established social order and individuals and on an overarching framework of consensus on societal health goals. And SHG seeks to address power inequalities through participation and consensus.

---

[38] Ibid., quoting S. O. Funtowicz and J. R. Ravetz, "Science for the Post-Normal Age," *Futures* 25, no. 7 (1993): 739.

[39] Fischer, "European Governance Still Technocratic?" 6.

[40] B. J. Zabawa, "Making the Health Insurance Flexibility and Accountability (HIFA) Waiver Work through Collaborative Governance," *Annals of Health Law* 12, no. 2 (2003): 379.

[41] G. Blakeley, "Governing Ourselves: Citizen Participation and Governance in Barcelona and Manchester," *International Journal of Urban and Regional Research* 34, no. 1 (2010): 139.

Additional variants of decentralized civic participation governance models also differ from SHG but share some important elements. Co-governance combines "a strong state, extensive market economies, and a lively civil society."[42] Local governments share power and govern with actors like local businesses, civic organizations, and neighboring cities, steering such efforts through network management or metagovernance. Like SHG, co-governance calls for collaboration among public, private, and civic actors within the public sector. However, co-governance lacks SHG's emphasis on social norms, which help hold cooperation together. Under co-governance, cooperation would be challenging in difficult situations, as actors may cease cooperating if further collaboration produces no common gains. Removing decisions from elected institutions also weakens accountability mechanisms.

Community governance and collaborative governance models both devolve governance to lower tiers of government, frequently the local and even institutional level. Under community governance, community representatives influence and specify policy, especially social welfare policy, to best serve local needs and to build capacity through community consultation, local adaptation of externally specified services, and greater awareness of resource use.[43] Collaborative governance emphasizes "problem-solving . . . information sharing and deliberation among knowledgeable parties," the "participation by interested and affected parties in all stages of the decision-making process," and the "development of temporary rules subject to revision" based on "continuous monitoring and evaluation."[44] Examples of collaborative governance include the public–private partnerships to expand health coverage under the US Health Insurance Flexibility and Accountability waiver, Seattle's neighborhood planning program, and US Environmental Protection Agency projects on watershed, Superfund, and environmental justice issues.[45]

Like SHG, collaborative governance emphasizes actors' interdependence and accountability, with the government or a designated agency at the center. SHG, however, sees government as more than simply a "facilitator of multistakeholder negotiations."[46] It allocates more authority to government in the mutual collective accountability framework, to enhance the legitimacy of both

[42] A. Røiseland, "Local Self-Government or Local Co-Governance?" *Lex Localis: Journal of Local Self-Government* 8, no. 2 (2010): 140.

[43] K. O'Toole, J. Dennis, S. I. Kilpatrick, and J. E. Farmer, "From Passive Welfare to Community Governance: Youth NGOs in Australia and Scotland," *Children and Youth Services Review* 32, no. 3 (2010): 430–6.

[44] Zabawa, "Making the Health Insurance Flexibility and Accountability (HIFA) Waiver Work," 378.

[45] M. I. Neshkova, "How to Share in Governance Effectively," *Public Organization Review* 10, no. 2 (2010): 201-4; Zabawa, "Making the Health Insurance Flexibility and Accountability (HIFA) Waiver Work."

[46] Zabawa, "Making the Health Insurance Flexibility and Accountability (HIFA) Waiver Work," 378.

government and non-government actors. SHG also calls for a reorientation of underlying norms and motivations for authentic joint problem solving.

The civic republican ideal envisions citizens connected in pursuit of the greater common good. One view of civic republicanism directs lawyers, for example, to identify the common good and to align their clients' endeavors with social justice; thus, within this tradition lawyers don't pursue only their clients' interests. Preferences develop "dialogically, through a process of engagement and discussion among citizens."[47] Other versions of civic republicanism permit lawyers, as representatives of their clients, to pursue client interests, but stipulate that lawyers work toward the greater good of the system on their own time. Deliberation does not merely present extant preferences; participants must be ready to amend their preferences according to the public good. Civic republicanism emphasizes citizen deliberation and a pursuit of the public good.

Finally, another decentralized model of governance is the boundary-spanning policy regime (B-SPR), for unruly cross-sector problems primarily at the domestic national level.[48] B-SPRs bridge multiple policy domains and encourage "integrative policies" by "pressur[ing]" actors in relevant domains to work "more or less in accord toward similar ends."[49] The goal is to achieve greater policy cohesion and to make up for governance fragmentation. Examples of B-SPRs include community empowerment and pollution abatement in the 1960s and 1970s; in the 1980s and 1990s, drug criminalization, disability rights, and welfare responsibility; and in the 2000s, homeland security. Civic republicanism, community and collaborative governance, and B-SPRs have features in common with SHG, but SHG places greater emphasis on metarules within a higher-level structure, assigning responsibility and stipulating authority for public and private actors in a joint collaboration for health, to which we turn now.

## 12.4 Shared Health Governance

Academic and policy work in social cooperation and governance helps illuminate efforts to organize collectively in health and health care. But despite progress in institutional design, many efforts have begun with a problematic orientation: to found a theory of cooperation and governance on the singular subject theory of rational individualistic thinkers and actors. Entities,

---

[47] W. Bradley Wendel, "Nonlegal Regulation of the Legal Profession: Social Norms in Professional Communities," *Vanderbilt Law Review* 54, no. 5 (2001): 2000.

[48] A. E. Jochim and P. J. May, "Beyond Subsystems: Policy Regimes and Governance," *Policy Studies Journal* 38, no. 2 (2010): 303–27.

[49] Ibid., 307.

individuals, or groups are seen as isolated agents, even if they act collectively. On the other hand, a focus solely on the common good, overriding individual interests, is equally unsatisfactory. We must integrate both the methodological and normative importance of individuals and the key role of collectives. A narrow lens cannot encompass continual interactions of individuals and groups in a cascade of iterative and cumulative processes. Even the most basic health care example—the doctor–patient relationship—demonstrates the inescapable jointness and interaction involved in health and health care. Producing an effective and efficient health system, and ultimately individual and population health, requires shared resources, shared sovereignty, and shared responsibility based on the specific functions and roles individuals and groups take on in this enterprise. Thus, rather than relying solely on individualistic rationality, SHG also incorporates social rationality in an alternative view of health governance, which seeks to help us better effectuate principles of health and social justice.

Six core premises underlie SHG. The first is a social scientific one: multiple societal actors, public and private, engage in a joint enterprise that coproduces the conditions for all to be healthy. SHG offers an alternative set of fundamental assumptions for collective action in health and health care.

The second core premise is both normative and social scientific: achieving justice in health requires individual and group commitments. SHG proposes public moral norms as both effective motivation and authoritative standard for individual and group action on health justice. Internalized public moral norms convey the shared values and goals of society and are important for SHG's successful realization. Implementation will involve working out issues related to this premise: Who frames the norms? What situations permit disagreement with them? How do we most effectively inculcate these norms? What are the requirements for adhering to them? Can we better understand how norms are internalized and followed? What proportion of people need to follow them? Lessons from public health (for example, vaccination) and environmental policy (for example, recycling) are instructive.

A third core premise advances that generating a shared commitment to ideals can motivate people to pay attention and fulfill roles across governance subsystems (for example, financing, organization, and delivery of health care). The constitutive ideas bind the subsystems together to achieve a common purpose. *Health and Social Justice* offers illustrations of such ideas. This shared commitment can in turn lead to political obligations and commitments. The actors then give legitimacy and power to that regime, forming the bases of support for SHG. No single decision accomplishes this, but concurrent and successive decisions together bring the SHG framework to fruition.

A fourth premise is shared resources. The social commitment to ensuring the conditions for all individuals to be healthy involves sharing individual and societal resources. This premise has three components. The first is a commitment to contribute one's fair share to fund the joint enterprise. The implementation of this principle involves progressive financing such that, on a sliding scale, wealthier individuals and groups pay a greater percentage. The second, on the receiving end, proposes that each individual is entitled to receive a fair share of resources. The implementation of this principle allocates resources based on health functioning needs and health agency needs. The third is the responsibility to use these shared resources wisely and parsimoniously and not to demand more than one's fair share, based on bona fide needs as opposed to desires or preferences. We all share in the benefits that accrue to society from achieving justice in health: a more healthy, stable, cared-for, productive population; cost containment; and reduced disease risk. Thus, we all share in mobilizing and using the resources necessary to achieve this end.

A fifth premise concerns enforcement and social sanctions created to hold actors responsible, apportioned symmetrically according to the responsibilities attached to SHG functions and roles. While SHG includes a role for incentives and external motivation, it does not rely solely on such mechanisms, and positions both individual health agency and public moral norms importantly in its framework. SHG recognizes that systems cannot micromanage all actors' health and health care behavior at all times, and also that such micromanagement may be less effective than social norm internalization. Internalized norms provide a shared authoritative basis on which individuals and groups can use their health agency to make effective decisions for optimal individual and societal health.

A sixth premise involves shared sovereignty and constitutional commitments. The extensive theorizing and empirical work about governance, and the oscillation between ends of the central–local, expert–layperson, scientific–political, and procedural–substantive spectra, demonstrate how difficult it is to fine-tune institutional designs to improve health governance. And regardless of the intention to rein it in, self-interest maximization can take hold and produce suboptimal results in virtually every governance model. SHG offers a holistic sense of what is to be shared and mutual: (1) actions and goals; (2) responsibility; (3) resources; (4) norms; and (5) sovereignty. An internalized and joint ethical commitment to ensure the conditions for all to be healthy undergirds SHG and serves as motivation to hold ourselves accountable for our respective roles and conduct.

### 12.4.1 *Duties at the State Level: Recapping* Health and Social Justice *and Other Works*

A theory of health justice indicates additional principles for distributing responsibility to specific actors and institutions. These principles involve functional and role-based requirements and voluntary commitments. Under functional and role-based requirements, SHG assigns functions and roles to those individuals and groups best situated by their positions and resources to fulfill them. The voluntary commitments principle advances that individuals and groups voluntarily embrace their role, share resources, and relinquish some autonomy through collective action to prevent and address health problems. This allocative approach links with a consensus on a shared authoritative standard for specific duties so that specific actors and institutions will fulfill their obligations. In other words, actors and institutions have a clear understanding of what they are to do and intend to be bound by these obligations. The process of reaching consensus on specific duties in turn depends on actors internalizing public moral norms of health equity, motivating them to act to prevent and reduce inequalities in health capabilities as efficiently as possible. Efforts to establish consensus amidst pluralism, through incompletely theorized agreements, for example, are important. Ethical commitments to this goal are important to motivating actors, both in sacrificing resources and autonomy and in discharging their duties. Voluntary commitments enhance individual liberty by appealing to individually agreed-upon and embraced principles.

### 12.4.2 *Public Moral Norms as a Shared Authoritative Standard*

The content of SHG's social norms is an important focal point. To unpack this idea, we differentiate between public and private norms. Public here means applicable to the public sphere. So a public norm is a form of social norm since it applies to the social sphere, as opposed to applying only to our private spheres. A public norm has more political heft, concerning what we do as a society with public resources in publicly created conditions. While it derives its content from the public and social, its internalization and application involve both public and private actors. The morality of the norm is important. Norms of behavior can in fact be immoral, such as infanticide, rape, pillage, and corruption. A moral norm, by contrast, involves a deep, shared conviction that it is right and good, or at the very least that it is not wrong. An example is the fairness norm known as the Golden Rule, which some have argued is engrained in human culture, having evolved with the human species.[50] SHG therefore employs public moral norms to create a standard for joint commitments and joint decision-making. Not all moral norms are equally desirable for health and health care, however. There are even some moral norms whose fairness is debatable as applied to health and health care, such as absolutist libertarian or individualist theoretical approaches.

---

[50] K. Binmore, *Natural Justice* (New York: Oxford University Press, 2005).

The SHG project continues the journey *Health and Social Justice* began: to set out for our global society which moral ideas can serve as guides, which ought to be favored or disfavored. Elizabeth Anderson argues that public moral norms motivate our behavior autonomously and do not necessarily require appeal to self-interest or even to the threat of social sanctions.[51] In many individual decisions about health and health care, it will not be possible or desirable to apply social or emotional sanctions for enforcement—on individuals failing to comply with AIDS medication instructions, for example, or on doctors recommending unnecessary treatments to patients. Rather, we require a more profound commitment to both the individual good, building on self-regard as a human motivation, and the common good, an understanding that we work together as a body to create the conditions for all (including ourselves) to be healthy.

The autonomy involved in the normative motivation under an SHG framework is important. Willingly living out the public moral norm is essential for achieving conditions for individual and population health, for reaching a steady state of enabling conditions. Millions of individual decisions to get vaccinated against H1N1 or to adhere to tuberculosis treatment regimens or to cover one's mouth when one sneezes or to wash one's hands illustrate this willing commitment. Internalized public moral norms also entail, like the Golden Rule, an understanding that we are all inseparable parts of the whole, that we are as likely to benefit from a society where all can be healthy as to contribute to it. Thus, the public moral norm incorporates individual interest as well as concern for others. It links and aligns individual and society. While sanctions, incentives, and punishments can be helpful (for example, in binding doctors to standards for treatment recommendations to patients or regulating what providers can discuss with patients), without the autonomous effect of internalized norms on individuals embracing their responsibility for themselves and society, there will likely be insufficient motivation to act, and the wisdom and skills underpinning action will not develop over time. These public moral norms are not magic bullets, but they can help improve effectiveness and achieve the goals of a just society. To achieve socially rational objectives, we need socially conscious individual judgments at every turn.

### 12.4.3 *Social Commitments, Shared Goals, and Respective Roles*

SHG's third premise entails a joint commitment among individuals and society to work together to secure the conditions for all to be healthy. Under this premise, individuals and groups will be committed to doing their fair share,

---

[51] E. Anderson, "Beyond *Homo Economicus*: New Developments in Theories of Social Norms," *Philosophy & Public Affairs* 29, no. 2 (2000): 170–200.

including serving allocated roles, in creating these conditions. This joint or societal commitment is an important component in the SHG framework. It shares elements of self-understanding and identity with frameworks of collective agency and group membership put forward in social theory.[52]

### 12.4.4 The "We" in Health and Health Systems: A Nod to Plural Subject Theory

"Plural subject" theory (PST)[53] helps flesh out this shared commitment premise. PST explores the self-understanding of individuals in a group who view themselves and one another as a body of people jointly committed to a shared objective. In the PST account, joint commitments create an external force that binds one to act or believe a certain way, counter to expected actions or beliefs absent the commitment. The joint commitment thus creates a binding rule that individuals follow even when the rule might conflict with short-term rational self-interest maximization. Individuals are answerable to others and to themselves for violations.

The plural subjects in SHG are all of us. As plural subjects acting and in many cases working together, we create (or fail to create) the conditions for all individuals (including ourselves) to be healthy. The PST understanding that social groups are plural subjects and that "plural subject phenomena" include "*social rules* and *conventions, group languages, everyday agreements, collective beliefs* and *values,* and *genuinely collective emotions*"[54] is highly relevant to SHG. Among the features PST stipulates for joint commitments and plural subjecthood are: (1) open expression of willingness or quasi-readiness to do X together, where X connotes a belief or action; (2) common knowledge among the plural subjects that others have expressed willingness to do X together (this constitutes an element of trust in the reciprocity of others' behavior and is akin to the sociological notion of "consciousness as the basis of unity");[55] and (3) obligations binding plural members of the group together, such that "[e]ach party is answerable to all parties for any violation of the joint commitment."[56] Under SHG, individuals need to express readiness to grant an individual or a group decision-making power or to accept a standard—health

---

[52] M. Gilbert, *On Social Facts* (Princeton, NJ: Princeton University Press, 1992); J. R. Searle, "Collective Intentions and Actions," in *Intentions in Communication*, ed. P. R. Cohen, J. Morgan, and M. E. Pollack (Cambridge, MA: MIT Press, 1990): 401–15; R. Tuomela, *A Theory of Social Action* (Dordrecht: D. Reidel, 1984).

[53] Gilbert, *On Social Facts.*

[54] M. Gilbert, "The Structure of the Social Atom: Joint Commitment as the Foundation of Human Social Behavior," in *Socializing Metaphysics: The Nature of Social Reality*, ed. F. F. Schmitt (Lanham, MD: Rowman & Littlefield, 2003), 55.

[55] F. F. Schmitt, "Socializing Metaphysics: An Introduction," in *Socializing Metaphysics: The Nature of Social Reality*, ed. Schmitt, 1–38, 10.

[56] Gilbert, "The Structure of the Social Atom," 49.

equity, for example. Then individuals are politically obligated to uphold these decisions; political obligations flow from such commitments.

SHG diverges somewhat from PST, however, in the content of the moral imperative. PST does not distinguish between types of political obligations. Political obligations related to health under PST, for example, might be differently binding as compared to political obligations in other domains. However, under SHG, if moral considerations can persuasively bolster political obligations related to health, they could entail a robust commitment as compared to other types of commitments. Taking health functioning and health agency as central to human flourishing could provide that persuasive underpinning. An extensive discussion of these points is beyond this book's scope; an examination of health capabilities vis-à-vis other capabilities and routes to consensus amidst pluralism appears elsewhere.[57]

But PST offers intellectual resources that support a SHG view. Although PST cannot define what would constitute a fair share, nor what constitutes a reasonable definition of health justice, it can buttress the idea that individuals in a society have a political obligation to one another. This political obligation could involve supporting laws or norms that strive to foster, for example, health capabilities. Another question is whether SHG could, at least temporarily, rely on a political obligation to inculcate certain norms and align behaviors with them. But even if individuals have a political obligation to do X, as theorized by PST, one must wonder how relevant this obligation is if individuals do not believe it to be legitimate, and if it is not enforced.

The SHG framework of internalizing norms and behaviors, while more time intensive, seems a sustainable approach. The conviction that norms are legitimate and controlling is important.

### 12.4.5 Division of Responsibility and Shared Responsibility

SHG involves individuals taking actions to improve their own health, building on self-regard as well as regard for others as a human motivation, and it encompasses duties to avoid harming others and the system as a whole. Individual level believing and thinking are a necessary part of the SHG framework, fundamental to the principle of responsibility allocation and sharing. SHG involves spontaneous convergence, since explicit agreements at every stage and every decision point are not possible. Specific responsibilities in the collective arrangement fall to those who, by their roles or resources, are best positioned to fulfill them.

---

[57] Ruger, *Health and Social Justice.*

375

Based on these principles, the primary responsibility for efficiently preventing and reducing shortfall inequalities in central health capabilities falls to the state, because national governments have the political authority, resources, and regulatory and redistributive abilities to create health system infrastructures, including health care, public health, and other systems affecting health, like food, drug, consumer, environmental, and work safety. They are also in the best position to create and disseminate public goods necessary for sustaining central health capabilities. State duties include developing and maintaining a national health care and public health system, guaranteeing a universal comprehensive benefits package of medically necessary and medically appropriate goods and services, and creating an environment, including the social determinants of health, that supports central health capabilities. State duties also involve delegating specific duties to specific actors based on these principles. Actors can be private or public, but SHG relies on empirical evidence about the most cost-effective route to desired ends.

Actors also have a duty to inculcate norms—for example, of health equity—in their own spheres of influence. Medical providers (the medical profession and hospitals, clinics, and other actors) have duties to provide high-quality goods and services to patients as efficiently as possible. Private and public insurers have a duty to insure all citizens with a universal, comprehensive benefits package of medically necessary and medically appropriate goods and services of high quality at the lowest possible costs. If these insurers cannot fulfill this duty more efficiently than the state, then the state will assume this duty. Empirical evidence from comparative health systems suggests that the national government is likely in the best position to insure the population equitably and efficiently.[58]

Individuals and families have duties to promote their own health, fostered by individual interest, and we all (patients and other actors) owe each other a commitment to use our shared resources as wisely as possible. We also all share a duty to refrain from harming others and the system as a whole (for example, through fraudulent claims or making irresponsible health choices that do not show care for the consequences of an action or inaction). Finally, the state should allocate the duties of research and education in a multistep process, first to governmental and nongovernmental institutions best positioned to undertake such activity (for example, the National Institutes of Health, National Academy of Sciences, and National Science Foundation), and then

---

[58] P. Hussey and G. F. Anderson, "A Comparison of Single- and Multi-Payer Health Insurance Systems and Options for Reform," *Health Policy* 66, no. 3 (2003): 215–28; U. E. Reinhardt, P. S. Hussey, and G. F. Anderson, "U.S. Health Care Spending in an International Context," *Health Affairs* 23, no. 3 (2004): 10–25.

to entities such as universities and research institutes that fulfill this duty by creating and disseminating knowledge.

### 12.4.6 *Shared Responsibility, Collective Responsibility: A Caveat*

Collective responsibility and shared responsibility have multiple meanings, and clarification of their application in SHG is warranted. In SHG, individuals' understanding of their roles leads them to assume responsibility for doing their part successfully, pursuing specific goals to achieve together the overarching social aim. Shared responsibility thus has quite specific functional and role-based meaning and entails particular commitments, unlike broader, more existential notions of shared responsibility. In essence, shared responsibility in SHG is a thin conception, linking explicit behavior and actions with values and attitudes to create conditions for all to be healthy. Existentialist responsibility has a more diffuse and general structure; as one scholar notes, "Even when there is seemingly nothing that one can *do* to prevent an evil in the world, one has a responsibility to distance oneself from that evil, at the very least by not condoning it."[59] Under SHG, actors can and must do something— they must pursue their role-specific activities effectively. Shared responsibility under SHG is thus more narrow and delimited.

SHG does share two ideas with the social existentialists—that both community membership and shared attitudes create responsibilities for all members,[60] and that individuals and groups are responsible for "joint actions to which one contributes."[61] A change in understanding is necessary so individuals and groups see themselves as sharing responsibility for creating the conditions for all to be healthy, whether they do so by their own individual actions or those actions they share with groups and institutions. Ethical commitments to a shared goal, health equity for example, focus responsibility; a basic premise for achieving the shared goal is that all parties accept responsibility for this joint endeavor. This entails not just group morality but individual morality as well, preserving the methodological and normative importance of individuals and adding to it that of collectives. Because SHG applies positive motivation to establish conditions in which all have the ability to be healthy, it differs from the traditional motivation for responsibility scholarship, which takes causation, blameworthiness, and guilt for harm as a point of departure. SHG is both an individual and group based construct; both individuals and groups can have health agency, intentions, and goals.

---

[59] L. May, *Sharing Responsibility* (Chicago: University of Chicago Press, 1992), 3.
[60] K. Jaspers, *The Question of German Guilt* (New York: Dial Press, 1947); May, *Sharing Responsibility*.
[61] May, *Sharing Responsibility*, 8.

### 12.4.7 *External and Internal Motivation: Failure to Commit, Positive Motivation, Social Sanctions, and Enforcement*

The challenge is for people to commit, share resources, and agree to be held collectively responsible. Thus, individuals and groups aren't internalizing just any social norm, but a set of public moral norms. The health capability paradigm sets forth normative principles, spelling out the reasons for equity in health and explaining why individuals and actors should find such norms socially and individually rational. It may very well be, for example, that many individuals in many societies see health as an individual responsibility rather than a social obligation. In this case the heavy lifting is in convincing people of the necessity of the joint enterprise. Positive motivation makes this task possible in many cases. A segment of the population will resist, and, once institutions and procedures are put in place, an effective system of sanctions, formal rules, and even laws and regulation may be necessary to ensure that actors are fulfilling prescribed duties. Thus, this fifth core SHG premise specifies primarily positive but in some cases negative motivation to support the joint enterprise. Even though virtually every health system worldwide has tried numerous incentives and mechanisms of external motivation, these efforts alone will not suffice to create justice in health.

Drawing on what Gilbert calls common knowledge, the task of positive motivation is to generate common knowledge, self-understanding, and societal understanding so that individuals are clear about both the empirical evidence and the values. Individual and population health are inextricably linked, and improving our own health and that of others requires the shared commitment of us all. Health is a unique individual and social good, different from other types of private goods, and requires a different magnitude of joint effort. Allowing self-interest maximization to run rampant throughout the health sector produces suboptimal outcomes for everyone. Redefining individuals' self-understanding and institutionalizing this common knowledge underlie the SHG framework. As it stands, in many health systems, even those fully nationalized, actors see themselves as interacting with the system, either on the supply or demand side, in an individualized, ad hoc capacity. What is needed is the understanding that together, we are the health business. Free rider problems and failures to comply are omnipresent in health and health care. SHG, drawing on PST, can help minimize them. Demonstrating interdependence among individuals as parties to a social group appeals to the individualistic, rational side of persons and to social rationality simultaneously, but it requires monitoring and sanctioning to maintain stability.[62]

---

[62] M. Hechter, *Principles of Group Solidarity* (Berkeley, CA: University of California Press, 1987).

### 12.4.8 *Shared Sovereignty and Constitutional Commitments*

A sixth core SHG feature is shared sovereignty. SHG depends on individuals and groups coming together to develop structures and procedures to make decisions, govern collectively, and set standards for self and societal regulation. While SHG rests on the overarching political economic philosophy put forth in *Health and Social Justice*, it employs a constitution of sorts to delineate the ends and means of health governance at the global level. An SHG framework based on its own constitution will provide a structure for different institutions as they relate to each other (for example, national and subnational governments, civil society, and individuals). As a superstructure, a health constitution will delineate the respective actors (institutions, organizations, groups, individuals) in health governance and specify their respective duties and powers, thus allocating specific responsibilities for creating a health society. The health constitution would set the framework and procedures, informed by authoritative standards and principles. Constitutional interpretation would then assess whether or not such duties are being fulfilled and whether actors are meeting their obligations to ensure conditions for all to be healthy. To date, the different actors in the health system (for example, providers and physicians, insurers, clinics and hospitals, and individuals themselves) have not known what their respective duties and powers are. Attempting to hold them accountable for unspecified responsibilities is both unfair and unworkable.

The intent is to define effective institutional arrangements and duty allocations to create the conditions for a health society. This enterprise requires empirical research and evidence. The health constitution is not a legal constitution—it would not be legally enforceable in the courts—nor does it overreach in governing every aspect of society. It sets out meta-level rules for health, but it neither replaces nor competes with legal constitutions. Rather, the two types of constitutionalism are complementary. The health constitution is constitutional in the sense of prescribing institutional arrangements and procedures and in assigning responsibilities and authorities to public and private actors. The principles set out in *Health and Social Justice* imply an obligation that falls on society as a whole. Under the health constitution, state governments, as the institutions that represent society at large, will need to spearhead the effort to map a plan for all entities.

### 12.4.9 *Reactions and Objections*

Reactions to the SHG model may come in a variety of forms. Responding to them will involve, among other things, a clear understanding of what SHG is not. First, SHG is not conventional solidarity. It is not nearly as communitarian and allows a more central role for individualism and self regarding behavior. While examples of conventional solidarity in health systems exist—for example, in universal coverage in countries throughout the world—SHG is not just universal coverage, does not require a common conscience across life, and recognizes realistically that actors conflict considerably (rather than cohere) in the division of labor.[63] While conventional solidarity meets the SHG idea of shared resources, it is less focused on people governing themselves to use resources parsimoniously. Conventional solidarity also doesn't emphasize individual action and individual responsibility. Nor does it embrace, to the extent in SHG, the opportunity to build a social system out of individual self and other regarding behavior. The Swiss and German systems, for example, exhibit solidarity in the form of universal coverage (in Switzerland there is universal coverage and one-third of individuals receive government subsidies to purchase health insurance).[64] The German system seeks to preserve conventional solidarity.[65] Yet the Swiss system spends a significant proportion of gross domestic product per capita on health care,[66] and both Germany and Switzerland likely have as much health care overutilization as the United States.[67] Conventional solidarity is thus not quite enough to contain costs and use shared resources wisely, nor are occupational or interest group affiliations sufficient for solidarity in the health system; indeed, they often require greater governmental oversight. The medical profession and health insurance industry are examples. Conventional solidarity further neglects many of the other elements of SHG, particularly those focused on responsibility, constitutionalism in health, and individual-level costs and benefits.

Second, SHG is not socialism. Socialist health systems are government funded and government run; the public sector controls both financing and service delivery. The United Kingdom and Cuba are examples. By contrast, one of SHG's distinguishing features is an emphasis on individuals, private entities, and their actions, which are driven by internalized norms promoting societal interests in addition to their own. SHG does not preclude public systems, though public funding and public service delivery must encompass active individual involvement in health decision-making.

---

[63] E. Durkheim, *The Division of Labor in Society* (New York: Macmillan, 1933).

[64] R. E. Herzlinger and R. Parsa-Parsi, "Consumer-Driven Health Care: Lessons from Switzerland," *Journal of the American Medical Association* 292, no. 10 (2004): 1213–20.

[65] T.-M. Cheng and U. E. Reinhardt, "Shepherding Major Health System Reforms: A Conversation with German Health Minister Ulla Schmidt," *Health Affairs* 27 no. 3 (May 2008): w204–13.

[66] OECD, "OECD Health Data 2004: Tables and Charts from News Release Issued 3 June 2004," *OECD Health Data 2004*.

[67] U. E. Reinhardt, "The Swiss Health System: Regulated Competition without Managed Care," *Journal of the American Medical Association* 292, no. 10 (2004): 1227–31; T. P. Weil, "Health Reform in Germany: An American Assesses the New Operating Efficiencies," *Health Progress* 75, no. 7 (1994): 24–9.

Third, SHG is not just stewardship. In a way, conventional solidarity and socialism can both be considered as manifestations of government steward-ship: governments (with various degrees of democratic backing) decide to implement solidarity-based or socialist policies. As highly centralized and hierarchical health care systems show us, government directives and designs are not enough to ensure good health outcomes, and laws are not always sufficient to achieve health goals if popular norms oppose them. SHG would seek to address pressure points where self-interest maximization and/or incom-patible social norms override government laws and projects. In Japan, for example, legislation to promote organ donation has failed to raise low donation rates, which had been falling since the mid-1990s. One barrier has been family members' reluctance to permit organ removal from the deceased.[68] Govern-ment action has not been able to overcome this normative opposition.

Fourth, SHG is not just enhanced autonomy, shared clinical decision-making, or enlightened self-interest. SHG is more than consumer-directed medicine or the patient taking an active role in her own care with her phys-ician or team of providers. Decisions should account for both individual and societal interests at every stage. Finally, following principles of enlightened self-interest or self-interest rightly understood,[69] while interesting in the abstract, has failed to curtail the emergence of, for example, the dysfunctional American health care system. Relying on enlightened self-interest as a guiding principle leaves us without an overarching social objective whose achieve-ment involves roles and responsibilities for all.

## 12.5 Conclusion

Achieving justice in health has eluded most nations. Economic rational choice theory based on *Homo economicus*, the dominant social theory of cooperation, has failed to ground an effective approach to health. Even when societies cooperate on a grand scale through national health policy and national health systems, they do so in vastly different and often inadequate ways. It is a daunting challenge to allocate responsibility, resources, and sovereignty to create conditions where all have the ability to be healthy. Some will object to SHG on the grounds that its conditions are too onerous and implausible. But existing global health threats and health governance problems are arguably much more onerous. SHG offers a promising way forward.

---

[68] H. Ishida and H. Toma, "Organ Donation Problems in Japan and Countermeasures," *Saudi Journal of Kidney Diseases and Transplantation* 15, no. 2 (2004): 125–8.

[69] A. de Tocqueville, *Democracy in America and Two Essays on America*, trans. G. E. Bevan (London: Penguin, 2003).

# Name Index

# General Index